**Advance Praise for the Second Edition:**

❧ "This second edition of David Hackett's reader in American religious history provides even more riches than what was already a very strong first edition. By leaving traditional topics in theology and formal church life to other books, Hackett and his crew of first-rate authors offer outstanding treatment of religious practices, especially from groups that were usually absent in the older, more church-centered histories."

**—Mark Noll, Wheaton College**

❧ "For the first edition, David Hackett compiled a set of wonderful essays that displayed some of the newer scholarly initiatives in studying religion in American culture while also delineating its shape as a field of inquiry. The new edition selectively adjusts the set so as at once to refine the emphases and enhance the overall utility of the collection. *Religion and American Culture* will excel as a stimulating introduction to the field for beginning students while also serving to help those who are more advanced as they develop their specializations."

**—John F. Wilson, Princeton University**

❧ "This outstanding book reveals the fascinating diversity of American religious experience. It is ideal for classroom use."

**—Catherine A. Brekus, University of Chicago**

**Praise for the First Edition:**

❧ "At last those of us who regularly teach courses in American religious history have readily available a set of readings that puts students in touch with the field as it is being constituted now. Here is all the best new scholarship in lively and accessible form. Hackett gives us multicultural religious America in a format that communicates. I'm delighted and will surely use the reader in my own courses."

**—Catherine L. Albanese, University of California, Santa Barbara**

❧ "Hackett has chosen splendid, sparkling examples of the kind of historical writing that draws our attention to previously marginalized groups. He has, wisely, not attempted to deal in one collection with both the "outsiders" and the putative mainstream. Instead we have, collected in one place, supplementary readings that will extend and enrich the accounts offered in the best textbooks on American religious history."

**—William R. Hutchison, The Divinity School at Harvard University**

❧ "This book should be read by all who teach and study in America because it models academic justice in its treatment of the broad range of cultural perspectives and religious traditions."

**—Peter Paris, Princeton University**

# RELIGION
# AND
# AMERICAN
# CULTURE

# RELIGION AND AMERICAN CULTURE

## A Reader
## Second Edition

*David G. Hackett*

*Editor*

Routledge
New York and London

Published in 2003 by
Routledge
29 West 35th Street
New York, NY 10001
www.routledge-ny.com

Published in Great Britain by
Routledge
11 New Fetter Lane
London EC4P 4EE
www.routledge.co.uk

**Library of Congress Cataloging-in-Publication Data**

Religion and American culture : a reader / David G. Hackett, editor. — 2nd ed.
    p.  cm.
Includes bibliographical references.

ISBN 0-415-94272-1 (alk. paper) — ISBN 0-415-94273-X (pbk. : alk. paper)
    1.  United States—Religion.  2.  United States—Church history.  3.  Religion and culture—United States.
I.  Hackett, David G.

BL2525.R447 2003
200'.973—dc21

                                                                                        2002155347

# CONTENTS 🦌

## ACKNOWLEDGMENTS

A NUMBER OF FRIENDS AND COLLEAGUES have taken the time to offer their thoughts on the organization and content of this book. For their helpful advice and encouragement with the first edition, I particularly want to thank: Mary Bednarowksi, Jim Bratt, Ann Braude, John Corrigan, Fred Denny, Jay Dolan, Diana Eck, Cynthia Eller, Tracy Fessenden, Will Gravely, Ramón Gutiérrez, Yvonne Haddad, David Hall, Nathan Hatch, Sam Hill, Brooks Holifield, Charles Joyner, Laurie Maffly-Kipp, Joel Martin, Colleen McDannell, Deborah Dash Moore, Azim Nanji, Stephen Nissenbaum, Bob Orsi, Amanda Porterfield, Steve Prothero, Al Raboteau, Elizabeth Reis, Dan Richter, Jonathan Sarna, Leigh Schmidt, Jan Shipps, Steve Tipton, Roberto Trevino, Tim Tseng, Tom Tweed, Chris Vecsey, Grant Wacker, Margaret Washington, David Watt, Jack Wertheimer, David Wills, Bob Wuthnow, Wendy Young and the 1994–95 members of Princeton's Center for the Study of American Religion Friday workshop.

For their advice in the preparation of the second edition I want to thank Beth Wenger and, again, Tom Tweed and Joel Martin. At Routledge, Tenessa Gemelke has been a consistently caring and attentive editor. Her efforts made the production of this second edition an enjoyable experience. Our son Ben was born during the preparation of this second edition. I thank him, our daughter Evelyn, and my wife Wendy Young for teaching me the pleasures of "gearing up" when arriving home.

# INTRODUCTION TO THE FIRST EDITION ✎

TODAY THE STUDY OF AMERICAN RELIGION continues to move away from an older, European American, male, middle-class, northeastern, Protestant narrative concerned primarily with churches and theology and toward a multicultural tale of Native Americans, African Americans, Catholics, Jews, and other groups. Many of these new studies cut across boundaries of gender, class, and region, and pay particular attention to popular religion. Most current textbooks remain wedded to the older Protestant narrative. The purpose of this reader is to expose students to a broad overview of the new work emerging from this rapidly changing field.

At the outset we need to recognize that the field of American religious history is in the midst of substantial revision. As recently as the 1970s what we knew about the American religious past came primarily from the study of formal theology and the histories of the established churches. The crowning achievement in this tradition was the publication of Sydney Ahlstrom's magisterial *A Religious History of the American People* in 1972.[1] The great and continuing strength of church history is its attention to the influence of religious ideas and to the relationship between religion and political affairs. All of the major textbooks are written by historians schooled in this genre and their narratives largely reflect the dominant Protestant point of view. It is, of course, foolish to simply ignore the importance of Protestant churches in American religion. Nevertheless, as a recent president of the American Society of Church History concluded in a review of the available textbooks: "There is a widespread feeling among professionals in the field that the text resources available in the past are unsuitable for the present."[2]

Religious history started breaking away from church history in the 1960s, when social historians began to see religion as playing a more active role in social change. Influential historians, such as E. P. Thompson and Eugene Genovese, emphasized the power of popular religion in helping ordinary people to oppose the institutional religion of the ruling classes. By the 1970s, this conflict model was largely superseded by the insights of anthropologists who directed historians' interest to the meaning and order conveyed to believers by religious symbols. In particular, Clifford Geertz's understanding of "religion as a cultural system" was widely read and appropriated throughout the discipline. By the late 1970s, this mixture of a social history and cultural anthropology led to the emergence of the new area of "popular religion." Works by Jon Butler on magic and the occult, Rhys Isaac on the religious culture of eighteenth-century Virginia, as well as new research on revivalism and slave religion, all suggested the arrival of a new "popular" approach to the American religious past.[3]

During the 1980s, and up to the present, the thrust of this work has dramatically expanded the area of research. Regional religious stories of the West and the South are coming into view. Native American religious history, non-existent as a field until the 1980s, is an exciting and rapidly emerging new discipline. Dramatic revisions are being made in our understanding of the African American religious past. Mormons, Masons, Pentecostals, ethnic Catholics, sunbelt Jews, followers of Islam, Asian religions, and Haitian Vodou are now on the scene. Attention is being given to the relationship between religion and commercial culture. The complex view of women in today's women's studies is echoed in new works on women across class and racial lines. In many of these studies we can see a new interest in ritual and ceremony.

The result of this scholarship is not to offer a new interpretation of the American religious past. It is still not at all clear what should be the proper subject matter of religious history nor which methods and theories ought to be applied. Still, the sheer number of new works that demonstrate the existence and vitality of religious peoples and practices outside the domain of the Protestant middle class is sufficient to throw into doubt the explanatory power of the older view. Because a new paradigm is not yet clear, it is not the time for a new textbook. The older texts are valuable for providing the Protestant narrative. But exactly because the field is currently so rich and diverse, now is the time for an anthology that gives clear voice to these new studies.

The organization of the following readings is loosely chronological: four broad periods, with a particular focus on recurrent themes. Two different organizational schemes, one chronological and the other thematic, are currently followed in American religion courses. Both of these schemes have advantages and limitations; many who teach these courses use a combination of the two.

The chronological approach has the great advantage of providing a coherent overview of the development of American religion. This approach also has the disadvantage of favoring a Protestant periodization of the American past, though recent scholars have incorporated the chronological stories of Native Americans, European Americans, and African Americans into a larger scheme.[4]

Advocates of the thematic approach, in contrast, hold that a focus on themes rather than chronology allows for a decisive break from the older Protestant narrative, leaving more room for other stories to emerge. The drawback to this approach is that it risks a presentism and impressionism, intriguing students with all sorts of interesting issues, but perhaps failing to explain these issues very well (where do they come from and why are they this way and how do they relate to the other elements of the course?).

The solution suggested by this reader is to combine these two approaches by employing a loose chronological framework while paying attention to recurrent themes. The Native American story, for example, is introduced at the beginning but, unlike most traditional histories, does not disappear. It returns as that story changes through each successive historical period. Similar attention is given to the African American story through each stage of the chronology. Themes like "women and religion" are given particular attention not only during the period in which they become prominent, but also when they recur at later times. Issues of region and class are similarly prominent in many of the readings.

The intention of the following readings is neither to provide a new narrative nor simply assemble a random assortment of readings. Rather, through a loose chronology, attention to recurrent themes, and brief introductions to each selection, this reader offers a selection of the new work emerging in this dynamic and changing field.

## NOTES

1. Sydney E. Ahlstrom, *A Religious History of the American People* (New Haven: Yale University Press, 1972).

2. Stephen J. Stein, " 'Something Old, Something New, Something Borrowed, Something Left to Do': Choosing a Textbook for Religion in America." *Religion and American Culture* 3:2 (Summer 1993), 224.

3. For a sustained treatment of these developments, see Thomas Kselman ed., *Belief in History: Innovative Approaches to European and American Religion.* (Notre Dame, IN: University of Notre Dame Press, 1991), 1–15.

4. See especially the inclusive chronological approaches used by Catherine L. Albanese, *America: Religions and Religion* (Belmont, CA: Wadsworth Publishing Company, 2nd edition, 1992) and Peter W. Williams, *America's Religions: Traditions and Cultures* (New York: Macmillan Publishing Company, 1990).

# INTRODUCTION TO THE SECOND EDITION ❦

THIS SECOND EDITION INCLUDES ADVANCES IN THE FIELD since the publication of the first edition in 1995. Though each of these new essays cuts across several disciplines, three are primarily in the area of gender, two concern Native Americans, two consider new immigrants, and there are contributions on African Americans, popular culture, and the sociology of religion.

If there is one approach that draws together the majority of these new essays it is that of "lived religion." Originating in the French tradition of the sociology of religion, the term "lived religion" is enlarged in these essays to include cultural and ethnographic approaches to the study of American religion. Inquiries that lie behind the term "lived religion" build upon earlier studies in the area of "popular religion." Especially among historians of the Reformation, the concept of popular religion has meant the space between official Christianity and "pagan" culture where lay people enjoyed some degree of autonomy. Lived religion embraces popular religion's emphasis on the actions of the laity in creating their own religious practices from the available cultural resources. This new approach goes its own way, however, in breaking down popular religion's characteristic oppositions between elite and popular, high and low culture in favor of close analyses of "meaning." Rachel Wheeler's article on women and Christian practice, for example, circumvents the conflict between missionary imperialism and "native" religion by unraveling the multiple meanings embodied in ritual practice. Her study demonstrates that Mahican women were as involved as missionaries in creating a distinctive Indian Christianity. Robert Orsi's analysis of Catholic women's devotion to the saint of hopeless causes, similarly, helps us to see devotionalism as shaped by both the intentions of the clergy and the needs and desires of lay women. In the same vein, Marie Griffith reveals how conservative Protestant women's prayers, stories, and changed behaviors provided them with a variety of ways of interpreting the ideal of female submission to male authority. As "theorists of a relative freedom," together these scholars participate in a larger contemporary debate over what Orsi has called "the nature and limits of autonomy within the permeable boundaries of culture."[1]

The overall direction here is away from the rational order of doctrine or all-encompassing theories—that impose a false harmony and coherence on the messiness of everyday life—and toward an historical hermeneutics attuned to the contradictions, ironies, and subversions of religious practice. This perspective is particularly well suited to the study of new immigrant groups whose struggles over religious identity are inscribed in the conflicted and contested meanings of their rituals and new houses of worship. In this volume, Tom Tweed's exploration of devotions to Our Lady of the Exile uncovers the many national and religious meanings of worship at this Miami shrine for Cuban immigrants; Joanne Waghorne's analysis of the construction of Washington, D.C.'s Sri Siva-Vishnu Temple, in turn, reveals a strongly contested struggle to define the emerging global Hinduism. David Chidester's assessment of the relative merits of established models of religion for understanding popular culture, furthermore, carries forward "lived religion's" suspicion of fixed meanings for "religious" activities in everyday life.

The remaining new articles explore new areas or raise significant new questions. Ann Braude's provocative assertion that "Women's History IS American Religious History" challenges male organizing themes that have structured the narrative of American religious history. David Hackett's essay on the Prince Hall Masons sheds light upon beliefs and rituals practiced by a majority of prominent African American men at the turn of the twentieth century. Christopher Jocks raises disturbing ethical questions about the practice of Native American scholarship. Finally, Robert Bellah ends this second edition by questioning the whole idea that we are living within an increasingly multicultural society at a time when a common culture, or cancer, of individualism runs increasingly rampant through all of our lives.

### NOTE

1. Robert A. Orsi, "Everyday Miracles: The Study of Lived Religion" in David D. Hall, ed., *Lived Religion in America: Toward a History of Practice* (Princeton University Press, 1997), 13–14.

# PART ONE

# EARLY AMERICA
# 1500–1750

# THE PUEBLO INDIAN WORLD IN THE SIXTEENTH CENTURY

## Ramón A. Gutiérrez

The triumph of America's first European settlers over the Indians is a tale often told. According to most textbooks, American history "begins" with the defeat of the Native Americans. This story is usually told from the colonists' point of view. Rarely are we given the Indians' perspective. Since the 1980s a new generation of scholars has shown that the European encounter with America's Indians was not as one-sided as historical accounts have led us to believe. There was actually a dialogue between cultures, each of which had many voices. One insight of these new studies is that the Indians had their own point of view, a distinct historical voice that previous historians had unconsciously denied them.

   In the following historical reconstruction of sixteenth-century Pueblo culture and society, Ramón Gutiérrez presents the worldview of one of the more than five hundred Indian tribal worlds. He does this by weaving together a variety of sources into a rich tapestry that depicts the ideological, economic, cosmic, spatial, ritual, and sexual relations within the Pueblo community. This story comes from the Acoma Pueblo, the oldest continuously settled community in the United States. Nestled atop a steep rock formation in western New Mexico, the town of Acoma has a history that reaches back to 1300. Since that time the town has resisted neighboring aggressors, defeat by the Spanish, annexation by the United States, and recently, the invasion of modern technology. The myth that begins this essay reveals the origins and structure of their Pueblo Indian world.

Adapted by permission from Ramón A. Gutiérrez, "The Pueblo Indian World in the Sixteenth Century," in his *When Jesus Came, the Corn Mothers Went Away: Marriage, Sexuality, and Power in New Mexico, 1500–1846.* Copyright 1991 by the Board of Trustees of the Leland Stanford Jr. University. Reprinted with the permission of Stanford University Press, www.sup.org.

*I am glad I have seen your nakedness; it is beautiful; it will rain from now on.*

—Talashimitiwa, Hopi Indian from Oraibi, 1920

# 1

# THE PUEBLO INDIAN WORLD IN THE SIXTEENTH CENTURY

## Ramón A. Gutiérrez

IN THE BEGINNING two females were born underneath the earth at a place called Shipapu. In total darkness Tsichtinako (Thought Woman) nursed the sisters, taught them language and gave them each a basket that their father Uchtsiti had sent them containing the seeds and fetishes of all the plants and animals that were to exist in the world. Tsichtinako told the sisters to plant the four pine tree seeds they had in their basket and then to use the trees to ascend to the light. One grew so tall that it pushed a hole through the earth. Before the sisters climbed up the tree from the underworld, Thought Woman taught them how to praise the Sun with prayer and song. Every morning as the Sun rose, they would thank him for bringing them to the light by offering with outstretched hands sacred cornmeal and pollen. To the tones of the creation song, they would blow the offering to the sky, asking for long life, happiness, and success in all their endeavors.[1]

When the sisters reached the earth's surface it was soft, spongy, and not yet ripe. So they waited for the Sun to appear. When it rose, the six directions of the cosmos were revealed to them: the four cardinal points, the earth below, and the four skies above. The sisters prayed to the Sun, and as they did, Thought Woman named one of the girls Iatiku and made her Mother of the Corn clan; the other she named Nautsiti, Mother of the Sun clan.

"Why were we created?" they asked. Thought Woman answered, "Your father Uchtsiti made the world by throwing a clot of his blood into space, which by his power grew into the earth. He planted you within it so that you would bring to life all the things in your baskets in order that the world be complete for you to rule over it."

When the first day ended, the girls slept. They awoke before dawn to greet the Sun with a prayer on their lips and an offering of cornmeal and pollen. When Sun rose and gave them warmth, the sisters were very happy. Tsichtinako then took several seeds from their baskets and showed the sisters how to plant corn. With a dig stick she poked holes into Mother Earth and deposited seeds in her womb. The corn germinated and grew. When its ears were ripe and plump, Thought Woman showed them how to pick it, how to collect its pollen, and how to mill its kernels into the meal they would offer their father daily.

That night a flash of brilliant red light fell from the sky and when it touched the earth, it exploded into fire. "Your father Sun gives you fire to cook your food and to keep you warm," explained Thought Woman. "The fire's tongues will stay alive if fed branches from the pine tree that gave you passage from the underworld." From that day forward, Iatiku and Nautsiti had fire with which to cook corn. They flavored the corn with the salt they found in their baskets and ate to their hearts' content.

Next, Thought Woman taught the sisters how to give life to the animal fetishes in their baskets so that the animals would give them life in return. Mice, rats, moles, and prairie dogs were created and were given grasses on which to forage and multiply. The sisters cast pebbles in various directions and from these emerged mountains, plains, mesas, and canyons. From the seeds they next strewed about, pine, cedar, oak, and walnut trees grew and underneath them beans and squash sprouted and yielded their fruit. Rabbits, antelope, bison, and deer were dispatched to the open plains. To the mountains went the elk with their predators the lions, wolves, wildcats, and bears. Eagle, hawk, and turkey were cast into the sky, but turkey fell back to earth and never learned to fly. In the earth's waters fish, water snakes, and turtles were placed, and there they flourished and multiplied. Now Thought Woman told the sisters to kill an animal. "Roast meat and corn together and flavor it with salt," she instructed. "Before you eat, always pray and offer morsels of these to your father Uchtsiti who created the world and lives in the fourth sky above."

Tsichtinako cautioned Iatiku and Nautsiti to handle their baskets carefully. At first they did. But as they were giving life to the snakes one fetish fell out of a basket unnoticed and came to life of its own power as the serpent Pishuni. Pishuni bred selfishness and competitiveness between the sisters. Soon Nautsiti became sullen and refused to associate with Iatiku. When this occurred, Pishuni asked Nautsiti: "Why are you lonely and unhappy? If you want what will make you happy, I can tell you what to do. If you bore someone like yourself, you would no longer be lonely. Tsichtinako wants to hold back this happiness from you," he said. Nautsiti believed Pishuni and agreed to meet him near a rainbow. On a rock near the specified rainbow, Nautsiti lay on her back, and as she did drops of rain entered her body. From this rain she conceived and bore twin sons. Father Sun had strictly forbidden the sisters to bear children, and when he learned that Nautsiti had, he took Thought Woman away.

When Nautsiti's sons grew up, the sisters separated. Nautsiti departed East with her favorite child; Iatiku remained with Tiamuni, the son Nautsiti disliked. Iatiku and Tiamuni eventually married and had many daughters to whom they gave clan names representing all the things that their father had given them at emergence: Sky, Water, Fire, and Corn.

After Thought Woman departed, Iatiku took earth from her basket and made the season spirits: Shakako, the ferocious spirit of winter, Morityema, the surly spirit of spring, Maiyochina, the warm spirit of summer, and Shruisthia, the grumpy spirit of fall. Iatiku told the people that if they prayed properly to these spirits they would bring moisture, warmth, ripening, and frost, respectively.

Next Iatiku, their Corn Mother, took dirt from her basket and created the katsina, the Cloud-Spirits or ancestor dead who were to live beneath a lake in the West at Wenimats. Tsitsanits (Big Teeth) was brought to life first as ruler of the katsina, then many other katsina were brought to life. Some looked like birds with long beaks and bulging eyes, others had large animal snouts, and still others were moon creatures with horns sticking out of their heads like lunar crescents. "Your people and my people will be combined," Iatiku told the katsina. "You will give us food from your world and we will give you food from our world. Your people are to represent clouds; you are to bring rain." Iatiku then took cornmeal and opened a road four lengths long so that the katsina could travel to Wenimats and along which they would return when called.[2]

"Now we are going to make houses," said Corn Mother. Suddenly a house made of dirt and trees grew out of the earth resembling in shape the mesa and mountain homes of the season deities. Each of Iatiku's daughters constructed a house for her children and when they were all ready, Iatiku laid them out into a town. "All is well but . . . we have no sacred place, we have no *kaach* [kiva]," Iatiku said. She taught the oldest man of the Oak clan how to build religious houses underneath the earth's surface to resemble Shipapu, the place of emergence.

The people did not have a father of the game animals, so Iatiku appointed a Shaiyaik (Hunt Chief), taught him the songs and prayers of the hunt, gave him an altar, and showed him how to make stone fetishes and prayer sticks to secure the power of the prey animals. Hunt Chief eventually became overburdened with work and so Corn Mother made Tsatia hochani (War Chief or Outside Chief) to rule over everything outside the pueblo. Iatiku gave him a broken prayer stick with four tails marked on four sides to extend from the earth to the sky. "When you hold [the prayer stick] clasped in your hands," Iatiku told Tsatia hochani, "you are drawing all the people together so they will not be scattered. With this you will have great power over all the rest of the people." Iatiku gave the War Chief twin sons, Masewi (Wren Youth) and Oyoyewi (Mocking Bird Youth), to assist him. The boys were the Twin War Gods, sons of Father Sun.

The people had never known sickness until the serpent Pishuni returned as a plague. The people tried to cure themselves, but could not. To break Pishuni's spell Iatiku created the *chaianyi*, the Medicine Man. The oldest man of the Oak clan was made Fire Medicine Man because fire was the strongest thing that Sun had given them and oak burned hottest. Corn Mother told Oak Man to go to North Mountain and there in a pine tree that had been struck by lightning he would find an obsidian arrowhead that would be his heart and his protection. She taught him how to make black prayer sticks as symbols of the night in which he would work, and then made him an altar. Iatiku taught the Medicine Man how to mix medicines and how to secure the power of bears to destroy disease-causing witches. "Now I will make you *honani* [corn fetish] so that you will remember me," Iatiku said to the chaianyi, "it will have my power." Into a corn cob she blew her breath along with a few drops of honey to symbolize all plant food. The cob was wrapped in four husks and dressed with the tail feather of a roadrunner and of a magpie to make it useful in prayers. Iatiku also placed turquoise on the corn fetish so that it would always have the power to make one attractive and loved.

Everything was ready for a cure so Iatiku said to Fire Medicine Man, "Let us try it out." For four days the medicine man did not touch women, salt, or meat, and only sang and prayed. On the fourth night he performed a cure. The people quickly recovered. When Iatiku saw this, she also created the Flint, Spider, and Giant Medicine Societies.

Eventually it came to pass that the young people no longer respected Iatiku. So she returned to Shipapu. After she departed, Outside Chief led the people in search of their home at Haako (Acoma), "the place where the echo returned clearest." They settled at White House for a while but the katsina refused to visit because the young had insulted Iatiku. Rain clouds would not form and famine came. Flint Medicine Man and an ordinary man worked very hard, prayed, and fasted, and finally got the katsina to visit, bearing rain and gifts.

Iatiku's people were happy for a long time until sickness again befell them. The War Twins believed that this was a sign from Iatiku that they should move to Haako, and so they did, gathering everything in four days and traveling until they reached Washpashuka. They settled there until the people began to quarrel. When this occurred, Outside Chief told the people that it was time to move again. They walked south for many moons until they reached Tule Lake. The people settled at Tule Lake for a while too. But after they suffered a severe famine there, they decided to continue their search for Haako.

They traveled south until they reached Dyaptsiam, a place of many turkeys and antelope. There they built a town. The people lived very happily until Outside Chief reminded the Medicine Men and the War Twins that they still had not reached Haako. The chiefs searched in the south and came upon a large rock. Outside Chief yelled out, "Haako!" and listened. Four more times he yelled and each time the echo came back clearly. After four days of preparation the people moved to Haako and were happy knowing that their journey had ended.

## PUEBLO IDEOLOGY

The origin myth of the Acoma Indians just presented likened human life to plant life. Seeds held the potential to generate life. When planted deep within Mother Earth and fertilized by the sky's vivifying rain, seeds germinated, grew into plants, and eventually bore seeds that repeated the cycle of life. Like a sprouting maize shoot rooted in the earth or a child coming forth from its mother's womb, so the Pueblo Indians described their emergence from the underworld.[3]

All of the Pueblos have origin myths that dramatically depict the ideological structure of their world. Myths express the values and ideals that organize and make people's lives meaningful. They explain how the universe was created, its various components, and the tensions and balances that keep it intact. Whether through the deeds of gods, the feats of heroes, or the abominations of monsters, the Pueblo origin myths expressed life's generic prospects: birth, marriage, sex, quarreling, illness, migrations, and death. The Pueblo Indians conceived their history as instances of these generic forms. When pestilence struck, when famine engulfed the land, or when invading warriors demanded submission, it was through comparison with patterns in remote mythological events that the particular was understood.

The Western mind's linear concept of time imposes chronology on all events and struggles to comprehend the causes and consequences of moments that have irrevocably altered history. Such a concept of time was alien to the Pueblo Indians until quite recently. Time to them was not linear but cyclic: in the words of Mircea Eliade, it eternally returned. No event was deemed unique or serendipitous; the particular was simply comprehended through those experiences of mythic progenitors. Like the life contained within a seed that sprouts, bears fruit, and dies, only to be reborn again from a seed, so the Pueblo Indians conceived of time and of their historical past.[4]

## PUEBLO RITES

From birth until death every phase of a Pueblo Indian's life was marked by rites of transition and incorporation. Before children of either sex could be considered adults they needed a host of essentials. Girls needed religious fetishes, esoteric knowledge in curing, pottery production, household construction, basket making, and a husband. Boys likewise needed sacred fetishes, knowledge in hunting, warfare, curing, rain-conjuring, and a wife. Boys and girls, however, were incapable of obtaining these goods for themselves. Seniors had to secure them for their children and did so by offering gifts to those seniors who could provide the required goods. For example, four days after a child was born at Acoma, a medicine man had to present the infant to the rising sun, to give it a name, and to endow it with a perfect ear of corn, and if a boy, also with a flint arrowhead. Early on the fourth day, with four arm-gathering motions, the medicine man presented the child to the sun and gave it the sun's strength saying: "Now you have become a member of the _____ clan." When the medicine man returned the child to its mother he would announce: "Here comes [child's name] . . . she is bringing food, beads, game, and a long life into her house." The mother welcomed the abundance and prosperity her daughter brought with four arm-gathering motions. Then the medicine man sprinkled the baby's cradle board with medicines, attaching a perfect ear of corn, and if it was a boy, a flint arrowhead too. For the blessing and gifts the medicine man gave the child, the parents reciprocated with gifts of cornmeal and food.[5]

Thus when girls and boys began life they were already indebted to their parents for the payment of gifts to the medicine man on their behalf. As a result of this debt and the many others they would incur to reach adulthood, juniors had to reciprocate with obedience and respect toward their parents. Concretely, respect meant that girls had to work for their mothers grinding corn, cooking, and tanning hides; boys had to tend to the corn crops, hunt, and weave cloth. Seniors, by appropriating the products of their children's labor, obtained gift stuff to offer seniors of other households so that their children could receive those blessings, knowledge, and gifts they needed to become adults.[6]

Gift exchange in Pueblo society created dyadic status relationships between givers and receivers. A gift properly reciprocated with a countergift established the exchanging parties as equals, there being no further claim one could make of the other. If a gift giver initiated an exchange with a highly respected or knowledgeable person to obtain blessings, religious endowments, or ritual knowledge, such as when a parent offered a medicine man gifts so that he would present their child to the rising sun, the obligation created was fulfilled through a proper countergift. But if only one side gave and the other side could not reciprocate, the receiver out of gratitude had to give the presenter unending obedience and respect.[7]

The rules of reciprocity that governed gift exchange among the Pueblos are revealed in a variety of historical sources. The Acoma origin myth explains that when Tsichtinako gave life to Iatiku and Nautsiti, she presented each with a basket their father Uchtsiti had given them containing the seeds and fetishes of all the plants and animals in the world. As a result of this paternal gift the girls had to welcome him daily with songs and prayers, offering him the products of their labor—maize ground into cornmeal and sacred pollen. From the moment of their creation the Corn Mothers were indebted to their father for the baskets he had given them. Since they had nothing to give him in return, they did as Tsichtinako instructed, daily singing his praises and offering him food.

The Acoma origin myth also describes what could happen if the rules of reciprocity that governed gifting and structured generational obligation faltered. These themes surface in reference to the katsina, the beneficent rain spirits that represented the ancestral dead. In Pueblo thought, with increasing age one approached the godliness of katsina. The myth explains that the katsina first fought with the people, abandoned them, refused to shower them with rain and happiness, and ultimately severed the ties that bound them with the people because the young no longer respected the katsina and instead mimicked their gestures, burlesqued their dances, and refused to call them properly with gifts. Seniors scolded juniors for their disrespect, but the juniors continued to misbehave. When the katsina discovered this, they became very angry and refused to accept the peoples' prayer sticks. When the katsina finally visited they killed many people. The Twin War Boys retaliated by killing many katsina, explaining that they did so because "the katsina on their part should care for the people." The town chief told the Twins that the people were at fault because they had not respected the katsina. He urged the War Twins to use their magical powers to bring the katsina back to life. The Twins agreed because it was "by them [i.e., the katsina] that we have lived and been happy." The magic worked. The katsina came back to life. To teach the young the respect they had to show the katsina, that is, the reciprocity which regulated generational relations and labor exchange between juniors and seniors, every adolescent had to be initiated into the katsina cult and learn what death and destruction awaited those juniors who did not observe these rules.[8]

Marriage, the mark of transition from junior to senior status, was similarly enmeshed in gift exchanges. Girls married when they were about seventeen years old, said Hernan Gallegos in 1582, boys when they were about nineteen. This occurred in the standard boy-meets-girl way. The young man would then inform his parents that he wanted to marry. If the parents and kin agreed to the match, the senior members of his household gathered the necessary marriage-validating gifts on the boy's behalf. The willingness of elders to gather these gifts testified that the boy had been respectful of his elders, had toiled for them tirelessly, and had been obedient. Had he not, they could withhold the gifts he needed to present to his prospective in-laws, reminding him of his past failures and of their anger at him, much like when the katsina became angry at disrespectful juniors and refused to bless them.[9]

When the boy's elders had gathered their marriage-validating gifts, they took them to the girl's household. If the girl's kin agreed to the marriage and accepted the gifts, each person that accepted a gift had to give one in return. The gifts the bride's kin collected for her in-laws were usually taken to them on the fourth day after the initial gifts were received. Jane Collier characterizes this marital system as one of "equal bride-wealth" because "equal" amounts of wealth are exchanged between the boy's and girl's households to validate the marriage. When these exchanges were complete, a marital rite followed.[10]

Marriage and procreation marked one as an adult. Children triggered a new cycle of indebtedness. But if because of few or sickly children a couple was unable to produce those socially desired goods exchanged as gifts, then these unsuccessful seniors would have to indebt themselves to successful seniors in order to provide their own children with the prerequisites for adulthood. Unsuccessful seniors who obtained gifts they could not reciprocate for their child from successful seniors were indebted to them and could be expected to render labor, respect, and obedience. Heads of successful households, by having numerous juniors as well as unsuccessful seniors whose labor they could appropriate to accumulate gift-stuff, were thus in a position to support large extended households consisting of secondary wives, widows, orphans, and strays.

Relationships of superordination and subordination among the Puebloans were based on age and personal characteristics. Such societies are often called egalitarian because theoretically all men and women had equal access to those things a person of either sex needed in life, be it ritual blessings, esoteric knowledge, tools, land, or seeds. "I have not seen any principal houses by which any superiority over others could be shown," said Francisco Vásquez de Coronado in 1540, as he tried to assess the differences between the Aztecs and the Pueblos. Diego Pérez de Luxán visited the Hopi and Zuñi Pueblos in 1582 and concluded that no discernible differences in material trappings existed between the caciques, or chiefs, and others: "They are all equal." Age grading was one source of inequality in the Pueblos, but as one advanced through life and married, became a parent, a household head, and finally an elder, one's power and prestige also grew. Senior men, successful or unsuccessful, controlled social well-being. Senior women likewise commanded great respect and authority through ownership of the household, of its sacred fetishes, and of its seeds, whatever the household's size or productivity. "The old men are the ones who have the most authority," reported Hernando de Alvarado and Fray Juan de Padilla in 1540. Pedro de Castañeda observed that same year that the Hopi were governed "by an assembly of the oldest men."[11]

According to Jane Collier, "leadership is a creation of followership" among tribesmen. When a chief died or became so senile that he was no longer able to accumulate the gift-stuff to stage ceremonials and to indebt others, his following dissolved. The chief's children might be advantaged in obtaining ritual knowledge, blessings, and gifts, but every person who aspired to leadership had to obtain his own ritual knowledge, his own bride, and his own following. Leadership was not hereditarily based in one household or matri-lineage until the eighteenth century, thus minimizing inherited inequalities. Additionally, the Pueblos prized generosity and equated conspicuous wealth with witchcraft. Chiefs were above all successful seniors who generously gifted those who sought their help and selflessly provided all the goods necessary to stage religious ceremonials through which the gods' blessings were obtained.[12]

The Pueblo Indians viewed the relations between the sexes as relatively balanced. Women and men each had their own forms of wealth and power, which created independent but mutually interdependent spheres of action. The corn fetish every child was given at birth and the flint arrowhead with which boys were endowed symbolized these relations and expressed the basic preoccupations of a people living in a semi-arid environment. Corn and flint were food and water, but they were also the cosmic principles of femininity and masculinity. Female and male combined as corn seeds and rain combined, to perpetuate life. Corn plants without rain would shrivel and die; water without corn was no life at all. The ear of corn infants received represented the Corn Mothers that had given life to all humans, plants, and animals. At Acoma Pueblo this corn fetish is still called Iatiku, because it contains her heart and breath. For this reason too the Hopi called this corn fetish "mother." "Corn is my heart, it will be to [you] . . . as milk from my breasts," Zia's Corn Mother told her people. Individuals kept this corn fetish throughout their entire lives, for if crops failed its perfect seeds held the promise of a new crop cycle.[13]

If the corn ear represented the feminine generative powers latent in seeds, the earth, and women, the flint arrowhead represented the masculine germinative forces of the sky. Father Sun gave men flint arrowheads to bring forth rain, to harness heat, and to use as a weapon in the hunt. The noise emitted by striking together two pieces of flint resembled the thunder and lightning that accompanied rain. Rain fertilized seeds as men fertilized their women. Without rain or semen, life could not continue. The flint arrowhead was the sign of the hunter and warrior. Sun gave his sons, the Twin War Gods, arrowheads with which to give and take away life. From flint too came fire. When men struck flint and created that gift Sun gave them at the beginning of time, they transformed that which was raw into that which was cooked. To the Pueblo Indians flint, rain, semen, and hunting were to male as corn, earth, and childbearing were to female. This idea is conveyed in the Hopi word *posumi*, which means both corn seed and nubile woman. We see this too in the ceremony Zuñi women perform to celebrate the sex of their babies. Over a girl's vulva the women place a large seed-filled gourd and pray that her sexual parts grow large and her fruit abundant. The boy's penis is sprinkled with water, and the women pray that it remains small. Men became very angry when they saw this ritual, for through it women asserted that their life-bearing capacity was immense in comparison to that of men. Men vigorously contested this claim in their rituals to vivify the earth, sporting large artificial penises to show women that their fructifying powers were really more immense, "singing about the penis being the thing that made the women happy."[14]

The natal home was the primary unit of affiliation in Pueblo society. Everyone belonged to a home. Humans, animals, deities, and even the natural forces were believed to each have a home within which they lived. In the sixteenth century the Pueblos were matrilineal, anchoring maternity to matrilocal households. "The houses belong to the women, they being the ones who build them," observed Espinosa in 1601.[15]

The typical household unit consisted of a grandmother and her husband, her sisters and their husbands, her daughters and their husbands, various young children, and perhaps an orphan, slave, or stray. Women were attached to their natal dwelling throughout their lives, said Hernán Gallegos in 1582, and did "not leave except when permitted by their mothers." Men moved from house to house according to their stage of life. During childhood boys lived with their mothers, and at adolescence they moved into a kiva to learn male magical lore. When they had mastered these skills, and were deemed worthy of marriage by their kin, they took up residence in their wife's home. A man nonetheless remained tied to his maternal home throughout his life. For important ceremonial events, men returned to their maternal households. When this occurred the household became a matrilineage. Matrilineages that acknowledged descent from a common ancestor, usually through ownership of a similar animal or spirit fetish, formed larger, primarily religious aggregations known as clans.[16]

Large portions of a woman's day were spent preparing meals for her household. Corn, beans, and squash were the main staples of the diet. Corn was the most important and symbolic of these. It was boiled whole, toasted on the cob, or dried and ground into a fine powder easily cooked as bread or gruel. Every day a woman and her daughters knelt before metates, grinding corn to feed their gods, their fetishes, and their kin. The women worked joyfully at this task, observed Castañeda in 1540. "One crushes the maize, the next grinds it, and the third grinds it finer. While they are grinding, a man sits at the door playing a flageolet, and the women move their stones, keeping time with the music, and all three sing together."[17]

> Oh, for a heart as pure as pollen on corn blossoms,
> And for a life as sweet as honey gathered from the flowers,
> May I do good, as Corn has done good for my people
> Through all the days that were.
> Until my task is done and evening falls,
> Oh, Mighty Spirit, hear my grinding song.

Within the household an age hierarchy existed, for as Hernán Gallegos observed in 1582, "Women, if they have daughters, make them do the grinding." The production of pottery (e.g., storage jars, cooking utensils, ritual medicine bowls), moccasins, ceremonial apparel, and turkey-down blankets was also women's household work. Men appropriated and circulated some of these goods throughout the Southwest. Pottery was widely coveted and brought a handsome barter in hides, feathers, and meat.[18]

After feeding, the activity of greatest cultural import to Pueblo women was sexual intercourse. Women were empowered through their sexuality. Through sex women bore the children who would offer them labor and respect in old age. Through sex women incorporated husbands into their maternal households and expected labor and respect from them. Through sex women domesticated the wild malevolent spirits of nature and transformed them into beneficent household gods. Accordingly, then, sexuality was deemed essential for the peaceful continuation of life.

Female sexuality was theirs to give and withhold. In marriage a woman gave her husband her love and her body because of the labor he gave her mother, and because of all the marriage-validating gifts that had been given on her behalf to her in-laws. When women gave the gift of their body to men with whom no obligational ties existed, they expected something in return, such as blankets, meat, salt, and hides. For a man to enjoy a woman's body without giving her a gift in return was for him to become indebted to her in a bond of obligation.[19]

Erotic behavior in its myriad forms (heterosexuality, homosexuality, bisexuality) knew no boundaries of sex or age. Many of the great gods—the Zuñi Awonawilona, the Navajo First Man/First Woman, the Hopi Kawasaitaka katsina—were bisexual, combining the potentialities of male and female into one—a combination equally revered among humans. If the Indians sang of sex, copulated openly, staged orgiastic rituals, and named landmarks "Clitoris Spring," "Girl's Breast Point," "Buttocks-Vagina," and "Shove Penis," it was because the natural world around them was full of sexuality.[20]

Sexuality was equated with fertility, regeneration, and the holy by the Pueblo Indians, a pattern Mircea Eliade has found to be common to many societies. Humanity was dependent on sexuality for its continuation. The Acoma Indians say they were conceived when Pishuni, the serpentine deity of water, entered Nautsiti's body as rain. At the beginning of time, too, Thought Woman taught the Corn Mothers that maize would give them life if planted deep within Mother Earth's womb. When the clouds (men) poured down their rain (semen), the seeds (women) would germinate and come to life. The reader will recall that this is why a boy's penis was sprinkled with water at birth and a girl's vulva was covered with a seed-filled gourd.[21]

With the onset of menses Hopi girls were initiated into the clan-based Marau, Lakon, or Oaqol societies. Since the Hopi say that the Lakon and Oaqol ceremonies are derived from the Marau ceremony, let us focus on it. According to myth, the Marau Society was created by the Sun. He met a woman in the underworld and abducted her, and from their union came many children. Sun taught one of his sons the mysteries of the Wuwutcim (men's society) and one of his daughters those of the Marau.[22]

Twice a year, in January and in September, the Marau Society conducted a ceremony at which women officiated; at no other time did this occur. The January ceremony, which celebrated female fecundity, sexuality, and reproduction, began with four days of prayer-stick making, songs, prayers, and smokes. On the fifth day the society's initiates were inducted with a hair-washing. Throughout the next two days the women danced to awaken the sky's (men's) desires so that it would pour forth its rain (semen). Dancing naked in a circle with their backs to the community, the women would fondle clay phalluses and taunt the men with lewd songs to the clouds (rain, semen) and lightning (penis), repeatedly bending over to expose their genitals to the men. "Iss iss, iss iss," the men would cry excitedly. "I wish I wish, I wish I wish!"—wishes the women satisfied at the dance's end, cooling the passion of the men through intercourse, the symbol of cosmic harmony.[23]

The September Marau celebration was identical except for a ritual confrontation between the society's women and two men who impersonated the Twin War Gods. While the women danced holding corn-stalks with young ears of corn on them, the War Twins approached the circle and shot arrows at a bundle of produce that represented the feminine reproductive earth. The arrows symbolized lightning (penis), and their strikes germination (intercourse). The dancers then encircled the Twins and fed them cornmeal, the substance of female labor, which when exchanged as a gift symbolized peace, established affinity, and incorporated individuals into a household. When the dance ended, the women deposited the arrows at the shrine of the war gods.[24]

Warfare was a male activity among the Pueblos that was outside and beyond the moral order of society. In the continuum of reciprocities that regulated a pueblo, the taking of human life through violence was at the negative end; gifting was at the positive end, signifying the avoidance of war. Through the gifting of food and the offering of hospitality in the form of intercourse women assured communal peace. Violence was domesticated and tamed through such female ritual. And through the issue of women's bodies—children—foreigners and natives became one and were incorporated into households.[25]

These ideas were expressed poignantly during the scalp dance performed by Pueblo women when their men returned from war. Women would jubilantly greet returning war parties outside the pueblo, reported Fray Atanasio Domínguez in 1776, and together with their men would carry the scalps of the enemy dead, "singing on the way about the events of the battle . . . [with] howls, leaps, shouts, skirmishes, courses back and forth, salvos, and other demonstrations of rejoicing." When the scalps entered the pueblo, said Domínguez, "the women scornfully touch their private parts with the scalp." Another observer said that the women "bared their buttocks to it [the scalp]. They said it was their second and third husband and lay down on it as if having sexual intercourse. All of this was to take power away from the enemy." After the scalps had been robbed of their power in this way, they were attached to a large wooden pole and a dance was performed for them, which included much singing about the feats of battle and the prowess of Pueblo warriors.[26]

The Pueblos believed that an enemy's head and scalp were invested with the person's spirit; if not properly adopted, they would wreak havoc. To forestall this possibility, after the scalps were robbed of their power through intercourse, they were entrusted to women who fed them cornmeal and thereby incorporated them into a household. Beneficent fetishes now, the scalps were considered potent rain makers. "We are going to have a little rain," the Keres say, "the scalps are crying."[27]

Finally, we see the cultural importance that feeding and sexual intercourse played in domesticating all those alien and dangerous forces outside the pueblo in the deer butchering practices of the Acoma Indians. After the men killed a deer, usually through suffocation, they began the butchering by splitting open the deer's cavity. Then they removed the deer's penis, if it was male, or the vulva, if female, and placed the genitals in the stomach. This joining of genitals and stomach in a wild animal that is about to enter the village underscores the close symbolic association between sexuality and feeding. Women performed a similar rite for the deer when it entered the pueblo. First the women sexually taunted the dead deer with lewd speech, they "had" intercourse with it, fed it, and finally welcomed it into their home.[28]

The power women enjoyed by virtue of their control over the household, feeding, and sexuality was rivaled by the power men enjoyed as a result of their control over the community's relationships with its gods, which made hunting, warfare, rain making, and trade possible.

The space outside and beyond the pueblo was authentically the province of men and gained meaning in opposition to the space men controlled at the symbolic center of the town. The male conceptualization of space outlined here comes from Pueblo origin myths. Bear in mind that such myths are products of the male imagination. They are sacred knowledge that men transmitted to other men and as such were profoundly political narratives. By outlining the organization of society in mythic times, detailing who helped whom emerge when and where, men asserted their spatial claims, their rights, and their precedence in their relationships both with women and with the members of other households and clans.[29]

The men of every pueblo considered their town to be the center of the universe and placed their main kiva at the vortex of a spatial scheme that extended outward to the four cardinal points, upward to the four skies above, and downward to the underworld. Kivas were usually round (sometimes square) subterranean structures that conjoined space and time to reproduce the sacred time of emergence. Located at the center of the kiva's floor was the shipapu, the earth's navel, through which the people emerged from the underworld and through which they would return.[30]

The kiva was circular to resemble the sky. A hole in the center of the roof, the only entrance and source of light, symbolized the opening through which the Corn Mothers climbed onto the earth's surface. The profane space outside and the sacred space within the kiva were connected by a ladder called "rainbow" made of the same pine tree the sisters had used to emerge. The kiva floor had a fire altar that commemorated the gift of fire, and a hollow, dug-out place that represented the door to the house of the Sun, the Moon, and the mountains of the four cardinal points. The walls had altars on which were placed stone fetishes representing all the animals and deities of the world. Around the entire base of the kiva was an elevated ledge covered with bear and lion skins known as "fog seats." When the spirits that lived outside the pueblo were invoked and came to participate in ceremonials, they sat on these. Men's claims to precedence over women lay precisely in this capacity to bring what was outside the village into its core during religious rituals, to communicate with the gods, and thereby to order and control an otherwise chaotic and hostile natural world.[31]

Radiating outward horizontally from the kiva toward the four cardinal points were a series of tetrads that demarcated the sacral topography. The outermost tetrad was formed by the horizontal mountain peaks in which the seasonal spirits lived. In between the horizon and the pueblo were the shrines of the outlying hills and mesas. Shrines were "heaps of small stones which nature [had] formed," reported Hernán Gallegos in 1582, or holes in the earth's surface that resembled navels. People "worshiped and offered sacrifices" at these places, said Diego Pérez de Luxán, when they were "weary from their journey or troubled with any other burdens." Within the town the tetrad was repeated as directional points that all ceremonial dance circuits touched. At the center of the pueblo, the kiva united the cosmic six directions. Men owned the kivas and the sacred fetishes, altars, masks, and ritual paraphernalia contained therein.[32]

The kiva, as the navel that tied the people to their gods, was the physical symbol of political society. Each pueblo was a theocracy. At the center of political life stood the cacique, the town chief or Inside Chief, who exercised broad authority over all matters. Around him stood men of superlative knowledge in hunting, warfare, medicine magic, and rain-conjuring who by virtue of their abilities had accumulated large followings as well as large amounts of gift-stuff with which they could stage communal rites and offer gifts to others on behalf of unsuccessful villagers. Next were the unsuccessful seniors, their veneration increasing with age. Young male aspirants to the religious knowledge that would translate into political power came next. And finally, at the margins, as men saw it, were women, children, slaves, and strays.[33]

The forces of dispersion that could destroy Pueblo society were centrifugal. The political discourse that religious ritual made possible was centripetal. Men mechanistically created cosmic harmony, a requisite for social peace, only by coming together in unison at the center. Junior men moved from the margins to the center to obtain the blessings and ritual knowledge that would bring them adult status, a wife, and social power. But unlike the path of the young toward the old, of the human toward the godly, which was symbolized by movement from the margins to the center, our journey through the male world of ritual goes in the opposite direction, from the center outward. This expository strategy helps us to localize social groups in space.

Presiding over the town's main kiva, the quasi-divine Inside Chief was simultaneously a lawgiver and a peacemaker, a war lord and a high priest. He symbolized cosmic harmony and the embodiment of those forces of attraction that constituted society. He conjoined the human and the divine, the cosmological and the political, the mythic and the historic, and organized those three functions on which Pueblo religio-political life depended: administration of the sacred, exercise of physical force, and control over well-being and fecundity.[34]

The Inside Chief controlled the sacred in Pueblo society. He was the town's chief priest, a direct descendant of the Sun, "the holder of all roads of men," and the person who brought order to an otherwise chaotic cosmos. The people "esteemed and venerated the sun above all things," said Hernando de Alarcón in 1540, "because it warmed them and made the seeds germinate." Associated with the sky's greatest deity, the cacique regulated life's rhythms and assured happiness, prosperity, and long life. Appropriately, the Zuñi town chief was called Sun Speaker (*Pekwin*), and the Hopi chief, Sun Watcher (*Tawawunitaka*).[35]

The religious system the Inside Chief administered was fundamentally monistic. Humans, animals, natural forces, and supernatural spirits were all intricately related in balanced ties of reciprocity. The cosmic harmony every person desired was subject to human mechanistic control. So long as people performed religious rites joyfully and precisely, careful that every prayer was word-perfect and full of verve, and that the ritual paraphernalia was exact to the last detail, the forces of nature would reciprocate with their own uninterrupted flow. The sun would rise and set properly, the seasons of the year would come and go, bringing rainfall and verdant crops in summer, and in the winter, game and snow.[36]

The cacique's central imperative was to keep the cosmos properly balanced so that humanity did not swerve from life's road. So long as the forces of evil that threatened to disrupt society were rendered impotent through ritual, peace and prosperity reigned. The Inside Chief accomplished this by calling together the men in the town's households and clans for ritual purposes and by acting as arbiter of law and order. As high priest, the cacique was the keeper of sacred time. From the heights of the town's dwellings he watched the courses of the sun and moon and with amazing accuracy announced the summer and winter solstices, the vernal and autumnal equinoxes, and all the dates for planting, harvest, initiations, and rain and curing rites. At appropriate points in the lunar year, the cacique entered the town's main kiva, and by ritually recreating the primordial time of emergence when humans and gods were one, and when all a town's clans, kivas, and esoteric societies were in harmony, he temporarily obliterated local enmities and tensions.[37]

*recreation of cosmogony*

If the Inside Chief's administration of the sacred was a harmonizing power, the antithesis—violence, human domination, and the negation of the community's moral order, what we will call physical force—was in the hands of the Outside Chiefs, war chiefs who protected the village from external, natural, and supernatural enemies.[38]

The Outside Chiefs were the divine sons of Father Sun, Masewi (Wren Youth) and Oyoyewi (Mockingbird Youth), also known as the Twin War Gods, say the Acoma Indians. The Twins were conceived miraculously when an ordinary woman ate two pine nuts the Sun gave her. As youngsters the Twins were fearless warriors, roving the countryside, causing mischief, terrorizing others, and killing with those instruments of war their father had given them: bows, arrows, and flint arrowheads.[39]

*Outside chiefs*

The mythic tales of the Twin War Gods explained the use of force in Pueblo life. Physical force was born of the godhead through an act of copulation with a woman who represented the land's people. The sons were of their father's essence but were also his antithesis. At the center of society such brutish and terrorizing boys would have wreaked havoc. And so they were pushed to the peripheries as the Outside Chiefs to rule over all that was outside of the village. There, their violence befitted external threats to tranquillity. Localizing functions and social groups in space, we find that warfare was conceived of as marginal, young, and outside the pueblo, while the sacred was at the center, old, and inside the town.

Warfare was the most generalized masculine task in Pueblo society. Before boys could become men, they had to establish themselves as competent warriors. To do this, young men sought out a "warrior father" (usually the war chief or Outside Chief) of great bravery and skill to teach them the prayers, songs, dances, and esoteric lore that would give them power over enemies. Through offering the warrior father numerous gifts, aspiring warriors were gradually taught how to harness the power of the prey animals for success in battle. I want to emphasize the word gradually here, because knowledge was power, and as such it was in the interest of the warrior father to dispense his knowledge slowly. By so doing he maintained a large following and acquired numerous gifts with which he could indebt others and gather the means to stage large raids.[40]

*young men as warriors*

Besides the town's main kiva, male ritual associations devoted to war, curing, hunting, and rain-making each had its own kiva that doubled as a lodge house. Warrior novices lived in the warrior society kiva and there their warrior father taught them bravery, endurance, and agility. Before the arrival of European horses in the Southwest, all warfare was conducted on foot, so running fast was also a cultivated skill.[41]

When men practiced war magic they had to have pure minds and hearts. For the four days before and after war, they refrained from sexual intercourse and purified themselves with sweat baths and emetic drinks. Offering smokes to the war gods and singing war songs, they prayed for success. To obtain the ferocity and strength of bears, the cunning of lions, and the sharp vision of eagles, the warriors took their war fetishes shaped in the likeness of animals, bathed them in human blood and fed them pieces of human hearts that had been torn from the breasts of enemies in previous victories. When all the ritual preparations for warfare were complete, the warriors marched into battle.[42]

Once a young man had proven himself by killing an enemy he was inducted into the warrior society through an ordeal. The Zuñi Bow War Society required its initiates to sit naked atop a large ant hill for a day and submit stolidly to the insects' bites. Members of the Hopi, Zuñi, and Tewa Cactus War societies whipped themselves with cacti. Such a benumbing ordeal also marked the installation of a war chief.[43]

The opposing forces harmonized by the town chieftaincy—Inside Chief versus Outside Chiefs, center versus margin, old versus young, native versus foreign, law versus force—were dependent on the existence of fecundity and well-being. This third essential component of religious life was controlled competitively by three chieftaincies: the rain chiefs, the hunt chiefs, and the medicine men.

The chiefs who directed the hunt, rain, and medicine societies knew well the godly transmitted mysteries of life and death. Women might know the life-giving secrets of Mother Earth, seeds, and child-bearing, but through ritual men controlled the key to the positive and negative reciprocities in their world, which at any moment could be turned to life or death. The heart (which contained the breath and spirit of humans, animals, and deities) and blood were the symbols of the rituals staged by men to assure communal peace and fertility. Just as feeding was a central part of female ritual, so too men regularly gave life to their fetishes, bathing them in nourishing blood and symbolically feeding them bits of heart. Men also fed the earth with their own blood, whipping themselves crimson when they sought those blessings that assured fertility.

Rain was the Pueblo Indians' central preoccupation and the essential ingredient for fecundity. Men recognized that Mother Earth and women had immense capacities to bring forth life, but to realize this potential the sky had to fructify the earth with rain and men their wives with semen. Thus what the people worshipped most, said Hernando de Alarcón in 1540, was "the sun and water." Why did they worship water? According to Coronado it was "because it makes the maize grow and sustains their life, and that the only other reason they know is that their ancestors did so."[44]

The rain chief was one of the most powerful men in every village because he knew how to conjure rain both by calling Horned Water Snake and the katsina. The Pueblos equated serpentine deities with rain. The Horned Water Serpent of the Pueblos united the vertical levels of the cosmos. He lived both upon the earth and below it and so combined the masculine germinative forces of the sky (rain) with the feminine generation power of the earth (seeds). The phallic representations of Horned Water Snake were cloaked in feathers as a god of lightning and rain. The earliest Pueblo rock drawings depict him as a zigzag line with a horned triangular head and as a lightning snake attached to a cloudburst.[45]

The Pueblo Dead—the katsina—were also potent rain spirits, tied to the living in bonds of reciprocity. It was the rain chief who knew how to call the katsina and did so by offering them prayer sticks and gifts, asking them to visit with rain, food, and fertility. Katsina lived at the place of emergence underneath lakes and on mountaintops. Missives to the katsina were dispatched as puffs of smoke, which as mimetic magic beckoned the cloud spirits to visit. At death Puebloans became clouds. That is why to this day the Hopi harangue their dead, saying: "You are no longer a Hopi, you are a Cloud. When you get yonder you will tell the chief to hasten the rain clouds hither."[46]

After warfare, hunting was the broadest male task in Pueblo society. Men contributed meat to the maize diet at every pueblo, but it was at those villages dependent exclusively on rainfall for crop irrigation that hunting magic was most important. Boys learned hunting techniques by observing renowned hunters and by listening to their animal stories. When a boy killed his first rabbit, he was initiated into a hunt society and apprenticed to a hunt father who gradually taught him the prayers, songs, and magical ways of the hunt in return for gifts of corn and meat. The novice became a full member of the society when he captured a large game animal (deer, antelope, or mountain sheep). If by chance he killed a prey animal (bear, lion, or eagle), he automatically became a member of the warrior society, because hunting and warfare were considered very similar activities.[47]

Hunting practices for rabbit, antelope, deer, and buffalo were all very similar. We focus here on deer hunting because deer meat was the most abundant and highly prized, and because men thought of women as two-legged deer. A deer hunt was organized whenever food reserves were low, when a ceremonial was to be staged, or when the katsina were going to visit.

For four days the hunt chief led the hunt society's members in song, prayer, prayer-stick making, and smokes. During this time the eldest male of each household brought his lineage "offspring" animal fetish to the kiva and placed it next to the hunt chief's "mother" fetish on the society's altar. There the hunt chief empowered the fetishes with animal spirits for a successful hunt by bathing them in nourishing blood and feeding them small bits of the animal they were going to hunt. These fetishes contained the living heart and breath of the animals they depicted. When the hunt chief empowered them, he unleashed the fetish's heart and breath. The fetish's breath immediately pierced the heart of the hunted animal, sapped its soul's energy, and immobilized it. In this state the hunted animal was easily overcome.[48]

During these four days, and for four days after the hunt, men were sexually continent. Hunters believed that animals disliked the smell of women and would not allow themselves to be captured by a man so contaminated. To rid himself of such odor, a hunter purified his body with emetic drinks and smokes. If a man was to accomplish his goal, neither his mind nor his heart could be dissipated by the thought of women.[49]

The hunt began on the fourth day. Transformed into the animals they hunted, the hunters donned deerskins with the head and antlers still attached. The hunt chief selected the hunting ground and dispersed the men around its edges, forming a large circle. Slowly the circumference of the circle tightened and the deer became exhausted. Finally the deer were wrestled to the ground and choked. A deer was suffocated so that its breath and spirit would be reborn as more game, and because only the skins of suffocated animals could be used as hunt costumes.[50]

The deer was immediately skinned and disemboweled. First its heart was cut out and its blood was fed to the animal fetishes the hunters carried in their pouches. Next the stomach was removed and opened. If a doe, its vulva was placed in the stomach and sprinkled with corn pollen; if a buck, the penis and testicles were similarly treated. The carcass was then carried back to the pueblo, where it was adopted into the hunter's maternal household through ritual intercourse and ritual feeding. "We are glad you have come to our home and have not been ashamed of our people," Acoma's women would tell the deer as they offered it cornmeal. The hunter's relatives rubbed their hands over the deer's body and then across their own faces to obtain its beauty and strength. Finally, the hunter purified himself with juniper smoke so that the deer spirit would not haunt him. The meat was divided between the hunt chief who had taught the boy how to hunt and the hunter's household of affilia-tion.[51]

A pueblo's prosperity was fundamentally dependent on the physical and psychological well-being of its members. Thus every village had several *chaianyi*, medicine men who cured illnesses and exorcised disease-causing witches who robbed human hearts of their breath and spirit. As knowledgeable herbalists, the *chaianyi* cured minor ailments; but if a disease seemed unique, longlasting, or particularly debilitating, witchcraft was its cause. Witches wrought calamities and illnesses by shooting objects into the body of their victim or by stealing their heart. Using tactics similar to those of hunters, witches sapped people of their strength by attacking their heart. Since witches plied their craft disguised as ani-mals, medicine men had to fight them as animals. That is why *chaianyi* were known as bears (the fiercest animal humans knew) and their magic as "bear medicine." In such form medicine men could help people regain their health, winning back their heart and sucking out the objects shot into them by the witch.[52]

When an individual or a community was afflicted by disease, a cure by the medicine man known to have power over that illness was requested through gifts. For four days the medicine man prepared himself, smoking, making prayer-sticks, reciting the necessary prayers and songs, and abstaining from meat, salt, and sex. He made offerings at appropri-ate shrines, obtained water for medicines from sacred springs, erected an altar, and arranged on it fetishes, medicine bowls, and curing paraphernalia. When all was ready, the sick individual was placed on the floor before the altar. Near the patient, the medicine man made a circular sand painting representing all the powerful forces in the cosmos. Then, to obtain the power to cure from the "real" medicine men, the animals, he prayed to the bear fetish for the power of all the animals on earth, to the eagle fetish for the power of the ani-mals in the air, and to the weasel fetish for the power of the animals in the ground. Each of these fetishes was fed and bathed in blood from the heart of the animal they represented. Wearing a bear claw necklace with four claws, and holding eagle plumes in each hand, the medicine man "whipped away" the disease with cutting motions. If a quartz crystal with which the person's body was examined revealed foreign objects, the medicine man sucked them out. If the patient's heart had been stolen, the *chaianyi* fought with the witches to re-trieve it. When the ceremony ended, the patient drank medicines and returned home cured. If for some reason the patient died, the presumption was that the ceremony had not been properly conducted or that the *chaianyi's* heart was impure.[53]

In sum, entering male ceremonialism from the edges and moving toward the center, we first find the chiefs who controlled well-being and fertility (rain, hunt, and medicine chiefs), then the Outside Chiefs who organized physical force, and finally, at the core, the Inside Chief who represented the sacred powers of attraction that constituted political so-ciety. Through apprenticeship in a town's various societies, junior men gradually learned the religious knowledge they needed to assure prosperity and guarantee their personal ad-vance to senior status. Religious knowledge allowed men to harness and control those nat-ural forces outside the pueblo which the gods ruled, and to bring them peacefully into the core; it gave them the power to kill, and by so doing assured life. By carefully executing pre-scribed ritual formulas, they preserved the relationship of reciprocity that existed between men and the spirit world and kept the fragile structure of the cosmos intact.

Men envisioned a cosmos in which masculinity and femininity were relatively balanced. But the social world really was not so. In a largely horticultural society women asserted and could prove that they had enormous control and power over seed production, child-rearing, household construction, and the earth's fertility. Men admitted this. But they made a counterclaim that men's ability to communicate with the gods and to control life and death protected the precarious balance in the universe by forestalling village factionalism and dissent. The tendency of women to overproduce had to be properly controlled through the religious activities of men. Women's voraciousness for semen and the earth's infinite capacity to soak up rain sapped masculinity of its potence. This was indeed the case, explains Jane Collier, regarding gender concepts in "equal bridewealth" societies. On a daily basis women appropriated men's vital energies: the crops they planted, the children they engendered, and the meat from their hunts. Men thus frequently renewed their energies by segregating themselves from women and staging ceremonials to assure successful hunts, war, curing, and rain-making. Because potent femininity polluted and rendered male magic impotent, men abstained from sex with women for a prescribed period before and after their rituals. It is easy to understand the roots of these gender concepts in the social division of labor. The ecological constraints of the habitat in which men pursued their productive activities made their world precarious. Who could predict defeat in battle, disease, factionalism, drought, or poor hunting?[54]

It is as part of this contestation between the sexes over the cosmic power of men and women, and the masculine assertion that ritual give them a dominant hand, that we can best understand the place and function of the "third sex" in Pueblo life, the half-men/half-women, as the natives still know them, or the berdache (from the Arabic *bradaj*, meaning male prostitute), as the sixteenth-century Europeans called them.[55]

The berdache were biological males who had assumed the dress, occupations, mannerisms, and sexual comportment of females as a result of a sacred vision or community selection. Hernando de Alarcón in 1540 observed that in those villages where he found berdaches, they numbered four. Four was a sacred number to the Pueblo Indians; there were four horizontal directions, four seasons, four lengths to Wenimats, four days of preparation before ritual, and so on. Alarcón was told that if one of the four berdaches died, "a search was made for all the pregnant women in the land, and the first born was chosen to exercise the function of women. The women dressed them in their clothes, saying that if they were to act as such they should wear their clothes."[56] Alvar Núñez Cabeza de Vaca observed berdaches during his 1523–33 trek across Texas and New Mexico: "I saw one man married to another and these are impotent, effeminate men and they go about dressed as women, and do women's tasks, and shoot with a bow, and carry great burdens . . . and they are huskier than the other men and taller."[57]

That the berdache were consistently described as men abnormally tall and heavy led Fray Juan Agustín de Morfi in the 1770s and Dr. William A. Hammond, the U.S. Surgeon-General, in the 1850s to wonder if they were intersexuals. Morfi pondered the matter and admitted uncertainty; Hammond uncovered the "facts," examining the genitals of an Acoma and a Laguna berdache. To Hammond's amazement, neither was a hermaphrodite. Both had large mammary glands, scant pubic hair, small penises ("no larger than a thimble," "not . . . over an inch in length"), and small testicles ("the size of a small filbert," "about the size of a kidney bean"). More significant were the comments Hammond elicited from the Acoma berdache: "He told me that he had nursed several infants whose mothers had died, and that he had given them plenty of milk from his breasts. I expressed my doubts of the truth of this assertion, but he persisted with vehemence that it was true . . . he informed me with evident pride, [that he] possessed a large penis and his testicles were 'grandes como huevos'—as large as eggs." Despite the physiological realities, the Acoma berdache believed herself (she was always referred to with the feminine pronoun) to possess the reproductive capacities of both male and female. Rising above the basic dualities that structured the world, she symbolized the *coincidentia oppositorum*, the joining of opposites that men created in ritual.[58]

Pre-menopausal women polluted male ritual and were thus excluded from active participation in all kiva-centered ceremonials. According to Gallegos, when men gathered to renew the universe or to recreate primordial time "only the men take part, the women never." The participants in these rituals "wore the masks and dress of both men and women even though they were all men," attested Don Esteban Clemente in 1660, even to the point of smearing the insides of their legs with rabbit blood to resemble menstrual discharge.[59]

Ritual female impersonators may not all have been berdaches, but the historical evidence does seem to indicate this. On the basis of the berdaches' role in Pueblo ritual we see again the male assertion that they controlled all aspects of human life. Women had power only over half of creation; through ritual men controlled its entirety—male and female—and were thus equal if not superior to women. Women obviously contested this claim.

The emphasis male ritual placed on village cooperation and social peace also explains in purely functional terms the meaning of the berdache. As sacred half-man/half-woman who conjoined all that was male and female, she was a living symbol of cosmic harmony. Castañeda witnessed a boy's initiation as a berdache in 1540 and described how the women endowed him with female clothing, turquoises, and bracelets:

> Then the dignitaries came in to make use of her one at a time, and after them all the others who cared to. From then on she was not to deny herself to any one, as she was paid a certain established amount for the service. And even though she might take a husband later on, she was not thereby free to deny herself to any one who offered her pay.

Alarcón added that the berdaches who dressed and behaved like women "could not have carnal relations with women at all, but they themselves could be used by all marriageable youths. . . . They receive no compensation for this work . . . although they were free to take from any house what they needed for their living." As noted earlier, bachelors were residentially segregated in kivas until they married, ostensibly to master male esoteric lore, but also to minimize conflicts between juniors and seniors over claims to female sexuality that adult married men enjoyed. Sex with a berdache served a personal erotic need and a religious (political) end. So long as bachelors were having sex with the half-man/half-woman, the social peace they represented was not beset with village conflicts between men over women. This may have been why the Spaniards called the berdaches *putos* (male whores). European prostitutes initiated young men to sexuality and gave married men a sexual outlet without disrupting family, marriage, or patrimony.[60]

These, then, were the contours of Pueblo Indian society in the sixteenth century. Each pueblo was an aggregation of sedentary horticulturists living in extended matrilineal households, supplementing their existence through hunting and warfare. Elders controlled the organization of production and, through the distribution of its fruits as gifts and ritual blessings, perpetuated the main inequalities of life; the inequality between juniors and seniors and between successful and unsuccessful seniors. The household and all the activities symbolically related to it belonged to women; the kivas and the pueblo's relationships with its gods were the province of men.

## NOTES

The following abbreviated note citations are based on the manuscript sources and bibliography found in Ramón A. Gutiérrez, *When Jesus Came, the Corn Mothers Went Away: Marriage, Sexuality, and Power in New Mexico, 1500–1846* (Stanford University Press, 1991), 343–345, 389–415.

1. Several versions of Acoma Pueblo's origin myth exist. Here I have used Stirling's *Origin Myth of Acoma*, which is a transcription of a 1928 Bureau of American Ethnology taped interview with several Acoma Indians. The chief Acoma informant learned the origin myth as a youth during his initiation to the Koshari Society, a group of sacred clowns to whom all religious knowledge was entrusted. Other versions of the Acoma emergence myth can be found in White, *The Acoma Indians*; Boas, *Keresan Texts*; D. Ford, "A Creation Myth from Acoma"; J. Gunn, *Schat-Chen*; PIR, 242–48; Tyler, *Pueblo Gods and Myths*.

2. Several transliterations of katsina appear in ethnographic literature, including kachina, katcina, cachina, and catzina. The origins and significance of the katsina in Pueblo religion can be found in Dockstader, *The Katchina and the White Man*; Anderson, "The Pueblo Kachina Cult"; Bunzel, *Zuñi Katcinas*; Ellis, "A Pantheon of Kachinas"; Fewkes, "An interpretation of Katcina Worship"; Schaafsma and Schaafsma, "Pueblo Kachina Cult."

3. C. Lévi-Strauss, *Structural Anthropology* (New York, 1963), 220–21.

4. Eliade, *The Myth of the Eternal Return*. My understanding of the relationship between myth and history has been greatly influenced by Sahlins, *The Islands of History*, 56–60; Dumézil, *The Destiny of the Warrior*, 3–II; Vansina, *Oral Tradition as History*, 13–25; Eliade, *Patterns in Comparative Religion*, 388–409.

5. Stirling, *Origin Myth of Acoma*, 41–42. White, *The Acoma Indians*, 133–34.

6. My understanding of the politics of gift comes largely from Collier, *Marriage and Inequality*, 79–92; R. Ford, "Barter, Gift or Violence"; W. Jacobs, *Wilderness Politics and Gifts*; Mauss, *The Gift*; Sahlins, *Stone Age Economics*, 149–276; Whitehead, "Fertility and Exchange in New Guinea"; Meeker, Barlow, and Lipset, "Culture, Exchange, and Gender."

7. Collier, *Marriage and Inequality*, 103–5.

8. Stirling, *Origin Myth of Acoma*, 50–59.

9. RNM, 86; PIR, 43.

10. Collier, *Marriage and Inequality*, 71–141.

11. NCE, 174. RNM, 193–94. NCE, 183, 215.

12. Collier, *Marriage and Inequality*, 76.

13. Parsons, "Hopi Mothers and Children," 100. PIR, 182. See also Sjö and Mor, *The Great Cosmic Mother*.

14. Niethammer, *Daughters of the Earth*, 11; Parsons, "Mothers and Children at Zuñi," 168; Haeberlin, *The Idea of Fertilization*; Collier, *Marriage and Inequality*, 131–33; Duberman, ed., "Documents in Hopi Indian Sexuality," 124.

15. Declaration of Marcelo Espinosa, 1601, OD, 636.

16. Eggan, *Social Organization of the Western Pueblos*, 231–32, 291–324; Benedict, *Patterns of Culture*, 75–76. RNM, 86. Fox, *Kinship and Marriage*, 90.

17. NCE, 256.

18. Qoyawayma, *No Turning Back*, 5; RNM, 85. On female domestic production, also see NCE, 158–59, 183, 252, 255; RNM, 85, 172.

19. The gifts women demanded for sex are mentioned numerous places. See NCE, 248; RNM, 206; RBM, 43–44; HD vol. 3, 149, 184; AGN-INQ, 587–1: 19, 60, 64, 140.

20. Tyler, *Pueblo Gods and Myths*, 81; Hill, "Hermaphrodite and Transvestite in Navaho Culture"; Titiev, *Hopi Indians*, 153, 214–15. Titiev, *Old Oraibi*, 206; Hay, "The Hammond Report," 20. Ritual copulation is described in PIR, 566–67, 644, 805; Affidavits of Kuanwikvaya (1920), Steve Quonestewa (April 14, 1921), Quoyawyma (April 16, 1921), and L.R. McDonald (May 11, 1915) in the National Anthropological Archives, the Smithsonian Institution (Washington, D.C.). Bestiality, fellatio, and phallic clowning are reported in the affidavits of Siventiwa (1920), William H. Pfeifer (November 13, 1920), Blas Casaus (November 7, 1915), Otto Lomauitu (1920), and Emory A. Marks (December 11, 1920) deposited at the National Anthropological Archives.

21. Eliade, *Patterns in Comparative Religion*, 239–64, 331–66. PIR, 428–31. Niethammer, *Daughters of the Earth*, 11.

22. Fewkes, "The Tusayan New-fire Ceremony," 447; Titiev, *Old Oraibi*, 164.

23. Titiev, *Hopi Indians*, 164–65; Voth, *The Oraibi Ceremony*, 32; Duberman, ed., "Documents in Hopi Sexuality," 108–13; *PIR*, 675–82.

24. Titiev, *Hopi Indians*, 166–67; Schlegel, "Male and Female in Hopi Thought and Action."

25. Sahlins, *Stone Age Economics*, 149–276; Whitehead, "Fertility and Exchange in New Guinea."

26. *MNM*, 257. Other scalp dances are described and analyzed in *PIR*, 624–25, 644–45; Bunzel, "Zuñi Ritual Poetry," 679; Parsons, *The Scalp Ceremonial of Zuñi*.

27. *PRI*, 350–51; White, *The Pueblo of Santo Domingo*, 144–48.

28. White, *New Material from Acoma*, 336.

29. I thank Jane Collier for bringing this point to my attention. See also Yava, *Big Falling Snow*; and Talayesva, *Sun Chief*.

30. This spatial model is best described by Ortiz in *The Tewa World*, 11–28; Stubbs, *Bird's-Eye View of the Pueblos*; Tyler, *Pueblo Gods and Myths*, 169–79.

31. White, *The Acoma Indians*, 132. Stephen, *Hopi Journal*, vol. 2, 119on.

32. *RNM*, 101; *RBM*, 43; *RNM*, 193–94.

33. White, *Pueblo of Santa Ana*, 187; Parsons, *Hopi and Zuñi Ceremonialism*, 53; Schroeder, "Rio Grande Ethnohistory," 51.

34. These three categories of male political life come from Dumézil, *The Destiny of the Warrior* and *The Destiny of a King*.

35. *NCE*, 135. *PIR*, 169; Titiev, *Old Oraibi*, 131.

36. Bellah, "Religious Systems," 227–64; Benedict, *Patterns of Culture*, 54–55; Dozier, *Pueblo Indians of North America*, 151.

37. Bellah, "Religious Systems," 230. McCluskey, "The Astronomy of the Hopi Indians."

38. Tyler, *Pueblo Gods and Myths*, 219; *PIR*, 125.

39. Stirling, *Origin Myth of Acoma*, 97. Tyler, *Pueblo Gods and Myths*, 213.

40. Ibid. Those interested in the role that secrecy and the distribution of esoteric knowledge plays in creating and perpetuating inequality should consult Brandt, "On Secrecy and the Control of Knowledge," and "The Role of Secrecy in a Pueblo Society."

41. Nabokov, *Indian Running*.

42. Ellis, "Patterns of Aggression"; Woodbury, "A Reconsideration of Pueblo Warfare." Pueblo war societies have been extinct since the seventeeth century. To understand what Pueblo warrior societies may have been like, I studied warfare in other Indian tribes. See Hill, *Navaho Warfare*; Guernsey, "Notes on a Navajo War Dance"; Parsons, "Notes on a Navajo War Dance"; Bandelier, "On the Art of War and Mode of Warfare"; Ellis, "Patterns of Aggression"; Farmer, "Defensive Systems of the Southwest"; Hadlock, "Warfare Among the Northeastern Woodland Indians"; Mishkin, *Rank and Warfare Among the Plains Indians*; M. Smith, "The War Complex of the Plains Indians," and "American Indian Warfare"; Stewart, "Mohave Warfare."

43. *NCE*, 249; Bandelier, *Final Report of Investigations*, Part I, 69–70; *RBM*, 44; R. Smith, "Mexican and Anglo-Saxon Traffic in Scalps, Slaves, and Livestock," *West Texas Historical Association Year Book* (1960), 98–115. *RMB*, 239n. *PIR*, 467, 875, 923; J. Green, ed., *Zuñi: Selected Writing of Frank Hamilton Cushing* (Lincoln, 1979), passim.

44. Collier, *Marriage and Inequality*, 131–32. *NCE*, 184. Ibid., 175.

45. Fewkes, "A Few Tusayan Pictographs," 16–17; N. Judd, *The Material Culture of Pueblo Bonito*, 278. On phallic/serpentine symbolism see León, "El Culto del Falo"; Stoddard, "Phallic Symbols in America"; Lejeal, "Rites Phalliques."

46. *PIR*, 173. *RNM*, 99; *NCE*, 184, 258; *PIR*, 171. Katsina is a Hopi word meaning "respect spirit" (*ka*, respect, and *china*, spirit); the word is used here generically to refer to those cloud-beings known at Taos as *thlatsi* or *thliwa*, at Isleta as *wenin* or *thliwa*, at Jémez as *k'ats'ana* or *dysa*, and to the Tewa as *oxuhwa*. To Frederick Dockstader katsina means "life father" or "spirit father" (from *kachi*, life or spirit, and *na*, father). See Dockstader's *The Kachina and the White Man*, 9.

47. Tyler, *Pueblo Animals*, 32–35; Beaglehole, *Hopi Hunting*, 4–7; Underhill, *Ceremonial Patterns*, 30; Scully, *Pueblo*, 67.

48. Cushing, *Zuñi Fetishes*, 15.

49. Tyler, *Pueblo Animals*, 35–36. Beaglehole, *Hopi Hunting*, 6.

50. Driving animals into pits, into natural culs de sac, or over mesa tops were also common hunting techniques. Beaglehole, *Hopi Hunting*, 8.

51. White, *New Material from Acoma*, 336. Stirling, *Origin Myth of Acoma*, 24–25. Beaglehole, *Hopi Hunting*, 7, 11, 13. See also Bonnegjea, "Hunting Superstitions"; Hill, *Agriculture and Hunting Methods*.

52. Schlegel, "Socialization of a Hopi Girl," 453.

53. The illnesses and curses associated with various curing societies can be found in *PIR*, 189–92 and Titiev, *Old Oraibi*, 241. White, *The Acoma Indians*, 107–27; Underhill, *Ceremonial Patterns*, 38; Tyler, *Pueblo Animals*, 184–202; Simmons,

*Witchcraft in the Southwest*, 69–95; Parsons, "Witchcraft Among the Pueblos." It should be noted that although women could and still do become *chaianyi*, the Spanish friars and explorers never mentioned them as such. Rather, as shown in chapters 2 and 10, they thought of native women with religious or magical powers as witches.

Most pueblos today have clown societies. They probably existed in the sixteenth century but were not mentioned by the Europeans. I suspect that the Spanish chroniclers could not differentiate between the medicine men and their assistants, the clowns. On Pueblo clowning see Stirling, *Origin Myth of Acoma*, 33; Hieb, "Meaning and Mismeaning"; Erodes and Ortiz, *American Indian Myths and Legends*, 333–86.

54. Collier, *Marriage and Inequality*, 131–33.

55. These "men-women" were known to the Zuñi as *la'mana,* to the Tewa as *quetho*, and to the Navajo as *nadle*. They existed among the Keres (Acoma, Laguna, and Santa Ana) and Hopi, but I have not been able to locate their indigenous names. Parsons, "The Zuñi La'Mana"; S. Jacobs, "Comment"; Hill, "The Status of the Hermaphrodite"; Gifford, "Cultural Elements Distribution"; Fewkes, "A Few Tusayan Pictographs," AA, 5 (1892), 11.

56. Male berdache status has been reported in 113 North American Indian cultures; female berdache in only 30. The Navaho, Western Apache, and Utes are the only Southwestern Indian groups known to have female berdache. The berdache tradition is best studied in Callender and Kochems, "The North American Berdache"; S. Jacobs, "Berdache"; Williams, *The Spirit and the Flesh*. On female berdaches see Whitehead, "The Bow and the Burden Strap." Those interested in the cross-cultural meaning of homoeroticism and homosexuality will find the following works illuminating: Herdt, *Guardians of the Flute, Rituals of Manhood, and Ritualized Homosexuality in Melanesia*; Sergent, *Homosexuality in Greek Myth*; Boswell, *Christianity*; Ariès and Béjin, *Western Sexuality*; J. Trevisan, *Perverts in Paradise: Homosexuality in Brazil, from the Colonial Period to the Present* (New York, 1986); E. Blackwood, ed., *The Many Faces of Homosexuality*.

57. *NCE*, 130, 148. "Naufrahios de Alvar Núñez Cabeza de Vaca," quoted in Jonathan Katz, *Gay American History*, 285.

58. Fray Juan Agustín Morfi cited in Newcomb, *The Indians of Texas*, 74; Hammond, "The Disease of the Scythians." Ibid., 334–36. Eliade, *Mephistopheles and the Androgyne*, 78–124, and *Patterns in Comparative Religion*, 356–61, 419–25.

59. *RNM*, 99–100. Declaration of Don Esteban Clemente, 1660, *AGN-INQ* 587–1:123. Duberman, ed., "Documents in Hopi Indian Sexuality," 116. Hay, "The Hammond Report," 18.

60. *NCE*, 248. Ibid., 147–48.

# A WORLD OF WONDERS

*David D. Hall*

Historians traditionally have presented the Puritan religion of seventeenth-century New Englanders as a rational and coherent intellectual system. In breaking with the superstitions of the past, and especially Catholicism, the Puritans apparently turned away from the "magic" of sacraments and sacred places. Recent work in colonial history, however, suggests that the colonists lived within a broader, older "world of wonders." Rather than initiating the world's disenchantment, seventeenth-century Puritans mixed together what we in "modern" times try to separate as Christianity, on the one hand, and as magical beliefs and practices, on the other.

In David Hall's rendering, the Europeans who settled North America brought with them a widespread belief in magic and the occult. Witchcraft, apparitions, and other unearthly phenomena as well as supernatural explanations of natural events such as comets, hailstorms, earthquakes, sudden deaths, and monster births pervaded New England culture. Unlike England, where the popular culture of the laity was frequently at odds with the "official" religion of the clergy, popular religion as described by Hall was accessible to everyone, providing a language that all groups shared. It is nothing new to assert that seventeenth-century New England was culturally homogeneous. What makes Hall's argument revisionist is his belief that this common culture did not derive from Puritan theology. Rather, what the clergy and educated laity held in common was a far more enchanted universe laced with the "debris" of other systems of thought, some older than Christianity.

Reprinted by permission from David D. Hall, "A World of Wonders: The Mentality of the Supernatural in Seventeenth-Century New England," in Hall and David Grayson Allen, eds., *Seventeenth-Century New England* (Boston: The Colonial Society of Massachusetts, 1984), 239–274.

# 2

# A WORLD OF WONDERS

## The Mentality of the Supernatural
## in Seventeenth-Century New England

*David D. Hall*

THE PEOPLE of seventeenth-century New England lived in an enchanted universe. Theirs was a world of wonders. Ghosts came to people in the night, and trumpets blared, though no one saw from where the sound emerged. Nor could people see the lines of force that made a "long staff dance up and down in the chimney" of William Morse's house. In this enchanted world, the sky on a "clear day" could fill with "many companies of armed men in the air, clothed in light-colored garments, and the commander in sad [somber]." Many of the townsfolk of New Haven had seen a phantom ship sail regally into the harbor. An old man in Lynn had espied

> a strange black cloud in which after some space he saw a man in arms complete standing with
> his legs straddling and having a pike in his hands which he held across his breast . . . ; after a
> while the man vanished in whose room appeared a spacious ship seeming under sail though
> she kept the same station.

Voices spoke from heaven, and little children uttered warnings. Bending over his son Joseph's cradle one evening, an astonished Samuel Sewall heard him say, "The French are coming."[1]

All of these events were "wonders" to the colonists, events betokening the presence of superhuman or supernatural forces. In seventeenth-century New England it was common to speak of the providence of God as "wonder-working."[2] Some wonders were like miracles in being demonstrations of God's power to suspend or interrupt the laws of nature. Others were natural events that God employed as portents or signals of impending change. The events that Cotton Mather described in *Wonders of the Invisible World* were the handiwork of Satan and his minions. A wonder could also be something unexpected or extraordinary, like a sudden death or freak coincidence.[3]

In the course of the seventeenth century, many of the colonists would experience a wonder and many others tell stories of them. Either way, these events aroused strong feelings. An earthquake in New England in 1638 had caused divers men (that had never known an Earthquake before) being at work in the fields, to cast down their working tools, and run with ghastly terrified looks, to the next company they could meet withall.[4]

Almost a century later, as an earthquake rocked Boston, the "young people" in Samuel Sewall's house "were quickly frighted out of the shaking clattering kitchen, and fled with weeping cries into" their father's bedroom, "where they made a fire, and abode there till morning." In responding to such "marvellous" events, people used words like "awful," "terrible," and "amazing" to describe what had happened.[5] Every wonder made visible and real the immense forces that impinged upon the order of the world. A wonder reaffirmed the insecurity of existence and the majesty of a supreme God.

This essay is about the wonder as the colonists would know and tell of it. At the outset, we may dispose of one false issue: the people in New England who heard voices and saw apparitions were not deluded fanatics or "primitive" in their mentality. The possibility of these experiences was widely affirmed as credible in the best science and religion of the early seventeenth century. We can never answer with complete satisfaction the question as to why some persons do see ghosts or witness apparitions. But for the people of seventeenth-century Europe and America, these were ordinary events that many persons encountered, and many more believed in.

This is an essay, therefore, about phenomena that occurred on both sides of the Atlantic, and among both Protestants and Catholics. We may speak of a lore of wonders, an accumulation of stock references and literary conventions that descended to the colonists from Scripture, antiquity, the early Church and the Middle Ages. People in the seventeenth century inherited a lore that stretched back to the Greeks and Romans. Chaucer had told of portents and prodigies in *The Canterbury Tales*, as had the author of *The Golden Legend*, a medieval collection of saints' lives. Whenever the colonists spoke or wrote of wonders, they drew freely on this lore; theirs was a borrowed language.

To speak of continuity is to raise two other questions: how did this lore pass to the colonists, and how did it consort with their doctrinal understanding of the universe? The key intermediaries in transmitting an old language to the colonists were the English printer-booksellers who published great quantities of wonder tales in the sixteenth and seventeenth centuries. They had allies in certain writers who put together collections of this lore to suit new purposes, like the emergence of Protestantism. Protestants drew freely on the lore of wonders, adapting it to indicate the merits of their cause. To this end Luther had retold the story of a "monster" fish found in the River Tiber, interpreting it as a portent of Rome's mistakes. And the wonder could serve to reinforce the concept of God's providence, a doctrine of importance to the early Reformers.

But what of all the "superstitions" that this lore reiterated? The language of the wonder was rich in motifs and assumptions that seem at odds with the mentality of the Puritans who colonized New England. In breaking with the past, and especially with Catholicism, the Puritan movement had turned against the "magic" of the sacraments and holy relics, of sacred places and saints' days. The religion of the colonists seems, in retrospect, to have forecast and initiated a "disenchantment" of the world.[6] The Puritan God was a God of order and reason, interpreted by learned men in the form of systematic theology. In such statements, Puritanism assumed the shape of a coherent world view, intellectually neat and tidy and swept clean of superstition.

Such, at least, is how we characteristically understand the religion of the colonists. But the lore of wonders as repeated and developed by the colonists cannot be reconciled with so static or so modernist an understanding. We may come instead to recognize that contradiction, or a kind of intellectual pluralism, was truer of the colonists than a uniform and systematic mode of thought. So too, we may come to recognize that these people were not hostile to a folklore that had roots in paganism. Indeed, the wonder tale would introduce them to a popular culture that drew on many sources and traditions. In reiterating these tales, the colonists would affirm their own participation in this wider, older culture.

The lore of wonders was popular culture in the sense of being accessible to everyone; it was a language that all groups in society shared, known not only to the "learned" but to ordinary folk as well. It was popular in being so pervasive, and in being tolerant of contradictions. A full history of this culture and its absorption into Protestantism would lead in several directions, including that of witchcraft. My purpose is more limited, to begin upon a history of this lore as it was received by the colonists, and to trace how it provided them with a mentality of the supernatural.

Portents and prodigies were routine events in English printed broadsides of the seventeenth century. "Strange news from Brotherton," announced a broadside ballad of 1648 that told of wheat that rained down from the sky. "A wonder of wonders" of 1663 concerned a drummer boy who moved invisibly about the town of Tidworth. In "Strange and true news from Westmoreland," a murder story ends with the devil pointing out the guilty person. Hundreds of such broadside ballads, stories told in verse and printed on a single sheet of paper, circulated in the England of Cromwell and the Stuarts. Newssheets, which began appearing with some regularity in the 1640s, carried tales of other marvels. Pamphlets of no more than eight or sixteen pages contained reports of children speaking preternaturally and offered *Strange and wonderful News . . . of certain dreadfull Apparitions*. The yearly almanacs weighed in with their accounts of mystic forces emanating from the stars and planets.[7]

The same prodigies and portents would recur again and again in broadside ballads, newssheets, chapbooks, and almanacs. Tales of witchcraft and the devil, of comets, hailstorms, monster births, and apparitions—these were some of the most commonplace. "Murder will out," as supernatural forces intervened to indicate the guilty. The earth could open up and swallow persons who tell lies. "Many are the wonders which have lately happened," declared the anonymous author of *A miracle, of miracles*,

> as of sodaine and strange death upon perjured persons, strange sights in the Ayre, strange births on the Earth, Earthquakes, Commets, and fierie Impressions, with the execution of God himselfe from his holy fire in heaven, on the wretched man and his wife, at Holnhurst. . . .

A single ballad spoke of blazing stars, monstrous births, a rainstorm of blood, lightning, rainbows, and the sound of great guns. Others told of dreams and prophecies that bore upon the future of kings and countries. Almanacs and other astrological compendia reported similar events: comets, eclipses, joined fetuses, infants speaking.[8]

All of these were cheap forms of print. Hawked by peddlars and hung up in stalls for everyone to see and gape at, they reached the barely literate and the lower orders as well as readers of more means and schooling. The stories they contained would also turn up in a very different kind of book that ran to several hundred pages. Big books—perhaps in the grand format of the folio—were too expensive to circulate in quantity and had authors who announced themselves as of the "learned." But these differences in form and audience did not extend into the contents. The lore of portents and prodigies appeared in books like Thomas Beard's *The Theatre of Gods Judgements* as well as in the cheapest pamphlet.

Thomas Beard was a learned man, a graduate of Cambridge who practiced schoolteaching and received ordination as a minister. Born in the early years of Elizabeth's reign, he published *The Theatre of Gods Judgements* in 1597. Three more editions followed, the last of these in 1648. That same year, Samuel Clarke, like Beard a graduate of Cambridge and a minister, brought out a rival collection: *A Mirrour or Looking-Glasse both for Saints and Sinners, Held forth in about two thousand Examples: Wherein is presented, as Gods Wonderful Mercies to the one, so his severe Judgments against the other.* Clarke's *Examples* (to call it by the title the colonists would use) went through five editions, the final one appearing in 1671. Clarke was a non-conformist after 1662, ejected from the Church of England because he would not recant his Presbyterianism. The sequel to his book was William Turner's folio *Compleat History of the Most Remarkable Providences, Both of Judgement and Mercy, which have hapned in this Present Age* (1697). To this series should be added another Elizabethan work, Stephen Batman's *The Doome warning all men to Judgmente: Wherein are contayned for the most parte all the straunge Prodigies hapned in the Worlde* (1581). Ministers all, Batman, Beard, Clarke, and Turner had a secular competitor in the hack writer Nathaniel Crouch. His *Wonderful Prodigies of Judgment and Mercy, discovered in above Three Hundred Memorable Histories* (1682) was one of a string of works on prodigies and strange wonders that Crouch would publish in the 1680s under his pen name of Robert Burton.

As in the ballads and chapbooks, so in these books nature offered up innumerable signs of supernatural intervention:

> Now according to the variety and diversity of mens offences, the Lord in his most just and admirable judgment, useth diversity of punishments: . . . sometimes correcting them by storms and tempests, both by sea and land; other times by lightning, haile, and deluge of waters . . . and not seldom by remedilesse and sudden fires, heaven and earth, and all the elements being armed with an invincible force, to take vengeance upon such as traytors and rebels against God.

Earthquakes, multiple suns, strange lights in the sky, rainbows, sudden deaths, monstrous births—these were other frequent signs or signals.[9]

Like the ballad writers, Beard and Batman reported esoteric, even violent, events: rats that ate a man, a crow whose dung struck someone dead, the agonies of martyrs. In one or another of these books, we hear of dreams and prophecies, of crimes detected by some form of sympathetic magic, of thieves who rot away, and of armed men in the sky.[10] Much too was made of Satan. He offered compacts to young men in need of money, while sometimes serving as God's agent for inflicting vengeance. Many tales revolved around the curse, "the devil take you," and its surprising consequences:

> Not long since a Cavalier in Salisbury in the middest of his health-drinking and carrousing in a Tavern, drank a health to the Devil, saying, That if the devil would not come, and pledge him, he would not believe that there was either God or devil: whereupon his companions strucken with horror, hastened out of the room, and presently after hearing a hideous noise, and smelling a stinking savour, the Vintner ran up into the Chamber: and coming in, he

missed his guest, and found the window broken, the Iron barre in it bowed, and all bloody, but the man was never heard of afterwards.

The devil might appear in several guises. Black bears, a favorite of the ballad writers, turned up again in stories told by Beard and Batman, as did black dogs.[11]

In telling of these wonders, the men who organized the great collections borrowed from the broadside and the chapbook; a ballad tale of a woman who sank into the ground was reported in Clarke's *Examples*, in Crouch's *Wonderful Prodigies*, and again in Turner's *Compleat History*.[12] This flow of stories meant that "learned" men accorded credibility to wonders as readily as any ballad writer. In this regard, the great folios were no more critical or selective than the cheapest forms of print. The one format was the work of learned men, the other of printers and their literary hacks. But the two shared a popular culture of portents and prodigies, a common lore that linked small books and great, the reader of the ballad and the reader of the folio.

This was a lore that other Europeans were collecting and reporting in the sixteenth and seventeenth centuries. Sixteenth-century German broadsides told of comets, multiple suns, monster births, and armies in the air. A Lutheran who wrote an introduction to an encyclopedia of portents "attempted to define the spectrum of such 'wonder works,'" listing "signs, miracles, visions, prophecies, dreams, oracles, predictions, prodigies, divinations, omens, wonders, portents, presages, presentiments, monsters, impressions, marvels, spells, charms and incantations."[13] In Catholic France the *livrets bleus*, those inexpensive books that circulated widely in the seventeenth century, were dominated by accounts of apparitions, miracles, witchcraft, and possession. Some of these continental stories would reappear in England. Certain ballads were translated or adapted from a foreign source.[14] Thomas Beard described *The Theatre* as "translated from the French," and though his source remains unspecified, his book was parallelled by Simon Goulart's *Histories admirables et memorables de nostre temps*, of which there was an English translation in 1607.[15] On the continent, as in the England of Beard and Clarke, the distinction between reading matter that was "learned" and reading that was "popular" did not apply to tales of wonders. Nor was this lore of more appeal to Catholics than to Protestants. Indeed it seemed to cut across the line between the pagan and the Christian worlds.

No better demonstration of this blending exists than the eclectic sources on which Beard, Clarke, and their contemporaries drew. Aside from newssheets and ballads, whether English or imported, most of their material was culled from printed books that subsumed the sweep of western culture. The classical and early Christian sources included Vergil, Pliny, Plutarch, Seneca, Cicero, Josephus (a favorite), Gildas, Eusebius, and Bede. Then came the historians and chroniclers of the Middle Ages: Geoffrey of Monmouth, Voragine's *The Golden Legend*. The sixteenth and seventeenth centuries supplied a host of chronicles and encyclopedias: *The Mirrour of Magistrates*, the *Magdeburg Centuries*, and others by such writers as Hollingshead, Polydore Vergil, Conrad Lycosthenes, Sleiden, Camden, and Heylin. No source was more important to the English writers than John Foxe's *Acts and Monuments*, itself a résumé of narratives and chronicles extending back to Eusebius. A final source was that great wonder book, the Bible. Its narratives of visions, voices, strange deaths, and witches lent credence to such stories of a later date.[16]

In plundering this great mass of materials, Beard, Batman, and their successors made modest efforts to be critical. As Protestants, they followed Foxe's lead in dropping from their histories most of the visions, cures, and other miracles associated with the legends of the saints. But otherwise the English writers were willing to reprint the stories that descended to them from the Middle Ages and antiquity. No one questioned the legitimacy of Pliny's *Natural History* and its kin, to which, indeed, these writers conceded an unusual authority. The parting of the ways between the "ancients" and the "moderns" lay in the future. In conceding so much to their sources, whether classical or of the early Church or even of the Middle Ages, Beard and Clarke admitted to their pages a strange mixture of ideas and themes. This was a mixture that requires closer scrutiny, for the stories in these books were charged with several meanings.

Wonder stories were interesting in and of themselves; even now, events that seem to defy nature attract our curiosity. But in the seventeeth century, each portent carried a large burden of meaning. Much of this burden was compounded out of three main systems or traditions of ideas—apocalypticism, astrology, and the meteorology of the Greeks. Each of these systems was in decay or disrepute by the middle of the century, under challenge either from an alternative, more up-to-date science or from a growing disenchantment with prophetic visionaries. But even in decay these systems continued to give meaning to the wonder tales.

The most widely used of these traditions was the meteorology of the Greeks and Romans. In Aristotle's physics, meteorology referred to everything occurring in the region of the universe between the earth and moon. As a science it encompassed blazing stars, comets (deemed to circle earth below the moon), rainbows, lightning, and thunder as well as fanciful or misinterpreted phenomena like apparitions in the sky. After Aristotle, the key commentator on meteorology was Pliny, whose *Natural History* "embellished Aristotle's rational theory with many elements of wonder and even superstition." Pliny had become available in translation by the 1560s, and most other major Roman writers who spoke of meteors—Seneca, Plutarch, Vergil—had been made available in English by the early seventeenth century. But English readers learned of blazing stars and comets chiefly from translated versions of a dozen medieval and Renaissance encyclopedias, or from poetic versions such as *La Sepmaine* (1578), the work of a French Huguenot and poet du Bartas. His long poem, which proved immensely popular in English translation, melded Protestant didacticism with the lore of meteors as "prodigious signs."[17]

No less commonplace to most Elizabethans was astrology, the science of celestial bodies. Elizabethans learned their astrology from a medley of Medieval and Renaissance handbooks. These books taught a Christian version of the science, affirming, for example, that the stars and planets had no independent power but depended on the will of God. Astrology reached a wide audience via almanacs and their "prognostications" as keyed to planetary oppositions and conjunctions. Weather lore was another common vehicle of astrological ideas and images.[18]

A third intellectual tradition was apocalypticism. Several different strands converged to form this one tradition. The Scripture offered up a vision of the end in the Apocalypse. The Old and New Testaments told of persons who could prophesy the future on the basis of some vision, or perhaps by hearing voices: "If there be a prophet among you, I the Lord will make myself known unto him in a vision, and will speak to him in a dream" (Numbers 12:6). The legends of the saints were rich in visions, as were the lives of martyrs in Eusebius.[19] Geoffrey of Monmouth, a thirteenth-century English writer, invented prophecies that he ascribed to Merlin. These would survive into the seventeenth century in the company of other legendary sayings—of "Mother Shipton," of the Sybilline oracles, or of obscure Germans whose manuscript predictions were always being rediscovered.[20] With the coming of the Reformation, apocalypticism gained new vigor as Protestants connected their own movement to the cryptic references in Revelation. The feeling was pervasive that contemporary history manifested the great struggle between Christ and Antichrist, and that some cataclysmic alternation was impending. In his influential explication of the Book of Revelation, Joseph Mede reaffirmed the prophetic significance of voices, thunder, lightning, hail, eclipses, blazing stars, and the rise and fall of kings. Mede regarded all the seals and trumpets in Revelation as forecasting real historical events, and in working out the parallels he made it seem that the Apocalypse would not be long postponed.[21]

But the more crucial contribution of the Reformation was the doctrine of God's providence. The doctrine antedated Luther and Calvin. Chaucer's Knight had spoken of "Destiny, that Minister-General/Who executed on earth and over all/That providence which God has long foreseen," and the Psalmist sang of a God who stretched out his protection to the ends of the earth. Nonetheless, the doctrine had a fresh importance in the sixteenth century. In reaffirming the sovereignty of God, the Reformers also wished to understand their own emergence as prefigured in God's grand providential design. John Foxe, the martyrologist, made providence the animating principle of his great book. In its wake, Thomas Beard would reassure his readers that God was immediately and actively present in the world, the ultimate force behind everything that happened: "Is there any substance in this world that hath no cause of his subsisting . . . ? Doth not every thunderclap constraine you to tremble at the blast of his voyce?" Nothing in this world occurred according to contingency or "blind chance." All of nature, all of history, displayed a regularity that men must marvel at, a regularity that witnessed to the "all-surpassing power of God's will." From time to time this "marvellous" order was interrupted by other acts of providence, for God had the power to suspend the laws of nature and work wonders that were even more impressive than the routine harmony of things. The providence of God was as manifest in the swift and unexpected as in the "constant" order of the world.[22]

Beard, Clarke, and Turner were aggressively Protestant in pointing out the significance of God's providence, especially as it affected evil-doers, papists, and persecutors of the Church. In doing so, they continued to rely on astrology, apocalypticism, and meteorology for motifs and evidence. No one viewed these systems as in contradiction with each other. Indeed they seemed to reinforce the patterns of a providential universe. Astrology taught men to regard the heavens as infused with law and order. The meteorology of the ancients rested on assumptions about natural law. Science, whether old or new, was still allied with religion,[23] and the synthesis of Christianity and classical culture remained intact. Then too, the sciences of Greece and Rome were rich in possibilities for disruption and disorder. The conjunction of two planets could send shock waves through the universe. Stars could wander out of their ordained paths, and storms arise as nature fell into imbalance. The world as pictured by astrologers and scientists was prone to violent eruptions. This sense of things was echoed in apocalypticism, and writers on the Apocalypse would cite comets and eclipses as signs of the portending end. Meanwhile Satan raged incessantly against God's kingdom, leading many into sin and tormenting seekers after truth. Sin, injustice, persecution—these disorders of the moral universe were mirrored in the conflict and disorder of the heavens. An angry God was the supreme agent of disruption. Astrologers, the Hebrew prophets, the oracles of Greece and Rome, all spoke alike of doom portended in the turmoil of the heavens and the earth. A teleological universe yielded incessant signals of God's providential plan and his impending judgments.

As emblem of God's providence in all of its variety, the wonder had a rich significance. Still more possibilities for meaning were provided by a set of themes that circulated widely in Elizabethan England. One of these was the theme of decay or dissolution. It was a commonplace assumption among Elizabethans that the world was running down and soon would be exhausted. Portents never seemed to hint at progress or improvement but at impending chaos.[24] Another theme was *De Causibus*, or the rise and fall of great men. In Beard, as in books like the *Mirrour of Magistrates*, Elizabethans read of kings and princes, of men of greed and overreaching ambition, who seemed propelled by some inevitable force to fall from their high rank.[25] A third theme concerned evil as a power operating almost on its own. Evil was not distant or abstract but something always present in the flow of daily life. A book like Beard's, with its grand metaphor of "theatre," made good and evil the main actors in the drama of existence.[26] Yet another motif was fortune, its symbol a great wheel that swept some people up and others down.[27] A final theme was the interpenetration of the moral and the natural orders. Disruptions of the moral order had their echo in nature, and vice versa. This sympathy or correspondence was why Elizabethans assumed that corpses bled when touched by guilty persons. Hence too this correspondence meant that ills of the body, like sickness and death, betokened spiritual corruption. All of the natural world was permeated by forces of the spirit, be they forces working for good or for evil.[28]

The wonder books incorporated all these themes without concern for how they might seem contradictory. Fortune and providence were, after all, competing if not antithetical interpretations. But the wonder books were remarkably tolerant. They made room for decayed systems of belief; in their pages the pagan coexisted with the Christian, the old science of the Greeks with the new Protestant emphasis on providence. The "learned" may have preferred more distinctions, and a man like Thomas Hobbes found the whole body of this lore distasteful.[29] But in the first half of the seventeenth century, the lore of wonders remained generously eclectic both in its themes and in its audience. Everyone in Elizabethan England had some access to this lore. Writers such as Shakespeare and Milton availed themselves of references and motifs that also were the stock of ballad writers. Conventional, familiar, tolerant and open-ended, the lore of wonders was a language that everyone could speak and understand.

To trace the uses of this language for two or three examples is to trace them for the whole repertory of signs and signals. For Beard and his contemporaries, comets were perhaps the most widely publicized of all the meteors described in ancient science. It was a commonplace of Renaissance discussions to view comets as portending drastic change if not disaster—"drought, the pestilence, hunger, battels, the alteration of kingdomes, and common weales, and the traditions of men. Also windes, earthquakes, dearth, landflouds, and great heate to follow." Du Bartas summed up this wisdom in his *La Sepmaine*:

> There, with long bloody Hair, a Blazing Star Threatens the World with Famine, Plague & War:
> To Princes, death; to Kingdomes many crosses: To all Estates, Inevitable Losses. . . . [30]

His idiom came straight from Pliny, who, in viewing comets as "a very terrible portent," had noted their appearance "during the civil disorder in the consulship of Octavius, and again during the war between Pompey and Caesar."[31]

Thunder and lightning were other portents that drew on ancient sources for their meaning. In Scripture, they were repeatedly the instruments of an avenging God: "Cast forth lightning, and scatter them: Shoot out thine arrows, and destroy them" (Psalm 144:6). The prophecies of St. John in Revelation evoked the "voice" of thunder, lightning, and earthquakes (8:5; 10:4). Pliny had viewed thunderbolts as "direful and accursed," associating them with many kinds of wonders such as prophecy. To writers of the Renaissance, lightning seemed especially to betoken destructive violence. But the prophetic context could be invoked in plays like Marlowe's *Tamburlaine*, where the hero saw himself as the scourge of "a God full of revenging wrath, From whom the thunder and the lightning breaks."[32]

As for apparitions in the sky, the would-be scientific description in writers such as Pliny yielded to interpretation of such sights as portents of impending conflict or defeat. Among Beard, Clarke, and their contemporaries, a much repeated apparition story concerned the fall of Jerusalem. Recounting the destruction of Jerusalem, Josephus had described at length "the strange signes and tokens that appeared" before the city's fall. "One while there was a comet in form of a fiery sword, which for a year together did hang over the city." There were voices, and a man who cried out, "Wo, wo unto Jerusalem." Iron chariots flew through the air, and an army became visible in the clouds. All of this seemed credible to Elizabethans, and no less so, as we shall see, to the people of New England.[33]

Apparitions were credible on the authority of Josephus and Pliny, but they also figured in the folk belief of the English people. Folk belief is not easily distinguished from popular culture in an age when both could circulate by word of mouth. Where such beliefs arose and how they were transmitted—and whether they were fragments of some "primitive" mentality—are questions that are difficult to answer. What remains clear is that the wonder books made room for folklore also: stories of the devil as black dog or bear, the legends of the saints and their "white magic," tales of fairies, ghosts, and apparitions, of "murder will out," of curses and their consequences.[34]

So many sources; so many possibilities for meaning! In their tolerance, the great collections ended up without a unifying order of their own. Clarke verged off into sensationalism. Ballads recounted fables of serpents and dragons. Writers such as Crouch felt free to invent stories—as if most ballads were not fiction to begin with.[35] This playfulness was nowhere more amusingly revealed than in a chapbook of the 1640s that mated the predictions of the legendary "Mother Shipton" with the prophecies of a radical Puritan. The new and the old lay side by side without apparent contradiction.[36]

But were the colonists this tolerant, or did they order and discriminate in keeping with their Puritanism?

The same wonder tales that Englishmen were buying circulated in the colonies, often via books imported from the London book trade. As a student at Harvard in the 1670s, Edward Taylor had access to a copy of Samuel Clarke's *Examples*, out of which he copied "An Account of ante-mortem visions of Mr. John Holland."[37] In sermons of the 1670s, Increase Mather quoted frequently from Clarke and Beard.[38] Imported broadsides made some of Beard's stories familiar to New England readers; the Boston printer, John Foster, published in 1679 a facsimile of a London broadside, *Divine Examples of Gods Severe Judgments against Sabbath-Breakers*, a set of warning tales drawn mostly from *A Theatre of Gods Judgements*. Hezekiah Usher, a Boston bookseller, was importing copies of Nathaniel

Crouch's *Wonderful Prodigies of Judgment and Mercy* in the 1680s,[39] and another of Crouch's books, *Delights for the Ingenious*, came into the hands of the children of the Goodwin family.[40] Many more such books and broadsides must have crossed the Atlantic in the seventeenth century, though leaving no specific trace of their presence.

In the absence of such evidence we may turn to books and pamphlets that the colonists were writing. Almanacs appeared each year as soon as the colonists had established a printing press. As in England, these local products included references to portents and wonders. The almanac for 1649 offered its readers a lengthy "prognostication" that played on the theme of earthquakes as a portent of impending catastrophe:

> Great Earthquakes frequently (as one relates)
> Forerun strange plagues, dearths, wars and change of states,
> Earths shaking fits by venemous vapours here,
> How is it that they hurt not, as elsewhere!

Like its European counterpart, the New England almanac contained cryptic clues to what the future held:

> The morning Kings may next ensuing year,
> With mighty Armies in the aire appear,
> By one mans means there shall be hither sent
> The Army, Citty, King and Parliament . . .
> A Child but newly born, shall then foretell
> Great changes in a winding-sheet; Farewell.[41]

The almanac for 1648 tucked portents and prodigies into a "Chronologicall Table" that later almanacs would update:

> Mr. Stoughton and all the souldiers returned home, none being slain.
> Mrs. Dier brought forth her horned-foure-talented monster.
> The great and generall Earth-quake.[42]

Soon enough, moreover, the colonists were writing commentaries on meteors. The first to appear was Samuel Danforth's *An Astronomical Description of the late Comet or Blazing Star . . . Together with a brief Theological Application thereof* (1665). The comets of 1680 and 1682 stirred the Reverend Increase Mather to publish *Heavens Alarm to the World . . . Wherein Is Shewed, That fearful Sights and Signs in Heaven are the Presages of great Calamities at hand* and *Kometographia or A Discourse Concerning Comets*. In 1684, Mather undertook a more ambitious project, a compendium that resembled Clarke's *Examples*. *An Essay for the Recording of Illustrious Providences* was at once a collection of wonder tales and a plea for greater efforts among the colonists to preserve such stories.

Reiterating the commonplaces of a literary tradition, these books—the almanacs, the works of meteorology—are proof of the transfer of culture. It should be noted that Danforth and Mather were learned men who had become aware of scientific challenges to Aristotle's meteorology, challenges that jeopardized some aspects of the portent lore. Yet the two men put aside these alternatives to address a general audience, using an old language and familiar references, and insisting that "blazing stars" remained portents of God's providence.[43]

This message had wide credibility in seventeenth-century New England. We have some measure of its popularity in the record-keeping that went on. Certain public bodies, like the churches in Dorchester and Roxbury, incorporated references to "remarkable providences"—fires, storms, eclipses, victories, sudden deaths—into their records.[44] Each of the Puritan colonies summoned their people repeatedly to days of fasting and thanksgiving, and the calling of these days was cued to the perception of God's providence.[45] Early on, William Bradford, Edward Johnson, and John Winthrop wrote works of history that were richly providential in their narratives of how the colonists had overcome adversity and conflict. These books noted the usual array of signs and portents—eclipses, monster births, strange deaths and storms, miraculous deliverances and reversals—while telling also of more puzzling events, like the lights in the form of a man that were seen in Boston harbor, followed by a voice "calling out in a most dreadful manner, boy, boy, come away, come away."[46] Second- and third-generation historians would reiterate many of these stories, notably in Cotton Mather's *Magnalia Christi Americana* (1702).

All of this public record-keeping or public history was paralleled in private journals that functioned as individual "memorials" of "remarkable providences."[47] The most extensive of these diaries were kept by John Hull, a Boston merchant and the mint master for Massachusetts Bay, and the magistrate Samuel Sewall, who was Hull's son-in-law. Hull seemed almost overwhelmed at times by the flow of prophetic signals, as in his entry for a year—1666—itself accorded apocalyptic significance because 666 was the mark of the beast (Revelation 13:18).

> At New Haven was distinctly and plainly heard the noise of guns, two, three, five at a time, a great part of the day, being only such noises in the air. The same day, at evening, a house at Northampton [was] fired by lightning; a part of the timber split; a man in it killed . . . At Narriganset, in Mr. Edward Hutchinson's flock of sheep, were several monsters. In July were very many noises heard by several towns on Long Island, from the sea, distinctly, of great guns and small, and drums.

Early on in Samuel Sewall's record-keeping, he responded strongly to an eclipse: "Morning proper fair, the weather exceedingly benign, but (to me) metaphoric, dismal, dark and portentous, some prodigie appearing in every corner of the skies." For more than fifty years he kept track of many kinds of portents, from thunderstorms and rainbows to sudden deaths and disturbing sounds. A faithful buyer of each year's almanac, he inserted notes on deaths and weather portents in each monthly calendar.[48]

Hull and Sewall had witnessed many of the portents they took note of in their diaries; news of many others reached them secondhand. Travellers dropped by to tell of strange events, and Sewall heard of more from correspondents. A fierce hail storm that struck while he was having dinner with Cotton Mather led to an exchange of stories; Sewall remembered that a hail storm coincided with the Duke of Monmouth's ill-fated invasion of England in 1685, and Mather knew of other houses that had been struck by hail or lightning. The stories that reached Hull and Sewall were being told and listened to all over New England.[49]

This trade in stories is revealed with unique vividness in two places, a notebook Edward Taylor kept at Harvard and the correspondence passing in and out of Increase Mather's household. In his notebook Taylor recorded the story of "magical performances by a jug-gler." He had heard the story from Jonathan Mitchel, the minister in Cambridge, who in turn had learned it from Henry Dunster, the president of Harvard, "during recitation." Dunster had it from the Reverend John Wilson—and here the chain is interrupted. In his notebook Taylor wrote down the essence of another story passed along by word of mouth. A minister and Harvard president, Urian Oakes, had done the telling:

> A child that was born at Norwich last Bartholomew-Day . . . being in the nurses arms last Eas-terday . . . being about 30 weeks old spake these words (This is a hard world): the nurse when she had recovered herselfe a little from her trembling, & amazement at the Extraordinariness of the thing, said Why dear child! thou hast not known it: the child after a pause, replied, But it will be an hard world & you shall know it.

To this same notebook Taylor added his extracts out of Clarke's *Examples* and, from some other printed source, the prophetic scaffold speech of an Englishman executed in 1651.[50]

The traffic in wonder stories was crucial to the making of Increase Mather's *Essay for the Recording of Illustrious Providences.* In the early 1680s Mather was soliciting his fellow min-isters for contributions to his impending book. John Higginson of Salem, an older man who came to Boston as a student in the 1630s, responded to this call for stories by sending him word of the Reverend Joshua Moodey's collection of annotated almanacs, "so that I doubt not but besides those [stories] he hath sent you, you may have many more from him. For instance,—he speaks of 26 men thereabouts, dying or cast away in their drunk-ennes which calls to mind some such case here."

The following year, having learned from Mather that he did not "confine" himself "to things done in N.E.," Higginson wrote out and dispatched two wonder stories attributed to "persons credible," and of events "I believe . . . to be certain." Both concerned the devil, the one a story of a book that acted strangely on its readers, the other of a man who covenanted with the devil to insinuate "that there was neither God nor Devil, no Heaven nor Hell." The informant who told Higginson of the magical book, a man no longer living, had been a ruling elder of the church in Salem. Long after the experience—it happened back in England—he could still remember that

> as he read in [the book], he was seized on by a strange kind [of] Horror, both of Body & minde, the hair of his head standing up, &c. Finding these effects severall times, he acquainted his master with it, who observing the same effects, they concluding it was a Conjuring Book, resolved to burn it, which they did. He that brought it, in the shape of a man, never coming to call for it, they concluded it was the Devil.

The other story Higginson had collected in his days as minister at Guilford "from a godly old man yet living."[51]

As Higginson predicted, Joshua Moodey had stories to pass on. One was of a house in-habited by evil spirits, as told by the man who lived there. All was relatively quiet now; "the last sight I have heard of," Moodey added, "was the carrying away of severall Axes in the night, notwithstanding they were layed up, yea, lockt up very safe." From a "sober woman" Moodey also had a story of a "monstrous birth" that he described at length, concluding with an offer to "goe up and discourse with the midwife" if Mather wanted more details.[52]

Meanwhile Mather had heard from several informants in Connecticut. The minister in Stamford, John Bishop, had written him some years earlier to answer his inquiries about "the noise of a great gun in the air." In his new letter, Bishop poured out a flood of stories:

> We have had of late, great stormes of rain & wind, & sometimes of thunder & lightning, whereby some execution hath been done by the Lord's holy Hand, though with sparing mercy to mankind. Mr. Jones his house at N[ew] H[aven] broken into, & strange work made in one room thereof especially, wherein one of his daughters had been a little before; & no hurt to any of the family, but the house only . . . A little after which, at Norwalk, there were nine working oxen smitten dead in the woods, in a few rods space of ground, & after that, at Greenwich (a small town neer us, on the west side) on the 5 mo. 13, (when we had great thunder & lightning), there were seven swine & a dog smitten all dead, & so found the next morning, very near the dwelling house, where a family of children were alone (their parents not then at home) & no hurt to any of them, more then amazing fear.[53]

More such stories came to Mather from other hands—a narrative of Ann Cole's bewitchment, together with the story of a man who drank too much and died, accounts of providential rainstorms and remarkable deliverances, and of "two terrible strokes by thunder and lightning" that struck Marshfield in Plymouth Colony.[54]

From his brother, finally, came a letter of encouragement. Nathaniel Mather had moved to England in the early 1650's and remained there. But he remembered many of the stories he had listened to while growing up in Dorchester, or as a Harvard student:

> Mrs. Hibbons witchcrafts, & the discovery thereof, as also of H. Lake's wife, of Dorchester, whom, as I have heard, the devil drew in by appearing to her in the likeness, & acting the part of a child of hers then lately dead, on whom her heart was much set: as also another of a girl in Connecticut who was judged to dye a reall convert, tho she dyed for the same crime: Stories, as I heard them, as remarkable for some circumstances as most I have read. Mrs. Dyer's and Mrs. Hutchinson's monstrous births, & the remarkable death of the latter, with Mr. Wilson's prediction or threatning thereof, which, I remember, I heard of in New England.

Flowing from the memories of a man long since departed from New England, these stories reveal how much was passed along in conversation, and how rapidly a stock of native wonder tales had been accumulated.[55]

Most of these local stories had counterparts in stories told by Clarke and Beard or by the ballad writers. Many of these older stories passed among the colonists as well, enriching and legitimizing their own testimonies of the supernatural. We may speak again of all this lore as constituting a form of popular culture. Everyone knew this lore. Its circulation was not limited to print, as the Mather correspondence indicates so clearly. Nor was it something the rude multitude but not the learned could appreciate. When presidents of Harvard told wonder tales in class, when ministers retold stories of "magical" books and freakish bolts of lightning, we can be sure that we are dealing with a culture shared, with few exceptions, by all of the colonists. One other aspect of this culture deserves emphasis. Its cast was thoroughly traditional, employing the same mix of intellectual traditions, the same references and conventions, as the lore in Beard, Clarke, and the ballad writers.

Consider Danforth and Mather's descriptions of the comets they had witnessed. Like so many other commentators before them, Danforth and Mather relied on the meteorology of the ancients, as mediated via medieval and Renaissance encyclopedias. In proving that comets were "Portentous and Signal of great and notable Changes," Danforth drew upon du Bartas while citing, as parallels, events such as the death of Julius Caesar, which, according to tradition, had been prefigured by a comet.[56] Mather cited Josephus, Cicero, du Bartas, Mede, and Scripture as authorities when preaching on the comet of 1680. The description he gave of a comet that appeared in 1527 was entirely derivative:

> On the eleventh day of August, a most terrifying Comet was seen, of an immense longitude, and bloody colour. The form of it, was like a mans arm holding an huge Sword in his hand with which he was ready to strike. Such terrour and horrour surprized the Spectators of this Prodigy, as that some died away with dread & amazement.[57]

So, too, the references in diaries and in histories to lightning and the phenomenon of three suns repeated elements of an old code of reference. All of the traditional associations between lightning, disorder, and prophecy lay in the background of Sewall's frequent diary entries on thunder and lightning, Cotton Mather's *Brontologia Sacra: The Voice of the Glorious God in the Thunder*, and Samuel Arnold's description of a storm that struck the town of Marshfield, in which "the most dismal black cloud . . . that ever" anyone had seen had passed overhead, shooting forth its "arrows."[58] The phenomenon of three suns, remarked on in Shakespeare's works and by medieval chronicles as signalling the overthrow of kings, remained a "wonder" to Edward Johnson, who linked the "unwonted sights" of "two Parlii, or images of the Sun, and some other strange apparitions," with the "desperate opinion" of persons who in New England "would overthrow all the Ordinances of Christ."[59]

From medieval handbooks the colonists also borrowed the language of astrology. For them it was a Christian science; the stars were signs not causes. New England almanacs retained the old combination of weather lore and astrological prediction, as in an essay Israel Chauncey inserted in his almanac for 1663 on "The Natural Portents of Eclipses, according to Approved Authors."[60] Just as commonplace were the allusions to the consequences of certain planetary motions: "On October the third will be celebrated a famous conjunction of Saturn and Mars, and wherein they are deemed the two Malevolent and Infortunate Planets, the conjunction thereof (say Astrologers) Imports no good."[61] The mixture of astrology and political prediction that had flourished amid civil war in England also reached the colonies in 1690, when a printer newly disembarked from London published an abridged edition of John Holwell's fiercely anti-Tory, anti-Catholic *Catastrophe Mundi: or, Europe's Many Mutations Until the Year 1701.*[62]

Even more appealing to the colonists was the apocalyptic tradition. Visions, dreams, unseen voices—all these were almost everyday experiences, talked about in private and, remarkably, in books. Little children who spoke preternaturally were, as in the ballad literature, accorded special notice, as Taylor indicated by preserving the story of the child who told his nurse it was "an hard world." Nathaniel Morton reported an unseen "voice" that had alerted the beleaguered colonists at Plymouth to arson in their storehouse.[63] The Reverend Noadiah Russell

> heard of a man in Connecticut . . . who was taken with a sudden shivering after which he heard a voice saying that four dreadful judgments should come speedily upon the whole world viz: sword, famine, fire and sickness which should, without speedy reformation prevented, begin at New England.[64]

To interpret dreams as prophecy was to participate in a long-established tradition. John Winthrop, to whom a minister had told a dream of his, responded with another of his own:

[C]oming into his chamber, he found his wife . . . in bed, and three or four of their children lying by her, with most sweet and smiling countenances, with crowns upon their heads, and blue ribbons about their eyes. When he awaked, he told his wife his dream, and made this interpretation of it, that God would take of her children to make them fellow heirs with Christ in his kingdom.[65]

The *Magnalia Christi Americana*, a veritable encyclopedia of New England wonder tales, included many dreams and other acts of prophecying. The Reverend John Wilson had prophetic dreams as well as a "certain prophetical afflatus" that made his prayers affect or forecast the future. Another minister, John Eliot, was gifted with "forebodings of things that were to come," and a third, John Brock of Marblehead, could predict success for fishermen and locate missing boats![66]

Here we sense ourselves approaching folk belief. The wonder tales that passed among the colonists were openly folkloric in certain of their themes and motifs. Stephen Batman had incorporated the folk tradition of spectral, shape-shifting black dogs into *The Doome warning to Judgemente*.[67] A century later, people in New England testified that they had seen the devil in the shape of a black dog. William Barker, Jr., a confessing witch at Salem in 1692, had seen "the Shape of a black dog which looked Very Fercly Upon him" as "he was Goeing into the Woods one Evening" in search of cows. Sarah Carrier, enticed into witchcraft by members of her family, was promised "a black dog."[68] Many of the witnesses at Salem had been visited at night by apparitions of persons crying out for vengeance on their murderers. Such stories were a staple of folk legend and also of the ballad literature.[69] Another folk belief expressed at Salem was the power of white—or in this case, black—magic to keep persons dry in rainstorms. A witness had become suspicious of a visitor whose clothes showed no signs of passing through a storm on muddy roads. Many centuries before Salem witchcraft, the legend had grown up of a saint who remained dry in spite of rain. His was the power of white magic. In some fashion that defies analysis, the colonists were able to repeat this story, though modifying its details and making it a devil story.[70]

Where many of these strands converge—folklore, apocalypticism, white magic, the meteorology of Pliny and Aristotle—is in Increase Mather's *Essay for the Recording of Illustrious Providences*; because it built upon the wonder tales that people told as stories, the *Essay* has something of the quality of a folk narrative. Yet it is also a "learned" book. Between his own books—he owned the largest private library in New England—and those he found at Harvard, Mather could pillage most of western culture for his lore of portents. In keeping with its bookish sources, the *Essay* borrowed widely from the ancients and their mediators of the Renaissance. It borrowed also from the English collectors, especially Samuel Clarke and his *Examples*. And since Mather was committed to the mystery of the supernatural, he spent portions of the *Essay* arguing the validity of wonders against contemporary Europeans who were growing skeptical. As proof of the reality of witchcraft, he would repeat the story of the invisible drummer boy of Tidworth, taking it as true on the authority of the English minister and proto-scientist Joseph Glanville, though knowing that the story was denounced by others as a fable.[71]

The man on the receiving end of stories from his fellow clergy made use of some of them but not of others. The book bears signs of haste, as though his printer were impatient and his own control of what he wished to do imperfect. Chapter one told of "sea-deliverances," some of them native, others taken from an English book. In chapter two, a potpourri of stories, Mather reached back to King Philip's War for a captivity narrative and two related episodes; after telling of another "sea-deliverance," he opened up his Clarke's *Examples* and began to copy from it. In chapter three, on "Thunder and Lightning," he quoted from John Bishop's letter and added several other stories of lightning in New England. But the chapter ended with two German stories, some references to Scripture, and several bits of pedantry. Chapters four, six, seven, and eight were meditations and general arguments on providence, using European sources. Chapter nine demonstrated how thin the line was between the wonder and the curiosity, for here he told of persons who were deaf and dumb but learned to speak.[72] Chapter ten, "Of remarkable tempests," covered hurricanes, whirlwinds, earthquakes, and floods; chapter eleven, "concerning remarkable judgements," related how the enemies of God—Quakers, drunkards, and other enemies of New England—had been punished. Mather added a letter from Connecticut as chapter twelve, and in chapter five drew together several stories of "things preternatural"— demons, apparitions, and evil spirits.

The many layers of the *Essay* included the esoteric. Like Beard and Clarke before him, Mather had an eye for the unusual event. Some of his stranger stories were borrowed from a manuscript, presumably of English origin, that he had inherited from John Davenport, the long-time minister of New Haven. From it he drew a Faust-type story of a young student who contracted with the devil for money. But the black magic of the devil yielded to the higher powers of a group of faithful ministers, whose prayers forced Satan

> to give up that contract; after some hours continuance in prayer, a cloud was seen to spread itself over them, and out of it the very contract signed with the poor creatures blood was dropped down amongst them.

From this manuscript Mather drew an even more sensational story of a minister who drank too much, went to a cockfight on the Lord's Day, and while "curses . . . were between his lips, God smote him dead in the twinkle of an eye. And though Juxon were but young . . . his carcase was immediately so corrupted as that the stench of it was insufferable."

From the same collection, finally, Mather copied out a "strange passage" concerning a man suspected of stealing sheep who swore his innocence and

> wished, that if he had stollen it, God would cause the horns of the sheep to grow upon him. This man was seen within these few days by a minister of great repute for piety, who saith, that the man has a horn growing out of one corner of his mouth, just like that of a sheep; from which he hath cut seventeen inches, and is forced to keep it tyed by a string to his ear, to prevent its growing up to his eye.

Here again we sense ourselves confronting folk belief. This story of the sheep's horn had its parallel or antecedent in a medieval legend of a man who stole and ate a sheep, and then found a sheep's ear growing out of his mouth. The story of a student who compacted with the devil had roots in legends of the saints and, more remotely, in lore of eastern cultures.[73]

How like it was for wonder tales to build on folk or pagan legends! With its mixture of motifs and sources, *An Essay for the Recording of Illustrious Providences* reaffirmed the traditional tolerance of the genre. The tolerance of the *Essay* was mirrored in broader patterns of response. As readers and book buyers, the colonists were caught up in the wonder tale as it appeared in Beard and Clarke. As storytellers, they repeated to each other a growing stock of local wonders. And in their almanacs and diaries they recorded the prodigies and portents that were the stuff of everyday experience—the voices and strange sounds, monster births and lightning bolts, apparitions in the sky and doings of the devil. In confirming the validity and significance of all of these phenomena, Mather's *Essay* summed up a popular culture that the colonists shared in common with most other Europeans. His book epitomized the transfer of old ways of thinking to the New World.

But still we need to ask what kind of worldview was it that accepted the reality of evil spirits and of sheep's horns growing out of someone's mouth? The answer to this question lies elsewhere than in the theology of John Calvin or William Perkins. We are so accustomed to inflating the significance of Puritanism that we easily forget how much else impinged upon the making of beliefs among the colonists. Indeed, the historians who have commented on Mather's *Essay* have actively resisted its complexity. A century ago, the rational-minded Moses Coit Tyler was irritated by Mather's "palpable eagerness . . . to welcome, from any quarter of the earth or sea or sky, any messenger whatever, who may be seen hurrying toward Boston with his mouth full of marvels." Tyler deemed the stories in the book variously "tragic, or amusing, or disgusting, now and then merely stupid," and in one sweeping statement he condemned the book as "at once a laughable and an instructive memorial of the mental habits" of the colonists. Fifty years later, Kenneth Murdock tried to rescue the *Essay*, and by implication, Puritanism, by insisting that Mather was up to date in his science and in his efforts to weigh and judge the evidence for marvels. Dismissing this interpretation, Perry Miller politicized the book, while admitting that it "seems a collection of old-wives tales and atrocity stories, at best hilariously funny and at worse a parade of gullibility." This indifference to the texture of the *Essay*—Miller did acknowledge that its roots lay "in a venerable tradition, stretching back to the medieval exempla"—was symptomatic of a larger indifference to traditional belief and popular culture in early New England.[74] Center stage was wholly occupied by the complexities of Puritanism as an intellectual system, and if certain other beliefs, like witchcraft, lingered in the wings, they could safely be ignored since they were headed for extinction.

But the mental world of the colonists was not really fashioned in this manner. High or low, learned or unlearned, these people had absorbed a host of older beliefs. A modern critic who has written on Milton and science remarks that everyone in the early seventeenth century relied on a body of common knowledge that stemmed from Pliny, Aristotle, and the encyclopedists. This old lore was being challenged by new theories of the planets; yet like Mather and the colonists, Milton "was not ever seriously interested in a contest of cosmological theories." As a Christian and a Puritan, Milton believed that the universe was theocentric and teleological. He was also quite at home with a "popular science" that included astrology, finding "no incompatibility between" this science and the doctrines of free will and providence. This eclectic synthesis supported a view of the everyday world as hovering between anarchy and order. Decay and corruption were constant, and disorder in the moral sphere of things was echoed in the disorder of nature. Such a mixture of science and religion in Milton was formed out of intellectual, or popular, traditions that long ante-dated Puritanism.[75] It is not important to give dates or exact boundaries to these traditions. The point is rather that certain deeper layers of belief—call them folklore, call them "popular"—flowed into Milton's worldview as into Increase Mather's.[76]

Armed with this insight, we come finally to understand that the mentality of the supernatural in seventeenth-century New England encompassed themes and motifs that owed little to formal theology or to Puritanism. The people of New England viewed the world about them as demonstrating pattern and order. This was the order of God's providence; their world, like Milton's, was theocentric. It was also teleological, its structure the grand scheme laid out in the Apocalypse, the war of Antichrist against the godly. The forces of evil were immensely strong and cunning, in such sort that the providential order could seem to be "overthrown and turned upside down, men speaking evil of good, and good of evill, accounting darkness light, and light darknesse."[77] Disorder was profound in other ways. The world was rife with violence—with wars and persecution, pestilence and famine, pride, greed and envy. A righteous God could strike with terrible swiftness, disrupting natural law to punish evildoers or afflict the godly. The devil too had powers to wreak havoc. Each kind of violence was attuned to every other, as were the forms of order. This correspondence enriched the meaning of portents and prodigies, making them more terrifying. The plan and order of the universe was, after all, not always visible or readily deciphered. If there were purpose and plan, there were also the marvelous, the inexplicable, and the wonderful:

> One providence seems to look this way, another providence seems to look that way, quite contrary one to another. Hence these works are marveilous. Yea, and that which does add to the wonderment, is, in that the works of God sometimes seem to run counter with his word: so that there is dark and amazing intricacie in the ways of providence.[78]

There was mystery at the heart of things. Death could strike at any moment, the devil could mislead, the earth begin to tremble. In dramatizing all these possibilities, the wonder tale evoked the radical contingency of a world so thoroughly infused with invisible forces.

This mentality of the supernatural reflects the syncreticism of the Christian tradition. Early in its history Christianity had come to terms with the pagan notion of the prodigy and with such systems as astrology. The mixture that resulted cannot arbitrarily be separated into distinct spheres, one "magical" or pagan, the other orthodox or Christian.[79] As one modern historian has noted, the early modern European was receptive to the wonder tale because he "believed that everybody, living or inanimate, was composed of matter and a spirit. This idea was shared by eminent minds right up to the scientific revolution in the seventeenth century; it underlay the neo-Platonic belief of the Renaissance in the souls of stars and justified the persistence of astrology." In this same period no one could "make a clear distinction between nature and supernature" or view the world as simply "ruled . . . by laws" and not "caprice."[80] This way of thinking made its way across the Atlantic with the colonists. Theirs too was a syncretic Christianity. In tolerating the wonder tale and all its underlying themes, the colonists demonstrated the capacity to abide contradiction and ambiguity. So too they demonstrated their attachment to an old mentality, a popular culture transmitted through the lore of wonders.

Before the century ended, this mentality began to fall apart. Witchcraft, prophecy, and portents came under attack from a coalition of scientists, freethinkers, and clergy (especially Anglicans) who wanted to discredit them as "superstitions." The world lost its enchantment as the realm of nature became separate from the realm of spirit. Comets lost their role as portents; a Harvard graduate of another generation spurned this old belief in an essay published in 1719. Wonder tales, and the mentality embedded in them, lived on but now more clearly in the form of fringe or lower-class beliefs.[81] No learned man dared take the point of view that Increase Mather had assumed in 1684. In its own day, the wonder tale united what became sundered in the eighteenth century. Living as we do on the further side of disenchantment, it is not easy to reenter a world where matter and spirit were interlinked, where "superstitions" remained credible. But therein lies the challenge of the wonder.

## NOTES

The research that led to this essay was supported by the John Simon Guggenheim Memorial Foundation, the American Council of Learned Societies, the National Endowment for the Humanities (via the American Antiquarian Society), and Boston University. I am very grateful to these agencies for their support. I want also to thank Richard L. Bushman, Barbara Diefendorf, James Henretta, Keith Thomas, D. P. Walker, and Sam Bass Warner, Jr., for their comments on a previous version of this essay.

1. See footnote 6; George Lincoln Burr, ed., *Narratives of the Witchcraft Cases* (New York, 1914), 175; Increase Mather, *Remarkable Providences, illustrative of the earlier days of American colonisation* (London, 1856), 101, cited hereafter as *Essay*; "The Diaries of John Hull," American Antiquarian Society, *Transactions and Collections*, III (1897), 218; Cotton Mather, *Magnalia Christi Americana*, 2 vols. (Hartford, Conn., 1853–1854), I, 84; "The Diary of Noahdiah Russell," *New England Historical and Genealogical Register*, VII (1853), 53–54; Nathaniel Morton, *New-Englands Memoriall* (Cambridge, Mass., 1670), 52; *The Diary of Samuel Sewall*, M. Halsey Thomas, ed., 2 vols., (New York, 1973), I, 281.

2. Edward Johnson, *The Wonder-Working Providence of Sions Saviour*, ed. J. Franklin Jameson, *Original Narratives of Early American History* (New York, 1910); John Sherman, "To the Reader," in Cotton Mather, *Wonders of the Invisible World* (Boston, 1692).

3. Kitty Scoular, *Natural Magic: Studies in the Presentation of Nature in English Poetry from Spenser to Marvell* (Oxford, 1965), 5; Increase Mather, *The Latter Sign Discoursed of*, bound with *Kometographia* (Boston, 1682), second pagination, 7–11; Michael McKeon, *Politics and Poetry in Restoration England: The Case of Dryden's Annus Mirabilis* (Cambridge, Mass., 1975), 155–161.

4. Johnson, *Wonder-Working Providence*, ed. Jameson, 185.

5. *Letter-Book of Samuel Sewall*, 2 vols., Massachusetts Historical Society, *Collections*, 6th Ser., I–II (1886–1888), II, 229; *Diary of Samuel Sewall*, Thomas, ed., I, 369; II, 796.

6. Keith Thomas, *Religion and the Decline of Magic* (London). This complex, subtle book depicts seventeenth-century Protestants, and especially the more radical of the Puritans, as hostile to "magic"; and argues that the rural poor preferred the older beliefs that Puritans were opposing. But Thomas also provides much evidence of beliefs, e.g., astrology, that were not limited to the rural poor, and he is quite aware that Protestantism remained in touch with prophecy, exorcism, and even certain folk beliefs. My argument inevitably runs counter to the main emphasis of his book, but much of what I have to say is also present in his pages, and I am deeply indebted to the references he provides to sixteenth- and seventeenth-century sources.

7. Hyder Rollins, ed., *The Pack of Autolycus or Strange and Terrible News of Ghosts, Apparitions . . . as told in Broadside Ballads of the Years 1624–1693* (Cambridge, Mass., 1927), 36, 114, 162, and passim; Joseph Frank, *The Beginning of the English Newspaper 1620–1660* (Cambridge, Mass., 1961), 17; Bernard Capp, *English Almanacs 1500–1800* (Ithaca, N.Y., 1979), chap. 6; *Strange and wonderful News from Chippingnorton . . . Of certain dreadful Apparitions* [London, 1679].

8. Rollins, ed., *Pack of Autolycus*, 37, 62, 139, 82, 23; *A miracle, of miracles* [London, n.d.], 5; John Gadbury, *Natura Prodigiorum or, A discourse touching the nature of Prodigies* (London, 1660).

9. *The Theatre of Gods Judgements* (London, 1648), 409; Stephen Batman, *The Doome warning all men to the Iudgemente* (London, 1581), 317, 379, 390, 397.

10. Beard, *Theatre of Gods Judgements* 37, 48, 195; Batman, *Doome warning all men to the Iudgemente*, 403; [Nathaniel Crouch], *Admirable Curiosi-*

*ties, Rarities, & Wonders in England* (London, 1682), passim; Rollins, ed., *Pack of Autolycus*, 219. Here as elsewhere in this essay, the references could run into the hundreds in imitation of the dense texture of the great collections.

11. Samuel Clarke, *A Mirrour or Looking-Glasse both for Saints, and Sinners*, 2nd. ed., (London, 1654), 92–93; Beard, *Theatre of Gods Judgements*, Bk I, chapter 30; Rollins, ed., *Pack of Autolycus*, 75.

12. Rollins, ed., *Pack of Autolycus*, 62.

13. Miriam Chrisman, *Lay Culture, Learned Culture: Books and Social Change in Strasbourg 1480–1599* (New Haven, Conn., 1982), 257, 369ff; R. W. Scribner, *For the Sake of Simple Folk: Popular Propaganda for the German Reformation* (Cambridge, U.K., 1981), 125–127, 131, 184.

14. Rollins, ed., *Pack of Autolycus*, 81.

15. Simon Goulart, *Admirable and Memorable Histories containing the wonders of our time* (London, 1607). The original French edition appeared in 1547. Batman's *Doome* was largely a translation of Lycosthenes' *De prodigiis liber*.

16. The best guides (in English) to the lore of wonders are the literary historians whom I came to refer to as "the Shakespeareans," the men and women who have patrolled the sweep of English literary culture from Chaucer to Shakespeare and Milton, and who were very conscious of Shakespeare's roots in medieval and classical culture. A book of great practical utility, as my citations from it indicate, is S.K. Heninger, Jr., *A Handbook of Renaissance Meteorology* (Durham, N.C., 1960), which opens with an important survey of the encyclopedias that codified and transmitted so much of the wonder lore. No less important is Kester Svendsen, *Milton and Science* (New York, 1969), with its superb discussion in Chapter 1 of "The Compendious Method of Natural Philosophy: Milton and the Encyclopedic Tradition." The notes and across references in Hyder Rollins's *Pack of Autolycus* remain the best guide to the print culture I describe briefly. Other studies of importance include: Don Cameron Allen, *The Star-Crossed Renaissance: The Quarrel about Astrology and Its Influence in England* (New York, 1966); Willard Farnham, *The Medieval Heritage of Elizabethan Tragedy* (Berkeley, 1936); J.S.P. Tatlock, *The Scene of the Franklin's Tale Revisited* (London, 1914), and his *The Legendary History of Britain* (Berkeley and Los Angeles, 1950); Robert W. Hanning, *The Vision of History in Early Britain from Gildas to Geoffrey of Monmouth* (New York, 1966); Paul H. Kocher, *Science and Religion in Elizabethan England* (New York, 1969); George Lyman Kittredge, *The Old Farmer and His Almanac*

(Boston, 1904); and Henry A. Kelly, *Divine Providence in the England of Shakespeare's Histories* (Cambridge, Mass., 1970). An exhaustive survey is Lynn Thorndike, *A History of Magic and Experimental Science*, 8 vols. (New York, 1923–1958), esp. vols. IV–VII.

17. Heninger, *Handbook of Renaissance Meteorology*, 12, and chaps. 2–3.

18. Ibid., 30–32; Allen, *Star-Crossed Renaissance*, chap. 5; Capp, *English Almanacs*, chap. 5.

19. Eusebius, *The Ancient ecclesiastical histories* (London 1619), 64, 80; Bede's *Ecclesiastical History of the English People*, Bertram Colgrave and R.A.B. Mynors, eds. (Oxford, 1969), 141, 361–363; G.R. Owst, *Literature and Pulpit in Medieval England* (Cambridge, U.K., 1937), 129–130.

20. Tatlock, *Legendary History of Britain*, chap. 17; Rupert Taylor, *The Political Prophecy in England* (New York, 1911); Thomas, *Religion and the Decline of Magic*, chap. 13.

21. Scribner, *For the Sake of Simple Folk*, 116–117, 140–147, 184; Katharine R. Firth, *The Apocalyptic Tradition in Reformation Britain, 1530–1645* (Oxford, 1979); Joseph Mede, *The Key of the Revelation, searched and demonstrated out of the Naturall and proper characters of the Visions* (London, 1643), Pt. 1, 88, 94.

22. Chaucer, *The Canterbury Tales*, trans. Nevill Coghill (Baltimore, 1952), 70; Peter Lake, *Moderate Puritans and the Elizabethan Church* (Cambridge, U.K., 1982), 119–120; Beard, *Theatre of Gods Judgements*, 88; Thomas, *Religion and the Decline of Magic*, chap. 4.

23. As Kocher proves at length in *Science and Religion in Elizabethan England*. The close ties between science and religion are evident in the letters that Cotton Mather sent to the Royal Society; many of them report events that previously had been described as "wonders" in his father's *Essay for the Recording of Illustrious Providences*. Cf. George L. Kittredge, "Cotton Mather's Scientific Communications to the Royal Society," American Antiquarian Society, *Proceedings*, N.S. XXVI (1916), 18–57.

24. Capp, *English Almanacs*, 165; Hershel Baker, *The Race of Time* (Toronto, 1967) 57–63; Joseph J. Morgan, Jr., *Chaucer and the Theme of Mutability* (The Hague, 1961); Victor Harris, *All Coherence Gone* (Chicago, 1949), chaps. 4–5.

25. Farnham, *Medieval Heritage of Elizabethan Tragedy*, chap. 7; Scribner, *For the Sake of Simple Folk*, 117; Beard, *Theatre of Gods Judgements*, 80.

26. Michael MacDonald, *Mystical Bedlam: Madness, Anxiety, and Healing in Seventeenth-Century England* (Cambridge, U.K., 1981), 175, 202.

"There hath ever been from the beginning an inveterate antipathy between Satan and his instruments, and the children of God." (Clarke, *Examples*, 35.)

27. Howard R. Patch, *The Goddess Fortuna in Medieval Literature* (Cambridge, Mass., 1927); J. G. A. Pocock, *The Machiavellian Moment: Florentine Political Thought and the Atlantic Republican Tradition* (Princeton, 1975), 349–350.

28. E. M. W. Tillyard, *The Elizabethan World Picture* (New York, n.d.), chap. 7.

29. Thomas Hobbes, *Leviathan*, ed. Michael Oakeshott (Oxford, 1957), Pt. IV. Hobbes was almost sui generis; but there was widespread criticism in seventeeth-century England of astrology and apocalypticism, as well as an awareness that protents and prodigies were often manipulated for political benefit. This politicizing is evident in the flood of publications in 1679 and 1680, most of them anti-Catholic, anti-Stuart tracts in disguise, and in books like *Mirabilis Annus Secundus; Or, The Second Year of Prodigies. Being A true and impartial Collection of many strange Signes and Apparitions, which have this last Year been seen in the Heavens, and in the Earth, and in the Waters* (London, 1662), which, despite its title, is a radical Puritan onslaught against the restored monarchy. We are dealing with a series of contradictions, or better, of paradoxes: belief in portents, joined with skepticism about them; a conviction that some portents were not really significant, and that others were. For examples of this selectivity at work in the late sixteenth century, cf. L. H. Buell, "Elizabethan Portents: Superstition or Doctrine," in *Essays Critical and Historical Dedicated to Lily B. Campbell* (Berkeley and Los Angeles, 1950), 27–41.

30. Heninger, *Handbook of Renaissance Meteorology*, 87–91; du Bartas, *La Sepmaine*, quoted on the reverse of the title page of Samuel Danforth, *An Astronomical Description of the late Comet or Blazing Star* (Cambridge, Mass., 1665).

31. Pliny, *Natural History*, trans. H. Rackham (Cambridge, Mass., 1949), I, 235 (Bk II. xxiii).

32. Ibid., I, 275 (Bk II. liii): Heninger, *Handbook of Renaissance Meteorology*, 72–87.

33. *The Famous and Memorable Workers of Josephus . . . Faithfully Translated . . . by Thomas Lodge* (London, 1620), 738; Heninger, *Handbook of Renaissance Meteorology*, 91–94; Rollins, ed., *Pack of Autolycus*, 38.

34. Katherine M. Briggs, *The Anatomy of Puck: An Examination of Fairy Beliefs among Shakespeare's Contemporaries and Successors* (London, 1959); C. Grant Loomis, *White Magic: An Introduction to the Folklore of Christian Legend* (Cambridge, Mass., 1948); Kittredge, *Old Farmer and His Almanac*, chap. 6; T. F. Thiselton Dyer, *Folk Lore of Shakespear* (London, 1884).

35. As Rollins, ed., *Pack of Autolycus*, points out repeatedly.

36. *Twelve Strange Prophesies, besides Mother Shiptons. With the Predictions of John Saltmarsh* (London, 1648).

37. William P. Upham, "Remarks," *Massachusetts Historical Society, Proceedings*, 2d Ser., XIII (1899–1900), 126–127.

38. Increase Mather, *Wo to Drunkards* (Cambridge, Mass., 1673), 28; "The Diary of Increase Mather," *Massachusetts Historical Society, Proceedings*, 2d Ser., XIII (1899–1900), 345.

39. Worthington C. Ford, *The Boston Book Market, 1679–1700* (Boston, 1917), 149.

40. Mather, *Magnalia Christi Americana*, I, 205.

41. Kenneth B. Murdock, ed., *Handkerchiefs from Paul being Pious and Consolatory Verses of Puritan Massachusetts* (Cambridge, Mass., 1927), 109–111.

42. [Samuel Danforth], *An Almanack for the Year of Our Lord 1648* (Cambridge, Mass., 1648). Mary Dyer's monstrous birth was perhaps the first New England wonder to receive international attention. Cf. *Newes from New-England of A most strange and prodigious Birth* [London, 1642].

43. "My chief design, is to inform and edifie the ordinary sort of Readers. Yet considering that God hath made me a debter to the wise as well as to the weak, I have added some things of the nature, place, motion of Comets, which only such as have some skill in Astronomy can understand" ("To the Reader," in *Kometographia*).

44. *Records of the First Church at Dorchester in New England 1636–1734* (Boston, 1891); Roxbury Land and Church Records, Boston Record Commissioners, *Reports*, VI (Boston, 1881), 187–212.

45. William Deloss Love, Jr., *The Fast and Thanksgiving Days of New England* (Boston, 1895).

46. James Kendall Hosmer, ed., *Winthrop's Journal History of New England, 1630–1649*, 2 vols. (New York, 1953 [orig. publ. New York, 1908]), II, 156.

47. A very large number of such journals or brief autobiographical sketches survive, and their authors include artisans and farmers as well as ministers and merchants. Two diaries kept by oridinary people are John Dane, "A Declaration of Remarkable Proudenses in the Corse of My Life," *New England Historical and Genealogical Register*, VIII (1854), 147–156; and Charles F. Adams, Jr., "Abstract of [John] Marshall's Diary," *Massachusetts Historical Society, Proceedings*, 2d Ser., I (1884–1885), 148–164, and its continuation, Samuel A.

Green, "Remarks," ibid., 2d. Ser., XIV (1900–1901), 13–34.

48. *The Diaries of John Hull*, 217–218; *Diary of Samuel Sewall*, Thomas, ed. I, 12. I have analyzed this diary at greater length in "The Mental World of Samuel Sewall," *Massachusetts Historical Society, Proceedings*, XCII (1980), 21–44.

49. *Diary of Samuel Sewall*, Thomas, ed., I. 330–331.

50. Upham, "Remarks," 127–128. Taylor had access to one of the several versions of Christopher Love's scaffold speech; e.g., *The true and perfect Speech of Mr. Christopher Love* (London, 1651).

51. *Mather Papers*, 282–287.

52. Ibid., 360–362.

53. Ibid., 306–310.

54. Ibid., 466–481. The Marshfield episode, told in a letter from the Rev. Samuel Arnold, was later published by N. B. Shurtleff as *Thunder & Lightning; and Deaths at Marshfield in 1658 & 1666* (Boston, 1850).

55. *Mather Papers*, 58–59. The Mary Dyer story had long since passed into print in several places; cf. note 6, p. 258 above.

56. Danforth, *An Astronomical Description*, 16–21.

57. Mather, *Kometographia*, 96. Quoting again the familiar lines from du Bartas, *La Sepmaine*, Mather also spoke approvingly of apparitions in the air. In keeping with tradition, the colonists were sensitive to the shape and direction of comets; cf. Johnson, *Wonder-Working Providence*, ed. Jameson, 40; *Mather Papers*, 312.

58. Mather, *Magnalia Christi Americana*, II, 363–372; Shurtleff, *Thunder & Lightning*. 13–15.

59. Johnson, *Wonder-Working Providence*, ed. Jameson, 243. Cf. "The Diaries of John Hull," 208; *Mather Papers*, 349; and for the tradition, Rollins, ed., *Pack of Autolycus*, 38; Batman, *Doome warning to Judgemente*, 304.

60. Israel Chauncy, *An Almanack of the coelestial motions for . . . 1663* (Cambridge, Mass., 1663).

61. Noadiah Russell, *Cambridge Ephemeris. An Almanac . . . for . . . 1684* (Cambridge, Mass., 1684).

62. *Holwell's Predictions: of many remarkable things, which probably come to pass* (Cambridge, Mass., [1690]).

63. Morton, *New-Englands Memoriall*, 52.

64. "The Diary of Noahdiah Russell," 54. The references to such experiences were many; and I mean to write about them elsewhere, as the discussions of millennium and eschatology in New England Puritanism do not pay adequate (if any)

attention to the everyday experience of prophecying. Anne Hutchinson was gifted with prophetic sight and visions; cf. David D. Hall, ed., *The Antinomian Controversy, 1636–1638: A Documentary History* (Middletown, Conn., 1968), 271–273.

65. Winthrop, *Journal*, I, 84, 121.

66. Mather, *Magnalia Christi Americana*, I, 314–316, 544; II, 37–38. As with visionary prophecying, I must pass by many other instances, as well as avoiding the stories provided by Beard, Clarke, and Turner.

67. The folklore of black dogs is summarized in Katharine M. Briggs, *British Folk Tales and Legends: A Sampler* (London, 1977), 115–120.

68. Paul Boyer and Stephen Nissenbaum, eds., *The Salem Witchcraft Papers*, 3 vols. (New York, 1977), I, 74, 202–203; III, 742; II, 568.

69. Ibid., I, 166, 246–247.

70. Ibid., II, 578. Cf. Loomis, *White Magic*, 39.

71. Joseph Glanville, *A Blow at Modern Sadducism in some Philosophical Considerations about Witchcraft*, 4th ed. (London, 1668); Rollins, ed., *Pack of Autolycus*, 115.

72. The same generosity is characteristic of Bread and Clarke, and has medieval precedents; Tatlock, *Legendary History of Britain*, 276–277.

73. Mather, *Essay*, "Introduction"; H. L. D. Ward, *Catalogue of Romances in the Department of Manuscripts in the British Museum*, 3 vols. (London, 1883–1910), I, 257, II, 595.

74. Moses Coit Tyler, *A History of American Literature during the Colonial Time*, rev. ed., 2 vols. (New York, 1897), II, 73; Kenneth B. Murdock, *Increase Mather: The Foremost American Puritan* (Cambridge, Mass., 1925), 170–174; Perry Miller, *The New England Mind: From Colony to Province* (Cambridge, Mass, 1953), 143; but for apparent approval of Murdock's arguments, cf. 180.

75. Svendsen, *Milton and Science*, 5, 44, 84.

76. In trying to account for attitudes toward the Negro in early America, Winthrop Jordan was driven to speaking of "deeper" attitudes that somehow formed and were perpetuated in Elizabethan culture: Jordan, *White over Black: American Attitudes Toward the Negro, 1550–1812* (Baltimore, 1969), viii–ix, and chap. 1. My problem is akin to his, in that the popular culture I am describing was remarkably tenacious and encompassing, even though its exact sources and lines of influence cannot readily be specified.

77. Beard, *Theatre of Gods Judgements*, 2.

78. Increase Mather, *The Doctrine of Divine Providence Opened and Applyed* (Boston, 1684), 43, 30–32, 34, 81, 133; and for the figure of the wheel and

the rise and fall of kings, cf. pp. 9, 16–17. The image of the wheel derives from Ezekiel 1:15–16, et seq.

79. As is suggested by Jon Butler, "Magic, Astrology, and the Early American Religious Heritage, 1600–1760," *American Historical Review*, LXXXIV (1979), 317–346, an essay that seems almost perverse in its refusal to acknowledge the syncretism of seventeenth-century religion and the commo interest of both clergy and laity in such "superstitions." The most important description of intellectual tolerance and syncreticism in seventeenth-century England is MacDonald, *Mystical Bedlam*, which in this regard serves to correct the impression that arises from Thomas, *Religion and the Decline of Magic*, of a clear line between the two. Anthropologists struggle to define the difference between magic and religion; literary and cultural historians by and large agree in de-emphasizing the distinction. "Our hard and fast distinction between the natural and the supernatural was unknown in the middle ages; there was no line between jug-glery . . . and magic, most people not knowing how either was performed; indeed any remarkable performance with a secular background . . . might be called a miracle." Tatlock, *Legendary History*, 362–363. "It is of course notoriously difficult . . . to say where religion becomes magic: the genuine Middle English charms (like many of their predecessors in Old English) use much religious imagery." Douglas Gray, *Themes and Images in the Medieval English Religious Lyric* (London, 1972), 34. See also Jean-Claude Schmitt, "Les Traditions Folkloriques dans la Culture Médiévale," *Archives de Sciences Sociales des Religions*, LII (1981), 5–20, a reference I owe to Keith Thomas.

80. Jean Delumeau, *Catholicism between Luther and Voltaire: A New View of the Counter-Reformation* (London, 1977), 63.

81. Thomas Robie, *A Letter to a Certain Gentleman, ec.* (Boston, 1719), 8; J.F.C. Harrison, *The Second Coming: Popular Millenarianism, 1780–1850* (London, 1979), chap. 3.

WAR AND CULTURE

*Daniel K. Richter*

In recent years, an older "clash of cultures" model for understanding Indian European relations has been replaced by the view that a "new world" was collectively created. The new model suggests that different Native American tribes and the diverse French, Dutch, English, and other European colonists in early America acted and interacted through a complex process of cultural accommodation and conflict. This perspective is helping us to see why and how the various peoples of early America acted in their own societies and with each other in cooperation, conflict, and often confusion.

As Daniel Richter's essay shows, Indians' motives for making war were quite different from those that led Europeans into combat. From the colonists' perspective, the importance that Indians gave to war confirmed their image as bloodthirsty savages. In contrast, Richter argues that the Iroquois went to war "for reasons rooted as much in internal social demands as in external disputes with their neighbors." For many Indian cultures the traditional institution known as the "mourning war," through which a dead person was replaced by capturing or adopting someone else, provided a means for maintaining the population and coping with death. As Richter explains, the Iroquois understood the need to restore their population in spiritual terms. When a person died, the power of the clan or nation was decreased in proportion to his or her individual spiritual power. During the last decades of the seventeenth century, the Iroquois faced the very real possibility of extinction through exposure to European diseases. Though the ravages of European disease and colonial warfare prevented the "mourning war" from fulfilling its intended purpose, throughout the late seventeenth century this traditional approach to war helped the Iroquois assuage the grief of mourners and address the loss of spiritual power in their ranks.

Adapted by permission from Daniel K. Richter, "War and Culture: The Iroquois Experience," *William and Mary Quarterly*, XL (1983), 528–559.

# 3

# WAR AND CULTURE
## The Iroquois Experience

*Daniel K. Richter*

"THE CHARACTER of all these [Iroquois] Nations is warlike and cruel," wrote Jesuit missionary Paul Le Jeune in 1657. "The chief virtue of these poor Pagans being cruelty, just as mildness is that of Christians, they teach it to their children from their very cradles, and accustom them to the most atrocious carnage and the most barbarous spectacles."[1] Like most Europeans of his day, Le Jeune ignored his own countrymen's capacity for bloodlust and attributed the supposedly unique bellicosity of the Iroquois to their irreligion and uncivilized condition. Still, his observations contain a kernel of truth often overlooked by our more sympathetic eyes: in ways quite unfamiliar and largely unfathomable to Europeans, warfare was vitally important in the cultures of the seventeenth-century Iroquois and their neighbors. For generations of Euro-Americans, the significance that Indians attached to warfare seemed to substantiate images of bloodthirsty savages who waged war for mere sport. Only in recent decades have ethnohistorians discarded such shibboleths and begun to study Indian wars in the same economic and diplomatic frameworks long used by students of European conflicts. Almost necessarily, given the weight of past prejudice, their work has stressed similarities between Indian and European warfare.[2] Thus neither commonplace stereotypes nor scholarly efforts to combat them have left much room for serious consideration of the possibility that the non-state societies of aboriginal North America may have waged war for different—but no less rational and no more savage—purposes than did the nation-states of Europe.[3] This article explores that possibility through an analysis of the changing role of warfare in Iroquois culture during the first century after European contact.

The Iroquois Confederacy (composed, from west to east, of the Five Nations of the Seneca, Cayuga, Onondaga, Oneida, and Mohawk) frequently went to war for reasons rooted as much in internal social demands as in external disputes with their neighbors. The same observation could be made about countless European states, but the particular internal motives that often propelled the Iroquois and other northeastern Indians to make war have few parallels in Euro-American experience. In many Indian cultures a pattern known as the "mourning-war" was one means of restoring lost population, ensuring social continuity, and dealing with death.[4] A grasp of the changing role of this pattern in Iroquois culture is essential if the seventeenth- and early eighteenth-century campaigns of the Five Nations—and a vital aspect of the contact situation—are to be understood. "War is a necessary exercise for the Iroquois," explained missionary and ethnologist Joseph François Lafitau, "for, besides the usual motives which people have in declaring it against troublesome neighbours . . . , it is indispensable to them also because of one of their fundamental laws of being."[5]

## I

Euro-Americans often noted that martial skills were highly valued in Indian societies and that, for young men, exploits on the warpath were important determinants of personal prestige. This was, some hyperbolized, particularly true of the Iroquois. "It is not for the Sake of Tribute . . . that they make War," Cadwallader Colden observed of the Five Nations, "but from the Notions of Glory, which they have ever most strongly imprinted on their Minds."[6] Participation in a war party was a benchmark episode in an Iroquois youth's development, and later success in battle increased the young man's stature in his clan and village. His prospects for an advantageous marriage, his chances for recognition as a village leader, and his hopes for eventual selection to a sachemship depended largely—though by no means entirely—on his skill on the warpath, his munificence in giving war feasts, and his ability to attract followers when organizing a raid.[7] Missionary-explorer Louis Hennepin exaggerated when he claimed that "those amongst the *Iroquoise* who are not given to War, are had in great Contempt, and pass for Lazy and Effeminate People," but warriors did in fact reap great social rewards.[8]

The plaudits offered to successful warriors suggest a deep cultural significance; societies usually reward warlike behavior not for its own sake but for the useful functions it performs.[9] Among the functions postulated in recent studies of non-state warfare is the maintenance of stable population levels. Usually this involves, in more or less obvious ways, a check on excessive population growth, but in some instances warfare can be, for the victors, a means to increase the group's numbers.[10] The traditional wars of the Five Nations served the latter purpose. The Iroquois conceptualized the process of population maintenance in terms of individual and collective spiritual power. When a person died, the power of his or her lineage, clan, and nation was diminished in proportion to his or her individual spiritual strength.[11] To replenish the depleted power the Iroquois conducted "requickening" ceremonies at which the deceased's name—and with it the social role and duties it represented—was transferred to a successor. Vacant positions in Iroquois families and villages were thus both literally and symbolically filled, and the continuity of Iroquois society was confirmed, while survivors were assured that the social role and spiritual strength embodied in the departed's name had not been lost.[12] Warfare was crucial to these customs, for when the deceased was a person of ordinary status and little authority, the beneficiary of the requickening was often a war captive, who would be adopted "to help strengthen the familye in lew of their deceased Freind."[13] "A father who has lost his son adopts a young prisoner in his place," explained an eighteenth-century commentator on Indian customs. "An orphan takes a father or mother; a widow a husband; one man takes a sister and another a brother."[14]

On a societal level, then, warfare helped the Iroquois to deal with deaths in their ranks. On a personal, emotional level it performed similar functions. The Iroquois believed that the grief inspired by a relative's death could, if uncontrolled, plunge survivors into depths of despair that robbed them of their reason and disposed them to fits of rage potentially harmful to themselves and the community. Accordingly, Iroquois culture directed mourners' emotions into ritualized channels. Members of the deceased's household, "after having the hair cut, smearing the face with earth or charcoal and gotten themselves up in the most frightful negligence," embarked on ten days of "deep mourning," during which "they remain at the back of their bunk, their face against the ground or turned towards the back of the platform, their head enveloped in their blanket which is the dirtiest and least clean rag that they have. They do not look at or speak to anyone except through necessity and in a low voice. They hold themselves excused from every duty of civility and courtesy."[15] For the next year the survivors engaged in less intense formalized grieving, beginning to resume their daily habits but continuing to disregard their personal appearance and many social amenities. While mourners thus channeled their emotions, others hastened to "cover up" the grief of the bereaved with condolence rituals, feasts, and presents (including the special variety of condolence gift often somewhat misleadingly described as *wergild*). These were designed to cleanse sorrowing hearts and to ease the return to normal life. Social and personal needs converged at the culmination of these ceremonies, the "requickening" of the deceased.[16]

But if the mourners' grief remained unassuaged, the ultimate socially sanctioned channel for their violent impulses was a raid to seek captives who, it was hoped, would ease their pain. The target of the mourning-war was usually a people traditionally defined as enemies; neither they nor anyone else need necessarily be held directly responsible for the death that provoked the attack, though most often the foe could be made to bear the blame.[17] Raids for captives could be either large-scale efforts organized on village, nation, or confederacy levels or, more often, attacks by small parties raised at the behest of female kin of the deceased. Members of the dead person's household, presumably lost in grief, did not usually participate directly. Instead, young men who were related by marriage to the bereaved women but who lived in other longhouses were obliged to form a raiding party or face the matrons' accusations of cowardice.[18] When the warriors returned with captured men, women, and children, mourners could select a prisoner for adoption in the place of the deceased or they could vent their rage in rituals of torture and execution.[19]

The rituals began with the return of the war party, which had sent word ahead of the number of captives seized. Most of the villagers, holding clubs, sticks, and other weapons, stood in two rows outside the village entrance to meet the prisoners. Men, but usually not women or young children, received heavy blows designed to inflict pain without serious injury. Then they were stripped and led to a raised platform in an open space inside the village, where old women led the community in further physical abuse, tearing out fingernails and poking sensitive body parts with sticks and firebrands.[20] After several hours, prisoners were allowed to rest and eat, and later they were made to dance for their captors while their fate was decided. Headmen apportioned them to grieving families, whose matrons then chose either to adopt or to execute them.[21] If those who were adopted made a sincere effort to please their new relatives and to assimilate into village society, they could expect a long life; if they displeased, they were quietly and unceremoniously killed.

A captive slated for ritual execution was usually also adopted and subsequently addressed appropriately as "uncle" or "nephew," but his status was marked by a distinctive red and black pattern of facial paint. During the next few days the doomed man gave his death feast, where his executioners saluted him and allowed him to recite his war honors. On the appointed day he was tied with a short rope to a stake, and villagers of both sexes and all ages took turns wielding firebrands and various red hot objects to burn him systematically from the feet up. The tormentors behaved with religious solemnity and spoke in symbolic language of "caressing" their adopted relative with their firebrands. The victim was expected to endure his sufferings stoically and even to encourage his torturers, but this seems to have been ideal rather than typical behavior. If he too quickly began to swoon, his ordeal briefly ceased and he received food and drink and time to recover somewhat before the burning resumed. At length, before he expired, someone scalped him, another threw hot sand on his exposed skull, and finally a warrior dispatched him with a knife to the chest or a hatchet to the neck. Then the victim's flesh was stripped from his bones and thrown into cooking kettles, and the whole village feasted on his remains. This feast carried great religious significance for the Iroquois, but its full meaning is irretrievable; most European observers were too shocked to probe its implications.[22]

Mourners were not the only ones to benefit from the ceremonial torture and execution of captives. While grieving relatives vented their emotions, all of the villagers, by partaking in the humiliation of every prisoner and the torture of some, were able to participate directly in the defeat of their foes. Warfare thus dramatically promoted group cohesion and demonstrated to the Iroquois their superiority over their enemies. At the same time, youths learned valuable lessons in the behavior expected of warriors and in the way to die bravely should they ever be captured. Le Jeune's "barbarous spectacles" were a vital element in the ceremonial life of Iroquois communities.[23]

The social demands of the mourning-war shaped strategy and tactics in at least two ways. First, the essential measure of a war party's success was its ability to seize prisoners and bring them home alive. Capture of enemies was preferred to killing them on the spot and taking their scalps, while none of the benefits European combatants derived from war—territorial expansion, economic gain, plunder of the defeated—outranked the seizure of prisoners.[24] When missionary Jérôme Lalemant disparaged Iroquoian warfare as "consisting of a few broken heads along the highways, or of some captives brought into the country to be burned and eaten there," he was more accurate than he knew.[25] The overriding importance of captive taking set Iroquois warfare dramatically apart from the Euro-American military experience. "We are not like you CHRISTIANS for when you have taken Prisoners of one another you send them home, by such means you can never rout one another," explained the Onondaga orator Teganissorens to Gov. Robert Hunter of New York in 1711.[26]

The centrality of captives to the business of war was clear in precombat rituals: imagery centered on a boiling war kettle; the war feast presaged the future cannibalistic rite; mourning women urged warriors to bring them prisoners to assuage their grief; and, if more than one village participated in the campaign, leaders agreed in advance on the share of captives that each town would receive.[27] As Iroquois warriors saw it, to forget the importance of captive taking or to ignore the rituals associated with it was to invite defeat. In 1642 missionary Isaac Jogues observed a ceremony he believed to be a sacrifice to Areskoui, the deity who presided over Iroquois wars. "At a solemn feast which they had made of two Bears, which they had offered to their demon, they had used this form of words: 'Aireskoi, thou dost right to punish us, and to give us no more captives' (they were speaking of the Algonquins, of whom that year they had not taken one . . .) 'because we have sinned by not eating the bodies of those whom thou last gavest us; but we promise thee to eat the first ones whom thou shalt give us, as we now do with these two Bears.'"[28]

A second tactical reflection of the social functions of warfare was a strong sanction against the loss of Iroquois lives in battle. A war party that, by European standards, seemed on the brink of triumph could be expected to retreat sorrowfully homeward if it suffered a few fatalities. For the Indians, such a campaign was no victory; casualties would subvert the purpose of warfare as a means of restocking the population.[29] In contrast to European beliefs that to perish in combat was acceptable and even honorable, Iroquois beliefs made death in battle a frightful prospect, though one that must be faced bravely if necessary. Slain warriors, like all who died violent deaths, were said to be excluded from the villages of the dead, doomed to spend a roving eternity seeking vengeance. As a result, their bodies were not interred in village cemeteries, lest their angry souls disturb the repose of others. Both in burial and in the afterlife, a warrior who fell in combat faced separation from his family and friends.[30]

Efforts to minimize fatalities accordingly underlay several tactics that contemporary Euro-Americans considered cowardly: fondness for ambushes and surprise attacks; unwillingness to fight when outnumbered; and avoidance of frontal assaults on fortified places. Defensive tactics showed a similar emphasis on precluding loss of life. Spies in enemy villages and an extensive network of scouts warned of invading war parties before they could harm Iroquois villagers. If intruders did enter Iroquoia, defenders attacked from ambush, but only if they felt confident of repulsing the enemy without too many losses of their own. The people retreated behind palisades or, if the enemy appeared too strong to resist, burned their own villages and fled—warriors included—into the woods or to neighboring villages. Houses and corn supplies thus might temporarily be lost, but unless the invaders achieved complete surprise, the lives and spiritual power of the people remained intact. In general, when the Iroquois were at a disadvantage, they preferred flight or an insincerely negotiated truce to the costly last stands that earned glory for European warriors.[31]

That kind of glory, and the warlike way of life it reflected, were not Iroquois ideals. Warfare was a specific response to the death of specific individuals at specific times, a sporadic affair characterized by seizing from traditional enemies a few captives who would replace the dead, literally or symbolically, and ease the pain of those who mourned. While war was not to be undertaken gladly or lightly, it was still "a necessary exercise for the Iroquois,"[32] for it was an integral part of individual and social mourning practices. When the Iroquois envisioned a day of no more wars, with their Great League of Peace extended to all peoples, they also envisioned an alternative to the mourning functions of warfare. That alternative was embodied in the proceedings of league councils and Iroquois peace negotiations with other peoples, which began with—and frequently consisted entirely of—condolence ceremonies and exchanges of presents designed to dry the tears, unstop the mouths, and cleanse the hearts of bereaved participants.[33] Only when grief was forgotten could war end and peace begin. In the century following the arrival of Europeans, grief could seldom be forgotten.

## II

After the 1620s, when the Five Nations first made sustained contact with Europeans, the role of warfare in Iroquois culture changed dramatically. By 1675, European diseases, firearms, and trade had produced dangerous new patterns of conflict that threatened to derange the traditional functions of the mourning-war.

Before most Iroquois had ever seen a Dutchman or a Frenchman, they had felt the impact of the maladies the invaders inadvertently brought with them.[34] By the 1640s the number of Iroquois (and of their Indian neighbors) had probably already been halved by epidemics of smallpox, measles, and other European "childhood diseases," to which Indian populations had no immunity.[35] The devastation continued through the century. A partial list of plagues that struck the Five Nations includes "a general malady" among the Mohawk in 1647; "a great mortality" among the Onondaga in 1656–1657; a smallpox epidemic among the Oneida, Onondaga, Cayuga, and Seneca in 1661–1663; "a kind of contagion" among the Seneca in 1668; "a fever of . . . malignant character" among the Mohawk in 1673; and "a general Influenza" among the Seneca in 1676.[36] As thousands died, ever-growing numbers of captive adoptees would be necessary if the Iroquois were even to begin to replace their losses; mourning-wars of unprecedented scale loomed ahead. Warfare would cease to be a sporadic and specific response to individual deaths and would become instead a constant and increasingly undifferentiated symptom of societies in demographic crisis.

At the same time, European firearms would make warfare unprecedentedly dangerous for both the Iroquois and their foes, and would undermine traditional Indian sanctions against battle fatalities. The introduction of guns, together with the replacement of flint arrowheads by more efficient iron, copper, and brass ones that could pierce traditional Indian wooden armor, greatly increased the chances of death in combat and led to major changes in Iroquois tactics. In the early seventeenth century Champlain had observed mostly ceremonial and relatively bloodless confrontations between large Indian armies, but with the advent of muskets—which Europeans had designed to be fired in volleys during just such battles—massed confrontations became, from the Indian perspective, suicidal folly. They were quickly abandoned in favor of a redoubled emphasis on small-scale raids and ambushes, in which Indians learned far sooner than Euro-Americans how to aim cumbersome muskets accurately at individual targets.[37] By the early 1640s the Mohawk were honing such skills with approximately three hundred guns acquired from the Dutch of Albany and from English sources. Soon the rest of the Five Nations followed the Mohawk example.[38]

Temporarily, the Iroquois' plentiful supply and skillful use of firearms gave them a considerable advantage over their Indian enemies: during the 1640s and 1650s the less well armed Huron and the poorly armed Neutral and Khionontateronon (Petun or Tobacco Nation) succumbed to Iroquois firepower. That advantage had largely disappeared by the 1660s and 1670s, however, as the Five Nations learned in their battles with such heavily armed foes as the Susquehannock. Once muskets came into general use in Indian warfare, several drawbacks became apparent: they were more sluggish than arrows to fire and much slower to reload; their noise lessened the capacity for surprise; and reliance on them left Indians dependent on Euro-Americans for ammunition, repairs, and replacements. But there could be no return to the days of bows and arrows and wooden armor. Few Iroquois war parties could now expect to escape mortal casualties.[39]

While European diseases and firearms intensified Indian conflicts and stretched the mourning-war tradition beyond previous limits, a third major aspect of European contact pushed Iroquois warfare in novel directions. Trade with Europeans made economic motives central to American Indian conflicts for the first time. Because iron tools, firearms, and other trade goods so quickly became essential to Indian economies, struggles for those items and for furs to barter for them lay behind numerous seventeenth-century wars. Between 1624 and 1628 the Iroquois gained unimpeded access to European commodities when Mohawk warriors drove the Mahican to the east of the Hudson River and secured an open route to the Dutch traders of Albany.[40] But obtaining the furs to exchange for the goods of Albany was a problem not so easily solved. By about 1640 the Five Nations perhaps had exhausted the beaver stock of their home hunting territories; more important, they could not find in relatively temperate Iroquoia the thick northern pelts prized by Euro-American traders.[41] A long, far-flung series of "beaver wars" ensued, in which the Five Nations battled the Algonquian nations of the Saint Lawrence River region, the Huron, the Khionontateronon, the Neutral, the Erie, and other western and northern peoples in a constant struggle over fur supplies. In those wars the Iroquois more frequently sought dead beavers than live ones: most of their raids were not part of a strategic plan to seize new hunting grounds but piratical attacks on enemy canoes carrying pelts to Montreal and Trois-Rivières.[42]

The beaver wars inexorably embroiled the Iroquois in conflict with the French of Canada. Franco-Iroquois hostilities dated from the era of Champlain, who consistently based his relations with Canada's natives upon promises to aid them in their traditional raids against the Five Nations. "I came to the conclusion," wrote Champlain in 1619, "that it was very necessary to assist them, both to engage them the more to love us, and also to provide the means of furthering my enterprises and explorations which apparently could only be carried out with their help."[43] The French commander and a few of his men participated in Indian campaigns against the Five Nations in 1609, 1610, and 1615, and encouraged countless other raids.[44] From the 1630s to the 1660s, conflict between the Five Nations and Canadian Indians intensified, and Iroquois war parties armed with guns frequently blockaded the Saint Lawrence and stopped the flow of furs to the French settlements. A state of open war, punctuated by short truces, consequently prevailed between New France and various of the Five Nations, particularly the Mohawk. The battles were almost exclusively economic and geopolitical—the Iroquois were not much interested in French captives—and in general the French suffered more than the Iroquois from the fighting.[45] Finally, in 1666, a French army invaded Iroquoia and burned the Mohawks' fortified villages, from which all had fled to safety except a few old men who chose to stay and die. In 1667, the Five Nations and the French made a peace that lasted for over a decade.[46]

While the fur trade introduced new economic goals, additional foes, and wider scope to Iroquois warfare, it did not crowd out older cultural motives. Instead, the mourning-war tradition, deaths from disease, dependence on firearms, and the trade in furs combined to produce a dangerous spiral: epidemics led to deadlier mourning-wars fought with firearms; the need for guns increased the demand for pelts to trade for them; the quest for furs provoked wars with other nations; and deaths in those conflicts began the mourning-war cycle anew. At each turn, fresh economic and demographic motives fed the spiral.

Accordingly, in the mid-seventeenth-century Iroquois wars, the quest for captives was at least as important as the quest for furs. Even in the archetypal beaver war, the Five Nations-Huron conflict, only an overriding—even desperate—demand for prisoners can explain much of Iroquois behavior. For nearly a decade after the dispersal of the Huron Confederacy in 1649, Iroquois war parties killed or took captive every starving (and certainly peltry-less) group of Huron refugees they could find. Meanwhile, Iroquois ambassadors and warriors alternately negotiated with, cajoled, and threatened the Huron remnants living at Quebec to make them join their captive relatives in Iroquoia. Through all this, Mohawks, Senecas, and Onondagas occasionally shed each other's blood in arguments over the human spoils. Ultimately, in 1657, with French acquiescence, most of the Huron refugees fled from Quebec—the Arendaronon nation to the Onondaga country and the Attignawantan nation to the Mohawk country.[47]

Judging by the number of prisoners taken during the Five Nations' wars from the 1640s to the 1670s with their other Iroquoian neighbors—the Neutral, Khionontateronon, Erie, and Susquehannock—these conflicts stemmed from a similar mingling of captive-taking and fur trade motives. Like the Huron, each of those peoples shared with the Iroquois mixed horticultural and hunting and fishing economies, related languages, and similar beliefs, making them ideal candidates for adoption. But they could not satisfy the spiraling Iroquois demand for furs and captives; war parties from the Five Nations had to range ever farther in their quest. In a not atypical series of raids in 1661–1662, they struck the Abenaki of the New England region, the Algonquians of the subarctic, the Siouans of the Upper Mississippi area, and various Indians near Virginia, while continuing the struggle with enemies closer to home.[48] The results of the mid-century campaigns are recorded in the *Jesuit Relations*, whose pages are filled with descriptions of Iroquois torture and execution of captives and note enormous numbers of adoptions. The Five Nations had absorbed so many prisoners that in 1657 Le Jeune believed that "more Foreigners than natives of the country" resided in Iroquoia.[49] By the mid-1660s several missionaries estimated that two-thirds or more of the people in many Iroquois villages were adoptees.[50]

By 1675 a half-century of constantly escalating warfare had at best enabled the Iroquois to hold their own. Despite the beaver wars, the Five Nations still had few dependable sources of furs. In the early 1670s they hunted primarily on lands north of Lake Ontario, where armed clashes with Algonquian foes were likely, opportunities to steal peltries from them were abundant, and conflict with the French who claimed the territory was always possible.[51] Ironically, even the Franco-Iroquois peace of 1667 proved a mixed blessing for the Five Nations. Under the provisions of the treaty, Jesuit priests, who had hitherto labored in Iroquois villages only sporadically and at the risk of their lives, established missions in each of the Five Nations.[52] The Jesuits not only created Catholic converts but also generated strong Christian and traditionalist factions that brought unprecedented disquiet to Iroquois communities. Among the Onondaga, for example, the Christian sachem Garakontié's refusal to perform his duties in the traditional manner disrupted such important ceremonies as dream guessings, the roll call of the chiefs, and healing rituals.[53] And in 1671, traditionalist Mohawk women excluded at least one Catholic convert from her rightful seat on the council of matrons because of her faith.[54] Moreover, beginning in the late 1660s, missionaries encouraged increasing numbers of Catholic Iroquois—particularly Mohawks and Oneidas—to desert their homes for the mission villages of Canada; by the mid-1670s well over two hundred had departed.[55] A large proportion of those who left, however, were members of the Five Nations in name only. Many—perhaps most—were recently adopted Huron and other prisoners, an indication that the Iroquois were unable to assimilate effectively the mass of newcomers their mid-century wars had brought them.[56]

Problems in incorporating adoptees reflected a broader dilemma: by the late 1670s the mourning-war complex was crumbling. Warfare was failing to maintain a stable population; despite torrents of prisoners, gains from adoption were exceeded by losses from disease, combat, and migrations to Canada. Among the Mohawk—for whom more frequent contemporary population estimates exist than for the other nations of the confederacy—the number of warriors declined from 700 or 800 in the 1640s to approximately 300 in the late 1670s. Those figures imply that, even with a constant infusion of captive adoptees, Mohawk population fell by half during that period.[57] The Five Nations as a whole fared only slightly better. In the 1640s the confederacy, already drastically reduced in numbers, had counted over 10,000 people. By the 1670s there were perhaps only 8,600.[58] The mourning-war, then, was not discharging one of its primary functions.

Meanwhile, ancient customs regarding the treatment of prisoners were decaying as rituals degenerated into chaotic violence and sheer murderous rage displaced the orderly adoption of captives that the logic of the mourning-war demanded. In 1682 missionary Jean de Lamberville asserted that Iroquois warriors "killed and ate . . . on the spot" over six hundred enemies in a campaign in the Illinois country; if he was even half right, it is clear that something had gone horribly wrong in the practice of the mourning-war. The decay of important customs associated with traditional warfare is further indicated by Lamberville's account of the return of that war party with its surviving prisoners. A gauntlet ceremony at the main Onondaga village turned into a deadly attack, forcing headmen to struggle to protect the lives of the captives. A few hours later, drunken young men, "who observed[d] no usages or customs," broke into longhouses and tried to kill the prisoners whom the headmen had rescued. In vain leaders pleaded with their people to remember "That it was contrary to custom to ill-treat prisoners on their arrival, when They had not yet been given in the place of any person . . . and when their fate had been left Undecided by the victors."[59]

Nevertheless, despite the weakening of traditional restraints, in the 1670s Iroquois warfare still performed useful functions. It maintained a tenuous supply of furs to trade for essential European goods; it provided frequent campaigns to allow young men to show their valor; and it secured numerous captives to participate in the continual mourning rituals that the many Iroquois deaths demanded (though there could never be enough to restock the population absolutely). In the quarter-century after 1675, however, the scales would tip: by 1700 the Anglo-French struggle for control of the continent would make warfare—as the Five Nations were practicing it—dangerously dysfunctional for their societies.

## III

By 1700 Iroquois warfare and culture had reached a turning point. Up to about 1675, despite the impact of disease, firearms, and the fur trade, warfare still performed functions that outweighed its costs. But thereafter the Anglo-French struggle for control of North America made war disastrous for the Five Nations. Conflict in the west, instead of securing fur supplies, was cutting them off, while lack of pelts to trade and wartime shortages of goods at Albany created serious economic hardship in Iroquoia.[60] Those problems paled, however, in comparison with the physical toll. All of the Iroquois nations except the Cayuga had seen their villages and crops destroyed by invading armies, and all five nations were greatly weakened by loss of members to captivity, to death in combat, or to famine and disease. By some estimates, between 1689 and 1698 the Iroquois lost half of their fighting strength. That figure is probably an exaggeration, but by 1700 perhaps 500 of the 2,000 warriors the Five Nations fielded in 1689 had been killed or captured or had deserted to the French missions and had not been replaced by younger warriors. A loss of well over 1,600 from a total population of approximately 8,600 seems a conservative estimate.[61]

At the turn of the century, therefore, the mourning-war was no longer even symbolically restocking the population. And, far from being socially integrative, the Five Nations' current war was splitting their communities asunder. The heavy death toll of previous decades had robbed them of many respected headmen and clan matrons to whom the people had looked for guidance and arbitration of disputes. As a group of young Mohawk warriors lamented in 1691 when they came to parley with the Catholic Iroquois settled near Montreal, "all those . . . who had sense are dead."[62] The power vacuum, war weariness, and the pressures of the imperial struggle combined to place at each other's throats those who believed that the Iroquois' best chance lay in separate peace with the French and those who continued to rely on the English alliance. "The [Five] Nations are full of faction, the French having got a great interest among them," reported the Albany Commissioners for Indian Affairs in July 1700. At Onondaga, where, according to Governor Bellomont, the French had "full as many friends" as the English, the situation was particularly severe. Some sachems found themselves excluded from councils, and factions charged one another with using poison to remove adversaries from the scene. One pro-English Onondaga headman, Aquendero, had to take refuge near Albany, leaving his son near death and supposedly bewitched by opponents.[63] Their politics being ordered by an interlocking structure of lineages, clans and moieties, the Iroquois found such factions, which cut across kinship lines, difficult if not impossible to handle. In the 1630s the Huron, whose political structure was similar, never could manage the novel factional alignments that resulted from the introduction of Christianity. That failure perhaps contributed to their demise at the hands of the Five Nations.[64] Now the Iroquois found themselves at a similar pass.

As the new century opened, however, Iroquois headmen were beginning to construct solutions to some of the problems facing their people. From 1699 to 1701 Iroquois ambassadors—in particular the influential Onondaga Teganissorens—threaded the thickets of domestic factionalism and shuttled between their country and the Euro-American colonies to negotiate what one scholar has termed "The Grand Settlement of 1701."[65] On August 4, 1701, at an immense gathering at Montreal, representatives of the Seneca, Cayuga, Onondaga, and Oneida, also speaking for the Mohawk, met Governor Callière and headmen of the Wyandot, Algonquin, Abenaki, Nipissing, Ottawa, Ojibwa, Sauk, Fox, Miami, Potawatomi, and other French allies. The participants ratified arrangements made during the previous year that provided for a general peace, established vague boundaries for western hunting territories (the Iroquois basically consented to remain east of Detroit), and eschewed armed conflict in favor of arbitration by the governor of New France. A few days later, the Iroquois and Callière reached more specific understandings concerning Iroquois access to Detroit and other French western trading posts. Mostly from the French standpoint, the Iroquois promised neutrality in future Anglo-French wars.[66]

On one level, this series of treaties represented an Iroquois defeat. The Five Nations had lost the war and, in agreement to peace on terms largely dictated by Callière, had acknowledged their inability to prevail militarily over their French, and especially their Indian, enemies.[67] Nevertheless, the Grand Settlement did secure for the Iroquois five important ends: escape from the devastating warfare of the 1690s; rights to hunting in the west; potentially profitable trade with western Indians passing through Iroquoia to sell furs at Albany; access to markets in New France and Pennsylvania as well as in New York; and the promise of noninvolvement in future imperial wars. The Grand Settlement thus brought to the Five Nations not only peace on their northern and western flanks, but also a more stable economy based on guaranteed western hunting territories and access to multiple

Euro-American markets. Henceforth, self-destructive warfare need no longer be the only means of ensuring Iroquois economic survival, and neither need inter-Indian beaver wars necessarily entrap the Five Nations in struggles between Euro-Americans.[68] In 1724, nearly a generation after the negotiation of the Grand Settlement, an Iroquois spokesman explained to a delegation from Massachusetts how the treaties, while limiting Iroquois diplomatic and military options, nevertheless proved beneficial. "Tho' the Hatchett lays by our side yet the way is open between this Place and Canada, and trade is free both going and coming," he answered when the New Englanders urged the Iroquois to attack New France. "If a War should break out and we should use the Hatchett that layes by our Side, those Paths which are now open wo[u]ld be stopped, and if we should make war it would not end in a few days as yours doth but it must last till one nation or the other is destroyed as it has been heretofore with us[.] . . . [W]e know what whipping and scourging is from the Governor of Canada."[69]

After the Grand Settlement, then, Iroquois leaders tried to abandon warfare as a means of dealing with the diplomatic problems generated by the Anglo-French imperial rivalry and the economic dilemmas of the fur trade. Through most of the first half of the eighteenth century the headmen pursued a policy of neutrality between the empires with a dexterity that the English almost never, and the French only seldom, comprehended. At the same time the Iroquois began to cement peaceful trading relationships with the western nations. Sporadic fighting continued in the western hunting grounds through the first decade and a half of the eighteenth century, as the parties to the 1701 Montreal treaty sorted out the boundaries of their territories and engaged in reciprocal raids for captives that were provoked by contact between Iroquois and western Indian hunters near French posts. Iroquois headmen quickly took advantage of Canadian arbitration when such quarrels arose, however, and they struggled to restrain young warriors from campaigning in the west.

In addition to its diplomatic benefits, the Grand Settlement of 1701 provided a partial solution to Iroquois factionalism. Iroquoian non-state political structures could not suppress factional cleavages entirely, and in the years after 1701 differences over relations with the French and the English still divided Iroquois communities, as each European power continued to encourage its friends. Interpreters such as the Canadian Louis-Thomas Chabert de Joncaire and the New Yorker Lawrence Claeson (or Claes) struggled to win the hearts of Iroquois villagers; each side gave presents to its supporters; and on several occasions English officials interfered with the selection of sachems in order to strengthen pro-English factions. As a result, fratricidal disputes still occasionally threatened to tear villages apart.[70] Still, in general, avoidance of exclusive alliances or major military conflict with either European power allowed Iroquois councils to keep factional strife within bounds. A new generation of headmen learned to maintain a rough equilibrium between pro-French and pro-English factions at home, as well as peaceful relations with French and English abroad. Central to that strategy was an intricate policy that tried to balance French against English fortified trading posts, Canadian against New York blacksmiths, and Jesuit against Anglican missionaries. Each supplied the Iroquois with coveted aspects of Euro-American culture—trade goods, technology, and spiritual power, respectively—but each also could be a focus of factional leadership and a tool of Euro-American domination. The Grand Settlement provided a way to lessen, though hardly eliminate, those dangers.[71]

The years following the Grand Settlement also witnessed the stabilization of Iroquois population. Though the numbers of the Iroquois continued to decline gradually, the forces that had so dramatically reduced them in the seventeenth century abated markedly after

1701. The first two decades of the seventeenth century brought only one major epidemic—smallpox in 1716[72]—while the flow of Catholic converts to Canadian missions also slowed. The missions near Montreal had lost much of the utopian character that had previously attracted so many Iroquois converts.

By the early eighteenth century, drunkenness, crushing debts to traders, and insults from Euro-American neighbors were no less characteristic of Iroquois life in Canada than in Iroquoia, and the Jesuit priests serving the Canadian missions had become old, worn-out men who had long since abandoned dreams of turning Indians into Frenchmen.[73]

As the population drain from warfare, disease, and migration to mission villages moderated, peaceful assimilation of refugees from neighboring nations helped to replace those Iroquois who were lost. One French source even claimed, in 1716, that "the five Iroquois nations . . . are becoming more and more formidable through their great numbers."[74] Most notable among the newcomers were some 1,500 Tuscaroras who, after their defeat by the English and allied Indians of the Carolinas in 1713, migrated north to settle on lands located between the Onondaga and Oneida villages. They were adopted as the sixth nation of the Iroquois Confederacy about 1722. There are indications that the Tuscarora—who, according to William Andrews, Anglican missionary to the Mohawk, possessed "an Implacable hatred against Christians at Carolina"—contributed greatly to the spirit of independence and distrust of Europeans that guided the Six Nations on their middle course between the imperial powers. The Tuscarora, concluded Andrews, were "a great Occasion of Our Indians becoming so bad as they are, they now take all Occasions to find fault and quarrel, wanting to revolt."[75]

## IV

The first two decades of the eighteenth century brought a shift away from those aspects of Iroquois warfare that had been most socially disruptive. As the Iroquois freed themselves of many, though by no means all, of the demographic, economic, and diplomatic pressures that had made seventeenth-century warfare so devastating, the mourning-war began to resume some of its traditional functions in Iroquois culture.

As the Five Nations made peace with their old western and northern foes, Iroquois mourning-war raids came to focus on enemies the Iroquois called "Flatheads"—a vague epithet for the Catawba and other tribes on the frontiers of Virginia and the Carolinas.[76] Iroquois and Flathead war parties had traded blows during the 1670s and 1680s, conflict had resumed about 1707, and after the arrival of the Tuscarora in the 1710s, Iroquois raiding parties attacked the Flatheads regularly and almost exclusively.[77] The Catawba and other southeastern Indians sided with the Carolinians in the Tuscarora War of 1711–1713, bringing them into further conflict with warriors from the Five Nations, who fought alongside the Tuscarora.[78] After the Tuscarora moved north, Iroquois-Flathead warfare increased in intensity and lasted—despite several peace treaties—until the era of the American Revolution. This series of mourning-wars exasperated English officials from New York to the Carolinas, who could conceive no rational explanation for the conflicts except the intrigues of French envoys who delighted in stirring up trouble on English frontiers.[79]

Canadian authorities did indeed encourage Iroquois warriors with arms and presents. The French were happy for the chance to harass British settlements and to strike blows against Indians who troubled French inhabitants of New Orleans and the Mississippi Valley.[80] Yet the impetus for raiding the Flatheads lay with the Iroquois, not the French. At Onondaga in 1710, when emissaries from New York blamed French influence for the campaigns and presented a wampum belt calling for a halt to hostilities, a Seneca orator dismissed their arguments: "When I think of the Brave Warriours that hav[e] been slain by the Flatheads I can Govern my self no longer. . . . I reject your Belt for the Hatred I bear to the Flatheads can never be forgotten."[81] The Flatheads were an ideal target for the mourning-wars demanded by Iroquois women and warriors, for with conflict channeled southward, warfare with northern and western nations that, in the past, had brought disaster could be avoided. In addition, war with the Flatheads placated both Canadian authorities and pro-French Iroquois factions, since the raids countered a pro-English trade policy with a military policy useful to the French. And, from the perspective of Iroquois-English relations, the southern campaigns posed few risks. New York officials alternately forbade and countenanced raids against southern Indians as the fortunes of frontier war in the Carolinas and the intrigues of intercolonial politics shifted. But even when the governors of the Carolinas, Virginia, Pennsylvania, and New York did agree on schemes to impose peace, experience with English military impotence had taught the Iroquois that the governors could do little to stop the conflict.[82]

While the diplomatic advantages were many, perhaps the most important aspect of the Iroquois-Flathead conflicts was the partial return they allowed to the traditional ways of the mourning-war. By the 1720s the Five Nations had not undone the ravages of the preceding century, yet they had largely extricated themselves from the socially disastrous wars of the fur trade and of the European empires. And though prisoners no longer flowed into Iroquois villages in the floods of the seventeenth century, the southern raids provided enough captives for occasional mourning and condolence rituals that dried Iroquois tears and reminded the Five Nations of their superiority over their enemies. In the same letter of 1716 in which missionary Andrews noted the growing independence of the Iroquois since the Tuscarora had settled among them and the southern wars had intensified, he also vividly described the reception recently given to captives of the Onondaga and Oneida.[83] Iroquois warfare was again binding Iroquois families and villages together.

## NOTES

A preliminary version of this article was presented at the Institute of Early American History and Culture's 41st Conference in Early American History at Millersville State College, Apr. 30–May 2, 1981, organized by Francis Bremer. For comments on various drafts the author thanks Aaron Berman, Elizabeth Capelle, Barbara Graymont, Francis Jennings, Sharon Mead, Diana Meisinger, Amy Mittelman, Linda Roth, Paula Rubel, Herbert Sloan, Alden Vaughan, Robert Venables, and Anthony Wallace.

1. Reuben Gold Thwaites, ed., *The Jesuit Relations and Allied Documents: Travels and Explorations of the Jesuit Missionaries in New France, 1610–1791* (Cleveland, Ohio, 1896–1901), XLIII, 263, hereafter cited as *Jesuit Relations*.

2. See, for example, George T. Hunt, *The Wars of the Iroquois: A study in Intertribal Trade Relations* (Madison, Wis., 1940); W.W. Newcomb, Jr., "A Re-Examination of the Causes of Plains Warfare," *American Anthropologist*, N.S., LII (1950), 317–330;

and Francis Jennings, *The Invasion of America: Indians, Colonialism, and the Cant of Conquest* (Chapel Hill, N.C., 1975), 146–170.

3. While anthropologists disagree about the precise distinctions between the wars of state-organized and non-state societies, they generally agree that battles for territorial conquest, economic monopoly, and subjugation or enslavement of conquered peoples are the product of the technological and organizational capacities of the state. For overviews of the literature see C. R. Hallpike, "Functionalist Interpretations of Primitive Warfare," *Man*, N.S., VIII (1973), 451–470; and Andrew Vayda, "Warfare in Ecological Perspective," *Annual Review of Ecology and Systematics*, V (1974), 183–193.

4. My use of the term *mourning-war* differs from that of Marian W. Smith in "American Indian Warfare," New York Academy of Sciences, *Transactions*, 2d Ser., XIII (1951), 348–365, which stresses the psychological and emotional functions of the

mourning-war. As the following paragraphs seek to show, the psychology of the mourning-war was deeply rooted in Iroquois demography and social structure; my use of the term accordingly reflects a more holistic view of the cultural role of the mourning-war than does Smith's. On the dangers of an excessively psychological explanation of Indian warfare see Jennings, *Invasion of America*, 159; but see also the convincing defense of Smith in Richard Drinnon, "Ravished Land," *Indian Historian*, IX (Fall 1976), 24–26.

5. Joseph François Lafitau, *Customs of the American Indians Compared with the Customs of Primitive Times*, ed. and trans. William N. Fenton and Elizabeth L. Moore (Toronto, 1974, 1977 [orig. publ. Paris, 1724]), II, 98–99.

6. Cadwallader Colden, *The History of the Five Indian Nations of Canada, Which Are Dependent on the Province of New-York in America, and Are the Barrier between the English and French in That Part of the World* (London, 1747), 4, hereafter cited as Colden, *History* (1747).

7. Gabriel Sagard, *The Long Journey to the Country of the Hurons*, ed. George M. Wrong and trans. H. H. Langton (Toronto, 1939 [orig. publ. Paris, 1632]), 151–152; *Jesuit Relations*, XLII, 139; William N. Fenton, ed., "The Hyde Manuscript: Captain William Hyde's Observations of the 5 Nations of Indians at New York, 1698," *American Scene Magazine*, VI (1965), [9]; Bruce G., Trigger, *The Children of Aataentsic: A History of the Huron People to* 1660 (Montreal, 1976), I, 68–69, 145–147.

8. Hennepin, *A New Discovery of a Vast Country in America . . .* , 1st English ed. (London, 1698), II, 88.

9. Newcomb, "Re-Examination of Plains Warfare," *Am. Anthro.*, N.S., LII (1950), 320.

10. Andrew P. Vayda, "Expansion and Warfare among Swidden Agriculturalists," *Am. Anthro.*, N.S., LXIII (1961), 346–358; Anthony Leeds, "The Functions of War," in Jules Masserman, ed., *Violence and War, with Clinical Studies* (New York, 1963), 69–82; William Tulio Divale and Marvin Harris, "Population, Warfare, and the Male Supremacist Complex," *Am. Anthro.*, N.S., LXXVIII (1976), 521–538.

11. J. N. B. Hewitt, "Orenda and a Definition of Religion," *Am. Anthro.*, N.S., IV (1902), 33–46; Morris Wolf, *Iroquois Religion and Its Relation to Their Morals* (New York, 1919), 25–26; Alvin M. Josephy, Jr., *The Indian Heritage of America* (New York, 1968), 94; Ake Hultkrantz, *The Religions of the American Indians*, trans. Monica Setterwall (Berkeley, Calif., 1979), 12.

12. *Jesuit Relations*, XXIII, 165–169; Lafitau, *Customs of American Indians*, ed. and trans. Fenton and Moore, I, 71; B. H. Quain, "The Iroquois," in Margaret Mead, ed., *Cooperation and Competition among Primitive Peoples* (New York, 1937), 276–277.

13. Fenton, ed., "Hyde Manuscript," *Am. Scene Mag.*, VI (1965), [16].

14. Philip Mazzei, *Researches on the United States*, ed. and trans. Constance B. Sherman (Charlottesville, Va., 1976 [orig. publ. Paris, 1788]), 349. See also P[ierre] de Charlevoix, *Journal of a Voyage to North-America . . .* (London, 1761 [orig: publ. Paris, 1744]), I, 370–373, II, 33–34, and George S. Snyderman, "Behind the Tree of Peace: A Sociological Analysis of Iroquois Warfare," *Pennsylvania Archaeologist*, XVIII, nos. 3–4 (1948), 13–15.

15. Lafitau, *Customs of American Indians*, ed. and trans. Fenton and Moore, II, 241–245, quotation on p. 242.

16. *Jesuit Relations*, X, 273–275, XIX, 91, XLIII, 267–271, LX, 35–41. On wergild see Lewis H. Morgan, *League of the Ho-dé-no-sau-nee, or Iroquois* (Rochester, N.Y., 1851), 331–333, and Jennings, *Invasion of America*, 148–149. The parallel between Iroquois practice and the Germanic tradition of blood payments should not be stretched too far; Iroquois condolence presents were an integral part of the broader condolence process.

17. Smith, "American Indian Warfare," *N.Y. Acad. Sci., Trans.*, 2d Ser., XIII (1951), 352–354; Anthony F. C. Wallace, *The Death and Rebirth of the Seneca* (New York, 1970), 101. It is within the context of the mourning-war that what are usually described as Indian wars for revenge or blood feuds should be understood. The revenge motive—no doubt strong in Iroquois warfare—was only part of the larger complex of behavior and belief comprehended in the mourning-war. It should also be noted that raids might be inspired by *any* death, not just those attributable to murder or warfare and for which revenge or other atonement, such as the giving of condolence presents, was necessary. Among Euro-American observers, only the perceptive Lafitau seems to have been aware of this possibility (*Customs of American Indians*, ed. and trans. Fenton and Moore, II, 98–102, 154). I have found no other explicit contemporary discussion of this phenomenon, but several accounts indicate the formation of war parties in response to deaths from disease or other nonviolent causes. See H.P. Biggar et al., eds. and trans., *The Works of Samuel de Champlain* (Toronto, 1922–1936), II, 206–208, hereafter cited as *Works of Champlain*; *Jesuit Rela-*

*tions*, LXIV, 91; Jasper Dankers [Danckaerts] and Peter Sluyter, *Journal of a Voyage to New York and a Tour in Several of the American Colonies in 1679–80*, trans. and ed. Henry C. Murphy (Long Island Historical Society, *Memoirs*, I [Brooklyn, N.Y., 1867]), 277; and William M. Beauchamp, ed., *Moravian Journals Relating to Central New York*, 1745–66 (Syracuse, N.Y., 1916), 125–126, 183–186.

18. *Jesuit Relations*, X, 225–227; E.B. O'Callaghan et al., eds., *Documents Relative to the Colonial History of the State of New-York . . .* (Albany, N.Y., 1856–1887), IV, 22, hereafter cited as *N.Y. Col. Docs.*; Lafitau, *Customs of American Indians*, ed. and trans. Fenton and Moore, II, 99–103; Snyderman, "Behind the Tree of Peace," *Pa. Archaeol.*, XVIII, nos. 3–4 (1948), 15–20.

19. The following composite account is based on numerous contemporaneous reports of Iroquois treatment of captives. Among the more complete are *Jesuit Relations*, XXII, 251–267, XXXIX, 57–77, L, 59–63, LIV, 23–35; Gideon D. Scull, ed., *Voyages of Peter Esprit Radisson: Being an Account of His Travels and Experiences among the North American Indians, from 1652 to 1684* (Boston, 1885), 28–60; and James H. Coyne, ed. and trans., "Exploration of the Great Lakes, 1660–1670, by Dollier de Casson and de Bréhant de Galinée," Ontario Historical Society, *Papers and Records*, IV (1903), 31–35. See also the many other portrayals in *Jesuit Relations*; the discussions in Lafitau, *Customs of American Indians*, ed. and trans. Fenton and Moore, II, 148–172; Nathaniel Knowles, "The Torture of Captives by the Indians of Eastern North America," American Philosophical Society, *Proceedings*, LXXXII (1940), 181–190; and Wallace, *Death and Rebirth of the Seneca*, 103–107.

20. The gauntlet and the public humiliation and physical abuse of captives also served as initiation rites for prospective adoptees; see John Heckewelder, "An Account of the History, Manners, and Customs of the Indian Nations Who Once Inhabited Pennsylvania and the Neighbouring States," Am. Phil. Soc., *Transactions of the Historical and Literary Committee*, I (1819), 211–213. For a fuller discussion of Indian methods of indoctrinating adoptees see James Axtell, "The White Indians of Colonial America," *William and Mary Quarterly*, 3d Ser., XXXII (1975), 55–88.

21. Usually only adult male captives were executed, and most women and children seem to have escaped physical abuse. Occasionally, however, the Iroquois did torture and execute women and children. See Scull, ed., *Voyages of Radisson*, 56, and *Jesuit Relations*, XXXIX, 219–221, XLII, 97–99, LI,

213, 231–233, LII, 79, 157–159, LIII, 253, LXII, 59, LXIV, 127–129, LXV, 33–39.

22. Several authors—from James Adair and Philip Mazzei in the 18th century to W. Arens in 1979—have denied that the Iroquois engaged in cannibalism (Adair, *The History of the American Indians . . .* [London, 1775], 209; Mazzei, *Researches*, ed. and trans. Sherman, 359; Arens, *The Man-Eating Myth: Anthropology & Anthropophagy* [New York, 1979] 127–129). Arens is simply wrong, as Thomas S. Abler has shown in "Iroquois Cannibalism: Fact Not Fiction," *Ethnohistory*, XXVII (1980), 309–316. Adair and Mazzei, from the perspective of the late 18th century, were on firmer ground; by then the Five Nations apparently had abandoned anthropophagy. See Adolph B. Benson, ed., *Peter Kalm's Travels in North America* (New York, 1937), 694.

23. Robert L. Rands and Carroll L. Riley, "Diffusion and Discontinuous Distribution," *Am. Anthro.*, N.S., LX (1958), 284–289; Maurice R. Davie, *The Evolution of War: A Study of Its Role in Early Societies* (New Haven, Conn., 1929), 36–38; Hennepin, *New Discovery*, II, 92.

24. *Jesuit Relations*, LXII, 85–87, LXVII, 173; Knowles, "Torture of Captives," Am. Phil. Soc., *Procs.*, LXXXII (1940), 210–211.

25. *Jesuit Relations*, XIX, 81.

26. *N.Y. Col. Docs.*, V, 274.

27. *Works of Champlain*, IV, 330; Charlevoix, *Voyage to North-America*, I, 316–333.

28. *Jesuit Relations*, XXXIX, 221.

29. *Works of Champlain*, 73–74; *Jesuit Relations*, XXXII, 159.

30. *Jesuit Relations*, X, 145, XXXIX, 29–31; J.N.B. Hewitt, "The Iroquoian Concept of the Soul," *Journal of American Folk-Lore*, VIII (1895), 107–116.

31. *Sagard, Long Journey*, ed. Wrong and trans. Langton, 152–156; *Jesuit Relations*, XXII, 309–311, XXXII, 173–175, XXXIV, 197, LV, 79, LXVI, 273; Hennepin, *New Discovery*, II, 86–94; Patrick Mitchell Malone, "Indian and English Military Systems in New England in the Seventeenth Century" (Ph.D. diss., Brown University, 1971), 33–38.

32. Lafitau, *Customs of American Indians*, ed. and trans. Fenton and Moore, II, 98.

33. Paul A. W. Wallace, *The White Roots of Peace* (Philadelphia, 1946); A. F. C. Wallace, *Death and Rebirth of the Seneca*, 39–48, 93–98; William M. Beauchamp, *Civil, Religious and Mourning Councils and Ceremonies of Adoption of the New York Indians*, New York State Museum Bulletin 113 (Albany, N.Y., 1907). For a suggestive discussion of Indian definitions of peace see John Phillip Reid, *A*

*Better Kind of Hatchet: Law, Trade, and Diplomacy in the Cherokee Nation during the Early Years of European Contact* (University Park, Pa., 1976), 9–17.

34. On the devastating impact of European diseases—some Indian populations may have declined by a factor of 20 to 1 within a century or so of contact—see the works surveyed in Russell Thornton, "American Indian Historical Demography: A Review Essay with Suggestions for Future Research," *American Indian Culture and Research Journal*, III, No. 1 (1979), 69–74.

35. Trigger, *Children of Aataentsic*, II, 602; Cornelius J. Jaenen, *Friend and Foe: Aspects of French Amerindian Cultural Contact in the Sixteenth and Seventeenth Centuries* (New York, 1976), 100. Most of the early Iroquois epidemics went unrecorded by Europeans, but major smallpox epidemics are documented for the Mohawk in 1634 and the Seneca in 1640–1641; see [Harmen Meyndertsz van den Bogaert], "Narrative of a Journey into the Mohawk and Oneida Country, 1634–1635," in J. Franklin Jameson, ed., *Narratives of New Netherland, 1609–1664* (New York, 1909), 140–141, and *Jesuit Relations*, XXI, 211.

36. *Jesuit Relations*, XXX, 273, XLIV, 43, XLVII, 193, 205, XLVIII, 79–83, L, 63, LIV, 79–81, LVII, 81–83, LX, 175.

37. *Works of Champlain*, II, 95–100; Malone, "Indian and English Military Systems," 179–200; Jennings, *Invasion of America*, 165–166. After the introduction of firearms the Iroquois continued to raise armies of several hundred to a thousand men, but they almost never engaged them in set battles. Large armies ensured safe travel to distant battlegrounds and occasionally intimidated outnumbered opponents, but when they neared their objective they usually broke into small raiding parties. See Daniel Gookin, "Historical Collections of the Indians in New England" (1674), Massachusetts Historical Society, *Collections*, I (1792), 162, and Cadwallader Colden, *The History of the Five Indian Nations Depending on the Province of New-York in America* (New York, 1727), 8–10, hereafter cited as Colden, *History* (1727).

38. *N.Y. Col. Docs.*, I, 150; "Journal of New Netherland, 1647," in Jameson, ed., *Narratives of New Netherland*, 274; *Jesuit Relations*, XXIV, 295; Carl P. Russell, *Guns on the Early Frontiers: A History of Firearms from Colonial Times through the Years of the Western Fur Trade* (Berkeley, Calif., 1957), 11–15, 62–66.

39. *Jesuit Relations*, XXVII, 71, XLV, 205–207; Elisabeth Tooker, "The Iroquois Defeat of the Huron: A Review of Causes," *Pa. Archaeol.*, XXXIII (1963), 115–123; Keith F. Otterbein, "Why the Iroquois Won: An Analysis of Iroquois Military Tactics," *Ethnohistory*, XI (1964), 56–63; John K. Mahon, "Anglo-American Methods of Indian Warfare, 1676–1794," *Mississippi Valley Historical Review*, XLV (1958), 255.

40. Bruce G. Trigger, "The Mohawk-Mahican War (1624–28): The Establishment of a Pattern," *Canadian Historical Review*, LII (1971), 276–286.

41. Harold A. Innis, *The Fur Trade in Canada: An Introduction to Canadian Economic History* (New Haven, Conn., 1930), 1–4, 32–33; Hunt, *Wars of the Iroquois*, 33–37; John Witthoft, "Ancestry of the Susquehannocks," in John Witthoft and W. Fred Kinsey III, eds., *Susquehannock Miscellany* (Harrisburg, Pa., 1959), 34–35; Thomas Elliot Norton, *The Fur Trade in Colonial New York, 1686–1776* (Madison, Wis., 1974), 9–15.

42. The classic account of the beaver wars is Hunt, *Wars of the Iroquois*, but three decades of subsequent scholarship have overturned many of that work's interpretations. See Allen W. Trelease, "The Iroquois and the Western Fur Trade: A Problem in Interpretation," MVHR, XLIX (1962), 32–51; Raoul Naroll, "The Causes of the Fourth Iroquois War," *Ethnohistory*, XVI (1969), 51–81; Allan Forbes, Jr., "Two and a Half Centuries of Conflict: The Iroquois and the Laurentian Wars," *Pa. Archaeol.*, XL, nos. 3–4 (1970), 1–20; William N. Fenton, "The Iroquois in History," in Eleanor Burke Leacock and Nancy Oestreich Lurie, eds., *North American Indians in Historical Perspective* (New York, 1971), 139–145; Karl H. Schlesier, "Epidemics and Indian Middlemen: Rethinking the Wars of the Iroquois, 1609–1653," *Ethnohistory*, XXIII (1976), 129–145; and Trigger, *Children of Aataentsic*, esp. II, 617–664.

43. *Works of Champlain*, III, 31–32; see also II, 118–119, 186–191, 246–285, III, 207–228.

44. Ibid., II, 65–107, 120–138, III, 48–81.

45. *Jesuit Relations*, XXI-L, passim; Robert A. Goldstein, *French-Iroquois Diplomatic and Military Relations, 1609–1701* (The Hague, 1969), 62–99. The actual Canadian death toll in wars with the Iroquois before 1666 has recently been shown to have been quite low. Only 153 French were killed in raids while 143 were taken prisoner (perhaps 38 of those died in captivity); John A. Dickinson, "La guerre iroquoise et la mortalité en Nouvelle-France, 1608–1666," *Revue d'histoire de l'amerique française*, XXXVI (1982), 31–54. On 17th-century French captives of the Iroquois see Daniel K. Richter, "The Iroquois Melting Pot: Seventeenth-Century War Captives of the Five Nations" (paper

presented at the Shelby Cullom Davis Center Conference on War and Society in Early America, Princeton University, March 11–12, 1983), 18–19.

46. *Jesuit Relations*, L, 127–147, 239; *N.Y. Col. Docs.*, III, 121–127; A.J.F. van Laer, trans. and ed., *Correspondence of Jeremias van Rensselaer 1651–1674* (Albany, N.Y., 1932), 388.

47. *Jesuit Relations* XXXV, 183–205, XXXVI, 177–191, XLI, 43–65, XLIII, 115–125, 187–207, XLIV, 69–77, 165–167, 187–191; A.J.F. van Laer, trans. and ed., *Minutes of the Court of Fort Orange and Beverwyck, 1657–1660*, II (Albany, N.Y., 1923), 45–48; Scull, ed., *Voyages of Radisson*, 93–119; Nicholas Perrot, "Memoir on the Manners, Customs, and Religion of the Savages of North America" (c. 1680–1718), in Emma Helen Blair, ed. and trans., *The Indian Tribes of the Upper Mississippi Valley and Region of the Great Lakes . . .* (Cleveland Ohio, 1911), I, 148–193.

48. *Jesuit Relations*, XLVII, 139–153

49. Ibid., XLIII, 265.

50. Ibid., XLV, 207, LI, 123, 187.

51. *N.Y. Col. Docs.*, IX, 80; Victor Konrad, "An Iroquois Frontier: The North Shore of Lake Ontario during the late Seventeenth Century," *Journal of Historical Geography*, VII (1981), 129–144.

52. *Jesuit Relations*, LI, 81–85, 167–257, LII, 53–55.

53. Ibid., LV, 61–63, LVII, 133–141, LVIII, 211, LX, 187–195.

54. Ibid., LIV, 281–283.

55. Ibid., LVI, 29, LVIII, 247–253, LX, 145–147, LXI, 195–199, LXIII, 141–189.

56. Ibid., LV, 33–37, LVIII, 75–77.

57. E.B. O'Callaghan, ed., *The Documentary History of the State New-York* octavo ed. (Albany, N.Y., 1849–1851), I, 12–14; *Jesuit Relations*, XXIV, 295. Reflecting the purposes of most Euro-Americans who made estimates of Indian population, figures are usually given in terms of the number of available fighting men. The limited data available for direct comparisons of estimates of Iroquois fighting strength with estimates of total population indicate that the ratio of one warrior for every four people proposed in Sherburne F. Cook, "Interracial Warfare and Population Decline among the New England Indians," *Ethnohistory*, XX (1973), 13, applies to the Five Nations. Compare the estimates of a total Mohawk population of 560–580 in William Andrews to the Secretary of the Society for the Propagation of the Gospel in Foreign Parts, Sept. 7, 1713, Oct. 17, 1715, Records of the Society for the Propagation of the Gospel, Letterbooks, Ser. A, VIII, 186, XI, 268–269, S.P.G. Archives, London

(microfilm ed.), with the concurrent estimates of approximately 150 Mohawk warriors in Bernardus Freeman to the Secretary of S.P.G., May 28, 1712, ibid., VII, 203; Peter Wraxall, *An Abridgement of the Indian Affairs. . . . Transacted in the Colony of New York, from the Year 1678 to the Year 1751*, ed. Charles Howard McIlwain (Cambridge, Mass., 1915), 69: *N.Y. Col. Docs.*, V, 272; and Lawrence H. Leder, ed., *The Livingston Indian Records, 1666–1723* (Gettysburg, Pa., 1956), 220.

58. The estimates of 10,000 for the 1640s is from Trigger, *Children of Aataentsic*, 1,98; the figure of 8,600 for the 1670s is calculated from Wentworth Greenhalgh's 1677 estimate of 2,150 Iroquois warriors, in O'Callaghan, ed., *Documentary History*, I, 12–14. Compare the late 1670s estimate in Hennepin, *New Discovery*, II, 92–93, and see the tables of 17th- and 18th-century Iroquois warrior population in Snyderman, "Behind the Tree of Peace," *Pa. Archaeol.*, XVIII, nos. 3–4 (1948), 42; Bruce G. Trigger, ed., *Northeast*, in William C. Sturtevant, ed., *Handbook of North American Indians*, XV (Washington, D.C., 1978), 421; and Gunther Michelson, "Iroquois Population Statistics," *Man in the Northeast*, No. 14 (1977), 3–17. William Starna has recently suggested that all previous estimates for 1635 and earlier of Mohawk—and by implication Five Nations—population are drastically understated ("Mohawk Iroquois Populations: A Revision," *Ethnohistory*, XXVII [1980], 371–382).

59. *Jesuit Relations*, LXII, 71–95, quotation on 83.

60. Richard Aquila, "The Iroquois Restoration: A Study of Iroquois Power, Politics, and Relations with Indians and Whites, 1700–1744" (Ph.D. dissertation, Ohio State University, 1977), 16–29.

61. A 1698 report on New York's suffering during the War of the League of Augsburg states that there were 2,550 Iroquois warriors in 1689 and only 1,230 in 1698. The report probably contains some polemical overstatement: the first figure seems too high and the second too low. By comparison, 2,050 Iroquois warriors were estimated by Denonville in 1685, 1,400 by Bellomont in 1691, 1,750 by Bernardus Freeman in 1700, and 1,200 by a French cabinet paper in 1701 (*N.Y. Col. Docs.*, IV, 337, 768, IX, 281, 725; Freeman to the Secretary, May 28, 1712, Records of S.P.G., Letterbooks, Ser. A, VII, 203). If the figure of 1,750 warriors cited by Freeman—a minister who worked with the Mohawk—is correct, the total Iroquois population in 1700 was approximately 7,000, calculated by the ratio in note 57.

62. *Jesuit Relations*, LXIV, 59–61.

63. *N.Y. Col. Docs.*, IV, 648–661, 689–690.

64. Trigger, *Children of Aataentsic*, II, 709–724. See also the discussions of Indian factionalism in Robert F. Berkhofer, Jr., "The Political Context of a New Indian History," *Pacific Historical Review*, XL (1971), 373–380; and Edward H. Spicer, *Cycles of Conquest: The Impact of Spain, Mexico, and the United States on the Indians of the Southwest, 1533–1960* (Tucson, Ariz., 1962), 491–501.

65. Anthony F. C. Wallace, "Origins of Iroquois Neutrality: The Grand Settlement of 1701," *Pennsylvania History*, XXIV (1957), 223–235. The best reconstruction of the Iroquois diplomacy that led to the Grand Settlement is Richard L. Haan. "The Covenant Chain: Iroquois Diplomacy on the Niagara Frontier, 1697–1730" (Ph.D. diss., University of California, Santa Barbara, 1976), 64–147.

66. Bacqueville de La Potherie, *Histoire de l'Amérique Septentrionale*, IV (Paris, 1722), passim; *N.Y. Col. Docs.*, IX, 715–725.

67. Leroy V. Eid, "The Ojibwa-Iroquois War. The War the Five Nations Did Not Win," *Ethnohistory*, XXVI (1979), 297–324.

68. Aquila, "Iroquois Restoration," 109–171; Richard Haan, "The Problem of Iroquois Neutrality: Suggestions for Revision," *Ethnohistory*, XXVII (1980), 317–330.

69. *N.Y. Col. Docs.*, V, 724–725.

70. *N.Y. Col. Doc.*, V, 545, 569, 632, IX, 816; Thomas Barclay to Robert Hunter, Jan. 26, 1713 (extract), Records of S.P.G., Letterbooks, Ser. A, VIII, 251–252. For examples of Claeson's and Joncaire's activities see Colden, "Continuation," 360–363, 432–434, and *N.Y. Col. Docs.*, V, 538, 562– 569, IX, 759–765, 814, 876–903.

71. *N.Y. Col. Docs.*, V, 217–227; Colden, "Continuation," 408–409; Wraxall, *Abridgement of Indian Affairs*, ed. McIlwain, 79n–80n.

72. Andrews to the Secretary, Oct. 11, 1716, Records of S.P.G., Letterbooks, Ser. A, XII, 241; *N.Y. Col. Docs.*, V, 484–487, IX, 878.

73. *Jesuit Relations*, LXVI, 203–207, LXVII, 39–41; *N.Y. Col. Docs.*, IX 882–884; George F.G. Stanley, "The Policy of 'Francisation' as Applied to the Indians during the Ancien Regime," *Revue d'historie de l'amerique française*, II III (1949–1950), 333–348; Cornelius J. Jaenen, "The Frenchification and Evangelization of the Amerindians in the Seventeenth Century New France" (sic), Canadian Catholic Historical Association, *Study Sessions*, XXXV (1969), 57–71.

74. *Jesuit Relations*, LXVII, 27.

75. Andrews to the Secretary, Apr. 20, 1716, Apr. 23, 1717, Records of S.P.G. Letterbooks, Ser. A, XI, 319–320, XII, 310–312.

76. Henry R. Schoolcraft, *Notes on the Iroquois: Or, Contributions to the Statistics, Aboriginal History, Antiquities and General Ethnology of Western New York* (New York, 1846), 148–149; Fenton, "Iroquois in History," in Leacock and Lurie, eds., *North American Indians*, 147–148; Beauchamp, *History of New York Iroquois*, 139.

77. On Iroquois-Flathead conflicts before 1710 see of Colden, *History* (1727), 3071, and "Continuation," 361–363, and Wraxall, *Abridgement of Indian Affairs*, ed. McIlwain, 50–61. References to raids after 1710 in Colden, *N.Y. Col. Docs.*, and other sources are too numerous to cite here; a useful discussion is Aquila, "Iroquois Restoration," 294–346.

78. Wraxall, *Abridgement of Indian Affairs*, ed. McIlwain, 94–96; *N.Y. Col. Docs.*, V, 372–376, 382–388, 484–493; Verner W. Crane, *The Southern Frontier, 1670–1732* (Durham, N.C., 1928), 158–161.

79. *N.Y. Col Docs.* V, 542–545, 562–569, 635–640.

80. Ibid., IX, 876–878, 884–885, 1085, 1097–1098.

81. Colden, "Continuation," 382–383, brackets in original.

82. For examples of shifting New York policies regarding the Iroquois southern campaigns see *N.-Y. Col. Docs.*, V, 446–464, 542–545, and Wraxall, *Abridgement of Indian Affairs*, ed. McIlwain, 123.

83. Andrews to the Secretary, Apr. 20, 1716, Records of S.P.G., Letterbooks, Ser. A., XI, 320.

# AFRICAN AMERICANS, EXODUS, AND THE AMERICAN ISRAEL

## Albert J. Raboteau

During the past two decades, research on African American religious beliefs and practices has challenged an older focus on the institutional and intellectual life of white, middle-class Protestantism. This research demonstrates that African religious life has been an integral part of American religious history. At the same time, an older scholarship that emphasized the deficiencies of black life, compared to the white middle-class ideal, has been overtaken by a new approach that, while underscoring the heavy toll of white racism, nevertheless stresses the capacity of African Americans to adapt creatively to their hostile environment. Perhaps more than any other scholar, Albert Raboteau has led this contemporary emergence of African American religious history. In the following essay, Raboteau demonstrates how African slaves found within European American Protestantism a theology of history that they adapted to help them make sense of their enslavement. In the Exodus story, in particular, African slaves found a narrative with broad implications for their own situation to which they gave a radically new meaning.

Reprinted by permission from Albert J. Raboteau, "African Americans, Exodus, and the American Israel," in *African American Christianity: Essays in History*, Paul E. Johnson, ed. (Berkeley: California, 1994), 1–17.

*Canaan land is the land for me,*
*And let God's saints come in.*
*There was a wicked man,*
*He kept them children in Egypt land.*
*Canaan land is the land for me,*
*And let God's saints come in.*
*God did say to Moses one day,*
*Say, Moses, go to Egypt land,*
*And tell him to let my people go.*
*Canaan land is the land for me,*
*And let God's saints come in.*

—Slave Spiritual

# 4

# AFRICAN AMERICANS, EXODUS, AND THE AMERICAN ISRAEL

*Albert J. Raboteau*

IN THE ENCOUNTER with European Christianity in its Protestant form in North America, enslaved Africans and their descendants encountered something new: a fully articulated ritual relationship with the Supreme Being, who was pictured in the book that the Christians called the Bible not just as the Creator and Ruler of the Cosmos, but also as the God of History, a God who lifted up and cast down nations and peoples, a God whose sovereign will was directing all things toward an ultimate end, drawing good out of evil. As the transplanted Africans reflected upon the evil that had befallen them and their parents, they increasingly turned to the language, symbols, and worldview of the Christian holy book. There they found a theology of history that helped them to make sense of their enslavement. One story in particular caught their attention and fascinated them with its implications and potential applications to their own situation: the story of Exodus. What they did with that ancient story of the Near East is the topic of this essay. I begin by surveying the history of evangelization among the slaves in order to situate and define the Christianity that confronted them in North America. Then I describe what slaves and free blacks made of Christianity by focusing on their interpretation of the Exodus story, an interpretation which differed drastically, as we shall see, from that of white Americans.

## CONVERSION

From the beginning of the Atlantic slave trade, Europeans claimed that the conversion of slaves to Christianity justified the enslavement of Africans. Yet the conversion of slaves was not a high priority for colonial planters. British colonists in North America proved especially indifferent, if not downright hostile, to the conversion of their slaves. At first, opposition was based on the suspicion that English law forbade the enslavement of Christians and so would require slaveholders to emancipate any slave who received baptism. Masters suspected that slaves would therefore seek to be baptized in order to gain freedom. These fears were quickly allayed by colonial legislation declaring that baptism did not alter slave status.

With the legal obstacles aside, slaveowners for the most part still demonstrated scant interest in converting their slaves. According to the common wisdom, Christianity spoiled slaves. Christian slaves thought too highly of themselves, became impudent, and even turned rebellious. Moreover, Anglo-Americans were troubled by a deep-seated uneasiness at the prospect that slaves would claim Christian fellowship with white people. Africans were foreign; to convert them was to make them more like the English and therefore deserving of better treatment. In fact religion, like language and skin color, constituted the colonists' identity. To Christianize black-skinned Africans, therefore, would confuse the distinctiveness of the races and threaten the social order based upon that distinctiveness. Finally, the labor, not the souls of the slaves, concerned most slaveholders. Peter Kalm, a Swedish traveler in America from 1748 to 1750, perceptively described the colonists' objections to religious instruction for slaves:

> It is . . . to be pitied, that the masters of these negroes in most of the English colonies take little care of their spiritual welfare, and let them live on in their Pagan darkness. There are even some, who would be very ill pleased at, and would by all means hinder their negroes from being instructed in the doctrines of Christianity; to this they are partly led by the conceit of its being shameful, to have a spiritual brother or sister among so despicable a people; partly by thinking that they should not be able to keep their negroes so meanly afterwards; and partly through fear of the negroes growing too proud, on seeing themselves upon a level with their masters in religious matters.[1]

A concerted attack on these obstacles to slave conversion was mounted by the Church of England in 1701 when it established the Society for the Propagation of the Gospel in Foreign Parts to support missionaries to the colonies. The first task was to convince masters that they had a duty to instruct their slaves in the truths of the gospel. In tract after tract, widely distributed in the colonies, officers of the Society stressed the compatibility of Christianity with slavery. Masters need not fear that religion would ruin their slaves. On the contrary, Christianity would make them better slaves by convincing them to obey their owners out of a sense of moral duty instead of out of fear. After all, Society pamphlets explained, Christianity does not upset the social order, but supports it: "Scripture, far from making an alteration in Civil Rights, expressly directs that every man abide in the condition wherein he is called, with great indifference of mind concerning outward circumstances."[2] To prove the point, they reiterated ad nauseam the verse from Ephesians (6:5): "Slaves be obedient to your masters." The missionaries thus denied that spiritual equality implied worldly equality; they restricted the egalitarian impulse of Christianity to the realm of the spirit. So, in effect, they built a religious foundation to support slavery. As the historian Winthrop Jordan aptly put it, "These clergymen had been forced by the circumstance of racial slavery in America into propagating the Gospel by presenting it as an attractive device for slave control."[3]

The success of missions to the slaves depended largely on circumstances beyond the missionaries' control: the proportion of African-born to Creole slaves, the geographic location and work patterns of the slaves, and the ratio of blacks to whites in a given locale. Blacks in the North and in the Chesapeake region of Maryland and Virginia, for example, experienced more frequent and closer contact with whites than did those of the lowland coasts of South Carolina and Georgia, where large gangs of African slaves toiled on isolated rice plantations with only limited and infrequent exposure to whites or their religion. Even if a missionary gained regular access to slaves, the slaves did not invariably accept the

Christian gospel. Some rejected it, according to missionary accounts, because of "the Fondness they have for their old Heathenish Rites, and the strong Prejudice they must have against Teachers from among those, whom they serve so unwillingly."[4] Others accepted Christianity because they hoped—colonial legislation and missionary pronouncements notwithstanding—that baptism would raise their status and ensure eventual freedom for their children, if not for themselves. One missionary in South Carolina required slaves seeking baptism to swear an oath that they did not request the sacrament out of a desire for freedom.[5] (Apparently he missed the irony.) Missionaries complained that, even after instruction and baptism, slaves still mixed Christian beliefs with the traditional practices of their African homelands.

Discouraging though the prospects were, colonial clergymen had established a few successful missions among the slaves by the early eighteenth century. When the Bishop of London distributed a list of questions in 1724 requiring ministers to describe their work among the slaves, several respondents reported impressive numbers of baptisms. The great majority, however, stated vague intentions instead of concrete achievements. During the first 120 years of black slavery in British North America, Christianity made little headway in the slave population.

Slaves were first converted in large numbers in the wake of the religious revivals that periodically swept parts of the colonies beginning in the 1740s. Accounts by George Whitefield, Gilbert Tennent, Jonathan Edwards, and other revivalists made special mention of the fact that blacks were flocking to hear the message of salvation in hitherto unseen numbers. Not only were free blacks and slaves attending revivals, but they were also taking active part in the services as exhorters and preachers. For a variety of reasons evangelical revivalists succeeded where Anglican missionaries had failed. Whereas the Anglicans had depended upon a slow process of indoctrination, the evangelicals preached the immediate experience of conversion as the primary requirement for baptism, thereby making Christianity more quickly accessible. Because of the centrality of the conversion experience in their piety, evangelicals also tended to de-emphasize instruction and downplay learning as prerequisites of Christian life. As a result, all classes of society were welcome to participate actively in prayer meetings and revival services, in which the poor, the illiterate, and even the enslaved prayed, exhorted, and preached.

After the Revolution, revival fervor continued to flare up sporadically in the South. More and more slaves converted to Christianity under the dramatic preaching of evangelical revivalists, especially Methodists and Baptists. The emotionalism of the revivals encouraged the outward expression of religious feeling, and the sight of black and white converts weeping, shouting, fainting, and moving in ecstatic trance became a familiar, if sensationalized, feature of the sacramental and camp meeting seasons. In this heated atmosphere slaves found a form of Christian worship that resembled the religious celebrations of their African heritage. The analogy between African and evangelical styles of worship enabled the slaves to reinterpret the new religion by reference to the old, and so made this brand of Christianity seem less foreign than that of the more liturgically sedate Church of England.

The rise of the evangelical denominations, particularly the Methodists and the Baptists, threatened the established Anglican church in the South. Because they appealed to the "lower sort," the evangelicals suffered persecution at the hands of the Anglican authorities. Baptist preachers were jailed, their services were disrupted, and they were even roughed up by rowdies such as those in Virginia who thought it humorous to immerse the Baptists in mud. They were thought of as different in an unsettling sort of way. "There was a company of them in the back part of our town, and an outlandish set of people they certainly were," remarked one woman to the early Baptist historian David Benedict. "You yourself would say so if you had seen them. . . . You could hardly find one among them but was deformed in some way or other."[6] The evangelicals seemed to threaten the social as well as the religious order by accepting slaves into their societies. An anti-Baptist petition warned the Virginia assembly in 1777 that "there have been nightly meetings of slaves to receive the instruction of these teachers without the consent of their masters, which have produced very bad consequences."[7]

In the 1780s the evangelicals' implied challenge to the social order became explicit. Methodist conferences in 1780, in 1783, and again in 1784 strongly condemned slavery and tried "to extirpate this abomination," first from the ministry and then from the membership as a whole, by passing increasingly stringent regulations against slave-owning, slave-buying, and slave-selling.[8] Several Baptist leaders freed their slaves, and in 1789 the General Committee of Virginia Baptists condemned slavery as "a violent deprivation of the rights of nature."[9] In the South, these antislavery moves met with strong, immediate, and, as the leadership quickly realized, irreversible opposition. In 1785, the Baltimore Conference of the Methodist Church suspended the rules passed in 1784 by the Methodist General Conference. Methodist leader Thomas Coke explained, "We thought it prudent to suspend the minute concerning slavery, on account of the great opposition that had been given it, our work being in too infantile a state to push things to extremity." Local Baptist associations in Virginia responded to the General Committee's attack on slavery by declaring that the subject was "so abstruse" that no religious society had the right to concern itself with the issue; instead, each individual should be left "to act at discretion in order to keep a good conscience before God, as far as the laws of our land will admit."[10] As for the slaves, the goal of the Church should be the amelioration of their treatment, not their emancipation.

Thus, the evangelical challenge to slavery in the late eighteenth century failed. The intransigence of slavery once again set the limits of the Christian egalitarian impulse, just as it had in colonial days for the Anglican mission. Rapid growth of the Baptist and Methodist churches forced an ineluctable accommodation to slaveholding principles rather than the overthrow of slavery. At the beginning of the nineteenth century, Robert Semple, another Baptist historian, described the change that came over the "outlandish" Baptists after 1790: "Their preachers became much more correct in their manner of preaching. A great many odd tones, disgusting whoops and awkward gestures were disused. . . . Their zeal was less mixed with enthusiasm, and their piety became more rational. They were much more numerous, and, of course, in the eyes of the world, more respectable. Besides, they were joined by persons of much greater weight in civil society; their congregations became more numerous. . . . This could not but influence their manners and spirit more or less."[11] Though both Methodists and Baptists rapidly retreated from antislavery pronouncements, their struggle with the established order and their uneasiness about slavery gave slaves, at least initially, the impression that they were "friendly toward freedom." For a short time, revivalist evangelicalism breached the wall that colonial missionaries had built between spiritual and temporal equality. Converting slaves to Christianity could have implications beyond the spiritual, a possibility slaves were eager to explore.

Methodists and Baptists backed away from these implications in the 1790s, but they had already taken a momentous step, and it proved irreversible. The spread of Baptist and Methodist evangelicalism between 1770 and 1820 changed the religious complexion of the South by bringing unprecedented numbers of slaves into membership in the church and by introducing even larger numbers to at least the rudiments of Christianity. During the antebellum decades, Christianity diffused throughout the slave quarters, though most slaves did not hold membership in regular churches. Those slaves who did attend church generally attended with whites, but some—in greater numbers than historians have realized—attended separate black churches, even in the antebellum South.

Thanks to the willingness of the evangelical churches to license black men to exhort and preach, during the 1770s and 1780s a significant group of black preachers had begun to pastor their own people. Mainly Baptist, since the congregational independence of the Baptists gave them more leeway to preach than any other denomination, the black preachers exercised a ministry that was mostly informal and extra-ecclesial. It would be difficult to overestimate the importance of these early black preachers for the development of an African-American Christianity. In effect, they mediated between Christianity and the experience of the slaves (and free blacks), interpreting the stories, symbols, and events of the Bible to fit the day-to-day lives of those held in bondage. And whites—try as they might—could not control this interpretation or determine its "accuracy." Slave preachers, exhorters, and church-appointed watchmen instructed their fellow slaves, nurtured their religious development, and brought them to conversion—in some cases without any active involvement of white missionaries or masters whatsoever. By nurturing Christian communities among slaves and free blacks, the pioneer black preachers began to build an independent black church.

We tend to identify the development of the independent black church with free blacks in the North, but the spirit of religious independence also created separate black churches in the South. Several "African" churches, as they were called, sprang up before 1800. Some of these black congregations were independent to the extent that they called their own pastors and officers, joined local associations with white churches, and sent their own delegates to associational meetings. However, this early independence of black preachers and churches was curtailed during the antebellum period when, in reaction to slave conspiracies, all gatherings of blacks for whatever purpose were viewed with alarm. For slaves to participate in the organization, leadership, and governance of church structures was perceived as dangerous. Nevertheless, unlikely as it may seem, black churches continued to grow in size and number in the slave South. Though nominally controlled by whites, these separate congregations were frequently led by black ministers, some free and some slaves. Often the black congregations outnumbered the largest white churches in the local church associations. Although never numerous in the South, the separate black churches were extremely important, if limited, institutional expressions of black religious independence from white control.

In the North, the abolition of slavery after the Revolution gave black congregations and clergy much more leeway to assert control over their religious lives. Federal and state disestablishment of religion created an environment of voluntarism in which church organization flourished. Between 1790 and 1820, black Episcopalians, Methodists, Baptists, and Presbyterians founded churches, exercised congregational control where possible, and struggled with white elders, bishops, and associations to gain autonomy. Among the first to succeed in doing so was Bethel African Methodist Episcopal Church in Philadelphia.

Founded in 1794 by Richard Allen, a former slave who had become a licensed Methodist preacher, Bethel was organized after discriminatory treatment drove black Methodists to abandon St. George's, the white church they had supported for years. When the white elders of St. George's tried to take control of the Bethel church property, the black congregation went to court to retain their rights to the church they had built themselves. They won.

Conflicts elsewhere between black Methodists and white elders prompted Allen to call for a convention of African Methodists to meet in Philadelphia in 1816. There, delegates organized an independent black denomination, the African Methodist Episcopal (A.M.E.) Church, and elected Richard Allen its first bishop. Two other African Methodist denominations had organized by 1821. Though the black Methodists were the first to take independent control of their church property, finances, and governance on the denominational level, northern blacks in other churches also demonstrated their spirit of independence. In all denominations, the black churches formed the institutional core for the development of free black communities. Moreover, they gave black Christians the opportunity to articulate publicly their own vision of Christianity, which stood in eloquent testimony to the existence of two Christian Americas.

Of course, independent religious institutions were out of the question for the vast majority of black Americans, who were suffering the system of slavery in the southern states. If they attended church at all, they did so with whites or under white supervision. Nevertheless, slaves developed their own, extra-ecclesial "invisible institution" of religious life. In the slave quarters and brush arbors, they held their own religious meetings, where they interpreted Christianity according to their experience. Conversely, they also interpreted their experience by means of the myths, stories, and symbols of Christianity. They were even willing to risk severe punishment to attend forbidden prayer meetings in order to worship God free of white control. A former slave, Lucretia Alexander, explained why:

> The preacher came and . . . he'd just say, "Serve your masters. Don't steal your master's turkey. Don't steal your master's chickens. Don't steal your master's hawgs. Don't steal your master's meat. Do whatsomever your master tell you to do." Same old thing all the time. My father would have church in dwelling houses and they had to whisper. . . . Sometimes they would have church at his house. That would be when they want a real meetin' with some real preachin'. . . . They used to sing their songs in a whisper. That was a prayer meeting from house to house . . . once or twice a week.[12]

Inevitably the slaves' Christianity contradicted that of their masters. For the slaves knew that no matter how sincerely religious the slaveowners might be, their Christianity was compatible with slavery, and the slaves' was not. The division went deep; it extended to the fundamental interpretation of the Bible. The dichotomy between the faiths of black and white Christians was described by a white Methodist minister who pastored a black congregation in Charleston, South Carolina, in 1862:

> There were near fourteen hundred colored communications. . . . [Their] service was always thronged—galleries, lower floor, chancel, pulpit, steps and all. . . . The preacher could not complain of any deadly space between himself and his congregation. He was positively breast up to his people, with no possible loss of . . . rapport. Though ignorant of it at the time, he remembers now the cause of the enthusiasm under his deliverances [about] the "law of liberty"

and "freedom from Egyptian bondage." What was figurative they interpreted literally. He thought of but one ending of the war; they quite another. He remembers the sixty-eighth Psalm as affording numerous texts for their delectation, e.g., "Let God arise, let his enemies be scattered"; His "march through the wilderness"; "The Chariots of God are twenty thousand"; "The hill of God is as the hill of Basham"; and especially, "Though ye have lain among the pots, yet shall ye be as the wings of a dove covered with silver, and her feathers with yellow gold." . . . It is mortifying now to think that his comprehension was not equal to the African intellect. All he thought about was relief from the servitude of sin, and freedom from the bondage of the devil. . . . But they interpreted it literally in the good time coming, which of course could not but make their ebony complexion attractive, very.[13]

What the preacher is describing is the end of a long process, spanning almost two hundred and fifty years, by which slaves came to accept the gospel of Christianity. But the slaves did not simply become Christians; they fashioned Christianity to fit their own peculiar experience of enslavement in America. The preacher, like many white Christians before and since, thought there was no distance between him and "his people," no possible loss of rapport. He learned belatedly that the chasm was wide and deep. As one freedman succinctly stated, "We couldn't tell NO PREACHER NEBER how we suffer all dese long years. He know'd nothin' bout we."[14]

## EXODUS

No single symbol captures more clearly the distinctiveness of Afro-American Christianity than the symbol of Exodus. From the earliest days of colonization, white Christians had represented their journey across the Atlantic to America as the exodus of a New Israel from the bondage of Egypt into the Promised Land of milk and honey. For black Christians, the imagery was reversed: the Middle Passage had brought them to Egypt land, where they suffered bondage under a new Pharaoh. White Christians saw themselves as the New Israel; slaves identified themselves as the Old. This is, as Vincent Harding remarked, one of the abiding and tragic ironies of our history: the nation's claim to be the New Israel was contradicted by the Old Israel still enslaved in her midst.[15]

American preachers, politicians, and other orators found in the story of Exodus a rich source of metaphors to explicate the unfolding history of the nation. Each section of the narrative—the bondage in Egypt, the rescue at the Red Sea, the wandering in the wilderness, and the entrance into the Promised Land—provided a typological map to reconnoiter the moral terrain of American society. John Winthrop, the leader of the great Puritan expedition to Massachusetts Bay, set the pattern in his famous "A Modell of Christian Charity" sermon composed on his ship in 1630. Having elaborated the covenantal obligations that the settlers had contracted with God, echoing the Sinai covenant of Israel with Yahweh, Winthrop concluded his discourse with a close paraphrase of Moses' farewell instruction to Israel (Deuteronomy 30):

Beloved there is now sett before use life, and good, deathe and evil in that wee are Commaunded this day to love the Lord our God, and to love one another, to walke in his wayes and to keepe his Commaundements and his Ordinance, and his lawes, and the Articles of our Covenant with him that wee may live and be multiplied, and that the Lord our God may blesse us in the land whither we goe to poses it: But if our heartes shall turne away soe that wee will not obey, but shall be seduced and worship . . . other Gods, our pleasures, and proffitts, and serve them; it is propounded unto this day, wee shall surely perish out of the good Land whither wee passe over this vast Sea to possesse it. . . . [16]

Notice the particular application that Winthrop draws from the Exodus story: possession of the land is contingent upon observing the moral obligations of the covenant with God. It is a mark of the greatness of Winthrop's address that the obligations he emphasizes are justice, mercy, affection, meekness, gentleness, patience, generosity, and unity—not the qualities usually associated with taking or keeping possession of a land. Later and lesser sermons would extol much more active and aggressive virtues for the nation to observe.

Already in Winthrop's address there is an explicit notion of reciprocity between God's Will and America's Destiny: God has made a contract with us; if we live up to our part of the bargain, so will He. This pattern of reciprocity between Divine Providence and American Destiny had tremendous hortative power, which Puritan preachers exploited to the full over the next century and more in the jeremiad. In sermon after sermon, a succession of New England divines deciphered droughts, epidemics, Indian attacks, and other misfortunes as tokens of God's displeasure over the sins of the nation. Unless listeners took the opportunity to humble themselves, repent, and reform, they might expect much more of the same.

Implicit in this relationship of reciprocity there lay a danger: the danger of converting God's Will into America's Density. Winthrop was too good a Puritan to succumb to this temptation. Protected by his belief in the total sovereignty of God, he knew that the relationship between God's Will and human action was one-sided and that the proper human attitude was trust in God, not confidence in man. God's Will was the measure of America's deeds, not vice versa. Of course, no American preacher or politician would have disagreed, but as time went on the salient features of the American Exodus story changed. As the actual experience of migration with all its fear and tenuousness receded, Americans tended to lose sight of their radical dependence upon God and to celebrate their own achievements as a nation.

We can catch sight of the change by comparing the tone of Winthrop's "A Modell of Christian Charity" with the mood of an election sermon entitled "The United States Elevated to Glory and Honor," preached by Ezra Stiles in 1783. Flush with excitement over the success of the Revolution, Stiles dwelled at length on the unfolding destiny of the new nation. Quoting, like Winthrop, from the book of Deuteronomy, Stiles struck a celebratory rather than a hortatory note:

> "And to make thee high above all nations which he hath made, in praise, and in name, and in honour; and that thou mayest be an holy people unto the Lord thy God . . ." I have assumed [this] text as introductory to a discourse upon the political welfare of God's American Israel, and as allusively prophetic of the future prosperity and splendour of the United States. Already does the new constellation of the United States begin to realize this glory. It has already risen to an acknowledged sovereignty among the republicks and kingdoms of the world. And we have reason to hope, and I believe to expect, that God has still greater blessings in store for this vine which his own right hand hath planted, to make us "high among the nations in praise, and in name, and in honour."[17]

Stiles went on at great length to identify the reasons for his optimism about America's present and future preeminence, including the fact that "in our civil constitutions, those impediments are removed which obstruct the progress of society towards perfection."[18] It's a long away from Winthrop's caution to Stiles' confidence, from an "Errand in the Wilderness" to "progress towards perfection." In Stiles' election sermon we can perceive God's New Israel becoming the Redeemer Nation. The destiny of the New Israel was to reach the pinnacle of perfection and to carry liberty and the gospel around the globe.

In tandem with this exaggerated vision of America's Destiny went an exaggerated vision of human capacity. In an increasingly confident and prosperous nation, it was difficult to avoid shifting the emphasis from divine sovereignty to human ability. Historian Conrad Cherry has succinctly summarized the change in perception of America's destiny: "Believing that she had escaped the wickedness of the Old World and the guilt of the past, God's New Israel would find it all too easy to ignore her vices and all too difficult to admit a loss of innocence."[19]

Among the realities this optimistic vision ignored was the presence of another, darker Israel:

> America, America, foul and indelible is thy stain! Dark and dismal is the cloud that hangs over thee, for thy cruel wrongs and injuries to the fallen sons of Africa. The blood of her murdered ones cries to heaven for vengeance against Thee. . . . You may kill, tyrannize, and oppress as much as you choose, until cry shall come up before the throne of God; for I am firmly persuaded, that he will not suffer you to quell the proud, fearless and undaunted spirits of the Africans forever; for in his own time, he is able to plead our cause against you, and to pour out upon you the ten plagues of Egypt.[20]

So wrote Maria Stewart, a free black reform activist in Boston, in 1831. Her words were addressed to an America that projected itself as the probable site of the coming Millennium, Christ's thousand-year reign of peace and justice. From the perspective of slaves, and of free blacks like Maria Stewart, America was Egypt, and as long as she continued to enslave and oppress Black Israel, her destiny was in jeopardy. America stood under the judgment of God, and unless she repented, the death and destruction visited upon Biblical Egypt would be repeated here. The retribution envisaged was quite literal, as Mary Livermore, a white governess, discovered when she overheard a prayer uttered by Aggy, the slave housekeeper, whose daughter had just been brutally whipped by her master:

> Thar's a day a comin'! Thar's a day a comin' . . . I hear de rumblin' ob de chariots! I see de flashin' ob de guns! White folks' blood is a-runnin' on de ground like a riber, an' de dead's heaped up dat high! . . . Oh, Lor'! hasten de day when de blows, an' de bruises, an' de aches, an' de pains, shall come to de white folks, an' de buzzards shall eat 'em as dey's dead in de streets. Oh, Lor'! roll on de chariots, an' gib de black people rest an' peace.[21]

Nor did slaves share the exaggerated optimism of white Americans about human ability. Trapped in a system from which there seemed little, if any, possibility of deliverance by human actions, they emphasized trusting in the Lord instead of trusting in man. Sermon after sermon and prayer after prayer echoed the words that Moses spoke on the banks of the Red Sea: "Stand still and see the salvation of the Lord." Although the leaders of the three principal slave revolts—Gabriel Prosser in 1800, Denmark Vesey in 1822, and Nat Turner in 1831—all depended upon the Bible to justify and motivate rebellion, the Exodus story was used mainly to nurture internal resistance not external revolution among the slaves.

The story of Exodus contradicted the claim made by white Christians that God intended Africans to be slaves. It seemed to prove that slavery was against God's will and that slavery would inevitably end, although the when and the how remained hidden in Divine Providence. Christian slaves thus applied the Exodus story, whose end they knew, to their own experience of slavery, which had not yet ended, and so gave meaning and purpose to lives threatened by senseless and demeaning brutality. Exodus functioned as an archetypal myth for the slaves. The sacred history of God's liberation of his people would be or was being reenacted in the American South. A white Union Army chaplain working among freedmen in Decatur, Alabama, commented disapprovingly on the slaves' fascination with Exodus: "There is no part of the Bible with which they are so familiar as the story of the deliverance of Israel. Moses is their *ideal* of all that is high, and noble, and perfect, in man. I think they have been accustomed to regard Christ not so much in the light of a *spiritual* Deliverer, as that of a second Moses who would eventually lead *them* out of their prison-house of bondage."[22]

Thus, in the story of Israel's exodus from Egypt, the slaves envisioned a future radically different from their present. In times of despair, they remembered Exodus and found hope enough to endure the enormity of their suffering. As a slave named Polly eloquently explained to her mistress, "We poor creatures have need to believe in God, for if God Almighty will not be good to us some day, why were we born? When I heard of his delivering his people from bondage, I know it means the poor Africans."[23]

By appropriating the story of Exodus as their own story, black Christians articulated their own sense of peoplehood. Exodus symbolized their common history and common destiny. It would be hard to exaggerate the intensity of their identification with the children of Israel. A.M.E. pastor William Paul Quinn demonstrated how literal the metaphor of Exodus could become when he exhorted black Christians, "Let us comfort and encourage one another, and keep singing and shouting, great is the Holy One of Israel in the midst of us. Come thou Great Deliverer, once more awake thine almighty arm, and set thy African captives free."[24] As Quinn's exhortation reveals, it was prayer and worship that made the identification seem so real. Sermons, prayers, and songs recreated in the imagination of successive generations the travail and triumph of Israel. Exodus became dramatically real, especially in the songs and prayer meetings of the slaves, who reenacted the story as they shuffled in the ring dance they called "the shout." In the ecstasy of worship, time and distance collapsed, and the slaves literally became the children of Israel. With the Hebrews, they traveled dry-shod through the Red Sea; they, too, saw Pharaoh's army "get drownded"; they stood beside Moses on Mount Pisgah and gazed out over the Promised Land; they crossed Jordan under Joshua and marched with him around the walls of Jericho. Their prayers for deliverance resonated with the experiential power of these liturgical dramas.

Identification with Israel, then, gave the slaves a communal identity as a special, divinely favored people. This identity stood in stark contrast with racist propaganda, which depicted them as inferior to whites, as destined by nature and providence to the status of slaves. Exodus, the Promised Land, and Canaan were inextricably linked in the slaves' minds with the idea of freedom. Canaan referred not only to the condition of freedom but also to the territory of freedom—the North or Canada. As Frederick Douglass recalled, "A keen observer might have detected in our repeated singing of 'O Canaan, sweet Canaan,/I am bound for the land of Canaan,' something more than a hope of reaching heaven. We meant to reach the *North*, and the North was our Canaan."[25] Slave owners, too, were well aware that the Exodus story could be a source of unflattering and even subversive analogies. It took no genius to identify Pharaoh's army in the slave song, "My army cross ober, My army cross ober/O Pharaoh's army drownded."

The slaves' faith that God would free them just as he had freed Israel of old was validated by Emancipation. "Shout the glad tidings o'er Egypt's dark sea/Jehovah has triumphed, his people are free!" the ex-slaves sang in celebration of freedom. But it did not take long for the freedmen to realize that Canaan Land still lay somewhere in the distance. "There must be no looking back to Egypt," a band of refugee slaves behind Union lines were instructed by a slave preacher in 1862. "Israel passed forty years in the wildnerness, because of their unbelief. What if we cannot see right off the green fields of Canaan, Moses could not. He could not even see how to cross the Red Sea. If we would have greater freedom of body, we must free ourselves from the shackles of sin. . . . We must snap the chain of Satan, and educate ourselves and our children."[26]

But as time went on and slavery was succeeded by other forms of racial oppression, black Americans seemed trapped in the wilderness no matter how hard they tried to escape. Former slave Charles Davenport voiced the despair of many when he recalled, "De preachers would exhort us dat us was de chillen o' Israel in de wilderness an' de Lord done sent us to take dis land o' milk and honey. But how us gwine-a take land what's already been took?"[27] When race relations reached a new low in the 1880s and 1890s, several black leaders turned to Africa as the black Promised Land. Proponents of emigration, such as Henry McNeal Turner, urged Afro-Americans to abandon the American wilderness for an African Zion. Few black Americans, however, heeded the call to emigrate to Africa; most continued to search for their Promised Land here. And as decade succeeded decade they repeated the story of Exodus, which for so many years had kept their hopes alive. It was, then, a very old and evocative tradition that Martin Luther King, Jr., echoed in his last sermon:

> We've got some difficult days ahead. But it really doesn't matter with me now. Because I've been to the mountaintop. Like anybody I would like to live a long life. Longevity has its place. But I'm not concerned about that now. I just want to do God's will. And He's allowed me to go up to the mountain. And I've seen the Promised Land. And I may not get there with you. But I want you to know tonight that we as a people will get to the Promised land.[28]

A period of over three hundred years stretches between John Winthrop's vision of an American Promised Land and that of Martin Luther King, Jr. The people whom Winthrop addressed long ago took possession of their Promised Land; the people whom King addressed still wait to enter theirs. For three centuries, white and black Americans have dwelt in the same land. For at least two of those centuries, they have shared the same religion. And yet, during all those years, their national and religious identities have been radically opposed. It need not have been so. After all, Winthrop's version of Exodus and King's were not so far apart. Both men understood that charity is the charter that gives title to the Promised Land. Both taught that mercy, gentleness, and justice are the terms for occupancy. Both believed that the conditions of the contract had been set by God, not by man. At times in our history, the two visions have nearly coincided, as they did in the antislavery stance of the early evangelicals, or in the abolitionist movement, or in Lincoln's profound realization that Americans were an "almost chosen people," or in the civil rights movement of our own era. Yet, despite these moments of coherence, the meaning of the Exodus story for America has remained fundamentally ambiguous. Is America Israel, or is she Egypt?

## NOTES

1. Peter Kalm, *Travels into North America*, 2d ed. (London: 1772), reprinted in vol. 13 of *A General Collection of the Best and Most Interesting Voyages and Travels*, ed. John Pinkerton (London: 1812), 503.

2. Thomas Secker, Bishop of London, *A Sermon Preached before the Incorporated Society for the Propagation of the Gospel in Foreign Parts . . . February* 20, 1740–1 (London: 1741), reprinted in Frank J. Klingberg, *Anglican Humanitarianism in Colonial New York* (Philadelphia: Church Historical Society, 1940), 223.

3. Winthrop D. Jordan, *White over Black: American Attitudes toward the Negro, 1550–1812* (Baltimore: Penguin, 1969), 191.

4. Secker, "A Sermon Preached," 217.

5. Edgard Legare Pennington, *Thomas Bray's Associates and Their Work among the Negroes* (Worcester, Mass.: American Antiquarian Society, 1939), 25.

6. David Benedict, *Fifty Years among the Baptists* (New York: Sheldon & Company, 1860), 93–94.

7. Charles F. James, ed., *Documentary History of the Struggle for Religious Liberty in Virginia* (Lynchburg, Va.: J. P. Bell, 1900), 84–85.

8. Donald G. Mathews, *Slavery and Methodism: A Chapter in American Morality, 1780–1845* (Princeton, N.J.: 1965), 293–99.

9. David Barrow, *Circular Letter* (Norfolk, Va., [1798]), 4–5; Robert B. Semple, *A History of the Rise and Progress of the Baptists in Virginia*, ed. George W. Beale (Philadelphia: American Baptist Publication Society, 1894), 105.

10. Francis Asbury, *The Journal and Letters of Francis Asbury*, ed. Elmer T. Clark, J. Manning Potts, and Jacob S. Payton, 3 vols. (Nashville, Tenn.: Abingdon, 1958), 2: 284; Wesley M. Gewehr, *The Great Awakening in Virginia, 1740–1790* (Durham, N.C.: Duke University Press, 1930), 240–41, 244–48.

11. Semple, *History of Baptists in Virginia*, 59.

12. George P. Rawick, ed., *The American Slave: A Composite Autobiography*, 19 vols. (Westport, Conn.: Greenwood, 1972), vol. 8, *Arkansas Narratives*, pt. 1, p. 35.

13. Abel McGee Chreitzberg, *Early Methodism in the Carolinas* (Nashville, Tenn.: Publishing House of the M[ethodist] E[piscopal] C[hurch], South, 1897), 158–59.

14. Austa Melinda French, *Slavery in South Carolina and the Ex-Slaves; or, The Port Royal Mission* (New York: W.M. French, 1862), 127.

15. Vincent Harding, "The Uses of the Afro-American Past," in *The Religious Situation, 1969*, ed. Donald R. Cutter (Boston: Beacon, 1969), 829–40.

16. John Winthrop, "A Modell of Christian Charity," in *Winthrop Papers* (Boston: Massachusetts Historical Society, 1931), 2: 282–84, 292–95. Reprinted in Conrad Cherry, *God's New Israel: Religious Interpretations of American Destiny* (Englewood Cliffs, N.J.: Prentice-Hall, 1971), 43.

17. Ezra Stiles, "The United States Elevated to Glory and Honor," in *A Sermon Preached before Gov. Jonathan Trumbull and the General Assembly . . . May 8th, 1783*, 2d. ed. (Worcester, Mass.: Isaiah Thomas, 1785), 5–9, 58–75, 88–92, 95–98. Reprinted in Cherry, *God's New Israel*, 82–84.

18. Ibid., in Cherry, *God's New Israel*, 84.

19. Cherry, *God's New Israel*, 66.

20. Marilyn Richardson, ed., *Maria W. Stewart, America's First Black Woman Political Writer: Essays and Speeches* (Bloomington: Indiana University Press, 1987), 39–40.

21. Mary A. Livermore, *My Story of the War: A Woman's Narrative of Four Years Personal Experience . . .* (Hartford, Conn.: A. D. Worthington, 1889), 260–61.

22. William G. Kephart to L. Tappan, May 9, 1864, American Missionary Association Archives, Decatur, Ala., Reel 2; also in *American Missionary 8*, no. 7 (July 1864), 179.

23. As cited in diary entry of 12 December 1857 by her mistress: Barbara Leigh Smith Bodichon, *An American Diary, 1857–1858*, ed. Joseph W. Reed, Jr. (London: Routledge & Kegan Paul, 1972), 65.

24. W. Paul Quinn, *The Sword of Truth Going "Forth Conquering and to Conquer"; The Origin, Horrors, and Results of Slavery Faithfully and Mi-*

*nutely Described. . . .* (1834); reprinted in *Early Negro Writing, 1760–1837,* ed. Dorothy Porter (Boston: Beacon, 1971), 635.

25. Frederick Douglass, *Life and Times of Frederick Douglass: Written by Himself* (1892; reprint, New York: Crowell-Collier, 1969), 159–60.

26. American Missionary 6, no. 2 (February 1862): 33.

27. Norman R. Yetman, ed., *Voices from Slavery* (New York: Holt, Rinehart and Winston, 1970), 75.

28. Martin Luther King, Jr., sermon of April 3, 1968, delivered at Mason Temple, Memphis, Tenn., reprinted in *A Testament of Hope: The Essential Writings of Martin Luther King, Jr.,* ed. James Melvin Washington (San Francisco: Harper & Row, 1986), 286.

# WOMEN AND CHRISTIAN PRACTICE IN A MAHICAN VILLAGE

*Rachel Wheeler*

Only recently have scholars acknowledged the complexity of Native American Christianity. The earliest mission histories attributed Christian conversions to the power of the gospel while explaining away "failures" to the "primitive" nature of Indian society. Later work understood native Christianity as but a thin veneer that hid from outsiders the continuation of traditional practices. Recent work, in contrast, challenges this preoccupation with authenticity by treating missionaries and Christian Indians as historical actors who lived within overlapping historical and cultural contexts. In this essay, Rachel Wheeler uncovers a distinctive, Indian Christianity that was literally incorporated through such rituals as communion, and such human experiences as pregnancy, birth, and nursing. She also shows the factionalizing power of Christianity to divide the very families these Mahican women were struggling to hold together. While Christian ritual provided native women with new resources of spiritual power, Wheeler concludes that their need for such new sources "testifies to the severe strains" the destructive forces of colonialism wrought on native cultures.

Reprinted by permission from Rachel Wheeler, "Women and Christian Practice in a Mahican Village," *Religion and American Culture* 13:1 (Winter 2003) 27–68. Copyright 2003 by the Center for the Study of Religion and American Culture.

# 5

# WOMEN AND
# CHRISTIAN PRACTICE
# IN A MAHICAN VILLAGE

## *Rachel Wheeler*

### SARAH

She saw nothing with her Eyes, but her heart believed so in the Saviour as if she had seen him and she had then such a feeling of it, that she thought that if any one should pull the flesh from her bones she would nevertheless abide with him, and said she, "I believe I should not have felt it neither, for my whole body and heart felt a power from his wounds and blood."[1]

### RACHEL

| | |
|---|---|
| wen ey giff mey scheyld | When I give my child |
| suck en ey tenck an die blot en | suck and I think about the blood and |
| wouns off auer söffger ey fühl mey | wounds of our Savior I feel my |
| hat sam teims were wet en | heart sometimes very wet and |
| so ey tenck mey scheyld saks de | so I think my child sucks the |
| blot off auer söffger en ey fähl | blood of our Savior and I feel |
| de ensels luck efter mey en | the angels look after me and |
| mey scheyld. | my child.[2] |

In August of 1742, a little known scene of the Great Awakening was unfolding in the Mahican villages that dotted the Housatonic Valley region of Connecticut, Massachusetts, and New York.[3] On August 10th, the colorful Moravian leader, Count Ludwig von Zinzendorf, arrived in the village of Shekomeko to check on the progress of the newly founded mission. Six months earlier, he had overseen the baptism of the first three villagers. Their baptized names—Abraham, Isaac, and Jacob—expressed the Moravians' grand hopes that the men would be patriarchs to a new nation of believers. Zinzendorf was now in Shekomeko to witness as these three men assumed the Christian offices of elder, teacher, and exhorter. Twenty miles away and two days later, melancholic missionary David Brainerd preached the Presbyterian gospel of salvation in hopes of saving the residents of Pachgatgoch from Moravian heresy.

But it is not the denominational rivalry of Moravians and Calvinists that is of interest here. Rather it is the emergence of a distinctive indigenous Christianity that grew up amidst the convulsions of religious enthusiasm sweeping the northern colonies. That August day in Shekomeko, Abraham's wife was baptized. From then on, she would be called Sarah.[4] And in Pachgatgoch a young woman named Amanariochque listened as Brainerd preached an emotional sermon from Job 14:14 while members of his audience "cried out in great distress."[5] Although Brainerd fanned the flames of revival in Pachgatgoch, it was the Moravians who established a mission in the village and who, in February of 1743, baptized Amanariochque, bestowing the name Rachel on the young woman. And it was a Moravian missionary, Christian Friedrich Post, who sought Rachel's hand in marriage just weeks after her baptism.

Sarah and Rachel lived out their lives as Indians and Christians, as wives and mothers. Temperamentally, Sarah and Rachel could not have been more different. Like her biblical namesake, Sarah was the matriarch, more advanced in years, devoted to her husband, her children, and her community. Rachel was just 21 at the time of her baptism, with a fiery temperament and a longing to be a mother. These differences of personality and lifestage are vividly reflected in the tenor of their Christian expressions. Despite these differences, a common thread links their Christian practice: both Sarah and Rachel engaged the Moravian blood and wounds theology and practiced Christian ritual in ways that sought to preserve, sustain, and nourish self, family, and community. While Christianity became a source of empowerment for some native Northeasterners, it was also a source of significant tension, within the individual and between themselves and their families and larger communities. An exploration of Sarah and Rachel's practice of Christian ritual begins to uncover a unique tradition of native Christianity, demonstrating the way Christianity was indigenized as it was literally incorporated through such rituals as communion, and such human experiences as pregnancy, birth, and nursing.[6] While Sarah and Rachel found new sources of power in Christian ritual, they also experienced the factionalizing power of Christianity as the newly drawn lines between Christian and non-Christian sometimes bisected the very families they were struggling to hold together.

Until recently, native Christianity received relatively little scholarly attention. Except for early treatments of mission history, which attributed missionary "successes" to the power of the gospel and "failures" to the "backward" nature of Indian society, all scholars of cultural encounters have had to struggle with how to relate the conditions of colonialism to the acceptance of Christianity.[7] Beginning in the 1960s, necessary correctives to triumphalism emerged as ethnohistory joined forces with revisionist and social history, stressing the high cost of colonization exacted on native peoples and cultures. With greater attention to the complexity of native cultures came a movement to depict native peoples as historical actors, not simply historical victims.[8] This interest in native resistance led to an emphasis on nativist "revitalization movements."[9] Recent decades have also seen substantial advances in illuminating the impact of colonialism on gender relations in native societies.[10] Together, these various strains of scholarship have added immeasurably to our understanding of native societies and the tragic consequences of colonialism. Yet one population has remained understudied: native Christians. Generally, native Christianity has been understood as a the result of a colonization of consciousness or a thin veneer that served to obscure the continuation of traditional practices from missionary view.[11] These interpretations fall short, however, by preserving a central element of the older, triumphalist scholarship they were reacting against. The categories of noble and ignoble remained (with the casting reversed) and, more significantly, the missionaries were unimpeached as sole definers of Christianity.[12]

What is needed, and what has been emerging in recent years, is a fresh look at mission communities that treats missionaries and Christian Indians as legitimate interpreters and practitioners of Christianity who lived, practiced, and believed within inextricably linked yet distinct historical and cultural contexts. By understanding Christianity as that which is constructed through ritual practice by those who identify as Christian, this approach circumvents the preoccupation with questions of authenticity and allows for an investigation of mission experience that gives full consideration to social context. This is nothing new of course, but something long known to students of popular and local religion. Methods used in studying the relationship of lay and clerical Christianity in the colonial context are particularly well suited for use with the Moravian mission sources.[13] A recent essay by Anne Brown and David Hall provides a useful model for studying Sarah and Rachel's Christian practice. In focusing on the practice of baptism and communion in early New England, the authors are able to identify where lay people assented to ministerial dictates and where they charted their own path. Whether lay people followed their minister's teachings or not, argue Brown and Hall, "their behavior reveals an insistence on aligning religious practice with family strategies of preservation and incorporation."[14] The same could be written of Sarah and Rachel. In the social ends to which Sarah and Rachel directed the spiritual power accessed through Christian ritual we can begin to identify a distinctly native, and distinctly feminine, Christianity.

Before returning to Sarah and Rachel, the Moravians need some introduction. The missionaries who arrived in Shekomeko in the 1740s traced their roots to followers of the fifteenth-century martyr, Jan Hus. Facing violent persecution in the fifteenth and again in the seventeenth century, the movement continued largely underground, until being rekindled in the 1720s when members gained asylum on the estate of the Lutheran Count Ludwig von Zinzendorf in Saxony. The Renewed Unity of the Brethren emerged as a unique combination of Pietist and pre-Reformation tendencies. Out of zeal and necessity (Zinzendorf was exiled from Saxony in 1736), the Brethren launched mission outposts from Greenland to the West Indies to Georgia. The mission at Shekomeko was begun in 1740 and by 1741, Bethlehem, Pennsylvania, had become the headquarters for the Moravians' North American missions.[15]

Perhaps the safest generalization to be made about Moravian missionaries is that they confound all generalizations about colonial missionaries.[16] Protestants preached little of the Word of God and much of the love of Jesus. They made extensive use of music and images, and thus came under suspicion as "papists" from their Anglo-Protestant neighbors.[17] Evangelicals experienced conversion as a loving union with the Savior, not a painful recognition of innate sinfulness and utter dependence on God.[18] Missionaries hardly fit the Edwardsian ideal of the lone, tortured laborer in the wilderness striving to first civilize then Christianize the heathens. Instead, they often worked in couples or pairs of couples, and on the whole seemed to quite enjoy life among their native hosts.[19] These differences from other missionaries were precisely what gained Moravians entry into native communities. Not only was their approach significantly less culturally aggressive than that of their Anglo-Protestant counterparts, but Moravians and Mahicans quickly discovered that they shared a dislike and suspicion of the general run of European colonists. Above all, however, it was the Moravians' distinctive "blood and wounds" theology and the concomitant ritual practice that generated sustained interest in native communities.

The blood and wounds of Christ formed the central pillar of mid-eighteenth-century Moravian theology. Volumes could be written about this era, known as the Sifting Time, but for purposes here, three central aspects of the blood and wounds theology deserve special attention: the pervasiveness of familial metaphors, the emphasis on physical and spiritual sustenance derived from the wounds of Christ, and finally, believers' experience of Christ's nearness. These elements resulted in a presentation of the Christian message that was readily incorporated into traditional Mahican religion and culture.

Moravians elaborated a kinship of Christian fellowship: God the father, the Holy Spirit as Mother, and Jesus the Son of God. Christ is both mother of the Church (born of the wound in Jesus' side), and bridegroom to the believer.[20] Earthly ties mirror these divine relations and are thereby sanctified. The distinctive choir system by which peer groups lived and worshipped together enacted Moravian kinship theology. While in theory Moravians did not believe in transubstantiation, in practice, they experienced the blood and body of Christ vividly and viscerally. They were baptized in the blood of Christ, they sang of swimming in the wounds of Christ, they desired to crawl into the side hole of Christ, they were revived and sustained by drinking Christ's blood. The wounds, experienced most immediately through communion, offered sustenance, respite, and often spiritual ecstasy, expressions of which can readily be found in hymns, litanies, letters, and diaries.[21] Not only was consumption and incorporation of Christ's body prominently featured in Moravian worship, but Christ's immediate presence was constantly invoked, so much so that some communities appointed Christ as Chief Elder. His guidance was sought through the use of the Lot on questions mundane and grand.[22]

While many colonists found Moravian religious culture dangerous, smacking as it did of "enthusiasm," its spiritual grammar was not unlike that of native religious practice, and Mahicans enlivened this grammar with the vocabulary of their experience, experience deeply marked by colonialism.[23] As historian John Webster Grant has written, for a missionary message to be communicated and appropriated, the message must provide sufficient continuity as to be readily comprehensible, yet it must also be different enough that the perceived shortcomings of the status quo are addressed.[24] More than a century of contact with Europeans had brought drastic changes to Mahican society prior to the arrival of the Moravian missionaries. Moravian ritual practice offered sufficient continuity with Mahican understandings of spiritual efficacy to be recognizable, yet offered a new theology that helped to naturalize societal changes already underway. While the sources available for early–historical era Mahican culture are sparse, especially when compared with neighboring Iroquois and coastal New England communities, it is possible to sketch the outlines of Mahican religious, social, and economic practices and some of the changes wrought by contact with European settlers.

The people of the middle Hudson River Valley were a horticultural, matrilineal, clan-based society. Economic activities were sharply divided along gender lines, with the men and women occupying largely distinct spheres. Women's sphere was the domestic: producing and processing food, raising children, and constructing homes. Men's activities often took them away from the village, whether to hunt, trade, or wage war.[25] Kathleen Bragdon suggests that during the early historical period riverine, horticultural, and matrilineal societies like the Mahicans tended to be less hierarchical than coastal Algonquian peoples and women likely had considerable power.[26] Deeds dating to the seventeenth and eighteenth centuries conveying land in traditional Mahican territory frequently were signed by women, suggesting that women maintained substantial power in community affairs into the colonial period, even as the social structures of Mahican society were adapting to the colonial realities of disease, trade, and European encroachment.[27]

The century of contact with Europeans prior to the arrival of the Moravian missionaries saw significant cultural change among the Mahicans and their neighbors. Henry Hudson had sailed directly into Mahican territory in 1609 and a lively trade was soon established. While the trade initially bolstered Mahican status among neighboring tribes, it also brought with it a host of problems, including disease, increasing demand for skins and furs, and increasing hostilities with neighboring tribes over access to the trade.[28] Diminished numbers and increasing pressures from encroaching Dutch settlers along the fertile banks of the Hudson River prompted many Mahicans to resettle to the eastern reaches of their historic hunting territory near the Housatonic River, consolidating with Housatonic Indians who had also suffered great population losses.

By the late seventeenth century, epidemic disease and economic pressures were spurring change in Mahican cultural patterns. On the one hand, women had less direct contact with the forces of change. On the other, increased trade and warfare elevated men's roles and likely disrupted the balance of gender roles. The need to travel farther to hunt and trap necessitated smaller social units, thus elevating the status of the nuclear family, transforming the localized clan system and prompting the development of centralized tribal leadership. Anthropologist Ted Brasser cites evidence of a shift to single family dwellings from the traditional longhouse, built to house 16–18 families, and now used primarily as the chief's residence and for ceremonial purposes.[29] Additionally, by the late seventeenth century, many Mahicans found it necessary to supplement hunting and agricultural production with wages earned as day laborers on nearby Dutch farms.[30] What these changes meant in concrete terms for Mahican women and their experiences of family life is impossible to know with any certainty. But it is clear that at the time Moravian missionaries arrived in Shekomeko, Mahican cultural traditions were in flux as individuals and families struggled to adapt to a rapidly changing world. Conference minutes from weekly meetings between missionaries and villagers testify to the strain on marriages and family relationships under the press of colonialism.[31]

Even more difficult to assess than the broad outlines of pre- or early-contact social structures is the shape and content of Mahican religious practice and ideology. Little direct evidence of non-Christian religious practice survives from the first years of the missions, although there are a few tantalizing pieces of evidence. Ebenezer Poohpoonuc, the first Mahican to be baptized at the nearby Congregational mission in Stockbridge, offered his commentary to missionary John Sergeant on the occasion of a religious ceremony. Sergeant asked about his people's religious beliefs, and Poohpoonuc replied that some believed that everything worked according to its own laws, and some believed the sun to be a god, or at least home to god. Most, he reported, believed there was one supreme invisible being who was the maker of all things. Sergeant watched as an old man stood over a recently killed deer and implored, "O great God pity us, grant us Food to eat, afford us good and comfortable sleep, preserve us from being devoured by the Fowls that fly in the Air. This Deer is given in Token that we acknowledge thee the Giver of all Things." Following the ceremony, the man received a payment of wampum, the meat was boiled and distributed to everyone, with an extra portion given to a widow. When asked about the origins of the tradition, Poohpoonuc answered that there had once been a man among them who came down from heaven with snow shoes. The prophet cleared the country of monsters and taught the people the religious customs from the land above. He then married a wife among the people and had two children. While he prayed during a ceremony, he began to

rise up through the wigwam and the people begged him to leave one of his children behind, which he did. The child also had extraordinary powers and taught the people many
things.[32] Community ceremonies, like the deer sacrifice witnessed by Sergeant, sought to
keep the world in balance by acknowledging the favor of the spirits and offering a sacrifice.

In saying that some believed that everything worked according to its own laws, Poohpoonuc may well have been referring to the individual element of native worship, in which
individuals, after a period of fasting or other trials, received in a dream a guardian spirit.
Missionary John Heckewelder affirmed that such beliefs were universal among the various
tribes he had encountered. Boys were led through a course of fasting and powerful medicines that brought on visions in which "he has interviews with the Mannitto or with spirits, who inform him what he was before he was born and what he will be after his death." As
a result, some come to believe themselves "under the immediate protection of the celestial
powers." Zeisberger offered a similar account, observing "there is scarcely an Indian who
does not believe that one or more of these spirits has not been particularly given him to assist him and make him prosper." The particular spirit was made known in a dream and
considered their "Manitto."[33] Through the dreams or visions, individuals entered into relationships with particular spirits who could ensure their safe passage through life. The evidence is suggestive, if not conclusive, that some Mahican women came to view the
Moravian Savior as a guardian spirit who offered protection and sustenance.

At first glance, the sources recording native Christian expression, mediated as they are
by missionaries, might easily be dismissed as the wishful thinking of eager missionaries or
the simple parroting of neophytes intent on pleasing (or deceiving) their Christian teachers. But a uniquely Mohican Christian voice (or voices, rather) begins to emerge with careful attention to the context of these expressions. While European Moravian expressions are
properly understood within a mystical Christian tradition whose goal is union with the divine, almost without fail Mahican evocations of the blood and wounds were intended to
bring about efficacious spiritual intercession toward the sustenance—spiritual and physical—of self, family, and community.[34] Sarah and Rachel turned to the blood of Christ in
precisely these ways.

First, to Sarah. Identified in the Moravian records as "Wampanosch," Sarah was likely a
member of the Paugusett or Potatuck Indians, who inhabited the lower Housatonic Valley.
This region had suffered drastic population losses in recent years, and remnant populations likely sought to secure their future through alliance and settlement with Mahicans
moving east to take up residence on their old hunting grounds, as their traditional homelands became increasingly crowded with Dutch settlers.[35] No mention is made in the
Moravian records of any living blood relatives Sarah may have had, suggesting that her
family may well have perished in the recent wave of smallpox to descend on the region.
Sarah's marriage to Mamma'tnikan (later Abraham) from nearby Shekomeko in the late
1710s or early 1720s might well have cemented ties between the villages or even joined the
two villages together. Mamma'tnikan was the grandson of Mammanochqua, probably a
woman sachem of the Esopus, who before her death in the early 1680s, had attempted to
ensure that the lands including Shekomeko remained under her family's control.[36] That
Sarah took up residence in her husband's village (contrary to matrilineal traditions) provides further evidence of the precarious position of her home community, for as Kathleen
Bragdon suggests, unilinear societies often become more flexible during stressful periods

of colonization and/or epidemic disease.[37] Despite the odds, by the time the Moravian missionaries arrived in 1740, Sarah and Mamma'tnikan had been married for probably close to twenty years, and together, the couple had raised several children to adulthood.[38]

Sarah and Abraham raised their children in an uncertain world, a world with few relatives and precarious community ties. Just as Sarah had lost many in her family and community to smallpox, so Abraham's grandmother, father, aunt, brother, and sister had died of the disease. His mother had been killed by Mohawks when Abraham was just 11.[39] Given the extent of such losses, the social fabric of Shekomeko and surrounding communities must have been extremely fragile. Traditional cultural patterns that rested much on kinship networks would have become virtually impossible to maintain. At the same time Sarah and Abraham were trying to build a new family and community, Abraham was struggling to secure rights to his ancestral lands that were increasingly encroached upon by New York settlers. It was out of this frustration that Abraham first considered Christianity. A drinking bout following yet another unsuccessful trip to the New York governor brought about a vision that prompted Abraham to visit the mission at Stockbridge. Apparently unimpressed, Abraham returned to Shekomeko, and a year later, in New York making yet another (futile) plea for justice, he and a companion were drunk when they encountered a Moravian missionary, Christian Heinrich Rauch, fresh off the boat from Europe.[40]

Despite initial reservations, Abraham found the Moravian message and mission program appealing in some measure. Moravians offered access to new sources of spiritual power, few demands of cultural change (especially in comparison to the thorough cultural conversion expected at Stockbridge), and the prospect of a continued presence on ancestral lands. Sarah too came to find the Moravian message and manner appealing, though for different reasons—reasons that corresponded to (and sometimes challenged) traditional gender roles. Sarah sought individual fortitude, spiritual sustenance, and new ties to bind together family and community, all through the vehicle of Christian ritual.

Sarah was baptized in August of 1742 and participated in communion for the first time in March of 1743. The first hint we have of Sarah's experience of Christian ritual can be found in a diary entry by missionary Gottlob Büttner on the eve of a celebration of the Lord's Supper in December of that year:

> She saw nothing with her eyes, but her heart believed so in the Saviour as if she had seen him and she had then such a feeling of it, that she thought that if any one should pull the flesh from her bones she would nevertheless abide with him, and said she, "I believe I should not have felt it neither, for my whole body and heart felt a power from his wounds and blood."[41]

Rachel had a similar experience, testifying that when she experienced the blood and wounds of Christ, someone could pour scalding water over her without her marking it. It was as though she "stood before God in his house" and could not tell whether she walked on the earth or floated in the air, but felt the Savior and his angels sitting beside her.[42] Sarah's talk of flesh being pulled from her bones and Rachel's of scalding water being poured over her at first glance seem to be of a piece with the graphic blood and wounds theology of the Moravians. But the imagery is altogether different than that commonly employed by European Moravians, evoking instead practices associated with ritualized torture among many Algonquian and Iroquois peoples. Sarah would certainly have known of such torture practices even if she had no firsthand experience; her mother-in-law had been tortured and killed by French-allied Indians and other villagers had surely suffered similar fates.[43]

While most commonly associated with the Iroquois, there is considerable evidence that ritual torture of captives was practiced by Mahican and Delaware peoples as well. Captives were seized from enemy tribes to appease the deaths of family members. The power, and the obligation, to quench the crying blood of lost relatives belonged to women, who could appease the death either by the adoption of the captive or by mandating torture and death. If the captive was to be killed—a more likely fate for men than women and children—the whole village gathered to participate in the ritualized torture, with women playing the central role. As captives endured the villagers' torments, which often included application of burning brands, removal of fingernails, or pouring hot liquids or sand over the victims, they strove to conceal their suffering, thereby displaying spiritual fortitude and power. Captors admired the stoic suffering of their captives for it testified to their great spiritual power, power that the captors could appropriate through ritual consumption after the victim expired. According to Dutch observer van der Donck, all the while being tortured, the captive "continues to sing and dance until life is extinct, reproaching his tormentors, deriding their conduct, and extolling the bravery of his own nation," thereby winning the respect of his captors.[44] Observations made by missionary John Heckewelder over a century later suggest a continuity of practice when he described the ritualized torture of an accused murderer, who "while undergoing the most dreadful tortures," will "rehearse all vile acts of the kind he had committed during his life time, without showing fear of death," employing "an haughty tone, and with a pride," in hopes that "at his death, his soul may be permitted, to reenter the body of some unborn infant."[45] The torture victim's stoic suffering brought with it a chance of rebirth.

Understanding Sarah and Rachel's words against this backdrop and the Moravian practice of communion suggests some intriguing possibilities about the intersection of gender, colonialism, and Christian ritual. The Moravian symbolism surrounding communion intersected in powerful ways with native rituals of torture. Moravians placed especial emphasis on Christ's gruesome death, describing in great detail the spear wounds, the blood that ran like sweat, and his stoic death upon the cross, which they often depicted as a tree. Further, the *Abendmahl*, or communion, in which Christ's flesh was symbolically consumed, was often referred to by the Moravians as "Streiter-Mahl" or "fighters' meal." Moravians attributed a transformative power to Christ's blood and wounds.[46]

While women were less likely to be the victims of ritual torture, they were its directors. It was women's responsibility to balance the spiritual forces after the disruption caused by a death. In their accounts of warfare and torture, neither Heckewelder nor Zeisberger call particular attention to the central role of women, suggesting either the authors' cultural bias, the waning of women's power, or perhaps both. Historian Theda Perdue's assessment of changing Cherokee gender roles might apply equally to the Mahican situation. The new motives for war introduced by the trade and French-English colonial rivalries "excluded women from the social and spiritual benefits that traditional warfare had brought them."[47] One source of spiritual power would have been less readily available to Mahican women.

The Moravian emphasis on the redemptive power of suffering and on the transformative power of Christ's blood fused with Mahican cultural traditions to create a ritual practice fully Christian and Mahican. By participating in communion, Sarah and Rachel laid claim to two types of spiritual power: that traditionally accorded women as they avenged the deaths of their kin, and that claimed by captive warriors who secured a chance at rebirth through stoic endurance of torture. Consuming Christ's flesh might have functioned as a substitute for the traditional spiritual power available to women as active participants in the practice of war. In turn, this spiritual force is translated into the ability to suffer stoically.[48] Communion was thus one means of acquiring the spiritual power to sustain self in an environment increasingly hostile to Indian existence. By combining Mahican elements of ritual associated with the torture of captives and the Christian message of redemptive suffering, Shekomekoans forged a powerful new symbolic universe that helped make sense of the new world of colonialism.

If Sarah found resources of personal strength in Christian practice, she also sought means to reinforce community and kinship ties through her work as a member of the "Indianer Conferenz." These conferences were weekly meetings between the missionaries and a small group of appointed villagers. The Indian men and women who served on the committee were to meet individually with all community members and report back to the missionaries on everything from spiritual state to marital relations to plans for hunting or harvesting. These meetings served both as a forum to discuss familial and social problems. Marital problems occupy a significant portion of the conference minutes. Somewhat surprisingly, very few of the problems brought before the conference seem to be the result of missionary attempts to impose a new morality of marriage on villagers. Rather, the minutes call attention to the difficulties average men and women had in securing domestic harmony.[49] These tensions were likely the result of a number of forces: economic, political, and social changes brought on by colonialism translated into increased emphasis on the nuclear family, at the same time that the kinship ties that once supported individuals were severely disrupted. Sometimes, too, the source of domestic discord lay in differing degrees of participation in the emerging Christian community. The conferences were at once a potentially divisive force in the community and at the same time a significant venue for native leadership.[50]

Sarah's frequent service on this committee might well have functioned to support the role she would have held by tradition as wife of the head man of the village. Women in native societies had traditionally maintained oversight of domestic village affairs. What to European observers often looked like the absence of a formal legal code was in fact the operation of powerful moral suasion that shaped behavior through public praise and scorn.[51] The social upheaval of the decades prior to the founding of the Moravian mission at Shekomeko may well have created a space for more formal structures of moral regulation that came to be filled by the weekly conferences in which a group of village delegates considered the problems faced by individuals and families and sought resolution. Sarah thus exercised considerable authority in regulating behavior and overseeing the entrance of new members into the Christian community.[52] She strove in her work to establish a new foundation for community stability and mutual obligation. Whether a prior system of kinship became the basis of the new Christian community is impossible to know, though it seems quite probable.

Some women found solace in Sarah's counsel while others bristled at her authority. During one conference in the spring of 1745 Sarah reported on her conversation with a sick, unbaptized woman from Pachgatgoch. The unnamed woman (known only as "Naskomschock's wife and Johannes' friend") had remained behind in Pachgatgoch when many villagers had moved to Shekomeko, but now felt drawn to the Christian community. In a poignant image, the woman likened the Christian community to a grove of chestnut trees and herself to a lone tree.[53] Whether or not this woman ultimately moved to Shekomeko, her report to Sarah suggests that part of the appeal of becoming a Christian was the fellowship offered by the nascent community. It was often through people like Sarah that prospective Christians found their way into the Christian community. Not all villagers, however, saw Sarah's role in such a positive light. Rebecca, wife of Jacob (who together with Abraham was among the first to be baptized), was baptized on the same day as Sarah. Rebecca resented that she was expected to confess the state of her heart to Sarah. She complained to the missionaries that she could not understand why Sarah should be her confessor and expressed disdain for the conferences altogether.[54]

Sarah's authority was not limited to other women. On one occasion, Sarah and Abraham reported that Isaac had recently spent an entire day at a nearby tavern, and in his drunken state threatened to shoot Johannes (a prominent leader of the Christian-Mahican community) and spouted derogatory words about the Moravians. The couple queried the missionary whether they should speak to Isaac on their own or accompanied by the missionary. After putting the question to the Lot the missionary answered that the Savior wished them to speak alone with Isaac. One suspects that the missionary sensed his involvement would only heighten tensions.[55]

In her work as a frequent conference member, Sarah strove to bring new members into the Christian fold and to regulate the behavior of Christians. But it is through her relationships with family that a fuller sense of her Christian practice emerges, together with the tensions that sometimes erupted between her familial and Christian identities. On one occasion, Sarah reported to missionary Johannes Hagen that she was well and thought much about the Savior and felt much love for him, but her heart was much concerned with her children and the world.[56] Sarah's confession of concern for her children suggests she knew the missionary would not approve. Yet at the same time, she seemed to be making the case that she was a good Christian, not in spite of her familial concerns but because of them. For Sarah, being a Christian meant attempting to secure the welfare of her family.

The link between Christian ritual and family in Sarah's life is yet more apparent in the events surrounding the birth of a son in the late spring of 1747. It was an uncertain time to bring a child into the world, not only because Sarah would have been at least 40. The couple had arrived in the newly formed Christian-Mahican settlement at Gnadenhütten, Pennsylvania, having completed the 150-mile journey from Shekomeko while Sarah was eight months pregnant.[57] Abraham had been determined to remain in Shekomeko, unwilling to leave his home village despite the continued refusal of the New York government to recognize his land claims, and the increasing hostility of colonists towards Moravians and their native allies. It might well have been his wife's desire to have her unborn child baptized that finally persuaded him to leave his home village.[58] Following the birth of their son, Sarah expressed her fear that the missionaries might refuse to baptize the child because the couple had not initially joined the migration of Shekomeko Christians to Pennsylvania. She explained how much she had cried over the child and how greatly she desired he might receive the Savior's grace. Missionary Martin Mack consented and baptized the child. He would be called Isaac.[59]

With her youngest safely baptized, Sarah began to worry about her older children. Two sons, Jonathan and Joachim, had recently left the Moravian community, though both would soon return.[60] The 1744 act forbidding Moravians from preaching within the borders of New York (many suspected them of "papist" leanings) made it eminently clear that an alliance with the Moravians counted for little in the colonial world. Jonathan and Joachim may well have thought it wise to investigate other native communities farther to the west. Whatever their reasons, Sarah was distraught, not knowing if and when her sons would return, and fearing that their rejection of the Christian community might keep them from meeting again in the next world.[61] Unable to console his wife, Abraham pleaded with the European sisters that they try to comfort her. Maria Spangenberg related to Sarah her own difficult experiences as a mother whose children had not accepted the Savior.[62] Sarah seemed to be somewhat relieved by Maria's efforts and resigned to the reality that not all of her children would follow in her footsteps. Resigned to separation, Sarah was surely elated when Jonathan and his wife Anna returned to the congregation and began building a house in February 1749. For the time, her family was reunited.

Several years later Sarah would again be faced with trying circumstances and this time she chose to follow family, while attempting to maintain ties with the Christian community and especially with the power of the Savior's blood. In 1753, Abraham was appointed as captain of the Mahican nation and was called to move to Wyoming, Pennsylvania, to carry out his duties.[63] Sarah did not want to leave the Brethren, but neither could she bear being separated from her husband.[64] Her daughter-in-law Anna faced the same painful decision in the winter of 1753–54. Clearly upset, Anna pleaded with Jonathan,

> My dear husband, decide soon what you want to do, and don't take long: I want to tell you, what I want to do, I am not going with you to Susquehanna. If you want to go, you can. But I and my children want to stay with the congregation, for when I think about what the Savior did for us and for our children, it is impossible for me to resolve to go away from the congregation, I would inflict severe judgement upon myself.

Anna attributed the well-being of her children to the Savior and feared that leaving the Christian community would jeopardize the protection offered by the Savior. Jonathan promised to think over the matter while on his hunting trip and to have an answer for her when he returned. Anna anxiously awaited Jonathan's return, confessing to Esther, "Oh how often have I thought of him, especially during Christmas and New Year's week and I wished with my heart that he still feels some of that grace and blessing the Savior let us feel."[65] Sarah too, prayed for her son. When in the woods collecting firewood, she prayed to God that "he have mercy on my husband and children, and that he sends them a new heart."[66] For the time being anyway, Anna and Sarah's wish for Jonathan was granted: he decided to stay with the Brethren.[67] Sarah's relief that Jonathan decided to stay with the congregation must have been mixed with the sadness of her own impending departure. While the Christian congregation helped to cement new ties of community, particularly for women, it could also force painful choices when the multiple layers of Sarah's identity—as Mahican, wife, mother, and Christian—did not fit easily together.

As Sarah and Abraham set off for Wyoming in April 1754, the couple promised to "stay with the Savior and to tell others about Him and His love whenever possible."[68] In a letter to "Liebe Schwester" Maria Spangenberg sent later that year from Wyoming, Sarah confessed the difficulty of living among non-Christian Indians, but found that "the Savior still comes through to me and I abide by him" and that she continued to feel "what love I have for the Savior, because he was wounded and his blood shed that melts my heart and makes me happy." She prayed often for the Savior to "give me a drop of the blood that flows from his side." Finally, she asked that Spangenberg "remember me to the Savior" and promised to visit if she ever had the chance.[69] Being separated from the Moravian community was clearly trying for Sarah, but she continued to find spiritual power through communion with the blood of Christ. The Savior seemed to function for Sarah in much the same way as a guardian spirit that came to her offering protection. Sarah would eventually return to the congregation, but only after her husband had died.

On his deathbed in 1762, Abraham encouraged Sarah to return to the Moravians. Although she was indeed eager to return, Sarah feared the move would mean painful family decisions. She delayed returning for nearly a year, held back by her sons. Eventually, her older sons decided to move further west and urged her to join them. She refused, saying she would rather go to the Brethren, but, she said, "Go where you will. I can't help you and I can't hold you back." Unable to compel her sons to stay with her, she turned to her daughter, Sarah[70], and pleaded,

> You are my only daughter. You have heard my thoughts. What will you do? If you want to abandon me, you can do that. You have your freedom. I have raised you to adulthood and you would be sad if I should die in the woods at your side and be forever lost.

The younger Sarah broke into tears and promised to follow her mother. The family was welcomed back into the congregation, and soon work was begun on a house for Sarah and her two children.[71]

One year later, in 1764, Sarah and Isaac were living in Philadelphia where dozens of Moravian Indians had sought refuge in the midst of the frontier upheavals of Pontiac's Rebellion and the Paxton Boys incident. In this climate, no one trusted Christian Indians. In the cramped quarters of the Philadelphia Barracks, Sarah succumbed to smallpox in June of 1764, and Isaac followed his mother in death several weeks later.[72] At times, Sarah had found in the personal experience of the Savior's blood and in the support of the Moravian community a means of sustaining herself and her family, but her identity as a Christian Indian often left her in the impossible position of choosing one child over another, her faith over her family, or her family over her faith.

Rachel's life was more openly dramatic than Sarah's, yet she faced many of the same struggles of negotiating family and faith. The few short years of her life recorded in Moravian records were intense: filled with intense spiritual experiences, anxiety, and sorrow. Because Rachel married a missionary, her life is better documented than perhaps any of her sister villagers.[73] Like Sarah, Rachel drew heavily on the Moravian imagery of the blood and wounds of Christ. And she too directed her practice of Christian ritual to the ends of creating and preserving family.

At the time of her baptism, Rachel was 21 and already separated from her first husband. She had been married to a man named Annimhard, a Mahican from Shekomeko, but she was apparently unhappy and left the marriage, perhaps because the relationship had yet to produce any children, or perhaps because the relationship was abusive.[74] Rachel seems to have been at once eager to escape from family, yet at the same time afraid to chart a new course. Among those attentive to David Brainerd's preaching, she then became among the first of her village to be baptized by the Moravians.[75] Within weeks of her baptism, she was contemplating marriage to a white man. Rachel was clearly a woman in search of what she thought would be a better life. Although there is little in the sources to suggest why Post and Rachel chose each other, it seems that Post was intent on marrying an Indian woman, and Rachel might have hoped marriage to a European man with an especially close relationship to the Savior would produce the children she had been unable to conceive in her first marriage.[76] The couple was engaged in early August 1743 and married later that month. Just four days after the betrothal, Rachel was headed home to her mother in Pachgatgoch, apparently having second thoughts about her marriage to Post. Two weeks later, she returned, apologizing for her flight from Shekomeko. A month later, Rachel was still struggling with her marriage, confessing that she wanted to love her husband but could not.[77]

By December, Post's fellow missionaries were deeply concerned at Rachel's erratic behavior. Although she had returned to Shekomeko, she refused to consummate the marriage. The missionaries, perhaps even Post himself, sought the help of the Savior through the Lot. The answer came that it was time for the couple to effect their union.[78] Although Rachel consented, missionary Büttner had reason to believe that all was still not well. He was right, and Rachel was soon headed for Pachgatgoch. When she returned two weeks later, she refused to enter the mission house. Büttner sent his wife to speak with Rachel, and Post himself went to attempt to placate his wife. They inquired if she wanted to live alone, and promised her her own house. But Rachel remained stubbornly silent. Other members of the congregation tried to appease her, but Rachel gave no answer and again ran away. When Büttner penned a worried letter to Bethlehem headquarters seeking advice, she had yet to return. At a loss, Büttner sent Post to Bethlehem bearing his letter and dispatched a member of the congregation to New York to bring back some cloth, hoping to win over the disgruntled bride. Two days later, Rachel returned to Shekomeko.[79] One week later, on December 22, 1743, she moved into the missionaries' house.[80] Nine months almost to the day, Rachel gave birth to a baby boy, named Ludwig Johannes, whom she called Hannes.[81]

Pregnancy seems to have settled Rachel's restless soul. A letter to her friend and spiritual mother, Maria Spangenberg relates the joy she experienced at the prospect of becoming a mother.[82] She described for Spangenberg how she had once wept when she saw children at play in Shekomeko because she herself was childless. But now, she wrote, during worship services "my babe leaped in my womb" and she thanked "our Savior continually, that he has given me one." The letter implies that it was the Savior working through Joseph Spangenberg, more than Post, who was responsible for the child Rachel carried. Wrote Rachel,

I never yet felt my heart so at the Lord Supper as this time. I can't express how it was with me when I received that Blood, muchraa haniseho pekachkanon . . . and when Br. Joseph gave it to me, my heart, glowing and filled with the Sap of Life and thought, Muchree onewe onewe, onewe.[83]

Doubt about the life-giving powers Rachel attributed to the blood of the Savior vanish when we read another letter, this one written in August of 1745. "O beloved Mother," wrote Rachel, "I was very poor [of spirit] in Bethlehem and while we [she and Post] were together in the cabinet and Brother Joseph prayed, I felt the great grace of the Savior flood my heart with blood."[84] It was probably on this occasion that Rachel conceived her second child. The sexual overtones of the letter are hard to ignore, yet again it seems that it is God's grace, mediated through Christ's blood and Spangenberg's prayer, that bestows a child on Rachel. Post, it seems, just happened to be present.

Another letter dictated by Rachel that year to the "Brethren and Sisters in Barbies" (Suriname) offers further testimony to the life-giving properties Rachel found in Christ's blood. Rachel's eight-month-old Hannes died that year, and she had lost three siblings in 1744, so she might well have felt an even greater pull to establish a new, spiritual family, one that transcended the precarious bonds of biological kinship.[85] She testified to the distant members of her new Christian family that the Savior had received her as his child and "washed my heart with his blood." Now that she felt the Savior's blood on her heart, she found she was better able to love her husband, something she had clearly struggled with before. In concluding her letter, she professed her love for her distant Brethren and Sisters although "I don't know all your names." The Savior's blood was the means for establishing a new community; having been adopted by the Savior, and enabled by his blood to love her new husband, Rachel now claimed membership in a community that transcended local boundaries.[86]

Rachel's letters offer testimony to the power she found in Moravianism: the power to love a prickly husband, the power to conceive children, and the comfort of a new spiritual family. But they also testify powerfully to the very real and personal impact of colonialism. She had lost not only her son and three siblings, but doubtless many other friends and neighbors. Moravian missionaries, including her husband, had been forbidden from preaching in all of New York. Shekomeko and Pachgatgoch were now divided between those who chose to stay behind and those who followed as the missionaries retreated to Pennsylvania. In September of 1746, she again turned to her "liebe Mutter" Maria Spangenberg, who Rachel felt loved her "a great deal more than my own mother."[87] She confessed her sense of powerlessness, "I know and feel that I am a poor little creature and only the blood of our savior gives me wellness. . . . Now I feel my heart [is] always more hungry and thirsty after the blood of our Savior." The more difficult life became, the stronger was her desire for sustenance from the Savior. In the same letter, she described for Spangenberg how she had a premonition that left her heart "very heavy." She pleaded with the Savior to identify the cause. Was it her husband's illness? No, said the Savior. Then what? "And then Joshua came home dancing and singing and it was as if my finger was cut off." Joshua, a friend from Pachgatgoch, had enlisted in the army that summer and had been off fighting in Canada. He returned in early September and went on a drunken spree.[88] Rachel experienced this threat to the solidarity of the Christian community as physical pain. She prayed for the Savior to help the wayward Joshua. Feeling uneasy, Rachel could not sleep and so she took the letter she had received from Maria and went to "the house of our Savior." Unable to read, Rachel found the physical presence of the letter cheered her considerably. In the meeting house with the letter, Rachel recounted, "It was just so as when the Savior gave me my Hannes, and I was so glad that I did cry."[89] The letter was a gift of Maria's presence from the Savior.

Finally, Rachel's thoughts turned to her young child, Maria, named after Spangenberg. It is here that the connection between self, family, community, and Christian practice are most clearly evident. Wrote Rachel, "My child grows well and strong but it has a great cough. I wish our Savior did make her well again. I can't help her at all. The Savior must do everything." Rachel felt powerless to ensure the health of her child and turned to the Heiland, imagining that rather than breast milk, she fed her child from the Savior's wounds, "when I give my child suck and I think about the blood and wounds of our Savior I feel my heart sometimes very wet and so I think my child sucks the blood of our Savior and I feel the angels look after me and my child." She closed her letter with a prayer for her fellow villagers "that the Savior would give them a feeling of his blood and wounds in their hearts." And finally, an entreaty to Spangenberg, "you must think about me that he gives much grace. . . . We are your poor children Rachel and Maria Post."[90] The next year, in December of 1747, Rachel delivered a stillborn baby boy. Rachel and her young Maria both died the following day.[91]

Rachel's letters capture both the powerlessness and the empowerment experienced by many native Moravians. They demonstrate the creative spirituality of native Christians who enlisted new sources of spiritual power to strengthen the bonds of family and community and the ways in which the encroaching colonialism challenged the efficacy of tradition to sustain self, family, and community. Childless from her first marriage, Rachel turned to Christ's blood and a European man she had difficulty loving to give her a child. Let down in some way by her own mother, Rachel found sustenance from her spiritual mother, whose strength she hoped to pass on to her own daughter. Fearing mother's milk alone was insufficient nourishment for her beloved child, she fed little Maria from the wounds of the Savior.

It was through the practice of Christian ritual by Sarah, Rachel, and others that an indigenous Christianity came into existence. While these women found new resources of spiritual power in Christian ritual, their need for such new sources testifies to the severe strains on native cultures. Christianity as lived by Sarah and Rachel is marked indelibly by the destructive forces of colonialism. But it does not necessarily follow that the Christian residents of Shekomeko and Pachgatgoch were victims to a colonization of consciousness. Nor does it follow that native Christianity was the result of a self-conscious, strategic manipulation of the oppressor's religion. Through study of the religious expressions of individuals like Sarah and Rachel and of communities like Shekomeko we can begin to uncover a distinctive, Indian Christianity that expressed both deeply rooted cultural values and the realities of a dramatically changed world.

## NOTES

1. Büttner Diary, December 11, 1743, box 111, folder 2, item 7 (hereafter given in x/x/x format), Records of the Moravian Mission to the Indians, Moravian Archives, Bethlehem, Pennsylvania (hereafter RMM). See also entry of same date, 111/1 RMM.

2. Rachel to Maria Spangenberg, September 9, 1746, 113/1/5 RMM. This letter is in the hand of Rachel's husband, Christian. It starts in a broken German and shifts to broken English written in German script and according to German phonetics. Rachel had probably learned some English growing up in close proximity to English settlers. Post, a carpenter by trade and native of Polish Prussia, knew little English at this time. For biographical information on Post, see Thomas Christopher Chase, *Christian Frederick Post, 1715–1785: Mis-*

*sionary and Diplomat to the Indians of America* (Ph.D. thesis: Pennsylvania State University, 1982).

3. The term Mahican will be used throughout, although the term is problematic, suggesting as it does cultural homogeneity and sharply drawn political boundaries. Mahican tribal identity emerged as a response to colonialism; River Indians, Housatonics, Highland Indians, and Hudson River Mahicans confederated politically to treat with colonial governments and villages consolidated in the wake of epidemic disease and encroaching white settlement. Shekomekoans called themselves Mahican; Pachgatgoch identity is more difficult to determine. The Moravians listed the tribal identity of Pachgatgoch residents as Wampanosch, which has sometimes been taken to mean Wampanoag. However, Wampano means "East-

erner" in most Algonquian languages and thus could refer to any individual or group who had come from the east. A nineteenth century manuscript by Moravian missionary John Heckewelder suggests that the Wampanos might have been a branch of the River Indian Mahicans who earlier branched off from their Hudson River location and relocated to the vicinity of New Haven, preferring to live by the shore. If Heckewelder's sources were correct, then the Wampano and the Mahicans of Shekomeko were more closely related than previously understood. Heckewelder, *Notes, Amendments and Additions to Heckewelder's History of the Indians*, 970.1 H35m, American Philosophical Society, Philadelphia, 3. Bert Salwen, "Indians of Southern New England and Long Island: Early Period," in Bruce G. Trigger, ed., *Handbook of North American Indians*, vol. 15 (Washington, D.C.: Smithsonian Institution, 1978), 175. Throughout this article, to avoid excessive qualifications, I use "Mahican" as an umbrella term meant to include not only Mahican, but also Wampanosh, Mennising, Sopus, and Highland, whose representatives could be found in these villages. While there were most certainly meaningful cultural distinctions represented by the different terms, it is very difficult to determine what these may have been.

4. Isaac's wife was also baptized that day and named Rebecca. Jacob's wife, Rachel, was baptized in December of that year. Shekomeko Diary, August 11 and December 12, 1742, 111/1 RMM.

5. Moravian records note that Amanariochque was first awakened by Brainerd's preaching. On that visit, Brainerd reported that God gave him "his presence and Spirit in prayer and preaching: so that I was much assisted, and spake with power from Job 14:14. Some Indians cried out in great distress, and all appeared greatly concerned," Jonathan Edwards, *Life of Brainerd*, edited by Norman Petit (New Haven: Yale University Press, 1985), 176.

6. The Moravian records contain very little that suggests one way or the other whether baptized villagers continued in the practice of traditional religion. There are occasional references to the continuation of traditional herbal healing and sweatlodges, neither of which the Moravians understood to be religious practices. Moravians generally tended to define Christianity in terms of feeling and ritual and less in terms of cultural practices, and so this restricted view of Christianity likely aided the coexistence of native and Christian religious practices, a coexistence that would not have been entirely unprecedented for most native peoples whose religions were non-exclusive. Reli-

gious "dimorphism," as Jace Weaver has termed it, has long been a characteristic of native religious practice. As much as we might like to know about the continuation of "traditional" religions in Moravian missions, the sources simply do not allow for such a study. My presumption is that many native "lifeways," such as hunting and healing continued as they had before the arrival of the missionaries, and that neither Mahican nor Moravian found contradiction in doing so. For references to the use of native remedies, see Moravian mission diary entries for November 3, 1750 114/2 RMM, March 30, 1751 114/3 RMM, and May 24, 1753 112/3 RMM; for references to use of sweatlodges by men and women see: July 11, 1745 111/1 RMM, October 11, 1750 114/2 RMM, November 1, 1750 114/2 RMM and November 29, 1750 114/2 RMM. Jace Weaver, *That the People Might Live: Native American Literature and Native American Community* (New York: Oxford University Press, 1997), vii–viii.

7. Among the most noteworthy of recent works on Native Americans and Christianity are: James B. Treat, ed. *Native and Christian* (New York: Routledge, 1995); Jace Weaver, *Native American Religious Identity: Unforgotten Gods* (Maryknoll, N.Y.: Orbis, 1998); Sergei Kan, *Memory Eternal: Tlingit Culture and Russian Orthodox Christianity through Two Centuries* (Seattle: University of Washington Press, 1999); Michael McNally, *Ojibway Singers: Hymns, Grief, and a Native Culture in Motion* (New York: Oxford University Press, 2000).

8. Robert F. Berkhofer, *Salvation and the Savage: An Analysis of Protestant Missions and American Indian Response, 1787–1862* (Lexington: University of Kentucky Press, 1965); R. Pierce Beaver, *Church, State and American Indians: Two and a Half Centuries of Partnership in Missions between Protestant Churches and Government* (St. Louis: Concordia Publishing House, 1966); Henry Warner Bowden, *American Indians and Christian Missions: Studies in Cultural Conflict* (Chicago: University of Chicago Press, 1981); William G. McLoughlin, *Cherokees and Missionaries, 1789–1839* (New Haven: Yale University Press, 1984).

9. The emphasis on resistance to imperialism is not surprising given that many of these scholars came of age in the Vietnam era. Much excellent scholarship has come out of this line of inquiry. Anthony F. C. Wallace launched the field with his article, "Revitalization Movements," *American Anthropologist* 58 (1956), 264–281, and his subsequent book, *The Death and Rebirth of the Seneca* (New York: Knopf, 1969). Several works have followed in the same rich vein, including Gregory Evans Dowd, *Spirited Resistance: The North American Indian*

*Struggle for Unity, 1745–1815* (Baltimore: Johns Hopkins University Press, 1992); Joel Martin, *Sacred Revolt: The Muskogees Struggle for a New World* (Boston: Beacon Press, 1991); R. David Edmunds, *The Shawnee Prophet* (Lincoln: University of Nebraska Press, 1983).

10. On native women, colonization and Christianity, the foremost works include Mona Etienne and Eleanor Leacock, ed. *Women and Colonization: Anthropological Perspectives* (New York: Praeger Press, 1980); Irene Silverblatt, *Moon, Sun, and Witches: Gender Ideologies and Class in Inca and Colonial Peru* (Princeton: Princeton University Press, 1987); Karen Anderson, *Chain Her by One Foot: The Subjugation of Women in Seventeenth-Century New France* (New York: Routledge, 1991); Carol Devens, *Countering Colonization: Native American Women and Great Lakes Missions, 1630–1900* (Berkeley: University of California Press, 1992); Nancy Shoemaker, ed. *Negotiators of Change: Historical Perspectives on Native American Women* (New York: Routledge, 1995); and Theda Perdue, *Cherokee Women: Gender and Culture Change, 1700–1835* (Lincoln: University of Nebraska Press, 1998). The fall 1996 issue of *Ethnohistory* (43:4) is devoted to the encounters of native women and Christianity. Paula Strong's article in this issue, "Feminist Theory and the 'Invasion of the Heart'" offers an especially cogent and useful review of work in the field. Etienne and Leacock's work employed a Marxist bent and interpreted the advent of capitalism as the end of gender equality in native communities. Anderson finds that Christianity was a key element in establishing the subjugation of women to men in Huron and Montagnais communities. Devens studies the missions to Great Lakes Indians as one aspect of the colonization process and finds three possible responses to Christianity: native peoples 1) rejected it as a threat to tribal lifeways, 2) accommodated Christianity grudgingly in the face of dire economic conditions, or 3) divided along gender lines when the mission or economic circumstances affected men and women differently. Women's engagement with Christianity is understood as the conscious manipulation of a tool. Devens, *Countering Colonization*, 3–4, 21.

11. Francis Jennings, *The Invasion of America: Indians, Colonialism, and the Cant of Conquest* (Chapel Hill: University of North Carolina Press, 1975); for a more concise summary of Jennings' views of missions see his "Goals and Functions of Puritan Missions to the Indians," *Ethnohistory* 18 (1971), 197–212. See also James Ronda, " 'We Are Well as We Are:' An Indian Critique of Seventeenth-Century Missions," *William and Mary Quarterly* 34

(1977), 66–82; Neal Salisbury, "Red Puritans: The 'Praying Indians' of Massachusetts Bay and John Eliot," *William and Mary Quarterly* 31 (January 1974), 27–54. James Axtell has written much on the subject of missions, the most encompassing of which is *The Invasion Within: The Contest of Cultures in Colonial North America* (New York: Oxford, 1986). For a relatively recent reevaluation of New England missions, see Harold W. Van Lonkhuyzen, "A Reappraisal of the Praying Indians: Acculturation, Conversion and Identity at Natick, Massachusetts, 1646–1730" *New England Quarterly* 63 (1990), 396–428.

12. This is not to suggest that the missionaries are not in fact legitimate definers of Christianity, but only that it is a mistake to attempt to measure the "authenticity" of native Christianity by the extent to which it reproduces the Christianity taught and practiced by the missionaries.

13. The Moravian sources are unique in allowing such a study of lay Indian Christianity in the eighteenth century. Even the rich Jesuit sources do not compare to Moravian sources for depth of detail about individual lives. David Hall has been at the forefront of the movements to study first "popular religion" and, more recently, "lived religion." His recent edited volume contains essays by many of his students. David D. Hall, *Lived Religion in America: Toward a History of Practice* (Princeton: Princeton University Press, 1997). Inga Clendinnen's work on colonial Mexico presents a fine model for the study of local and lived religion in a native context. She argues against a "belief analysis" approach to the study of religion and proposes instead to seek religion in action and observances, or "religion as performed." Clendinnen, "Ways to the Sacred: Reconstructing 'Religion' in Sixteenth-Century Mexico," *History and Anthropology* 4 (1990), 105–41 (quote p. 110).

14. Brown and Hall, "Family Strategies and Religious Practice: Baptism and the Lord's Supper in Early New England," in Hall, ed. *Lived Religion*, 41–68, quote p. 50.

15. For a history of the Moravian Church from its Hussite origins, see Edmund De Schweinitz, *The History of the Church Known as the Unitas Fratrum* 2nd ed. (Bethlehem, Penn.: Moravian Publication Concern, 1901); and Rudolf Rican, *The History of the Unity of Brethren: A Protestant Hussite Church in Bohemia and Moravia*, C. Daniel Crews, trans. (Bethlehem, Penn., and Winston-Salem: The Moravian Church in America, 1992). For general treatments of the German Pietist movement, see F. Ernest Stoeffler, *German Pietism during the Eighteenth Century* (Leiden: Brill, 1973); Stoeffler,

*Continental Pietism and Early American Christianity* (Grand Rapids, Mich.: Eerdmans, 1976); and W. R. Ward, *The Protestant Evangelical Awakening* (Cambridge: Cambridge University Press, 1992). On Pietism and the Moravians see John Jacob Sessler, *Communal Pietism among the Early American Moravians* (New York: H. Holt and Company, 1933). Sessler and Ward both suggest that the Moravian missions were in part the result of their strained relations with princes and pulpits at home. For more recent studies of the Moravian movement in America, see Gillian Lindt Gollin, *Moravians in Two Worlds: A Study of Changing Communities* (New York: Columbia University Press, 1967), and Beverly Prior Smaby, *The Transformation of Bethlehem: From Communal Mission to Family Economy* (Philadelphia: University of Pennsylvania Press, 1988).

16. Early Moravian histories of the missions tend not to be as triumphalist as their Anglo-Protestant counterparts. On Moravian mission efforts in America, see George H. Loskiel, *History of the Mission of the United Brethren among the Indians of North America,* Christian Ignatius La Trobe, trans. (London: Brethren's Society for the Furtherance of the Gospel, 1794); John Heckewelder, *A Narrative of the Mission of the United Brethren among the Delaware and Mohegan Indians, from its Commencement, in the Year 1740, to the Close of the Year 1808* (Philadelphia: McCarty and Davis, 1820). More recent scholarship on the missions includes Elma Gray, *Wilderness Christians: The Moravian Mission to the Delaware Indians* (New York: Russell and Russell, 1953); Earl P. Olmstead, *Blackcoats among the Delaware: David Zeisberger on the Ohio Frontier* (Kent, Ohio: Kent State University Press, 1991). Jon Sensbach's recent book explores Moravian relations with African Americans, in Sensbach, *A Separate Canaan: The Making of an Afro-Moravian World in North Carolina, 1763–1840* (Chapel Hill: University of North Carolina Press, 1998). A couple of recent dissertations and recent articles have made substantial use of the Moravian mission sources in the writing of Indian history. Amy Schutt, "Forging Identities: Native Americans and Moravian Missionaries in Pennsylvania and Ohio, 1765–1782" (Ph.D. diss., Indiana University, 1995); and Schutt, "Tribal Identity in the Moravian Missions on the Susquehanna," *Pennsylvania History* 66 (1999), 378–98; Jane Merritt, "Kinship, Community and Practicing Culture: Indians and the Colonial Encounter in Pennsylvania, 1700–1763" (Ph.D. diss., University of Washington, 1995); Merritt, "Dreaming of the Savior's Blood: Moravians and the Indian Great Awakening in Pennsyl-

vania," *William and Mary Quarterly* 54 (1997), 723–46; and Merritt, "Cultural Encounters along a Gender Frontier: Mahican, Delaware and German Women in Eighteenth-Century Pennsylvania," *Pennsylvania History* 67 (2000), 502–531.

17. When missionary Christian Rauch went on a scouting trip to Mohawk territory in January of 1743, he found "it was common talk every where that we were papists." It was feared the Moravians' missionary work was simply a ruse and a way to win the natives to their side, which, once effected, the Moravians would "war with them [the Indians] against the other inhabitants and help deliver the land into the hands of the Spaniards." Christian Rauch, undated recollections of a journey into Mohawk country, 221/4/1 RMM. Several missionaries were arrested in Connecticut in 1743. During questioning, an Anglican minister took issue with Moravian methods of instructing the Indians, claiming they were "erroneous, dangerous and papist-like." The minister feared Moravians made "ignorance the Mother of Religion as the Romans do." John Christopher Pyrlaeus' account of his arrest and trial, June 1743, 111/9/1 RMM. Shekomeko missionary Gottlob Büttner was held in New York in 1744 following the renewal of hostilities between England and France. During his trial, Büttner was asked why he had not gone to teach among the papists. Rumor circulated that the Moravians had received a shipment of guns and powder from the French. English translation of a report of Gottlob Büttner's trial at New York in a letter to Peter Böhler, August 13, 1744, 112/3/5 RMM. Gottlob Büttner's diary entry June 5, 1744, 112/2/3 RMM. For another reference to Büttner and charges of papacy, see Büttner's diary entry October 17, 1744, 112/19/5 RMM.

18. This issue was in fact a major cause of Zinzendorf's break with the Pietists. For Zinzendorf's views on love as the primary experience of faith, see his lecture "Concerning Saving Faith," in Nicholaus Ludwig Count von Zinzendorf *Nine Public Lecures on Important Subjects in Religion,* George W. Forell, translator and editor (Iowa City: University of Iowa Press, 1973), 34–42. See also Sessler, *Communal Pietism,* 142.

19. Missionary Martin Mack recorded his feelings as he neared Shekomeko, "my heart longed very much after Checomeco so that I could not sleep in the night being so near to it." Mack's colleague, John Pyrlaeus, reported that his heart nearly broke when he met his Mahican hosts, "one cannot help loving them. . . . I am heartily willing even to remain among them." "A Short Acc't of Brother Martin Mack's Journey to Checomeco and

Back to Bethlehem," November 1745, 217/12b/2 RMM. Pyrlaeus, June 1743, 111/9/1 RMM. Although Moravian mission policy accords better with modern sensibilities, it would be misguided to uphold these missionaries as proto-multiculturalists. Their relatively non-aggressive proselytizing stemmed less from an appreciation of the innate worth of Indian culture than from the particular historical and political circumstances in which they labored.

20. Gary Kinkel has explored Zinzendorf's feminine imagery in *Our Dear Mother the Spirit: An Investigation of Count Zinzendorf's Theology and Praxis* (Lanham, Md: University Press of America, 1990). Much of this imagery can be found throughout Christian history. Caroline Walker Bynum has argued for an understanding of Medieval Christian art as centrally tied to ideas of family and sustenance, especially as indicated by the association of Mary's breast milk and Jesus's spilled blood as nourishment. See especially, Bynum, "The Body of Christ in the Middle Ages: An Answer to Leo Steinberg," in her collection of essays, *Fragmentation and Redemption: Essays on Gender and the Body in Medieval Religion* (New York: Zone Books, 1991).

21. A recent and balanced treatment of this rich body of Moravian religious expression is Craig Atwood, *Blood, Sex and Death in Zinzendorf's Bethlehem* (Ph.D. dissertation: Princeton Theological Seminary, 1995). Sessler's *Communal Pietism* contains many lengthy quotes from original Moravian sources. A few verses from hymns used in the Mahican missions aptly illustrate Moravian wounds theology as presented at the missions:

> Make thou for these dear little
> Souls a fine soft bed in thy wound
> Holes and in the wound within
> thy side, there let them sleep,
> eat, drink and hide.

Fürbitte für Kinder," 331/3 RMM.

> My Lamb! I thank thee heartily
> that thou didst die upon the Tree,
> and wert so wounded for my soul
> and gotst within thy Side a Hole
>
> Where now a sinner rests so
> well, and can with Tears of
> Pleasure tell "he on the Cross,
> my Lamb God! And I live
> only thro' his Blood."
>
> O wounded Head, o through-bor'd
> Feet, O hands and Side, you
> are so sweet! Be only still
> more dear to me. O Lamb!
> Where is a Lamb like Thee!

English verses #26, 331/3 RMM.

22. A common Moravian practice through which the will of the Savior was sought on issues mundane and grand. On the use of the Lot, see Beverly Smaby, *The Transformation of Moravian Bethlehem from Mission to Family Economy* (Philadelphia: University of Pennsylvania Press, 1988), 23–4.

23. Numerous anti-Moravian tracts were published in the 1740s that often called attention to the Moravian "delusion" of experiencing the nearness of Christ. See especially, Samuel Finley, *Satan Strip'd of his Angelick Robe: Being the Substance of several Sermons Preach'd at Philadelphia, January 1742–3 from 2 Thessalonians 2.11,12. Shewing, the Strength, Nature and Symptoms of Delusion. With an Application to the Moravians* (Philadelphia: W. Bradford, 1743); Gilbert Tennent, *The Necessity of Holding Fast the Truth* (Boston, 1742); and Gilbert Tennent, *Some Account of the Principles of the Moravians: chiefly collected from several conversations with Count Zinzendorf; and from some sermons preached by him at Berlin, and published in London* (London, 1743).

24. John Webster Grant, *Moon of Wintertime: Missionaries and the Indians of Canada in Encounters since 1534* (Toronto: University of Toronto Press, 1984), chapter 11.

25. The most complete ethnography of the Mahicans remains Ted Brasser's, *Riding on the Frontier's Crest: Mahican Indian Culture and Cultural Change* (Ottawa: National Museums of Canada, 1974). Kathleen Bragdon discusses the marriage practices of southern New England native peoples. Bragdon, *Native People of Southern New England, 1500–1650* (Norman: University of Oklahoma Press, 1996), see especially chapters 3 and 7.

26. Bragdon, *Native People*, especially chapter 1.

27. Robert Steven Grumet discusses women's signatures on deeds among Coastal Algonquians in "Sunksquaws, Shamans, and Tradeswomen: Middle Atlantic Coastal Algonkian Women during the 17th and 18th Centuries," in Mona Etienne and Eleanor Leacock, eds. *Women and Colonization: Anthropological Perspectives* (New York: Praeger, 1980), 43–62. A 1735 deed from Mauhammetpeet and Mequnnisqua, women of Scaticook, to the Province of Massachusetts Bay conveyed a significant parcel of land that would eventually sprout ten towns. A confirmation of the women's ownership of the land was signed by 19 men of the Scaticooks three days before the deed itself. Another deed from Nechehoosqua, a Scaticook woman, deeded land "north of Fort Dummer" for $100 in bills of credit to Jeremiah Allen of Boston "and to his Successor or Successors in Trust for the use and Benefit of Said Province for ever." Henry Andrew Wright,

*Indian Deeds of Hampden County* (Springfield, 1905), 120–30.

28. Van der Donck noted, "the Indians also affirm, that before the arrival of the Christians, and before the small pox broke out amongst them, they were ten times as numerous as they now are, and that their population had been melted down by this disease, whereof nine-tenths of them have died." Van der Donck, *A Description of the New Netherlands* (Syracuse: Syracuse University Press, 1968), 64. Almost a century later, in 1734, Ebeneezer Poohpoonuc, the first to be baptized at the Stockbridge mission, lamented that "since my remembrance, there were Ten Indians, where there is now One" while "the Christians greatly increase and multiply, and spread over the Land." Nathaniel Appleton, *Gospel Ministers Must Be Fit for The Master's Use* (Boston: S. Kneeland & T. Green, 1735), iv.

29. Brasser, *Riding on the Frontier's Crest*, 29. Adraien van der Donck's account of the Mahican and Delaware was first published in 1655. Van der Donck, *A Description of the New Netherlands*, 79. A sketch of Shekomeko done in 1745 by Moravian missionary Johannes Hagen seems to confirm this pattern. All of the dwellings depicted are single family. 112/17/1 RMM.

30. In 1722, the Mahican chief Ompamit lodged a complaint with Governor Burnet of New York "that many of our people are obliged to hire land of the Christians at a very dear rate, and to give half the corn for rent, and the other half they are tempted by rum to sell." Edmund Bailey O'Callaghan and Berthold Fermow, *Documents Relative to the Colonial History of the State of New York* (Albany: 1856–1887), vol. 5, 661–3. Missionary John Sergeant of Stockbridge noted the small numbers assembled to hear him preach, explaining "the men were gone into New York Government, to reap for the Dutch people there." Samuel Hopkins, *Historical Memoirs Relating to the Housatonic Indians* (Boston: S. Kneeland, 1753), 31. The early Moravian records make frequent reference to village residents working for the Dutch and selling mats, baskets, wooden bowls, and canoes to European neighbors. Interestingly, a scan of the Index to the Moravian records demonstrates that there are far more references to selling manufactured goods than game or skins.

31. On marriage practices among the seventeenth-century Delaware and Mahican, see van der Donck, *A Description of the New Netherlands*, 84. David Zeisberger reported on late eighteenth-century Delaware marriage customs in his *History of the North American Indians*, Archer Butler Hulbert, ed. (Ohio State Archeological and Historical Society, 1910), 78–82. John Heckewelder comments on the nature of Delaware marriage customs in *History, Manners and Customs of the Indian Nations Who Once Inhabited Pennsylvania and the Neighbouring States*, rev. ed. by W. C. Reichel (Philadelphia: Historical Society of Pennsylvania, 1876), 154–158.

32. Hopkins, *Historical Memoirs*, 10–12.

33. Both Heckewelder and Zeisberger depict these guardian spirits as the province of boys and men and it is unclear whether women had similar experiences, though it is unclear whether Zeisberger was using the male pronouns to include men and women. It seems likely that both men and women could have guardian spirits, though they would presumably function to quite different ends. Heckewelder, *History, Manners and Customs*, 245–248. Hulbert, *Zeisberger's History*, 132–33.

34. For a discussion of Moravian mysticism, see F. Ernest Stoeffler, *Mysticism in the German Devotional Literature of Colonial Pennsylvania* (Allentown, Penn.: Schlechter's for The Pennsylvania German Folklore Society, 1950), especially chapter 4, "Mysticism among the Moravians."

35. Brasser, *Riding on the Frontier's Crest*, 29.

36. The grandmother's identity as sachem cannot be fully proved, but the evidence is highly suggestive. A document in the Moravian records, written in support of Abraham's efforts to persuade the New York officials to make good on a previous transaction, details the tragic history of Abraham's family and how he came to be among the sole surviving heirs of the land. His grandmother, Mammanochqua, was cited as the owner of the lands including Shekomeko, who during a great epidemic of 60 years ago (1683) was prompted to try to secure land for her descendants. Robert Grumet cites evidence of a woman sachem of the Esopus named Mamanuchqua who signed several deeds in the 1670s and 1680s. Additionally, it makes more sense that, as sachem, Abraham's grandmother was attempting to preserve tribal lands, rather than family lands. The land including Shekomeko may well have been traditional hunting territory of the Esopus. Brasser suggests a date of 1711 for the founding of the village of Shekomeko. Further, one of the witnesses to Abraham's right to the land cited in the Moravian records was Cornelius, or Gadrachseth, listed as the "Old Captain," likely the former chief of Shekomeko, who often traveled to the Hudson to confer with other Mahican leaders. Memorandum dated October 1743, 113/5/3 RMM. Grumet, "Sunksquaws, Shamans, and Tradeswomen: Middle

Atlantic Coastal Algonkian Women during the 17th and 18th Centuries," in Mona Etienne and Eleanor Leacock, eds. *Women and Colonization: Anthropological Perspectives* (New York: Praeger, 1980), 43–62. Brasser, *Riding on the Frontier's Crest*, 67. See Shekomeko records dated February 15 and February 21, 1743, 111/2/1 RMM.

37. It might also suggest the differing traditions of the Wampano, as Bragdon suggests that the record is unclear on whether coastal southern New England peoples were matrilineal or patrilineal. Bragdon, *Native People*, 158–160. Additionally, there would have been quite a mix of varying tribal traditions among the residents of Shekomeko. According to the Moravian records, residents at Shekomeko included Mahican as well as "Wampanosch," "Sopus," "Highland," and "Mennissing." See Fliegel's translation of the Moravian catalogues of Indian residents, located at 3191/2/1 RMM.

38. If David Zeisberger's account of Delaware practices holds true for Mahican society as well, Sarah was likely born around 1705 at the latest. According to Zeisberger, Delaware men generally married when they were 18–20 and women at 14 or 15. Sarah and Abraham had several sons of marriageable age when the Moravians arrived in Shekomeko. Their son David himself had a son who died in 1744 (no date is given for his birth). Son Jonathan married Anna in 1744. Son Joachim married Catharina sometime in the early 1740s. So, if the oldest of Sarah's children was 20 in 1740 and she had married at 14, she would have been born in 1705. Hulbert, *Zeisberger's History*, 82–83. Carl John Fliegel, *Index to Records of the Moravian Mission among the Indians of North America* (New Haven: Research Publications, Inc., 1970).

39. Memorandum dated October 1743, 113/5/3 RMM.

40. John Sergeant reported on Mamma'tnikan's visit to Stockbridge in April of 1739. In Mamma't-nikan's vision, as reported to Sergeant, a roar of rushing water filled his ears and he saw before him a group of Indians drunk and naked and unable to escape the onrushing water. A voice told him he must give up all wickedness. The vision continued, a strong light shone all about him, and he heard "a noise like the blowing of a pair of bellows" followed by "a violent blast of wind which dispersed the Indians into the air." Awakening from the vision, Mamma'tnikan resolved to give up drink and seek knowledge of Christianity. John Sergeant diary entries dated April 14 and June 17, 1739, Stiles Papers, Beinecke Library, New Haven, Conn. John Sergeant made at least one visit to Shekomeko, as recorded in the Shekomeko Diary for October 1743, 111/1 RMM. The first meeting between Mamma'tnikan and the Moravians is found in the Shekomeko diary, July 1740, 111/1 RMM.

41. Büttner Diary [Eng], December 11, 1743, 111/2/7 RMM. "Erzehlte Sara, daß ihr ganz besonders etliche Tage daher gewesen sie wäre nämlich zu erst sehr bekümmert gewesen wie sie doch mit dem Heylande stünde, und hätte ihn gebetten 3 nachten hinter einander. Er möchte ihr doch zu erkennen geben wie ihr Herze mit ihm stünde endlich wären, ihr ein mahl die Wunden des Heylandes, so klar und so lebendig geworden, und hätten ihr ein solch gefühl im Herzen verursacht daß sie dächte wenn ihr zu der Zeit iemand Stücke vom Leibe Geißre, sie hätte es nicht gefühlt, ihr Augen hätten zwar die Wunden nicht gesehen aber ihr Herze hätte eine solche Kraft daran gefühlt als ob sie selbige wircklich sähe." December 11, 1743, 111/1 RMM.

42. This account was taken down by Rachel's husband, Christian Post, who was a joiner by trade and wrote with little punctuation, capitalization, or attention to grammar. "Sie sagt sie wäre so sehr sindig und elend sie wiste nicht warums sie der Heiland so lieb hätte es wäre wohl umb seines Blut und der Wunden willen womit er sie erkauft hat beim eintrit in den sahl ists ihr gewesen als hät einer mit heissen wasser übergossen sie hat nicht gefühlt ob sie auf den boden trete oder in der luft schwebte es ist ihr so gewesen als wen sie vor gott treten in sein haus. Sie hat gefült als wen der lieb heiland mit seinem engelkens bey sie gesessen wir wohin zeit und Ewigkeit eure armen sinder sein." Letter from Rachel, 219/1/7 RMM.

43. "Die Manhat [Abraham's mother] selbsten wurde in den damaligen krigen zwischen denen Englishen und Franzen, von denen Franz Maquaischen Indianen gefangen und Todt geschlagen." Memorandum on Abraham's Land, 113/5 RMM.

44. Van der Donck, *A Description of the New Netherlands*, 99–101; Heckewelder, *History, Manners and Customs*, 217–19; Hulbert, ed. *David Zeisberger's History*, 102–108. Daniel Richter discusses the meaning of this practice extensively in *The Ordeal of the Longhouse: The Peoples of the Iroquois League in the Era of European Colonization* (Chapel Hill: University of North Carolina Press, 1992), 33–36, 66–71, and in an article, "War and Culture: The Iroquois Experience," *William and Mary Quarterly* XL (1983), 528–559. John Steckley has written provocatively and persuasively of the ways in which Jesuit missionaries used Iroquois and Huron torture practices as a basis for conveying Christian

themes. Steckley, "The Warrior and the Lineage: Jesuit Use of Iroquoian Images to Communicate Christianity," *Ethnohistory* 39:4 (1992), 478–509. On stoic suffering, see especially Steckley, "The Warrior," 491–94. For a discussion of women's roles in torture, see Karen Anderson, *Chain Her by One Foot*, 169–78. Anderson interprets women's participation in the torture of captives as a means of releasing pent up aggression fueled by a restrictive society in which expressions of anger were forbidden. Theda Perdue offers an insightful analysis of the changing meaning of Cherokee women's participation in war, especially their central role in deciding the fate of captives. Perdue, *Cherokee Women*, 49–55, 66–69.

45. Quoted from Heckewelder's notes for a never published revised edition of his *An Account of the History, Manners and Customs of the Indian Nations*. Heckewelder, *Notes, Amendments and Additions to Heckewelder's History of the Indians*, 11–12, 970.1 H35m, American Philosophical Society, Philadelphia.

46. An entry of the Shekomeko diary reads in part "die geschwister im Hauße hatten heute ein sehr geseegnetes Streitermahl." October 2, 1743, 111/1 RMM. In hymns written for use in the Mahican missions (often with the assistance of the Mahican couple, Josua and Bathseba), Christ's cross is frequently referred to as a tree. This booklet of hymns contains German, English, and Mahican versions. There seems to be some correspondence between the European language and Mahican language hymns. A few of the Mahican hymns have the German translation interlineated, while many are written in Mahican alone.

> Behold the loving son of God
> Strech'd out upon the Tree,
> Behold him shedding forth his blood
> For all of you and me."

Englische Verse #25, 331/3 RMM.

> 2) The Blood Sweat trickling down thy Face,
> Assure my Heart of purchased Grace.
> Thy Cross, thy suffrings and thy Pain
> my everlasting Strength Remain.
> 3) Cleanse me and wash me in thy Blood,
> Then only Thine I'll be;
> Create me Thine, and I will
> have no other Lord but thee.

English Verses #28, 331/3 RMM.

There is some evidence that such depictions resonated with Indian neophytes. Nicodemus, a Wampano Indian from Shekomeko who made the move to Gnadenhütten near Bethlehem, reported to the missionaries a dream in which he saw Jesus in a tree and kissed his wounds. "Nicodemus und Eva besuchten uns und erzehlten unterschiedliche Instanzen der Arbeit des Lämleins an ihren Herzen, sonderlich auch wie letztere in Träume den Heiland am Baume gesehen und seine durchstochene Seite geküßet haben." January 6, 1748, Gnadenhütten Diary, 116/3/1 RMM.

47. In a chapter on war, Theda Perdue explores the changes to traditional Cherokee gender roles in the pursuit of war that accompanied the economic and political transformations begun during the colonial era. She suggests that women were often vulnerable to raiding warriors as they worked in the fields. If they were not immediately killed, they were more apt to be adopted than tortured. On the other side of the battle lines, women had once "avenged the deaths of their relatives personally through torture, but by the late eighteenth century torture had waned." Perdue, *Cherokee Women*, chapter 4 (quote 90).

48. Traditionally, women too likely placed a high value on stoicism, though the occasions for demonstrating stoicism and gaining power thereby would have been private (childbirth) rather than public (warfare and torture). Some scholars have suggested that the nearly universal European assumption that Indian women gave birth with far less pain than European women is largely a function of a cultural imperative of stoicism. James Axtell, ed. *The Indian Peoples of Eastern America: A Documentary History of the Sexes* (New York: Oxford University Press, 1981), 3. Roger Williams noted of the Narragansett that "most of them count it a shame for a Woman in Travell to make complaint, and many of them are scarcely heard to groane." Quoted in Bragdon, *Native People*, 175. On the spiritual powers gained through suffering, Perdue writes, "although women could not avoid the physical and spiritual dangers brought on by menstruation, pregnancy and childbirth, they could gain a spiritual power through these trials." Perdue, *Cherokee Women*, 32–36.

49. For Moravian conference minutes from Shekomeko, see for example, 112/5/3 RMM which contains conference minutes from June 1744–January 1745. One entry dated September 20, 1744, reads, "Ruth sagte sie feilte in Ihren Herzen das Boas so lange er so wäre sie nicht könde lieben und sie wolte nicht mehr zu ihnen, sondern alleine bleiben;" several days later, the minutes noted, "Cornelius hat gestern Ruth in seinem Hause gefunden und erfahren daß sie wieder von ihrem Mann geschlagen und weg gejagt worden;" December 9, 1744 reads, "Cornelius seine Fr. hat bey der

Sara sich sehr beklagt über ihren Mann;" January 1, 1745 reads, "Petrus wurde verklagt das er sich auf der Jagt gegen sein Weib schlecht hat mit gefahrtet."

50. I have yet to find any discussion of the process by which delegates were chosen to serve on the committee, but it is apparent that it was the Christian members in good standing who most often served. At times, these were people who were apparently prominent members of the community even before the arrival of the Moravians. But it is also clear that the Moravians helped to disrupt traditional patterns of authority. Many native communities experienced a new factionalism between Christians and non-Christians. See, for example, Daniel K. Richter, "Iroquois Versus Iroquois: Jesuit Missions and Christianity in Village Politics, 1642–1686," *Ethnohistory* 32:1 (1985), 1–16. James Axtell also deals extensively with this question in *The Invasion Within.*

51. For example, Heckewelder comments, "although the Indians have no code of laws for their government, their chiefs find little or no difficulty in governing them." And further, he writes, "it may justly be a subject of wonder, how a nation without a written code of laws or system of jurisprudence, without any form or constitution of government, and without even a single elective or hereditary magistrate, can subsist together in peace and harmony, and in the exercise of the moral virtues." He goes on to attribute the smooth operation of society to "the pains which the Indians take to instill at an early age honest and virtuous principles upon the minds of their children, and to the method which they pursue in educating them." In this task, parents were assisted by all members of the community, who employed public praise and scorn to shape behavior. Such education would have been largely the province of women. Heckewelder, *History, Manners and Customs,* 107, 113–4.

52. Conference minutes from 1744 show Sarah particularly active in domestic disputes. On June 10, Sarah recommended that Eva continue to live in the house with Sarah's son David and his wife Anna. On June 17, she reported on Martha's desire to move to Shekomeko from Potatik in order to find a husband. On December 16, Sarah brought forward Rebecca's complaint that Susanna was her husband's "kebs weib" (concubine). She also reported on Esther's spiritual condition, saying sometimes she was very happy and others, she was "sehr elend" and that her mother often bothered her. On December 23, Sarah's daughter-in-law, Anna, reported that she had often prayed to the Savior for her husband Jonathan to return. Worker's Conference Minutes, 112/5/3 RMM.

A sampling of the Gnadenhütten diary for 1752 for all references to Sarah suggests Sarah's continued community work. On January 12, she is listed as conference member. January 17, she visits homes of Christians. February 7 she offers advice to parents on education of children. February 12, March 11, and June 4 Sarah serves as "Jungerin" or disciple. July 26 she reports the spiritual desires of a relative. August 15, she helps a sick woman. September 14 she visits Christians. September 29 she pleads on behalf of an old friend. September 20, she makes house calls. Gnadenhütten diary, January–December 1752, 117/3 RMM.

53. "Sie wolte gerne des heyland sein, und warum sie sich nicht lange schon hingegeben, als die brüder von hier abgereist sind und ihr man auch hier war ist sie allein in Potatcoch geblieben, ist aber unruhig gewesen, das sie den aus gangen in der unruhe hat sie eine kastangen baum gesehen so ist die gemein in Schecomeko wie die viele baumchen von einer art und sie war so alleine mit solchen schweren Herzen soll sie den verlangte her getaufft zu werden, wen sie auch solte nach bethlehem gehen, es mächte ihr auch kosten was es wolle." March 31, 1745, 112/15 RMM.

54. One suspects that the missionaries in selecting conference members tended to give precedence to those villagers who were respected Christians and whom they perceived as holding political sway in the community. Rebecca and Jacob would have met the first criterion, but not the second. "Rebecca hat gesacht was das sein solte sie kennte es nicht verstehen, daß Sara solte die Perschon sein der sie solte ihr Herz sagen, und wiste auch nicht was die Konferenz wäre." Conference minutes, April 11, 1745, 112/15 RMM.

55. "Abraham, Jacob, Sara kommen zu mir und sagten das Isaac d. 29 May den ganzen tag in WirtsHause gewesen wäre und gesoffen als er war zu Hause gekommen hatte er sehr [illeg] und geruffen daß er wolte der Johannes tod schiessen, und gegen die Gemeine in Bethl. gerrede. Abraham sagte mir auch das mir Johannes viel schäme sagte erzehlte es weren aber alles [illeg] sie fragten mich ob sie solten mit Isaac alleine reden oder ob ich auch wolte dar bey sein. Ich sagte ihnen aber das sei alleine solten mit ihm reden, (der Heyl. woltens das sie solten alein mit ihm reden)." Conference Minutes, June 4, 1745, 112/8 RMM.

56. "Sarah ging mit ihren herzen heraus, nemlich daß sie allezeit die Gedancken von sich gehabt, sie hätte den Heiland lieb, und stünde gut mit ihr:

Nun aber sehe sie daß ihr herz an der Erde und ihren Kindern gehangen." Shekomeko Diary, August 7, 1745, 111/1 RMM.

57. The community had been in flux as the Moravians came under increasing suspicion due to the renewal of colonial hostilities and as Shekomeko residents felt ever greater pressure from an increasing population of New Yorkers. The Moravians secured land from the Delaware about 30 miles from Bethlehem, and most Shekomekoans eventually relocated to the Pennsylvania site. The dislocation and cramped quarters facilitated a devastating epidemic which claimed the lives of many Shekomekoans. Pachgatgoch Diary, April 22, 1747, 116/1 RMM.

58. Actually, he sought to stay in Wechquadnach, another Mahican village in New York, near Shekomeko where some of the villagers moved following the dissolution of Shekomeko.

59. "Die Abrahams Sarah wurde mit einem Söhngen entbunden . . . Abraham verlangte auch daß sein Kind möchte getaufft werden, desgleichen äusserte sich auch die Sara gegen die Esther und sagte, sie wäre wohl sehr arm und hätte sich versundigt am Heiland und der Gemeine als sie noch in Shecomeko gewesen wäre, doch würde sie vor eine große Gnade halten wenn ihr Kind könte getaufft werden ihr Herz und Sinn wäre, es solte des Hlds ganz seyn . . . Die Sarah sagte sie hätte schon viel geweint über die Kind, und weil sie so schlecht stände, so hätte sie immer gedacht, daß Kind würden wir wol nicht tauffen. Sie würde aber den Heiland sehr davor dancken, wenn es die Gnade haben könnte." Pachgatgoch Diary, May 6–8, 1747, 116/1 RMM.

60. A 1749 list of farmland assigned in Gnadenhütten includes Abraham and his three sons, David, Joachim, and Jonathan. September 2, 1749, 119/1/4 RMM.Lists of communicants from the same year include Abraham and Sarah, David and Sarah, Jonathan and Anna, but not Joachim. December 17, 1749 119/2/1 RMM. A similar list from 1752 includes all three couples. January 15, 1752 119/2/3 RMM.

61. "Jonathan aber läge ihr sehr am Herzen und er habe sie in Shecomeco recht zur Gemeine getriben und gesagt: Mutter wenn wir hier bleiben, so werden wir alle verdammnt: und nun komme er nicht, so fürchte sie, er werde verdammt werden." May 29, 1747 116/1 RMM. The Moravian records contain numerous references to a dying parent exhorting family members to remain faithful after their death so that they would be reunited. Jonathan himself had once found comfort when his premature child died by believing "it's near to the wounds,

and if we continue faithful to our Savior we shall see it again with him." Letter from Brother Jonathan, 319/2/19 RMM. Similarly, Gideon of Pachgatgoch sent his greetings to his daughter Christina and other friends and family, exclaiming "what a blessed and happy time this will be when we shall come together and meet one another there above, when we are gone home to our Savior for to live with him for ever. That will be a great happiness to us." Letter from Gideon, 319/3/9 RMM.

62. "Maria und Mackin liessen sie rufen, die Mary bezeugte ihr herzliches mitleiden, und daß sie es selbst erfahren wie einen Mutter Herzen sey wenn ihre Kinder den Hld nicht annehmen wolten. Sie erzehlte ihr wie sie von Lämmlein sey getröstet vor den, nemlich sie habe ihr Kind dem der sie gemacht und denn gekauft, in seine Hand gegeben, weil er die Seelen doch lieber habe als alle Väter und alle Mütter. Denn wurde ihr von den 2 Kindern gesagt, und wie der größte den kleinen weg geführt. Man konte es ihr ansehen wie nah es ihr ging." Pachgatgoch Diary, May 29, 1747, 116/1 RMM. Johanna (Jannetje) Rau Mack was the daughter of Johannes Rau whose farm lay just two miles from Shekomeko. As a child, Jannetje had spent enough time with her Mahican neighbors to learn their language. Martin Mack was sent to Shekomeko in 1742 to assist missionaries Rauch and Büttner. He and Jannetje were soon married.

63. For a discussion of the duties of a captain, see Zeisberger. Hulbert, *Zeisberger's History,* 100–101. The Iroquois had been seeking for some time to settle allied Indians in this area. In 1745, Abraham had decided not to move to Wyoming for fear that it lay on the warpath of the Flatheads (Catawbas) and that the Indians there lived immoral lives. For Abraham's view of the move, see Shekomeko diary entries dated, May 30, June 1, and June 16, 1745, 111/1 RMM. In the fall of 1753, Abraham was named to be a Mahican captain. In a conference between Delaware and Mahicans in April 1753, Abraham deposited several strings of wampum, the first of which read: "Ich bin 7 Jahr wie ein Kind herumgegangen und habe keine Chiefs gehabt und habe euch meine Freunde auch nicht gesehen. Ich habe auf euren alten Plaz die 7 Jahr beym Kleinen feuer gewohnt. Dieser Herbst aber bin ich zu meinen alter Plaz beym Mahikan hingegangen da habe ich einer Chiefs gesehen. Die Mahikander haben dran gedacht daß hier in Gnadenh. auch ein Chief seyn soll mit Nahmen Mamanetthekan [Abraham]. Dieser Mamanetthekan hat um sich der Zeit beym feuer gesaßen und den Weg hinaufgesehen der diesen Sommer gemacht ist und da hat er

meine Freunde die Nantikoks Schawanohs und
Deleware gesehen." April 5, 1753 119/1/9 RMM.
Abraham felt he must go, though he feared the conditions there would not be conducive to a Christian
community. "Den Vormittag sprach Br. Martin mit
dem Alten Abraham, der unter andern erzehlte, daß
seine Gedancken doch ein bißgen stärcker nach Wajomick gingen als in Gnadenhütten, und das darum,
weil sies den Nantikoks und Shawanohs ver-
sprochen hätten, er fürchte, es möchte sonst was
schlimmes geraus kommen, wenn sie nicht gingen."
Gnadenhütten diary, March 2, 1754 118/1 RMM.
Abraham knew his wife did not want to accompany
him and he requested that the Brethren let her stay
with them. Sarah insisted on following her husband. "Nachhero brachte br. Abraham seine Worte
daß er nun resolvirt wäre, nach Wajomick zu
ziehen, und bat zugleich wehmüthig ab, womit er
bishero die Brr. betrübt hätte. Er höfte, wenn er
nach Wajomick käme, würde er nichts anders
treiben als die lehre von Jesu Marter, wir solten ihn
lieb behalten, seine Frau könte er mit guten Gewis-
sen nicht mitnehmen weil sie auch lieber wolte hier
bleiben. Er bat auch, die Gemeinen wolte sich seiner
Frau annehmen, und sie in ihrer Pflege behalten. Er
wünschte nur noch eins, daß ihm die Brr. möchten
von thun, wenn er nach Wajomick käme, wo er
wohnen solte, ob er unter den Shawanos, die jezo da
wohnten, wohnen solte, oder aber alleine wo an
einen Ort wohnen solte." Gnadenhütten Diary,
March 13, 1754, 118/1 RMM.

64. "Sarah sagte: ich will beym Hld bleiben,
und Ihn lieb behalten, dabey vergoß sie noch viel
Thränen. dann namen sie von uns Herzl. Abschied,
und gingen mit ihren Kindern zu Mittag am ersten
fort. Die mehresten folgten ihnen bald nach, einige
aber blieben nach der Tag hier. Der Abzug war betrübt zu sehen." Gnadenhütten Diary, April 24,
1754 118/1 RMM; Meniolagomekah Diary, June
13, 1763, 124/2 RMM.

65. "Die Esther fragte sie warum sie denn
weinte, die Anna antwortete: Sie hätte Ursach
genug zu weinen, sie dächte viel an ihren Mann.
Vor etl. Tagen, ehe er auf die Jagd wäre gegangen,
hätte sie gesagt: Mein Lieber Mann, beschiene dich
doch bald, was du thun wilt, und mache nicht so
langeö Ich will der sagen, was ich thun will, ich gehe
nicht mit dir an die Susquehanna. Wenn du gehen
wilt, du kanst. Ich aber und meine Kinder wollen
bei der Gem. bleiben: denn wenn ich bedanke, was
Hld an uns und an uns Kindern gethan hat, so kan
ich mich unmögl. dazu resolviren, von der Gemeine zu ziehen, ich würde mir ein scheres Ge-
richte zuziehen. Darauf sagte Jonathan: liebe Frau,

habe noch ein wenig Geduld mit mir, und wenn ich
werde von der Jagd zu Hause kammen, denn will
ich dir eine Antwort sagen. denn sagte die Anna:
darüber denke und weine ich, und warte mit Ver-
langen auf meinen Mann, zu was er sich wird resolvirt haben, ach wie ofte habe ich an ihn gedacht,
besonders in der Christnacht und Neu-Jahrs
Woche, und habe ihm von Herzen gewünscht,
wenn er doch auch etwas fühlen mägte von der
Gnade und Seligkeit, dir uns Hld hat fühlen laßen.
Den Abend kam er euch von der Jagd zu Haus."
January 9, 1754, Gnadenhütten Diary, 118/1 RMM.

66. "Jonathan ging heute zu seinen Vater und
Mutter, und that Wederuf, was er die Zeit in senen
schlechten Umständen gegen die Gemeine geredet
hatte, und bat mit Thränen, sie solten ihm verge-
ben. Womit er ihnen Schaden gethan hätte, es wäre
ihm iezu ganz anders, und seine Augen würden
nicht viel trocken, wenn er darüber dächte. Die
Sarah hub die Hände auf, und danckte dem Hld,
der ihr Gebet erhöret hat, und sagte, wenn ich im
Busch ginge Holz zu holen, so bin ich alle mal auf
meine Knien niedergefallen, und habe zu Gott
geschreyen, er soll sich doch erbarmen über
meinen Mann und Kinder, und ihnen wieder einen
andern Sinn und Herz schencken, und Gott hat
mich erhört, dafür dancke ich ihm." January 16,
1754, Gnadenhütten Diary, 118/1 RMM

67. "Er [Jonathan] sagte: ezo wollen wir wieder
aufs neue dem Herzen nach mit einander bekannt
werden; und seine Anna danck dem Hld der ihr
Gebet für ihren Mann erhört hat." January 15,
1754, Gnadenhütten Diary, 118/1 RMM.

68. "Kam Br. Abraham mit seiner Sarah nach
zu uns, sie versprachen beym Hld zu bleiben, und
den andern bey gelegenheit auch manch Wörtigen
von Ihn und seiner Liebe zu sagen." Gnadenhütten
diary, April 24, 1754 118/1 RMM.

69. "Ich grüße dich Herzlich. Wie wohl ich
dich noch nicht gesehen habe, so habe ich dich
doch lieb. Ich bin sehr arm hier in Wajomic, der
Heiland thut sich aber doch zu mir, und ich halte
mich an ihn darum halte ich immer am Heiland,
weil ich mein herz fühle, darum lieb ich den Heiland, weil er Wunden hat, und sein Blut vergoßen
hat, das schmolzt mein Herz und macht mich auch
freudig. Ich bitte allezeit, daß der Heiland mir ein
Tröpfen Blut in mein herz mag schencken, das aus
der Seite und seinen füßen gefloßen ist, daß ichs
einmal vergoßen möge. Ich bitte dich meine
Schwester, denck vorm Heiland an mich, ich habe
es nötig, denn ich bin unter Indianern die noch in
Sünden leben. Ich grüse und küse dich jezo abwe-
send, wenn ich aber einmal werde zu dir kommen,

und dich sehe, so will ichs auch lieblich thun. Ich bin die arme Sara. Ich grüße auch Martins und Schmicks frau und all." Sarah to Sister Spangenberg, August 31, 1754 319/4/9 RMM.

70. No birthdate is given for young Sarah, but she was baptized September 17, 1749, and was likely born around the same time.

71. "Zu ihrer Tochter hat sie gesagt: du bist meine einige Tochter, du hast nun meinen Sinn gehört, was willstu nun machen . . . Wilstu mich verlaßen, du kanst es thun, du hast deine Freyheit, ich bin lange mit euch gegangen und habe euch gros gezogen, und ihr würdet euch betrüben, wenn ich bey euch im Busch sterben sollte, und ginge verloren, darum haltet euch nicht auf. Die Tochter fing an sehr zu weinen, und sagte, ich will mit dir gehen, wie wohl ich noch nicht einen solchen Sinn habe wie du, und kan nicht sagen ob ich bey dir bleiben werde." Meniolagomekah Diary, June 13–20, 1763, 124/4 RMM.

72. Philadelphia Diary, June 10, 1764, 127/2 RMM.

73. Much of the information on Rachel's life is in the form of conference minutes and letters from Rachel to Maria Spangenberg, whom she often turned to for comfort and support. Rachel dictated these letters and her husband transcribed them.

74. Later baptized Boas, Annimhard was accused of beating his second wife, Ruth. Conference minutes note "Cornelius hat gestern Ruth in seinem Hause gefunden und erfahren daß sie wieder von ihrem mann geschlagen und weg gejagt worden." One week later, the minutes report "Ruth sagte sie feilte in Ihren Herzen das Boas so lange er so wäre sie nicht könder lieben und sie wolte nicht mehr zu ihnen, sondern alleine bleiben." September 23 and 30 1744 112/5/3 RMM.

75. Her father, Lucas, was baptized March 27, 1743. Her mother, Priscilla, was baptized August 2, 1743. Her sister, also named Priscilla was baptized August 7, 1743. Her brother, Lucas was baptized March 14, 1749.

76. The other three candidates were Tachtamoa (daughter of Johannes and later baptized Debora); a 32-year-old unbaptized widow, and 18-year-old Maria (daughter of Gideon, the chief of Pachgatgoch, and also object of affection of the chief of Stockbridge, probably Umpachenee), Büttner's diary, February 21, 1743, 111/2/1 RMM.

77. "Rahel hat gesagt sie wolte ihren Mann lieb haben, könte aber nicht." Shekomeko Diary, August 13, 24, 28 and September 10, 1743, 111/1 RMM and Conference Minutes, September 19, and October 16, 1743, 111/6 RMM. Apparently, Rachel was not alone in having difficulty liking Post. He had a tendentious personality and seldom won many admirers. The only full length biography of Post is Chase's dissertation, *Christian Frederick Post, 1715–1785.*

78. "*Mittlerzeit wolte der Heyland sie solten ihre vereinigung haben, welches sie ihm aber eineige mahl nicht erlaubte.*" Büttner to Anton Seiffert, December 9, 1743, 111/8/7 RMM. The Lot was not to be used by individuals, but only by Elders acting in the interest of the Gemeine, or congregation. Smaby, *Transformation,* 24.

79. Büttner to Anton Seiffert, December 9, 1743, 111/8/7 RMM.

80. Conference Minutes, December 22, 1743, 111/6 RMM.

81. The boy was born September 24, 1744. Rachel often confided in Johannes, one of the first four men to be baptized by the Moravians. Her child is likely named after Zinzendorf and Johannes. Many couples named their children after their own family members. That Rachel didn't suggests there may well have been tensions between her and her family.

82. That Rachel addressed Maria as "Liebe Mutter" rather than the more common "Schwester" (as Sarah and others called her) suggests the uncommon bond between the women and Rachel's desire for a spiritual mother. Maria Spangenberg's given name was Eva-Maria, but she was known as Maria and her husband, Augustus, as Joseph. Referring to Spangenberg as Mother might also suggest that Rachel viewed Spangenberg as the embodiment of Mary, mother of Jesus, or as the Holy Spirit, commonly referred to as Mother by Moravians. Native understanding of selfhood was quite different from prevailing European notions, stressing the relational basis of identity over inborn essence. For example, when an individual was named after an important person, the individual shared in the personhood of their namesake. Rachel may well have seen Maria Spangenberg as the present embodiment of the Heiland's mother. She would have been encouraged in this belief by the European Moravians who clearly put great store in the power of names, so clearly evident in the baptisms of Abraham and Sarah, Isaac and Rebecca, and Jacob and Rachel. See Richard White, "'Although I Am Dead, I Am Not Entirely Dead. I Have Left a Second of Myself': Constructing Self and Persons on the Middle Ground of Early America," in *Through a Glass Darkly: Reflections on Personal Identity in Early America,* ed. Ronald Hoffman, Mechal Sobel, and Fredrika J. Teute

(Chapel Hill: University of North Carolina Press, 1997), 404–418. See also Daniel K. Richter, *The Ordeal of the Longhouse: The Peoples of the Iroquois League in the Era of European Colonization* (Chapel Hill: University of North Carolina Press, 1992).

83. Rachel to Maria Spangenberg, 319/2/1 RMM. The original German letter can be found at 219/1/7 RMM. Neither letter is dated, but presumably this letter refers to her first pregnancy.

84. Moravians believed sex to be a sacrament and allegedly newly married couples were often enjoined to consummate their marriage while others waited outside the small room [Kabinet]. "O liebe muter. Ich wahr sehr arm in Bethlehem und weill wir zu sammen waren im Kabinet und Bruder Joseph bätte fühlt ich große Gnade der Heiland begoß mein Hertz recht mit Blutt daß er hielt mich alle zeit wohl und vergnicht im Herzen ob ich gleich noch so elend bin." Rachel to Maria Spangenberg, October 1745, 319/1/10, RMM. On Moravian attitudes toward sexuality and marriage, see Craig Atwood, "Sleeping in the Arms of Christ: Sanctifying Sexuality in the Eighteenth-Century Moravian Church," *Journal of the History of Sexuality* 8 (1997), 25–51 and Peter Vogt, " 'Ehereligion': The Moravian Theory and Practice of Marriage as Point of Contention in the Conflict between Ephrata and Bethlehem," forthcoming.

85. Hannes died May 13, 1745. Rachel's sister Priscilla (named after their mother) was baptized August 7, 1743. Her brother, Lucas (named after their father) was baptized March 14, 1749. Three other children, Benigna, Salome, and Esther were also baptized. Three of the children (likely Benigna, Esther, and Priscilla) all died in 1744.

86. Rachel Post to Brethren and Sisters in Berbies, 1745, 319/3/5 RMM. Another letter further suggests reconciliation with her husband. In a letter to her fellow villagers, Rachel assured them that she loved her husband and her child (one-year-old Maria) was well. Rachel to Gnadenhütten, A. (April? August?) 1746, 219/1/7 RMM.

87. "En dis mey moder dus laf mie so mus en gret del mor den mey ohn moder." Rachel to Maria Spangenberg, September 9, 1746 113/1/5 RMM.

88. For references to Josua see Post's Pachgatgoch diary, July 22, 1746, September 1, 1746 and September 9, 1746, 113/1/5 RMM.

89. "Mey hart was won dey were heffe ey did not noh wat did key so heffe mey hart ey was alwes kreyin Ples aur söfger hi schut scho mie wat it was eff mey men was sick mey hart did sey noh it is som oder tinks en den did Josua kom hohm tensing en schringin o mey hart did krey were mutz et was as iff was kot won off mey finger aff en ey did krey were mutz dat aur söfger mut help him egin ey kut not schlip hohlneit beloved moder ey tuckt iur letter aut de heus off aur söfger it was ius so es wen de söfger giwid mey hens en ey was so gled dat ey did krey." Rachel to Maria Spangenberg, September 9, 1746 113/1/5 RMM.

90. A similar, but more fragmentary, bit of evidence suggests that other women experienced a similar power in giving birth and nursing their children. The Gnadenhütten diary reports, "Die Aeimel erzehlte bei der Gelegenheit wie ihrs in ihren Herzen wäre wenn sie Kinder vor den Hld trüge und wenn sie gebähre und säugete." June 7, 1747 116/6 RMM. Rachel's letter reads, "mey scheyld gros well en strang but it hes eh gret kaff ey wist auer söffger did meg him well egen. ey ken help him noting de söffger muß du alting . . . wen ey giff mey scheyld suck en ey tenck an die blot en wouns off auer söffger ey fühl mey hat sam teims were wet en so ey tenck mey scheyld saks de blot off auer söffger en ey fähl de engels luck efter mey en mey scheyld . . . ey em puhr but ey krey en pre vor dem dat de söffger wut giff dem eh fühling off his blot en wouns in de harts. beluvet moder ie mus tenck an mie dat hie giefs mutz gres . . . wie er iur pur schilderen Rahel und Maria Post." Rachel to Maria Spangenberg, September 9, 1746 113/1/5 RMM.

91. Pachgatgoch Diary, December 26, 1747, 116/2 RMM.

PART TWO

# REVOLUTION AND SOCIAL CHANGE 1750–1865

# THE DIALECTIC OF DOUBLE-CONSCIOUSNESS IN BLACK AMERICAN FREEDOM CELEBRATIONS, 1808–1863

*William B. Gravely*

During the past two decades a number of scholars have argued that racism did not emerge with slavery but rather with the Revolution, when Africans and their descendants were incorporated into a new society in which they lacked the rights of equality that were given to white people. Racism explained why some people could be denied the liberty that the Declaration of Independence guaranteed to all of the new nation's citizens as a matter of self-evident natural law. By labeling African Americans an inferior race, European Americans resolved the contradiction between slavery and equality; African Americans, in contrast, called for resolution through an end to slavery.

Between the Revolution and the Civil War the "double-consciousness" of being African and being American became an issue for free blacks in the Northern states. Unlike the slaves in the South, Northern blacks were supposedly "free." Yet they remained shackled by a complex set of racial ideas, which evolved over the nineteenth century until they were systematically "proven" by late nineteenth-century "scientific" depictions of African people's less evolved and immutable physical traits. In William Gravely's analysis, the black American freedom celebrations that emerged in the early nineteenth century ritualized this dialectic of "double-consciousness" in Northern free black experience. Not surprisingly, many blacks rejected the patriotic nationalism that regularly marked the celebration of the Fourth of July. Instead, through their participation in the commemoration of specific events in the African pilgrimage in the New World, the freedom celebrations gave roots to black peoples' emerging African American identity.

Reprinted by permission from William B. Gravely, "The Dialectic of Double-Consciousness in Black American Freedom Celebrations, 1808–1863," *Journal of Negro History* (Winter 1982), 302–317. Courtesy of The Association for the Study of African American Life and History, Inc.

# 6

# THE DIALECTIC OF DOUBLE-CONSCIOUSNESS IN BLACK AMERICAN FREEDOM CELEBRATIONS, 1808–1863

*William B. Gravely*

IN A CELEBRATED PASSAGE in *The Souls of Black Folk*, W. E. B. Du Bois characterized black American existence in terms of "a peculiar sensation" of "double-consciousness." "One ever feels his two-ness," he wrote, "—an American, a Negro; two souls, two thoughts, two unreconciled strivings; two warring ideals in one dark body, whose dogged strength alone keeps it from being torn asunder. The history of the American Negro is the history of this strife. . . ."[1]

In the period from the Revolution to the Civil War, the "double-consciousness" of being black and being American, of which Du Bois spoke, came into sharp focus for free blacks in the northern states. Residing in a radically-based, slave-holding republic, their national identity was perenially challenged. The prevailing sentiment of the white majority, North and South, proclaimed the United States a white man's country. From individual incidents of discrimination to "black laws" which proscribed all "quasi-free Negroes," as John Hope Franklin terms the caste, that sentiment was dramatically reinforced.[2]

For some free blacks—especially after new reminders of American racism like the Fugitive Slave Law of 1850 or the Dred Scott decision of the Supreme Court seven years later—the dilemma of double-consciousness grew into an irreconcilable and unbearable paradox. Emigration became a way to resolve the dilemma—as a dream, if not always a reality.[3] More often, however, free blacks maintained a dialectical existence—black and American—and created a culture of alternative institutions which reflected both aspects of the dialectic. They made a viable community life by building schools and churches, forming literary societies and library companies, and organizing voluntary associations for mutual assistance and benevolence. They joined vigilance committees which aided fugitive slaves and convened protest meetings to counter racial injustice locally and nationally. By their presence and their persistence, Northern free blacks contradicted the white vision of America and in its place articulated and lived out an image of the country which could accommodate the dialectic—being blacks and being Americans.[4]

Their freedom celebrations ritualized the dialectic of double-consciousness in northern free black experience, and interpreted it in oration and song. Begun to commemorate three specific events in the black pilgrimage in the New World, the freedom celebration told a story of peoplehood and gave roots to an emerging black identity "within the embrace of American nationality."[5]

The tradition of black freedom celebrations predated general emancipation by more than a half century.[6] Of the three most important holidays of black freedom before 1863, the first was New Year's Day, commemorating the abolition of the foreign slave trade by England, Denmark, and the United States. On January 1, 1808, free blacks in two cities where their numbers were greatest—New York and Philadelphia—gathered to salute the occasion.[7]

The program for the day in New York set a pattern that was duplicated in subsequent New Year's Day festivals, as well as in other freedom celebrations later in the century. The morning service at the African church (historic Mother Zion Church) opened with "A solemn address to Almighty God," offered by Abraham Thompson, an African Methodist Episcopal Zion minister. A choir under the direction of William Hamilton, who would be the speaker in 1809 and in 1815, then sang "an appropriate anthem," otherwise unidentified. Henry Sipkins, who gave an oration the next year, read the congressional act of abolition and made a brief introductory statement. He was followed by Peter Williams, Jr., a twenty-one-year-old student preparing for the ministry in the Protestant Episcopal church, who delivered the formal address of the day. After a congregational hymn, Thomas Miller, Sr. (a Methodist local preacher) concluded the exercises with another prayer. In the afternoon there was a similar order of service, mixing prayer with song and highlighting a sermon by James Varick, who later became the first A. M. E. Zion bishop in America.[8]

For at least eight years, blacks in New York kept New Year's Day in this manner. In Philadelphia, the practice continued as late as 1830.[9] Boston's smaller free black community also commemorated the end of the foreign slave trade between 1808 and 1822, but on July 14. The date for the anniversary was selected "for convenience, merely," an official explanation stated, but it also acknowledged "the abolition of *slavery* in [the] Commonwealth [of Massachusetts]."[10]

As far as current evidence indicates, other black communities did not keep New Year's Day as a holiday of freedom. Nor is it entirely clear when and why the celebration ceased. One possible factor, as Benjamin Quarles has suggested, was a loss of enthusiasm for commemorating the end of the foreign slave trade, since there were wholesale violations of the law.[11] The growing domestic traffic in slaves probably had an impact as well, undermining the earlier optimism of January First orators that the proscription of the foreign trade spelled the end of slavery. In Boston, at least, the end of the celebrations was attributed to white opposition and ridicule and the apparent inability of the political authorities to protect blacks, especially as they marched through the city streets on the holiday.[12]

Despite the decline of New Year's Day as a freedom holiday, until the Emancipation Proclamation of 1863 marked January First with even greater significance, the tradition of celebrations remained vital. The end of slavery in New York on July 4, 1827, spawned a new black holiday.[13] For the next eight years, New York State Abolition Day was commemorated in five states. There are records of eighteen separate celebrations, beginning with the original observance in eight locations. In four of these places (New York City, Baltimore, Cooperstown, New York, and Fredericksburg, Virginia), Independence Day, the actual date on which the legislation abolishing slavery took effect, was used. For a second celebration in New York City, however, and for festivities in Albany, Rochester, and New Haven, blacks chose the next day for the commemoration. The desire for a separate black holiday favored the fifth, though there was considerable debate at the time over which day to set aside.[14]

Like the January First celebration, most July Fifth festivals were held in black churches. At the same time they included more outdoor activities. Parades became typical, though not without a hot dispute concerning whether public processions were appropriate or not.[15] Other symbolic acts—the firing of gun salutes, the display of banners, and community dinners with formal toasts—expressed the mood of jubilation for this summer holiday. The entire celebration at Rochester in 1827 was out of doors, culminating in an address in the Public Square by the fugitive slave Austin Steward.[16]

New York Abolition Day was observed in some localities as late as 1859, but it was kept the most consistently between 1827 and 1834.[17] As in the case of the New Year's freedom celebration, July Fifth was replaced in the tradition by a new event, the emancipation of 670,000 bondsmen and bondswomen in the British West Indies in 1834. In recognition of their freedom, August First became the most widely commemorated and most enduring of the antebellum freedom holidays in America.[18]

The new abolitionism of the 1830s encouraged a broader white participation in the annual August First observances than was true of the two earlier holidays.[19] Blacks often joined with whites to celebrate, but they also continued separate exercises, yet without prohibiting whites from attending. The decision to hold separate celebrations was prompted by the sentiment which the A. M. E. Zion pastor, Jehiel C. Beman, expressed in 1843. "He insisted that the colored man, as he was the injured party, could alone *feel* on this occasion," the *Liberator* reported. "Freely acknowledging all the sympathies of our white friends, he considered they *could not*, having never been placed in the same circumstances with the colored people, *feel* as they do in celebrating this great event."[20]

Dating from 1834 through 1862, there are nearly 150 recorded black observances of West Indies Emancipation Day in the United States.[21] Geographically, those August First gatherings produced by blacks represented fifty-seven different places in thirteen states. According to newspaper accounts there were additional celebrations by fugitive slaves in London (1851, 1853) and by black American expatriates in Liberia (1859) and in Canada (1852, 1854–55, 1857, 1859–60).[22]

The format for August First festivities also expanded beyond the pattern of the two earlier celebrations. Some crowds, numbering as many as 7,000 people, could only be accommodated out of doors.[23] For that reason, and because the ceremonies took on a less restrictive religious atmosphere, fewer celebrations occurred in black churches. The growing number of organizations which wished to display their banners and the benefit of the summer climate made processions routine. Some, with local black militia companies and brass bands, added a martial atmosphere to the parade.[24] Since the celebration lasted most of the day, and when the weather was favorable, outdoor picnics and community dinners provided the necessary refreshments. The early black historian, William C. Nell, amusingly described one such "feast" at which "about eighty ladies and gentlemen 'proclaimed liberty' to their masticating machinery, and manifested quite an industrious spirit while engaged in discussing the fare of various kinds with which the table was bountifully supplied."[25] Teetotal reformers at some dinners attested to their convictions either by using lemonade or cold water for toasts or by sponsoring separate Temperance Festivals on August First.[26] Black groups in Albany (1836), Boston (1838), Detroit (1854), and Cincinnati

(1855) spent part of the holiday on steamboat excursions, earning, in the initial instance, a rebuke from other celebrants in Catskill, New York.[27]

As early as 1846, August First activities featured an Emancipation Ball, at which "the light fantastic toe was kept in motion till 'break of dawn,'" according to one account. The ball in Geneva, New York's Temperance House was restrained—"comfortable and quiet"— but more sober-minded blacks still objected, without success, to the innovation of dancing on August First. The practice spread, so that in 1853 Rochester's celebration witnessed "the 'mazy dance.'" Two years later, the San Francisco correspondent to the leading black weekly commented that dancing "was evidently more enjoyed than anything else" on the holiday. Disapprovingly, he noted that "with a majority of the colored people of this city, [it] is the acme of human happiness."[28]

Other commentators were more indulgent of the need for "a day of freedom," as Frederick Douglass put it in 1859, "when every man may seek his happiness in his own way, and without any very marked concern for the ordinary rules of decorum." With "no Fourth of July here, on which to display banners, burn powder, ring bells, dance and drink whiskey," Douglass added on another occasion, blacks turned to "the First of August." As always, he admitted, there were "a few . . . who carried this 4th of Julyism a little too far."[29] Describing the New Bedford, Massachusetts, celebration of 1851, William C. Nell pronounced, with similar tolerance, "prayer or speech, song or dance" as "acceptable garlands, hung on the altar of Freedom."[30]

With West Indies Emancipation Day the freedom celebration reached its zenith before the Civil War. The three freedom holidays—January First, July Fifth, and August First— did not, of course, exhaust the possibilities of public ritualization of the black experience.[31] Nor did all blacks support the celebrations or acknowledge the three holidays. Some objected to commemorating West Indies emancipation, since it compensated slaveholders as well as gave blacks their freedom. "Let us seek some day in which some enslaved black man in our land swelled beyond the measure of his chains and won liberty or death," exclaimed J. McCune Smith, a medical graduate of the University of Glasgow, who had, by 1856, become disaffected with the August First tradition. He nominated the date of Denmark Vesey's death in South Carolina in 1822, after his plot against slavery was uncovered, or the date of Nat Turner's rebellion in Virginia in 1831.[32] The Cleveland correspondent for the *Weekly Anglo-African* (New York) recommended Turner's birthday or the date of the downfall of slavery in Haiti.[33] Other blacks complained that the freedom holidays wasted time and money.[34] By the 1850s, however, the appeal of the freedom celebration had grown beyond the point where individual dissent could effectively challenge its continuity. Long before the observance of the abolition of slavery in the District of Columbia in 1862 or of a national emancipation day, it had become an institution in northern free black life.[35]

In its development over fifty years certain features of the form of the freedom celebration remained constant, despite the improvisation and innovation that accompanied the commemoration of the holidays. That form had its roots in the black church's style of worship, using choirs, congregational singing, prayers, readings, and sermons. In the freedom festivals the sermons became formal orations and the readings were taken as frequently from legislative acts related to the observance or from the Declaration of Independence as from the Bible.[36] Some of the church's music was sung as part of the celebration, as when one August First concluded with a sacred concert, but it was characteristic to perform new compositions especially written for the occasion or to sing "those soul-stirring freedom songs" that were familiar in anti-slavery circles.[37] The basic liturgical unit, which joined the spoken word, with the sung word, the word of prayer and the written word, remained much the same.[38]

Likewise, there was, from the first, an explicit rationale stated for the functions and meanings of the annual rituals which the freedom celebrations became. Unquestionably, the desire to "remember, with gratitude and rejoicing, the day of deliverance to so many of our long-abused race," as Frederick Douglass observed, was an initial purpose for keeping the freedom holiday.[39] The same logic governed the recommendation by Absalom Jones, the first black Episcopal priest in America, that "the day of the abolition of the slave trade in our country, be set apart in every year, as a day of publick thanksgiving."[40]

The celebrative nature of the freedom holiday did not obscure a second reason for public commemoration—to remember those who were still enslaved. "The cheerless condition of our southern brethren," as Joseph Sidney described it in 1809, sharply contrasted with the "day of festivity."[41] Because "our brethren in this land are in slavery still," Solomon R. Alexander announced at Boston in 1840, "we come . . . to show how we feel for [them], and to show our opposers that we feel how much their redemption depends on us."[42] Such a mood of empathy was not difficult to evoke. The audiences were full of those, the *Colored American* reported of Newark's observance in 1839, "who had once wore [sic] the galling yoke of slavery." On the platform that day were two who had escaped bondage, Samuel R. Ward and James W. C. Pennington.[43] When they, or other fugitives like Douglass, Jermain W. Loguen, William Wells Brown, or Lunsford Lane, spoke of slavery to black gatherings, they lent an experiential depth that no white abolitionist could manage. Hence, Loguen affected his Geneva, New York, audience when he "revered the memory of a mother, who was black as she could cleverly be made," as did Douglass when he said, "While I am addressing you, four of my own dear sisters and one brother are enduring the frightful horrors of American slavery."[44]

These two complementary motives for the freedom celebrations drew on the countervailing feelings of joy and sorrow, of despair and hope. As Austin Steward stated in 1827, "we will rejoice, though sobs interrupt the songs of our rejoicing, and tears mingle in the cup we pledge to Freedom."[45] But there was still another reason to keep the "annual jubilee."[46] It was, to quote a committee of the Banneker Institute of Philadelphia in 1858, an occasion which "keeps before the minds of the American people *their* duty to the millions of slaves upon the Southern plantations, and, coming right in the wake of the 4th of July, gives abolitionists a fine opportunity to expose the hollow-heartedness of American liberty and Christianity, and to offset the buncombe speeches made upon our national anniversary."[47]

The culminating factor to keep alive the tradition of freedom celebrations was their function in expressing a feeling of community among free blacks. "They bring our people together," Douglass remarked in 1857, "and enable us to see and commune with each other to mutual profit."[48] The elaborate planning for the anniversaries already indicated a high degree of community spirit, but the orators appealed for ever greater unity and for common courses of action by free blacks. They admonished blacks to identify with each other, to use every advantage for social and intellectual improvement, to uphold high standards of conduct in order not to provoke charges of immorality or irresponsibility upon the race.[49] As a fourth reason, then, the freedom holidays imparted a sense of the collectivity, to which the speakers gave historical roots.

"It has always been, and still is, customary for nations to set apart some day, or days in the year," Amos Gerry Beman observed in 1839, "when their orators recount the glory of their ancestors." The Congregationalist pastor bemoaned the fact that blacks, "as a people," had "no such day to celebrate."[50] Ironically, in the same address Beman demonstrated how the First of August functioned to fill the void. When he surveyed in rough outline an historical tradition for Africans in America, he was engaged, as were most orators before and after him, in the process of telling the black American story.

At Philadelphia's original celebration, Absalom Jones recognized that the meaning of the event being commemorated depended on an historical consciousness and the sense of belonging to a tradition. Citing the example of the people of Israel, whose Passover liturgy required every Jew to think of himself as having come forth from Egyptian bondage, Jones contended, "Let the history of the sufferings of our brethren and of their deliverance descend by this means to our children, to the remotest generations."[51] In spite of Jones' allusion to the Hebrew exodus, the freedom celebration's orators seldom directly compared the black and the Jewish experiences.[52] Their consciousness of belonging to a distinct people rather depended on two interlocking images, of Africa and of a racially-based enslavement against which the struggle for freedom was fought in the New World.[53] Even Jones recognized as much when he admonished, "It becomes us, publickly and privately, to acknowledge, that an African slave, ready to perish, was our father or our grandfather."[54]

The idea of Africa as a single reality, and of a psychic tie with it as the source of black peoplehood, appeared in the earliest of the freedom addresses.[55] Peter Williams' oration of 1808 identified him as "A Descendent of Africa," even though he was born in this country and actually referred to himself later in the speech "as an American."[56] A year later Henry Sipkins spoke of Africa as "our parent-country," a phrase similar to William Hamilton's allusion in 1815, "the country of our parents."[57] To Russell Parrott, Africa was "the native land of our fathers" while to George Lawrence it was "the mother country."[58] Moreover, when black spokesmen on January First addressed their compatriots, they commonly employed designations that linked them with Africa.[59]

Besides this collective identity with Africa, the earliest speeches contained romanticized pictures of the continent prior to the coming of the white European. It was, according to Hamilton in 1809, "the country of our forefathers [which] might truly be called paradise."[60] The speech by Sipkins the same year depicted a state of perfection in portraying Africa. "It exhibits the most blissful regions," he declared, "productive of all the necessaries and even luxuries of life, almost independent of the arm of husbandry. Its innocent inhabitants regardless of, or unacquainted with the concerns of busy life, enjoyed with uninterrupted pleasure the state in which, by the beneficent hand of nature, they were placed."[61]

The Fifth of July celebrations continued to emphasize African origins and employed equivalent titles to refer to blacks. The term "Ethiopian" was freely heard at Cincinnati's commemoration in 1831, and the poetic phrase "Afric's sons" or "sons of Afric" occurred in two separate speeches in 1827.[62] One toast offered in 1828 paid tribute to "the fair daughters of Africa," while another saluted "Our Colored Brethren throughout the universe."[63]

While the theme of African identity dominated the oratory of the first two freedom holidays, the dialectic of double-consciousness still remained. The same speakers who ritualized African origins also reiterated the advantages of being born in America. As early as 1808 Peter Williams claimed the revolutionary heritage of the republic for himself, referring to "the sons of 76" whose "inspired voice" gave mankind the "noble sentiments" of the Declaration of Independence.[64] Because the "black bore his part" in two wars with the British, Russell Parrott did not hesitate to commend "the pure love of country."[65] On the one hand, George Lawrence complained, "Many are the miseries of our exiled race in this land," but on the other, he praised "the land in which we live" because it gave the "opportunity rapidly to advance the prosperity of liberty."[66]

Up to the time of West Indies emancipation, therefore, the characteristic form of black double-consciousness in the freedom celebration was an explicit "Afri-American" identity, as New Haven's Peter Osborne termed it.[67] In the oratory of August First the dialectic shifted in emphasis from African origins to the crucible of American slavery. The speakers paid less attention to the people's beginnings and made fewer references to an African past. They concentrated instead on how American slavery originated and on the struggle for freedom in America. They demonstrated that as a people they were committed to the liberation of blacks in slavery. In the process they affirmed that they had American as well as African roots, that the full meaning of the black saga, encompassing both sides of the dialectic, summed up the cultural transformation of Africans into "colored Americans."[68]

The corporate consciousness among Northern free blacks, which all the freedom celebrations assumed as well as fostered, expressed itself assertively in the texts of the oratory of all three holidays of black freedom. The addresses, taken as a whole, confronted and challenged white racial ideologies in religious and political guises. The freedom orators found that it was necessary from the first to oppose the "reproach," as Adam Carman put it in 1811, that branded blacks "an inferior species of human beings," who were "incapable of reason and virtue."[69] In a continuing polemic against white racism the connection to an African past had, they discovered, strategic uses as well as deep resonances of collective meaning. On January First and July Fifth, they called upon the glories of the ancient Egyptian and Ethiopian civilizations to disprove the charge, to quote William Hamilton in 1809, "that we have not produced any poets, mathematicians, or any to excel in any science whatever."[70] With obvious pride, Owen B. Nickens told an Ohio audience that Africa was "the birthplace and cradle of the arts and sciences."[71] Likewise, William Miller contended that the Bible and classical history confirmed each other in acclaiming "that the first learned nation, was a nation of blacks."[72]

The major difficulty with proclaiming the greatness of the African past was the necessity to explain the fall of the race from its originally elevated status in learning and culture. That problem, and the need to refute the religious pro-slavery outlook which pervaded white American theology and church life,[73] required a consideration of the ultimate cause of black bondage, that led, in turn, to the issue of theodicy—how to reconcile the suffering of Africans with a belief in divine benevolence. The orators did not turn away from the issue.

"Ye peaceful people, what have ye done, to merit this?" Russell Parrott burst forth with the agonizing question.[74] Portraying "the middle passage," black Baptist Nathaniel Paul asked the ocean and the "winds" why they aided the process of enslavement. Then he inquired how God could "look on with the calm indifference of an unconcerned spectator" when "a portion" of his "own creatures" were "reduced to a state of mere vassalage and misery."[75] The fact of black suffering prompted William Miller to lament his existence like the biblical figure Job, by cursing the day of his birth and the time of conception. Yet, among all freedom orators, only Miller was willing to risk saying that God was punishing Africans for their sins. "Our progenitors, after arriving at the plentitude of prosperity, and the pinnacle of national greatness," he explained, "forgot Jehovah's benignity, and dared to defy his wrath." Applying a literalist view to the prophecies of Isaiah concerning Egypt and Ethiopia, he found them "astonishingly fulfilled, even to a very late period, upon the unhappy Africans."[76] By contrast, all other speakers maintained the tensions within the problem of theodicy, confirming the divine intention for and origination of human freedom while reflecting, without a final explanation, upon the mystery of evil and the destructive potential in human nature.

The consensus in the oratory supported a belief that the nature and will of God was benevolent and that justice would ultimately reign in history. "The fugitive blacksmith," James W. C. Pennington, claimed "God's agency in our behalf," even as Frederick Douglass described "the spirit of God commanding the devil of slavery to go out of the British West Indies."[77] They shared the sentiment of Presbyterian preacher and editor Samuel Cornish, who confessed "the cause of the oppressed" as "the cause of God."[78] It was God's nature, Absalom Jones preached, to intervene "in behalf of oppressed and distressed nations, as the deliverer of the innocent, and of those who call upon his name." Nonetheless, Jones confided to his Philadelphia congregation, "it has always been a mystery, why the impartial Father of the human race should have permitted the transportation of so many millions of our fellow creatures to this country, to endure all the miseries of slavery."[79]

Although there were a few blacks who thought that God's designs might encompass slavery as a means to Christianize, civilize, and restore modern Africa to her original greatness,[80] the more basic tendency in the oratory left the final explanation for the oppression of blacks unresolved in the mystery of divine providence. Holding on to the hope for ultimate vindication while disavowing any "attempt to justify the cruelty, the avarice and injustice of those who dragged our forefathers from their native land," Joseph Sidney told his audience, "God's ways are not as our ways, nor his thoughts as our thoughts."[81] Any alternative was unthinkable. To denounce God seemed to surrender the transcendent basis for moral judgment, and to sanction slavery as divinely ordained required that blacks agree with the "blasphemy" of their "enemies" who maintained, William Hamilton explained, "*God hath made [us] to be slaves.*"[82]

When the orators sought to explain the human cause of slavery, they had less difficulty. Some said it lay in "the desire of gain" or in the "heart of avarice."[83] Others, like Russell Parrott, pondered the connection between "the commencement of the sufferings of the Africans, and the discovery of the new world; which, to one portion of the human family, has afforded such advantages, to the unfortunate African, has been the source of the greatest misery."[84] Anticipating the theme of his famous "Address to the Slaves" four years later, Henry Highland Garnet told the Troy, New York, celebration of 1839, "Let the time come when the traders in human flesh cannot fill their pockets with the wages of those who have reaped down their fields, and the system will fly as upon the wings of the wind."[85] An inability to account for the divine purpose in slavery, thus, did not relieve "the oppressors" who were "culpable for their savage treatment to the unoffending Africans," as William Miller stated it.[86]

The final mystery was, therefore, less theodicy than anthropodicy, less the inexplicable character of God than of man, and more particularly of white Europeans and Americans who were "destitute of those generous and noble sentiments that dictated our emancipation," as Russell Parrott charged.[87] In the end, however, William Hamilton could not even fathom the human source of the scourge of slavery. "We stand confounded," he remarked in 1809, "that there could be found any . . . so lost to their nature and the fine feelings of man, as to commit, unprovokedly commit, such acts of cruelty on an unoffending part of the human family." Six years later, recounting the barbarities associated with slavery, he concluded sarcastically, "If these are some of the marks of superiority, may heaven in mercy always keep us inferior."[88]

The problems of theodicy and anthropodicy had a counterpart in the conflict over how to reconcile a commitment to democratic ideals as found in American republicanism with the reality of slavery and racial prejudice. Early and often in the freedom celebrations, orators invoked the Declaration of Independence and its principles of freedom and equality in a valiant attempt to salvage the democratic faith from pro-slavery, racist perversion.

The great American contradiction as "a slaveholding Republic,"[89] black spokesmen made clear, did not come after the beginning of the nation. It predated, coexisted with, and endured after the Revolution. "While the siren song of liberty and equality was sang [sic] through the land," William Hamilton observed in 1809, "the groans of the oppressed made the music very discordant, and . . . America's fame was very much tarnished thereby."[90] On July Fifth, 1827 Nathaniel Paul mused over the "palpable inconsistencies" of America. He queried how slavery could "ever have found a place in this otherwise happiest of all countries—a country, the very soil which is said to be consecrated to liberty, and its fruits the equal rights of man."[91]

The paradox from the beginning of the nation was nowhere more exposed than in the career of the author of the Declaration of Independence, Thomas Jefferson. In his speech of January 1, 1814, Joseph Sidney, a Federalist in politics, inquired "Is the great idol of democracy our friend?" Responding negatively, Sidney accused the "Virginian Junto" of disrespecting "the rights of our African brethren; several hundreds of whom he keeps as slaves on his plantation."[92] In a New York Abolition Day address, a year after Jefferson's death, William Hamilton described him as "an ambidexter philosopher." Recalling the ex-president's comments about black inferiority in his *Notes on Virginia*, Hamilton asked how it was possible to reconcile the egalitarian claims of the Declaration with an argument "that *one class of men are not equal to another*." Then, he went on, "Suppose that such philosopher should keep around him a number of slaves, and at the *same* time should tell you, that God hath no attribute to favour the cause of the master in case of an insurrection of the slaves."[93] The implication was clear. Jefferson's dilemma was, in microcosm, the national contradiction.

Not surprisingly, many blacks rejected the mainstream tradition of patriotic nationalism which regularly marked the celebration of the Fourth of July. It would be, David Nickens argued in 1832, "a mock pretence" and "a want of sound understanding" for blacks to acknowledge a day which "causes millions of our sable race to groan under the galling yoke of bondage."[94] On August First in Newark, seven years later, James W. C. Pennington agreed. "We cannot rejoice in an event in which our case is made an exception," he proclaimed, and "we cannot exult in what is termed the blessing of the nation, when this blessing is positively denied to one sixth of the community."[95]

To reject "all the unmeaning twaddle of Fourth of July orators,"[96] in William Watkins' words, did not mean that Northern free blacks had conceded to those who denied them American citizenship or ignored their plight and the contradiction which it posed to the democratic dream. They did dissent, radically, from a version of the nation which, through racism, had all but destroyed that dream, but they simultaneously and fervently affirmed an alternative vision of America. In it, new heroes replaced the founding fathers. Praising the charter members of the New York State Manumission Society, William Hamilton advised his listeners that "the names of WASHINGTON and JEFFERSON should not be pronounced *in the hearing of your children* until they learned who were the true defenders of American liberty."[97]

The black counter-version of the national story, however, included more than white heroes. Referring to Crispus Attucks, August First speakers noted "that the first blood spilt for independence in this country was by a colored man."[98] The "fathers" in the black story were still the descendants of African slaves, but the emphasis was on the struggle in America, instead of the people's beginnings. They were black patriots in America's wars and those who resisted bondage, like Nat Turner, the insurrectionists in New York in 1741, and the fugitives whose escapes attested that they belonged to "a people determined to be free."[99]

As a vocal and determined minority, Northern free blacks did not choose to be known as "colored Americans" from a groveling mentality or self-deprecating need for white acceptance.[100] That designation, which replaced the more self-conscious African terminology by the 1830s, was a bold challenge to a society which had cynically accommodated itself to human bondage and created a social system of racial caste. The black declaration of American faith was not a request "for sympathy" or "favors at the hand of [the] country," but a pressing "demand" for essential "rights," which, because they were given "by the Creator," as William Wells Brown contended in 1858, "they cannot be taken from us by any Congress or Legislature."[101]

The new "colored American" form of double-consciousness required an identity with "the millions . . . quivering in the rice swamp, or the cottonfield, beneath the oppressor's lash," as William Watkins put it, "for we are one people."[102] It encompassed the defiance of Charles L. Remond, who told the New Bedford August First observance in 1858, "that he was prepared to spit upon the [Dred Scott] decision of Judge [Roger D.] Taney," and that he was willing to be branded "a traitor to the government and the Union, so long as his rights were denied him for no fault of his."[103] It provoked the determination by free blacks, in the words of a committee in New York on August 1, 1836, to "fill every continent and island with the story of the WRONGS done to our brethren, by the *Christian, church-going, psalm-singing, long prayer-making, lynching, tar and feathering, man-roasting, human-flesh-dealers of America!*" and "to *preach* the DECLARATION OF INDEPENDENCE, till it begins to be put in PRACTICE."[104] Finally, it included a consistent opposition to colonization and emigration because blacks were, as Abraham D. Shadd stated it in 1840, "Americans in common with others." Peter Osborne agreed, when he told a July Fifth assembly, "this is our native country" and "our forefathers planted trees" in it "for us, and we intend to stay and eat the fruit."[105]

From the same perspective, George Downing spoke against the emigrationist sentiment among blacks following the Dred Scott decision. "We have," he confirmed, "a hopeful, and I will add, an inseparable providential identity with this country; with its institutions—with the ideas connected with its formation, which were the uplifting of man—universal brotherhood." Then, formulating a remarkable statement of national mission with reference to the black experience, Downing declared: "We, the descendants, to a great extent, of those most unjustly held in bondage [have become] the most fit subjects to be selected to work out in perfection the realization of a great principle, *the fraternal unity of man.* THIS

IS AMERICA'S MISSION. We suffer in the interim; but we can, as is abundantly proven, endure. We can and do hope."[106]

With Downing's assertion the last step in the evolution of antebellum free black "double-consciousness" had been taken. The stage was set, in Frederick Douglass's words in the summer of 1861, "for an event which shall be for us, and the world, more than West Indies Emancipation; and that would be the emancipation of every slave in America."[107] In this sense the freedom celebrations had all along been a "harbinger of American emancipation," as William C. Nell expressed it in 1840—a ritualization by free blacks of their own freedom, however proscribed, and a dramatic expression of hope for "a national jubilee." "America will yet become," Nell told his Boston audience, "what she is now on paper— 'The asylum for the free and home of the oppressed.'"[108]

Identifying both with the slave and with what the New England convention of August 1, 1859, called "our own loved but guilty land," northern free blacks were prepared to see the forthcoming Civil War, with all its ambiguities, in terms of the struggle for black freedom.[109] The same points of contact—with the emancipated slave and with the democratic faith for which they had assumed a unique custody—carried them into the era of Reconstruction with the conviction that being black was a distinctive way of being American.

## NOTES

The author acknowledges the support of the University of Denver and the National Endowment for the Humanities which aided the research for this study.

1. W. E. B. Du Bois, *The Souls of Black Folk in Three Negro Classics*, intro. by John Hope Franklin (New York, 1965), 215. The passage originally appeared in "Strivings of the Negro People," *Atlantic Monthly*, 80 (1897), 194–95.

2. John Hope Franklin, *From Slavery to Freedom*, 3d. ed. (New York, 1967), 220. See also Leon F. Litwack, *North of Slavery: The Negro in the Free States 1790–1860* (Chicago, 1961).

3. Floyd J. Miller, *The Search for a Black Nationality: Black Colonization and Emigration 1787–1863* (Urbana, Ill., 1975).

4. Leonard I. Sweet, *Black Images of America 1784–1870* (New York, 1976), 5–6, 89, 147. See also Jane H. and William H. Pease, *They Who Would Be Free: Blacks' Search for Freedom, 1830–1861* (New York, 1974).

5. Paul C. Nagel, *This Sacred Trust: American Nationality 1798–1889* (New York, 1971), xii. This suggestive study, however, makes no references to blacks.

6. William H. Wiggins has done an impressive study of the folk tradition of emancipation celebrations beginning in 1863. See his dissertation, "Free at Last!': A study of Afro-American Emancipation Day Celebrations" (University of Indiana, 1974) and his essay, " 'Lift Every Voice': A Study of Afro-American Emancipation Celebrations," in Roger D. Abrahams and John F. Szwed, eds., *Discovering Afro-America* (Leiden, Netherlands, 1975), 46–57.

7. In 1810 there were 9,823 blacks in New York City and 40,350 in the state. The same census reported 23,287 blacks in Pennsylvania with the largest concentration in Philadelphia. Leo H. Hirsch, "The Negro and New York, 1783–1865," *Journal of Negro History*, 16 (1931), 415; *Negro Population in the United States 1790–1915* (New York, 1968 reprinted.), 45.

The following black and abolitionist newspapers and periodicals were consulted in this study: *Aliened American* (Cleveland); *Anglo-African Magazine* (New York City); *Anti-Slavery Bugle* (Salem, Ohio); *Colored American* (New York City): *Christian Recorder* (Philadelphia); *Douglass' Monthly* (Rochester, New York); *Emancipator* (New York City); *Frederick Douglass' Paper* (Rochester, New York); *Freedom's Journal* (New York City); *Genius of Universal Emancipation* (various places of publication); *Herald of Freedom* (Concord, New Hampshire); *The Liberator* (Boston): *Mirror of the Times* (San Francisco); *National Anti-Slavery Standard* (New York City); *National Enquirer and Constitutional Advocate of Universal Liberty* (Philadelphia); *National Principia* (New York City); *National Reformer* (Philadelphia); *Northern Star and Freeman's Advocate* (Albany, New York); *Palladium of Liberty* (Columbus, Ohio); *Pennsylvania Freeman* (Philadelphia); *Provincial Freeman* (Toronto); *Repository of Religion and Literature, and of Science and Art* (Indianapolis and Baltimore); *Rights of All* (New

York City); *Union Missionary* (New York City); *Union Missionary Herald* (Hartford, Connecticut); *Weekly Anglo-African* (New York).

8. The Program was printed in Peter Williams, Jr., *An Oration on the Abolition of the Slave Trade: Delivered in the African Church, in the City of New-York, January 1, 1808* (New York, 1808), unnumbered, 3. Daniel Coker listed a sermon by "Rev. James Varrick" on this occasion, but without indicating its published status. See *A Dialogue Between a Virginian and an African Minister* (Balitmore, 1810), 40–42 as reprinted in Dorothy Porter, ed., *Negro Protest Pamphlets* (New York, 1969).

9. Benjamin Quarles erroneously states that New York Negroes ceased the celebrations within three years. See *Black Abolitionists* (New York, 1969), 119. From the thirteen celebrations in New York and six in Philadelphia, for which there is primary evidence, fifteen orations have survived in published form.

10. Thomas Gray, *A Sermon Delivery in Boston Before the African Society. On the 14th day of July, 1818: The Anniversary of the Abolition of the Slave Trade* (Boston, 1818), unnumbered, 2. Orations by four other white guest speakers, all area clergymen (Jedidiah Morse, Paul Dean, Thaddeus M. Harris, John S. J. Gardiner), survive from the Boston celebrations of 1808, 1810, 1819, 1822. All were sponsored by the African Society of Boston, a black organization formed in 1796. See Dorothy Porter, ed., *Early Negro Writing 1760–1837* (Boston, 1971), 9–12.

11. *Black Abolitionists*, 119.

12. For a retrospective account of Boston's July 4th celebrations, see *The Liberator*, August 13, 1847. There are in the Boston Public Library five broadsides which were published as satirical attacks by whites from 1816 through 1825 (the latter date is an estimate).

13. By statute the state legislature of New York began to abolish slavery by gradual means in 1799. After July 4, 1827, no other persons could be born into or subjected to slavery who were not finishing out defined terms of servitude. It was still legal for non-resident slaveholders to bring their chattels into the state for periods not exceeding nine months. Arthur Zilversmit, *The First Emancipation: The Abolition of Slavery in the North* (Chicago, 1967), 180–82, 208–14.

14. *Freedom's Journal*, April 20, June 22, 29, July 6, 13, 20, 27, 1827.

15. Samuel Cornish and John Russwurn, editors of the first black newspaper, opposed parades, as did the national Negro convention of 1834. Ibid., April 27, June 29, July 13, 1827; July 18, August 1, 15, 1828; *Minutes of the Fourth Annual Convention, for the Improvement of the Free People of Colour, in the United States, Held by Adjournments in the Asbury Church. New-York, From the 2d to the 12th of June Inclusive* (New York, 1834), 14, as reprinted in Howard Holman Bell, ed., *Minutes of the Proceedings of the National Negro Conventions 1830–1864* (New York, 1969).

16. *Freedom's Journal*, July 27, 1827. Steward gave the locations as "Johnson's Square" in his autobiography, which contains a full text of his speech: *Twenty-two Years a Slave, and Forty Years a Freeman* (Rochester, 1857), 150–63.

17. Quarles claims that the emancipation day observance "lasted only three or four years," and that "it was resurected for a single time" in 1856 in Auburn, New York (*Frederick Douglass' Paper*, July 18, 1856 as cited in *Black Abolitionists*, 121, 274). I have no evidence of celebrations between 1834 and 1856, although William C. Nell wrote in 1859 of the continued recognition of July Fifth while acknowledging that it was a declining practice "for many reasons." That same year William J. Watkins delivered the oration for festivities at Jefferson, New York, which included the firing of 100 guns and the performance of the Mannsville Saze Horn Band. *Weekly Anglo-African*, June 9, 23, 30, 1859.

18. The original abolition law of August 1, 1834, retained an apprenticeship system which functioned as another kind of forced labor until finally outlawed by Parliament, effective August 1, 1838. Some black celebrations dated from the former, others from the latter date. The figure 670,000 revises the older general estimate of 800,000 and is based on recent scholarship. Stiv Jakobsson, *Am I Not a Man and a Brother? British Missions and the Abolition of the Slave Trade and Slavery in West Africa and the West Indies 1786–1838* (Uppsala, 1972), 511–14, 572–76; W. L. Mathieson, *British Slavery and Its Abolition* (London, 1926), 230ff., 243–46, 300–06.

19. The American Anti-Slavery Society recommended that all abolitionists keep August First. *Liberator*, July 18, 1835.

20. Ibid., August 11, 1843.

21. This number does not include more than a hundred other celebrations during the same period which were organized by white abolitionists and which featured racially mixed audiences and black speakers on the program.

22. *Liberator*, Sept. 1, 1851; Aug. 20, 1852; Aug. 26, 1859; Aug. 23, 1861; *Frederick Douglass' Paper*, Aug. 11, 1854; *Provincial Freeman*, Aug. 5, 19, 1854; Aug. 2, 1855; Aug. 15, 1857; *National Anti-Slavery*

*Standard*, Aug. 20, 1853; Aug. 19, 1854; Aug. 13, 1859; *Weekly Anglo-African*, Oct. 15, 1859.

23. Some of the larger crowds were at New Bedford, Mass.: 7,000 in 1855; Staten Island, N.Y.: 500 in 1855; Urbana, Ohio: 5,000 in 1856; Canadaigua, N.Y.: 4,000 in 1847.

24. For some of the names of military companies and bands, see *Liberator*, Sept. 1, 1843; Aug. 7, 1846; Aug. 15, 1851; Aug. 19, 1853; *Frederick Douglass' Paper*, Aug. 12, 1853; *National Anti-Slavery Standard*, Aug. 11, 1855.

25. *Liberator*, Aug. 14, 1840.

26. Ibid., Aug. 10, 1838; July 26, 1839; *Colored American*, Aug. 31, 1839; Aug. 15, 1840; *National Enquirer and Constitutional Advocate of Universal Liberty*, Aug. 31, 1836; *Pennsylvania Freeman*, Aug. 15, 1839.

27. *Liberator*, Aug. 10, 1838; July 27, 1855; *Emancipator*, Aug. 11, 1836; *Frederick Douglass' Paper*, Aug. 11, 1854.

28. *National Anti-Slavery* Aug. 20, 1846; Aug. 13, 1859; *Frederick Douglass' Paper*, Aug. 21, 1851; Aug. 5, 1853; Sept. 28, 1855; *Liberator*, Aug. 26, 1859.

29. *Douglass' Monthly*, 2 (1859), 113; 3 (1860), 323.

30. *Liberator*, Aug. 15, 1851.

31. In a few instances Northern free blacks turned traditional Independence Day and Thanksgiving observances into protests against the inconsistencies of white America. In at least one other state, New Jersey, they kept state emancipation day (September 5) though with what frequency is not clear. In 1825 blacks in Baltimore commemorated Haitian independence. Two new celebrations evolved in the 1850s. One in Massachusetts on March 15 beginning in 1858 honored Crispus Attucks' death in the pre-Revolutionary Boston Massacre. After 1851 in and around Syracuse, New York, Jerry Rescue Day was an anniversary in October, marking the successful revolt to free, by force, a fugitive slave. Northern blacks also conducted memorial services for and sometimes kept the anniversaries of the deaths of prominent leaders of the race and anti-slavery heroes. Public ceremonies of certain black Masonic orders performed some of the same functions as the freedom celebration.

32. *Frederick Douglass' Paper*, Aug. 16, 1856 as quoted in Quarles, *Black Abolitionists*, 128, 275. Even though Smith had earlier participated in August First celebrations, he argued, "We, the colored people, should do something ourselves worthy of celebration, and not be everlastingly celebrating the deeds of a race by which we are despised." Frederick Douglass answered him by citing examples of black resistance as having forced, through "outbreaks and violence," the end of slavery in the West Indies. Philip S. Foner, ed., *The Life and Writings of Frederick Douglass* (New York, n.d.), II, 434, 439. Martin Delany, a leading black emigrationist, made the same point at a First of August observance in Liberia in 1859. See *Liberia Herald*, as quoted in *Weekly Anglo-African*, Oct. 15, 1859.

33. *Weekly Anglo-African*, Aug. 6, 1859.

34. See Andrew B. Slater's complaint in *Frederick Douglass' Paper*, Apr. 8, 1853.

35. *National Principia*, May 27, 1862; *Douglass' Monthly*, 5 (1862), 676, 769–70, 796–97; *Christian Recorder*, Jan. 3, 17, 1863; James M. McPherson, *The Negro's Civil War* (New York, 1965), 48–52.

36. For examples of the order of service for freedom celebrations, see William Hamilton, *An Address to the New York African Society, for Mutual Relief, Delivered in the Universalist Church, January 2, 1809* (New York, 1809) in Porter, *Early Negro Writing*, 33–34; Adam Carman, *An Oration Delivered at the Fourth Anniversary of the Abolition of the Slave Trade, in the Methodist Episcopal Church, in Second-Street, New York, January 1, 1811* (New York, 1811), 4–5; Joseph Sidney, *An Oration, Commemorative of the Abolition of the Slave Trade in the United States; Delivered in the African Asbury Church, in the City of New-York, on the First of January, 1814* (New York, 1814), 16; Russel Parrott, *An Oration of the Abolition of the Slave Trade, Delivered on First of January, 1812 at the African Church of St. Thomas* (Philadelphia, 1812), unnumbered, 1; *Liberator*, Aug. 20, 1834; July 27, 1855; *National Anti-Slavery Standard*, Aug. 1, 1844; *Frederick Douglass' Paper*, Aug. 12, 1853; *Weekly Anglo-African*, July 30, 1859.

37. Examples of texts of songs are in Carman, *Oration* (1811), 21–23; Sidney, *Oration* (1814), 13–15; Absalom Jones, *A Thanksgiving Sermon, Preached January 1, 1808, In St. Thomas' or the African Episcopal Church, Philadelphia: On Account of the Abolition of the African Slave Trade, On That Day, by the Congress of the United States* (Philadelphia, 1808), 5–6; Nathaniel Paul, *An Address, Delivered on the Celebration of the Abolition of Slavery, In the State of New-York, July 5, 1827* (Albany, 1827) in Porter, *Negro Protest Pamphlets*, 24; *Liberator*, Nov. 21, 1835; July 26, Aug. 16, 23, 1839; July 22, Aug. 19, 1842; Aug. 4, 11, 1843; Aug. 1, 8, 1845; Aug. 19, 1853; Aug. 19, 1859; *National Anti-Slavery Standard*, Sept. 11, 1851; Aug. 13, 1853; *Weekly Anglo-African*, Aug. 6, 1859; June 2, 1860; *Colored American*, Aug. 5, 1837; Aug. 18, 25, 1838; Aug. 24, Sept. 28, 1839; *Frederick Douglass' Paper*, Aug. 10, 1855.

38. In a remarkable address before the American Academy of Religion in Atlanta in 1971, Vincent Harding contended: "We are a people of the spoken word, we are a people of the danced word, we are a people of the sung word, we are a people of the musical word." From a tape-recording of "The Afro-American Experience as a Source of Salvation History."

39. *National Anti-Slavery Standard*, Aug. 19, 1847.

40. Jones, *Sermon*, 19.

41. Sidney, *An Oration Commemorative of the Abolition of the Slave Trade in the United States; Delivered before the Wilberforce Philanthropic Association, in the City of New York on the Second of January, 1809* (New York, 1809) in Porter, *Early Negro Writing*, 358.

42. *Liberator*, Aug. 24, 1839.

43. *Colored American*, Aug. 24, 1839.

44. Geneva Courier in *Frederick Douglass' Paper*, Aug. 21, 1851; Foner, *Works of Douglass*, I, 328; *Liberator*, Aug. 8, 1845.

45. Sidney, *Oration* (1809) in Porter, *Early Negro Writing*, 358; Steward, *Twenty-two Years a Slave*, 157.

46. Sidney, *Oration* (1814), 5.

47. American Negro Historical Society Papers, Leon Gardiner Collection, Pennsylvania Historical Society, file 5G, folio 9.

48. Foner, *Works of Douglass*, II, 433.

49. Jones, *Sermon*, 17–18; Williams, *Oration* (1808), 26; Steward, *Twenty-two Years a Slave*, 158–61; Paul, *Address* (1827), 18–21 and *An Address, Delivered at Troy, on the Celebration of the Abolition of Slavery, in the State of New-York, July 6, 1829—Second Anniversary* (Albany, 1829), 13–16; Amos Gerry Beman, *Address Delivered at the Celebration of the West India Emancipation, in Davis' Hall, Hudson, N.Y., on Monday; August 2, 1847* (Troy, 1847), 15–16; *Colored American*, Aug. 22, Sept. 26, Oct. 3, 1840. The emphasis on morality and self-improvement, common to free black literature of the period, leads Frederick Cooper to make an erroneous distinction between abolitionism and civil rights on the one hand, and social uplift on the other. He fails to see that in a racist society, self-improvement and success can be one form of asserting equal rights. See "Elevating the Race: The Social Thought of Black Leaders, 1827–50," *American Quarterly*, 24 (1972), 604–25 and Sweet's caveat in *Black Images*, 129–30, n. 12 (which is in contrast with comments on 108).

50. *Colored American*, Sept. 26, 1840; James W. C. Pennington, *An Address Delivered at Newark,*

N.J. at the First Anniversary of West India Emancipation, August 1, 1839 (Newark, 1839), 9.

51. Jones, *Sermon*, 19–20; Paul, *Address* (1827), 3.

52. Other direct allusions, besides Jones' references, are in *Liberator*, Aug. 11, 1843; *Frederick Douglass' Paper*, Aug. 4, 1854; Steward, *Twenty-two Years a Slave*, 156–57.

53. On Africa as "a religious image," see Charles H. Long, "Perspectives for a Study of Afro-American Religion in the United States," *History of Religions*, 11 (1971), 56–58.

54. Jones, *Sermon*, 17.

55. On the tendency to view the African continent as a unitary image, see Sterling Stuckey, *The Ideological Origins of Black Nationalism* (Boston 1972), 1–2, n. 1.

56. Williams, *Oration* (1808), 1, 21; Parrott, *Oration* (1812), 3; Sipkins, *An Oration on the Abolition of the Slave Trade; Delivered in the African Church, in the City of New York, January 2, 1809* (New York, 1809) in Porter, *Early Negro Writing*, 365.

57. Williams, *Oration* (1808), 9; Sipkins, *Oration* (1809) in Porter, *Early Negro Writing*, 367; William Hamilton, *An Oration, on the Abolition of the Slave Trade, Delivered in the Episcopal Asbury African Church, in Elizabeth-St. New York, January 2, 1815* (New York, 1815) in Porter, *Early Negro Writing*, 391.

58. Parrott, *Oration* (1812), 6; George Lawrence, *Oration on the Abolition of the Slave Trade, Delivered on the First Day of January, 1813, in the African Methodist Episcopal Church* (New York, 813) in Porter, *Early Negro Writing*, 375–76.

59. Examples are "Africans," "beloved Africans," "descendants of Africans," "descendants of African forefathers," "African brethren," and "natives of Africa." William Miller, *A Sermon on the Abolition of the Slave Trade: Delivered in the African Church, New-York, on the First of January, 1810* (New York, 1810), 3; Russell Parrott, *An Oration of the Abolition of the Slave Trade. Delivered on the First of January, 1814. At the African Church of St. Thomas* (Philadelphia, 1814) in Porter, *Early Negro Writing*, 384; Sidney, *Oration* (1814), 6; Lawrence, *Oration* (1813) and Sipkins, *Oration* (1809) in Porter, *Early Negro Writing*, 371, 375, 380; Williams, *Oration* (1808), 11, 18–19; Jones, *Sermon*, 15.

60. Hamilton, *Address* (1809) in Porter, *Early Negro Writing*, 35.

61. Williams, *Oration* (1808), 12–13; Sipkins, *Oration* (1809); Lawrence, *Oration* (1813); Parrott *Oration* (1814), and Hamilton. *Oration* (1815) in

Porter, *Early Negro Writing*, 367–68, 376–77, 384ff., 391–94.

62. *Liberator*, July 30, 1831; Paul, *Address* (1827), 21; William Hamilton, *An Oration Delivered in the African Zion Church, on the Fourth of July, 1827, in Commemoration of the Abolition of Domestic Slavery in This State* (New York, 1827), 5.

63. *Liberator*, July 30, 1831; *Freedom's Journal*, July 11, 1828.

64. Williams, *Oration* (1808), 21; Hamilton, *Address (1809)* in Porter, *Early Negro Writing*, 39; Russell Parrott, *An Address, on the Abolition of the Slave-Trade, Delivered before the Different African Benevolent Societies. On the 1st of January, 1816* (Philadelphia, 1816), 12.

65. Parrott, *Oration* (1814) in Porter, *Early Negro Writing*, 390.

66. Lawrence, *Oration* (1813) in Porter, *Early Negro Writing*, 379, 382.

67. *Liberator*, Dec. 1, 1832.

68. Charles Long has contended that "the history of the names by which [the black] community has chosen to call itself . . . can be seen as a religious history." See "Perspectives for a Study of Afro-American Religion in the United States," 60–61.

69. Carman, *Oration* (1811), 18.

70. Hamilton, *Address* (1809), in Porter, *Early Negro Writing*, 36.

71. *Liberator*, July 30, 1831.

72. Miller, *Sermon*, 4.

73. H. Shelton Smith's study of southern religion and race is set in a national context, especially in the antebellum era. See *In His Image, But . . . Racism in Southern Religion 1790–1910* (Durham, 1972).

74. Parrott, *Oration* (1812), 6.

75. Paul, *Address* (1827), 10–11.

76. Miller, *Sermon*, 5–6. Timothy Smith treats Miller as a representative black preacher who dealt with the problem of suffering and evil, but he neglects to notice the implications of Miller's literalism for attributing collective guilt to Africans. See "Slavery and Theology in the Emergence of Black Christian Consciousness in Nineteenth-Century America," *Church History*, 41 (1972), 501–2.

77. James W. C. Pennington, *The Reasonableness of the Abolition of Slavery at the South, a Legitimate Inference from the Success of British Emancipation. An Address, Delivered at Hartford, Conn., on the First of August, 1856* (Hartford, 1856), 14, 16, 18; Foner, *Works of Douglass*, II, 27; Williams, *Oration* (1808), 11, 20; Miller, *Sermon*, 3; Paul, *Address* (1827), 3, 5, 8, 18; Paul, *Address*

(1829), 4; Sidney, *Oration* (1814), 6, 9; Parrott *Oration* (1812), 7; Sidney, *Oration* (1809), Sipkins, *Oration* (1809), Lawrence, *Oration* (1813), and Parrott, *Oration* (1814) in Porter, *Early Negro Writing*, 362–63, 366, 372, 375, 387; *Frederick Douglass' Paper*, August 5, 1853. See also Sweet, *Black Images of America*, 70–71.

78. *Colored American*, July 28, Aug. 11, 1838; *Frederick Douglass' Paper*, Aug. 18, 1854.

79. Jones, *Sermon*, 10–11, 18.

80. *Liberator*, July 30, 1831; Miller, *Sermon*, 13–14; Parrott, *Oration* (1812), 10; Parrott, *Oration* (1814) in Porter, *Early Negro Writing*, 390; Paul, *Address* (1826), 22.

81. Sidney, *Oration* (1814), 11.

82. Hamilton, *Oration* 11; Paul, *Address* (1829), 7, 11.

83. Williams, *Oration* (1808), 12, 17; Sipkins, *Oration* (1809) and Hamilton, *Oration* (1815) in Porter, *Early Negro Writing*, 367, 395; Foner, *Works of Douglass*, II, 431–32.

84. Parrott, *Oration* (1814) in Porter, *Early Negro Writing*, 384.

85. Henry Highland Garnet, "An Oration Delivered Before the Citizens of Troy, N.Y. *On the First of August*, 1839," *National Reformer*, 1 (Oct., 1839), 156. Garnet's "Address to the United States of America" in 1843 is available in several reprint editions and anthologies like Ruth Miller, ed. *Black American Literature 1760–Present* (Beverly Hills, Calif., 1971), 129–37.

86. Miller, *Sermon*, 8.

87. Parrott, *Address* (1816), 3.

88. Hamilton, *Address* (1809) and *Oration* (1815) in Porter, *Early Negro Writing*, 35, 398.

89. Foner, *Works of Douglass*, I, 324. See August Meier, "Frederick Douglass' Vision of America: A Case-Study in Nineteenth-Century Negro Protest," in Harold M. Hyman and Leonard W. Levy, eds., *Freedom and Reform* (New York, 1967), 127–48.

90. Hamilton, *Address* (1809) in Porter, *Early Negro Writing*, 39.

91. Paul, *Address* (1827), 11–12.

92. Sidney, *Oration* (1814), 7–8; Sidney, *Oration* (1809), and Hamilton, *Oration* (1815) in Porter, *Early Negro Writing*, 361–62, 399.

93. Hamilton, *Oration* (1827), 12.

94. *Liberator*, Aug. 11, 1832.

95. Pennington, *Address* (1839), 10; Foner, *Works of Douglass*, II, 181–205; *Liberator*, Dec. 1, 1832.

96. *Frederick Douglass' Paper*. Aug. 10. 1855.

97. Hamilton, *Oration* (1827), 8.

98. *Liberator* as quoted in *Colored American*. Aug. 31, 1839.

99. *Liberator*, Aug. 14, 1840; Aug. 13, 1858; *Frederick Douglass' Paper*, Aug. 26, 1853; *Weekly Anglo-African*, Aug. 20, 1859; Foner, *Works of Douglass*, I, 328; II, 437–39.

100. *Weekly Anglo-African*, Aug. 6, 1859; *Liberator*. Aug. 14, 1840; Aug. 19, 1842; Aug. 15, 1851; Aug. 19, 1853; Aug. 13, 1858; Pennington, *Address* (1839), 9–10, 12.

101. *Liberator*, Aug. 13, 1858; *Frederick Douglass' Paper*, Aug. 26, 1853.

102. *Frederick Douglass' Paper*, Aug. 10, 1855.

103. *Liberator*, Aug. 13, 1858.

104. *Address in Commemoration of the Great Jubilee, Of the 1st of August, 1834* (n.p. [New York?], n.d. [1836]) issued by "Committee of Arrangements: Samuel E. Cornish, Theodore S. Wright, Henry Sipkins, Thomas Downing, Thomas Van Ransalaer," 2–3.

105. *Colored American*, Aug. 22, 1840; *Liberator*, Dec. 1, 1832. On the resurgence of emigrationist views among blacks in the 1850s, see Hollis R. Lynch, "Pan-Negro Nationalism in the New World, Before 1862," in August Meier and Elliott Rudwick, eds., *The Making of Black America* (New York, 1969), I, 42–65.

106. *Liberator*, Aug. 15, 1859.

107. *Douglass' Monthly* IV (1861), 500.

108. *Liberator*, Aug. 14, 1840.

109. *Weekly Anglo-African*, Aug. 6, 1859.

# FROM "MIDDLE GROUND" TO "UNDERGROUND"

*Joel W. Martin*

Despite the fact that most histories of American religion exclude Native Americans from all but the beginning of their narratives, throughout American history Native American religious traditions continued not only to exist but to improvise and adapt to the new European American culture. As Joel Martin demonstrates, during the period of the early Republic the emergence of the southeastern Indians' cultural "underground" signalled a new phase in European-Indian cultural interaction. Prior to the Revolution, the southeastern Indians in the interior had created a "middle ground" of contact with the English and the French through which they were able to accommodate the new European ways within their traditional patterns of life. In ways reminiscent of the "mourning-wars" described by Daniel Richter, Native Americans intensified their traditional rituals in response to European challenges. By the beginning of the 1800s, however, the systematic exploitation characteristic of complete colonization was well underway. Now Native Americans not only reacted against their captors, they also created new traditions and adapted old ones in the new world created by colonization. What Joel Martin calls the Indians' cultural "underground" represented a "hidden set of beliefs and practices that reinforced their identity as Indians and strengthened their will to survive and resist." As Martin emphasizes, these innovative responses to European colonizing were neither reactionary nor non-traditional; instead, they provided a resource for the continual reformulation of beliefs and ritual practices to meet new circumstances.

Reprinted by permission from Joel W. Martin, "From 'Middle Ground' to 'Underground': Southeastern Indians and the Early Republic," in *Native Americans and the Early Republic*, Ronald Hoffman and Frederick Hoxie, eds. (Charlottesville: University of Virginia, 1996).

# 7

# FROM "MIDDLE GROUND" TO "UNDERGROUND"

## Southeastern Indians and the Early Republic

*Joel W. Martin*

DURING THE PERIOD of the early Republic, unprecedented numbers of white settlers invaded the southeastern interior and introduced a new order hostile to the existence of Indians in the region. Southeastern Indians responded with a variety of strategies. Some emigrated. A small and highly visible elite turned toward white ways and became commercial planters and slave owners. A much larger number pursued alternative paths designed to prevent the extinction of their cultures. As residents of homelands being occupied by a hostile, alien force, this group relied increasingly upon a kind of cultural "underground," a hidden set of beliefs and practices that reinforced their identity as Indians and strengthened their will to survive and resist. This essay unearths the "underground" developed by Cherokees and Muskogee Creeks.

The necessity for a cultural "underground" emerged earlier among the Cherokees, a people who, unlike the Creeks, were defeated militarily during the American Revolution. Before the American Revolution, Cherokees, like other large groups of southeastern Indians in the interior, had succeeded fairly well in requiring the English to accommodate indigenous cultural and political expectations. Cherokee men and women traded frequently and successfully with the English. While Cherokee men traded deerskins, human captives, and horses for guns, paint, rum, mirrors, looking glasses, and many other items that they adapted to their own ends, Cherokee women traded food, herbs, and cane baskets for clothes, money, bread, and butter. Cherokee women formed sexual liaisons with English traders, and gave birth to and raised métis children who later played a very important role in Cherokee society. In sum, Cherokee men and women had handled cross-cultural contact and exchange very successfully. They had accommodated material, economic, social, and political changes within traditional patterns and routines.[1]

If it required several generations of English and Cherokee efforts to build this "middle ground," a set of relationships, interactions, and altered identities, it took only a single generation to destroy it.[2] Two wars did the fatal damage. During the first, the Cherokee-Carolina war of 1759–1761, white troops burned many Cherokee towns and destroyed their stores of corn and beans. This caused Cherokees to reappraise their relationship with Carolinians. After the war, the Cherokees curtailed their economic contact and political engagement with Carolinians.[3] Meanwhile, Carolinians also devalued trade with Cherokees, their former enemies. During the 1760s, English refugees from Indian attacks in Virginia settled in great numbers in Carolina's backcountry. They had no tolerance for Indians or those who traded with them. They ostracized and attacked traders. Intercultural exchange, the main bridge between Carolinians and Cherokees, was dismantled as new forms of cultural and racial hatred became the norm. How the Cherokees responded to this new situation was shaped in large measure by their decentralized form of governance.[4]

Throughout the eighteenth century, Cherokee villages operated with considerable autonomy. While the Cherokees seemed closer than other southeastern Indians to creating a centralized and coercive political organization at a national level, no state existed. Cherokees gave their primary loyalties to individual villages. Villages had a great say in shaping their relations with the rest of the world. Influenced by regionalism, local leadership, unique historical experiences, and a host of other variables, villages frequently adopted divergent stances toward the English. Within any given village, no individual leader or governing body could coerce people to obey their decisions. Headmen might decide to promote neutrality, but villagers might decide for war.[5]

During the 1760s and '70s, Cherokee headmen ceded great quantities of land to the English to cover trade debts. Not surprisingly, Cherokees who disliked these cessions did not hesistate to express themselves.[6] The most bitter opposition came from young Cherokee men. Treaties signed in 1771, 1775, and 1777 ceded millions of acres of Cherokee lands north of the Cumberland river, including prime hunting lands. Young Cherokee men said additional loss of territory would be fatal to the Cherokee people. To give their hunting lands away would force a change in Cherokee subsistence, a shift from hunting and toward raising livestock. Such a change was equated with cultural death by a Cherokee leader named Dragging Canoe. "It seemed to be the intention of the white people to destroy them from being a people," he said, emphasizing how whites nearly surrounded Cherokees.[7] Young Cherokee men did not want to rely upon domesticated animals for subsistence. The Maker had given tame animals to whites, and wild ones to Indians. Not wanting to be penned up like hogs by encircling white settlers, they determined to maintain open access to traditional hunting grounds. During the mid-1770s followers of Dragging Canoe went on the offensive. They left their respective villages and formed Chickamauga, a new settlement on the Tennessee River.[8]

Chickamauga people maligned those Cherokees who did not join them with the hated name of "Virginians," and called themselves *Ani-yuníwiya*, or "real people."[9] Because they opposed white domination, emphasized the cultural division between whites and Indians, and rejected certain aspects of European civilization, we might call them "nativists." Yet, that label is too simplistic and it is pejorative.[10] The Chickamaugans showed considerable openness to cultural pluralism. They fostered direct ties to other indigenous groups and to the British in Pensacola. Chickamauga's inhabitants included Cherokees, Cherokee métis, Muskogees, and British loyalists. In 1776, the Chickamaugans attacked the Virginians who had settled in the Watauga Valley. During subsequent years, many bloody exchanges followed.[11]

Most Cherokees did not join the Chickamaugans. Nevertheless, they were caught up in the warfare of the American Revolution. During the summer of 1776, thousands of Whig troops invaded Cherokee country. Motivated by the rhetoric of genocide and enslavement, they destroyed Cherokee habitations, orchards, and crops. Several subsequent campaigns attested to the determination of whites to destroy the Cherokee people. While they did not succeed in this goal, whites did destroy the middle ground once and for all. By 1777, the old patterns of mutual accommodation were gone. Whites no longer showed Cherokees respect, and Cherokees could not forget how whites had stained their hands with the blood of Cherokee women and children.[12]

After their defeat in the American Revolution, most Cherokees in the Carolinas adopted a strategy of non-militant separatism. They developed a cultural "underground," a set of practices and beliefs that reinforced linguistic, cultural, ethical, and religious boundaries between themselves and whites. If they could not preserve physical distance and political independence, they could at least bolster symbolic distinctions in many areas of life and protect the core of their identity. For instance, Cherokees fluent in English pretended they did not understand it when addressed by Americans. As they had long done, Cherokees continued to keep their sacred rituals secret. Additionally, it may have been around this time that they began performing a dance that satirized negative traits associated with whites. Among themselves, Cherokees danced the Booger dance, in which masked Cherokee men pretended to be Europeans: "awkward, ridiculous, lewd, and menacing."[13]

Just as the dance dramatized the difference between whites and Indians, myths describing the separate creation of human races became widely popular among the Cherokees. Originating among Indian prophets in the eighteenth century, the theory of racial polygenesis held that "red" people were fundamentally different from "white" people. Some Cherokees were proponents of the theory as early as 1799. In 1811, a Cherokee prophet promoted a small revitalization movement saying the following: "You yourselves can see that the white people are entirely different beings from us; we are made of red clay; they, out of white sand." Evidently, by that time at a popular level Cherokees had come to assume the difference between whites and Indians to be ontological: sacred and permanent.[14]

On a less metaphysical plane, many post-Revolutionary Cherokees created distance between themselves and whites by relying increasingly upon métis individuals to serve as cultural intermediaries. These individuals were perfectly poised to play such a role. Bicultural progeny of English fathers and Cherokee mothers, they owned a disproportionate number of slaves and increasingly modeled their lifestyle on that of white planters. At a time when many Cherokees were trying to differentiate themselves symbolically from whites, these individuals were identifying more openly with white ways. Their role as cultural brokers was crucial for several decades.[15]

The métis elite accepted Protestant missionaries into their midst, became producers of crops and livestock for white markets, and eventually reorganized the Cherokee polity by forming a constitutional government (1827).[16] During the 1820s, the Cherokee elite attracted national praise. Anglo writers heralded their agrarian, mercantile, religious, and social achievements. In his *Remarks on the Practicability of Indian Reform* (1828), Isaac McCoy, eager to convince policymakers and church officials that Indians could be civilized, pointed to the Cherokee countryside.

> Numerous flocks of sheep, goats, and swine, cover the vallies and hills. . . . The natives carry on a considerable trade with the adjoining States. . . . Apple and peach orchards are quite common, and gardens are cultivated. . . . Butter and cheese are seen on Cherokee tables. There are many publick roads in the nation, and houses of entertainment kept by natives. Numerous flourishing villages are seen in every section of the country. . . . The population is rapidly in-

creasing. . . . Some of the most influential characters are members of the church, and live consistently with their professions. Schools are increasing every year; learning is encouraged and rewarded. The female character is elevated and duly respected.[17]

McCoy concluded that the Cherokees as a whole were "a *civilized* people." Another commentator agreed, saying that the "Cherokees have the aspect, and the elements, at least, of a regular, civilized, Christian nation."[18] The Cherokees, it was implied, were exceptional Indians.

But when white commentators like McCoy described Cherokee society, they were really only describing the lifestyle and values of the Cherokee elite. As one missionary admitted, he worked primarily with "persons who speak both languages; as half-breeds, whites brought up in the nation, or married into Indian families, or otherwise dependent on them. This class of people have always been *the connecting link* between the Indians and the whites."[19] Dependent upon this class of mediators, whites inevitably knew the members of that class better than they knew the majority of Cherokees with whom they had less direct contact. This state of affairs may have been precisely the one ordinary Cherokees desired. Métis mediators provided them with a very useful and effective screen behind which they could continue to lead traditional lives beyond the gaze of whites. In effect, Cherokees used the métis to connect them to and shield them from a dominant public order organized around threatening values.

A comparison of elite and non-elite responses to Christianity underscores the difference between the two groups. During the 1820s, Cherokees were missionized more than any group of interior Indians. Four denominations (Presbyterian, Moravian, Baptist, and Methodist) vied for converts. In 1827 these denominations supported eight Indian schools and seventy-one teachers who directly affected the lives of two hundred Cherokee boys and girls. Nevertheless, in 1830, these denominations could only claim 1,300 members out of total Cherokee population exceeding 15,000. Within the pool of converts, one would find almost all of the members of the Cherokee elite.[20]

Ninety percent of the Cherokee people did not have significant contact with Christian missionaries. Among the ten percent of Cherokees who were exposed directly to Christianity, many were persuaded by arguments circulating among the Cherokees against the alien religion. An epistemological argument held that Christians' stories were "mere legendary tales." An ontological argument reasoned that because "the Cherokees were a different race from the whites," they could have "no concern in the white people's religion." And an ethical argument, after observing how Christians acted, concluded that Christians were hypocrites. Rather than adopt the new religion, they continued to tell sacred stories, participate in rituals, and practice values cherished by their ancestors. Even among the small number of Cherokees who attended Christian services regularly, most refused to entirely forsake their traditional practices.[21]

The great majority of Cherokees did not convert to Christianity, attend school, hold elected office, run houses of entertainment, own slaves, or publish newspapers.[22] Literacy, another aspect of "civilization" embraced by the elite, also elicited negative responses from ordinary Cherokees. Cherokees and other southeastern Indians experienced literacy as an essential part of white domination. Literacy was associated primarily with missionaries, government agents, treaty negotiators, land speculators, and powerful traders. Literacy was linked to people who routinely denigrated Cherokee religion, tried to control Cherokee politics, and defrauded Cherokees of their lands. Given these associations, it is not surprising that most Cherokees did not try to learn to read and write. As one of their myths revealed, they felt that literacy, like Christianity, belonged exclusively to white people. According to the myth, in the beginning, the Maker had given the book to the Indian, the real or genuine man. When the Indian was not paying attention, however, the tricky white man stole the book. As a consequence of that primordial theft, the white man has since had an easy life, and the Indian has been compelled to gain his subsistence by hunting.[23]

All of this changed when Sequoyah, the son of a European man and a Cherokee woman, created in 1821 a syllabary, a set of written symbols representing the basic sounds of the Cherokee language.[24] The syllabary was a cultural hybrid. It was European in form (the symbols were written and read) and Cherokee in content (the symbols represented the spoken Cherokee language). But if we would appreciate fully Sequoyah's achievement we need to go beyond noting its bicultural roots. Sequoyah's syllabary precipitated a movement of significant cultural renewal in the early 1820s among common Cherokee men and women.[25]

When Sequoyah through his syllabary made literacy in Cherokee possible, Cherokee men and women thought initially he had done something magical. Because they associated literacy with a use of power for destructive purposes, they thought Sequoyah's efforts were delirious or idiotic.[26] Soon, however, Sequoyah convinced them through public demonstrations that he had done nothing magical or crazy, that anyone could learn to write the Cherokee language. Cherokees realized that here was new power that could be employed to preserve the core of Cherokee identity. From that point on, they showed zeal in learning and teaching the syllabary. White observers were astounded at how the new mode of writing caught on. In 1824, they reported that "the Knowledge of Mr. Guess's Alphabet is spreading through the nation like fire among the leaves." By 1825, the majority of Cherokees had learned the system, and "letters in Cherokee were passing in all directions."[27] With every letter written, non-elite Cherokees strengthened their own culture and implicitly refuted white claims to superiority. White culture was no more sacred than was the culture of the Cherokees. Or to put it another way, Cherokee culture was no less sacred than that of whites. By taking the tools and symbols associated with the invading culture and turning them to counter-colonial purposes, Sequoyah produced a written language that served as "virtually a code to sustain the traditional community *beyond the perception of the authorities, red or white.*" Sequoyah had given non-elite Cherokees a valuable way to nurture and preserve Cherokee identity during the very period when whites were invading their lands in unprecedented numbers. Though in theory whatever was written was public and could be read by whites literate in Cherokee, in practice the overwhelming majority of letters were never seen by whites. In effect, this kind of literacy nurtured, without betraying, the Cherokee underground, the set of beliefs and practices, cultural values and affiliations, that defined the Cherokees as a distinct people.[28]

Literate or not, all Cherokees, including the elite, could not prevent the invasion of their land by thousands of outsiders. Whichever strategy of resistance or accommodation they employed, they were unable to overcome the fundamental power relations shaping their world during the period of the early republic. Whites entered their land by the thousands during the Gold Rush of 1829; Georgia extinguished Cherokee sovereignty June 1, 1830; whites stole Cherokee property with impunity and drove Cherokees from their farms. In 1838, the great majority of Cherokees (sixteen thousand people) were forced to move west in a murderous march that cost the people thousands of lives.[29] Two years earlier, their native neighbors to the south, the Muskogees, had been compelled to travel their own "Trail of Tears."[30] In essence, both southeastern peoples were forced to leave their ancestral homes by whites who wanted Indian lands for cotton culture.

If Muskogee and Cherokee experiences of dispossession and removal in the 1830s seem very similar, their earlier experiences with the white invasion were distinct in some very important ways. Geography was key. Because the Muskogees were much farther away from Carolina's backcountry and because their trade was essential to backcountry Georgia, the Muskogees, unlike the Cherokees, were not targeted for massive intercultural violence during the 1760s or during the American Revolution. Muskogee towns survived the entire eighteenth century without being attacked by Europeans or Euro-Americans, a very remarkable record for the eastern half of North America.

Nevertheless, if they successfully avoided the wars with whites that hurt Cherokees so badly, the Muskogees had faced some tough challenges during the eighteenth century. Beginning in the 1760s, Augusta merchants and traders had dramatically expanded the rum trade to the Muskogees. Over the next five decades, this trade increased the Muskogees' economic dependency, encouraged violence among villagers, promoted overhunting, precipitated an ecological crisis, and increased intertribal conflicts.[31] Eventually, the trade would provide whites with the means to force large cessions of land, cessions which would in turn inspire a movement of violent resistance among the Muskogees, the Redstick revolt of 1812–14. Only then did the Muskogees experience the kind of crushing military invasion that the Cherokees had faced decades earlier. This difference in timing is very significant. It underscores the fact that the stories of Cherokee and Muskogee resistance are not identical. Rather, these stories converge and diverge in ways that warrant closer examination.[32]

Before the Redstick revolt, most Muskogees avoided massive conflicts by employing a rich range of small-scale modes of resistance. While less spectacular than the Redstick movement, these forms of resistance were very important throughout the period of the early Republic, a time when domination was on the rise, but not yet complete. Many elementary forms of resistance were performed in secret, in the woods, under the cover of darkness, or in a state of intoxication. During the 1790s, for example, as white encroachment made hunting on the Georgia-Muskogee frontier more difficult and dangerous, "gangs" of young Muskogee men began stealing whites' horses and slaves, and selling them to complicit traders in Tennessee and Florida. Young men explicitly justified their acts as retaliation for white encroachment. When white hunting parties poached their game, the Muskogees responded by killing the settlers' cattle. In a few instances, they murdered individual whites, took women and children captive, plundered the stores of traders, and burned settlers' farm buildings and houses. When white authorities demanded justice, headmen said they were powerless to provide it. They blamed the unruliness of young men whose "mischief" they could not prevent. Furthermore, many of the accused men said they had committed their crimes while drunk and therefore were not accountable.[33]

Muskogees found creative ways to frustrate dominating whites. Proselytized by Moravian missionaries, they dissembled and said they already knew everything about the Savior. Lectured by the United States agent on the merits of patrilineal kinship patterns or commercial agriculture, they turned silent or pretended they could not understand. Advised to cede land at treaty conferences, they recalled the great quantity of lands already lost, reminded U.S. officials of the promises of previous presidents, invoked the ways of their own ancestors, and pled the future needs of their progeny. Acts of theft, arson, and murder; the strategic use of flattery, equivocation, procrastination, lies, and dissimulation; careful appeals to high moral principles or the exonerating circumstance of intoxication—these were but a few ways Muskogees resisted white aggression and settler incursions without risking everything in a direct conflict.[34]

What is striking is that many of these less dramatic and small-scale modes, because they were performed in secret or involved purposeful obfuscation, allowed Muskogees and other southeastern Indians to express deep-seated resentments while keeping the wellsprings of resistance "underground," partially hidden from whites and collaborating Indians. Unfortunately for us, this had the additional effect of insuring that the full depth and range of the Muskogees' responses to domination would not be clearly recorded in the historical documents. Because most of these documents were written by whites who were kept partially in the dark, it is difficult to establish precisely the Muskogees' true feelings, motivations, ideas, and rationales. In anthropologist James Scott's terms, the documents do a good job of showing us the "public transcript," the ways Muskogees and other southeastern Indians acted in the presence of power. The documents do a much less satisfactory job of revealing the "hidden transcript," the discourses, gestures, rituals, and symbols southeastern Indians cultivated among themselves to justify, promote, and perpetuate resistance.[35] Like other scholars who deal with documents produced in situations of domination, we find there are no transparent windows into the consciousness of the oppressed.[36] This lack, however, should not lead to skepticism or agnosticism. If not exactly transparent, some windows nonetheless exist. The Redstick revolt is such a window. Because the Redsticks risked everything and dared to resist openly, their movement provides historians with one of our best glimpses at the hidden transcript developed by southeastern Indians resisting domination.

Like the Chickamaugan movement, the Redstick movement attracted people who were angry with their headmen for authorizing massive land cessions to whites. Intended to cover debts incurred in the deerskin trade, these cessions signaled for Muskogees a profound change in Indian-white relations. Everything hinged on the interpretation and handling of debt. Essential to the everyday transactions of the deerskin trade, debt for generations had signified ties between individual hunters and traders. Hunters went into debt to obtain what they needed for a season's hunt and to supply their kin with goods. They negotiated with traders whom they knew personally. In the new system, debt was abstracted from personal relationships and made into a commodity that could itself be traded on the market. The debts owed small traders were purchased at discount by the largest trading firm in the region, Panton, Leslie and Company—later John Forbes and Company. This firm then aggregated the debts of entire communities of hunters, indeed of all Muskogee hunters, to produce one astronomical lump sum which the firm charged against the Muskogee people. By 1803, the firm claimed the Muskogees owed $113,000.[37]

This extraordinary debt would have been impossible for the firm to collect, if not for the cooperation of the United States. Such cooperation was novel. In previous years, hostility and competition had characterized the relations of United States officials and Pensacola merchants. In 1793, for instance, William Panton of Pensacola encouraged the Muskogees to resist the advance of the Georgians through whatever means possible, including violence. United States officials said Panton "would rather see the whole state of

Georgians in flames, and women and children massacred by the savages, than lose one hundred deer skins."[38] By 1803, Panton was dead, and the interests of the United States and the Pensacola merchants coincided. During the first decade of the nineteenth century, United States agents compelled Muskogee headmen to cede millions of acres of land to the United States. In exchange for the land, the United States paid off some of the Indians' aggregate debt. Thus, thousands of small, face-to-face exchanges between traders and hunters were transmuted by a multinational company and an expanding nation-state into massive land cessions that affected an entire people. These cessions signaled the end of play-off politics, expanded United States sovereignty, took from the Muskogee people many of their best hunting grounds, and undermined the deerskin trade, the central economic basis of the middle ground.[39]

This example shows how Americans, working with Pensacola merchants, exploited an established practice, the giving of credit, for new ends antithetical to the existence of the middle ground itself. A similar tale of ex post facto transmutation can be told by examining what happened to the institution of alliance chiefs after the departure of the French and the defeat of the British. During the 1790s and 1800s, intercultural diplomacy did not work as it had in the past. Earlier alliance chiefs like Malatchi had struggled to find a compromise between European demands and the expectations of his people. Later alliance chiefs did the same thing, but now the white side of the balance weighed far more heavily upon them. The Americans, too numerous and too strong, no longer needed to listen to or compromise with their Indian interlocutors. Chiefs found themselves compelled to execute or legitimize policies that signified not mutual accommodation, but U.S. domination. They were required to sign treaties permanently ceding massive quantities of land, to authorize the building of roads through their people's territories, and to enforce justice against their own peoples even when this meant violating sacred cultural values. Some chiefs such as Hopoithle Miko of Tallassee refused to comply, and tried to set up alternative governments. Others chiefs such as Tustunnuggee Thlucco (Big Warrior) of Tuckabatchee promised to comply, but dissimulated in speech or procrastinated in action. Still others, such as William McIntosh of Coweta, profited personally from their mediating role and adopted the lifestyle of white settlers or planters. Was a chief like McIntosh a true intermediary or a colonial collaborator? It was becoming hard to tell.[40]

As Americans and complicit Indians corrupted the institutions that supported cross-cultural exchange and mutual accommodation, and as white populations increased and settled closer to the Indians of the interior southeast, white authorities and intellectuals developed a coherent narrative that legitimated and depoliticized these great changes. According to this narrative, the United States was the great benefactor of southeastern Indians, and if Indians could only make a few adjustments, they would be much happier. The old system of gift-giving was dead, the rules of the market applied now, and cessions were necessary to pay trade debts. Although these cessions deprived the Muskogees and other Indians of ancestral game lands, hunters need not despair. They could cease "savagery" to become commercial agriculturalists and raise livestock. Men should stay home, accumulate property, and pass it on to their children. Chiefs should police their people and enforce white justice. All would benefit. Whites would gain and use the land to its full potential, and Indians would become civilized. The plan of civilization, as represented to the Muskogees by U.S. Agent Benjamin Hawkins, was for the Muskogees' own good.[41]

Muskogees did not have to obey the U.S. agent, but they had to listen to him and show respect. Because Hawkins controlled the federal annuities paid to Muskogees, could materially reward and punish villagers, and increasingly monopolized the execution of justice in Muskogee country, he could enter Muskogee villages with impunity and presume to tell the Muskogees how they had to change. His influence signaled that a new set of power relations was shaping Indian-white encounters. The United States, and for that matter individual states such as Georgia, possessed vastly more economic and military power than the Muskogee people. By the turn of the century, Muskogees could no longer compel cultural, political, or economic reciprocity.

As Muskogees experienced the rise of domination and witnessed its effects on subsistence, commerce, politics, and intercultural relations, they created their own narratives to explain what was happening. Just as whites told stories, proposed plans, and developed institutions to impose their will, Muskogees told stories, created movements, and developed practices to resist the loss of territory, economic dependency, political domination, and cultural imperialism. Usually this subversive cultural activity went on out of the sight of whites, in the southeastern "underground." However, in the Redstick revolt it came into almost full view when thousands of Muskogees decided to revolt against the United States. Because Muskogee resistance took a massive and open form in the Redstick prophetic movement, study of this movement provides one of our best documented glimpses of the otherwise hidden transcript of southeastern Indians.

When the New Madrid earthquake violently shook their lands in 1811–1812, Muskogees cast about for a meaningful and useful interpretation of the unprecedented events.[42] In shaping their interpretations, the Muskogee people, unlike whites, did not turn to the Book for guidance.[43] As a Muskogee man put it, "White people have the old book from God. We Indians do not have it and are unable to read it."[44] Even so, he averred, his people still possessed insight into the order of things. "The Indians know it without a book; they dream much of God, and therefore they know it." Instead of turning to Scriptures, Muskogees turned to their spiritual leaders, their shamans. Inspired shamans trembled and convulsed as if vibrated by an earthquake or seized by a spirit. These shamans or "shakers" traveled to and from the spirit worlds.[45] They declared a charismatic event revelatory of sacred forces was at work, and interpreted historical events and the earthquake through the template of Muskogean religious myth.

Muskogees imagined the cosmos divided into three primordial worlds: the Upper World, This World, and the Lower World. Just as the Sun and Moon illuminated the earth, manifested order in their movements, and helped demarcate temporal boundaries, the Upper World released the powers of perfection, order, permanence, clarity, periodicity. Pitted against the Upper World and releasing exactly contrary powers was the Lower World, the realm of reversals, madness, creativity, fertility, chaos. In the Lower World, there lived a major class of sacred beings. It was not taken lightly, for it included the most dangerous spirit beings. Foremost among these was the Tie-Snake, a primeval dragon-like antlered monster snake. Although most Europeans denied the existence of Tie-Snakes, some traders like James Adair were not sure. Adair accepted southeastern Indians' accounts of snakes "of a more enormous size than is mentioned in history" that could bewitch their prey with their eyes and tongues, change color, and dazzle spectators with "piercing rays of light that blaze from their foreheads."[46] Muskogees strongly affirmed the

reality of these creatures. According to Muskogees, these great snakes could stretch themselves across the channel and practically dam the stream. During the early nineteenth century in Muskogee, the Tie-Snake was closely associated with a particularly dangerous rocky
stretch of the Chattahoochee river and could often be seen there. "It had the appearance,
when floating on the water, of a large number of barrels strung together, end to end, and
could, almost at any time, be seen catching its prey by folding its helpless victims in the
coils or 'tie' of its tail and instantly destroying life by a deadly hug."[47] In addition to making
water travel dangerous, these Snakes brought numerous sicknesses to humans. Merely
looking at the creature could cause insanity or death. And yet, it was very difficult for a
human not to look, for the Tie-Snake was strangely beautiful. Dreadfully alluring, its body
was armored with crystalline scales that shone iridescently, its forehead crowned with an
extraordinarily bright crystal. Highly prized as aids in divination, these dazzling scales and
crystals could only be obtained by a shaman purified for contact with the dangerous powers of the Lower World.

In 1812, a Muskogee shaman Captain Sam Isaacs related to Upper Muskogees his vision
of "diving down to the bottom of the river and laying there and traveling about for many
days and nights receiving instruction and information from an enormous and friendly serpent that dwells there and was acquainted with future events and all other things necessary
for a man to know in this life."[48] As Captain Isaacs revealed, it was the powerful Tie-Snake
who recklessly shook the earth and unleashed a new force for recreating the world. Based
upon this vision, the special knowledge and power that it provided him, and his familiarity
with Tecumseh and the Shawnee prophets, Isaacs acquired the veneration of several hundred people.[49] As the movement grew, however, a younger group of shamans came to the
fore. Borrowing from the fiery tales of apocalypse told by runaway Afro-Christian slaves,
they said the Upper World power known as the Maker of Breath was about to destroy the
present colonial order. This prophecy of cosmological upheaval provided the metaphors,
symbols, and values that justified revolt against seemingly insurmountable odds. By identifying with these cosmic forces, the Muskogee rebels gained courage and felt they could
purge their land of colonizers. Allied with the Shawnees and other Indians, they would
"make the land clear of the Americans or lose their lives."[50]

Just as the Muskogees interpreted earthly events through the symbolic template of sacred stories, so they acted politically in a way directly patterned after rituals of purification and world renewal. Homologies between rituals and revolutionary acts were strong.
When they attacked an enemy town, the shamans said it would fall on the eighth day, for
eight was a sacred number. Eight days was also the length of time it took the Muskogees to
perform their most important collective ceremony, the *póskita* or Busk, an annual ritual
celebrating the primordial origins of corn and the rebirth of the social order. Muskogee
rebels performed a dance borrowed from the Shawnees to symbolize solidarity with other
Indians and their utter determination to resist white civilization's hegemonic power. If
this meant attacking collaborating Muskogees or coercing people to join their movement,
the Redsticks were willing to do so. "The declaration of the prophets [was] to destroy
every thing received from the Americans, all the Chiefs and their adherents who are
friendly to the customs and ways of the white people." They were directed by the prophets
"to kill any of their own People if they do not take up the war Club."[51] The rebels ritually
assassinated collaborating chiefs and targeted Hawkins and his assistants for execution.
They waged war on cattle. Central to the subsistence base of invading settlers, cattle sym-

bolized white civilization itself. The Muskogee rebels agreed with their Chickamaugan predecessors. These tame animals were the very antithesis of the wild animals given to real Indians by the Maker of Breath. As they had always done in traditional initiation ceremonies, the rebels withdrew to the woods, fasted, consumed purifying beverages, and danced. Through these and many other acts, Muskogee rebels turned an upside-down world right side up. With prophetic declarations, new dances, purification ceremonies, wars on certain animals and people, and humorous inversionary gestures, the Muskogee rebels rejected domination and showed that they were indeed the masters of the land and all of its symbols.[52]

As historian Gregory Dowd notes in his study of earlier Indian revolts, prophetic messages spread very fast in Indian country.[53] One of the main ways prophecies were disseminated was through rumors. As scholars of anti-colonial movements have shown, rumors can elaborate, distort, and exaggerate information regarding events of vital importance, can spread with incredible speed, and can give voice to popular utopian longings. Rumors have no identifiable authors, so people can spread them while disavowing responsibility for their contents and effects. Rumors circulated rapidly in the southeastern underground. After the New Madrid earthquake, among the Muskogees, "flying tales daily multiplied and were exaggerated in all parts of the [Muskogee] nation, told and received as truth by every one. . . . [These] Tales had no Father for they were said to be told by first one and then another and nobody could ascertain who, but the relators were at a distance in general and hard to be detected." In many of these "flying, fatherless tales," Tecumseh, the great Shawnee leader of pan-tribalism, figured prominently. Indeed, according to some of the popular narratives, Tecumseh had stomped his foot and caused the earth to shake. In others, Tecumseh did not cause the earthquakes, but he prophesied how the Lower World would release awesome power, collapse the old order, and allow a new one to emerge. Responding to these rumors and other stories, seven to nine thousand Muskogees revolted against the United States.[54]

An equal number did not revolt. Why not? If several thousand Muskogees living on the Chattahoochee (Lower Muskogees) did not take up the red club, it does not mean that they were not religious or even less religious than the Redsticks. People can share the same religion but interpret its implications differently. They can cherish the same myths and rituals, and still come to blows. When the Redsticks called for revolt, the Lower Muskogees listened, hesitated, and decided against joining their more militant cousins. They felt there were better ways to resist white domination. Since Lower Muskogees lived very close to Georgians, they feared they would suffer catastrophic losses if they joined the revolt. But fear was not the only factor shaping their response. By 1811, Lower Muskogees had already dealt with the major economic and social challenges caused by the loss of their ancestral hunting lands. Like their Cherokee neighbors, they had shifted their secondary subsistence cycle away from hunting towards the raising of livestock and the trading of agricultural products. Women gained greater direct access to the market. Old men also benefited. A Coweta chief said he had "more pleasure . . . in carding and dying his cotton and making his clothing [with a loom] than he ever had in his young days hunting. 'I am old . . . and as such according to our old ways useless but according to the new way more useful than ever.'"[55] As for the young men, the Lower Muskogees most directly affected by the loss of hunting lands, many of them had emigrated, relocating in northern Florida. A region where settlers were rare and game was plentiful, northern Florida had served as a kind of escape valve for generations of Lower Muskogees frustrated with white encroachment. As a consequence, in 1811, among Lower Muskogees living on the Chattahoochee, there was no critical mass of angry young men determined to keep the traditional hunting grounds free of whites. Excepting the ethnically distinct town of Yuchis, Lower Muskogee towns determined to side with the Georgians against the Upper Muskogees. They expected to be amply rewarded for this alliance.[56]

Neither the Upper or Lower Muskogees saw their expectations fulfilled. The Redsticks were devastated utterly by their war with the United States. The Lower Muskogees, although the allies of the victorious United States, were forced by Andrew Jackson to cede millions of acres of their land. After the war, the influx of white settlers accelerated. Nevertheless, Upper and Lower Muskogees continued to resist. Muskogees had employed a wide range of subtle and not so subtle forms of resistance before the Redstick movement. They did so afterwards as well, and learned much from the Cherokees. In the decades following the Redstick war, Muskogees increasingly relied upon métis individuals, including educated Cherokees, to serve as cultural intermediaries. Cherokee métis involved themselves quite visibly in Muskogee affairs during the 1820s. For instance, in 1826, John Ridge and David Vann provided counsel and served as secretaries to Muskogee headmen during treaty negotiations with the United States.[57]

There is also evidence that Muskogees, like Cherokees, made special efforts to hide their culture of the sacred from Anglo scrutiny. For instance, during the 1820s, the Tuckabatchees would not let any white person see their ancient copper plates, sacred items displayed during that town's Busk ceremony. Although Lee Compere, a Baptist missionary, lived among the Tuckabatchees from 1822 to 1828, he "would never get to see them. . . . The Indians were reluctant to talk about them." Compere did succeed in persuading Tustunnuggee Thlucco to relate some of the Muskogees' sacred history, including how they had defeated the indigenous inhabitants of the southeast. However, when Compere made an insensitive comparison between this ancient story of conquest and the ongoing Anglo-American invasion, the chief turned silent. Compere had crossed the line. "From that time I could never after induce him or any of the other chiefs to give me any more of their history."[58]

In addition to hiding their most sacred relics and keeping much of their oral tradition secret, Muskogees tried to protect their ceremonies from white civilization. They created new rules governing the consumption of alcohol and the use of manufactured goods during the Busk. In some towns, both were banned. At least in one square ground, it was "considered as a desecration for an Indian to allow himself to be touched by even the dress of a white man, until the ceremony of purification is complete."[59] This could have been the case earlier, but the fact that the rule was enforced in 1835 reveals an active concern to protect sacred ceremonies from white meddling.

In addition to protecting their own religion, Muskogees tried to check the influence of the Christian religion in their country. Most chiefs would not permit preaching in their towns. When Compere (through a Muskogee interpreter named John Davis) began conversing on the Gospel in the square ground of Tuckabatchee, the men ignored him and concentrated on cutting sticks and rubbing their pipes. On another occasion, they protested that they were too old to learn such things, and "did not want to hear them." In another town, Muskogees told Compere to avoid the square altogether as many Indians were intoxicated and would cause trouble.[60]

Not surprisingly, Compere's mission was not very successful. Except for Davis, he converted almost no "full-bloods." He simply did not have access to the Muskogees' inner lives. They kept their sacred life secret, as an incident in the spring of 1828 revealed. When clearing land for cultivation, Compere killed a hickory, unwittingly violating a Muskogee rule of propriety. A Muskogee woman informed him that he had "broke in upon some of the secrets of the Indians' superstition . . . which is that the Indians consider such trees when they happen to be found in the Townfield as sacred to the Great Spirit." Informed of his error, Compere was "not very sorry." Aware that he was being kept in the dark about major aspects of Muskogee life, Compere was pleased the accident had happened. It had served as "the means of dragging out a secret which I might never have learned without."[61] Muskogees simply did not trust Compere. Not surprisingly, the mission failed. Within a few years, the Muskogees were forcibly removed from Alabama.

In the decades prior to removal, Muskogees and Cherokees alike had experienced the invasion of their lands by missionaries, miners, government agents, settlers, and slaves. Although they had occasionally responded with violence, much more common were the everyday non-violent means they used to protect their feelings, rituals, identities, and cultures. Confronted with hostile whites in their midst, Muskogees and Cherokees consciously kept important things, values, beliefs, practices, and ideas secret. They developed alternative stories and myths to explain the origins of the diverse races, performed rituals and dances that celebrated their identities as Indians, and carefully controlled whites' access to their interior lives. By developing and hiding an underground cultural life, they retained their sense of their separate identity even as their land was being invaded.

To be sure, sometimes the Cherokees and Muskogees used violent means to repel whites, most spectacularly in the Chickamaugan and Redstick revolts. Even these revolts, however, were linked to the southeastern underground. The revolts simply concentrated in a vivid, explicit manner what was already present in a more diffuse, less visible way among the Cherokees and Muskogees. In the revolts, symbols, practices, and narratives emphasizing Indian distinctiveness were underscored, exaggerated, dramatized, and, most important, made public. Like geysers, the violent character of the Chickamauga and Redstick revolts attracted a lot of attention from shocked whites. But also like geysers, these revolts owed their existence to larger underground currents flowing out of sight. If the revolts deserve attention, surely deserving equal or greater attention is the cultural underground that made them possible. Southeastern Indians found much of value there: powerful symbols of a separate Indian identity, opportunities to vent frustrations, and a rich repertoire of strategies to resist domination. Although purposefully hidden by its creators and long overlooked by historians, the southeastern Indians' underground should be unearthed at last and ignored no longer, for it exercised significant influence during the period of the early Republic.

## NOTES

This essay benefited from comments by Mary Young, Frederick Hoxie, Peter Wood, Stephen Aron, and James Merrell.

1. James Merrell, " 'Our Bond of Peace': Patterns of Intercultural Exchange in the Carolina Piedmont, 1650–1750," in *Powhatan's Mantle*, 198–204; Gary Goodwin, *Cherokees in Transition: A Study of Changing Culture and Environment Prior to* 1775 (Chicago: University of Chicago Press, 1977), 94; Marvin Thomas Hatley, "The Dividing Paths: The Encounters of the Cherokees and the South Carolinians in the Southern Mountains, 1670–1785," (Ph.D. diss., Duke University, 1989), 96, 103, 137, 139, 144, 146, 156.

2. Richard White, *The Middle Ground Indians, Empires, and Republics in the Great Lakes Region,*

*1650–1815* (New York: Cambridge University Press, 1991), x, 38–40, 79, 84–90, 114–115, 179–180, 175, 202, 312–313.

3. John R. Alden, *John Stuart and the Southern Colonial Frontier* (Ann Arbor: University of Michigan Press, 1944), 208, 298–301; Hatley, "The Dividing Paths," 606–621.

4. David Cockran, *The Cherokee Frontier, 1540–1783* (Norman: University of Oklahoma Press, 1962), 194, 256–65; Hatley, "The Dividing Paths," 391, 395–396, 443, 456–464, 483–484, 533, 535, 538, 539, 54, 560.

5. Duane Champagne, *Social Order and Political Change: Constitutional Governments among the Cherokee, the Choctaw, the Chickasaw, and the Creek* (Stanford: Stanford University Press, 1992), 25, 28, 39, 57–59, 74–77.

6. Alden, *Southern Frontier*, 187, 208, 298, 303; Louis DeVorsey, *The Indian Boundary in the Southern Colonies, 1763–1775* (Chapel Hill: University of North Carolina Press, 1966), 102, 116, 126, 128, 133, 135; Duane H. King, "Long Island of the Holston: Sacred Cherokee Ground," *Journal of Cherokee Studies* (Fall 1976): 113–127. Hatley, "The Dividing Paths," 606–621, 627, 658–661.

7. Henry Stuart, "Account of his Proceedings with the Indians, Pensacola, August 25, 1776," [PRO, CO 5/7, 333–378], in William L. Saunders, ed., *The Colonial Records of North Carolina, 1662–1776* (10 vols., Raleigh, 1886–1890), x, 764.

8. Samuel Coles Williams, ed., *Adair's History of the American Indians*, (Johnson City, Tenn.: The Watauga Press, 1930), 138–139; DeVorsey, *Indian Boundary*, 74–85; Hatley, "The Dividing Paths," 631–642, 648–672.

9. James Paul Pate, "The Chickamauga: A Forgotten Segment of Indian Resistance on the Southern Frontier," Ph.D. diss., Mississippi State University, 1969, 81; John Brown, *Old Frontiers: The Story of the Cherokee Indians from Earliest Times to the Date of Their Removal to the West, 1838* (Kingsport, Tenn.: Southern Publishers, Inc., 1938), 165–167.

10. "Nativism" has negative connotations. Contemporary scholars associate nativism with closed-mindedness, ethnocentrism, racist attitudes, and a surrender of reason. See the way the word is used in current abstracts in *Dissertation Abstracts International, A, Humanities and Social Sciences* (Ann Arbor: University Microfilms International, 1991), passim.

11. Gregory Evans Dowd, *A Spirited Resistance: The North American Struggle for Unity, 1745–1815*

(Baltimore: The Johns Hopkins University Press, 1992), 48–56.

12. For the 1776 intercolonial expedition and its consequences, see James H. O'Donnell, *Southern Indians in the American Revolution* (Knoxville: University of Tennessee Press, 1973), 34–69, 118–119; Hatley, "The Dividing Paths," 571, 573, 578, 674, 675. For the rhetoric of genocide and enslavement, ibid., 567, 570, 582, 593, 648, 665. For the end of the Cherokee middle ground, ibid., 684, 718.

13. For the Booger Dance and secret rituals, see Frank G. Speck and Leonard Broom, *Cherokee Dance and Drama* (Berkeley: University of California Press, 1951), 36–39; Raymond D. Fogelson and Amelia B. Walker, "Self and Other in Cherokee Booger Dances," *Journal of Cherokee Studies* 5 (Fall 1980): 88–102; Hatley, "The Dividing Paths," 680–695, 698–699, 702–706.

14. For stories of separate creation and distinct destinies, see Bishop Edmund de Schweinitz, ed. and trans. "The Narrative of Marie Le Roy and Barbara Leiniger," in *Pennsylvania Archives 7* (1878); James Mooney, *The Ghost-Dance Religion and Wounded Knee* (Dover Publications, New Publications, 1973), 677; William G. McLoughlin, *Cherokees and Missionaries, 1789–1839* (New Haven: Yale University Press, 1984), 91, 97; McLoughlin, *The Cherokee Ghost Dance: Essays on the Southeastern Indians, 1789–1861* (Macon, Ga.: Mercer University Press, 1984), 253–260; Gregory Evans Dowd, *A Spirited Resistance: The North American Indian Struggle for Unity, 1745–1815* (Baltimore: Johns Hopkins University Press, 1992), 21, 63.

15. For métis mediators, see Ronald N. Satz, "Cherokee Traditionalism, Protestant Evangelism, and the Trail of Tears, Part II," *Tennessee Historical Quarterly* XLIV (Winter 1985): 380–402; Hatley, "The Dividing Paths," 695–697. For métis slaveowning, see Theda Perdue, *Slavery and the Evolution of Cherokee Society, 1540–1866* (Knoxville: University of Tennessee Press, 1979), 57–60.

16. See William G. McLoughlin, "Who Civilized the Cherokees?," *Journal of Cherokee Studies* 1988 (13): 55–81; Douglas C. Wilms, "Cherokee Acculturation and Changing Land Use Practices," *Chronicles of Oklahoma*, 1978 56(3): 331–343; Marguerite McFadden, "The Saga of 'Rich Joe' Vann," *Chronicles of Oklahoma*, 1983 61(1): 68–79; Michelle Daniel, "From Blood Feud to Jury System: The Metamorphosis of Cherokee Law from 1750 to 1840," *American Indian Quarterly*, 1987 11(2): 97–125. Cherokee slaveowners, like Muskogees, were usually lenient when compared to whites. See

Theda Perdue, "Cherokee Planters, Black Slaves, and African Colonization," *Chronicles of Oklahoma* 1982 60(3): 322–331; William G. McLoughlin, *Cherokee Renascence in the New Republic* (Princeton: Princeton University Press, 1986); Duane Champagne, *Social Order and Political Change: Constitutional Governments Among the Cherokee, the Choctaw, the Chickasaw, and the Creek* (Stanford: Stanford University Press, 1992).

17. Isaac McCoy, *The Practicability of Indian Reform, Embracing Their Colonization* (Boston: Lincoln and Edmands, 1827), 27–28.

18. Review of *The Practicability of Indian Reform, Embracing Their Colonization,* in *The American Baptist Magazine* 137 (May, 1828), 151. See also, William G. McLoughlin, *Cherokee Renascence in the New Republic* (Princeton: Princeton University Press, 1986), 277–301.

19. Letter from Evan Jones, May 1, 1828, *American Baptist Magazine* 139 (July, 1828), 213 [emphasis mine].

20. "Official Statement of Indian Schools," *The American Baptist Magazine* 134 (February, 1828), 64; McLoughlin, *Cherokees and Missionaries,* 175.

21. For mere legends and hypocrites, see *The American Baptist Magazine* 132 (December 1827), 364. For a different race, see *The American Baptist Magazine,* 100 (April, 1825), 111. For majority participation in a traditional rite (a new year ceremony), see *The American Baptist Magazine* 141 (September, 1828), 269. For simultaneous participation in Christianity and traditional religion, see Isaac Proctor to Jeremiah Evarts, December 11, 1827, American Board of Commissioners for Foreign Missions, Houghton Library, Harvard University [henceforth: ABCFM].

22. Journal of Lee Compere, postscript, March 1828, American Indian Correspondence, American Baptist Foreign Mission Societies, Records, 1817–1959, American Baptist Historical Society, Rochester, New York.

23. The myth is related in Grant Foreman, *Sequoyah* (Norman: University of Oklahoma Press, 1938), 21. Another version of the myth, recorded by a Moravian in 1815, is reprinted in Clemens de Baillou, "A Contribution to the Mythology and Conceptual World of the Cherokee Indians," *Ethnohistory* 8 (1961): 100–102. See also Hatley, "The Dividing Paths," 698–99.

24. See Albert V. Goodpasture, "The Paternity of Sequoya, The Inventor of the Cherokee Alphabet," *The Chronicles of Oklahoma* 1 (January, 1921): 121–130; Samuel C. Williams, "The Father of Sequoyah: Nathaniel Gist," *The Chronicles of Oklahoma* 15 (March, 1937): 3–20; William G. McLoughlin, *Cherokees and Missionaries,* 183.

25. See McLoughlin, *Renascence,* 350–354. During a conversation in July, 1991, in Lexington, Kentucky, Theda Perdue directed my attention to this subject.

26. "Invention of the Cherokee Alphabet," August, 13, 1828, the *Cherokee Phoenix;* see also the comments of Samuel Lorenzo Knapp, quoted in Foreman, 24–25.

27. McLoughlin, *Renascence,* 352–353. For knowledge of the alphabet, William Chamberlain's Journal, October 22, 1824, ABCFM; for letters in Cherokee, Isaac Proctor to Jeremiah Evarts, January 25, 1825, ABCFM.

28. McLoughlin, *Cherokees and Missionaries,* 185–186 [emphasis mine].

29. Harold David Williams, "The North Georgia Gold Rush" (Ph.D. dissertation, Auburn University, 1988); Mary Young, "Racism in Red and Black: Indians and Other Free People of Color in Georgia Law, Politics, and Removal Policy," *Georgia Historical Quarterly* 73 (Fall 1988): 492–518; Russell Thornton, "The Demography of the Trail of Tears Period: A New Estimate of Cherokee Population Losses," in *Cherokee Removal: Before and After,* ed. William L. Anderson (Athens: University of Georgia Press, 1991); David Kleit, "Living Under the Threat and Promise of Removal: Conflict and Cooperation in the Cherokee Country During the 1830s," unpublished paper presented at the 1993 Conference of the Society for Historians of the Early American Republic, July 22, 1993, Chapel Hill, North Carolina.

30. Mary Elizabeth Young, *Redskins, Ruffleshirts, and Rednecks: Indian Allotments in Alabama and Mississippi, 1830–1860* (Norman: University of Oklahoma Press, 1961); idem, "Tribal Reorganization in the Southeast, 1800–1842," 59–82; Marvin L. Ellis, III, "The Indian Fires Go Out: Removing the Creeks From Georgia and Alabama, 1825–1837," (M.A. thesis, Auburn University, 1982).

31. Williams, ed., *Adair's History,* 35; Edmond Atkin, *Indians of the Southern Colonial Frontier: The Edmond Atkin Report and Plan of 1755,* ed. by Wilbur Jacobs (Columbia, S.C., 1954), 35; William Bartram, *Travels Through North and South Carolina, Georgia, East and West Florida, the Cherokee Country, the Extensive Territories of the Muscogulges, or Creek Confederacy, and the Country of the Chactaws* (1791, rpt. New York: Penguin, 1988),

53–62; David Taitt, "Journal of David Taitt's Travels from Pensacola, West Florida, to and through the Country of the Upper and Lower Creeks, 1772," in *Travels in the American Colonies*, edited by Newton D. Mereness (New York: Macmillan Company, 1916), 507, 513, 524–525; Joel W. Martin, *Sacred Revolt: The Muskogees' Struggle for a New World* (Boston: Beacon Press, 1991), 65–69; Samuel J. Wells, "Rum, Skins, and Powder: A Choctaw Interpreter and The Treaty of Mount Dexter," *Chronicles of Oklahoma* 1983–84 61(4): 422–428; Blue Clark, "Chickasaw Colonization in Oklahoma," *Chronicles of Oklahoma* 1976 54(1): 44–59; White, *Roots of Dependency*, 69–92, 122.

32. Peter H. Wood, "The Changing Population of the Colonial South: An Overview by Race and Region, 1685–1790," 35–103, in *Powhatan's Mantle*, ed. Peter H. Wood, Gregory A. Waselkov, and Thomas M. Hatley, 59–60; Martin, *Sacred Revolt*, 46–113.

33. For stealing horses, abducting slaves, and killing cattle, see Timothy Barnard to Gov. George Hanley, January 18, 1789, May 27, 1789, November 6, 1789, Unpublished Letters, 86, 94, 98; Timothy Barnard to James Seagrove, July 13, 1792, April 19, 1793, June 20, 1793, Unpublished Letters, 120, 149, 174; Timothy Barnard to Major Henry Gaither, March 4, 1793, Unpublished Letters, 130; Daniel Stewart to General Gunn, November 2, 1796, Creek Indian Letters, Talks, and Treaties, 1705–1839, 420, Department of Archives and History of the State of Georgia, Atlanta, Georgia. For white traders dealing in stolen horses, see "A talk delivered by Mr. Barnard to the Indians assembled at the Cussetahs," March 22, 1793, Unpublished Letters, 132; Timothy Barnard to Major Henry Gaither, April 20, 1793, Unpublished Letters, 154; "A talk from the Big Warrior of the Cussetahs," May 2, 1793, Unpublished Letters, 164. For white poaching of Indian game and plundering of Indian property, see Timothy Barnard to James Seagrove, March 26, 1793, Unpublished Letters, 136; Proceedings of the Court of Enquiry, July 22, 1794, Creek Indian Letters, 387–390. For murder of individual whites, see Timothy Barnard to James Seagrove, May 10, 1792, Unpublished Letters, 116; Timothy Bernard to James Seagrove, April 9, 1793, Unpublished Letters, 142. For captives, see Timothy Barnard to James Seagrove, June 20, 1793, Unpublished Letters, 172. For the plunder of traders' stores, see Timothy Barnard to Major Henry Gaither, April 10, 1793, Unpublished Letters, 143. For intoxication as exonerating circumstance, "Journal of Thomas Bosomworth," August 25, 1752, 286.

34. For dissimulation with missionaries, see Carl Mauelshagen and Gerald H. Davis, trans., *Partners in the Lord's Work: The Diary of Two Moravian Missionaries in the Creek Indian Country*, Research Paper Number 21 (Atlanta: Georgia State College, 1969), 22; see also 30, 72. For silence and feigned ignorance, see Hawkins, *Letters, Journals, and Writings*, I: 47–48. For negotiating strategies, see ibid., II: 562; James F. Doster, *The Creek Indians and Their Florida Lands, 1740–1823* (New York: Garland Publishing, 1974), II: 16; Hoboheilthlee Micco [Hopoithle Miko] to the President of the United States, May 15, 1811, Letters Received by the Office of the Secretary of War on Indian Affairs, 1800–1823, Microcopy #M271 Roll #1 Frame 554, U.S. National Archives, Washington.

35. See James C. Scott, *Domination and the Arts of Resistance: Hidden Transcripts* (New Haven: Yale University Press, 1990). Scott defines the "*public transcript* as a shorthand way of describing the open interaction between subordinates and those who dominate"(2). Hidden transcripts, in contrast, are not expressed so openly. On the one hand, "every subordinate group creates, out of its ordeal, a 'hidden transcript' that represents a critique of power spoken behind the back of the dominant." On the other, "the powerful, for their part, also develop a hidden transcript script representing the practices and claims of their rule that cannot be openly avowed" (xii).

36. See *Subaltern Studies: Writings on South Asian History and Society, III*, ed. Ranajit Guha (Oxford: Oxford University Press, 1984); Gayatri Spivak, "Subaltern Studies: Deconstructing Historiography," 197–221, in *In Other Worlds: Essays in Cultural Politics* (New York: Methuen, 1987); Ranahit Guha and Gayatri Chakravorty Spivak, eds., *Selected Subaltern Studies* (New York: Oxford University Press, 1988).

37. William Simpson, August 20, 1803, Letters Received by Sec. of War, Indian Affairs, 1800–1823, Microfilm M-271, Reel 1, NARG 75; William S. Coker and Thomas D. Watson, *Indian Traders of the Southeastern Spanish Borderlands, Panton, Leslie and Company and John Forbes and Company, 1783–1847* (University of West Florida Press: Pensacola, 1986), 228.

38. Timothy Barnard to James Seagrove, July 2, 1793, Unpublished Letters of Timothy Barnard, 1784–1820, 188, Department of Archives and History of the State of Georgia, Atlanta, Georgia.

39. For U.S. collection efforts, see Hawkins, *Letters, Journals and Writings*, 476, 483, 505, 526–527, Coker and Watson, *Indian Traders of the*

*Southeastern Spanish Borderlands*, 227–30, 243–72; Florette Henri, *The Southern Indians and Benjamin Hawkins, 1796–1816* (Norman: University of Oklahoma Press, 1986), 219–220, 244–253; White, *Roots of Dependency*, 95–96; Samuel J. Wells, "Federal Indian Policy: From Accommodation to Removal," 181–213, in *The Choctaw Before Removal*, 186–87, 208n17.

40. Hassig, "Internal Conflict in the Creek War of 1813–1814," 256; Waselkov and Wood, "The Creek War of 1813–1814," 7; Hawkins, *Letters, Writings and Journals*, 631–632, 632–634; Frank Lawrence Owsley, Jr., *The Struggle for the Gulf Borderlands: The Creek War and the Battle of New Orleans, 1812–1815* (Gainesville: University Presses of Florida, 1981), 15–16. See also Douglas Barber, "Council Government and the Genesis of the Creek War," *Alabama Review* 1985 (3): 163–174; Martin, *Sacred Revolt*, 125.

41. Martin, *Sacred Revolt*, 87–113; Henri, *The Southern Indians*, 83–111.

42. Halbert and Ball, *The Creek War*, 71. Geologists refer to this event as the New Madrid earthquake and estimate that it would have measured 8.2 on the Richter scale, thus making it the largest such event to have occurred in North America in the last several centuries. See Moravian Mission Diary entry, Springplace, Georgia, February 10, 1811, Moravian Archives, Winston-Salem, North Carolina, quoted in McLoughlin, *The Cherokee Ghost Dance*, Appendix E, 142; Francis Howard to Dr. Porter, Jefferson, Georgia, February 14, 1812, "Creek Indian Letters, Talks and Treaties, 1782–1839," ed. Louise Frederick Hays, Georgia Department of Archives and History, Atlanta, Georgia; Mauelshagen and Davis, trans. and eds., *Partners in the Lord's Work*, 68; Moravian Mission Diary entry, Springplace, Georgia, December 17, 1811, Moravian Archives, Winston-Salem North Carolina, quoted in McLoughlin, *The Cherokee Ghost Dance*, Appendix E, 143; R. A. Eppley, *Earthquake History of the United States, Part I* (Washington: Government Printing Office, 1965), 67–68; Yamaguchi, "Macon County, Alabama," 197; *Niles Weekly Register*, Jan. 4, 1812.

43. Homi Bhabha theorizes the problematic of the Book in the colonial context in his articles, "Signs Taken for Wonders: Questions of Ambivalence and Authority under a Tree Outside Delhi, May 1817," *Critical Inquiry* 12 (1985), 144–165; and idem, "Of Mimicry and Man: The Ambivalence of Colonial Discourse," *October* 28 (1984), 125–133; See also Peter Worsley, *The Trumpet Shall Sound*, 241.

44. Mauelshagen and Davis, trans. and eds., *Partners in the Lords' Work*, 53.

45. The following discussion of shamans is based upon Bartram, *Travels*, 390; Jean Bernard-Bossu, *Travels*, 149; Wiliams, *Adair's History*, 90; Swanton, "Creek Ethnographic and Vocabulary Notes"; idem, *The Indians of the Southeastern United States*, 774; Wright, *Creeks and Seminoles*, 157–159; Waselkov and Wood, "The Creek War of 1813–1814," 4.

46. Williams, ed., *Adair's History*, 250 [237].

47. F. L. Cherry, "History of Opelika," *The Alabama Historical Quarterly* Vol. 15, No. 2 (1953): 184; See also, Charles Hudson, "Uktena: A Cherokee Anomalous Monster," *Journal of Cherokee Studies* 3/2 (Spring 1978): 62–75; Raymond D. Fogelson, "Windigo Goes South: Stoneclad among the Cherokees," in *Manlike Monsters on Trial: Early Records and Modern Evidence*, eds. Marjorie M. Halpin and Michael M. Ames (Vancouver: University of British Columbia Press, 1980): 132–151.

48. Nunez, "Creek Nativism," 149.

49. Isaacs had visited Tecumseh in the northwest. According to Woodward, Isaacs was a Muskogee from the town of "Coowersortda [Coosaudee]" (*Woodward's Reminiscences*, 36–37).

50. John Innerarity to James Innerarity, July 27, 1813, Creek Indian Letters, 797. For a much fuller development of the different shamans' interpretations, see Martin, *Sacred Revolt*, 114–149.

51. Hawkins, *Letters, Journals and Writings*, 652. "Testimony of James Moore," July 13, 1813, Creek Indian Letters, 785. For Redstick coercion, see Hawkins, *Letters, Journal and Writings*, 666, 669, 673.

52. "Report of Alexander Cornells, interpreter, to Colonel Hawkins," June 22, 1813, *American State Papers: Indian Affairs* (Washington: Gales and Seaton, 1832), I, 845–846; Hawkins, *Letters, Journals and Writings*, II: 641; Frank Lawrence Owsley, Jr., *The Struggle for the Gulf Borderlands: The Creek War and the Battle of New Orleans, 1812–1815* (Gainesville: University Presses of Florida, 1981), 17; Martin, *Sacred Revolt*, 114–149.

53. Dowd, *A Spirited Resistance*, 34, 138.

54. Nunez, "Creek Nativism," 146. For the importance of rumor in anti-colonial movements, see Kenelm Burridge, *New Heaven, New Earth: A Study of Millenarian Activities* (New York: Schocken Books, 1969), 106–107; Shahid Amin, "Gandhi as Mahatma: Gorakhpur District, Eastern UP, 1921–22," 1–61, in *Subaltern Studies: Writings on South Asian History and Society, III*, ed. Ranajit Guha (Oxford: Oxford University Press, 1984); James Scott, *Domination and the Arts of Resistance*, 144–148.

55. Hawkins, *Letters, Journals and Writings*, 562.

56. Ibid., 612, 636, 646, 648, 650–51, 654–57, 664, 666, 672. For the migration of Lower Muskogees to Florida, see William C. Sturtevant, "Creek Into Seminole," In *North American Indians in Historical Perspective*, ed. Eleanor Burke Leacock and Nancy Oestreich Lurie (New York: Random House, 1971); Bartram, *Travels*, 181–182. For descriptions of ample game in Florida, see ibid., 165, 170, 172.

57. McLoughlin, *Cherokee Renascence*, 372–375; Edwin C. McReynolds, *Oklahoma: A History of the Sooner State* (Norman: University of Oklahoma Press, 1954), 122–23.

58. Notes Furnished A. J. Pickett by the Rev. Lee Compere of Mississippi relating to the Creek Indians among whom he lived as a Missionary, Albert J. Pickett Papers, Notes upon the History of Alabama, section 24, Alabama Department of Archives and History, Montgomery, Alabama.

59. For "considered as a desecration," John Howard Payne, "The Green-Corn Dance," *Continental Monthly*, Vol. 1 (1862), 24.

60. For ignoring, protesting, and delaying, *The American Baptist Magazine* 125 (May 1827): 143–146.

61. Journal of Lee Compere, April 25, 1828, American Indian Correspondence.

# WOMEN'S HISTORY *IS* AMERICAN RELIGIOUS HISTORY

*Ann Braude*

For more than two decades, scholars in the field of women's studies have been working to establish the importance of women's experience in place of the assumption that men adequately represent the human norm. In the area of American religious history this new scholarship has made clear that women have constituted the majority of participants in religious activities and institutions throughout American history. In this essay Ann Braude employs this essential insight to challenge three organizing themes that have been used to structure the narrative of American religious history—that religion: declined in the colonial period; was feminized in Victorian America; and gave way to a secular order in the twentieth century. Braude argues that all three of these influential motifs are historical fictions driven by the assumption that the public influence of the Protestant clergy is the most important measure of the role of religion in American society. In contrast, Braude holds that focusing on the increasing vigor of women's religious lives and roles is a more useful theme for narrating the story of American religion. Rather than religion declining in the colonial period, Braude argues that during this period women moved toward a greater spiritual equality with men. Instead of religion becoming more privatized during the nineteenth century, she sees women assuming more public roles as guardians of private morality and piety. Finally, differing from the dominant view that religion has become more secularized in the twentieth century, the author sees religious women exercising more public authority, first as voters and as shapers of the welfare state during the Progressive Era, then as members of the ordained clergy following the rise of feminism in the 1970s. Instead of continuing to employ the established narrative that focuses on the absence of men, Ann Braude concludes that a better theme for the story of American religion may be found in the presence of women.

Reprinted by permission from Ann Braude, "Women's History *Is* American Religious History," in *Retelling U.S. Religious History*, Thomas A. Tweed, ed. (Berkeley: California, 1997), 87–107.

# 8

# WOMEN'S HISTORY *IS* AMERICAN RELIGIOUS HISTORY

*Ann Braude*

IN AMERICA, women go to church. This essay explores how we would tell the story of American religion if we took as our point of departure the fact that women constitute the majority of participants in religious activities and institutions. It reexamines from this vantage point three influential motifs that have been used to structure the narrative of American religious history—declension, feminization, and secularization. Each of these, in turn, rests on the respective historical claims that religion declined in the colonial period, was feminized in Victorian America, and gave way to a secular order in the twentieth century. I believe that attention to gender helps to explain why these motifs, and the historical claims that ground them, have held such explanatory power for historians even though, from an empirical perspective, they never happened. Interpreters have turned to these themes to narrate American religious history not because they point to demonstrable demographic or institutional shifts. Rather, their popularity as organizing ideas seems to reveal more about historians' and churchmen's anxieties about the role of religion in American society, anxieties closely tied to women's numerical dominance in churches, synagogues, and temples. From this perspective, the historical developments that these three themes attempt to explain concern increase, not decrease. To put it differently, the motif of the story I narrate is female presence rather than male absence. The plot, which I can only suggest here, traces the increasing vigor of women's religious lives and roles, discerning some of the same chronological shifts as older narratives, but interpreting them differently. The story shifts, I argue, as women move toward spiritual equality with men in the colonial period, as they assume public roles because of their positions as guardians of private morality and piety during the nineteenth century, and, in the twentieth, as women exercise public moral authority first as voters and as shapers of the welfare state during the Progressive Era, then as members of the ordained clergy following the rise of feminism in the 1970s. This essay suggests that narratives focusing on the absence of men reflect theological concerns of Reformed Protestantism, and that a more useful theme for the story of American religion may be found in the presence of women.[1]

## THE FEMALE MAJORITY

One cannot tell a story unless one knows who the characters are. Women constitute the majority of participants in religion in the United States, and have wherever Christianity has become the dominant faith in North America. Indeed, the numerical dominance of women in all but a few religious groups constitutes one of the most consistent features of American religion, and one of the least explained. Beginning in the early seventeenth century, more women than men could give convincing accounts of the rigorous dealings between God and the soul prerequisite to membership in Puritan churches. Women have outnumbered men in Protestant churches among whites and blacks, in the North and the South, and across denominations.[2] Among Catholics, women's vocations to the religious life have far outnumbered men's, while lay women have participated disproportionately in diverse devotional practices.[3] Women's religiosity still exceeds men's when studies control for educational level and workforce participation. While there is no comprehensive study analyzing sex ratios in religious affiliation, all of the available case studies indicate female majorities: there is no counter-example in which men are found to sustain a substantial religious group over a significant period of time. Studies documenting increases in male participation usually show only a temporary decrease in the size of a consistent female majority.[4] The only exceptions are groups in which religious affiliation is contiguous with membership in an organic community (Hasidic Jews, Native American tribal groups), or small groups that draw unusually sharp boundaries between themselves and the larger culture (Unification Church, International Society for Krishna Consciousness, Nation of Islam).

These exceptions go a long way toward proving the rule: they define group identity by rejection of the dominant values and structures of American society, explicitly dissenting from American gender roles. Likewise, for some immigrant groups increased participation by women in religious institutions has been an important feature of Americanization (for example, Reform and Conservative Jews).[5] We do not yet have adequate information about the response of Muslim, Hindu, and Buddhist immigrant groups to American gender norms for religious participation. However, already there are indications that women's participation in mosque services (discouraged or prohibited in many Islamic countries) plays an increasingly important role in the religious identity of American Muslim women in immigrant communities. It also is clear that among non-Asian Americans who have adopted Buddhism, Asian gender norms have been rejected in favor of American expectations for women's institutional participation.[6]

To say that women go to church in the United States is not to say that other national cultures may not present similar or even more extreme patterns, but the goal of this essay is to examine the significance of women's numerical dominance for telling the story of American religious history.[7] Women have made religious institutions possible by providing audiences for preaching, participants for rituals, the material and financial support for religious buildings, and, perhaps most important, by inculcating faith in their children to provide the next generation of participants. There could be no lone man in the pulpit without the mass of women who fill the pews. There would be no clergy, no seminaries to train them, no theology to teach them, and no hierarchies to ordain them, unless women supported all of these institutions from which they historically have been excluded—and still are by Catholics, conservative Protestants, and Orthodox Jews. To understand the history of religion in America, one must ask what made each group's teachings and practices meaningful to its female members.

While women have been the mainstays of the largest and most powerful American religious groups, they also have been leaders of dissent. Throughout most of American history, women have been barred from leadership as clergy, elders, or theologians, or, until the twentieth century, as lay leaders. Because women have been excluded from religious leadership at the same time that they have been elevated for their natural piety, it is not surprising that they have played a prominent role in religious dissent. Well-known leaders such as Mary Baker Eddy, Ellen Gould White, Ann Lee, Helena Blavatsky, and Aimee Semple McPherson played key roles as religious innovators.[8] It is precisely the consistency of the religious establishment in restricting women's leadership and confining their self-expression that ensures that the rejection of conventional gender roles and of conventional religious beliefs often will go hand in hand. From Anne Hutchinson to Ann Lee to Starhawk, examples abound in which women's articulation of distinctive religious views have been perceived as presenting fundamental threats to the well-ordered (patriarchal) society. Thus women's religious leadership, itself a dissent from prevailing norms, will be especially visible among dissident religious groups. Elsewhere I have explored the role of such groups in encouraging women's leadership and the role of women in promoting religious dissent.[9] This essay, in contrast, focuses on women's role as the backbone of the vast majority of well-established religious groups whose values constitute the status quo of American morality. Women's significance in groups considered marginal must not be allowed to obscure their centrality in maintaining what scholars traditionally have called the "mainstream." Women's history *is* American religious history.

Having established that women will be the main characters, the task of constructing a narrative of American religious history remains extremely difficult. Women are present in every class, race, and ethnicity: they are immigrants and natives, old and young, educated and illiterate, northern and southern, Mexican and Canadian. They reside in every geographical area, they are urban and rural, single and married, theologians and devotees. They belong to every American religious group. In short, American women are as diverse as the country itself, and as difficult to categorize. They stand somewhere within every "site" from which American religion can be viewed. What women share is a differential in power between themselves and their male peers, and the common experiences of the roles to which society has assigned them. American religious history is founded on a paradox: its institutions have relied for their existence on the very group they have disenfranchised. The willingness of women to participate in the institution that enforces their subordination and provides the cosmological justification for it requires explanation, but women have done more than participate. They have embraced the churches and the belief systems they teach, finding special meaning there for their lives as women and defending them against a variety of threats from without.

If women are to be the main characters, then, power must be the subplot, whatever the main event. The numerical dominance of women among the laity always must be viewed in tandem with the exclusion of women from institutional religious authority. Robert A. Orsi's observation about devotional Catholicism—that it is practiced *by* women in the presence of male authority—has relevance to a broad spectrum of American religion. The theme of many stories of American religion is a strong association of lay piety with

femininity and of clerical roles with masculinity. As Mary Maples Dunn puts it, "passive females, ruled over by ministers . . . personify Christian virtue."[10] Church structures reified
gender hierarchies: just as women failed to receive recognition, authority, or remuneration
for domestic labor that made the household possible, their role as the backbone of the
church went unnoticed and unrewarded. The wealth of scholarship produced over the last
twenty years showing the centrality of women in sustaining American Christianity cannot
be interpreted as demonstrating publicly acknowledged female dominance. The conceit of
male dominance has been essential to the logic of American religion.

This is not to suggest that women did not exert other types of power as a result of their
religious beliefs and activities. For example, the biographies of exceptional female historical figures are filled with accounts of how personal piety led to spiritual empowerment.
Piety also has provided ordinary women with a source of moral power in the family, in the
community, and most important, in their own lives, where religious practice has enabled
generations of women to endure apparently unendurable situations. In assessing women's
involvement in religion, we should not limit our perception of power to those forms that
are publicly recognized within religious institutions. New narratives then must both expand accepted notions of power *and* deal seriously with the meaning and consequences of
women's exclusion from official or institutional power. Furthermore, we must not confuse
the ability to endure with the opportunity to influence. Religion may provide one without
the other—and to understand women's experience we must distinguish between them.

For the most part, scholars of religion have accepted the claims made by church hierarchies that it is the types of power that men wield that are important, and that men's monopoly on institutional authority means that the characters of the story of American
religion should exclude the majority of participants. Over and over, studies have perpetuated through their subject matter the contention that the views of one man in the pulpit
are more important than those of the many women in the pews. Ironically, this characterization applies equally to recent accounts focused on "democratic" religious movements
that "empowered ordinary people."[11] No survey history of American religion has taken
women's presence into account in structuring its narrative; most have ignored women's
role completely.[12]

This essay takes both women's centrality in American religion and their lack of authority as its points of departure. The first step required by this reorientation is a simple one—
to view the story of religion in America as the story of women's presence. The story begins
when women are there. Where women are present, religion flourishes; where they are absent, it does not. While this formula seems overly simple, it is a necessary corrective to the
distortions caused by the absence of the central characters from standard narratives. Such
a crude statement cannot tell the whole story of any American religion, but few stories can
be told without it. Similarly, once women's presence is acknowledged, few stories can be
told without reference to the gendered power dynamics of religious systems. This does not
mean that women have been passive victims of religious ideologies. Rather, it means that
the way women negotiated their roles within the ideologies always must be kept in view.
Holding these two lenses simultaneously before the data of history requires a reevaluation
of nearly every story of American religion. To illustrate how such reevaluation can proceed, I begin by examining influential narrative motifs derived from the "master narrative"
of American religion, the story of reformed Anglo-Protestantism. The lens of women's his-

tory brings into focus both the gender specificity and the cultural and religious particularity of the themes.

## THE HISTORY OF THE MINORITY

The story of Anglo-Protestantism in North America has been told as a story of linear progress and, conversely, as a tale of constant decline since an edenic Puritan moment when religious and civil authority combined in perfect harmony. Here I focus on the second interpretive tradition, the ideological agenda of which is less transparent than that of the first. I turn the lens of gender on three interrelated narrative fictions that have been used to structure accounts of American religious history: declension, feminization, and secularization. I call these "narrative fictions" because the processes they describe cannot be discerned from empirical data about church membership or structures. Churches did not decline in Puritan New England; they did not experience a new female majority in the nineteenth century; nor did they disappear in the twentieth. All three fictions result from the assumption that the public influence of the Protestant clergy is the most important measure of the role of religion in American society. All assert that there was a time (immediately before whatever period is being studied) when Protestant ministers enjoyed a degree of authority that has since been undermined, and that this constitutes a stage in the decline of religion in the modern world.

Mary Maples Dunn has suggested of Puritan New England that "what was seen as a 'declension' was only a loss of *male* piety."[13] Numerous additional studies document that concerns about declension among both seventeenth-century divines and twentieth-century historians correlate not with decreases in church membership but rather with decreases in the proportion of men among church members. What needs to be added to Dunn's statement is that female majorities are the norm in American religious groups, so the perception that they constitute a "declension" is a normative assertion about the superior value of male church membership rather than an empirical observation. It is the temporary gender equity characterizing some first-generation Puritan churches, not the development of a predominantly female laity, that departs from American norms. Gender balance in religion seems to result from gender imbalance in the population. The disproportionate number of men among the first generation of English immigrants artificially inflated the proportion of male church members, a pattern that was repeated in many immigrant and frontier populations.[14] Permanent female majorities appear within twenty years in New England churches, and their stability has been documented for the subsequent three hundred years. While the size of the female majority may vary, its presence is a constant, not a trend.[15]

Declension has been a primary theme of American religious history since Cotton and Increase Mather merged historical narrative and jeremiad to criticize the "great and visible decay in the power of Godliness among many professors in these Churches."[16] Even Perry Miller, who made declension a central theme of modern Puritan studies, warned that we should not take literally accounts of religious decline penned by clergy who used self-denunciation as an exhortation to piety.[17] Nevertheless, the term entered the historiography to connote a falling away from the intellectual rigors of a consistent Calvinism expressed in relaxed standards for church membership indicating a loosening of the doctrine of predestination. While subsequent generations of historians contested particulars of Miller's account, they accepted the fundamental dynamic that fueled it—the view that the primary threat to religion in American culture came from the marketplace, and from a Protestant ethic that placed worldly endeavors in competition with otherworldly concerns. This way of telling the story of American religion anticipates the notion of "separate spheres," so widely debated among historians of American women, and the concept of "feminization."

The term *feminization* has been used to describe a refashioning of church teachings in response to a rise in the female membership, usually identified as occurring between the Revolution and the Civil War. Barbara Welter applied the term *feminization* to American religion, explaining that after the American Revolution the critical importance of political and economic activity made them "more competitive, more aggressive," that is, more "masculine." At the same time, "Religion, along with the family . . . was not very important, and so became the property of the ladies . . . more domesticated, more emotional, more soft and accommodating—in a word, more 'feminine.'" The most influential use of the term was in Ann Douglas's *The Feminization of American Culture*, where the word referred to a loss of nerve on the part of the Protestant ministry who conspired with their female supporters to cut the spine out of American culture. Just as her teacher Perry Miller coined the term *declension* to describe a falling away from the difficult doctrines of Calvinist theology during the Puritan period, Douglas found the same process in the nineteenth century, but blamed it on women. As we have seen, however, female majorities were nothing new in the nineteenth century. Nor were they a secret. Cotton Mather knew that "there are far more godly women in the world than godly men" in the seventeenth century, and he made sure his congregation did too. So if female majorities alone could lead to a specific type of theological change, they ought to have done so before the nineteenth century. What Richard Shiels describes as "the feminization of American Congregationalism" consists of an increase in the size of the female majority from 60 percent during most of the eighteenth century to 70 percent during the early national period. This was a notable change, but was it a "feminization"? His finding that the "final decades of the Second Great Awakening checked the feminization process but did not reverse it" is characteristic of historians' use of the term to describe something like a contagious disease.[18] The term *feminization*, then, is a misnomer when applied to religious demographics. Like the term *declension*, it expresses a nostalgia for a religious landscape that never existed.

Once we have severed feminization from its demographic implications, we still must ask whether it has utility in describing ideological change. Here the concept has been used to join together the rise of domesticity and the rise of liberal theology in Protestantism. While this link does seem to hold true for the liberal denominations studied by Ann Douglas, those denominations were losing ground to other groups during the nineteenth century, and so cannot be said to represent American culture. But domestic ideology never was limited to advocates of a single theological persuasion. American Catholics adopted all the accoutrements of domesticity without notable theological change, and conservative Protestants took to it at least as well as liberals. If the historiography of the nineteenth century has not demonstrated amply that religious groups can laud domesticity and conservative theology, then the data of the twentieth makes it abundantly clear. Betty De Berg, for example, has argued that the rise of Fundamentalism in the 1920s may be seen as an attempt to provide a theological foundation for the preservation of domestic values.[19] Since the 1960s, domestic values have been associated much more closely with religious conservatives than with liberals. Perhaps this simply reflects liberals' greater receptivity to change:

when domesticity was new it was championed by liberals; when it had become the status quo it found favor with conservatives. Nevertheless, the sympathy between domestic values and certain theological doctrines cannot adequately explain its rise and persistence in American culture.

Of the three themes I have proposed to view through the lens of gender, secularization is the most far-reaching in its implications. It also has been the most influential among American intellectuals and has by far the largest scholarly literature. It forms an aspect of the theory of modernization that lies at the basis of modern sociology. Secularization theory has been called a myth by some contemporary sociologists, defended by others, and reinterpreted with ever-increasing subtlety.[20] It lies far beyond the scope of this essay to offer a full (or even brief) treatment of the debate over secularization. However, I include it here because it continues the tradition of discerning declines in the influence of religion that are not reflected in declines in church membership or institutional strength. In contrast to the expectations of sociologists, statistics show that per capita church membership in the United States increased steadily throughout the nineteenth century, beginning at less than 10 percent and reaching stunningly high rates (67 to 76 percent) that have persisted throughout the twentieth century.[21]

Does the discrepancy between the perception of secularization and rising rates of church membership have anything to do with gender? The apparent paradox often is explained by describing a relocation of religion's influence from the public realm to the private. The theme of secularization is thus closely related to another narrative fiction—the highly gendered concept of "separate spheres," in which a public/private dichotomy is used to describe the distinctive roles of men and women in society. While the terms *public* and *private* have been used to mean different things by historians debating the existence of a "woman's sphere" and by sociologists trying to describe the process of modernization, both depend on a dichotomy that has strongly gendered associations. John Murray Cuddihy, for example, has described the process of assimilation for nineteenth-century Jews as learning to be "private in public" by adopting the decorum and respectability of bourgeois culture.[22] In other words, the price of admission to the public realm of civil society was leaving one's religion at home, where it would influence only private behavior. Secularization can mean the same thing as feminization, a decline in religion's efficacy in a public realm associated with men's activities, concurrent with persistent or increased influence in a private realm associated with women and the family.

I have argued that declension, feminization, and secularization never happened, if the terms are understood in their most overt sense. They can be said to have happened only if they are understood as referring not to demographic shifts but rather to anxieties caused by the belief that such shifts were occurring or the fear that they might occur. In each case, the term expresses nostalgia for a world that never existed, a world in which men went to church and were as moved as women by what they heard there, a world in which the clergy felt they had precisely as much public influence as they should. Perhaps it is not women who have sentimentalized American Protestantism, but rather the male clergy who have cherished a romantic notion of a patriarchal past.

## THE HISTORY OF THE MAJORITY

If American religious history is viewed from a perspective in which women are assumed to hold the central position in the narrative, the possibility arises that the aforementioned anxieties result not from declines in religion but rather from advances, advances in both the quality and the quantity of women's participation in American Protestantism. Attention to power discrepancies further reveals that all three narrative fictions incorporate a judgment that the health and integrity of a religious group are seriously threatened by any increase in the visibility or influence of its female members. Because women are viewed as the less powerful half of society, their numerical dominance is interpreted as a decline in power for a religious institution. Thus declension, feminization, and secularization incorporate into the story of American religion assumptions about women's powerlessness derived from the value systems of American Protestantism. If the assumption of women's powerlessness is rejected (or at least bracketed), and women's participation is viewed as a neutral or conceivably even as a positive contribution to a religious institution, then the story of American religion might have a very different shape. The cultural transitions referred to as declension, feminization, and secularization might be seen as positive developments in American Protestantism: the colonial period saw an increase in the spiritual status and role of women; the nineteenth century saw a vast increase in the activities and influence of the female laity; and the twentieth century, in a process that is still ongoing, has witnessed the rise of female clergy and a reorientation of liturgy and theology based on women's experience.

Historians of American women have interpreted these transitions primarily in terms of a shift away from the longstanding Christian view of women as temptresses in league with the devil toward a view of women as models of Christian virtue. Throughout Christian history women have been associated both with Eve, symbol of human disobedience to God, and with Mary, model of Christian submission. Puritan scholars have argued that reformed theology's rejection of celibacy and elevation of the family marked a watershed, shifting the balance toward a positive view of women's nature. If grace was to be attained within marriage and the family, mothers must join fathers as religious exemplars. While the newly spiritualized family elevated the authority of the father, it did so at the expense of the church hierarchy, increasing the role of the laity in general, so that women's religious role also was enhanced. Likewise, women shared in the religious empowerment of a newly literate laity, who could read the Bible for themselves. Puritan ministers portrayed women as formed by God in order to serve as helpmates to their husbands, in both material and spiritual goals. To support such a view, they had to defend women against the charge that they drew men into sin, and argue instead for women's spiritual equality with men.[23]

On an institutional level, the Puritan notion of church membership demonstrated the importance of women's religious role. Church membership was in itself a new concept. Before the advent of Protestantism all residents of a geographical area surrounding a church belonged to that parish, saints and sinners alike. The Puritan notion of a church gathered out of the world, composed only of those few whom God had predestined for salvation, drew attention to the fact that more women than men could meet the membership requirements, providing a convincing account of the evidence for their own salvation.

During the eighteenth century, the rise of Evangelicalism enshrined a religious style that elevated qualities associated with femininity as normative. The model conversion experience of the Great Awakening encouraged an emotional and sensual surrender in which both male and female saints became "brides" of Christ. The relative spiritual equality of the period produced remarkably similar accounts of the conversion experience from men and women—but both partook of qualities considered feminine.[24]

By the nineteenth century, the balance between Eve and Mary in Protestant prescriptive literature had tipped so far that women were portrayed as inherently pious by nature. A society nervous about the implications of moving production and economic activity out of the home elevated domestic virtues into a religious calling for women. In Barbara Welter's classic formulation, a True Woman of the nineteenth century was pure, pious, passive, and domestic. Each of these characteristics was seen as mutually reinforcing: women were believed to protect their purity by restricting their activities to the so-called domestic sphere. There they could maintain pristine homes untainted by the men's sphere of the marketplace, where competition and self-interest would breed immorality if not tempered by the influence of pure wives and mothers. In the home, mothers provided a Christian atmosphere through loving example and self-sacrifice, not through the exercise of authority. For women, teachings about family life and social relations harmonized exactly with religious instruction. "Thy will, not mine, be done" summarized the appropriate attitude for the ideal wife and daughter as well as for the ideal Christian.[25]

While more subtle observers acknowledge that positive and negative valuations of women's nature have coexisted throughout American religious history, many agree that among Protestants the balance had shifted in favor of a positive view by the Victorian period. Rather than assigning this shift to a particular demographic moment, Nancy Cott sees it as a gradual transition occurring between the seventeenth and nineteenth centuries. Most important, she sees the religious notion that women as a group shared a positive moral "nature" as a prerequisite to the gender consciousness that allowed the rise of women's movements. While domestic ideology reflected Protestant anxieties about religious, cultural, and racial diversity, it was by no means limited to a single social or religious group. Historians most frequently associate domesticity with middle-class Anglo-Protestants in the mid-nineteenth century, but substantial evidence indicates that its impact crossed economic, racial, and ethnic boundaries and continued into the twentieth century, reasserting itself in a modern version following World War II. A growing literature documents domestic ideology among Catholics, Jews, African American Protestants, Asian American immigrants, and white working-class Protestants.[26]

Yet the story of religion in nineteenth-century America cannot be told simply by replacing "feminization" with "domesticity." Domestic ideology, as I argued earlier, ran wide and deep through American culture, and did not require a specific theological outlook. It could be—and was—used to argue for or against the ordination of women, for or against women's education, for or against suffrage. The rise of Evangelicalism both reinforced and challenged the notion that a woman's place was in the home. The urgency of evangelical imperatives in revivalist denominations authorized new roles for women both within and outside the home.[27] Even as women departed daily from the unrealistic ideology of the Cult of True Womanhood, they used its assumptions about women's natural piety to assert authority in the home and in the public realm. From the antebellum American Female Moral Reform Society to Another Mother for Peace in the 1960s, women embraced claims about moral superiority based on religious gender ideologies.[28] In the ideology of separate spheres for men and women, the church occupied an awkward indeterminate status: while it was clearly beyond the privacy of the home, it was a religiously sanctioned place for women.

Evangelical morality allowed women to criticize, and sometimes control, men's behavior. It extended the sphere of women's influence far beyond the home. But women also had to live by the values through which they asserted public authority, so the transition from temptress to moral model was not without cost. In the old view of woman as temptress her power to threaten male virtue resulted from her sexuality. Consequently, women's moral elevation required their sexual disempowerment. Frank acknowledgment of sexual desire in women during the colonial period gave way to a vigorous denial of its existence in the nineteenth century. Nancy Cott has argued that women gained a great deal by accepting the restrictions on their behavior required by an evangelical moral code. "Passionlessness," in her view, "was on the other side of the coin which paid, so to speak, for women's admission to moral equality."[29]

But women's sexuality (and the religious problems it posed to men) did not, of course, disappear when it was denied in prescriptive literature; nor did all women live up to Protestant ideals of femininity. The view of woman as temptress, then, did not dissolve with the rise of Evangelicalism and domestic ideology. In fact, the more responsibility the churches assigned to women for the spiritual welfare of their families, the greater the repercussions of any lapses in feminine purity. Any moral failing on the part of husband or child might ultimately be laid on a woman who failed to be "true." Thus women's moral ascendence did not mark the demise of negative views of women. As Carol Karlsen has shown in the context of colonial New England, the two views needed each other. The risk of being found guilty of witchcraft for evincing traits such as anger or avarice, which were unfeminine and un-Christian, functioned to encourage obedient Christian character in all women. Likewise, in the nineteenth and twentieth centuries, demonic images of women who fail to live up to their "nature" play a crucial role in defining normative Christian roles by contrast. While Puritan scholars have demonstrated that the idea of women as "Handmaidens of the Lord" was not a Victorian invention, scholars of twentieth-century Fundamentalism have shown that a view of women as "Handmaidens of the Devil" could be applied to a World War II pin-up girl as easily (if not as harshly) as to a seventeenth-century woman accused of witchcraft.[30] While the shift toward positive views of woman's nature is a major event in the story of American religion, it is crucial to remember that it remains by definition incomplete, that it is not a positive valuation of women qua women, but rather of an ideal that few women ever can attain.

Nevertheless, the increased emphasis on women's presumed natural piety marked a major transition in American religious history, because it meant that women could begin to use religion to assert moral authority. Rather than a decline in religious institutions, this shift inaugurated a stunning proliferation of organizations composed exclusively of women intent on promoting Protestant values. These were the groups that facilitated the existence of religious institutions by supporting the training of clergy, sponsoring missionaries and evangelists, maintaining the sanctuary, and providing a host of other unglamorous services. While some, such as the ubiquitous Maternal Associations, had private goals like praying for the conversion of members' children, even this served an institutional function, because converted children would become church members, supplying the most fundamental institutional need. But many of the new women's groups hoped to have a direct impact on public life. Antebellum Female Moral Reform Societies, for example, organized not only to rescue fallen women but also to control the behavior of men who patronized prostitutes. In contrast to the prescriptions of domestic literature urging women to rely on private influence to change men's behavior, religiously motivated reform women understood the public sphere as an appropriate arena of activity and as a site where they might promote their moral agenda. The New York Society, for example, published the names of men who patronized prostitutes or seduced unmarried women.[31]

Beyond these more subtle evidences of women's centrality to the progress of religious institutions in the nineteenth century, women's organizations were crucial to the three most important reform movements of the nineteenth century—antislavery, temperance, and missions. Each of these movements effectively promoted evangelical Protestant values as a basis for political action, the first two resulting in constitutional amendments and the third becoming intertwined with United States foreign policy. In each case, organizations of Protestant women developed influential gender-based theoretical justifications for the reform, as well as providing financial support. Leaders like Frances Willard articulated a "social gospel" to a broader spectrum of Christians than those affected by the later, male liberals more identified with the term. Women's religious activism advanced the presence of Protestantism in public political discourse and advanced new priorities that would transform the denominations.[32]

By the beginning of the twentieth century, women's organizations had become so successful as promoters of Protestant churches that they were perceived as a threat by male church leaders. With membership far outnumbering that of denominational counterparts led by men, women's missionary societies pursued a distinctive agenda based on women's values, support for women missionaries, and social services for women in the mission field. Because women's missionary societies were organized on a national level, they offered a female alternative to the exclusively male hierarchies of their denominations. Denominations occasionally acknowledged that these groups represented the disenfranchised majority of members by turning to missionary societies when they wanted to communicate with the women of the church. In the early decades of the twentieth century, male church hierarchies moved to take control by subsuming women's organizations into "general" missionary societies. Although this change was touted as a move toward equality, the result for the most powerful women's groups was a loss of control of their organizations, budgets, and programs.[33] In spite of the efforts of denominations to restrict women's public roles, the early twentieth century saw significant success for women's public promotion of Protestantism. The maternalist values that contributed to Progressive reform and the rise of the welfare state built on the foundations of nineteenth-century women's religious culture.[34]

In the second half of the twentieth century, women's religious commitments have contributed remarkable vitality to the churches during a presumably secular age. With the rise of feminism in the 1970s women flooded the ranks of ministerial candidates. While even those denominations that ordained women had few female candidates before the 1970s, women have comprised 50 percent or more of seminary students in the liberal denominations (including Reform and Conservative Judaism) since the early eighties. In addition, the women's movement spurred debates leading to the ordination of women among additional religious bodies, most notably Lutheran, Episcopal, and Jewish. The Catholic Church, which continues to limit ordination to men, has had a drastic shortage of priests, and has been forced to shift a variety of religious functions to laypeople (most often women).[35]

According to the secularization thesis, the increasing presence of women in religious leadership could be seen as an indication of a decline in the status and influence of religious institutions. If one looks at the internal impact of feminism on the denominations, however, it is difficult to portray it as a symptom of decline. The feminist movement has served as a catalyst to liturgical creativity, inspiring new inclusive-language hymnals, prayerbooks, and lectionaries. It has rekindled interest in theology, giving rise to whole new areas of theological inquiry and to a new generation of women theologians. Names like Rosemary Radford Ruether and Elisabeth Schussler-Fiorenza have become household words among American church women who may not be able to name a single male theologian.

In addition to the new leadership roles assumed by women clergy, the ordination of women may be significant in breaking down the longstanding association of the clergy with men and the laity with women—an association that may inhibit religious participation by men in lay roles. There are some indications that the gender gap in church membership is declining, not because fewer women go to church but because more men do.[36]

It also can be argued that debates about gender roles have increased the vigor of conservative religious groups. Some studies suggest that women are attracted to conservative religious communities precisely because they offer access to traditional roles of wife and mother.[37] Opposition to changing roles for women and to specific feminist proposals such as abortion rights and the Equal Rights Amendment has galvanized religious commitment among conservative Catholics, Mormons, and, especially, Evangelicals. Antifeminist or pro-family positions have inspired new attempts by women and men to promote Christian values in public.

## RELIGION AND MASCULINITY

In spite of the ideological difficulties presented by the identity between piety and femininity in American culture, many men do go to church. But the presence of men does not negate cultural associations between women and religion, rather it allows them to be acted out in a public arena. The dual identification of Christian women with both Eve and Mary made patriarchal authority essential. If women could be either good or bad, male authority was necessary to assure that they chose to be good, and that they did not tempt men toward sin.

Which men go to church? Biographies of America's famous theologians frequently attribute their subject's religious concern to their mother's piety.[38] But it is not only great divines who profess the faith of their mothers rather than their fathers. Mary Ryan's study of the Second Great Awakening in Utica, New York, found converts were twice as likely to follow a female relative into church membership as a male relative. Theodore Dwight Weld's account of how he experienced conversion after his aunt "followed with several ladies and shut me in" to a pew to hear evangelist Charles Finney supports Ryan's picture of revivals at which women literally led their husbands and children into church by the hand. Her findings have been confirmed by other studies.[39]

Because the men who do go to church most often do so in the presence of female relatives, men's participation in religion can be illumined if it is seen in relation to women's. Men may attend church as heads of families, whose ability to coerce attendance from dependents reinforces their authority. Or men may agree to worship at the behest of more involved wives or mothers, in which case their participation is a secondary effect of women's piety. Gay men or men without families also may embrace lay religious roles incompatible with conventional masculinity. In general, however, the strong association of clergy with men and laity with women seems to have a chilling effect on the participation of male laity. One recent study documented the paucity of male youth in African American denominations, suggesting that the identification of piety and femininity continues to expand today.[40]

Because women's dominance in the laity has been accompanied by a devaluation of female participation, male church members have been highly valued and well rewarded for attending church. The most visible and powerful lay roles have been reserved for them. In most denominations women could not vote as members of the laity until the twentieth century. This meant that Protestant churches had a greater power discrepancy between male and female laity than in the Catholic Church, in which no lay members had substantial authority. In many denominations women could not vote until long after they were enfranchised by the Nineteenth Amendment to the Constitution in 1920. Men who did attend church enjoyed a setting in which their participation—especially as heads of family—was highly valued, regardless of contrary evidence. In assuming that female dominance is an aberration to be explained or a problem to be solved, historians have accepted the theological and institutional traditions' privileging of men's participation.

Men who assumed lay roles as religious leaders were bolstered by a tradition of muscular Christianity that portrayed religious virtue as compatible with normative masculinity.[41] The gender ratio of church membership, however, suggests that this tradition never held the influence of the association of piety with femininity. For men, ideals of masculinity often conflicted with Christian virtues rather than reinforcing them. American men frequently have found themselves in the position of abrogating religious values to make it possible for their women and children to practice them. Whether exemplifying manhood by competing in the marketplace, the battlefield, or the playing field, the goal for men was to win, not to offer examples of self-sacrificial love. (Although winning often required self-sacrifice, this was the means, not the end, of normative masculinity.) The numerical dominance of women in the churches as well as the identification of piety with femininity reinforced the idea that the church was not part of men's world. Following disestablishment of the Protestant churches during the early National period, clergy had less and less appeal as role models for American men.[42]

Impediments to men's religious participation sometimes have been offered as explanations for the presence of female majorities. C. Eric Lincoln and Lawrence H. Mamiya, authors of the massive sociological study *The Black Church in the African-American Experience*, entitle a three-page section on the numerical dominance of the female laity "Where Have All the Black Men Gone?" The section says nothing about women, but focuses on the devastating demographic realities that remove men from the black community, as well as the cultural factors that discourage them from going to church.[43] Assuming that a female majority could be the result only of racist violence is disturbing for several reasons. First, as the reader probably has wearied of being reminded, such a view ignores the prevalence of this pattern throughout American religious groups. Second, and more important, it assumes that there is something wrong with a majority female church, and that it is a symptom of social dysfunction. If this is the case, it will require a broad reevaluation of American religious history.

## CATHOLICISM AND FEMINIZATION

The limitations of narrative devices equating women's presence with a decline in religion resulting from a loss of male authority become even clearer if they are applied beyond the Protestant groups from which they derive. The term *feminization* rarely has been applied to American Catholicism, although it espoused many of the same gendered religious norms that characterized nineteenth-century Protestantism. Rosemary Ruether has used the term *secularized mariology* to refer to domestic ideology among nineteenth-century Catholics—a term indicating continuity rather than decline in religious beliefs. The Marian Century, from 1850 to 1950, coincided in many ways with the Cult of True Womanhood. From the point of view of Protestant historiography, Catholicism always was "feminized." Nineteenth-century Catholics, after all, had never stripped their churches of the rich sensual environment or intercessory figures whose absence constituted the "masculine" style of reformed theology and worship. The concept of "feminization" expresses the normative claims of the Protestant reformation. The cult of the saints and especially the veneration of the Virgin presented just the type of loving mediators that "feminized" Protestantism presented in the figure of Jesus. It is not surprising that the greatest "feminizer" of them all, Harriet Beecher Stowe, hung paintings of Italian Madonnas over her fireplaces and abandoned the extreme anti-Catholicism of her family to laud the virtues of *Agnes of Sorrento* (1862). The term *feminization*, then, retains the anti-Catholic as well as the antiwoman bias of the standard narratives of American religion.

The significance of the presence of women in American Catholic history is less studied than the Protestant case, but the data are quite suggestive. The Irish, who came to dominate American Catholicism during the nineteenth century, had a greater rate of female immigration than any other group. These women quickly became the economic backbone of the American Catholic Church.[44] The Irish immigration was especially remarkable for the large number of single women it included.[45] Single religious women made the parochial school system possible by providing a labor force whose subsistence wages constituted a massive economic subsidy. Following 1884, when the Third Plenary Council made the establishment of parochial schools the priority of every diocese in the country, female vocations skyrocketed. Teaching in parochial schools became the primary occupation of women religious, and sisters became the primary educators of Catholic children. Because contact between student and teacher far exceeds that between priest and parishioner, nun's roles as teachers made them central as religious socializers of Catholic children. Sisters instructed children in the rudiments of their faith, and prepared them to receive the sacraments and to establish Catholic homes. By the end of the nineteenth century there were 40,000 nuns in the United States, outnumbering priests by four to one. By 1950, there were 177,000 American women in 450 religious congregations. Without the women who felt a vocation to the religious life, the Third Plenary Council could not have made parochial education the hallmark of preconciliar American Catholicism.[46]

Girls were much more likely than boys to attend Catholic school before the Third Plenary Council, because immigrant families often relied on their sons' labor to survive. Thus girls who would grow up to raise Catholic families were likely to be more thoroughly imbued with the values of the church than the men they married. For instance, the number of boys enrolled in Catholic schools in Massachusetts did not approach the number of girls until well into the twentieth century when child labor had been outlawed. Once again women's presence and lack of authority must be viewed in tandem. Catholics placed a higher priority on educating girls in a milieu that would in many ways encourage their subordination.[47]

## CONCLUSION

In my analysis of Catholics, as in my treatment of other groups, I have argued that the historiography of American religion depends on a host of undocumented normative assumptions about religion and gender. As a corrective, in this essay I have sketched the outlines of a narrative of U.S. religion that is organized around the themes of female presence and male power. Many questions remain. For instance, it is unclear exactly why women, more than men, have found religions to be effective avenues for understanding their experiences and constructing their identities. Informed readers will notice omissions. Many groups do not appear in my abbreviated account. My aim was to be suggestive, not exhaustive; provocative, not conclusive. If I am right, however, focusing on the cluster of motifs that concern gender—especially female presence—promises to allow other characters to come into view. And we cannot expect to understand the history of religion in America until we know at least as much about the women who have formed the majority of participants as we do about the male minority who have stood in the pulpit.

## NOTES

1. I would like to thank members of the Comparative Women's History Seminar at the University of Minnesota, especially Riv-Ellen Prell and M. J. Maynes, and members of the American Religion and Culture Workshop at Princeton University, especially Marie Griffith, as well as Colleen McDannell for helpful comments on drafts of this essay and Michael McNally for research assistance. Tom Tweed provided inspiration, insight, persistence, and expert editing through many drafts.

2. Robert G. Pope, *The Half-Way Covenant: Church Membership in Puritan New England* (Princeton: Princeton University Press, 1969), chap. 8; Mary Maples Dunn, "Saints and Sisters: Congregational and Quaker Women in the Early Colonial Period," and Gerald Moran, "'Sisters' in Christ: Women and the Church in Seventeenth-Century New England," both in Janet Wilson James, ed., *Women in American Religion* (Philadelphia: University of Pennsylvania Press, 1980); Richard D. Shiels, "The Feminization of American Congregationalism, 1730–1835," *American Quarterly* 39 (1981): 45–62; Donald Mathews, *Religion in the Old South* (Chicago: University of Chicago Press, 1977), 47; Mary Ryan, *The Cradle of the Middle Class: The Family in Oneida County, New York, 1790–1865* (New York: Cambridge University Press, 1983), 75–83; C. Eric Lincoln and Lawrence H. Mamiya, *The Black Church in the African-American Experience* (Durham, N.C.: Duke University Press, 1990).

3. Because the Catholic Church counts as members all who receive baptism, its membership in the United States has the same proportion of females as the general population, 51 percent. This figure tells little about involvement with or sustenance of the church, so categories such as vocations and participation in religious practice are more useful. Larger female majorities in these categories are documented in Mary J. Oates, "Organized Voluntarism: The Catholic Sisters in Massachusetts, 1870–1940," in *Women in American Religion*, and idem, "Organizing for Service: Challenges to Community Life and Work Decisions in Catholic Sisterhoods, 1850–1940," in Wendy E. Chmielewski, Louis J. Kern, and Marlyn Klee-Hartzell, eds., *Women in Spiritual and Communitarian Societies in the United States* (Syracuse: Syracuse University Press, 1993); Robert Anthony Orsi, "'He Keeps Me Going': Women's Devotion to Saint Jude and the Dialectics of Gender in American Catholicism, 1929–1965," in Thomas Kselman, ed., *Belief in History* (Notre Dame, Ind.: University of Notre Dame Press, 1991).

4. Robert Wuthnow and William Lehrman, "Religion: Inhibitor or Facilitator of Political Involvement among Women?" in Louise A. Tilly and Patricia Gurin, eds. *Women, Politics, and Change* (New York: Russell Sage Foundation, 1990), 300–322; Rodney Stark and William Sims Bainbridge, *The Future of Religion: Secularization, Revival, and Cult Formation* (Berkeley: University of California Press, 1985); Roger Finke and Rodney Stark, *The Churching of America, 1776–1990* (New Brunswick, N.J.: Rutgers University Press, 1992), 33–35, 66–71; Cedric Cowing, "Sex and Preaching

in the Great Awakening," *American Quarterly*, 30 (fall 1968): 624–44; Barbara E. Lacey, "Gender, Piety, and Secularization in Connecticut Religion, 1720–1775," *Journal of Social History* 24 (summer 1991): 799–821.

5. Beverly Thomas McCloud, "African-American Muslim Women," in Yvonne Haddad, ed., *The Muslims of America* (New York: Oxford University Press, 1991), 177–87; Marshall Sklare, *Conservative Judaism: An American Religious Movement* (Glencoe, Ill.: Free Press, 1955), 86–88; Leon A. Jicks, *The Americanization of the Synagogue, 1820–1870* (Hanover, N.H.: Brandeis University Press, 1976).

6. Marcia K. Hermansen, "Two-Way Acculturation: Muslim Women in America between Individual Choice (Liminality) and Community Affiliation (Communitas)," in *Muslims of America*, 199; Rita Gross, *Buddhism after Patriarchy: A Feminist History, Analysis and Reconstruction of Buddhism* (Albany: SUNY Press, 1993); Anne Carolyn Klein, *Meeting the Great Bliss Queen: Buddhists, Feminists, and the Art of the Self* (Boston: Beacon Press, 1995). See also Thomas A. Tweed, *The American Encounter with Buddhism, 1844–1912* (Bloomington: Indiana University Press, 1992), 85–87.

7. Many studies support similar findings for Europe. See, for example, Suzanne Desan, *Reclaiming the Sacred: Lay Religion and Popular Politics in Revolutionary France* (Ithaca, N.Y.: Cornell University Press), 210–15; William A. Christian, Jr., *Person and God in a Spanish Valley* (New York: Seminar Press, 1972); Olwen Hufton, "The Reconstruction of a Church 1796–1801," in Gwynne Lewis and Colin Lucas, eds., *Beyond the Terror: Essays in French Regional Social History, 1794–1815* (Cambridge: Cambridge University Press, 1983), 21–52; Hugh McLeod, *Religion and the People of Western Europe, 1789–1970* (Oxford: Oxford University Press, 1981), 28–35, found that female majorities characterize both Catholic and Protestant countries. Michel Vovelle locates the rise of a female majority to the eighteenth century, but he documents gender parity in enthusiasm for the mass only for a brief moment in 1710, with female majorities in evidence both before and after. Michel Vovelle, *Piété baroque et déchristianisation en province au XVIII siècle* (Paris: Editions du Seuil, 1978), 134. Beyond Europe comparative data are currently difficult to obtain.

8. Mary Farrell Bednarowski, "Outside the Mainstream: Women's Religion and Women Religious Leaders in Nineteenth-Century America," *Journal of the American Academy of Religion* 48 (June 1980): 207–31; Catherine Wessinger, ed., *Women's Leadership in Marginal Religions: Explorations Outside the Mainstream* (Urbana: University of Illinois Press, 1993).

9. Ann Braude, *Radical Spirits: Spiritualism and Women's Rights in Nineteenth-Century America* (Boston: Beacon Press, 1989); idem, "The Perils of Passivity: Women's Leadership in Spiritualism and Christian Science," in *Women's Leadership in Marginal Religions*.

10. Dunn, "Saints and Sisters," 37; Orsi, "'He Keeps Me Going.'"

11. Nathan O. Hatch, *The Democratization of American Christianity* (New Haven: Yale University Press, 1989), 10.

12. References to women and gender that affect the narrative are so infrequent in surveys on American religion that there is no need to list particular texts. A survey text that mentions women more frequently than most is Peter W. Williams, *America's Religions: Traditions and Cultures* (New York: Macmillan, 1990). A thematic (rather than narrative) text that includes women is Mary Farrell Bednarowski, *American Religion: A Cultural Perspective* (Englewood Cliffs, N. J.: Prentice Hall, 1984).

13. Dunn, "Saints and Sisters," 37.

14. Shiels, "Feminization of American Congregationalism."

15. Harry S. Stout and Catherine A. Brekus, "Declension, Gender, and the 'New Religious History,'" and Gerald Moran, "'Sinners Are Turned into Saints in Numbers': Puritanism and Revivalism in Colonial Connecticut," both in Philip R. Vandermeer and Robert P. Swierenga, eds., *Belief and Behavior: Essays in the New Religious History* (New Brunswick, N.J.: Rutgers University Press, 1991). Stout and Brekus conclude that feminization *did* occur following the Revolutionary War. However, the membership statistics they present for the First Church of New Haven reveal a relatively constant sex ratio in which women outnumber men by more than two to one from 1680 to 1980. The only years in which they found male majorities were 1639 to 1659.

16. Perry Miller, *The New England Mind: From Colony to Province* (1953; Boston: Beacon Press, 1961), 34.

17. Ibid., chap. 2.

18. Barbara Welter, "The Feminization of American Religion: 1800–1860," in Mary Hartman and Lois Banner, eds., *Clio's Consciousness Raised* (New York: Harper Torchbooks, 1973), 138; Ann Douglas, *The Feminization of American Culture* (New York: Knopf, 1977); Cotton Mather, *Ornaments of the Daughters of Zion* (Boston: Samuel

Phillips, 1691), 56; Shiels, "Feminization of American Congregationalism."

19. Betty A. De Berg, *Ungodly Women: Gender and the First Wave of American Fundamentalism* (Minneapolis: Fortress Press, 1990).

20. See, for example, Jeffrey K. Hadden and Anson Shupe, eds., *Secularization and Fundamentalism Reconsidered* (New York: Paragon House Books, 1989), and Stark and Bainbridge, *Future of Religion*.

21. Paul E. Johnson, *A Shopkeeper's Millennium* (New York: Hill and Wang, 1978), 4–6; George Gallup, Jr., "Fifty Years of Gallup Surveys on Religion," *Gallup Report* 236 (May): 4–14.

22. John Murray Cuddihy, *The Ordeal of Civility: Freud, Marx, Lévi-Strauss and the Jewish Struggle with Modernity* (1974; New York: Delta, 1976), 34 and passim; see also idem, *No Offense: Civil Religion and Protestant Taste* (New York: Seabury Press, 1978).

23. Edmund S. Morgan, *The Puritan Family: Religion and Domestic Relations in Seventeenth-Century New England* (New York: Harper and Row, 1966); Laurel Thatcher Ulrich, "Virtuous Women Found: New England Ministerial Literature, 1668–1735," in *Women in American Religion*; Lona Malmsheimer, "Daughters of Zion: New England Roots of American Feminism," *New England Quarterly* 50 (September 1977): 484–504; Carol F. Karlsen, *The Devil in the Shape of a Woman: Witchcraft in Colonial New England* (New York: Vintage Books, 1989); David Hall, *Worlds of Wonder, Days of Judgment* (New York: Knopf, 1989), 32–34, 128–30.

24. Susan Juster, *Disorderly Women: Sexual Politics and Evangelicalism in Revolutionary New England* (Ithaca, N.Y.: Cornell University Press, 1994); Margaret Mason, "The Typology of the Female as a Model for the Regenerate in Puritan Preaching, 1690–1730," *Signs* 2 (1976): 304–15; Barbara Leslie Epstein, *The Politics of Domesticity: Women, Evangelism and Temperance in Nineteenth-Century America* (Middletown, Conn.: Wesleyan University Press, 1981).

25. Barbara Welter, "The Cult of True Womanhood: 1829–1860," *American Quarterly* 18 (1966): 151–74.

26. Colleen McDannell, "Catholic Domesticity, 1860–1960," in Karen Kennelly, C.S.J., ed., *American Catholic Women: A Historical Exploration* (New York: Macmillan, 1989), 48–80; Ann Braude, "The Jewish Woman's Encounter with American Culture," in Rosemary Ruether and Rosemary Keller, eds., *Women and Religion in America* (San Fran-

cisco: Harper and Row, 1981), 1:156; Evelyn Brooks Higginbotham, *Righteous Discontent: The Women's Movement in the Black Baptist Church, 1880–1920* (Cambridge, Mass.: Harvard University Press, 1993); Peggy Pascoe, *Relations of Rescue: The Search for Female Moral Authority in the American West, 1874–1939* (New York: Oxford University Press, 1990); Margaret Lamberts Bendroth, *Fundamentalism and Gender: 1875 to the Present* (New Haven: Yale University Press, 1993); Cott, "Passionlessness," 163.

27. Christine L. Krueger, *The Reader's Repentance: Woman Preachers, Woman Writers, and Nineteenth-Century Social Discourse* (Chicago: University of Chicago Press, 1992).

28. The literature documenting this tendency is legion. See, for example, Carroll Smith-Rosenberg, "Beauty, the Beast, and the Militant Woman: A Case Study in Sex Roles and Social Stress in Jacksonian America," in *Disorderly Conduct* (New York: Oxford University Press, 1985), 109–28; Epstein, *Politics of Domesticity*; Mary Ryan, "A Woman's Awakening: Evangelical Religion and the Families of Utica, New York, 1800–1840," in *Women and Religion in America*, and idem, "The Power of Women's Networks: A Case Study of Female Moral Reform in Antebellum America," *Feminist Studies* 5 (spring 1979): 66–88; Nancy F. Cott, *The Bonds of Womanhood: "Woman's Sphere" in New England, 1780–1835* (New Haven: Yale University Press, 1977); Patricia R. Hill, *The World Their Household: The American Women's Foreign Mission Movement and Cultural Transformation, 1870–1920* (Ann Arbor: University of Michigan Press, 1985); Elaine J. Lawless, *Handmaidens of the Lord: Pentecostal Women Preachers and Traditional Religion* (Philadelphia: University of Pennsylvania Press, 1988).

29. Nancy F. Cott, "Passionlessness: An Interpretation of Victorian Sexual Ideology, 1790–1850," *Signs: Journal of Women in Culture and Society* 4 (1978): 219–36.

30. Ulrich, "Virtuous Women Found"; Bendroth, *Fundamentalism and Gender*, 110; Karlsen, *The Devil in the Shape of a Woman*; De Berg, *Ungodly Women*.

31. Ryan, "Power of Women's Networks"; Smith-Rosenberg, "Beauty, the Beast, and the Militant Woman," 109–28.

32. Jean Fagin Yellin, *Women and Sisters: The Anti-Slavery Feminists in American Culture* (New Haven: Yale University Press, 1989); Jean Fagin Yellin and John C. Van Horne, eds., *The Abolitionist Sisterhood: Women's Political Culture in Antebellum*

*America* (Ithaca, N.Y.: Cornell University Press, 1994); Epstein, *Politics of Domesticity.*

33. R. Pierce Beaver, *American Protestant Women in World Mission: A History of the First Feminist Movement in North America* (Grand Rapids, Mich.: Eerdmans, 1980); Barbara Welter, "She Hath Done What She Could: Protestant Women's Missionary Careers in the Nineteenth-Century," in *Women in American Religion*; Elizabeth Howell Verdesi, *In but Still Out: Women in the Church* (Philadelphia: Westminster Press, 1976), chap. 3; Hill, *The World Their Household.*

34. Sonya Michel and Seth Koven, eds., *Mothers of a New World: Maternalist Politics and the Origins of the Welfare State* (New York: Routledge, 1993).

35. Barbara Brown Zikmund, "Women and Ordination," in Rosemary Skinner Keller and Rosemary Radford Ruether, eds., *In Our Own Voices* (San Francisco: Harper San Francisco, 1995), 292–340.

36. Wuthnow and Lehrman, "Religion: Inhibitor or Facilitator?"

37. Lynn Davidman, *Tradition in a Rootless World: Women Turn to Orthodox Judaism* (Berkeley: University of California Press, 1991).

38. See, for example, Marie Caskey, *Chariot of Fire: Religion and the Beecher Family* (New Haven: Yale University Press, 1977).

39. Ryan, "A Woman's Awakening," 91; Stout and Brekus, "Declension, Gender, and the 'New Religious History,'" in *Belief and Behavior,* 29.

40. Lincoln and Mamiya, *The Black Church,* 304–6.

41. Gail Bederman, "'The Women Have Had Charge of the Church Work Long Enough': The Men and Religion Forward Movement of 1911–1912 and the Masculinization of Middle-Class Protestantism," *American Quarterly* 41 (September 1989): 432–65.

42. Mark C. Carnes, *Secret Ritual and Manhood in Victorian America* (New Haven: Yale University Press, 1989); Douglas, *Feminization of American Culture*; E. Anthony Rotundo, *American Manhood* (New York: Basic Books, 1993), 172.

43. Lincoln and Mamiya, *The Black Church,* 304–6.

44. Colleen McDannell, "Going to the Ladies' Fair: Irish Catholics in New York City, 1870–1900," in Timothy Meagher and Ronald Baylor, eds., *The New York Irish* (Baltimore: Johns Hopkins University Press, forthcoming).

45. James J. Kenneally, *The History of American Catholic Women* (New York: Crossroads, 1990), 66.

46. Oates, "Organized Voluntarism," and idem, "Organizing for Service"; Mary Ewens, O.P., *The Role of the Nun in Nineteenth-Century America* (1971; Salem, N.H.: Ayer, 1984), 35–64.

47. Oates, "Organized Voluntarism," 150.

## "BELIEVER I KNOW"

*Charles Joyner*

Charles Joyner believes that what is original about African American Christianity "lies neither in its African elements nor in its Christian elements, but in its unique and creative synthesis of both." Joyner reminds us that the slaves did not simply become Christians; instead, they imaginatively fashioned their faith from the available cultural resources. In the following essay, Joyner enters the inner world of the slaves who lived on the South Carolina and Georgia lowcountry plantations during the antebellum period in order to explore the transformation of their diverse African cultures into an emerging African American Christianity. Joyner notes that most mature lowcountry slaves came directly from different ethnic groups in Africa and the Carribean and were aware of their roots. He argues that to underestimate the retention and adaptation of those African behavior patterns most meaningful to these slaves is to deprive them of their past. Yet to overestimate the African contribution to African American Christianity is to take from the slaves their creativity. Rather, the emergence of African American Christianity is an evolving story that includes both the retention of African traditions as well as innovative adaptations to American Christianity.

Reprinted by permission from Charles Joyner, " 'Believer I Know': The Emergence of African American Christianity" in *African American Christianity: Essays in History*, Paul E. Johnson, ed. (Berkeley: California, 1994), 18–46.

*Suffering produces endurance,*
*endurance produces character,*
*and character produces hope.*

—Romans 5: 3–4

*Glory Hallelujah*
*Believer I know*
*I done cross Jorden*
*Believer I know*

—Georgia slave song sung by Katie Brown

# 9

## "BELIEVER I KNOW"
### The Emergence of African American Christianity

*Charles Joyner*

THE LITTLE SHIP with its human cargo sailed up the Altamaha River. Major Pierce Butler had purchased a large number of Africans for his Georgia plantation in 1803. When the vessel arrived at Butler's Island, the Major's plantation manager informed him, "You have no people that can talk with them but they are so smart your young Wenches are Speculating very high for husbands."[1] In the new physical and social environment of the lowcountry, African men and women of various ethnic groups mixed in ways that did not occur in Africa. Similarly, the varied African cultures were increasingly fused in combinations that did not exist in Africa. A new culture, predominantly African in origin, but different from any *particular* African culture, began to take shape.

During the formative years of African American culture, most of the mature slaves on many South Carolina and Georgia lowcountry plantations came either directly from Africa or from the Caribbean. According to a Georgia slave, "Doze Africans alluz call one annudduh 'countryman' . . . Dey know ef dey come frum duh same tribe by duh mahk dey hab. Some hab a long mahk an some hab a roun un. Udduhs weah eahring in duh eah. Some weahs it in duh lef eah an doze from anudduh tribe weahs it in duh right eah."[2]

There was a great mixture of African ethnic groups in the lowcountry, but African ethnic distinctions continued to be made among the slaves as long as slavery lasted. Coromantees from the Gold Coast were said to be ferocious and unforgiving, but hardy and therefore favored as field hands. Congos and Angolas were alleged to be handsome and docile, but weak and predisposed to run away. And Ibos from the Niger delta were considered sickly, melancholy, and suicidal. On any given morning in a lowcountry rice field, an enslaved African would meet more Africans from more ethnic groups than he or she would have encountered in a lifetime in Africa.[3]

To underestimate the Africanity of African American Christianity is to rob the slaves of their heritage. But to overestimate the Africanity of African American Christianity is to rob the slaves of their creativity. Africans were creative in Africa; they did not cease to be creative as involuntary settlers in America. The African American Christianity that developed was neither a dark version of the Christianity preached by slaveholders nor a continuation of African religion disguised as Christianity. The story of the emergence of African American Christianity is a story of an emergent African American culture as well as of residual

African cultures, a story of innovation as well as of tradition, a story of change as well as of continuity.

## MUSLIM SLAVES

The old man always wore a fez and a long coat, just as he would have done in Africa. He was the driver on Thomas Spalding's Sapelo Island plantation, near Darien, Georgia. A Georgia rice planter's daughter who visited the Spalding plantation in the 1850s wrote of the old man and his family many years later: "They were all tall and well-formed, with good features. They conversed with us in English, but in talking among themselves they used a foreign tongue that no one else understood. . . . These Negroes held themselves aloof from the others as if they were conscious of their own superiority." The old man's name was Bilali Mohomet, and he was the great-grandfather of Katie Brown and Shadrach Hall. According to Shad, Bilali and his wife "pray at sun-up and face duh sun on duh knees an bow tuh it tree times, kneelin on a lill mat." Katie added, "Dey wuz bery puhticluh bout duh time dey pray an dey ber regluh bout duh hour. Wen duh sun come up, wen it straight obuh head and wen it set, das duh time dey pray. Dey bow tuh duh sun an hab lill mat tuh kneel on. Duh beads is on a long string. Bilali he pull bead an he say, 'Belambi, Hakabara, Mahamadu.' Phoebe she say, 'Ameen, Ameen.'" When Bilali died, he was buried with his prayer rug and his Koran. Many former Gullah slaves remembered their ancestors praying in the Muslim fashion.[4]

Bilali and other Muslim slaves on the Georgia coast carefully observed Muslim fasts and feast days. Katie Brown recalled the Muslim rice cakes made by her grandmother: "She make funny flat cake she call 'saraka'. She make um same day ebry yeah, an it big day. Wen dey finish, she call us in, all duh chillun, an put in hans lill flat cake an we eats it. Yes'm, I membuh how she make it. She wash rice, an po off all duh watuh. She let wet rice sit all night, an in mawnin rice is all swell. She tak dat rice an put it in wooden mawtuh, an beat it tuh paste wid wooden pestle. She add honey, sometime shuguh, an make it in flat cake wid uh hans. 'Saraka' she call um." Shad Hall remembered that his grandmother made the pieces of saraka into dumplings. Katie Brown said her grandmother rolled the rice paste into balls "the size of small fowls' eggs" and set them aside to harden. When the saraka was ready, the children were lined up so that the grandmother could make certain their hands were clean. Any child whose hands were not clean had to go wash them. The other children had to wait until everyone was ready. As she handed each child some of the saraka, the grandmother would say either "Saraka dee" or "Ah-me, Ah-me."[5]

It is important to note that Christianity enjoyed no religious monopoly among Gullah slaves. Christianity had to compete in a religiously diverse environment. African-born slaves, for instance, often maintained their traditional religious outlooks. "At the time I first went to Carolina, there were a great many African slaves in the country," recalled fugitive slave Charles Ball. "Many of them believed there were several gods; some of whom were good, and others evil." Other African-born slaves embraced Islam. There was a considerable Muslim presence in the Georgia and South Carolina lowcountry. "I knew several who must have been, from what I have since learned, Mohammedans," Ball noted. "There was one man on this plantation who prayed five times every day, always turning his face to the east." It has been estimated that as many as twenty percent of the enslaved Africans in America embraced Islam. There is evidence that Muslim slaves in coastal Georgia deliberately sought marriage partners of the same faith as late as the second generation. On some lowcountry plantations, Muslim slaves were given a ration of beef instead of pork.[6]

## THE SLAVEHOLDERS' MISSION TO THE SLAVES

The Reverend Charles Colcock Jones stood in his Savannah pulpit and, in his ringing voice, delivered an eloquent sermon urging slaveholders to instruct their slaves in the principles of the Christian religion. Not only would religious instruction save the slaves' souls, he said, but it would also create "a greater subordination" among the slaves and teach them "respect and obedience [to] all those whom God in his providence has placed in authority over them." The Reverend Jones was not only pastor of Savannah's First Presbyterian Church but also the master of three rice plantations and more than one hundred slaves in Liberty County, Georgia. While he seemed genuinely concerned for the salvation of his slaves' souls, there is no question that he consciously and deliberately used religion as an instrument of discipline and control. A faithful servant, Jones believed, was more profitable than an unfaithful servant. So he attempted to tailor Christianity to keep bondsmen reconciled to their bondage. Jones and similarly inclined slaveholders wanted their slaves delivered from "savage heathenism" to the true light of the Christian gospel, preferably of the Episcopal or Presbyterian persuasion.[7]

Early lowcountry planters were reluctant to tolerate missionary efforts among their slaves. "There has always been a strong repugnance amongst the planters, against their slaves becoming members of any religious society," Charles Ball wrote in 1837. "They fear the slaves, by attending the meetings and listening to the preachers, may imbibe the morality they teach, the notions of equality and liberty, maintained in the gospel." Planters doubted that preachers could be depended upon to defend the Peculiar Institution. "The abolition measures have excited such a spirit of jealousy and suspicion that some planters will not listen to the introduction of religion on their places," wrote a Charleston clergyman in 1836. Gradually, however, at least some ministers won the trust of the slaveholders and began missionary work among the slaves. Henry Brown, a former slave near Charleston, recalled that his master's slaves "went to meeting two nights a week and on Sunday they went to Church, where they had a white preacher Dr. Rose hired to preach to them."

Masters came more and more to believe that religion sustained rather than threatened slavery, and slave churchgoing came to seem less and less threatening. By the 1830s, lowcountry masters were giving increased attention to controlling the *content* of slave religion. A Georgia planter's daughter remembered her father's efforts to evangelize his slaves. "There was Sabbath School each Sunday afternoon, under the big live oaks," she recalled. "My Father would read from the Bible and we would tell simple stories to the children and many grownups, who came with them."[8] In 1837 the Reverend Jones published a *catechism* especially for slaves. One section was devoted to "Duties of Masters and Servants." In it Jones, too fastidious to call a slave a slave, addressed a series of questions to the "servants":

Q. What are the Servants to count their Masters worthy of?

A. All honour.

Q. How are they to try to please their Masters?

A. Please them well in all things, not answering again.

Q. Is it right for a Servant when commanded to do anything to be sullen and slow, and answering his master again?

A. No.

Q. But suppose the Master is hard to please, and threatens and punishes more than he ought, what is the Servant to do?

A.    Do his best to please him.

Q.    Are Servants at liberty to tell lies and deceive their Masters?

A.    No.

Q.    If servants will faithfully do their duty and Serve God in their stations as Servants, will they be respected of men, and blessed and honoured of God, as well as others?

A.    Yes.[9]

Slaveholders supported religious instruction partly out of sincere Christian concern for the salvation of the slaves. On his deathbed one Charleston master instructed his children, "I wish you also to give all the indulgence you possibly can to the negroes in going to Church, and making them repeat their questions, for this reason that if neglected we will have to answer for the loss of their souls." The Christianity disseminated by slaveholders, however, was very selective, emphasizing obedience in the here and now as much as salvation in the hereafter. The slaves were going to get religion whether their masters liked it or not, many masters reasoned, so making religion safe for slavery became a matter of high priority. South Carolina planter Robert F. W. Allston described his slaves as "attentive to religious instruction, and greatly improved in intelligence and morals, in domestic relations, etc. . . . Indeed, the degree of intelligence which as a class they are acquiring is worthy of deep consideration." If the planters evidence a genuine concern for their slaves' spiritual welfare, they also recognized that religion was a more subtle, more humane, and more effective means of control than the whip.[10]

There are incessant references in the Jones family correspondence to the spiritual as well as physical welfare of the slaves. Sandy Maybank, then working as the head carpenter at Montevideo plantation in coastal Georgia, received a letter from the man who claimed to own him. "I trust," Charles Colcock Jones wrote to Maybank, "that you are holding on to your high profession of the Gospel of our Lord and Saviour Jesus Christ at all times, and constantly watch and pray." "You know our life and health are in His hands," Jones constantly counseled his driver Catoe, "and it is a great comfort to me to have a good hope that you love Him, and do put all your trust in our Lord and Saviour Jesus Christ, who is a precious Saviour to us in life and in death." And Jones was quite pleased when Catoe sent back such replies as "Your people all seem to be doing very well. They attend praise and go to church regularly whenever there is preaching in reach." Another Jones driver, Andrew, wrote, "About a month ago Revd Mr Law administered the sacraments in Sunbury and among several black people that joined the church was my daughter Dinah, and I trust that she may practice what she professes, for as Mas John says it is no light thing to be a Christian, for we may play with the lightning and the rattle snake, but dont trifle with Almighty God 'lest he tear you to pieces in his anger and then be never to deliver you.'"[11]

To suggest that lowcountry slaveholders cynically reduced Christianity to patience, humility, and the fear of sin, or that they were more concerned with the discipline of slaves than with the salvation of souls, would be untrue to history. "In our philosophy, right is the highest expediency," James Henley Thornwell insisted, "and obedience to God the firmest security of communities as well as individuals. We have not sought the protection of our property in the debasement of our species; we have not maintained our own interests in this world, by the deliberate sacrifice of the eternal interests of the thousands who look to us for the way to salvation." Nevertheless, it would also be untrue to history not to point out that much of the slaveholders' missionary motivation was their understanding that preaching had a significant effect on slave discipline. Ministers went out of their way to appease the slaveholders by approaching slave religion with the utmost discretion. Masters knew that so long as the slaves were listening to a trusted white preacher, they could not (at least for the moment) be listening to a subversive black one.[12]

Some slaveholders opposed the religious education of slaves as useless. Certainly not all slaveholders believed that slave religion would promote slave control. One reason for doubt was their belief in black Christians' excessive propensity for backsliding. In fact, black Christians were no more and no less immune to backsliding than were white Christians, even with the constant religious instruction that was the stock-in-trade of such slaveholders as the Reverend Charles Colcock Jones. Others maintained that the slaves were not fully human creatures and were therefore incapable of reasoning and of learning the truths of the Christian religion. Still others feared the intense emotionalism preferred by the slaves as the appropriate form of worship. The Reverend Jones encountered considerable opposition from his fellow slaveholders until he was able to prove to their satisfaction that he favored only quiet and sedate worship services. Others, such as the Georgia slaveholders Pierce Butler and James Hamilton Couper, were simply indifferent to the religious education of their slaves. At Couper's showplace Georgia plantation, Swedish visitor Fredericka Bremer tried to teach a gathering of the slave children to recite the Lord's Prayer. "The children grinned, laughed, showed their white teeth," she said, "and evinced very plainly that none of them knew what that wonderful prayer meant nor that they had a Father in heaven."[13]

White preachers had to face the dilemma that their Christianity was—at least potentially—subversive of slavery. During the 1834 South Carolina legislative debate over the prohibition on teaching slaves to read and write, Whitemarsh Seabrook noted that anyone who wanted slaves to read the *entire* Bible belonged in "a room in the Lunatic Asylum." To be fair, the ministers were more than mere sycophants of cynical slaveholders. They did not select only the texts that promoted order and discipline among the slaves. But they could not fail to realize that while Christianity promoted order among the slaves, it also contained the seeds of disorder. They certainly would not preach to their congregations that Pharoah had enslaved the children of Israel and had held them in bondage in Egypt, that the Lord had then visited plagues on the slaveholders, or that Moses had led the slaves in a mass escape out of bondage in Egypt to the Promised Land.[14]

If the white ministers shied away from scriptural passages with clear analogies to the condition of the slaves, they did preach the equality of all in the sight of God and the equality of human sinfulness. The Reverend James Henley Thornwell put it thus:

It is a publick testimony to our faith, that the Negro is of one blood with ourselves—that he has sinned as we have, and that he has an equal interest with us in the great redemption. Science, falsely so-called, may attempt to exclude him from the brotherhood of humanity. Men may be seeking eminence and distinction by arguments which link them with the brute; but the instinctive impulses of our nature, combined with the plainest declarations of the word of God, lead us to recognize in his form and lineaments—in his moral, religious, and intellectual nature—the same humanity in which we glory as the image of God. We are not ashamed to call him our brother. Christianity, such ministers preached, imposed obligations not just on the slaves but on their earthly masters as well. Both master and slave on this earth would be held to the same account before the heavenly Master. As the Bible taught servants to obey their masters, these ministers preached, so it required masters to rule their servants wisely, and it required the rich to use their riches to do good.[15]

Thus was the slaveholders' theological dilemma posed: as Christians, they were committed to the religious instruction of their slaves, but the religion preached to the slaves also called the masters to account. Masters were as subject as slaves were to the requirements of Christianity. The idea of equality before God created a problem of role boundaries and emphasized tensions and anomalies within the institution of slavery that could not easily be ignored. Governor Robert F. W. Allston believed that the "best inducement to keep the slaves both Christian and quiescent" was "example on our part; next a just, consistent, systematic administration of domestic government."[16]

### SLAVE WORSHIP

The preacher began softly and conversationally, his voice cool and level. But slowly and gradually he built toward a more pronounced, more powerful rhythm. The slaves in the congregation did not receive his words passively. As the rhythm rose and fell, they became participants as well. The congregational response was essential to worship, a religious requirement. Just as in Africa, such antiphony exemplified the solidarity of the community even as the sermon called forth the profoundest expression of the individual: neither I-Thou nor I-You, but the sacred link between the individual and the social body. The slaves *had* to talk back to the sermon. The preacher had not come to give his own opinions; he had come to preach the word of God to a people who refused to be passive and uncritical receptors. "Amen!" "Yes, Lord!" "Yes, Jesus!" "Yes! Yes!" Feet began to pat. Under the influence of congregational response, the preacher built steadily.

> An dem buckra dat beat dem nigger onjestly an onmusefully, jes kase de po nigger cant help e self, dems de meanest buckra ob all, an berry much like de sheep-killin dog dat cowud to take sumpn dat cant help a self.

"Preach the sermon!" someone shouted. "Yes, Lord!" "Yes, Jesus!" "Yes!" The preacher began to pace back and forth, raising his hands. Someone began to hum a mournful air, and the humming spread through the congregation. The slaves' bodies rocked, their heads nodded, their hands clapped, and their feet stamped a steady rhythm, pushing the preacher onward.

> Dat berry ting dat de nigger cant fend e self an helpless, mek de gentleman buckra berry pashunt an slow to punish dem nigger.

The preacher told them to put all their faith in the Lord. The Lord would deliver them from the House of Bondage as He had delivered the children of Israel from bondage in Egypt. The preacher also likened his flock of slave Christians to a flock of sheep.

> An de berry fack dat de Lawd sheep is po helpless ting, mek de Lawd pity an lub we mo, an mek we pen pun Him an cry fur Him in de time ob trouble an danejur. An dat wha de Lawd want, fur we feel we own weakness an trust in Him strenk. De mudder lub de morest de chile dats de weakest an dat need um de morest, and so wud de Sabeyur an e lettle wuns dat pend only pun Him.

As he moved his congregation toward a crescendo of exaltation, the preacher broke into a chant. The response was no longer confined to antiphonal amens but also included shouts and cries, the clapping of hands and the stamping of feet, and the indescribable sounds of religious transcendence. The congregation worshiped with soul and body in unison. Relying heavily on tone, gesture, and rhythm, the preacher preached a sermon defiant enough to release pent-up frustrations among the slave community, although neither so incendiary as to stir hopeless revolts nor so blatant as to bring down the wrath of the masters upon their heads. But expressing even such mild sentiments could be dangerous. Who could tell when slaves might begin to ask the Lord not merely to deliver them in the next world, but to aid them in casting off the shackles of those who claimed to own them in this one?[17]

Slave preachers achieved renown in the slave community as "men of words." They delivered sermons and prayers with memorable Biblical imagery, imagery that seemed especially relevant to the slaves' own situations. "We're down here, Lord," they preached, "chewin' on dry bones an' swallerin' bitter pills!" The slaves could identify with Moses leading the children of Israel out of enslavement in Egypt after the Lord had visited seven years of plagues upon the slaveholders. They could identify with the crucified Jesus, suffering through his time on the cross, as the slave preacher chanted:

> They led him from hall to hall!
> They whipped him all night long!
> They nailed him to the cross!
> Don't y'u hear how the hammer ring?

It is not difficult to understand why the slaves preferred their own preachers to the emotionless and self-serving platitudes of the white missionaries.[18]

To Christian slaves, the slave preachers were men of status. "My pa was a preacher why I become a Christian so early," testified one. "He used to tell us of hell an' how hot it is. I was so afraid of hell 'till I was always tryin' to do the right thing so I couldn't go to that terrible place." The slave preachers' continuing importance as men of words exemplified another adaptation of African traditions to African American Christianity. The linguistic inventiveness of the slave preachers was related to the ancient concept of *nommo*: the properly spoken word that results in appropriate action. Utilizing ritualized language and behavior as symbolic action, they transformed religious ritual through transcendental ecstasy into structured meaning, renewing and recycling the energies of the slave community. Such "gifted" men, straddling the sacred and secular worlds, were believed to exercise sacred powers within the secular domain. They often mediated between the slaves' Christian beliefs and the workaday world of the lowcountry. The role they played as arbiters in settling disputes among the slaves was itself a product of their African heritage of the involvement of religion in everyday life. Through such mediation the preachers not only promoted social order but also played a major role in solidifying a sense of community among the slaves. In addition, as strong cultural personalities whose identities did not depend upon their positions as slaves, they served younger slaves as important role models.[19]

Slave preachers also sowed the seeds of discontent. The slaves' spiritual life was largely hidden from white observation. Often the slave preachers held services apart from the whites and without their knowledge. The major slave insurrections of the Old South—those of Gabriel Prosser, Nat Turner, and Denmark Vesey—were planned under the cover of such religious associations. According to Charleston's official account of the Vesey plot, "among the conspirators a majority of them belonged to the African church," a recently formed Methodist church described as "composed wholly of persons of color and almost entirely of blacks." The importance of the slaves' religion thus rested upon its capacity to serve them as a source not only of cultural values but also of an understanding of themselves, of their world, and of the relations between themselves and their world. It served them, in other words, both as a model *for* behavior and as a model *of* behavior. The power of African American Christianity in supporting the social values of Gullah slaves rested upon its ability to make plain a world in which those values, as well as the forces opposing them, were primal elements.[20]

## THE SPIRITUALS

The theological orientation of African American Christianity is strikingly revealed in African American spirituals collected in South Carolina in the 1860s. Because the spirituals were transmitted orally, it may be assumed that whatever did not correspond to the slaves' shared religious and poetic sensibilities was eliminated. Deriving their raw materials from Biblical passages, nature, work patterns, and other songs, slave poets often used material objects as poetic devices in the spirituals to amplify their artistry with the resonance of hidden meanings. In the spirituals, for instance, gates symbolically lead to a new and better life. "Children Do Linger," for instance, promises a reunion in the next world when "we'll meet at Zion Gateway." Gates imply passage into the new life for some, but exclusion for others. Not everyone will be allowed through the gates of heaven. In the spiritual "Heaven Bell A-Ringing," the slaves sang, "I run to de gate, but the gate shut fast." In this verse the anonymous slave poet voices the despair of the downtrodden sinner with little hope, a downtrodden sinner barred from entry into heaven. The same theme echoes through yet another spiritual, "Bell Da Ring." Sinners are excluded from the new life, for "the gates are all shut, when de bell done ring."[21]

Streets and roads undergo poetic transformation into symbols of deliverance in the spirituals. Streets are used to suggest that if one walks and lives in the right path, one will find redemption and success: "If you walk de golden street and you join de golden band/ Sing glory be to my Emanuel," the slaves sang in "King Emanuel." One who lives on or walks down the golden street is on the path to deliverance. But the verses, by beginning with "if" clauses, also imply that not everyone will walk down the golden street or join the golden band. Roads fulfill a similar poetic function in the spirituals. Singers announce that they are traveling down the right road, the golden road—set apart from common, ordinary roads—because "I know de road, Heaven bell a'ring, I know de road." But roads in the spirituals are not always as "golden" as streets. Sometimes roads are ordeals, expressing the slaves' belief that one must travel the dark and stormy road of life—full of trials, tribulations, and temptations—if one hopes to reach the golden road to heaven. The road is long ("O walk Jordan long road") and hard ("Road so stormy, Bell da ring"). But the spirituals offer hope to the sinner, reminding believers that the golden road is farther along, beyond the misery of life in bondage ("If you look up de road you see Fader Mosey, join the Angel Band"). If the road is long and dark, "Sister Dolly light the lamp, and the lamp light the road." The road is long and hard, but it leads to Paradise ("I'se been on de road into heaven, My Lord!").[22]

A road itself implies movement, and the slaves always seem to be on the move in the spirituals. In "I Wish I Been Dere," the singer's family has died, and the singer expresses the desire to go with them to Heaven. "I wish I been dere to climb Jacob's ladder." The ascending motion of the spiritual was transcendent to slaves held down too long. The ladder, usually depicted as the Biblical Jacob's ladder, is another poetic transformation in the spirituals. It symbolizes social, economic, or religious climbing. To ascend the ladder is to reach a higher and better level of existence. The line "I wish I been dere to climb Jacob's ladder" reflects the slaves' aspirations to climb to a better place.[23]

Slave poets use ships, boats, and arks in the lowcountry spirituals to symbolize the transfer of people or souls from one place to another over impassable terrain. The Sea Island rowing song "Michael Row the Boat Ashore" utilizes this poetic transformation several times: "Michael row the boat ashore, Hallelujah. . . . Michael boat a music boat. . . . Sister help for trim dat boat. . . . Michael haul the boat ashore, then you'll hear the horn they blow." The boat that carries the souls of men and women into heaven is recalled in such lines as "When de ship is out a-sailin, Hallelujah" and "O brudder will you meet us when de ship is out a-sailin?"[24]

Whereas many spirituals express a desire for change symbolized by traveling roads or climbing ladders, "Fare Ye Well" expresses a feeling that a new life must begin by sweeping the old life clean ("Jesus gib me a little broom, for to sweep 'em clean"). Brooms symbolize the power to become new and better by the act of cleansing, therefore leading the slave upward and forward toward God and a good life.[25]

Through the spirituals slaves were striving to climb higher, to get to a better place, to find a happier life. One way they might fulfill their desire for accomplishment was to build something with their own hands, something they could call their own. The act of building appealed to the slaves. When they sang "Build a house in Paradise/Build it widout a hammer or a nail," they added another dimension to their desire to build houses of their own. A house built without hammer or nail is more than just a house; it is transformed into something miraculous. The hammer and the nail recall Jesus on the cross. And the spiritual assured the slaves that there are many mansions in heaven built not with hammers and nails but with faith.[26]

All of these poetic transformations symbolize deliverance, the passage of souls from this world into the next. Believers either cross through the gates of heaven, enter heaven by sweeping their souls clean with a broom, ride in a boat to heaven, or enter heaven by passing over the streets and roads of righteousness. For some slaves, at least, these devices must also have symbolized the end of slavery and their passage into freedom.[27]

## SPIRIT POSSESSION

African American Christianity emerged from the fragmentation of a unified African religious outlook into separate streams in America. Fragmentation and re-formation were especially marked among the Gullah-speaking slaves of the South Carolina and Georgia lowcountry. One stream of inherited African cosmology included polytheism, the concept of rebirth, and spirit possession in religious ritual. In the South Carolina and Georgia lowcountry, far from the African context of their sacred cosmos, the slaves worshiped their new Christian God with the kind of expressive behavior their African heritage taught them was appropriate for an important deity: a high degree of spiritualism in worship, including the use of chants and bodily movement to rhythmic accompaniment, leading to trances and spirit possession. The phenomenon of spirit possession, one of the most significant features in African religion (especially pronounced among the Bantu, the Yoruba, and the

Fante-Ashanti), was reinterpreted in Christian terms to become a central feature of expressive behavior in African American Christianity and a necessary part of the conversion experience. Conversion was the climax of a spiritual journey called "seeking." A prolonged period of praying "in the wilderness" induced an ecstatic trance without which conversion was not considered authentic. On Sapelo Island, Georgia, Katie Brown sang:

> The way to get to Heaven
> Believer I know
> Go in the wil'erness
> Believer I know
> Cry Lord have mercy
> Believer I know
> Cry Lord have mercy
> Believer I know
> Glory Hallelujah
> Believer I know
> I done cross Jorden
> Believer I know.

Not until one had actually experienced spirit possession was one accepted as a church member; those who had not experienced it were still regarded as sinners.[28]

Slave Christians often held secret meetings at night to pray, to sing, and to "shout." "Shouting" was not the same as yelling or making a loud noise. "Shouting" denoted bodily movements accompanied by singing, handclapping, and foot-stomping. As late as the 1930s, the folklorist John A. Lomax reported that in Murrells Inlet, South Carolina, he had seen "young girls dive through the air and fall headlong on the hard floor in defiance of bruised flesh and broken bones. The men were more careful of bodily injuries, seemingly content to 'hold' the riotous females temporarily under the influence of the words of the minister." White observers often mistook shouting for dancing. In shouting, however, the feet were not supposed to cross each other or to leave the floor; such acts would be dancing, and dancing was regarded as sinful. Frederika Bremer reported having heard that "the Methodist missionaries, who are the most influential and effective teachers and preachers among the negroes, are very angry with them for their love of dancing and music, and declare them to be sinful." Such hostility seemed to her "a very unwise proceeding on the part of the preachers. Are not all God's gifts good, and may they not be made use of in His honor? . . . I would, instead, let them have sacred dances, and let them sing to them joyful songs of praise in the beautiful air, beneath the blossoming trees. Did not King David dance and sing in pious rapture before the ark of God?" Exemplifying the creative adaptation of the West African ring "dance," which was performed to complex drum rhythms, the shout consisted of body motions performed to the accompaniment of spirituals. Slaves improvised a substitute for the drums, with polyrhythmic hand-clapping and foot-stomping. While slave Christians often deprecated dancing, they shouted with great enthusiasm.[29]

When slave Christians gathered for praise meetings at one another's quarters, the soaring rhetoric of the prayers, the antiphonal singing, and the ecstatic shouts provided a release for pent-up emotions. For the slaves, religious services constituted not a relationship between a performer and an audience but a mutual performance. Just as the spirituals were marked by the strong call-and-response antiphony of African music, so prayers and sermons were punctuated by congregational responses.[30]

## HAGS, HAUNTS, AND PLAT EYES

Her hair was plaited and tightly wrapped with white twine. Her garments hung loosely about her gaunt frame. Her name was Addie, and she came out of slavery times. Her windowless cabin had but one room. Her table consisted of a board and four sticks, her china of clam shells. A blue milk-of-magnesia bottle served as a flower vase. But in this cabin Addie had reared fourteen grandchildren and great-grandchildren. In her yard redbirds visited, sunflowers turned their faces to the sun, and crape myrtles displayed their colorful finery. Wild plum trees hugged the sides of her house, and green corn waved a bright promise in the fields beyond. In March of 1936, Addie sat on the porch of her cabin at Murrells Inlet, South Carolina, with Genevieve Willcox Chandler, a fieldworker for the Federal Writers Project, spinning out her memories of life in bondage. Addie's nose crinkled with the effort to put her life into words, to leave behind her testimony so that future generations could know what the slaves had been forced to live through. She was asked about "Plat Eyes," the most hideous and most malevolent of the occult spirits of the Georgia and South Carolina coast, evil spirits that changed shapes at will in order to lure victims into danger and rob them of their sanity. "De ole folks is talk bout Plat Eye," Addie recalled.

Dey say dey takes shape ob all kind da critter—dawg, cat, hawg, mule, varmint and I is hear tell ob Plat Eye takin form ob gator. I ain see dem scusing wan lettle time. You know dat leetle swamply place hind de Parsonage? Well, wan time—I hab meh bloom on me [was in her prime] een dem days. . . . En I bawg tru dat deep white sand en I passes de grabe yard entrance en I leabes de open en enters dem dahk woods whey de moss wabe low en brush een yuh face. En I been tink bout Plat Eye. De min come tuh me it wuz good time tuh meet um.

Den I bresh dem weepin moss aside en I trabble de wet mud een meh bare feets en my shoe been tie tuh meh girdle string. En wen I been come tuh de foot lawg . . . a cootuh [small turtle] slide offen de lawg at meh feets. En, clare tuh Gawd, I been fuh look up at dat cootuh en den I turn meh eye up en der wuz a cat—black cat wid he eye lak balls ob fire en he back all arch up en he tail twissin en er switchin en he hair stan on end. E move backward front ob me cross dat cypress lawg. En he been big. E been large ez meh leetle yearlin ox.

En I talk tuh 'em en try fuh draw close. En I say tuh um, "I ain fuh feah nuttin! Ain no ghos'! Ain no hant! Ain no Plat Eye! Ain no nuttin'!" En I'se try fuh sing,

> E carry me tru many ob danger
> Because he fus lubb me.
> E guard gainst hant en Plat Eye
> Because he fus lubb me.

En dat Plat Eye ain gib me back meh word. E mobe forward en he tail swish en swish same lak big moccasin tail wen e lash de rushes.

En de mind come to me, "Chile ob Gawd, doan you show no fear!" En I is brace up. En meh short handle leetle clam rake been een meh han', en I sing,

> Gawd will take care ob me.
> Walkin' tru many of dangers,

Gawd will take care ob me.

En den de min [mind] come tuh me, "De Lawd heps dem wut heps deyself!" En I raise up meh rake en I come right cross dat critter head.

Ef dat had uh been a real cat, I'd uh pin um tuh dat lawg. Meh rake been bury deep, en de lawg hold um. En I clare tuh Gawd, e up en prance right under meh feets, dem eyes burnin holes een me en e tail swish, swish lak ole Sooky tail wen de flies bad.

En I gits mad. I fuh struggle wid meh rake en de lawg loosen e grip en I fuh pray, "Gib Addie strenth, O Gawd!" En down I come straight tru dat critter middle . . . But dat critter ain feel meh lick.

En I'se rassel lak Jacob wid de angel. I been strong en hab meh bloom on me. It ain 'vail nuttin. No man! Mr. Plat Eye jes ez pert en frisky as fore he been hit. En I'buse um en I cuss um en I say, "You debbil! Clare mah path!" En if dat critter didn't paw de air en jus rise up dat big bamboo vine an me fuh hit um ebry jump!

So, I tink, "Sinner, lebel dat lawg." De min' come to me, "Chile ob Gawd, trabbel de woods path!" En I tuhn back en I hit dat path. En I ain been tarry en jes ez I wuz gibbin Gawd de praise fuh delivuh me, DERE DAT CAT! Dis time he big ez meh middle size ox en he eye been BLAZE!

En I lam [strike at] en I lam. En dat rake handle been wire en been nail on. En jus ez I mek meh las' lam, dat critter rise up for my eyes en dis time e been big ez cousin Andrew full grown ox. En he vanish up dat ole box pine ez yuh quits de deep woods.

I ain b'lieve een Plat Eye 'twell den, but I min's meh step since dem days. En wen I trabbles de deep woods whey de moss wabe low . . . en de firefly flickuh, I'se ready fuh um.

Uncle Murphy, e witch doctuh en e been tell me how fuh fend um off. Gunpowder en sulphur. Dey is say Plat Eye can't stan' dem smell mix. Dat man full ob knowledge. E mus hab Gawd min' een um. So I totes meh powder en sulphur en I carries meh stick een meh han en I puts meh truss een Gawd.[31]

Addie's plat eye narrative illustrates a second stream of African cosmology, a stream that proved less compatible with African American Christianity than rebirth and spirit possession. Many slaves in the South Carolina and Georgia lowcountry continued to embrace African supernatural beliefs that were not incorporated into African American Christianity but instead persisted in a kind of parallel stream. Addie's defense against plat eyes, in its ingenious blend of creativity, tradition, and common sense, may be seen as a metaphor for the emergence of African American Christianity.[32]

"Hags"—or "boo hags"—were one example of these supernatural beliefs. Hags were the disembodied spirits of witches or "conjure men" who were believed to leave their skins behind in order to fly through the air and give people nightmares, or "ride" them. Especially bothersome creatures, hags were believed able to fly through the air to midnight rendezvous, and to sail through keyholes by placing the bone of a black cat in their mouths. It was said that hags could bewitch people merely by looking at them. Even accusations of cannibalism attached to those suspected of witchcraft. Old Grace, an elderly slave on St. Simons Island, was rumored by her neighbors to be a hag. Local children were warned to stay away from her cabin because she allegedly boasted that she had eaten children in her native land. Slaves could take precautions, however, to keep hags from riding them: "conjure balls" (hair balls filled with roots, herbs, and other substances) were sometimes successful in keeping them at bay. But the only certain preventive was to eliminate the hag. That could best be done by the traditional African method of salting and peppering the skin while she had left it behind to go out "hagging."[33]

"Haunts"—the spirits of the dead—returned from time to time to trouble the living, in a modified version of the Congo *zumbi* or the Haitian *zombi*. The process of dying, according to West African belief, was not complete for up to five years. The spirits of the ancestors—the living dead—were the closest link between the world of the living and the world of the spirits, because they straddled both worlds.[34]

Haunts were most likely to appear at certain times, such as during a full moon or on Friday nights when the moon was young, although they were believed also to show themselves in broad daylight at certain places. Some believed that haunts rose up in every graveyard on the stroke of twelve; one haunt—the spirit of the oldest dead—would stay behind to guard the vacated graves while the others roamed the roads and entered houses. At slave funerals, efforts were made to contain the spirits of the ancestors; the living sought to prevent the dead from remaining behind as malign spirits.[35]

## CONJURATION

Many features of African religion thus either converged or coexisted with Christianity. A third stream of African cosmology maintained a subterranean existence outside of and inimical to African American Christianity. This element of slave religion continues to be largely unknown and at least partly unknowable. Documentation of voodoo, or hoodoo (as African conjuration was called in the New World), is inevitably scanty, as such magical shamanism was practiced clandestinely. Still, sufficient evidence remains to testify to the existence of an underground stream of magical shamanism, not only throughout the slavery period, but long beyond.[36]

Illness was regarded as supernatural in origin; thus it was necessary, through sorcery, to summon the spirits of the dead to offer advice or to perform cures. Voodoo, or hoodoo, could be used for either protective or malevolent purposes: it could cure an illness, kill an enemy, or secure someone's love. All misfortune, including (presumably) slavery, was regarded as the result of magical shamanism. The only way a slave could gain protection from sorcery was by stronger countersorcery. With some variation, voodoo was known throughout the slave societies of the New World.[37]

The survival of African sorcery seems to have been most pronounced in the South Carolina and Georgia lowcountry, where slaves were concentrated in significant numbers. Voodoo grew with the arrival of slaves from the West Indies or directly from Africa, who adapted African snake cults to a new environment. High in the African pantheon, the snake god of the Ewe, Fon, Bantu, Dahomey, Ouidah, and Yoruba symbolized the cosmic energy of nature, the dealer of fortune or misfortune. The African names for the voodoo gods were lost; their personalities converged with those of Judeo-Christian prophets and saints, demons and devils. They continued to comfort believers and to wreak havoc on the wicked. Only the snake god's sorcerers could invoke his protective power. Snakeskins were prominent in initiation rituals. Snake charming was featured in some rites. All sorts of supernatural might were attributed to serpents in the snake lore of lowcountry slaves.[38]

Voodoo in the lowcountry never approached the complexities of Haitian Vodun; nevertheless, it achieved a distinctive character above the level of simple, unorganized sorcery. Gullah slaves took their physical or personal problems more often to local conjurers—the priests of the old religion—than to their masters. Such conjurers often enjoyed considerable power within the slave community, even among some of the Christians. They were spoken of with great awe, and some were considered invulnerable. No feat of black magic was considered beyond their ability to perform. Conjurers gained and held their influence over the slaves by various methods and especially by fear. Their patrons relied upon them both for protection and relief from spells and for casting spells upon their enemies.[39]

The sorcerer's spells could be benign as well as malign. If conjurers were considered the source of most misfortunes, they were also held in high esteem as healers. The positive role played by the sorcerers in treating slave illnesses demonstrates the role religion played in every aspect of life among the slaves. Voodoo allowed the slaves the exalted feeling of direct contact with the supernatural in attempting to cope with their ailments.[40]

Not all Gullah slaves believed in magical shamanism; the sorcerers neither commanded universal adherence nor approached the political power of the priests of Obeah, Myalism, or Vodun in the West Indies. Most Christian slaves—if they did not summarily reject the appeal of sorcery—considered the shaman's powers to be evil, hostile to the spirit of Christianity. Nevertheless, conjurers exercised an extraordinary influence over the lives of other slaves that they could have neither gained nor maintained if they had not fulfilled a real function. Even if they are often considered frauds and extortionists, sorcerers served their fellow slaves in times of suffering. They were interpreters of those unobservable spirits whose activities directed everyday life; they were awesome beings whose supernatural powers could be enlisted in the redress of grievances. Gullah Jack, one of the organizers of the Denmark Vesey plot, enlisted his occult powers in the cause of the slave revolt. Sorcerers in the lowcountry bridged for Gullah slaves the precarious life of servitude in this world and the mysteries of the spirit world. They turned human behavior into a perceived cosmic order and projected images of that order onto the plane of the slaves' everyday experience. They created a buffer against mental and emotional submission for the slaves who believed in them. Many—perhaps most—of the slaves abandoned shamanistic traditions, but those who held on tenaciously to their beliefs helped to preserve and extend an autonomous African heritage, making an important contribution to community and survival.[41]

## THE CREATIVITY OF SLAVE CHRISTIANITY

Thus the once-unified religious cosmology fragmented. Adherence to the various components was by no means uniform. Some Gullah slaves abandoned belief in all forms of non-Christian supernaturalism; many selectively adhered to some beliefs and abandoned others. Some undoubtedly continued African religious practices under cover of Christianity. What may have appeared to the slaveholders to be the Christian cross may well have referred, in the mind of a given slave, to the Yoruba belief in sacred crossroads or the Kongo symbol for the four points of the sun. How easily Christianity might be interpreted in the same "primitive" terms that Western scholars apply to African religions is pointed up by Zora Neale Hurston in a letter she wrote, with mock naïveté, to her anthropological mentor, Franz Boas:

> Is it safe for me to say that baptism is an extension of water worship as a part of pantheism just as the sacrament is an extension of cannibalism? Isn[']t the use of candles in the Catholic chu[r]ch a relic of fire worship? Are not all the uses of fire upon the altars the same thing? Is not the christian ritual rather one of attenuated nature-worship, in the fire, water, and blood?

Might not the frequently mentioned fire of the Holy Ghost not be an unconscious fire worship. May it not be a deification of fire?"[42]

Despite a large number of "survivals" of African cultural patterns, what is most obvious from a truly Afrocentric perspective is the creativity of slave culture in the lowcountry. Most of the slaves' culture was neither "retained" from Africa nor "adopted" from white slaveholders. Rather, it was created by the slaves from a convergence of various African cultural patterns, white cultural influence, and the necessities demanded by new environment.[43]

The religion created by enslaved Africans shaped as much as it reflected their worldview. The Christianity of African Americans reveals both their mental picture of the unalterable shape of reality and their deepest, most comprehensive concepts of cosmic order. For them, religion functioned to portray their ethical and aesthetic preferences as normative—given the imposed conditions of reality—while it also supported such preferences by invoking deeply felt ethical and aesthetic beliefs as evidence of their truth. The African contribution to African American Christianity was enormous. The slaves did not simply adopt the God and the faith of the white missionaries. In establishing a spiritual life for themselves, they reinterpreted the elements of Christianity in terms of deep-rooted African religious concerns. Africa was not culturally homogeneous, nor did it bequeath to its exiles in the African diaspora a legacy of static survivals. In fact, religious expression in Africa was diverse, and borrowings among ethnic groups were common. Rising above the variety of beliefs and practices, however, was a shared bond—a concept of the sacred cosmos in which virtually all experience was religious, from the naming of children to planting, hunting, and fishing practices. Underlying the various African cultures were shared cognitive (or "grammatical") orientations—mental rules governing appropriate behavior—that profoundly affected the slaves' adoption, adaptation, and application of Christianity.[44] The originality of African American Christianity, then, lies neither in its African elements nor in its Christian elements, but in its unique and creative synthesis of both. Examination of the selective Christianity evangelized to the slaves may provide some perspective on the process by which lowcountry slaves mixed both elements and adapted both to the realities of slave life.

Despite unusually strong continuities of Islam and of traditional African religions, most Gullah slaves embraced Christianity. In their praise meetings, in their ecstatic prayers and exuberant shouts, and especially in their transcendent spirituals, they found a source of strength and endurance that enabled them to triumph over the collective tragedy of enslavement.

## NOTES

Part of this essay was written while the author was an associate of the W. E. B. Du Bois Institute for Afro-American Research at Harvard University. The support of the Du Bois Institute is gratefully acknowledged. Earlier versions of this paper were presented in the New Christianities series at the University of Utah and in the symposium on the History of African American Christianity at the Harvard Divinity School, Cambridge, Mass., December 8–9, 1989. I am grateful to Randall Burkett, Ronald Coleman, Robert L. Hall, Paul Johnson, Albert Raboteau, Margaret Washington, and David Wills for their helpful comments.

1. Roswell King to Pierce Butler, May 13, 1803, quoted in Malcolm Bell, Jr., *Major Butler's Legacy: Five Generations of a Slaveholding Family* (Athens: University of Georgia Press, 1987), 132.

2. Interviews with Robert Pinckney, Wilmington Island, and Ryna Johnson, St. Simons Island, in Savannah Unit, Federal Writers Project

[eds.], *Drums and Shadows: Survival Studies among the Georgia Coastal Negroes* (Athens: University of Georgia Press, 1940; reprint, 1987), 106, 176. Cf. Daniel C. Littlefield, *Rice and Slaves: Ethnicity and the Slave Trade in Colonial South Carolina* (Baton Rouge: Louisiana State University Press, 1981).

3. One of the most controversial topics in the controversial literature of American slavery is the nature and origin—the intellectual and spiritual sources—of the religion of the slaves. One school of thought, deriving from the work of the black sociologist E. Franklin Frazier, emphasizes the influence of white culture upon enslaved Africans. Some leading contemporary scholars of slavery emphasize that the values and practices of white Christians penetrated deeply into black Christianity, and the black church became perhaps the most important agency in "Americanizing" enslaved Africans and their descendants. See John Boles, *Black Southerners, 1619–1869* (Lexington: University of Kentucky Press, 1983), 153–68; John Boles, ed., *Masters and Slaves in the House of the Lord* (Lexington: University of Kentucky Press, 1988); and John Blassingame *The Slave Community: Plantation Life in the Antebellum South*, 2d ed. (New York: Oxford University Press, 1979), 98. An opposite school of thought, emphasizing the "Africanity" of slave religion, derves from the work of the white anthropologist Melville J. Herskovits. Sterling Stuckey, for example, argues that the Christianity of the slaves was "shot through with African values." A leading contemporary spokesman for Africanity, Stuckey interprets the culture of the African diaspora using African rather than European ideals. "By operating under cover of Christianity," Stuckey writes, "vital aspects of Africanity, which were considered eccentric in movement, sound, or symbolism, could more easily be practiced openly." As Stuckey sees it, slave Christianity was simply "a protective exterior beneath which more complex, less familiar (to outsiders) religious principles and practices were operative." Writing from an Afrocentric critical perspective, Stuckey insists that the distinctive attributes of slave Christianity were outward and visible manifestations of inward and invisible African cognitive orientations, reflecting "a religious outlook toward which the master class might otherwise be hostile." What John Blassingame describes as "the 'Americanization' of the bondsman" Stuckey calls the "Africanization of Christianity." See Sterling Stuckey, *Slave Culture: Nationalist Theory and the Foundations of Black America* (New York: Oxford University Press, 1987), 35–36, 54, 57. Cf. Blassingame, *Slave Community*, 98. A third school

of thought, exemplified by Mechal Sobel, sees the emergence of slave religion as a convergence of European and African religious values. In her study of the colonial Chesapeake, Sobel contends that stressing the relative autonomy of slave culture overlooks the cultural interaction of Africans and Europeans. Enslaved Africans, she argues, adopted Christian eschatology, while their white neighbors adopted African practices of spirit possession and the African sense of life as a spiritual pilgrimage. Thus, not only was black culture shaped by exposure to white culture, but emergent forms of white culture were also shaped by close association with bearers of African tradition. See Mechal Sobel, *The World They Made Together: Black and White Values in Eighteenth-Century Virginia* (Princeton, N.J.: Princeton University Press, 1987), esp. 11, 137, 221, 233. To acknowledge the convergence of African and European elements in African American Christianity, however, is not to imply that Europe and Africa always converged in relatively equal proportions. In such places as the South Carolina and Georgia lowcountry, enslaved Africans and their descendants constituted 80 to 90 percent of the population for most of the eighteenth and nineteenth centuries. In such places, African cultural influences necessarily outweighed European ones.

4. Georgia Bryan Conrad, "Reminiscences of a Southern Woman," *Southern Workman* 30 (1901): 13; see also her *Reminiscences of a Southern Woman* (Hampton, Va., [1901]). Interview with Shad Hall, Sapelo Island, Georgia, in Savannah Writers Project, *Drums and Shadows*, 166; interview with Katie Brown, Sapelo Island, Georgia, ibid., 161. The name is transcribed Bi-la-li, Bu Allah, or Ben Ali in various sources. See also Clyde Ahmad Winters, "Afro-American Muslims from Slavery to Freedom," *Islamic Studies* 17 (1978), 187–90; Alan D. Austin, *African Muslims in Antebellum America* (New York: Garland, 1984).

5. Katie Brown, in Savannah Writers Project, *Drums and Shadows*, 162; Katie Brown, quoted in Lydia Parrish, *Slave Songs of the Georgia Sea Islands* (New York: Creative Age Press, 1942; reprint, Athens: University of Georgia Press, 1991), 27; Shad Hall, in Savannah Writers Project, *Drums and Shadows*, 166.

6. Charles Ball, *Slavery in the United States: A Narrative of the Life and Adventures of Charles Ball, A Black Man, Who Lived Forty Years in Maryland, South Carolina and Georgia, as a Slave* (New York: John Taylor, 1835), 164–65; Ball Family Papers, South Carolina Library, University of South Carolina, Columbia. According to Sterling Stuckey,

"the great bulk of the slaves were scarcely touched by Christianity": *Slave Culture*, 37–38.

7. Charles Colcock Jones, *Suggestions on the Religious Instruction of the Negroes in the Southern States* (Philadelphia: Presbyterian Board of Publication, 1847), quoted in Robert S. Starobin, ed., *Blacks in Bondage: Letters of American Slaves* (New York: New Viewpoints, 1974), 42.

8. Ball, *Slavery in the United States*, 164–65, 201–3; Rev. Edward Thomas to Rt. Rev. R. W. Whittingham, March 10, 1836, quoted in Eugene D. Genovese, *Roll, Jordan, Roll: The World the Slaves Made* (New York: Pantheon, 1974), 187; Paul Trapier, *The Religious Instruction of the Black Population: The Gospel To Be Given to Our Servants* (Charleston, S.C., 1847), 14; Henry Brown, Charleston, interviewed by Jessie A. Butler, in *The American Slave: A Composite Autobiography*, ed. George P. Rawick (Westport, Conn.: Greenwood, 1972), vol. 2, sec. 1, 120; Sarah Hodgson Torian, ed., "Antebellum and War Memories of Mrs. Telfair Hodgson," *Georgia Historical Quarterly* 27 (1943), 351. Cf. William W. Freehling, *Prelude to Civil War* (New York: Harper and Row, 1966), 336–37; Luther P. Jackson, "Religious Instruction of Negroes, 1830–1860, With Special Reference to South Carolina," *Journal of Negro History* 15 (1930), 72–114.

9. Charles Colcock Jones, *A Catechism of Scripture, Doctrine and Practice for Families and Sabbath Schools. Designed Also for the Oral Instruction of Colored Persons* (Savannah and New York: Observer Office Press, 1844), 127–30, quoted in Bell, *Major Butler's Legacy*, 152–63.

10. John Rogers, "My Dear Children," April 5, 1842, quoted in Genovese, *Roll, Jordan, Roll*, 190; Robert F. W. Allston, quoted by Ulrich B. Phillips, "Racial Problems, Adjustments, and Disturbances," in *The South in the Building of the Nation*, ed. Julian A. C. Chandler, Franklin L. Riley, James C. Ballagh, John Bell Henneman, Edwin Mims, Thomas E. Watson, Samuel Chiles Mitchell, and Walter Lynwood Fleming, (Richmond, Va.: Southern Historical Publishing Society, 1909–12), 4: 210.

11. Charles Colcock Jones to Sandy Maybank, quoted in Starobin, *Blacks in Bondage*, 42; Charles Colcock Jones to Catoe, January 28, 1831, ibid., 44; Catoe to Charles Colcock Jones, September 3, 1852, ibid., 48; Andrew to Charles Colcock Jones, September 10, 1852, ibid., 51–52.

12. James Henley Thornwell, *The Rights and Duties of the Masters: A Sermon Preached at the Dedication of a Church Erected in Charleston, S.C. for the Benefit and Instruction of the Colored Population* (Charleston, S.C.: Walker and James, 1850), 11;

Public Proceedings Relating to Calvary Church and the Religious Instruction of Slaves* (Charleston, S.C.: Walker and James, 1805), 19.

13. Frederika Bremer, *Homes in the New World: Impressions of America* (New York: Harper, 1853), 1:491.

14. Whitemarsh Seabrook, quoted in Freehling, *Prelude to Civil War*, 335; Whitemarsh Seabrook, *Essay on the Management of Slaves* (Charleston, S.C.: Miller and Brown, 1834), 15, 28–30. On the revolutionary potential of African American Christianity, see Orville Vernon Burton, *In My Father's House Are Many Mansions: Family and Community in Edgefield, South Carolina* (Chapel Hill: University of North Carolina Press, 1985), 152–58.

15. Thornwell, *Rights and Duties of Masters*, 11; Alexander Glennie, *Sermons Preached on Plantations to Congregations of Slaves* (Charleston, S.C.: 1844), 1–5, 21–27. Cf. John Blassingame, *The Slave Community: Plantation Life in the Anti-Bellum South* (New York: Oxford University Press, 1972), 170.

16. Robert F. W. Allston, *Essay on Sea Coast Crops* (Charleston, S.C.: A. E. Miller, 1854), 41. On the problem of role boundaries in culture, see Mary Douglas, *Purity and Danger: An Analysis of Concepts of Pollution* (London: Praeger, 1966), 143.

17. This is a composite of descriptions of slave religious services in Bremer, *Homes in the New World*, 1: 289–90; William Wyndham Malet, *An Errand to the South in the Summer of 1862* (London: Richard Bentley, 1863), 49–50, 74; Laurence Oliphant, *Patriots and Filibusters; or Incidents of Political and Exploratory Travel* (Edinburgh: Blackwood, 1860), 140–41; Sir Charles Lyell, *A Second Visit to the United States of America* (London: John Murray, 1849), 1: 269–70, 2: 213–14; A. M. H. Christensen, "Spirituals and Shouts of the Southern Negroes," *Journal of American Folk-Lore* 7 (1894), 154–55; H. G. Spaulding, "Under the Palmetto," *Continental Monthly* 4 (1863), 196–200; Daniel E. Huger Smith, "A Plantation Boyhood," in *A Carolina Rice Plantation of the Fifies*, ed. Alice R. Hugher Smith and Herbert Ravenel Sass (New York: William Morrow, 1936), 75; C. Vann Woodward, ed., *Mary Chestnut's Civil War* (New Haven, Conn.: Yale University Press, 1981), 213–14; and John G. Williams, *De Ole Plantation: Elder Coteney's Sermons* (Charleston, S.C.: Walker, Evans, and Coggswell, 1895), 2–11. The text is quoted from Williams, *De Ole Plantation*, 40. I recorded a similar African American religious service at New Bethel Baptist Church on Sandy Island, S.C., January 16, 1972. William Faulkner includes a literary description of such a

service in the "Dilsey" section of *The Sound and the Fury* (New York: Jonathan Cape and Harrison Smith, 1929). See also analyses of African American preaching styles in W. E. B. Du Bois, "Religion of the Southern Negro," *New World* 9 (1900); Grace Sims Holt, "Stylin' Outta the Black Pulpit," in *Rappin' and Stylin' Out*, ed. Thomas Kochman (Urbana: University of Illinois Press, 1972), 189–95; Le Roi Jones, *Blues People: Negro Music in White America* (New York: William Morrow, 1963), 45–46; Henry H. Mitchell, *Black Preaching* (Philadelphia: J. B. Lippincott, 1970); Bruce A Rosenburg, *The Art of the American Folk Preacher* (New York: Oxford University Press, 1970), 7, 10, 14, 17, 40, 47, 51, 115–16; Gerald L. Davis, *I Got the Word in Me and I can Preach It, You Known* (Philadelphia: University of Pennsylvania Press, 1987); W. D. Weatherford, *American Churches and the Negro: An Historical Study from early Slave Days to the Present* (Boston: Christopher Publishing House, 1957), 114–15; Carter G. Woodson, *History of the Negro Church* (Washington, D.C.: Association for the Study of Negro Life and History, 1921), 41; Clarence E. Walker, *A Rock in a Weary Land: The African Methodist Episcopal Church during the Civil War and Reconstruction* (Baton Rouge: Louisiana State University Press, 1982), 61. On the status of the slave preachers in the slave community, see John W. Blassingame, "Status and Social Structure in the Slave Community," in *The Afro-American Slaves: Community or Chaos*, ed. Randall M. Miller (Malabar, Fla.: Robert Krieger, 1981), 114, 120–21. *Buckra* means white person.

18. Parrish, *Slave Songs*, 166.

19. Henry Brown interview in Rawick, *The American Slave*, vol. 2, sec. 1, 126. Cf. Albert J. Raboteau, Jr., *Slave Religion: The "Invisible Institution" in the Antebellum South* (New York: Oxford University Press, 1978), 136–37; Roger Bastide *African Civilisations in the New World*, trans. Peter Green (New York: Harper and Row, 1971), 92. On the social position of the preacher in the slave community, see Blassingame, "Status and Social Structure," 114, 120–21. On the social position of the man of words elsewhere in the African diaspora, see Roger D. Abrahams, *The Man of Words in the West Indies* (Baltimore, Md.: Johns Hopkins University Press, 1983). On the social position of the man of words in African societies, see S. A. Babalola, *The Content and Form of Yoruba Ijala* (Oxford: Clarendon Press, 1966), 40–55; Dan Ben-Amos, *Sweet Words: Storytelling Events in Benin* (Philadelphia: Institute for the Study of Human Issues, 1975), and his "Two Benin Storytellers," in Richard M. Dorson, ed., *African Folklore* (Garden City, N.Y.: Doubleday, 1972), 103–14; Ruth Finnegan, *Limba Stories and Storytelling* (Oxford: Clarendon Press, 1966), 64–85; and Judith Irvine, "Caste and Communication in a Woloj Village" (Ph.D. dissertation, University of Pennsylvania, 1973). For a discussion of the "phenomenon of mid-transition"—of one who straddles sacred and secular worlds—see Victor W. Turner, *The Forest of Symbols: Aspects of Ndembu Ritual* (Ithaca, N.Y.: Cornell University Press, 1967), 110; and Victor W. Turner, ed., *Celebration: Studies in Festivity and Ritual* (Washington, D.C.: Smithsonian Institution, 1982). See also Kenneth Burke, *Language as Symbolic Action: Essays in Life, Literature, and Method* (Berkeley and Los Angeles: University of California Press, 1971), 391; and Peter Berger and Thomas Luckmann, *The Social Construction of Reality: A Treatise in the Sociology of Knowledge* (Garden City, N.Y.: Doubleday, 1966), 47–49.

20. Lionel H. Kennedy and Thomas Parker, *An Official Report of the Trials of Sundry Negroes Charged with an Attempt to Raise an Insurrection in the State of South Carolina* (Charleston, S.C.: James R. Schenk, 1822), 14–15, 50, 54, 61. Other contemporary accounts include Edwin C. Holland, *A Refutation of the Calumines against Southern and Western States: An Account of the Late Intended Insurrection among a Portion of the Blacks of this City*, 3d ed. (Charleston, S.C.: A. E. Miller, 1822), 22–23, 30; [James Hamilton, Jr.], *Narrative of the Conspiracy and Intended Insurrection among a Portion of the Blacks in the State of South Carolina in the Year 1822* (Boston: Joseph W. Ingram, 1822); and [Thomas Pinckney,] *Reflections, Occasioned by the Late Disturbances in Charleston* (Charleston, S.C.: A. E. Miller, 1822). There is a manuscript trial transcript in [Thomas Bennett], Governor's Message No. 2, November 2, 1822, Governor's Papers, South Carolina Department of Archives and History, Columbia. Book-length secondary accounts of the Vesey plot include John Lofton, *Denmark Vesey's Revolt: The Slave Plot that Lit a Fuse to Fort Sumter* (Kent, Ohio: Kent State University Press, 1983); and Robert S. Starobin, ed., *Insurrection in South Carolina: The Slave Conspiracy of 1822* (Englewood Cliffs, N.J.: Prentice-Hall, 1970). Cf. Clifford Geertz, *The Interpretation of Cultures* (New York: Basic Books, 1973), 123–31.

21. William Francis Allen, Charles P. Ware, and Lucy McKim Garrison, eds., *Slave Songs of the United States* (Boston: A. Simpson, 1867), 51, 55, 20, 34. Cf. John Lovell, Jr., *Black Song: The Forge and The Flame. The Story of How the Afro-American Spiritual Was Hammered Out* (New York: Macmillan, 1972), 244–50.

22. Allen, Ware, and Garrison, *Slave Songs of the U.S.,* 6, 13, 26, 28, 34, 39, 42, 50, 63, 66, 75, 81.

23. Ibid., 67, 29.

24. Ibid., 23, 50–51.

25. Ibid., 93.

26. Ibid., 68, 29.

27. Charles Joyner, *Folk Song in South Carolina* (Columbia, S.C.: University of South Carolina Press, 1971), 62–95.

28. Katie Brown, in Parish, *Slave Songs,* 131–32; Chalmers S. Murray, "Edisto's Ghosts Fond of Whiskey," Chalmers S. Murray Papers, South Carolina Historical Society, Charleston (hereinafter abbreviated SCHS). Cf. Julia Peterkin, *Green Thursday* (New York: Alfred A. Knopf, 1924), 94–101; and Roland Steiner, "Seeking Jesus," *Journal of American Folklore* 14 (1901): 672. For comparative examples of the convergence of African spirit possession with Christianity in African American cultures, see Erika Bourguignon's "Ritual Dissociation and Possession Belief in Caribbean Negro Religion," in Norman E. Whitten, Jr., and John F. Szwed, eds., *Afro-American Anthropology: Contemporary Perspectives* (New York: Free Press, 1970), 87–101; Elsa Goveia, *Slave Society in the British Leeward Islands at the End of the Eighteenth Century* (New Haven, Conn.: Yale University Press, 1965), 247–48; Edward Brathwaite, *The Development of Creole Society in Jamaica, 1770–1820* (Oxford: Clarendon Press, 1971), 219; George E. Simpson, " 'Batismal,' 'Mourning,' and 'Building' Ceremonies of the Shouters of Trinidad," *Journal of American Folklore* 79 (1965): 537–50; and George E. Simpson, *The Shango Cult in Trinidad* (San Juan, P.R.: Institute of Caribbean Studies, 1965), 155.

29. John A. Lomax, *Field Notes 1935–1937,* John A. Lomax Papers, Archive of Folk Culture, Library of Congress; Bremer, *Homes in the New World,* 1: 290; Chalmers S. Murray, "Tom-Toms Sound for Edisto Rites," in Murray Papers, SCHS; Smith, "A Plantation Boyhood," 75–76; Charlotte Forten, "Life on the Sea Islands," *Atlantic Monthly* 13 (1864): 593–94, and *The Journal of Charlotte L. Forten,* ed. Ray L. Billington (New York: Dryden Press, 1953), 153, 184, 190, 205; Allen, Ware, and Garrison, *Slave Songs of the U.S.,* xiv; Thomas Wentworth Higginson, "Negro Spirituals," *Atlantic Monthly* 19 (1867): 685–94, and his *Army Life in a Black Regiment* (Boston, 1870), 197–98; Elizabeth Ware Pearson, ed., *Letters from Port Royal* (Boston: W. B. Clarke, 1906), 22–28; Rupert S. Holland, ed., *Letters and Diary of Laura M. Towne: Written from the Sea Islands of South Carolina, 1862–1884* (Cambridge, Mass.: 1912), 20–23; Society for the Preservation of Spirituals, *The Carolina Low Country* (New York: William Morrow, 1931), 198–201; Zora Neale Hurston, "Shouting," in Nancy Cunard, ed., *Negro: An Anthology* (London: Wishart, 1934), 49–50; Willie Lee Rose, *Rehearsal for Reconstruction: The Port Royal Experiment* (Indianapolis, Ind.: Bobbs-Merrill, 1964), 91. The symbolic significance of drums to both blacks and whites is illustrated in Edward G. Mason, "A Visit to South Carolina in 1860," *Atlantic Monthly* 53 (1884): 244. The importance of shouting in African American Christianity is underlined by an exchange between a Gullah preacher and a white folklorist in 1936. After a field trip to All Saints Parish in the South Carolina lowcountry, John A. Lomax wrote in his field notes, "Once I asked the Reverend Aaron Pinnacle of Heavens Gate Church, South Carolina, why he deliberately attempted in his sermons to influence his congregation to 'shout'. . . . The Reverend Pinnacle, coal black [illegible] replied without hesitation: 'If I did not preach shoutin' sermons, my congregation would pay me nothing.' Even in religious matters, the economic factor is dominant. We can't get away from it." See Lomax, Field Notes, 1935–1937, Lomax Papers, Library of Congress.

30. Trapier, *Religious Instruction,* 4; Almira Coffin to Mrs. J. G. Osgood, May 10, 1851, in J. Harold Easterby, ed., "South Carolina through New England Eyes: Almira Coffin's Visit to the Low Country in 1851," *South Carolina Historical Magazine* 45 (1944): 131.

31. "Truss Gawd or Ad's Plat Eye," collected by Genevieve Willcox Chandler, Murrells Inlet, South Carolina, WPA Manuscript Collection, South Caroliniana Library (hereafter, SCL), University of South Carolina, Columbia. "Memories of an Island," 90–94; "Conjure Horses Have Passed," "Edisto Treasure Tales Unfruitful," and "Negroes Plagued by Edisto Ghosts," in Murray Papers, SCHS; John Bennett Papers, MS vol., 60, 63–64, SCHS; Ben Washington, Eulonia, Georgia, in Savannah Writers Project, *Drums and Shadows,* 136; Peterkin, *Green Thursday,* 77–78. Cf. Henry C. Davis, "Negro Folk-Lore in South Carolina," *Journal of American Folklore* 27 (1914), 248; Newbell Niles Puckett, *Folk Beliefs of the Southern Negro* (Chapel Hill: University of North Carolina, 1926), 130; and Ambrose E. Gonzales, *The Black Border: Gullah Stories of the Carolina Coast* (Columbia, S.C.: The State Company, 1922), 33.

32. MS vol. 10–17, 61–76, 103–104, 112, in Bennett Papers, SCHS; "Boo-Hags," "Conjer-Horsed," and "Edisto Reveres Old Time Magic," in Murray Papers, SCHS. Cf. Davis, "Negro Folk-Lore," 247; Puckett, *Folk Beliefs,* 147; William R.

Bascom, "Acculturation among the Gullah Negroes," *American Anthropologist* 43 (1941): 49. In Josephine Pinckney's novel *Great Mischief* (New York: Viking Press, 1948), a retelling of the Faust legend, a nineteenth-century Charleston apothecary becomes enmeshed in black magic and is lured to his doom by a charming hag. For a comparative perspective, see Bastide, *African Civilisations*, 108–10. For an African derivation, see E. E. Evans-Pritchard, *Theories of Primitive Religion* (Oxford: Clarendon Press, 1965), 17.

33. MS vol. 10–17, 61, 76, 103, 112, in Bennett Papers, SCHS; "Conjer Horses Have Passed," "Edisto's Ghosts Fond of Whiskey," and "Edisto Reveres Old Time Magic," in Murray Papers, SCHS. Cf. Bascom, "Acculturation among Gullah Negroes," 49; F. C. Bartlett, *Psychology and Primitive Culture* (New York: Macmillan, 1923), 63, 110, 117–18.

34. Jack Wilson, Old Fort, Georgia, in Savannah Writers Project, *Drums and Shadows*, 7; Shad Hall, Sapelo Island, Georgia, ibid., 167.

35. Solbert Butler, Hampton County, interviewed by Phoebe Faucette, in Rawick, *The American Slave*, vol. 2, sec. 1, 161–65; Isaiah Butler, Hampton County, interviewed by Phoebe Faucette, ibid., vol. 2, sec. 1, 160; MS vol. in Bennett Papers, SCHS; "Gullahs Nearer to Spirit World," "Edisto Negroes Close to Spirits," and "Voodoo Gods Yet Alive on Islands," in Murray Papers, SCHS. Cf. Bastide, *African Civilisations*, 108–10.

36. "Voodoo Survivals Traced on Edisto," "Tom-Toms Sound for Edisto Rites," and "Edisto Reveres Old Time Magic," in Murray Papers, SCHS; James R. Sparkman, "The Negro," in Sparkman Family Papers, SCL. For a similar portrayal of the fragmentation of African religion in Jamaica, see Bastide, *African Civilizations*, 103. That all three streams should be considered aspects of slave religion is suggested by Anthony F. C. Wallace's definition of religion as "that kind of behavior which can be classified as belief and ritual concerned with supernatural beings, powers, and forces" in his *Religion: An Anthropological View* (New York: Random House, 1966), 5; and by Mary Douglas, in her *Edward Evans-Pritchard* (New York: Viking, 1980), 25–26.

37. MS vol., 18–24, 39A, 81–87, 158 in Bennett Papers, SCHS; "Voodoo Gods Yet Alive on Island," "Voodoo Survivals Traced on Edisto," and "Memories of an Island," 193–96, in Murray Papers, SCHS. Cf. George Eaton Simpson, "The Shango Cult in Nigeria and Trinidad," *American Anthropologist* 54 (1962): 1204–29, and his *Shango Cult in Trinidad*, Harold Courlander, *The Dream and the Hoe: The Life and Lore of the Haitian People* (Berkeley and Los Angeles: University of California Press, 1960); Alfred Metraux, *Voodoo in Haiti,* trans. Hugo Charteris (New York: Oxford University Press, 1959); Melville J. Herskovits, *Life in a Haitian Valley* (New York: Alfred A. Knopf, 1937); John Mbiti, *African Religions and Philosophy* (Garden City, N.Y.: Doubleday, 1979), 83; Bastide, *African Civilisations* 59–60, 101–3; Martha Beckwith, "Some Religious Cults in Jamaica," *American Journal of Psychology* 34 (1923): 32–45; Donald Hogg, "The Convince Cult in Jamaica," in Sidney Mintz, ed., *Papers in Caribbean Anthropology* (New Haven, Conn.: Yale University, Department of Anthropology, 1960); George Eaton Simpson, "Jamaica Revivalist Cults," *Social and Economic Studies* 5 (1956): 321–42; Puckett, *Folk Beliefs,* 167–310; E. Horace Fitchett, "Superstitions in South Carolina," *Crisis* 43 (1936): 360–71; Monica Shuler, "Afro-American Slave Culture," in Michael Craton, ed., *Roots and Branches: Current Directions in Slave Studies* (Toronto: Pergamon Press, 1979), 129–37.

38. "Voodoo Gods Yet Alive On Islands," "Edisto Overrun by Rattlesnakes," "Voodoo Survivals Traced on Edisto," and "Conjer-Men Keep Den of Reptiles," in Murray Papers, SCHS: *Account of the late Intended Insurrection,* 23 Cf. Davis, "Negro Folk-Lore in South Carolina," 245; Benjamin A. Botkin, "Folk-Say and Folk-Lore," in William T. Couch, ed., *Culture in the South* (Chapel Hill: University of North Carolina Press, 1934), 590; Bastide, *African Civilizations,* 134–47; Paul D. Escott, *Slavery Remembered: A Record of Twentieth-Century Slave Narratives* (Chapel Hill: University of North Carolina Press, 1979), 105; Genovese, *Roll Jordon, Roll,* 220; John Blassingame, *The Slave Community,* 41; Zora Neale Hurston, *Mules and Men* (Philadelphia: J.B. Lippincott, 1935), 247, and her "Hoodoo in America," *Journal of American Folklore* 44 (1931), 317–417; Leonora Herron and Alice Bacon, "Conjuring and Conjure-Doctors," *Southern Workman* 24 (1895): 118. Julia Peterkin's novels of African American folk life in South Carolina are veritable catalogs of such folk beliefs: see, e.g., *Black April* (Indianapolis, Ind.: Bobbs-Merrill, 1927), 147–48, 245, and *Bright Skin* (Indianapolis, Ind.: Bobbs-Merrill, 1932), 59.

39. Kennedy and Parker, *Official Report,* 15–16, 78; "Memories of an Island," 108, 193–97, and "Edisto Reveres Old Time Magic," in Murray Papers, SCHS; MS vol., 18–24, and "Edisto Negroes Close to Spirits" in Bennett Papers, SCHS. Cf. Davis, "Negro Folk-Lore," 245–48; Fitchett, "Superstitions," 360–71; Puckett *Folk Beliefs,* 200; Herron and Bacon, "Conjuring and Conjure-Doctors,"

193–94; Blassingame, *Slave Community*, 109; Gilbert Osofsky, ed., *Puttin' On Ole Massa* (New York: Harper and Row, 1969), 37; Du Bois, "Religion of the Southern Negro," 618; W. E. B. Du Bois, *The Souls of Black Folk* (Chicago: A.C. McClurg, 1903), 144; "Lizard in the Head," collected by Genevieve Willcox Chandler, WPA Manuscript Collection, SCL; Peterkin, *Green Thursday*, 158–63, *Black April*, 123, and *Bright Skin*, 114.

40. "Edisto Reveres Old Time Magic," in Murray Papers, SCHS. Cf. Peterkin, *Black April*, 7; Julia F. Morton, *Folk Remedies of the Low Country* (Miami, Fla.: E.A. Seaman, 1974), Davis, "Negro Folk-Lore," 247; Wayland D. Hand, *Popular Beliefs and Superstitions from North Carolina* (Durham, N.C.: Duke University Press, 1961), 858–62; Roland Steiner, "Breziel Robinson Possessed of Two Spirits," *Journal of American Folklore* 13 (1900), 226–28; Charles W. Chesnutt, "Superstitions and Folklore of the South," *Modern Culture* 13 (1901), 231–35; Herron and Bacon, "Conjuring and Conjure-Doctors," 210–11. The distrust of white medicine is well portrayed in Peterkin, *Black April*, 71, 275, 281–83. For a comparative perspective, see Metraux, *Voodoo in Haiti*.

41. Isaiah Butler, Hampton County, interviewed by Phoebe Faucette, in Rawick, *American Slave*, vol. 2, sec. 1, 160; "Edisto Negroes Close to Spirits," in Murray Papers, SCHS; Kennedy and Parker, *Official Report*, 76.

42. Zora Neale Hurston, Eau Gallie, Florida, to Franz Boas, New York, April 21, 1929, in Zora Neale Hurston Papers, American Philosophical Society Library, Philadelphia, Pa. I am grateful to Amy Horowitz for bringing this letter to my attention. A quilter on Johns Island, South Carolina, explained to folklorist Mary Arnold Twinning in the 1970s that the cross in her quilt pattern was not a Christian cross. Instead, "it represented danger, evil, and bad feelings." See Mary Arnold Twinning, "An Examination of African Retentions in the Folk Culture of the South Carolina and Georgia Sea Islands" (Ph.D. dissertation, Indiana University, 1977), 188. Cf. Peterkin, *Bright Skin*, 51; Leland Ferguson, "The Cross Is a Magic Sign: Marks on Pottery from Colonial South Carolina," paper presented at "Digging the Afro-American Past: A Research Conference on Historical Archaeology and the Black Experience," (University of Mississippi, May 18, 1989).

43. I have elsewhere described this process of convergence as the *creolization* of slave culture. See Charles Joyner, *Down by the Riverside: A South Carolina Slave Community* (Urbana: University of Illinois Press, 1984); my "The Creolization of Slave Folklife: All Saints Parish, South Carolina, as a Test Case," *Historical Reflections/Reflexions Historiques* (Waterloo, Ontario) 6 (1979): 435–53; and my "Creolization," *Encyclopedia of Southern Culture*, ed. William R. Ferris and Charles Reagan Wilson (Chapel Hill: University of North Carolina Press, 1989), 147–49.

44. Cf. Geertz, *Interpretation of Cultures*, 89–90; 119; Darryl Forde, ed., *African Worlds: Studies in the Cosmological Ideas and Social Values of African Peoples* (London: Oxford University Press, 1954); Meyer Fortes, *Oedipus and Job in West African Religion* (Cambridge: Cambridge University Press, 1951); Geoffrey Parindeer Parrinder, *African Traditional Religion* (Westport, Conn.: Greenwood Press, 1962); William R. Bascom, *Ifa Divination: Communication between Gods and Men in West Africa* (Bloomington: Indiana University Press, 1969); E. E. Evans-Pritchard, *Nuer Religion* (Oxford: Clarendon Press, 1956), and his *Witchcraft, Oracles, and Magic among the Azande* (Oxford: Clarendon Press, 1937); W. E. Abraham, *The Mind of Africa* (Chicago: University of Chicago Press, 1962), chap. 2; R. S. Rattray, *Religion and Art in Ashanti* (Oxford: Clarendon Press, 1926); Mbiti, *African Religions and Philosophy*, chap. 3; Melville J. Herskovits and Frances S. Herskovits, *An Outline of Dahomean Religious Belief* (Menasha, Wisc.: American Anthropological Association, 1933); Martha Warren Beckwith, *Black Roadways: A Study of Jamaican Folk Life* (Chapel Hill: University of North Carolina Press, 1929), chaps. 2, 6; Dominique Zahan, *The Religion, Spirituality, and Thought of Traditional Africa*, trans. Kate E. Martin and Lawrence M. Martin (Chicago: University of Chicago Press, 1979); Mechal Sobel, *Trabelin' On: The Slave Journey to an Afro-Baptist Faith* (Westport, Conn.: Greenwood Press, 1979). The importance of a continuing Yoruba and Ashanti influence and declining Bantu religious influence in African American religion, despite Bantu demographic dominance in the New World, is discussed in Bastide, *African Civilizations*, 104–15.

PART THREE

# THE MODERN WORLD
# 1865–1945

# THE RELIGION OF THE LOST CAUSE

*Charles Reagan Wilson*

Students of southern history know that the South's separate cultural identity did not die after the Civil War. Charles Reagan Wilson identifies how this southern civil religion, represented by a fusion of evangelical Protestantism and southern white culture, emerged after 1865 in response to the need for defeated southerners to nurture their distinct spiritual and cultural values. After the Civil War, southern preachers portrayed Dixie as a godly society violated by marauding Yankees. The Southern military leaders (especially Robert E. Lee, Jefferson Davis, and "Stonewall" Jackson) were depicted as prophets and martyrs whose Christian virtues and military valor were signal traits of the southern character. In southern churches stained glass windows depicting Confederate sacrifices evoked thoughts of the suffering Christ, museums housed "sacred relics," and battlefields were dedicated as the people sang religious hymns. Of course this sanctification of southern society posed a difficult theological problem. Preachers never quite resolved why the righteous South had fallen to the infidel Yankees. Instead they gave solace to their people by recalling how, like Christ crucified, the South could be defeated while its ideals lived on. By remembering the Civil War as a holy cause and mythologizing their past, Wilson argues, southerners "tried to overcome their existential worries and to live with their tragic sense of life."

Reprinted by permission from Charles Reagan Wilson, "The Religion of the Lost Cause: Ritual and Organization of the Southern Civil Religion, 1865–1920," *The Journal of Southern History* XLVI, no. 2 (May 1980): 219–238.

# 10

## THE RELIGION OF THE LOST CAUSE

Ritual and Organization of the Southern
Civil Religion, 1865–1920

*Charles Reagan Wilson*

SCHOLARS HAVE LONG NOTED the importance of religion in the South. The predominant evangelical Protestantism and the distinct regional church structures have been key factors in a "southern identity" separate from that of the North. Historians of southern religion have noted the close ties between religion and southern culture itself. Denominational studies have pointed out the role of the churches in acquiescing to the area's racial orthodoxy and in imposing a conservative, moralistic tone on the South since the late nineteenth century, while other works have posited the existence of two cultures in Dixie, one of Christian and one of southern values. At times, it is clear, the churches have been in "cultural captivity," rather than maintaining a judgmental distance, to southern values. The ties between religion and culture in the South have actually been even closer than has so far been suggested. In the years after the Civil War a pervasive southern civil religion emerged. This common religion of the South, which grew out of Confederate defeat in the Civil War, had an identifiable mythology, ritual, and organization. C. Vann Woodward noted long ago that the southern experience of defeat in the Civil War nurtured a tragic sense of life in the region, but historians have overlooked the fact that this profound understanding has been expressed in a civil religion which blended Christian and southern values.[1]

The religion of the Lost Cause originated in the antebellum period. By 1860 a religious culture had been established, wherein a religious outlook and tone permeated southern society. The popular sects (Methodists, Baptists, and Presbyterians) provided a sense of community in the individualistic rural areas, which helped to nurture a southern identity. At a time when northern religion was becoming increasingly diverse, the southern churches remained orthodox in theology and, above all, evangelical in orientation. Despite a conversion-centered theology, ministers played a key role in defending the status quo, and by 1845 the Methodists and the Baptists had split from their northern counterparts, supplying an institutionalized foundation for the belief in southern distinctiveness. The proslavery argument leaned more heavily on the Bible and Christian ministers than on anything else, thus tying churches and culture close together. Because of the religious culture, southern life seemed so Christian to the clerics that they saw threats to their society as challenges to the last bastion of Christian civilization in America.

During the Civil War religion played a vital role in the Confederacy. Preachers nourished Confederate morale, served as chaplains to the southern armies, and directed the intense revivals in the Confederate ranks. As a result of the wartime experience the religious culture became even more deeply engrained in the South. Preachers who had been soliders or chaplains became the celebrants of the Lost Cause religion after the war. By 1865 conditions existed for the emergence of an institutionalized common religion that would grow out of the antebellum-wartime religious culture.[2]

Judged by historical and anthropological criteria, the civil religion that emerged in the postbellum South was an authentic expression of religion. The South faced problems after the Civil War which were cultural but also religious—the problems of providing meaning to life and society amid the baffling failure of fundamental beliefs, offering comfort to those suffering poverty and disillusionment, and encouraging a sense of belonging in the shattered southern community. Anthropologist Anthony F. C. Wallace argues that religion originates "in situations of social and cultural stress," and for postbellum southerners such traditional religious issues as the nature of suffering, evil, and the seeming irrationality of life had a disturbing relevance. Scholars stress that the existence of a sacred symbol system and its embodiment in ritual define religion. As Clifford Geertz has said, the religious response to the threat of disorder in existence is the creation of symbols "of such a genuine order of the world which will account for, and even celebrate, the perceived ambiguities, puzzles, and paradoxes in human experience." These symbols create "long-lasting moods and motivations," which lead men to act on their religious feelings. Mythology, in other words, is not enough to launch a religion. Ritual is crucial because, as Geertz has said, it is "out of the context of concrete acts of religious observance that religious conviction emerges on the human plane." As Wallace concisely expresses it, "The primary phenomenon of religion is ritual." Not all rituals, to be sure, are religious. The crucial factors are rhetoric and intent: whether the language and motivation of a ritual are religious. The constant application of Biblical archetypes to the Confederacy and the interpretation of the Civil War experience in cosmic terms indicated the religious importance of the Lost Cause.[3]

The southern civil religion assumes added meaning when compared to the American civil religion. Sociologist Robert Neelly Bellah's 1967 article on the civil religion and his subsequent work have focused scholarly discussion on the common religion of the American people. Bellah argued that "an elaborate and well-institutionalized civil religion" existed that was "clearly differentiated" from the denominations. He defined "civil religion" as the "religious dimension" of a "people through which it interprets its historical experience in the light of transcendent reality." Like Sidney Earl Mead, Bellah saw it as essentially prophetic, judging the behavior of the nation against transcendent values. Will Herberg has suggested that the civil religion has been a folk religion, a common religion emerging out of the life of the folk. He argues that it grew out of a long social and historical experience that established a heterogeneous society. The civil religion came to be the American Way of Life, a set of beliefs that were accepted and revered by Protestants, Catholics, and Jews. "Democracy" has been the fundamental concept of this civil religion. Scholars have identified the sources of the American public faith in the Enlightenment tradition and in the secularized Puritan and Revivalist traditions. It clearly was born during the American Revolution, but the American civil religion was reborn, with the new theme of sacrifice and renewal, in the Civil War.[4]

In the post–Civil War South the antebellum religious culture evolved into a southern civil religion, differing from the national faith. A set of values arose that could be designated a Southern Way of Life. Dixie's value system differed from that which Herberg discussed—southerners undoubtedly were less optimistic, less liberal, less democratic, less tolerant, and more homogeneously Protestant. In their religion southerners stressed "democracy" less than the conservative concepts of moral virtue and an orderly society. Though the whole course of southern history provided the background, the southern civil religion actually emerged from the Civil War experience. Just as the revolution of 1776 caused Americans to see their historical experience in transcedent terms, so the Confederate experience led southerners to a profound self-examination. They understood that the results of the war had clearly given them a history distinct from the northern one. Southerners thus focused the mythic, ritualistic, and organizational dimensions of their civil religion around the Confederacy. Moreover, the Enlightenment tradition played virtually no role in the religion of the Lost Cause, but the emotionally intense, dynamic Revivalist tradition and the secularized legacy of idealistic, moralistic Puritanism did shape it.

As a result of emerging from a heterogeneous, immigrant society, the American civil religion was especially significant in providing a sense of belonging to the uprooted immigrants. As a result of its origins in Confederate defeat, the southern civil religion offered confused southerners a sense of meaning, an identity in a precarious but distinct culture. One central issue of the American public faith has been the relationship between church and state, but, since the Confederate quest for political nationhood failed, the southern civil religion has been less concerned with that question than with the cultural issue of identity.

The mythology of the American civil religion taught that Americans are a chosen people, destined to play a special role in the world as representatives of freedom and equality. The religion of the Lost Cause rested on a mythology that focused on the Confederacy. It was a creation myth, the story of the attempt to create a southern nation. According to the mythmakers a pantheon of southern heroes, portrayed as the highest products of the Old South civilization, had appeared during the Civil War to battle the forces of evil as symbolized by the Yankees. The myth enacted the Christian story of Christ's suffering and death with the Confederacy at the sacred center. But in the southern myth the Christian drama of suffering and salvation was incomplete. The Confederacy lost a holy war, and there was no resurrection.[5]

As Mircea Eliade has said, "it is not enough to *know* the origin myth, one must *recite* it. . . ." While other southern myths could be seen in literature, politics, or economics, the Confederate myth reached its true fulfillment after the Civil War in a ritualistic structure of activities that represented a religious commemoration and celebration of the Confederacy. One part of the ritualistic liturgy focused on the religious figures of the Lost Cause. Southern Protestant churches have been sparse in iconography, but the southern civil religion was rich in images. Southern ministers and other rhetoricians portrayed Robert Edward Lee, Thomas Jonathan ("Stonewall") Jackson, Jefferson Davis, and many other wartime heroes as religious saints and martyrs.[6] They were said to epitomize the best of Christian and southern values. Their images pervaded the South, and they were especially aimed at children. In the first two decades of the last century local chapters of the United Daughters of the Confederacy undertook successfully to blanket southern schools with portraits of Lee and Davis. Lee's birthday, January 19, became a holiday throughout Dixie, and ceremonies honoring him frequently occurred in the schools.[7]

An explicit link between Confederate images and religious values was made in the stained-glass windows placed in churches to commemorate Confederate sacrifices. One of the earliest of these was a window placed in Trinity Church, Portsmouth, Virginia, in April 1868, while Federal troops still occupied the city. The window portrayed a Biblical Rachel weeping at a tomb, on which appeared the names of the members of the congregation who had died during the war. In Mississippi, Biloxi's Church of the Redeemer, "the Westminister of the South," was particularly prominent in this endeavor at the turn of the century. St. Paul's Episcopal Church in Richmond, which had been the wartime congregation of many Confederate leaders, established a Lee Memorial Window, which used an Egyptian scene to connect the Confederacy with the stories of the Old Testament. Even a Negro Presbyterian church in Roanoke, Virginia, dedicated a Stonewall Jackson memorial window. The pastor had been a pupil in Jackson's Sunday school in prewar Lexington, Virginia.[8]

Wartime artifacts also had a sacred aura. Bibles that had been touched by the Cause were especially holy. The United Daughters of the Confederacy kept under lock and key the Bible used when Jefferson Davis was sworn in as President of the Confederacy. More poignantly, a faded, torn overcoat belonging to a young Confederate martyr named Sam Davis was discovered in 1897, and when shown to a United Daughters of the Confederacy meeting the response was, said an observer, first "sacred silence" and then weeping. Presbyterian preacher James Isaac Vance noted that, "like Elijah's mantle of old, the spirit of the mighty dwells within it." Museums were sanctuaries containing such sacred relics. The Confederate Museum in Richmond, which had been the White House of the Confederacy, included a room for each seceding state. These rooms had medals, flags, uniforms, and weapons from the Confederacy, and the Solid South Room displayed the Great Seal of the Confederate States.[9]

The southern civil religion had its reverent images and its sacred artifacts, and it also had its hymns. One group of hymns sung at postwar Confederate gatherings was made up of Christian songs straight from the hymnal. "Nearer My God to Thee," "Abide with Me," and "Praise God from Whom All Blessings Flow" were popular, but the favorite was "How Firm a Foundation." Another group of Confederate sacred songs was created by putting new words to old melodies. The spirit of "That Old-Time Religion" was preserved when someone retitled it "We Are Old-Time Confederates." J. B. Stinson composed new verses for the melody of "When the Roll is Called Up Yonder I'll Be There." A change from the original lyric was the phrase "let's be there," rather than "I'll be there," indicating a more communal redemption in the Lost Cause version. The song used Confederates as evangelical models of behavior: "On that mistless, lonely morning when the saved of Christ shall rise,/In the Father's many-mansioned home to share;/Where our Lee and Jackson call to us [sic] their homes beyond the skies,/When the roll is called up yonder, let's be there."[10] Of special significance was the hymn "Let Us Pass Over the River, and Rest Under the Shade of the Trees," which was officially adopted by the Southern Methodist Church. The words in the title were the last words spoken by the dying Stonewall Jackson. Two other hymns, "Stonewall Jackson's Requiem" and "Stonewall Jackson's Way," made a similar appeal. At some ceremonial occasions choirs from local churches sang hymns. In 1907 southerners organized the United Confederate Choirs of America, and soon the young belles from Dixie, clad in Confederate gray uniforms, were a popular presence at ritual events.[11]

These liturgical ingredients appeared during the ritualistic expressions of the Lost Cause. In the years immediately after the war southern anguish at Confederate defeat was most apparent during the special days appointed by the denominations or the states for humiliation, fasting, prayer, or thanksgiving. These special days could be occasions for jeremiads calling prodigals back to the church, prophesying future battles, or stressing submission to God's mysterious providence in the face of seemingly unwarranted suffering.[12] Southerners, however, usually ignored the national Thanksgiving Day, complaining that northerners used the day to exploit the war issue and to wave the bloody shirt. D. Shaver, the editor of the *Christian Index*, a Baptist newspaper in Atlanta, noted in 1869 that such days too often evoked in the Yankee "the smell (if they do not wake the thirst) of blood." He characterized the northern Christian's behavior on Thanksgiving Day as like that of a Pharisee of old who stood "pilloried through the ages as venting a self-complacent but empty piety." Southerners did celebrate thanksgiving days designated by their denominations, but in general the days of humiliation, fasting, and prayer were more appropriate to the immediate postwar southern mood.[13]

Southern reverence for dead heroes could be seen in the activities of yet another ritual event—Confederate Memorial Day. Southern legend has it that the custom of decorating the graves of soldiers arose in Georgia in 1866 when Mrs. Charles J. Williams, a Confederate widow, published an appeal to southerners to set apart a day "to be handed down through time as a religious custom of the South to wreathe the graves of our martyred dead with flowers." Like true Confederates, southern states could not at first agree among themselves as to which day to honor, but by 1916 ten states had designated June 3, Jefferson Davis's birthday, as Memorial Day. Women played a key role in this ritual since they were in charge of decorating the graves with flowers and of organizing the day's events. It was a holy day, "the Sabbath of the South." One southern woman compared her sisters to the Biblical Mary and Martha, who "last at the cross and first at the grave brought their offerings of love. . . ." Another southern woman noted that the aroma of flowers on Memorial Day was "like incense burning in golden censers to the memory of the saints."[14]

A third ritual was the funeral of a wartime hero. The veterans attending the funerals dressed in their gray uniforms, served as active or honorary pallbearers, and provided a military ceremony. Everything was done according to the "Confederate Veteran's Burial Ritual," which emphasized that the soldier was going to "an honorable grave." "He fought a good fight," said the ritual, "and has left a record of which we, his surviving comrades, are proud, and which is a heritage of glory to his family and their descendants for all time to come." These ceremonies reiterated what southerners heard elsewhere—that despite defeat the Confederate experience proved that they were a noble, virtuous people. Moreover, the Confederate funeral included the display of the Confederate flag, the central symbol of the southern identity. Often, it was dramatically placed over the hero's casket just before the box was lowered into the ground, while at other times the folded battle flag was removed from the coffin and placed at the head of the grave. Even after southerners began again to honor the American flag, they continued to cherish the Stars and Bars as well.[15]

The dedication of monuments to the Confederate heroes was the fourth ritualistic expression of the Lost Cause. In 1914 the *Confederate Veteran* magazine revealed that over a thousand monuments existed in the South, and by that time many battlefields had been set aside as pilgrimage sites with holy shrines. Preachers converted the innumerable statues dotting the southern countryside into religious objects, almost idols, that quite blatantly taught Christian religious and moral lessons. "Our cause is with God" and "In hope of a joyful resurrection" were among the most directly religious inscriptions on monuments, but they were not atypical ones. El Dorado, Arkansas, erected a marble drinking fountain to the Confederacy, and its publicity statement said—in a phrase culled from countless hymns and sermons on the sacrificial Jesus—that the water in it symbolized "the loving stream of blood" that was shed by the southern soldiers. Drinkers from the fount were thus symbolically baptized in Confederate blood. The dedication of such monuments became more elaborate as the years went on. Perhaps the greatest monument dedication came in 1907, when an estimated 200,000 people gathered in Richmond for the dedication of a statue to Jefferson Davis on Monument Boulevard. Richmond was the Mecca of the Lost Cause, and Monument Boulevard was the sacred road to it containing statues of Lee, James Ewell Brown ("Jeb") Stuart, George Washington, and Stonewall Jackson, as well as Davis.[16]

Rituals similar to these existed as part of the American civil religion. In both instances, they were, to use Claude Lévi-Strauss's categories, partly commemorative rites that re-created the mythical time of the past and partly mourning rites that converted dead heroes into revered ancestors. Both civil religions confronted the precariousness and instability of collective life. They were ways for communities to help their citizens meet their individual fears of death. As sociologist William Lloyd Warner has said: "Whenever the living think about the deaths of others they necessarily express some of their own concern about their own extinction." By the continuance of the community, the citizens in it achieve a measure of immortality. For southerners the need for such a symbolic life was even greater than for northerners. Union soldiers sacrificed, but at least the success of their cause seemed to validate their deaths. Postwar southerners feared that the defeat of the Confederacy had jeopardized their continued existence as a distinctively southern people. By participating in the Lost Cause rituals southerners tried to show that the Confederate sacrifices had not been in vain. Similar rituals existed to honor the Grand Army of the Republic, but the crucial point was that southern rituals began from a very different starting point and had a different symbolic content. Thus, within the United States there was a functioning civil religion not dedicated to honoring the American nation.[17]

The permanence of the Lost Cause religion could be seen in its structural-functional aspect. Three institutions directed its operations, furnishing ongoing leadership and institutional encouragement. One organizational focus was the Confederate veterans' groups. Local associations of veterans existed in the 1870s and 1880s, but southerners took a step forward in this activity with the establishment of the United Confederate Veterans in New Orleans in 1889. The heirs of the Lost Cause formed another group in 1896, the United Sons of Confederate Veterans, which supplied still more energy for the movement. The local chapters of these organizations held frequent meetings, which were an important social activity for southerners, especially those in rural areas. They also had their sacred elements, mostly in the rhetoric used in orations. The highlight of the year for the veterans was the annual regionwide reunion, which was held in a major southern city. It was one of the most highly publicized events in the South. Railroads ran special trains, and the cities gave lavish welcomes to the grizzled old men and their entourage of splendidly dressed young women sponsored by the local chapters. Tens of thousands of people flocked into the chosen city each year to relive the past for a few days. The earliest reunions were boisterous gatherings, but that spirit did not subdue an equally religious tone, especially as the veterans aged. In 1899 the reunion was in Charleston, and a city reporter noted that the veterans were lighthearted at times but that they also were as devout as any pilgrim going "to the tomb of the prophet, or Christian knight to the walls of Jerusalem."[18]

Each day of the reunion began with a prayer, which usually reminded the aging Confederates that religion was at the heart of the Confederate heritage. Presbyterian clergyman Peyton H. Hogue, in a prayer at the tenth reunion in 1900, was not subtle in suggesting his view of the typical Confederate's afterlife. He prayed that those present "may meet in that Heavenly Home where Lee, Jackson and all the Heroes who have gone before are waiting to welcome us there."[19] A hymn was usually sung after the invocation. One favorite was the "Doxology," which ended with the explicitly Christian reference, "Praise Father, Son, and Holy Ghost." A memorial service was held each year at a local church as part of the official reunion program, and it was here that the most direct connections were made between Christianity and the Confederacy. At the 1920 reunion, for example, the Baptist cleric B. A. Owen compared the memorial service to the Christian sacrament, the Holy Communion. In the Communion service, he said, "our hearts are focused upon Calvary's cross and the dying Lamb of God," and in the Confederate sacrament "we hold sweet converse with the spirits of departed comrades." In order to coordinate their work at memorial services and elsewhere the ministers of the Lost Cause organized a Chaplains' Association before the Atlanta reunion in 1898.[20]

The Nashville reunion of 1897 was probably the single most religiously oriented Confederate meeting. The veterans met that year at the downtown Union Gospel Tabernacle, later known as Ryman Auditorium, the home of southern music's Grand Old Opry. A new balcony was added to the tabernacle for the 1897 convention, and it was dedicated as a Confederate memorial. Sitting on hard church pews facing the altar and the permanent baptismal font, the veterans had a rollicking but reverent time in 1897 in the sweltering summer heat of the poorly ventilated tabernacle. Each reunion ended with a long parade, and the 1897 procession was one of the most memorable. The reviewing stand was set up on the campus of the Methodists' Vanderbilt University, where the old veterans paused before continuing their march. The reunion coincided with Tennessee's centennial celebration and included the unveiling in Nashville's new Centennial Park of the Parthenon, the replica of the ancient Greek temple, and a mammoth statue to the goddess Athena. The Confederate parade ended in Centennial Park, and as the old soldiers entered the grounds the bells from a nearby tower chimed the old hymn, "Shall We Gather at the River?" Apparently unintentionally, the ceremony evoked comparisons with the annual Panathenaic procession in ancient Athens from the lower agora to the Acropolis, and then to the Parthenon, the temple of Athena.[21]

If religion pervaded the United Confederate Veterans, it saturated the United Daughters of the Confederacy. The importance of Christianity to the Daughters could be seen in the approved ritual for their meetings. It began with an invocation by the president: "Daughters of the Confederacy, this day we are gathered together, in the sight of God, to strengthen the bonds that unite us in a common cause; to renew the vows of loyalty to our sacred principles; to do homage unto the memory of our gallant Confederate soldiers, and to perpetuate the fame of their noble deeds into the third and fourth generations. To this end we invoke the aid of our Lord." The members responded, "From the end of the Earth will I cry unto Thee, when my heart is overwhelmed; lead me to the rock that is higher than I." After similar chanted exchanges, the hymn "How Firm a Foundation" was sung, followed by the reading of a prayer composed by Episcopal bishop Ellison Capers of South

Carolina, who had been a Confederate general before entering the ministry. After the prayer the president then read the Lord's Prayer, and the meeting or convention began its official business.[22]

The Daughters provided an unmatched crusading zeal to the religion of the Lost Cause. The members rarely doubted that God was on their side. Cornelia Branch Stone entitled her 1912 pamphlet on Confederate history a *U. D. C. Catechism for Children*, a title that suggested the assumed sacred quality of its contents. The Daughters took an especially aggressive role in preserving the records of the southern past. These were sacred documents that were viewed by the women in a fundamentalist perspective. Mrs. M. D. Farris of Texas urged the organization in 1912 to guard its records and archives, "even as the children of Israel did the Ark of the Covenant."[23]

The Christian churches formed the second organizational focus for the southern civil religion. The postwar development of the religion of the Lost Cause was intimately related to developments in the churches themselves. Before the war an evangelical consensus had been achieved in the South, but it had not been institutionalized. Not until after the war did church membership become pervasive. The evangelical denominations that profited from this enormous expansion of what Samuel S. Hill, Jr., calls a "single-option religious culture" taught an inward, conversion-centered religion. Fundamental beliefs on such matters as sin, guilt, grace, judgment, the reality of heaven and hell, and the loving Jesus were agreed upon by all without regard to denominational boundaries. The concept of a civil religion at first glance seems contrary to this inward theology, but the southern churches were not so otherwordly as to ignore society entirely. A southern social gospel existed, as did successful attempts to establish moral reform through state coercion. The combination of a societal interest and the dynamic growth of an evangelical Protestantism was not antithetical to the development of a civil religion.[24]

Unlike the American civil religion, the religion of the Lost Cause did not entirely stand apart from the Christian denominations. They taught similar religious-moral values, and the southern heroes had been directly touched by Christianity. The God invoked in the Lost Cause was a distinctly Biblical, transcendent God. Prayers at veterans' gatherings appealed for the blessings of, in John William Jones's words, the "God of Israel, God of the centuries, God of our forefathers, God of Jefferson Davis and Sidney Johnston and Robert E. Lee, and Stonewall Jackson, God of the Southern Confederacy." Prayers invariably ended in some variation of "We ask it all in the name and for the sake of Christ our dear Redeemer." At the 1907 veterans' reunion the Reverend Randolph Harrison McKim, like other preachers before and after him, invoked the third person of the Christian godhead, praying for "the blessing of the Holy Ghost in our hearts." The references to Christ and the Holy Ghost clearly differentiated the southern civil religion from the more deistic American civil religion. The latter's ceremonies rarely included such Christian references because of potential alienation of Jews, who were but a small percentage of the southern population. In the South, in short, the civil religion and Christianity openly supported each other.[25]

Certainly, the most blatant connections between Christianity and the Confederacy were made during Confederate rituals. Though they praised their society and its customs, it is clear that in their normal Christian services southerners did not worship the Confederacy. Nevertheless, southern religious journals, books, and even pulpits were the sources of Lost Cause sentiments. Church buildings were the most frequently used sites for Memorial Day activities, funerals of veterans, and memorial observances when prominent Confederates died. Such gatherings were interdenominational, with pastors from different religious bodies participating. A spirit of interdenominationalism had existed in the wartime Confederate armies, and it survived in the postbellum South in the ceremonies of the Lost Cause. The overwhelmingly Protestant character of southern religion facilitated the growth of an ecumenical Lost Cause religion. It, in turn, furthered Protestant ecumenicism. Although predominantly Protestant, southern religion was not manifested in any one denomination but was ecclesiastically fragmented. The Lost Cause offered a forum for ministers and laymen from differing churches to participate in a common spiritual activity. References to particular denominational beliefs were occasionally made, but since southerners shared so many of the same doctrines there was a basis for cooperation.[26]  Moreover, despite the Protestant orientation of the Lost Cause, Catholics and Jews were not excluded from it. Members of these faiths joined the Confederate groups, and rabbis and priests occasionally appeared at Lost Cause events. Undoubtedly, with some discomfort, Catholics and Jews accepted the Protestant tinge of the southern civil religion and made their own contributions to it.[27]

The southern churches proved to be important institutions for the dissemination of the Lost Cause. Despite the opposition of some clerics, on Sunday morning, November 27, 1884, congregations across the South contributed to a well-promoted special collection to finance a Robert E. Lee monument in Richmond. The denominational papers approvingly published appeals of Confederate organizations for support, editorially endorsed Lost Cause fund raising, recommended Confederate writings, and praised the Lost Cause itself. The Confederate periodicals, in turn, printed stories about Christianity seemingly unrelated to the usual focus on the Civil War. Richmond was the center of Lost Cause activity, and the city was also a religious publishing center. The Episcopalians, Baptists, Methodists, and Presbyterians all published periodicals there, and the Southern Presbyterian Publishing House was located in the Confederate capital. Nashville was a religious publishing center as well, and it had the same Confederate-Christian mixture. The *Confederate Veteran* magazine, the most important organ of the Lost Cause after 1890, had its offices in and was published by the Publishing House of the Southern Methodist Church in the city.[28]

The close connection between the churches and the Confederate organizations could be seen in terms of the central experience of southern Protestantism—evangelicalism. Confederate heroes were popular choices to appear at southern revivals. The most influential southern evangelist, iconoclastic Georgia Methodist Samuel Porter ("Sam") Jones, was a master at having Confederates testify to the power of Christianity in their lives, preferably its inspirational effect on the battlefield. At the same time, a significant feature of the religious rhetoric of the reunions was the insistence on a response by the veterans. The invitation to follow Christ, which was made during the memorial services, was also an invitation to follow once again Robert E. Lee, Stonewall Jackson, and Jefferson Davis. Some reunions thus resembled vast revivals, with tens of thousands of listeners hearing ministers remind them of the imminence of death for the aged veterans and of the need to ensure everlasting life.[29]

The third organizational embodiment of the Lost Cause, the educational system, directed the effort to pass the Lost Cause religion on to future generations. Confederate veterans and their widows and daughters dominated the schools, serving as teachers and administrators, and they had no reticence in teaching the southern tradition. The year

1907 was especially observed in the southern schools. It was the centennial of General Lee's birth, and state boards of education issued pamphlets providing guidelines to encourage appropriate celebrations in the schools. In addition, the latter-day Confederates were sought to maintain a pro-southern interpretation of the Civil War in the textbooks used in southern schools. The United Daughters of the Confederacy directed this endeavor, pressuring school boards to adopt textbooks from an approved list compiled by the organization. The same concern motivated the later southern Fundamentalists who campaigned to keep the doctrine of evolution out of textbooks. The most direct Christian-Confederate connections were not in the public schools but in the private academies, particularly in the denominational schools. Typical of these were the Episcopal High School of Alexandria, Virginia, and the Stonewall Jackson Institute, a Presbyterian female academy, in Abingdon, Virginia. Confederate leaders like Lee and Jackson were the explicit models of behavior for the students, and the ex-Confederate teachers served as living models of virtue. The students wore Confederate-style uniforms and drilled on campus, and the advertisements for these religious schools played upon the Confederate theme to attract young people. The United Daughters of the Confederacy supported the Stonewall Jackson Institute by financing scholarships to the school.[30]

Two colleges existed as major institutional shrines of the Lost Cause. The first was the University of the South, an Episcopal college located like an isolated retreat in the mountains at Sewanee, Tennessee. Bishop Leonidas Polk, who would later die at the Battle of Pine Mountain in Georgia while serving as a brigadier general, founded the school in the sectionally divisive 1850s, conceiving of it in part as a place to educate young southerners in regional as well as Christian values. The nascent institution was all but destroyed during the Civil War, but Bishop Charles Todd Quintard, himself a Confederate chaplain and active member of postwar Confederate veterans' groups, resurrected it. The most potent Lost Cause influence came from the faculty he assembled. They were "a body of noble men," said Sarah Barnwell Elliott, daughter of Bishop Stephen Elliott, in 1909, "with the training, education, and traditions of the Old South and whose like we shall never see again." They included William Porcher DuBose, a captain in Lee's Army of Northern Virginia and later a respected theologian; Major George Rainsford Fairbanks of the Army of Tennessee; Brigadier General Francis Asbury Shoup of Florida; Brigadier General Josiah Gorgas, the Confederacy's chief of ordnance; and General Edmund Kirby Smith, commander of the Trans-Mississippi Department of the Confederate armies, who had the honor of being known as the last general to surrender. Women also contributed to the inculcation of Lost Cause religious values. The University of the South gave free tuition to the children of Confederate widows who boarded college students. The Sewanee matrons purposely chose names to connect their homes to the South; thus, one could find a Palmetto Hall, a Magnolia Hall, and an Alabama Hall. They re-created and fostered the culture of the Old South that had produced the heroes of the war.[31]

Sewanee was also an institutional center for Lost Cause orations, dedications, and other rituals. These events adapted Lost Cause themes to the student audience. When Lee died in 1870, for example, the Episcopal bishop of Louisiana, Joseph Pere Bell Wilmer, preached a sermon on the general's moral and religious virtues for the edification of the students. Moreover, when one of the heroes on campus died, regional attention concentrated on Sewanee, prompting the appearance of the ritualistic trappings of the civil religion. Confederate monuments and plaques still dot the campus, serving as devotional points on the holy ground.[32]

Washington and Lee University reflected a different aspect of the southern civil religion than that at the University of the South. Located at Lexington in the Virginia valley, it was more Virginian in its Confederate orientation, and its Christian influence was predominantly Presbyterian. Stonewall Jackson had taught in Lexington at the Virginia Military Institute before the war, and the town provided recruits for his famed Stonewall Brigade. Washington College itself, like Sewanee, suffered during the war, but the choice in 1865 of Robert E. Lee to head the school gave it a new start and a new fame as a center of the Lost Cause. In a sermon, Baptist preacher Edwin Theodore Winkler described the sacred atmosphere of the campus in evocative phrases: "Lexington is the parable of the great Virginia soldiers. In that quiet scholastic retreat, in that city set upon a hill and crowned with martial trophies, they, being dead, yet speak."[33]

The presence of prominent Confederates was again the key factor in fostering a Lost Cause aura in Lexington. Among the residents of the town were Colonel William Preston Johnston, son of the martyred General Albert Sidney Johnston; Colonel William Nelson, chief ordnance officer for Stonewall Jackson's command; John Letcher, wartime governor of Virginia; Confederate Judge John White Brockenbrough; General Francis Henney Smith, superintendent of Virginia Military Institute; Colonel John Mercer Brooke, builder of the *Merrimac*, Commander Matthew Fontaine Maury, famed geographer who taught at the institute; and Brigadier General William Nelson Pendleton, rector of the Grace Memorial Episcopal Church, where Lee worshiped. The Lost Cause religious orientation came most directly from the influence of one man—Lee. A deeply religious man himself, he encouraged spiritual activities, including revivalism, at his school. He helped launch the town's Young Men's Christian Association, supervised the erection of a chapel on campus, organized daily interdenominational devotionals conducted by the town's pastors, and invited preachers from across the South to deliver baccalaureate sermons.[34]

As at Sewanee, Lexington was a focus for orations, dedications, and funerals. The chapel was one of the most holy of all Lost Cause shrines. Lee was buried there in a limestone mausoleum, and the site was marked by a recumbent statue of white marble resting on a sarcophagus. The unveiling of the monument on June 23, 1883, was a media event throughout the South. In 1907, the year of the centennial of Lee's birth, the entire region looked to Lexington for the major commemoration of the birth. Stonewall Jackson was also buried in the town, in the cemetery of the Presbyterian church. Lexington came to be so full of Lost Cause shrines that one could take an organized walking tour, which bore some resemblance to a medieval processional of the Stations of the Cross.[35]

All these rituals and institutions dealt with a profound problem. The southern civil religion emerged because defeat in the Civil War had created the spiritual and psychological need for southerners to reaffirm their identity, an identity which came to have outright religious dimensions. Each Lost Cause ritual and organization was tangible evidence that southerners had made a religion out of their history. As with all ritualistic repetition of archetypal actions, southerners in their institutionalized Lost Cause religion were trying symbolically to overcome history. By repetition of ritual, they recreated the mythical times of their noble ancestors and paid tribute to them.[36] Despite the bafflement and frustration of defeat, southerners showed that the time of the myth's creation still had meaning for them. The Confederate veteran was a living incarnation of an idea that southerners tried to defend at the cultural level after Confederate defeat had made political success impossible. Every time a Confederate veteran died, every time flowers were placed on graves on Southern Memorial Day, southerners relived and confronted the death of the Confederacy. The religion of the Lost Cause was a cult of the dead, which dealt with essential religious concerns. Having lost what they considered to be a holy war, southerners had to face suffering, doubt, guilt, a recognition of what seemed to be evil triumphant, and above all death. Through the ritualistic and organizational activities of their civil religion, southerners tried to overcome their existential worries and to live with their tragic sense of life.

## NOTES

1. Kenneth K. Bailey, *Southern White Protestantism in the Twentieth Century* (New York and other cities, 1964); Rufus B. Spain, *At Ease in Zion: Social History of of Southern Baptists, 1865–1900* (Nashville, 1967); Hunter D. Farish, *The Circuit Rider Dismounts: A Social History of Southern Methodism, 1865–1900* (Richmond, 1938); Ernest T. Thompson, *Presbyterians in the South* (3 vols., Richmond, 1963–1974); Samuel S. Hill, Jr., *Southern Churches in Crisis* (New York and other cities, 1966); Hill et al., *Religion and the Solid South* (Nashville and New York, 1972); John L. Eighmy, *Churches in Cultural Captivity: A History of the Social Attitudes of Southern Baptists* (Knoxville, 1972); H. Shelton Smith, *In His Image, But . . . : Racism in Southern Religion, 1780–1910* (Durham, N.C., 1972); Woodward, *The Burden of Southern History* (Baton Rouge, 1960), especially chap. I.

2. Hill, *Southern Churches*, 12–14, 52, 56–59; John B. Boles, *The Great Revival, 1787–1805: The Origins of the Southern Evangelical Mind* (Lexington, Ky., 1972); Boles, *Religion in Antebellum Kentucky* (Lexington, Ky., 1976), 123–45; Dickson D. Bruce, Jr., "Religion, Society and Culture in the Old South: A Comparative View," *American Quarterly*, XXVI (October 1974), 399–416; Donald G. Mathews, *Religion in the Old South* (Chicago and London, 1977). For the wartime role of the churches there is no synthesis, but see James W. Silver, *Confederate Morale and Church Propaganda* (Tuscaloosa, Ala., 1957); Herman Norton, *Rebel Religion: The Story of Confederate Chaplains* (St. Louis, 1961); John Shepard, Jr., "Religion in the Army of Northern Virginia," *North Carolina Historical Review*, XXV (July 1948), 341–76; and the special issue of *Civil War History*, VI (December 1960).

3. Wallace, *Religion: An Anthropological View* (New York, 1966), 30 (first quotation), 102 (fifth quotation); Geertz, "Religion as a Cultural System," in Michael Banton, ed., *Anthropological Approaches to the Study of Religion* (New York, 1966), 4 (third quotation), 8–12, 14, 23 (second quotation), 28 (fourth quotation). See also Andrew M. Greeley, *The Denominational Society: A Sociological Approach to Religion in America* (Glenview, Ill., 1972), 28, and Mircea Eliade, *Myth and Reality* (New York and Evanston, Ill., 1963), 8, 17–18.

4. Bellah, "Civil Religion in America," in Russell E. Richey and Donald G. Jones, eds., *American Civil Religion* (New York and other cities, 1974), 21–44 (first two quotations on p. 21); Bellah, *The Broken Covenant: American Civil Religion in Time of Trial* (New York, 1975), 3 (last two quotations); Mead, "The 'Nation with the Soul of a Church,'" in Richey and Jones, eds., *American Civil Religion*, 45–75; Herberg, "America's Civil Religion: What It Is and Whence It Comes," ibid., 76–88; Herberg, *Protestant Catholic Jew: An Essay in American Religious Sociology* (Garden City, N.Y., 1955); Catherine L. Albanese, *Sons of the Fathers: The Civil Religion of the American Revolution* (Philadelphia, 1976); James H. Moorhead, *American Apocalypse: Yankee Protestants and the Civil War, 1860–1869* (New Haven, 1978).

5. For the political, economic, intellectual, and literary aspects of the Lost Cause myth see Rollin G. Osterweis, *The Myth of the Lost Cause, 1865–1900* (Hamden, Conn., 1973); Daniel Aaron, *The Unwritten War: American Writers and the Civil War* (New York, 1973); Paul M. Gaston, *The New South Creed: A Study in Southern Mythmaking* (New York, 1970); Richard M. Weaver, *The Southern Tradition at Bay: A History of Postbellum Thought* (New Rochelle, N.Y., 1968), Richard B. Harwell, "The Confederate Heritage," in Louis D. Rubin, Jr., and James J. Kilpatrick, eds., *The Lasting South: Fourteen Southerners Look at Their Home* (Chicago, 1957), 16–27; William B. Hesseltine, *Confederate Leaders in the New South* (Baton Rouge, 1950); Susan S. Durant, "The Gently

Furled Banner: The Development of the Myth of the Lost Cause, 1865–1900" (Ph.D. dissertation, University of North Carolina, 1972); and Sharon E. Hannum, "Confederate Cavaliers: The Myth in War and Defeat" (Ph.D. dissertation, Rice University, 1965).

6. Eliade, *Myth and Reality*, 17; "Robert E. Lee," and "Innocence Vindicated," Atlanta *Christian Index, October* 20, 1870, 162; August 23, 1866, 135; "Robert E. Lee," Richmond *Southern Churchman*, January 19, 1907, 2; T. V. Moore, "Memorial Discourse on the Death of General Robert E. Lee," and "Jefferson Davis," in Nashville *Christian Advocate*, November 5, 1870, 2; December 12, 1889, 8; and James P. Smith, "Jackson's Religious Character: An Address at Lexington, Va.," Southern Historical Society, *Papers*, XIIII (September 1920), 67–75. The *Papers* will be cited hereinafter as SHSP.

7. United Daughters of the Confederacy, *Minutes of the Fourteenth Annual Convention . . .* 1907 (Opelika, Ala., 1908), 6; ibid., 1915 (Charlotte, N.C., n.d.), 357; "The South's Tribute to General Lee," *Confederate Veteran*, XXII (February 1914), 62. The minutes of conventions of the United Daughters of the Confederacy will hereinafter be cited as UDC, Minutes along with the proper years. The *Confederate Veteran* will hereinafter be cited as CV.

8. "The Memorial Window in Trinity Church, Portsmouth, Va., to the Confederate Dead of Its Congregation," SHSP, XIX (January 1891), 207–12; "Pegram Battalion Association," ibid., XVI (January–December 1888), 194–206; J. William Jones, "The Career of General Jackson," ibid., XXXV (January–December 1907), 97; "A Memorial Chapel at Fort Domelson," CV, V (September 1897), 461; Elizabeth W. Weddell, *St. Paul's Church, Richmond, Virginia . . .* (2 vols., Richmond, 1931), 1, frontispiece, 224–25.

9. CV, VIII (November 1900), 468; "Sermons Before the Reunion," ibid., V (July 1897), 351 (quotation); ibid., XXII (May 1914), 194; Herbert and Marjorie Katz, *Museums, U.S.A.: A History and Guide* (Garden City, N. Y., 1965), 181.

10. United Confederate Veterans (hereinafter UCV), *Minutes of the Ninth Annual Meeting and Reunion . . . 1899* (New Orleans, 1900), 17, 32; UCV, *Minutes of the Twenty-first Annual Meeting and Reunion . . . 1911* (New Orleans, n.d.), 111; UCV, *Minutes of the Nineetenth Annual Meeting and Reunion . . . 1909* (New Orleans, n.d.), 64; UDC, *Minutes . . . 1912* (Jackson, Tenn., n.d.), 321, 407; UDC, *Minutes . . . 1914* (Raleigh, N. C., 1915), 406; UDC, *Ritual of the United Daughters of the*

*Confederacy* (Austin, Texas, n.d.); "Burial of Margaret Davis Hayes," CV, XVII (December 1909), 612; "Old Time Confederates," ibid., VIII (July 1900), 298; Joseph M. Brown, "Dixie," ibid., XII (March 1904), 134; "Memorial Ode," ibid., IX (December 1901), 567.

11. CV, IX (April 1901), 147; UDC, *Minutes . . . 1909* (Opelika, Ala., 1909), 56. See also C. H. Scott, "The Hymn of Robert E. Lee," SHSP, N.S., II (September 1915), 322; A. W. Kercheval, "The Burial of Lieutenant-General Jackson: A Dirge," *New Eclectic*, V (November 1869), 611; "The Ohio Division," CV, XXVI (August 1918), 368; Harold B. Simpson, *Hood's Texas Brigade in Reunion and Memory* (Hillsboro, Texas, 1974), 76; "The Confederate Choir No. 1," CV, XV (April 1907), 154–55; "United Confederate Choirs of America," ibid., XV (July 1907), 304; "Stonewall Jackson's Way," ibid., XXV (November 1917), 528–29; "Our Confederate Veterans," ibid., V (August 1897), 439; ibid., VI (November 1898), cover.

12. Southern Presbyterian General Assembly, *Minutes of the General Assembly of the Presbyterian Church in the United States* (Columbia, S.C., 1867), 137; Stephen Elliott, "Forty-fifth Sermon: On the State Fast-day," in Elliott, *Sermons by the Right Reverend Stephen Elliott . . .* (New York, 1867), 497, 505, 507; "Day of Fasting, Humiliation and Prayer," Atlanta *Christian Index*, March 9, 1865, 3.

13. "Thanksgiving Day: Its Afterclaps," Atlanta *Christian Index*, December 16, 1869, 2. See also "Day of Thanksgiving," Columbia (S.C.) *Southern Presbyterian*, November 14, 1872, 2; "The Two Proclamations," Atlanta *Christian Index*, November 22, 1866, 1; and Elliott's sermon "On the National Thanksgiving day," in Elliott, *Sermons*, 514–15.

14. James H. M'Neilly, "Jefferson Davis: Gentleman, Patriot, Christian," CV, XXIV (June 1916), 248; "Our Memorial Day," ibid., XXII (May 1914), 195; Lizzie Rutherford Chapter, UDC, *A History of the Origin of Memorial Day . . .* (Columbus, Ga., 1898), 24 (first quotation); Mrs. A. M'D. Wilson, "Memorial Day," CV, XVII (April 1919); 156 (second and third quotations); UDC, *Minutes . . . 1901* (Nashville, 1902), 112.

15. UCV, Texas Division, James J. A. Barker Camp, No. 1555, *Burial Ritual* (n.p., n.d.); "Burial Ritual for Veterans," CV, III (February 1895), 43 (first and second quotations); "Burial Ritual. Suitable for Confederates Everywhere," ibid., XVII (May 1909), 214; Arthur B. Kinsolving, *Texas George: The Life of George Herbert Kinsolving . . .* (Milwaukee and London, 1932), 130; "Rev. Romulus Morris Tuttle," CV, XII (June 1904),

296–97; and "Summer Archibald Cunningham," ibid., XXII (January 1914), 6–8.

16. "The Monumental Spirit of the South," CV, XXII (August 1914), 344; Confederate Monumental Association, *Tennessee Confederate Memorial* (Nashville, n.d.); 44; "Dedicatory Prayer of Monument," CV, IX (January 1901), 38; "Confederate Monument at San Antonio," ibid., VII (September 1899), 399 (first quotation); "Confederate Monument at Bolivar, Tenn.," ibid., VIII (August 1900), 353 (second quotation); "Fourth Report of Monumental Committee," UCV, *Minutes of the Twenty-first Annual Meeting and Reunion*, 52; *Historic Southern Monuments: Representative Memorials of the Heroic Dead of the Southern Confederacy* (Washington and New York, 1911), 53–54 (third quotation), 133, 265, 426–27; UCV, *Minutes of the Seventeenth Annual Meeting and Reunion* 1907.

17. Warner, *The Living and the Dead: A Study of the Symbolic Life of Americans* (New Haven, 1959), 280. See also Claude Lévi-Strauss, *The Savage Mind* (Chicago, 1962), 236–37; Warner, "An American Sacred Ceremony," in Richey and Jones, eds., *American Civil Religion*, 89–111; Catherine Albanese, "Requiem for Memorial Day: Dissent in the Redeemer Nation," *American Quarterly*, XXVI (October 1974), 386–98; Conrad Cherry, "Two American Sacred Ceremonies: Their Implications for the Study of Religion in America," ibid., XXI (Winter 1969), 739–54.

18. For background on the veterans groups see William W. White, *The Confederate Veteran* (Tuscaloosa, Ala., 1962). The reporter's quotation was in UCV, *Minutes of the Ninth Annual Meeting and Reunion*, 8.

19. UCV, *Minutes of the Tenth Annual Meeting and Reunion . . . 1900* (New Orleans, 1902), 70 (quotation). For examples of this revealing theme in other forums see UCV, *Minutes of the Twelfth Annual Meeting and Reunion . . . 1902* (New Orleans, n.d.), 10; "The Confederate Dead of Mississippi: Prayer," SHSP, XVIII (January–December 1890), 297; "The Monument to General Robert E. Lee: The Prayer," ibid., XVII (January–December 1889), 301–302.

20. For hymns at the reunions see UCV, *Minutes of the Seventh Annual Meeting and Reunion . . . 1897* (New Orleans, 1898), 15; UCV, *Minutes of the Tenth Annual Meeting and Reunion*, 40; UCV, *Minutes of the Thirteenth Annual Meeting and Reunion . . . 1903* (New Orleans, n.d.), 50. For the memorial services see UCV, *Minutes of the Tenth Annual Meeting and Reunion*, 95–101; UCV, *Minutes of the Seventeenth Annual Meeting and Reunion*,

110; UCV, *Minutes of the Thirtieth Annual Meeting and Reunion . . . 1920* (New Orleans, n.d.), 41.

21. "The Reunion: The Seventh Annual Convention of the U. D. C.," CV, V (July 1897), 338–39; ibid., V (June 1897), 243; "Comment on Nashville Reunion," ibid., V (September 1897), 463; "About the Nashville Reunion," CV, V (August 1897), 427–28.

22. UDC, *Ritual of the United Daughters of the Confederacy* (Austin, Texas, n.d.), 1–2 (quotations); UDC, *Minutes . . . 1905* (Nashville, 1906), 265–66. Local women's groups in 1900 formed an organization similar to the U. D. C., the Confederated Memorial Associations of the South. See *History of the Confederated Memorial Associations of the South* (New Orleans, 1904), 32–34.

23. *Poppenheim, History*, 1–12; Some, *U. D. C. Catechism for Children* (n.p., 1912); UDC, *Minutes . . . 1912*, 398.

24. Hill et al., *Religion and the Solid South*, 18–19, 26–28, 36–37 (quotation on 37); Hill, *Southern Churches*, xvii, 18, 201; Bailey, *Southern White Protestantism*, 2–3.

25. "Chaplain Jones' Prayer," UCV, *Minutes of the Eighteenth Annual Meeting and Reunion . . . 1908* (New Orleans, n.d.), 49–50 (first quotation); UCV, *Minutes of the Twentieth Annual Meeting and Reunion . . . 1910* (New Orleans, n.d.), 53–54, 121; "Prayer," UCV, *Minutes of the Seventeenth Annual Meeting and Reunion . . . 1907*, 64 (third quotation). See also "The Confederate Dead in Stonewall Cemetery, Winchester, Va." SHSP. XXII (January–December 1894), 42; Hoge's Prayer," ibid., 352–53; "Confederate Dead of Florida . . . ," ibid., XXVII (January–December 1899), 112. The failure to make specifically Christian references is noted by Bellah, "Civil Religion in America," and Martin E. Marty, "Two Kinds of Civil Religion," in Richey and Jones, eds., *American Civil Religion*, 23, 28, 148; and by Conrad Cherry, *God's New Israel: Religious Interpretations of American Destiny* (Englewood Cliffs, N.J., 1971), 9–10.

26. For examples of the interdenominational character of the Lost Cause see John L. Johnson, *Autobiographical Notes* (Boulder, Colo., 1958), 279; Moses D. Hogue to Peyton Hogue, May 22, 1891; January 20, 1893, Moses Drury Hogue Papers (Historical Foundation of the Presbyterian and Reformed Churches, Montreat, N.C.); "Gordon Memorial Service at Nashville," CV, XII (June 1904), 293; J. William Jones, *The Davis Memorial Volume; or, Our Dead President, Jefferson Davis, and the World's Tribute to His Memory* (Waco, Texas, 1890), 590–91, 595, 598.

27. For examples of Catholic and Jewish involvement in the Lost Cause see "Monument to Father Ryan in Mobile," CV, XXI (October 1913), 489–90; "The Reunion," ibid., V (July 1897), 340–41; "Address of Rabbi J. K. Gutheim," SHSP, X (June 1882), 248–50; "Sir Moses Ezekiel," CV, XXV (May 1917), 235–36.

28. Thomas I., Connelly, *The Marble Man: Robert E. Lee and His Image in American Society* (New York, 1977), 45; "Appeal to the South," Atlanta *Christian Index*, February 28, 1884, 4; CV, V (July 1897), 359; Edward P. Humphrey, "Moses and the Critics," *Southern Bivouac*, N.S., I (August 1885), 134–39; "Bishop John James Tigert," CV, XV (January 1907), 25; ibid., V (August 1897), 401.

29. Laura M. Jones and Walt Holcomb, *The Life and Sayings of Sam P. Jones* . . . Atlanta, 1907), 142–48, 447–48; George C. Rankin, *The Story of My Life* . . . Nashville and Dallas, 1912), 227; J. William Jones, *Personal Reminiscences, Anecdotes and Letters of Gen. Robert E. Lee* (New York, 1874), 333; UCV, *Minutes of the Tenth Annual Meeting and Reunion*, 102 104, 108.

30. A. D. Mayo, "The Woman's Movement in the South," *New England Magazine*, N.S., V (October 1891), 257; White, *Confederate Veteran*, 59–60; UDC, *Minutes* . . . 1901 (Nashville, 1902), 127–28; J. William Jones, *School History of the United States* (Baltimore, 1896): Arthur B. Kinsolving, *The Story of a Southern School: The Episcopal High School of Virginia* (Baltimore, 1922), 79–80, 102, 132; C. D. Walker, "A Living Monument," CV, VIII (July 1900), 334; advertisement for Stonewall Jackson Institute, ibid., XII (July 1904), back cover; ibid., XXV (July 1917), back cover; UDC, *Minutes* . . . 1915 (Charlotte, N.C., n.d.), 142.

31. Arthur B. Chitty, "Heir of Hopes: Historical Summary of the University of the South," *Historical Magazine of the Protestant Episcopal Church*, XXIII (September 1954), 258–60; Chitty, *Reconstruction at Sewanee: The Founding of the University of the South and Its First Administration*, 1857–1872 (Sewanee, Tenn., 1954), 45, 54–55, 73, 83; George R. Fairbanks, *History of the University of the South at Sewanee, Tennessee* (Jacksonville, Fla., 1905), 38–59, 70, 394; Richard Wilmer, *In Memoriam: A Sermon in Commemoration of the Life and Labors of the Rt. Rev. Stephen Elliott* . . . (Mobile, 1867),

13–14; Elliott, *An Appeal for Southern Books and Relics for the Library of the University of the South* (Sewanee, 1921), no pagination (quotation); Moultrie Guerry, *Men Who Made Sewanee* (Sewanee, Tenn., 1932), 73, 89, 92, 49–71; Queenie W. Washington, "Memories,"; Louise Finley, "Magnolia Hall"; and Monte Cooper, "Miss Sada," in Lily Baker et al., eds., *Sewanee* (Sewanee, Tenn., 1932), 61–63, 100–101, 142–43.

32. Wilmer, *Gen'l Robert E. Lee: An Address Delivered Before the Students of the University of the South, October 15, 1870* (Nashville, 1872), 5, 9–12; "Funeral of Gen. E. Kirby-Smith," CEI (April 1893), 100–101; "Monument of Gen. E. A. Shoup," ibid., XI (July 1904).

33. The Winkler quotation is in Jones, *Personal Reminiscences*, 130–31. See also Henry A. White, *The Scotch-Irish University of the South: Washington and Lee* (Lexington, Va.; 1890), 21–22; W. G. Bean, *The Liberty Hall Volunteers: Stonewall's College Boys* (Charlottesville, Va., 1964); Walter C. Preston, *Lee, West Point and Lexington* (Yellow Springs, Ohio, 1934), 48–51, 53–57; Ollinger Crenshaw, *General Lee's College: The Rise and Growth of Washington and Lee University* (New York, 1969), 152–54.

34. Franklin L. Riley, ed., *General Robert E. Lee After Appomattox* (New York, 1922), 19–20, 22–23, 62; Marshall W. Fishwick, "Robert E. Lee Churchman," *Historical Magazine of the Protestant Episcopal Church*, XXX (December 1961), 251–58, 260–63; Archibald T. Robertson, *Life and Letters of John Albert Broadus* (Philadelphia, 1910), 224–26; Francis H. Smith, *The Virginia Military Institute, Its Building and Rebuiding* (Lynchburg, Va., 1912); and Susan P. Lee, *Memoirs of William Nelson Pendleton* (Philadelphia, 1893), 422–38.

35. *Ceremonies Connected with the Inauguration of the Mausoleum and the Unveiling of the Recumbent Figure of General Robert Edward Lee at Washington and Lee University, Lexington, Va., June 28, 1883* (Richmond, 1883); Thomas N. Page, *The Old South: Essays Social and Political* (New York, 1894), 3, 51–54; Crenshaw, *General Lee's College*, 282–89; Charles F. Adams, *Lee's Centennial: An Address* (Boston, 1907), 2, 6, 8, 14, 57; "The Old Virginia Town, Lexington," CV, I (April 1893), 108.

36. Mircea Eliade, *Patterns in Comparative Religion* (New York, 1958), 216–35.

THE EASTER PARADE

*Leigh Eric Schmidt*

At least since the beginning of the nineteenth century, Christianity has been deeply involved in the American commercial culture. This relationship has only recently been
carefully examined. In the following essay, Leigh Schmidt considers the "complementary yet contested relationship" between Christianity and commercial culture when
the relationship became particularly apparent in the late nineteenth century. At that
time the commercialization of religious holidays suggested both the pervasive influence of Christianity on American culture and a profound transformation of Christian
symbols from earlier ideals of self-denial to a new gospel of prosperity. Schmidt inves-
tigates the growth of this "devout consumption" through the elaborate displays of
Easter flowers and the parade of Easter fashions both inside and outside of churches.
Though the churches helped to create this new Easter, critics saw the growing com-
mercialism as a cultural contest over the very meaning of Christianity. This was a struggle that pitted Christ against culture, religious hopes of heavenly salvation against
secular desires for earthly pleasure. "But the critics," Schmidt observes, "rarely fathomed the complexity of the drama that so disturbed them."

Reprinted by permission from Leigh Eric Schmidt, "The Easter Parade: Piety, Fashion, and Display,"
*Religion and American Culture* 4:2 (Summer 1994): 135–164. Copyright 2003 by the Center for the
Study of Religion and American Culture.

# 11

## THE EASTER PARADE

## Piety, Fashion, and Display

*Leigh Eric Schmidt*

IRVING BERLIN'S POPULAR MUSICAL of 1948, *Easter Parade*, starring Fred Astaire and Judy Garland, opens with a wonderful shopping scene. It is the day before Easter, 1911. Astaire's character, Don Hewes, sings and dances his way along the streets of New York past a drygoods store and through millinery, florist, and toy shops. "Me, oh, my," he sings, "there's a lot to buy. There is shopping I must do. Happy Easter to you." In the millinery store saleswomen model elaborate Easter bonnets and mellifluously offer their wares: "Here's a hat that you must take home. Happy Easter. . . . This was made for the hat parade on the well-known avenue. This one's nice and it's worth the price. Happy Easter to you." Everywhere Hewes goes he buys things—a bonnet, a large pot of lilies, a toy bunny. By the time he leaves the florist, he has purchased so many gifts that he is followed by three attendants who help carry all the packages. Don Hewes is a consumer on a spree, and Easter is the occasion for it.[1]

With a boyish exuberance, Hewes prepares for Easter by shopping. His efforts are aimed not at readying himself for church or sacrament but at insuring that his companion will make a fine appearance in New York's fashion parade. The opening chorus chirrups this theme: "In your Easter bonnet with all the frills upon it, you'll be the grandest lady in the Easter parade. I'll be all in clover, and when they look you over, I'll be the proudest fellow in the Easter parade." Fulfillment consists of having his consort admired with envious gazes. When Hewes and his new dance partner, a humble show girl who doubles as a barmaid, actually encounter the promenade the next day, she is overawed. "I can't believe I'm really here," she gasps. "You know, I used to read about the Easter parade in New York, and then I'd look at the pictures of the women in their lovely clothes and dream that maybe someday I'd . . . " Her voice trails off in wonder and dreamy aspiration. The only religious image in the film appears in the last scene when the Easter parade has returned for another year. A Gothic church looms as a dim backdrop for the fancily dressed couples who stroll by in a streaming concourse of affluence.

The film is not primarily about Easter, of course, but about Astaire and Garland and their marvelous dancing and singing. But the movie and Berlin's popular theme song are illuminating texts about the American Easter all the same. From at least the 1880s through the 1950s, this dress parade was one of the primary cultural expressions of Easter in the

United States, one of the fundamental ways that the occasion was identified and celebrated. The holy day blossomed in the late nineteenth century into a cultural rite of spring with elaborate floral decorations, new clothes, fancy millinery, chocolate bunnies, greeting cards, and other gifts. The movie, like the Easter parade itself, embodied an expansive public faith in American abundance, a gospel of wealth, self-gratification, and prosperity: "Everything seems to come your way," the chorus lilts, "Happy Easter!"

In his recent novel *Operation Shylock*, Philip Roth celebrates Irving Berlin's *Easter Parade* for its creative de-Christianization of the festival, for its promotion of a "scholockified Christianity" in which the bonnet overthrows the cross.[2] But, in many ways, Berlin was merely offering a catchy, hummable benediction for the fashionable modern festival that American Christians had been busily creating for themselves over the previous century. This consumer-oriented Easter actually had deep religious wellsprings, and the juxtapositions of Christian devotion and lavish display were as richly polychromatic as the holiday flowers and fashions themselves. Fathoming the growing significance attached to church decoration in the second half of the nineteenth century is of first importance in making sense of this modern Easter. These religious patterns of embellishment, in turn, fed commercial holiday displays and spectacles of Easter merchandising. Lushly adorned churches provided the backdrop for finely appareled congregants and for the efflorescence of the Easter parade in New York City and elsewhere. All along, this Easter fanfare elicited sharp criticism from devotees of simplicity and plainness; that is, from those who were alienated from this faith of comfortable materialism, an estrangement that was often etched in sharply gendered terms. A complementary yet contested relationship between American Christianity and the modern consumer culture became increasingly evident in the second half of the nineteenth century, and that conjunction found performance in the Easter festival.

## THE ART OF CHURCH DECORATION AND THE ART OF WINDOW DISPLAY
The Gothic church that flickers in the last frames of *Easter Parade* stands very much in the background, perhaps a nostalgic image—distant, unobtrusive, evanescent. Yet, to understand the development of the Easter parade as a cultural and religious event, this neo-Gothic edifice and others like it have to be brought into the foreground. Churches such as Trinity Episcopal Church, St. Patrick's Cathedral, and St. Thomas's Episcopal Church in New York City, with their rich Gothic ornament, are central, not peripheral, to this story. The elaborate decorations that these splendid urban churches created for ecclesiastical festivals such as Christmas and Easter are crucial for fathoming the emergence of a fashionable Easter in the second half of the nineteenth century. The newly cultivated art of church decoration, in turn, helped inspire inventive window trimmers and interior designers in their creation of holiday spectacles for merchandising purposes.

Easter, even more than Christmas, remained under a Puritan and evangelical cloud in the antebellum United States. Though various denominations all along preserved the holiday—most prominently Episcopalians, Roman Catholics, Lutherans, and Moravians—their celebrations were, until mid-century, localistic, parochial, and disparate. The festival became a well-nigh ubiquitous cultural event only in the decades after 1860, as low-church Protestant resistance or indifference gave way to approbation and as Episcopalian, Roman Catholic, and new immigrant observances became ever more prominent. Middle-class Victorians, fascinated with the recovery of fading holiday traditions and the cultivation of new home-centered festivities, discovered lush possibilities in this spring rite. The *New*

*York Herald*, in a report on "Eastertide" in 1881, proclaimed that "A few years ago and Easter as a holiday was scarcely thought of, except by the devout; now all are eager to join in the celebration." Between about 1860 and 1890, Easter took distinctive religious and cultural shape as an American holiday.[3]

In an 1863 article on Easter, *Harper's New Monthly Magazine* suggested the growing embrace of the feast in American culture. "It is one of the obvious marks of our American religion," the article related, "that we are noticing more habitually and affectionately the ancient days and seasons of the Christian Church." Easter, following Christmas's rising popularity, showed "unmistakable signs that it is fast gaining upon the religious affection and public regard of our people." "We have carefully noted the gradual increase of observance of the day," the journal continued, "and can remember when it was a somewhat memorable thing for a minister, not Catholic or Episcopal, to preach an Easter sermon." What the magazine found most revealing of "this new love for Easter," however, was the increasing use of elaborate floral decorations for the festival. "Easter flowers are making their way into churches of all persuasions," the magazine applauded. "One of our chief Presbyterian churches near by decked its communion-table and pulpit with flowers for the third time this Easter season." The writer praised Easter floral displays for their artistic taste and devotional symbolism their "ministry of the beautiful." The splendor of Easter flowers embodied the new compelling allure of the festival.[4]

In lauding Easter flowers, the *Harper's* piece was celebrating the expanding art of church decoration. As a liturgical movement, this art effloresced in England and the United States in the middle decades of the nineteenth century. An outgrowth of the ritualist or Catholic turn within Anglican and Episcopalian circles, the new forms of church decoration meshed with the Gothic revival in Victorian church architecture and ornament. English writers such as William A. Barrett and Ernest Geldart led the way in formalizing the rubrics of modern church decoration in a number of handbooks that helped foster and guide the burgeoning art on both sides of the Atlantic. These writers codified a new aesthetic for church adornment, nostalgically medieval and Gothic in its vision but decidedly Victorian and modern in its elaboration. They cultivated what T. J. Jackson Lears has called "the religion of beauty"—a devotional love of liturgical drama, material symbolism, polychromatic color, sumptuous music, and graceful ornament. They wanted to fill the churches, as one handbook attested, with "sermons in stones, in glass, in wood, in flowers, and fruits, and leaves."[5]

Much of this ritual adornment focused on the high holy days of Christmas and Easter. Festooning the interior of churches with evergreens, flowers, vines, mosses, berries, leaves, wreaths, illuminated texts, emblems, tracery, and other devices became holiday staples. Indeed, such festal decorations reached modish proportions among Victorian churchgoers. "Few fashions," Edward L. Cutts commented in 1868 in the third edition of his handbook on church decoration, "have made such rapid progress within the last few years as the improved fashion of Decorating our Churches with evergreens and flowers for the great Church festivals." By 1882, another leading advocate of the "new fashion," Ernest Geldart, could remark that "it requires an effort of memory to recall the days when, save a few ill-set sprigs of holly at Christmas, none of these things were known."[6]

Christmas initially led the way in church decoration, but Easter soon came to rival, if not surpass, the winter feast for special adornment. Ernest R. Suffling commented on Easter's ascent in his manual *Church Festival Decorations*:

> Decorating the church at Easter, which a generation ago was but feebly carried out, has now
> become a recognized and general institution, and at no season of the year is it more appropri-
> ate. The joy of our hearts at the Resurrection of our Saviour—the seal of the completion of
> His work on earth—must surely be even greater than on the festival of His birth. The festival,
> coming as it does in early spring, is best commemorated by the use of as many flowers as
> possible.[7]

Weaving garlands around pillars, covering fonts and reading desks with fresh blooms,
hanging wreaths from arches and rails, erecting floral crosses on the altar or communion
table, filling windowsills with bouquets, setting up vine-covered trellises, and creating
pyramids of lilies—in short, putting flowers everywhere—became an Easter vogue of dazzling proportions.

One way to render specific the rising importance of floral decorations at Easter is
through diaries. The journal of Henry Dana Ward, rector of St. Jude's Episcopal Church in
New York City, survives for the years 1850 to 1857, and it suggests the budding interest in
Easter flowers. He mentioned no special floral displays for his Easter services from 1850 to
1854, but, in 1855, he noted that "the recess behind the Table was furnished with three pots
of flowers in full bloom and the Font with the same in partial bloom." Ward thought that
the flowers, all "Egyptian lilies," were pretty and pleasing, adding to the solemnity of the
service. Of these decorations, as well as new coverings for the communion table and the
pulpit, he took comfort that "no one was offended by these small novelties." He also made
clear that his forays into festal decoration were tame compared to those of some other
Episcopal churches. Visiting an afternoon Easter service at Trinity in 1857, he found the
ritualism and decorations excessive: "They make *too much* of a good thing—chant the Anthems to death—and make a show of flowers on the Font & the reading Desk."[8] Decades
before "the concept of show invaded the domain of culture" in the form of showplaces,
showrooms, and fashion shows, churches like Trinity were cultivating a festive, luxuriant,
and dramatic religious world through the increasingly ornate art of church decoration.[9]
This sense of Easter decorations as a show or spectacle would become all the more evident
in the decades after the Civil War.

The diary of a young man who worked as a clerk at Tiffany's in New York City in the
early 1870s suggests the dramatic impression that Easter decorations made. For Easter
1873, he went to a morning service at Christ Church and an afternoon service at St.
Stephen's, both of which he found "magnificent," if fearfully crowded. The two churches,
"well trimmed with beautiful flowers," were stunning in their decorations. He continued:

> At Christs Church the burning star they had Christmas was over the alter [sic] besides the dec-
> orations of flowers. At St Stephens was arranged in the same manner—gas jets[.] Over the
> alter [sic] (as if it was there without anything to keep it there) was suspended a cross and
> above over it a crown. The effect was very good[,] the flaming of the gas making it so
> brilliant.[10]

The decorations clearly made a lasting impression on this young man (here at Easter he
still remembers the blazing star from the previous Christmas). Indeed, he seemed far more
overawed by the decorations that he saw in New York's Episcopal and Catholic churches
than anything he came across in New York's stores. For theatrical effect, the stores in the
1870s still had much to learn from the churches.

The special floral decorations for Easter received particular attention in women's diaries. An active Baptist laywoman in New York City, Sarah Todd, commented in her diary on a visit to an Episcopal church for an Easter service in 1867: "Being Easter Sunday the Church was handsomely dressed with flowers." Likewise, in her diary, New Yorker Elizabeth Merchant often made note of the Easter display of flowers: "Our church was beautifully dressed with flowers," she wrote of Easter 1883; "The church was lovely with flowers," she recalled of Easter worship in 1886; "Flowers perfectly beautiful & Mr Brooks splendid," she eulogized of two Easter services at Trinity Episcopal that she and her son enjoyed in 1887. Another New York woman made similar notations about Easter in her diary, writing in 1888: "Easter Day, Communion Sunday. Flowers in church. Alice & I took the children to the Church to see the flowers." Decorations seen, as much as sermons heard or eucharistic elements received, stood out in the memories that these women recorded. Perhaps for women especially, who often took charge of these floral displays, Easter in the churches became preeminently a time of flowers.[11]

The implications and consequences of the new fascination with Easter decorations were manifold. Certainly, and perhaps quintessentially, this art constituted an important new medium for religious expression. The decorations were devotional; their "double purpose" was to glorify God and edify wayfaring Christians. At Trinity Episcopal in 1861, the *New York Sun* reported, the Easter floral decorations were "in fine taste": "Flowers suggestive of the fundamental doctrines of Christianity composed the ornaments, and were so grouped as to indicate the cardinal truths of religion. In the centre of the altar was a floral globe mounted by a cross, and expressive of the redemption of the world." Floral decorations, testifying to the promise of new life, became for Victorians one of the dominant ways of communicating the Christian message of resurrection. To make certain that the devotional significance of the decorations remained clear, the churches often prominently displayed illuminated scriptural texts, usually drawn in intricate Gothic lettering. Arches and altars, chancels and choirs, brimmed with monumental affirmations: "He is risen"; "I am the Resurrection and the Life"; "Now is Christ risen from the dead, the first-fruits of them that slept"; "O death, where is thy sting? O grave, where is thy victory?" Easter decorations were a form of popular piety that evoked the ancient coalescence of the rebirth of spring and the resurrection of Christ.[12]

In their devotional dimensions, Easter decorations also suggested a sentimental and domestic version of Christian piety. Easter, *Harper's* said, was "winning our household feeling as well as our religious respect"; it served as a liturgical affirmation of the eternality of "family affections," as a celebration of "the great sentiment of home love." This domestic tenor was evident in the increasing overlap of church and home decorations: lilies, floral crosses, and distinctive Easter bouquets, for example, all ornamented Victorian altars and parlors alike. The decorative result was to join the church and the home in a shared, overarching design—"the House Beautiful."[13] Moreover, flowers suggested how Easter was becoming preeminently "the festival of sacred remembrance." Easter blooms, lilies especially, were presented in the churches as personal memorials for "departed kindred and friends"; they were hopeful, powerful tokens of the restored wholeness of familial circles. Indeed, the new love of Easter flowers was at one level the liturgical counterpart to Elizabeth Stuart Phelps's Victorian best-seller *The Gates Ajar*—a sentimental, consoling portrayal of heaven in terms of home, family, and friends: The new Easter helped reinforce the Victorian predilection for picturing heaven more as a place of human relationships and domestic reunions than as a God-centered realm of divine praise, light, and glory.[14]

The new passion for floral decoration clearly carried consequences that were not only devotional and domestic. For one thing, issues of competition and emulation crept into the Easter displays. The handbooks warned against the tendencies toward extravagance and rivalry: "Never try to beat the record," Ernest Geldart instructed. "Pray don't let it be your ambition that prompts you to 'beat' anything you have ever done, and above all, don't try to beat your neighbour's efforts." Admonitions notwithstanding, competition became an acknowledged undercurrent in holiday decoration. Who would have the most beautiful and extensive floral displays? Who would have the most inspiring music, the most solemn, dramatic, and crowded services? As the *New York Herald* observed in 1881, "The Catholics and Episcopalians are, of course, the foremost in the observance of the season, but other denominations are not far behind, and all vie with each other to make their house the most attractive to the worshipper." In America's free-market religious culture, church decoration became another way of attracting parishioners and gaining attention. Less ritualistic denominations—Presbyterians, Methodists, and even Baptists—learned to emulate Episcopalian and Catholic forms of holiday celebration in order to hold the allegiance of their people at these seasons of the year. Thorstein Veblen was wrong to view the "devout consumption" of the churches in the 1890s—their increasingly elaborate "ceremonial paraphernalia"—simply in terms of "status" and "conspicuous waste" (such an interpretation was irredeemably monochromatic and reductionistic). But he was right to see competition and emulation as component parts of Victorian church furnishing and decoration.[15]

Another unintended consequence of holiday church decoration was how it fostered modishness and exoticism. In 1867, the *New York Herald*, in commenting on the "elaborate floral decorations" for Easter at St. John the Baptist Episcopal Church, noted that the display included "one of the only three genuine palms known to exist in the United States." Similarly, the *Herald's* 1873 report on the Easter decorations in the Church of the Divine Paternity struck the same chord of rarity: "Surmounting the reredos was a magnificent cross made of lilies, on either side of which were two recumbent beds of roses. The altar was profusely covered with the rarest of exotics." Ernest Suffling, summarizing this trend toward floral exoticism—if not colonialist rampage—observed that where a few "indigenous evergreens" had formerly satisfied the church decorator, now "we ransack the whole world, for our grasses, flowers, and palms, or fruits and mosses." There was little that was traditional, antimodern, or medieval, the *New York Sun* declared, in searching out "rare evergreens," "choice tropicals," or "calla lilies of remarkable size and beauty, sent hermetically sealed from California." Style, taste, abundance, and novelty—the very values of the burgeoning consumer culture—became defining features of Easter decorations in the churches. The fashionable Easter given expression in the Easter parade and in turn-of-the-century department stores had its roots in the religious culture, which itself was becoming progressively more consumerist in its modes of celebration. At Easter, devout consumption fed its more worldly counterpart.[16]

A final, portentous consequence of the new art of church decoration was that it provided a model or repertory for holiday displays outside the churches in the marketplace. With Easter, even more than with Christmas, the commercial culture built its enterprise directly on the religious culture—on Christian patterns of decoration, display, and celebration. Church music, flowers, ornaments, banners, and other decorations all found their way into show windows and interior displays in late-nineteenth- and early twentieth-century department stores. Easter decorations were clearly very attractive for commercial appropriation; their associations with the church, with women and the home, with fashion and affluence, were all useful connections for merchandising. With multiple layers of meaning, Easter emblems, popularized through church decoration, provided retailers with rich and redolent symbols. More broadly, the art of church decoration offered a useful aesthetic for the art of store decoration. Church decorators, like their commercial counterparts after them, stressed the power of visual representation, the importance of harmonizing form and color, the careful planning of designs, and the expressive potentialities of lighting and glass. Church decorators also provided a principle of innovation, regularly experimenting with new decorative materials and warning against "sameness," "feeble repetition," and "distasteful monotony" in beautifying the sanctuary. This outlook intermeshed with the mounting desire of window trimmers and store decorators to bring seasonal variety and originality to their display of goods. Thus, in surprising and hitherto little seen ways, the art of church decoration helped generate what William Leach has called "the display aesthetic" that came to characterize the modern consumer culture.[17]

The movie *Easter Parade* in itself suggests the migration of church decoration into the marketplace: Don Hewes passes the show window of a dry-goods store that is trimmed with Easter lilies, as is the interior of the millinery shop he patronizes. The transformation of church decorations into store embellishments was evident as early as the 1880s and 1890s. "Make a gala week of the week before Easter," the *Dry Goods Chronicle* exhorted in 1898. "Tog your store out until it shines with the Easter spirit. . . . Blossom with the Easter lily, give your store a dress in keeping with this Easter festival." This kind of advice was regularly put into practice. "The store is in harmony with the occasion," Wanamaker's Easter catalogue boasted in 1893; "Easter Symbols are everywhere in the decorations. . . . Easter merchandise is all over the store." By the turn of the century, such Easter displays and embellishments had become standard trade preparations: lavish store decorations were considered essential for imparting and evoking the Easter spirit and for attracting holiday shoppers.[18]

All along, trimming a store for Easter meant a profusion of seasonal folk symbols such as rabbits, chicks, and eggs. It also meant a surplus of Christian iconography—miniature churches, choirs, pipe organs, stained glass, crosses, lilies, religious banners, and devotional mottoes. The *American Advertiser* offered this description of a "delicate and pleasing" Easter window in a Chicago jewelry store in 1890:

> The window floor was covered with white jewelers' cotton in sheets, looking pure as snow. A cross of similar material and whiteness was slightly raised above the level of the window-floor, in the middle rear part of the window. On each side of the window was a calla lily blossom, the flower being cut short off below the bloom. Inside the lily, like a drop of purest dew, sparkled a diamond—just one on each lily. The cross was slightly twined with smilax, which also bordered the back of the window. A white rose was scattered here and there, and on the cross and on the white window floor were displayed a few gems and trinkets,—not enough to distract the attention or give the appearance of crowding. . . . Taken altogether the display was the perfection of good taste and artistic skill.

The cross and lilies, staples of church decoration, became mainstays of the window dresser's art—repeated centerpieces for the display of goods, whether millinery, greeting cards, or even groceries. In this case, jewelry and other items were actually attached to the lilies and the cross, making their linkage direct and tangible.[19]

Designs for show windows also played upon the sentimental, domestic dimensions of Victorian Easter piety. One window trimmer bragged in 1896 of a crowd-stopping Easter display that proved pleasing to patrons and proprietor alike. Entitled "Gates Ajar," the window was trimmed from floor to ceiling "with spotless white silk handkerchiefs entwined with ferns and smilax from the millinery stock and plants from the hot-house." The focal point of the window was "a flight of five steps, at the head of which was a large double gate, partially opened, so as to show one large figure in white silk and pretty little cherubs (dolls with wings of gold and silver paper) as if in the act of flying." This show-window glimpse of silky white seraphs and everlasting life dovetailed with the alluring domestic heaven depicted in Elizabeth Stuart Phelps's *Gates Ajar* and its sequels. In *The Feminization of American Culture*, Ann Douglas wryly comments that reading Phelps's novels about heaven with all their luminous detail about domestic furnishings and possessions "is somewhat like window-shopping outside the fanciest stores on Fifth Avenue." Window trimmers and store decorators had the same intuition. In their appropriation of Phelps's themes, they made explicit the otherwise implicit interconnections between this domestic piety and consumerist ideals.[20]

Store decorations for Easter were often more elaborate than such relatively modest show windows and sometimes rivaled the churches in what one window trimmer called "cathedral effect[s]." This decorative intricacy was epitomized in the Easter adornment in Wanamaker's in Philadelphia. As was the case at Christmas, Wanamaker's Grand Court was transformed at Easter into a religious spectacle. Statues of angels, thousands of lilies and ferns, displays of ornate ecclesiastical vestments, religious banners and tapestries, and mottoes proclaiming "He is Risen!" and "Alleluia!" all found place in Wanamaker's during the Easter season in the early decades of this century. The store's grandest Easter spectacle, however, was the annual display, beginning in the mid-1920s, of two monumental canvases by the Hungarian artist Michael de Munkacsy—one painting (20'8" by 13'6"), entitled *Christ before Pilate*, and the other (23'4" by 14'2"), entitled *Christ on Calvary*. Painted respectively in 1881 and 1884, these works had been widely exhibited and heralded in this country and had achieved international repute in their day as grand masterpieces. Purchased by John Wanamaker as favored treasures for his own impressive collection of art, the paintings were eventually put on display in the Grand Court each year during Lent and Easter. The exhibition of paintings with this level of acclaim was something that the churches could rarely match or duplicate. Easter displays like these brought into sharp relief the dynamic interplay of art, piety, and commerce in the American marketplace. Easter in Wanamaker's epitomized the translation of the Gothic revival and the art of church decoration into a commercial idiom.[21]

Discerning the meaning and significance of the varied Christian emblems that found their way into show windows and department stores is no easy task. What did religious symbols—such as the cross, lilies, church replicas, or the Agnus Dei—come to symbolize when placed within the context of Easter displays? In the ersatz, artful, and cunning world of the marketplace, the meanings of symbols were particularly unstable, uncertain, and slippery. Perhaps such religious emblems became quite literally so much window dressing, that is, artificial, distracting, and illusory fluff, little more than splashes of color and attractive packaging, a vapid and insincere mimicry of liturgical art. Certainly, the employment of religious symbols as merchandising icons carried an undeniable artifice and double-ness, a sharp edge of deception. In their intramural discussions of display techniques, win-dow trimmers were often quite candid about their purposes. L. Frank Baum, who started in the fantasy world of show windows before moving on to the *Wizard of Oz*, commented matter-of-factly on the place of the cross in Easter displays: "The cross is the principal em-blem of Easter and is used in connection with many displays, being suitable for any line of merchandise. To be most effective it should be a floral cross." The essential object in win-dow dressing was, after all, to sell goods, and religious symbols, as with all display props, were used self-consciously to maximize this effect. Creatively negotiating the borderland between commerce and Christianity was part of the window trimmer's calling, and these Easter icons were, at one level, simply another trick of the trade.[22]

But these displays represented more than commercial artifice. The widespread infusion of religious symbols into the marketplace also suggested the deep hold of Christianity on the culture and indicated anew how "adaptable" American religion was to "popular com-mercial forms."[23] Far from eschewing Christian emblems, retailers seized the opportunity to consecrate their stores through holiday decorations. Often enough, churchgoing mer-chants employed these emblems straightforwardly to evoke and affirm the old-time piety; certainly John Wanamaker, YMCA leader and Sunday school titan, understood his cathe-dral-like decorations and his in-store choir concerts in religious terms. The density of spir-itual referents was, after all, what made these symbols so powerful; it is also, of course, what made them so useful. Still, the manipulation, misappropriation, or displacement of Chris-tian symbols was rarely the issue for merchants or customers: in these displays, Christian hopes and consumerist dreams regularly merged into a cohesive cultural whole. Rather than shunting aside the church, the department stores (and the emergent mass culture that these institutions represented) accorded Christianity considerable cultural authority dur-ing the holidays. And, in some ways, merchants seemed to be doing exactly what liberal Protestant pundits had been calling for; namely, the wholesale sacralization of the market-place. Social gospeller George Herron exhorted "the Christian business men of America" to "make the marketplace as sacred as the church. . . . You can draw the world's trades and traffics within the onsweep of Christ's redemptive purpose," Herron insisted. Wanamaker and other merchants like him were seen by many Protestants as the consummate consecra-tors of wealth and the market. In the "one undivided Kingdom of God," commerce and Christianity would harmoniously support one another. The turn-of-the-century celebra-tions of Christmas and Easter in the department stores were the festivals of that liberal cul-tural faith. Indeed, in some ways, they represented a re-visioning in modern Protestant guise of the "festive marketplace" of the Middle Ages and the Renaissance in which church celebration met the "brimming-over abundance of the fair."[24]

This seemingly happy convergence of Christianity and consumption suggested in itself, however, a profound transformation in the meaning of Christian symbols. The stores all too clearly presented a new prosperity gospel that was far removed from traditional Chris-tian emphases on self-abnegation. "When I survey the wondrous cross on which the Prince of glory died," Isaac Watts had versified in the eighteenth century, in lines his Victo-rian heirs still sang, "My richest gain I count but loss, and pour contempt on all my pride. . . . All the vain things that charm me most, I sacrifice them to his blood." Surveying the wondrous cross within a show window or a department store effectively shifted the foundations of this crucicentric piety from self-denial to self-fulfillment. The very context in which these symbols appeared suggested a substantial revision of the faith—a new image of piety at peace with plenty and at home in the new "dream world" of mass consumption. This was no small subversion. Traditional Christian symbols of self-abnegation had come to legitimate luxury, elegance, and indulgence. The cross itself had become one of the charms of the merchandiser's art, its religious power absorbed into the new magic of modern commodities and advertising.[25]

## PIETY, FASHION, AND A SPRING PROMENADE

The vogue for Easter flowers and church decoration intertwined with other Easter fashions—those in clothing and millinery. Of an Easter service at Christ Church, an Episcopal congregation on Fifth Avenue, the *New York Herald* wrote in 1873: "More than one-half of the congregation were ladies, who displayed all the gorgeous and marvelous articles of dress which Dame Fashion has submitted to be the ruling idea of Spring, and the appearance of the body of the church thus vied in effect and magnificence with the pleasant and tasteful array of flowers which decorated the chancel." In a similar vein, a reporter compared "the costumes of the ladies" at St. Patrick's Cathedral for Easter 1871 with "a parterre of flowers." Since spring millinery fashions actually tended to include various flora and fauna, such comparisons were not mere similes. Fashions in flowers and dress, indeed, interpenetrated one another. In 1897, for example, the *New York Times* reported that violets were in greater demand than any other Easter flower "because the violet, in all its various shades, is the predominating color in dress." The very development of the Easter parade along Fifth Avenue was in part connected with the popularity of visiting the different churches to see their elaborate floral decorations. "Many will go to church to-day to see the flowers," the *New York Times* observed in 1889, "and not a few are accustomed to join the parade on Fifth-avenue from church to church, just to look at the beautiful productions of nature." The Victorian love of Easter flowers and church decoration blossomed naturally into the famous promenade of fashions.[26]

Having new clothes for Easter or dressing up in special ways for the festival was never simply about modern fashions or modern forms of consumption and display. The practice had deep roots, or at least resonances, in European religious traditions and folk customs at Easter. Sacred times—baptisms, weddings, funerals, fasts, and feasts—warranted special forms of dress, material markers of holiness and celebration. Uncommon or distinctive garb for Easter, as with the Sunday best of the sabbatarian or the special vestments of priests, had long communicated the solemnity, sacrality, and seriousness of the occasion. The special raiment might be as simple as wearing new gloves, ribbons, or stockings or as stunning as dressing wholly in white. Conventions were localistic and diverse, but the overarching point was captured in an Irish adage: "For Christmas, food and drink; for Easter, new clothes." A frequently recited maxim from Poor Robin distilled such holiday expectations into a couplet:

> At Easter let your clothes be new,
> Or else be sure you will it rue.

This old English saying itself became part of the Victorian memory about Easter, a selective slice of Easter folklore that helped people situate their own interest in new attire for the holiday within the comforting framework of tradition. As the *New York Herald* noted in

1855, "There is an old proverb that if on Easter Sunday some part of your dress is not new you will have no good fortune that year."[27]

The parade of Easter fashions in New York City emerged as a distinct religious and cultural event in the 1870s and 1880s, and the Easter services of the churches were at the center of it. An account in 1873 in the *New York Herald* of "the throngs of people" going to and from church suggested the parade's incipient form:

> They were a gaily dressed crowd of worshippers, and the female portion of it seemed to have come out *en masse* in fresh apparel, and dazzled the eye with their exhibition of shade and color in the multitudinous and variegated hues of their garments. Fifth avenue, from Tenth street to the Central Park, from ten o'clock in the morning till late in the afternoon, was one long procession of men and women, whose attire and bearing betokened refinement, wealth and prosperity, and nearly all these were worshippers of some denomination or another, as the crowds that poured in and out of the various religious edifices along the line of the avenue amply testified.

By the end of the 1870s, the "fashionable promenade" was more clearly defined in terms of the early afternoon, ensuing at the conclusion of the morning church services: "In the afternoon," the *Herald* reported in 1879, "Fifth avenue was a brilliant sight when the thronging congregations of the various churches poured out upon the sidewalks and leisurely journeyed homeward." *Le beau monde* flowed out of the churches into a vast concourse of style, affluence, and luxury.[28]

In the 1880s, the afternoon promenade of Easter churchgoers became all the more "the great fashion show of the year." By 1890, the procession had achieved standing as a recognized marvel on New York's calendar of festivities and had taken on its enduring designation as *the Easter parade*. As the *New York Times* reported in 1890, "It was the great Easter Sunday parade, which has become such an established institution in New York that the curious flock to Fifth-avenue almost as numerously and enthusiastically as they do to see a circus parade." A spectacle of new spring fashions, prismatic colors, Easter bouquets and corsages, elaborate and ever-changing millinery, New York's "great Easter parade" was an occasion for people "to see and be seen." By the mid-1890s, day-trippers from New Jersey and Long Island as well as other visitors flocked to the Fifth Avenue pageant to survey the fashions and to join in the promenade. Thus having begun as a procession of fashionable and privileged churchgoers, the parade quickly became a jostling, crowded scene—"a kaleidoscope of humanity that changed incessantly and presented a new picture with every change."[29]

The emergence of the Easter parade presented a choice opportunity for dry-goods and millinery establishments. Surprisingly, however, retailers were not overly quick to push the promotional connection between Easter and seasonal fashions. While Christmas was already garnering the advertising attention of New York's emergent dry-goods palaces in the 1840s and 1850s as well as attracting the humbug of smaller shopkeepers even earlier, Easter went unnoticed. Spring openings were a merchandising staple for New York firms by the mid-nineteenth century, yet no advertising efforts were fabricated to link spring bonnets or other spring fashions explicitly to Easter. In the 1850s and 1860s, newspaper advertisements for seasonal apparel remained the same before and after Easter. Through the mid-1870s, few, if any, attempts were made to create a specific market for the holiday, even though the connection between Easter and new spring styles was already apparent in New York's most fashionable churches. Only in the late 1870s did New York's merchants begin to exploit the growing religious linkage between Easter and fashion. According to Ralph M. Hower, Macy's first began to promote goods specifically for Easter in its newspaper advertising in 1878, and this coincides with the early efforts of other retailers. For example, in the *New York Sun* in 1878, E. Ridley & Sons advertised "Trimmed Bonnets and Round Hats, Manufactured for Easter," and Lord & Taylor made a similar pitch. In the 1880s, almost all the leading department stores would join in this kind of advertising, thus bringing spring fashions and the Easter festival into explicit and deepening alliance.[30]

By the 1890s, promotion of Easter within the dry-goods industry was in full swing. There was no bigger event in the trade's calendar. "Easter is pre-eminently the festival of the dry goods trade," the *Dry Goods Economist* concluded in 1894. "Much of the success of the year's business hangs upon the demand experienced during the weeks just preceding Easter." Retailers did all they could to stoke the desire for Easter fashions. "Everything is done during these days to influence the shopper to buy," the *Dry Goods Economist* observed of the Easter season in 1894. "Windows are trimmed with all the art at the dresser's command and with as much study as the Royal Academician gives to a magnificent painting." Merchants had clearly come to see their role in the Easter festival as more than one of simply responding to a demand for seasonal goods. Instead, their goal was to expand the market, to deepen and widen these holiday customs. "Women may be induced to think more and more of something special for Easter by telling insinuations judiciously put in your advertising," the *Dry Goods Chronicle* theorized in 1898. "Women may be induced to forego the satisfying of some actual need in order to gratify an Easter fancy, provided you prod their vanity with suggestive advertising and supplement it with a fetching store display." As was the case with so many other dimensions of the expanding consumer culture, women were condescendingly cast as the arch-consumers at Easter and received most of the attention in its promotion. If merchants had been slow to get on the Easter bandwagon in the 1860s and 1870s, they were among its loudest trumpeters and trombonists by the 1890s. Through their tireless promotions, they helped define Easter as "a time for 'dress parade' and 'full feather.'"[31]

A spectacle of vast proportions, the Easter parade was assuredly a multivalent ritual, a multilayered cultural performance. For the devout, the season's new clothes were part of a synthesis of piety and material culture. As the gray of winter and the darkness of Lent and Good Friday gave way to the rebirth of spring and the Resurrection, the sumptuous hues of Easter fashions reflected these transitions. New Yorker Elizabeth Orr suggested this interplay of themes in her diary entry about Easter in 1871:

> Easter Sunday came in bright and beautiful[,] has been one of the most beautiful Spring days I ever experienced. Every one seemed to be influenced by the weather, bright happy faces. Most every one out in their holiday clothes gotten up for the occasion. Dr Eddy gave us one of his good discourses on the reserection [sic] of Christ and his followers. Oh that I may be one of that number! 'Am I his or Am I not' should be a question with us. I know and feel my sinfulness, and he came to save just such a sinner. I repent every day, and trust I am forgiven. Oh that happy day when we will have no more sin to repent of, but constantly [be] in the presence of our Lord and Master.[32]

In her recollections of the day's activities, the beautiful spring weather led naturally to promenading in holiday clothes, which connected seamlessly, in turn, with pious reflections on sin, repentance, and resurrection. Easter devotion was part of a rich mix or jumble of experiences in which impressions of clothes and sunshine and smiles flitted alongside the ringing words of the pastor's sermon.

Elizabeth Merchant's diary entries for Easter displayed the same sort of tangled synthesis of seasonal rejoicing, new clothes, and resurrection. The Saturday before Easter in 1881 she noted: "Went to town looking for Easter cards & buying myself a dress . . . with linings &c. [T]hen went to Bible class & heard a lovely lecture from Dr. Hall on the resurrection." In another passage she waxed eloquent on the interconnections between the new life of Easter and the vernal revival:

> Oh! Such a perfect day! trees budding birds singing—grass is green & sky so beautiful with its fleecy clouds. All the air full of sweet Spring sounds. I long to be out Enjoying every Moment at this season of so much beauty. There is an immense Robin red breast hopping and flying over the lawn! Oh God will the resurrection of our frail bodies be glorious like this waking of nature from the cold death of Winter?

Elizabeth Merchant readily combined the simple satisfactions of Easter shopping with the deeper mysteries of Christianity and nature. The same overlay of experiences was captured in Clara Pardee's clipped entry for Easter 1883: "A lovely Easter day—Out to church & walked up 5th Ave. Crowds of people—spring hats." Marjorie Reynolds was similarly terse in her notes about Easter in 1912: "Robed in new white corduroy. To the Brick [Church] with Oliver & a bunch of flowers. I don't know [what] I enjoyed more . . . a packed church . . . beautiful music & a good sermon . . . on the Av. afterwards w[ith] O[liver] & Mr. M[iddle] up to 59th St." The clear reconfiguring of Easter by the burgeoning consumer culture did not necessarily lessen the feast's religious power; instead it added to its sensuous richness and complexity. In these women's diaries, there was no necessary movement away from salvation to self-fulfillment, no hard-and-fast opposition between Christian soteriology and cosmopolitan display. For religious and cultural critics, it would prove all too easy to associate the feminized domains of church decoration and Easter fashion with vanity and immodesty (one trade writer tellingly spoke of the "masculine contempt" for dress and millinery). In these women's jottings, however, church and parade, fashion and festival, coalesced into an undivided whole.[33]

As the movie suggests, not all the spring promenaders and curious onlookers cared about this synthesis of piety and materiality. As with any festival, a wide range of motivations and expectations animated those in attendance. Thousands and eventually hundreds of thousands clogged New York's fashionable thoroughfares for the Easter parade, and people took their bearings from various sources, sometimes divergent, often overlapping. Some went forth from the churches on errands of benevolence, making their way to hospitals and orphanages with flowers to brighten up the holiday for others. Others were abroad mostly to court and flirt and ogle; almost all were seeking diversion and entertainment of one kind or another. Not a few came out to work the milling crowds: thieves and pickpockets with fleet hands, hucksters and hawkers with various wares. At the same time, many of Veblen's leisure class graced the avenue, showcasing their status, urbanity, and importance, perhaps most interested in the occasion as a theater of social prestige. Also, many who were frankly indifferent to religion joined in the procession—those, as the *New York Herald* groused in 1890, who had heard "no Easter benediction" and whose holiday glow "came from a brandy cocktail with a dash of absinthe in it." In all, the parade presented a pluralistic melange of characters who processed to various rhythms.[34]

Certainly among the loudest drummers was fashion: lovers of new spring apparel and millinery, devotees of the latest style and vogue, peopled Fifth Avenue. The Easter parade, as the movie highlighted, was indeed a celebration of the consumer culture—its capitalistic abundance, its unfettered choices, its constantly changing styles. If there was ever a holiday spectacle that apotheosized the American Way of Life, this was it. New York's dress parade was a tableau of American prosperity. Eventually, it even came to be seen as a parable about the bounties of American enterprise that contrasted sharply with the failures of Soviet communism. "Fifth Avenue on Easter Sunday," a *New York Times* columnist wrote in 1949, "would probably irritate Stalin more than he is already exasperated with the United States. . . . It will take a long series of five-year plans before the Soviet woman can buy a dress, a hat or a pair of shoes for anything near the price a New York working girl paid for her Easter outfit."[35] In 1955, the *Saturday Evening Post* was even more blunt about the parade's cultural meaning: New York's springtime pageant stood as "a reflection of the American Dream—that a person is as good as the clothes, car and home he is able to buy." In this writer's reckoning, the church's celebration of Easter was "incidental" to this wider public affirmation of American abundance and prosperity. The Easter parade's essential trademark was, to be sure, a gospel of wealth.[36]

Still, the parade remained all along a polysemous event, hardly reducible to a surface of fashion, respectability, and buttoned-up conventionality. Beneath its consumerist credo were carnivalesque tinges reminiscent of old Easter Monday traditions of mummery, which, as at New Year's, included outlandish costumes and boisterous conviviality. (How else but in terms of the fantastical and improvisational could one explain the large hat worn by one woman in 1953 that contained both a replica of the Last Supper and a live bird in a cage?) In many ways, the Easter parade was an unstructured, boundless, liminal event; there was "no apparent beginning, ending, organization or purpose." People flowed in and out of it—something of a leisurely free-for-all where fashionable promenaders, idle spectators, and publicity mongers merged into a closely commingled throng. The Easter parade may have begun in the 1870s as a parade of refinement—a middle- and upper-class staging of gentility, a sort of ritual primer for immigrants and the working class on the accoutrements of respectability—but by the turn of the century it had far more of the crowded, unpredictable energy of a street fair in which both Lenten and bourgeois strictures often melted into Easter laughter. Certainly, the residual form of the parade that survives today in New York City is more masked frolic than fashion show.[37]

The creative, playful possibilities were also seen in the role women assumed in this public performance. With their elaborate dresses and millinery, they took center stage. In a culture in which men and their civic associations had long dominated formal street parades and in a culture in which rowdy male youths had long made carnivalesque festivity and masking their special domain, the Easter parade was decidedly different. In contrast to the home-centered celebrations that so often prevailed among middle-class Victorian women and in contrast to the commonly minimal role of women as spectators on the edges of civic ceremony, Easter was about women in public procession. Whereas most nineteenth-century parades revolved quite literally around the *man* in the street, the Easter parade turned this convention on its head. Also, women's parading in Easter millinery served as a subversion of Pauline (and evangelical Protestant) views about head-coverings as emblematic of female modesty and meekness. The new world of Easter millinery was, in part, about the assertion of the self; about a world of mirrors and studied appearances ("You cannot have too many mirrors," one book on the art of millinery advised); about self-transformation through bewitching lines, fabrics, and colors; about the fashioning of the self in a parade of protean styles.[38]

Among the most far-reaching consequences of New York's dress parade was that it became a cultural model for spin-off observances around the country. Parallel events cropped up in other major cities, such as Philadelphia and Boston, and appeared in smaller towns as well. The cultural diffusion of New York's great Easter procession became especially evident in satellite resorts such as Coney Island, Asbury Park, and Atlantic City, where the entrepreneurs of commercialized leisure reproduced facsimiles for their own purposes. In these places the Easter parade was transformed into an excursion, a tourist attraction. At Coney Island in 1925, for example, the *New York Herald* reported that the local chamber of commerce had organized, with the help of several manufacturers, "a fashion show and Easter parade." To augment the proceedings the promoters had hired fifty show girls to parade in bathing suits; the crowds were overwhelming. No less hucksterish were the proceedings at Atlantic City, where, by the 1920s, the Easter parade was attracting annual crowds of 200,000 and more. Like Coney Island, Atlantic City was an excursionist's wonderland, and the parade there presented a kaleidoscopic scene of lolling, laughing pleasure-seekers—a Boardwalk carnival of costuming and consumption. Easter, like other American holidays, became a vacation. Begun in an outflow of the churches, the Easter parade climaxed in an amusement for that ultimate consumer, the tourist.[39]

## RAINING ON THE EASTER PARADE:
## PROTEST, SUBVERSION, AND DISQUIET

All the display and fashion of the modern American Easter bewildered various people and inspired recurrent cultural criticism. Distressed commentators presented a wide range of intellectual perspectives from social gospel principles about economic justice to bedrock Puritan and republican convictions about simplicity and plainness. Above all, critics saw this as a cultural contest over the very meaning of Easter. Could the age-old Christian message of redemptive sacrifice and resurrection at the heart of Holy Week shine through the modern fanfare of style, novelty, and affluence? It was a struggle in ritual, liturgy, and performance to define what the values of the nation were and what Christianity demanded of its adherents. Seen from the perspective of the long history of the church, the struggle embodied perennial strains between Christ and culture, God and mammon. Viewed from the narrower span of American religious history, the conflict evoked familiar tensions between Puritan theocentrism and Yankee anthropocentrism, between otherwordly hopes of redemption and consumer dreams of material abundance, and between republican notions of male virtue and the corresponding fears of effeminacy and foppery.

Critics worried regularly over Easter extravagance. This "vaunting of personal possessions" in a parade of fashions abraded deep-seated cultural values of simplicity, frugality, and self-denial. If waning in the face of the expanding consumer culture, these principles continued to hold considerable allegiance, and concerns over Easter fashions brought these cultural tensions into sharp relief, perhaps particularly so since, as a religious event, Easter was expected to undergird, not subvert, the traditional values of thrift and moderation. Challenges to Easter indulgence took various forms. One Nazarene minister in Illinois in 1930, for example, gained notice with a bit of evangelical showmanship: he protested the predilection for turning Easter into "a fashion show" and a time of luxury by leading worship "attired in overalls." A Methodist minister in New Jersey in 1956 made the same point by wearing old clothes to conduct his Easter service. The worldliness of the Easter parade, the swaggering of "supreme ego, self-interest, [and] self-conceit," the searing contrast between Jesus' suffering and humiliation on the road to Calvary and the modern "fanfaronade of women in silks and furs" jarred a writer for the *Christian Century* in 1932. Two decades later another contributor to the same weekly wondered at the Fifth Avenue procession in which all seemed to cry "Look at me!" To its critics, the Easter parade was seen as a giant spectacle of vain self-assertion.[40]

Commentary on the American Easter sometimes cut deep to fundamental issues of social and economic justice. Like the Christmas rush, Easter preparations put huge burdens on workers to meet the surging demand for holiday goods and to satisfy the throng of holiday shoppers. Edwin Markham, poet of the social gospel whose "The Man with the Hoe" (1899) launched him to fame as a prophet against dehumanizing labor, spotlighted the crushing hardships of the holiday seasons in a series of blistering, reform-minded essays on child labor. Fired in part by his understanding of Jesus as a socialistic and progressivist visionary, Markham laid into "this generation of the colossal factory and the multitudinous store and the teeming tenement-house," all of which darkened even the joys of Christmas and Easter. "To thousands of those who depend on . . . the fashion-plate for light and leading," he blasted, "Easter means only a time of changing styles—a date on which to display new spring gowns and bonnets—a sort of national millinery opening. But to the workers in the shadow, . . . it means only a blind rush and tug of work that makes this solemn festival a time of dread and weariness. They might truly say in tears, 'They have taken away my Lord, and I know not where they have laid him.'"[41]

Markham aimed his sharpest attacks at sweatshops where children labored late into the night at piecework wages over artificial flowers for millinery to satisfy "the season's rush." He estimated that three-quarters of those making this production in New York City, the center of the industry, were children under age fourteen. "There is no other Easter preparation," he concluded, "where children are so cruelly overworked as in the making of artificial flowers." These "vampire blossoms" robbed children of education, health, and play:

> I lately visited a factory where a group of girls were making artificial roses. They were working ten hours a day, some of them getting only a dollar and a half a week. . . . Swiftly, rhythmically, the ever-flying fingers darted through the motions, keeping time to the unheard but clamorous metronome of need. Many of the girls had inflamed eyes. . . . The faces were dulled, the gaze was listless. Here was another illustration of the tragedy in our civilization—the work that deadens the worker.

The sweatshop exploitation of women and children, raised to feverish levels during the holiday rush, was, to Markham, "the tragedy behind the flaunting festoons of our Easter Vanity Fair."[42]

With stinging directness, Markham raked the muck on Easter fashions. Writing with a second-person bluntness that indicated again the gendered nature of this contest, he blasted: "Perhaps, last Easter, you, my lady, wore one of those pretty things of lace and chiffon trimmed with shining beads and made at midnight by your starved-down sister."[43] Like Washington Gladden, Walter Rauschenbusch, and other social reformers, Markham pressed the middle class to see their complicity in the suffering of the urban poor, to recognize that their choices as consumers were deeply interwoven with issues of economic justice, and to understand that their festive indulgence intensified city sweatshops and tenements. But since, in the gendering of consumption, women were seen as the chief devotees of fashion and novelty, these attacks were always directed far more at women than men. In raining on the Easter parade, critics inevitably aimed their sharpest barbs at the supposed vanity and folly of women.

Issues of social justice were also raised within the Easter parade itself as New York's colossal spectacle became the occasion for turning grievance into ritual. Protesters exploited the carnivalesque or fantastical potentialities within the procession to create a platform for various causes. During the Great Depression, groups of the unemployed, for example, paraded in "battered top hats, lumberjack coats, frayed trousers and broken shoes." If their social commentary was not clear enough, some carried placards or banners: "ONE FIFTH AVENUE GOWN EQUALS A YEAR OF RELIEF." Inverting the fashionableness and capitalistic excesses of New York's Easter procession was often used as a tool for labor and socialist protests. The Easter parade as an embodiment of American complacency and abundance called forth protesters and critics who used it as occasion to question the very values that underpinned this rite of spring. The meanings of the festival were thus never univocal, but contested and challenged, always subject to inversion and antithesis. The very modishness of the Easter parade provided the wedge for critics to open up issues of economic fairness and social justice—the lever by which to turn the whole ritual upside down.[44]

It is important, though, to see that these cultural contests over the meaning of Easter were never simply a matter of polarities: anxious critics versus unabashed celebrants; clear-eyed prophets versus profit-seeking merchants; ascetics versus sybarites. When people faced consumerist tensions in their own celebrations of Easter, they resolved them variously or simply lived with them. For example, the Reverend Morgan Dix, rector at Trinity Episcopal Church in New York, a parish as fond as any of elaborate floral decorations and the display of Easter finery, found himself wondering in 1880 if festal ornamentation had become too extravagant. Was the church turning into "a hot-house"? One writer in 1883 considered Easter floral adornments in the churches attractive and appropriate, but still questioned whether the churches had, "even without intention, become but poor imitations of the theatre in their efforts at exhibition." The writer praised "simple" floral decorations but rejected costly ones which displayed a "foolish pride and a selfish ambition to out-do all others." Some suggested that Easter flowers should be distributed after church to the poor; still others recommended forgoing them and giving the money to charity. Unresolved tensions, ambiguities, and contradictions were evident also in Edwin Markham's career. At once critic of the "multitude of baubles" and "unmeaning trinkets" of the commercialized Easter—the "flimsy cards," the "glass eggs," the "paste chickens," the "plaster rabbits"—Markham turned around and happily sold his verses for sentiments on greeting cards. Not even the sharpest critics were exempt from the tensions that they highlighted.[45]

Some experienced these polarities and sought self-consciously to harmonize them. Reflecting on the Easter parade in 1905, a writer in *Harper's* recognized the tensions that many felt between mere "outward adornment" and the religious meaning of the festival. "I have known," he reported, "women to say that they avoided springing new frocks on an admiring world on Easter Sunday because they did not wish to intrude so trivial a thing as millinery upon a religious festival of such deep significance." But it "seems to me," he said, "that if one gets the right point of view, all the outward tokens of Easter are harmonious with the inner spiritual meanings of it." The flowers and clothes had sacramental importance; they were "outward manifestations" of Easter's religious solemnity and significance. One minister, writing in 1910, summarized both the tensions and their potential resolution:

> One dislikes the element of fashionable frivolity which has come to mark some people's keeping of the Easter feast; but, apart from that, as the city shops and streets break out into fragrant and beautiful bloom, one realizes the close kinship between heavenly and spiritual things and things material and earthly.

All along this was the core concern—how to mediate piety and materiality, flesh and spirit, faith and riches, the inward and the outward in a world of proliferating goods.[46]

Easter, even more than Christmas, disclosed the role of the churches in the rise of consumer-oriented celebrations. The enlarging scope of "devout consumption" was seen in the elaborate displays of Easter flowers and other church decorations. The conflux of consumption and Christianity was nowhere more evident than in the streaming parade of Easter fashions as stylish celebrants poured into and out of the churches. Even as the churches helped facilitate this new Easter, cultivating a modern synthesis of piety and display, some critics demonstrated considerable wariness about where this alliance between Christian celebration and the consumer culture was headed. They foresaw the dim outlines of Irving Berlin's *Easter Parade* or Philip Roth's "schlockified Christianity," in which the holiday became a synonym for shopping and abundance, a ritual display of consumerist plenty. But the critics rarely fathomed the complexity of the drama that so disturbed them. They failed to see the hybridized commingling of faith and fashion, renewal and laughter, piety and improvisation that paraded before them.

## NOTES

1. These and subsequent quotations have been transcribed from the movie itself, which is widely available on videocassette. I have also consulted a copy of the screenplay at the Lilly Library, Indiana University.

2. Philip Roth, *Operation Shylock: A Confession* (New York: Simon and Schuster, 1993), 157.

3. *New York Herald*, April 16, 1881, 5. Existing secondary literature focuses more on the holiday's folk beliefs and customs than on historical shifts or modern reconfigurations of the festival. See Theodore Caplow and Margaret Holmes Williamson, "Decoding Middletown's Easter Bunny: A Study in American Iconography," *Semiotica* 32 (1980): 221–32; Nada Gray, *Holidays: Victorian Women Celebrate in Pennsylvania* (University Park: Pennsylvania State University Press, 1983), 54–67; Elizabeth Clarke Kieffer, "Easter Customs of Lancaster

County," *Papers of the Lancaster Historical Society* 52 (1948): 49–68; Venetia Newall, *An Egg at Easter: A Folklore Study* (Bloomington: Indiana University Press, 1971); and Alfred L. Shoemaker, *Eastertide in Pennsylvania: A Folk Cultural Study* (Kutztown: Pennsylvania Folklife Society, 1960). For a notable exception, see James H. Barnett, "The Easter Festival: A Study in Cultural Change," *American Sociological Review* 14 (1949): 62–70.

4. "Easter Flowers," *Harper's New Monthly magazine* 27 (July, 1863): 189–94.

5. T. J. Jackson Lears, *No Place of Grace: Antimodernism and the Transformation of American Culture, 1880–1920* (New York: Pantheon, 1981), 183–215; Ernest Geldart, ed., *The Art of Garnishing Churches at Christmas and Other Times: A Manual of Directions* (London: Cox Sons, Buckley and Co., 1882), 12. See also William A. Barrett, *Flowers and*

*Festivals: Or, Directions for the Floral Decoration of Churches* (New York: Pott and Amery, 1868).

6. Edward L. Cutts, *An Essay on the Christmas Decoration of Churches: With an Appendix on the Mode of Decorating Churches for Easter, the School Feast, Harvest Thanksgiving, Confirmation, a Marriage, and a Baptism*, 3rd ed. (London: Horace Cox, 1868), 12; Geldart, ed., *Art of Garnishing Churches*, 11.

7. Ernest R. Suffling, *Church Festival Decorations: Being Full Directions for Garnishing Churches for Christmas, Easter, Whitsuntide, and Harvest*, 2d ed. (New York: Charles Scribner's Sons, 1907), 74.

8. Henry Dana Ward, "Diary," April 8, 1855; March 23, 1856; April 12, 1857, New York Public Library, Rare Books and Manuscripts.

9. On this invasion, see William R. Leach, "Transformations in a Culture of Consumption: Women and Department Stores, 1890–1925," *Journal of American History* 71 (1984): 325.

10. Unidentified Author, "Dairy, 1872–1873," April 13, 1873, New York Historical Society, Manuscripts.

11. Sarah Anne Todd, "Diary," April 21, 1867, New York Historical Society, Manuscripts; Elizabeth W. Merchant, "Diary," March 25, 1883; April 25, 1886; April 10, 1887, New York Public Library, Rare Books and Manuscripts; Mrs. George Richards, "Diary," April 1, 1888, New York Historical Society, Manuscripts. For the initiative of women in church decoration, see, for example, "How Some Churches Looked Last Easter," *Ladies' Home Journal* 21 (March 1904): 32–33.

12. Geldart, ed., *Art of Garnishing Churches*, 12, 44; *New York Sun*, April 1, 1861, 2; Suffling, *Church Festival Decorations*, 85–86.

13. "Easter Flowers," 190; Suffling, *Church Festival Decorations*, 2. On this domestic and sentimental piety, see Ann Douglas, *The Feminization of American Culture* (New York: Knopf, 1977); and Colleen McDannell, *The Christian Home in Victorian America, 1840–1900* (Bloomington: Indiana University Press, 1986).

14. "Easter Flowers," 190. On Phelps's novel and "the new domestic heaven," see Douglas, *Feminization of American Culture*, 214–15, 223–26.

15. Ernest Geldart, *A Manual of Church Decoration and Symbolism Containing Directions and Advice to Those Who Desire Worthily to Deck the Church at the Various Seasons of the Year* (Oxford: A. R. Mowbray and Co., 1899), 17–18; *New York Herald*, April 16, 1881, 5; Thorstein Veblen, *The Theory of the Leisure Class: An Economic Study of Institutions* (New York: Macmillan, 1899; repr., New York: Random House, 1934), 119, 307–9. On

the narrow limits of Veblen's model, see T. J. Jackson Lears, "Beyond Veblen: Rethinking Consumer Culture in America," in *Consuming Visions: Accumulation and Display of Goods in America, 1880–1920*, ed. Simon J. Bronner (New York: Norton, 1989), 73–97.

16. *New York Herald*, April 21, 1867, 4; April 14, 1873, 4; Suffling, *Church Festival Decorations*, 32–33; *New York Sun*, April 22, 1878, 3. Here I am playing off Lears's argument in *No Place of Grace* about the antimodernism in Anglo-Catholic aesthetics. As Lears suggests, this antimodernist, medievalist stance often had modernist, therapeutic consequences. This was at no point clearer than in the Victorian elaboration of the art of church decoration.

17. Geldart, ed., *Art of Garnishing Churches*, 12, 19; William Leach, "Strategists of Display and the Production of Desire," in Bronner, ed., *Consuming Visions*, 104. Leach's conclusions about this "display aesthetic" are offered in expanded and far more critical form in his *Land of Desire: Merchants, Power, and the Rise of a New American Culture* (New York: Pantheon, 1993).

18. *Dry Goods Chronicle*, March 26, 1898, 19; John Wanamaker (Philadelphia), "Easter, 1893," Dry Goods Scrapbook, Bella Landauer Collection, New-York Historical Society.

19. "News from the Cities," *American Advertiser* 4 (April 1890): unpag. For other examples, see [Charles A. Tracy], *The Art of Decorating Show Windows and Interiors*, 3rd ed. (Chicago: Merchants Record Co., 1906), 199–206, 314–15; Alfred G. Bauer, *The Art of Window Dressing for Grocers* (Chicago: Sprague, Warner & Company, [1902]), 30–32; "Robinson Window," *Greeting Card* 8 (March 1936): 28; "Lilies, a Cross, Lighted Candles," *Greeting Card* 5 (March 1933): 5; and "The Cross Was Illuminated," *Greeting Card* 5 (March 1933), 8.

20. Robert A. Childs, *"The Thoughful Thinker" on Window-Dressing and Advertising Together with Wholesome Advice for Those in Business and Those about to Start* (Syracuse, N.Y.: United States Window Trimmer's Bureau, [1896], 21; Douglas, *Feminization of American Culture*, 225.

21. Tracy, *Art of Decorating Show Windows*, 315. For Wanamaker's Easter displays, see box 11B, folders 10 and 23; box 12D, folder 2, Wanamaker Collection, Historical Society of Pennsylvania, Philadelphia. On the paintings of Michael de Munkacsy, see box 55, folder 14; box 63, folder 3, Wanamaker Collection. See also Leach, *Land of Desire*, 213–14, 222–23.

22. L. Frank Baum, *The Art of Decorating Dry Goods Windows and Interiors* (Chicago: Tile Show

Window Publishing Co., 1900), unpag. intro., 181, 185. On Baum, see Leach, *Land of Desire*, 55–61.

23. This is R. Laurence Moore's conclusion about the varied blendings of Protestant values with commercial amusements and popular literature in the first half of the nineteenth century. See Moore, "Religion, Secularization, and the Shaping of the Culture Industry in Antebellum American," *American Quarterly* 41 (1989): 236.

24. George D. Herron, *The Message of Jesus to Men of Wealth* (New York: Fleming H. Revell Co., 1891), 29–31. The "one undivided Kingdom of God" is a phrase from Washington Gladden, *Things New and Old in Discourses of Christian Truth and Life* (Columbus, Ohio: A. H. Smythe, 1883), 260. On the "festive marketplace," see the classic evocation in Mikhail Bakhtin, *Rabelais and His World*, trans. Helene Iswolsky (Cambridge, Mass.: M.I.T. Press, 1968), 19, 92. For Wanamaker as the consummate sacralizer of prosperity, see "The Power of Consecrated Wealth: John Wanamaker—What the Rich Can Do," *Christian Recorder*, March 15, 1877, 4–5. On liberal Protestantism and the consumer ethos, see Susan Curtis, *A Consuming Faith: The Social Gospel and Modern American Culture* (Baltimore: Johns Hopkins University Press, 1991).

25. For the Watts hymn within the context of a Victorian Easter service, see Jennie M. Bingham, *Easter Voices* (New York: Hunt and Eaton, 1891), 2. On the consumer culture as a dream world, see Rosalind H. Williams, *Dream Worlds: Mass Consumption in Late Nineteenth-Century France* (Berkeley: University of California Press, 1982). On the new therapeutic gospel, see especially T. J. Jackson Lears, "From Salvation to Self-Realization: Advertising and the Therapeutic Roots of the Consumer Culture, 1880–1930," in *The Culture of Consumption: Critical Essays in American History, 1880–1980*, ed. Richard Wightman Fox and T. J. Jackson Lears (New York: Pantheon, 1983), 3–38. On the wider absorption of religious symbols into modern advertising, see Roland Marchand, *Advertising the American Dream: Making Way for Modernity, 1920–1940* (Berkeley: University of California Press, 1985), 264–84.

27. For the Irish adage, see Francis X. Weiser, *The Easter Book* (New York: Harcourt, Brace and Co., 1954), 159–61. For Poor Robin's maxim, see John Brand and W. Carew Hazlitt, *Popular Antiquities of Great Britain: Comprising Notices of the Moveable and Immoveable Feasts, Customs, Superstitions and Amusements Past and Present*, 3 vols. (London: John Russell Smith, 1870), 1:93. On Easter clothes, see A. R. Wright, *British Calendar Customs: England*, 3 vols., ed. T. E. Lones (London: The

Folk-Lore Society, 1936–1940), 1:101; and Shoemaker, *Eastertide in Pennsylvania*, 24. For the *Herald's* version of the proverb, see *New York Herald*, April 8, 1855, 1.

28. *New York Herald*, April 14, 1873, 4; April 14, 1879, 8.

29. *New York Herald*, April 26, 1886, 8; *New York Times*, April 7, 1890, 2.

30. Ralph M. Hower, *History of Macy's of New York, 1858–1919: Chapters in the Evolution of the Department Store* (Cambridge: Harvard University Press, 1943), 170, 451n.37; *New York Sun*, April 17, 1878, 4; April 16, 1878, 4. It is important to underline that my analysis of Easter's commercialization is confined to the United States. It is likely that merchants in Paris or London, where the growth of the consumer culture was somewhat ahead of the United States and where Easter traditions were far less encumbered by low-church Protestant sentiments, were significantly in advance of their American counterparts. For a hint of this, see Neil McKendrick, John Brewer, and J. H. Plumb, *The Birth of a Consumer Society: The Commercialization of Eighteenth-Century England* (Bloomington: Indiana University Press, 1982), 74.

31. *Dry Goods Economist*, March 24, 1894, 36, 37; *Dry Goods Chronicle*, March 26, 1898, 19; *Dry Goods Economist* March 18, 1893, 55.

32. Elizabeth Schuneman Orr, "Diary," April 9, 1871, New York Public Library, Rare Books and Manuscripts.

33. Merchant, "Diary," April 16, 1881; April 21, 1867; Clara Burton Pardee, "Diary," March 25, 1883, New-York Historical Society, Manuscripts; Majorie R. Reynolds, "Diary," April 7, 1912, New-York Historical Society, Manuscripts; "New York Millinery," *Millinery Trade Review* 7 (April 1882): 56.

34. *New York Herald*, April 7, 1890, 3.

35. Anne O'Hare McCormick, quoted in "The Easter Parade," *Time*, April 25, 1949, 19.

36. Rufus Jarman, "Manhattan's Easter Madness," *Saturday Evening Post*, April 9, 1955, 103.

37. Ibid. On Easter conviviality and costuming, see Shoemaker, *Eastertide in Pennsylvania*, 43–45; and Bakhtin, *Rabelais and His World*, 78–79, 146. For the woman's outlandish hat, see *New York Times*, April 6, 1953, 14.

38. Anna Ben Yusuf, *The Art of Millinery* (New York: Millinery Trade Publishing Co., 1909), 227. On the male domination of nineteenth-century parades and public ceremonies as well as the efforts of women to gain a foothold in these rituals, see Mary P. Ryan, *Women in Public: Between Banners and Ballots, 1825–1880* (Baltimore: Johns Hopkins University Press, 1990), 19–57; and Susan G. Davis, *Pa-*

*rades and Power: Street Theatre in Nineteenth-Century Philadelphia* (Philadelphia: Temple University Press, 1985; repr., Berkeley: University of California Press, 1986), 47, 149, 157, 190.

39. *New York Herald*, April 13, 1925, 3. For representative accounts of Easter parades in the resorts, see *New York Times*, April 16, 1906, 9; John Steevens, "The Charm of Eastertide at Atlantic City," *Harper's Weekly*, April 18, 1908, 20–22; *New York Times*, April 20, 1908, 3; *New York Herald*, April 8, 1912, 4; and *New York Times*, April 22, 1935, 11. On Coney Island and Atlantic City, see respectively, John F. Kasson, *Amusing the Million: Coney Island at the Turn of the Century* (New York: Hill and Wang, 1978); and Charles E. Funnell, *By the Beautiful Sea: The Rise and High Times of That Great American Resort* (New York: Alfred A. Knopf, 1975), esp. 46, 89. Barnett noted in 1949 of New York's Easter parade: "The pattern appears to be diffusing as an *American* practice." See Barnett, "Easter Festival," 69.

40. *New York Times*, April 23, 1946, 25; April 19, 1930, 9; April 2, 1956, 14; Raymond Kresensky, "Easter Parade," *Christian Century*, March 23, 1932, 384–85; Dorothy Lee Richardson, "Easter Sunday, Fifth Avenue," *Christian Century*, April 28, 1954, 511.

41. Edwin Markham, "The Blight on the Easter Lilies," *Cosmopolitan* 42 (April 1907): 667–68. Markham's essays on child labor were collected in *Children in Bondage* (New York: Hearst's International, 1914).

42. "Blight on the Easter Lilies," 670–73.

43. Ibid., 669.

44. *New York Times*, March 28, 1932, 1; Jarman, "Manhattan's Easter Madness," 104.

45. *New York Times*, March 28, 1880, 2; "Proper Observance of Easter," *Concert Quarterly* 1 (March 1883): 1; *New York Times*, March 18, 1894, 18; Markham, "Blight on the Easter Lilies," 668; Louis Filler, *The Unknown Edwin Markham: His Mystery and Its Significance* (Yellow Springs, Ohio: Antioch Press, 1966), 140.

46. E. S. Martin, "New York's Easter Parade," *Harper's Weekly*, April 22, 1905, 567; William C. Doane, *The Book of Easter* (New York: Macmillan, 1910), vii.

# THE DEBATE OVER MIXED SEATING IN THE AMERICAN SYNAGOGUE

*Jonathan D. Sarna*

A new generation of scholars is employing innovative methods to uncover the "inner" history of American Jews. Until recently, American historians have either paid little attention to Jewish religious history or focused their attention on the "external" history of Jewish interaction with American society. The new scholarship, in contrast, enters into the world of the synagogue and the experiences of ordinary people in order to tell the story of American Jewish religious life.

In the following essay, Jonathan Sarna demonstrates that throughout most of American Jewish religious history debates over separate (male and female) seating and mixed (family) seating were visible expressions of a host of more deep-seated differences over Jewish social and religious values. The issue first emerged in the Reform congregations of the nineteenth century, divided Reform from Orthodox in the early twentieth century, and remains a division between Conservatism and Orthodoxy in the contemporary period. Those congregations that advocated the end to separate seating of women in the gallery and men on the ground floor justified this change in traditional practices on the multiple grounds of family unity, women's equality, improved decorum, modernization, and keeping young people involved in religious life. For opponents the same changes signaled assimilation, Christianization, violation of Jewish law, and the abandonment of tradition. By closely attending to this seemingly mundane issue, Sarna provides insight into both the changing American synagogue and the changing relationship between Jewish religious life and the surrounding American society.

Adapted by permission from Jonathan D. Sarna, "The Debate Over Mixed Seating in the American Synagogue," in Jack Wertheimer, ed., *The American Synagogue: A Sanctuary Transformed* (New York: Cambridge University Press, 1987), 363–393. Reprinted with the permission of Cambridge University Press.

# 12

# THE DEBATE OVER MIXED SEATING
# IN THE AMERICAN SYNAGOGUE

## Jonathan D. Sarna

"PUES HAVE NEVER yet found an historian," John M. Neale complained, when he under-took to survey the subject of church seating for the Cambridge Camden Society in 1842.[1] To a large extent, the same situation prevails today in connection with "pues" in the Amer-ican synagogue. Although it is common knowledge that American synagogue seating pat-terns have changed greatly over time—sometimes following acrimonious, even violent disputes—the subject as a whole remains unstudied, seemingly too arcane for historians to bother with.[2] Seating patterns, however, actually reflect down-to-earth social realities, and are richly deserving of study. Behind wearisome debates over how sanctuary seats should be arranged and allocated lie fundamental disagreements over the kinds of social and reli-gious values that the synagogue should project and the relationship between the syna-gogue and the larger society that surrounds it. As we shall see, where people sit reveals much about what they believe.

The necessarily limited study of seating patterns that follows focuses only on the most important and controversial seating innovation in the American synagogue: mixed (fam-ily) seating. Other innovations—seats that no longer face east,[3] pulpits moved from center to front,[4] free (unassigned) seating, closed-off pew ends, and the like—require separate treatment. As we shall see, mixed seating is a ramified and multifaceted issue that clearly reflects the impact of American values on synagogue life, for it pits family unity, sexual equality, and modernity against the accepted Jewish legal (*halachic*) practice of sexual sep-aration in prayer. Discussions surrounding this innovation form part of a larger Jewish de-bate over Americanization, and should really be viewed in the overall context of ritual reform.[5] By itself, however, the seating issue has taken on a symbolic quality. It serves not only as a focus on the changing nature of the American synagogue, but also on the chang-ing nature of the larger society—American and Jewish—in which the synagogue is set.

## I

The extent to which men and women were separated in the synagogues of antiquity has been disputed. There can, however, be no doubt that separate seating of one form or an-other characterized Jewish worship from early medieval times onward. The idea that men and women should worship apart prevailed in many Christian churches no less than in synagogues—although the latter more frequently demanded a physical barrier between the sexes—and separate seating remained standard practice in much of Europe down to the contemporary period.

In 1845, the Reform Congregation of Berlin abolished the separate women's gallery in the synagogue and the traditional *mechitsa* (partition) between men and women. Although mandating "the seating of men and women on the same floor," the congregation continued to preserve the principle of sexual separation during worship: men occupied the left side of the auditorium, women the right.[7] As late as the early twentieth century, the Hamburg temple, the cradle of German Reform, refused a donation of one million marks from the American banker Henry Budge, who had returned to settle in Hamburg following his father's death, because the sum was conditional on "men and women sitting together" in the new edifice. To Dr. Jacob Sonderling, then rabbi of the temple, that idea was shocking. "In the Hamburg Temple," he reports, "men and women remained separated up to the last moment."[8]

Mixed synagogue seating, or to use the more common nineteenth-century term, "family seating," first developed in Reform Jewish circles in the United States. Rabbi Isaac Mayer Wise, the leading nineteenth-century exponent of American Reform, took personal credit for this particular innovation, claiming to have introduced Jewry's first family pews "in 1850 [sic] . . . in the temple of Albany."[9] Wise, however, did not *invent* family seating. To understand what he did do, and why, requires first a brief digression into the history of church seating in America.

The earliest New England churches and meetinghouses, following the then-traditional British practice, separated men, women, and children in worship. Men and women sat on opposite sides of a central aisle, and children, also divided according to sex, sat in the back or upstairs. As John Demos points out, "Family relationships were effectively discounted, or at least submerged, in this particular context . . . the family community and the religious community were fundamentally distinct."[10] Churches sought to underscore the role of the individual as the basic unit in matters of faith and prayer. "God's minister," according to Patricia Tracy, "superseded the role of any other agent; each heart was supposed to be unprotected against the thunder of the Gospel."[11]

Beginning in the mid-eighteenth century, church seating patterns began to change. Families at first won permission to sit together in church on a voluntary basis, and subsequently family seating became the norm.[12] Outside of New England, the history of church seating has not been written, and the pattern may have been more diverse. Missouri Synod Lutherans, for example, maintained separate seating in their churches (which were heavily influenced by German practice) down to at least the end of the nineteenth century. For the most part, however, the family pew won rapid and widespread acceptance in church circles, and Americans, forgetting that there were other possibilities, came to believe that "the family that prays together stays together."[13]

The overwhelming move to adopt family seating stems from great changes in the history of the family that have been amply detailed elsewhere. The growing differentiation between home and work saw families take on a new symbolic role, termed by Demos "the family as refuge," the image being that of family members clustering together for protection against the evils of anomic industrial society. Fear of family breakdown naturally led to a host of new rituals and forms (including the cult of domesticity) designed to "strengthen the family" against the menacing forces threatening to rend it asunder.[14] The family pew was one of these new forms. By raising the family's status over that of the single individual, and by symbolically linking family values to religious values, the family pew demonstrated, as separate seating did not, that the church stood behind the family structure one hundred percent. Family burial plots,[15] which came into vogue at about the same time as family pews, carried the same message of family togetherness on into eternity.

Whether Rabbi Isaac Mayer Wise appreciated the symbolic significance of family pews when he introduced them in 1851 cannot be known. His biographer waxes enthusiastic about how the new system, "enable[d] families to worship together and to have the warmth of togetherness . . . in the deepest and most sacred of moments,"[16] but Wise himself never said anything of the sort. Instead, as he related the story, family pews became a feature of Congregation Anshe Emeth in Albany almost as an afterthought.

Wise had first come to Albany in 1846 to serve as the rabbi of Congregation Beth El. He was a new immigrant, twenty-seven years old, and thoroughly inexperienced, but he dreamed great dreams and displayed boundless energy. Before long he introduced a series of reforms. Like most early reforms, Wise's aimed mainly at improving decorum and effecting changes in the liturgy. He abolished the sale of synagogue honors, forbade standing during the Torah reading, eliminated various medieval liturgical poems (*piyyutim*), introduced German and English hymns into the service, initiated the confirmation ceremony, and organized a mixed choir.[17] But his effort to effect Berlin-style changes in synagogue seating to make room for the choir ("I suggested to apportion the seats anew, and to set apart half of the floor, as well as of the gallery, for the women") raised a howl of protest and got nowhere, and even within the mixed choir "the girls objected strenuously to sitting among the men."[18] Wise never even raised the issue of family pews.

A series of tangled disputes between Wise and his president, Louis Spanier, led to Wise's dismissal from Beth El Congregation two days before Rosh Hashanah in 1850. Wise considered his firing illegal, and on the advice of counsel took his place as usual on New Year's morning. As he made ready to remove the Torah from the ark, Louis Spanier took the law into his own hands and lashed out at him. The assault knocked off the rabbi's hat, wounded his pride, and precipitated a general melee that the police had to be called out to quell. The next day, Wise held Rosh Hashanah services at his home. The day after that, he was invited to a meeting consisting of "prominent members of the congregation together with a large number of young men,"[19] where a new congregation, Anshe Emeth, came into being with Wise as its rabbi. Anshe Emeth dedicated its new building, formerly a Baptist church, on October 3, 1851. Wise served the congregation there until 1854, when he journeyed west to Cincinnati to assume his life-long position at Bene Yeshurun.[20]

Anshe Emeth is usually credited with being the first synagogue with mixed seating in the world. As Wise relates the circumstances in his *Reminiscences*: "American Judaism is indebted to the Anshe Emeth congregation of Albany for one important reform; viz., family pews. The church-building had family pews, and the congregation resolved unanimously to retain them. This innovation was initiated later in all American reform congregations. This was an important step, which was severely condemned at the time."[21] According to this account, and it is the only substantial one we have, family pews entered Judaism for pragmatic reasons: Members voted to make do with the (costly) building they had bought, and not to expend additional funds to convert its American-style family pews into a more traditional Jewish seating arrangement. Had members considered this a particularly momentous action on their part, they would surely have called attention to it in their consecration proceedings, and Isaac Mayer Wise would have said something on the subject in his dedication sermon. Nothing at all was said, however, and only the sharp eye of Isaac Leeser detected in the description of the synagogue "another reform of the Doctor's, one by no means to be commended." Far from being "severely condemned at the time," the reform seems otherwise to have been uniformly ignored.[22] Pragmatic reforms aimed at improving decorum and bringing the synagogue more closely into harmony with the prevailing American Christian pattern were nothing new, even if this particular reform had not previously been introduced. Nor was there any organized opposition to Wise within his own congregation to generate adverse publicity against him. The "loud remonstrations of all orthodoxy," which Wise purported to remember, actually came later. Anshe Emeth's family pews met with scarcely a murmur.[23]

The introduction of family seating at New York's Temple Emanu-El in 1854 attracted no more notice. When Emanu-El was established in 1845, the very year of the Berlin seating reform, its sanctuary provided for separate seating, women behind the men, in one room. The move to family pews took place, as at Anshe Emeth, when the congregation moved into a new building (the Twelfth Street Synagogue), a former church, and there found enclosed family pews already set up.[24] Although they had no known ideological basis for introducing mixed seating, members presumably found the thought of families worshipping together as a unit in the American fashion far more appealing than the thought of introducing separate seating where none had been before. Convenience triumphed, and justifications followed.

## II

Ideological defenses of mixed seating, when they came, concentrated not on family worship, an American innovation, but rather on an older, European, and more widely contended Jewish issue of the day: women's status in the synagogue. Rabbis versed in the polemics of Reform Judaism in Germany felt more at home in this debate, having argued about the status of women at the rabbinical conferences in Frankfurt (1845) and Breslau (1846),[25] and they viewed the principle involved as a much more important one than mixed seating, which they had never before seen, and which seemed to them at the time to be just another case of following in the ways of the gentiles.[26] As a result, the same basic arguments that justified the abolition of the gallery and "separate but equal" seating in Germany came to be used to justify mixed family seating in the United States. Critical differences between these two new seating patterns proved less important in the long run than the fact that Jews and non-Jews on both sides of the Atlantic came to view the debate over the synagogue seating of women as a debate over the synagogue status of women, and they followed it with interest.

The status of women in the synagogue, and in Judaism in general, attracted considerable attention in early America, much of it negative. As early as 1744, Dr. Alexander Hamilton, a Scottish-born physician, compared the women's gallery in New York's Shearith Israel to a "hen coop." Dr. Philip Milledoler, later president of Rutgers, told a meeting of the American Society for Evangelizing the Jews in 1816 that the "female character" among Jews "holds a station far inferior to that which it was intended to occupy by the God of nature." *The Western Monthly Review*, describing "The Present State of the Jews" in 1829, found that "the Jewess of these days is treated as an inferior being." That was putting it mildly, according to James Gordon Bennett, editor of the *New York Herald*. After visiting Shearith Israel, on Yom Kippur 1836, he attacked the status of women in Judaism as one of the most lamentable features in the entire religion—and one that Jesus improved:

The great error of the Jews is the degradation in which their religion places woman. In the services of religion, she is separated and huddled into a gallery like beautiful crockery ware, while the men perform the ceremonies below. It was the author of Christianity that brought her out of this Egyptian bondage, and put her on an equality with the other sex in civil and religious rites. Hence, have sprung all the civilization, refinement, intelligence and genius of Europe. The Hebrew prays "I thank thee, Lord, that I am not a woman"—the Christian—"I praise thee, Lord, that I and my wife are immortal."[27]

There were, of course, other, more positive images of American Jewish women available, including not a few works of apologetica penned by Jews themselves. These explained the traditional rationale behind Jewish laws on women and enumerated long lists of Jewish women "heroes" from the biblical period onward.[28] Literary treatments of Jewish women also offered occasional positive images, usually of noble, alluringly exotic, Semitic maidens, who functioned more as "erotic dream figures," manifestations of romantic ideals, than anything else.[29] Still, to many Americans, Judaism's "mistreatment" of "the weaker sex" was an established fact: evidence of Judaism's "Oriental" and "primitive" character, in stark contrast to "modern" Christianity. By visibly changing the position of women in the synagogue, Jews sought to undermine this fact, to buttress their claims to modernity, and to fend off the embarrassing Christian charges that they had otherwise to face. In abolishing the women's gallery, synagogue leaders thus sought to elevate not only the status of women in Judaism, but also the status of Judaism itself.

The first Jewish leader in America to stress the relationship between changes in synagogue seating and changes in the status of Jewish women seems to have been Rabbi David Einhorn, who immigrated to America in 1855 and rapidly came to dominate the radical wing of the nascent Reform Movement. Einhorn had agitated for "the complete religious equality of woman with man" at the 1846 Breslau Reform Rabbinical Conference, where he declared it his "mission to make legal declaration of the equal religious obligation and justification of women in as far as this is possible."[30] Within the first few years of his tenure at Temple Har Sinai in Baltimore, he endeavored to put this principle into effect, abolishing what he called the "gallery-cage," and bringing women down to share the same floor as men, though apparently not, at first, the same pews.[31]

In discussing the women's issue in *Sinai*, his German-language magazine, Einhorn characteristically stressed the higher "principle" behind his action, in this case abandonment of what he considered to be misguided Oriental rabbinic strictures against women, and a return to what he identified as the more proper biblical lesson of sexual equality. Gallery seating, he sneered, originally stemmed from unseemly acts of levity that marred the celebration of *simchat bet hashoeva* (the water-drawing festival) in temple times. Since staid Occidental modes of worship held forth no similar dangers to modesty, the gallery could be dispensed with. Although clearly less comfortable with the proprieties of completely mixed seating, Einhorn nevertheless allowed that when a husband sat next to his wife and children nothing untoward could be expected. The essential principle, he repeated, was "religious equalization of women." Everything else connected with seating reforms was of secondary importance.[32]

Einhorn's rationale for mixed seating won wide acceptance, perhaps because it offered a specifically Jewish as well as ethically motivated reason to adopt an American practice, and also perhaps because it made a virtue out of what many were coming to see as a practical necessity. Whatever the case, family seating spread. Chicago Sinai, ideologically linked to its Baltimore namesake, never had a gallery and wrote into its basic propositions (1859) that "in the public worship of the congregation, there should be no discrimination made in favor of the male and against female worshippers."[33] A year later, in San Francisco, Rabbi Elkan Cohn, newly appointed to Congregation Emanu-El, introduced mixed seating as one of his first acts, complaining, as he did so, that Judaism "excluded women from so many privileges to which they are justly entitled."[34] The next fifteen years saw mixed seating develop at a rapid pace. In some cases, proponents exclusively stressed women's inequality and the bad image it projected. Rabbi Raphael D'C Lewin, for example, denounced separate seating as "a relic of the Dark Ages."[35] More frequently, pragmatic considerations—purchase of a new synagogue building (perhaps a church containing pews), the need to use the gallery for a choir, the inability of women in the gallery to hear what was going on, or the "undignified" appearance presented by a synagogue where the gallery was far more crowded than the main sanctuary below—worked hand in hand with ideological factors in bringing about reform.[36] In at least one case, Sherith Israel in San Francisco, mixed seating came about because, as the minutes report, "the existing custom of separating the sexes during Divine Services is a cause of annoyance and disturbance in our devotion."[37] Whatever the real reason, however, most synagogues eventually came to justify mixed seating on the basis of women's equality. Isaac Mayer Wise led the way, quite misleadingly retrojecting the women's issue back into his Albany reforms:

> The Jewish woman had been treated almost as a stranger in the synagogue; she had been kept at a distance, and had been excluded from all participation in the life of the congregation, had been relegated to the gallery, even as was the negro in Southern churches. The emancipation of the Jewish woman was begun in Albany, by having the Jewish girls sing in the choir, and this beginning was reinforced by the introduction of family pews.[38]

Although mixed seating looked like an imitation of gentile practices, no proponent of reform would admit that it was. In seeking to modernize Judaism, Reform leaders always insisted that they were strengthening the faith and preventing defections to Christianity; assimilation was as much anathema to them as to their opponents. Knowing how sensitive they were on this issue, critics of mixed seating regularly coupled their references to the innovation with terms like "Gentile fashion," "semblance of a church," and "Christian."[39] They knew that such charges struck home.

Otherwise, traditionalists generally contented themselves to defend their time-honored practices on the basis of Jewish legal precedents and religious prooftexts, chief among them the Talmudic discussion of temple seating practices in Tractate Sukkah 51b. "This is the direct and forcible language of the Talmud," the learned Laemmlein Buttenwieser insisted after quoting his source at length, "and on it we are content to rest our case without further argument."[40]

Proponents of change naturally put forward different interpretations of these texts.[41] Even those most eager to introduce reforms still continued to seek the legitimacy that textual roots provided. The never-ending textual arguments, however, are less important than the fact that the two sides in the seating controversy unwittingly talked past one another. Proponents defended mixed seating as a test of Judaism's ability to meet modernity's challenge to Jewish survival. Opponents defended traditional seating as a test of Judaism's ability to parry modernity's threats to Jewish distinctiveness. Although the two sides seemed only to be debating laws and practices, the words they used and the passions behind them indicate that the central arguments really reached deeper. Ultimately, they touched on the most basic values—traditional ones and Enlightenment ones—that each side held dear.

## III

One of the most historically interesting clashes over mixed seating took place at the venerable B'nai Jeshurun synagogue in New York City in 1875. The dispute eventually reached civil court—one of comparatively few such cases to do so—and involved many of the leading rabbis of the period. It serves as a valuable case study of the whole mixed seating issue as it developed in, disrupted, and ultimately split an individual congregation.

B'nai Jeshurun was the second synagogue founded in New York City (1825) and has proudly boasted of being New York's "oldest Ashkenazic Congregation." From its founding, it followed the path of traditional Judaism, maintaining close ties with the Great Synagogue in London. It grew steadily, various schisms notwithstanding. From 1825 to 1850, its membership increased fivefold to nearly 150, and during the same period its financial condition strengthened appreciably. An even more dynamic period of growth began in 1849 when it elected Rabbi Morris J. Raphall, then rabbi and preacher of England's Birmingham Hebrew Congregation, to serve as its "Lecturer and Preacher." Raphall's salary reputedly was "the most munificent salary received by any preacher in the country"—an investment that handsomely paid off. As America's first "glamour rabbi," he attracted large numbers of new members to the congregation and won B'nai Jeshurun a position of high regard both in the Jewish and the non-Jewish communities. This position was enhanced in 1851 when the congregation dedicated its magnificent new edifice, the Greene Street Synagogue.[42]

As is so often the case, the new situation at B'nai Jeshurun created pressures for ritual reform. Decorum became the watchword as trustees worried more and more about the image projected by the congregation to the world at large. In 1851 and again in 1856 the interests of decorum ("that high standing of respectability which the world has a right to expect and which should correspond with this noble edifice") motivated changes in the distribution of synagogue honors, and in the method of announcing synagogue offerings.[43] Subsequent changes affected the saying of the priestly blessing, henceforward to be repeated "without singing and chanting," and of the Mourner's Kaddish, which mourners were instructed to recite "in unison with the Reader." The institution of a choir, and the introduction of special attire for the cantor and rabbi underlined B'nai Jeshurun's transformation into a showpiece synagogue with a performance-oriented ritual: a move that the congregation's new membership, new building, and new community status had made inevitable.[44]

Once begun, the pressure for reform at B'nai Jeshurun did not so easily abate. The needs and desires of members, coupled with contemporary trends favoring liberalization in synagogues and churches, motivated board members to initiate discussion of seating changes (abolition of the gallery and mixed pews) as early as 1862. At the rabbi's urging, they were not followed up. In 1868, following the death of Rabbi Raphall, the trustees formed a joint committee on ritual, charged with investigating a wide range of possible "improvements" to the synagogue service, alterations in the "internal arrangement of the Synagogue" being only one of them. As a first step, the reader's desk was moved from its traditional place at the center of the synagogue to the front, a move that three years earlier had been voted down. In 1869, the board introduced a confirmation ceremony. Some sixty-three other changes also came up for consideration that year: most dealt with abolition of liturgical poems (*piyyutim*); a few went further, suggesting such things as doing away with the priestly blessing and ending the traditional calling up of seven men to the Torah. After consultation with their new rabbi, Dr. Henry Vidaver, and with Rabbi Jonas Bondi, editor of the *Hebrew Leader*, both of whom evaluated the proposed changes from the perspective of Jewish law, many of these changes, though not the most radical ones, were put into effect.[45]

In November 1871, the congregation took another step along the road to reform. It voted fifty to thirty-one to include women in the choir. Although sanctioned by Rabbi Vidaver, and widely practiced elsewhere, this move by one of America's oldest and most distinguished congregations generated considerable controversy. In spite of Rabbi Vidaver's insistence that Jewish law had not been breached, everyone realized that a mixed choir involved a more substantial departure from Jewish tradition than had previously been allowed. The choir was subsequently abandoned, "as it was found impracticable without an organ," but further steps in the direction of reform seemed inevitable.[46] Nobody should have been surprised when, on November 8, 1874, four months after Rabbi Vidaver had left the congregation for a more lucrative position in San Francisco, B'nai Jeshurun's members met to consider "the propriety of altering the present seats into Pews and also to add an Organ to the Choir."[47]

In reviewing the many changes that took place during this trying period in B'nai Jeshurun's history, Rabbi Israel Goldstein stressed the uncertainty of the congregation, the inner struggle between competing values that pulled members simultaneously in two directions, toward tradition and toward change: "The Congregation's decisions were made and unmade, amidst turbulent sentiment. Many of the members threatened to resign if the changes were not introduced. Others threatened to resign if the changes were introduced. Questions were repeatedly resubmitted and reconsidered, and the sentiment shifted as each faction in turn gained ascendancy."[48]

Even those most favoring change in congregational ritual aimed to stay within the bounds of "our established [Jewish] laws." They wanted the bountiful benefits that they thought reform would bring without sacrificing the comforting legitimacy that they knew tradition provided. Ideally, they somehow sought to be both Orthodox and modern at the same time, enjoying the benefits of both positions, and satisfying everyone.[49]

Although all members of B'nai Jeshurun may have prayed for this Utopia, younger and newer members nevertheless spearheaded the movement for change. One wishes that available evidence on this point were more substantial. Still, of the identifiable members who signed the petition calling for a special congregational meeting to consider instituting family pews and an organ, all five were members of ten years' standing or less (two additional signers cannot be identified). The fact that Joseph Aden, a member of B'nai Jeshurun, laid special stress on his being sixty-two years old when he declared himself in favor of the proposed changes—as if most reformers were far younger—offers additional corroborative evidence.[50]

Reforms in the 1870s all over the American Jewish community stemmed, at least in part, from fears that the young, American-born children of Central European immigrants were being lost to Judaism. Many Jews worried for their faith's future survival. Some foresaw a merger with Unitarianism. Young William Rosenblatt, in an article entitled "The Jews: What They Are Coming To" printed in the widely read *Galaxy*, openly predicted impending doom: "Of that ancient people only the history of their perils and their sufferings will remain."[51] Although various Jews resigned themselves to this "inevitable" fate, others looked to reforms that promised to win the young people back. When, as at B'nai Jeshurun, younger members took upon themselves the initiative to bring about change, their elders usually agreed to support them. They feared, as B'nai Jeshurun's president, Moses Strasburger, candidly admitted, that without changes the congregation would "become disbanded."[52]

Support for reform was by no means unanimous at B'nai Jeshurun: at the tumultuous special meeting called to discuss the question, fifty-five members voted for seating changes and installation of an organ, thirty members remained opposed. The majority viewed the changes they sanctioned as permissible and necessary next steps in the long process of internal transformation that had been going on for a quarter of a century. They believed that by modernizing B'nai Jeshurun—bringing it into harmony "with the requirements of modern taste and culture"—they were saving it for the next generation.[53] The minority, which had grown increasingly restive as the pace of reform quickened, viewed the same changes as confirming evidence of the congregation's final abandonment of Jewish law and tradition. They wondered aloud if the reforms would have been promulgated had an "orthodox lecturer" stood at the congregation's helm.[54]

The B'nai Jeshurun experience illustrates the major issues raised by mixed seating controversies from the late nineteenth century onward. For supporters, the proposed seating change translated into terms like family togetherness, women's equality, conformity to local norms, a modern, progressive image, and saving the youth—values that most Jews viewed positively. For opponents, the same change implied abandonment of tradition, violation of Jewish law, assimilation, Christianization, and promiscuity—consequences that most Jews viewed with horror. Pulled simultaneously in two directions that both seemed right—directions that reflected opposing views on modernity—many of those seeking compromise in the middle took solace in assurances from their leaders that Judaism and mixed seating were fully compatible. Rabbinic arguments and the adoption of mixed seating in synagogue after synagogue made the case for the "Jewishness" of the practice that much more compelling. Feeling reassured that they could reconcile modernity and tradition and still have mixed seating, majorities at congregations like B'nai Jeshurun opted for change. Minorities opposed to the change, meanwhile, found in separate seating a visible and defensible issue around which they could rally. Separate seating imparted just that sense of detached protest against modernity that, supporters felt, Judaism needed to express in order to survive. By exhibiting their reverence for tradition through the basic spatial arrangement of the synagogue, traditionalists made their point of disagreement with innovators plain for all to see. In time, "separate seating" and "mixed seating" became shorthand statements, visible expressions of differences on a host of more fundamental issues that lay beneath the surface.

## IV

Mixed seating generally ceased to be a controversial issue in Reform Judaism after the 1870s. By 1890, Isaac Mayer Wise, who was in a position to know, wrote that "today *no* synagogue is built in this country without family pews."[55] Applied to Reform temples, the statement seems to be correct. Orthodox synagogues, of course, continued to separate men and women, and this remained true in the new Orthodox "showpiece" congregations erected, particularly in New York, in the wake of large-scale East European Jewish immigration.[56] In 1895, a proposal for mixed seating did agitate the nation's leading Sephardic Synagogue, Shearith Israel, but the trustees unanimously voted it down. They resolved that in the new synagogue, then under construction, seating would remain, "men in the auditorium and women in the galleries as in the present synagogue." Ninety-six women submitted a resolution supporting the maintenance of this "time-honored custom."[57]

Over the next two decades, debates over mixed seating took place at a good many other modern Orthodox synagogues, especially those that sought to cater to young people. But for the most part—Congregation Mount Sinai of Central Harlem, founded in 1904, being a noteworthy exception—separate seating held. Modernity in these congregations came to mean decorum, use of the English language, and weekly sermons. Proposed seating reforms, by their nature far more divisive, were effectively tabled.[58]

Between the two world wars, the issue of mixed seating arose again, this time in the rapidly growing Conservative Movement. Living in what Marshall Sklare has identified as "areas of third settlement"—younger, more aware of surrounding non-Jewish and Reform Jewish practices, and more worried about the Jewishness of their children—Conservative Jews sought a form of worship that would be "traditional and at the same time modern." Gallery seating for women was not what they had in mind. It violated the American norm of family seating. It ran counter to modern views on the position of women. And it proved dysfunctional to synagogue life, since in America, Jewish women played an increasingly important part in all religious activities, and felt discriminated against by the gallery. Seating reforms thus ranked high on the Conservative Jewish agenda.[59]

In 1921, the question of "whether family pews would be a departure from traditional Judaism" came before the Rabbinical Assembly's [Conservative Jewish] Committee on the Interpretation of Jewish Law. Professor Louis Ginzberg, chairman of the committee, responded that gallery seating was unnecessary, but that "the separation of the sexes is a Jewish custom well established for about 2000 years, and must not be taken lightly."[60] The "separate but equal" seating pattern that Ginzberg advocated failed to satisfy proponents of family togetherness in worship, and most Conservative synagogues introduced mixed seating instead, in some cases preserving sexually segregated areas in the synagogue for those who wanted them ("compromise seating")[61]. In 1947, Ginzberg himself told a congregation in Baltimore that if "continued separation of family units during services presents a great danger to its spiritual welfare, the minority ought to yield to the spiritual need of the majority."[62] Privately he admitted that "when you live long enough in America you realize that the status of womanhood had changed so much that separating women from men has become obsolete."[63] By 1955, according to Marshall Sklare, mixed seating featured in "the overwhelming majority of Conservative synagogues," and served "as the most commonly accepted yardstick for differentiating Conservatism from Orthodoxy."[64]

Although recognized Orthodox leaders did indeed tout mixed seating as the "great divide"—the action that put a congregation beyond the pale of Orthodox tradition—many members of Orthodox congregations apparently disagreed. Congregations that both professed to be Orthodox and employed rabbis who graduated from Orthodox rabbinical seminaries still introduced family pews, defending them in one case, on the basis of the "spirit, traditions and procedure of Orthodox Judaism," and in another on the pragmatic grounds that they would "be inviting to the younger members."[65] One source claims that in 1961 there existed "perhaps 250 Orthodox synagogues where family seating is practiced."[66]

A different estimate, from 1954, holds that "90% of the graduates of the Chicago Hebrew Theological Institution, which is Orthodox, and 50% of the graduates of the Yeshiva, the Orthodox institution in New York, have positions where family seating or optional family seating prevails." How accurate either estimate was remains unclear, but at least according to one (perhaps biased) observer family seating had "definitely become a form and tradition of Orthodox Israelites adopted and practiced by an overwhelming number of Orthodox Synagogues." Certainly rabbis who served mixed-seating congregations continued to belong to the Orthodox Rabbinical Council of America without fear of expulsion.[67]

Synagogue practices notwithstanding, Yeshiva University continuously opposed mixed seating. It nominally revoked the ordination of its graduates if they continued to serve mixed-seating congregations after having been warned to leave them. The only temporary justification allowing a graduate to accept a mixed-seating position was if Yeshiva's then president, Bernard Revel, felt that "an able, diplomatic man" could bring the errant congregation "back to the fold."[68] Although in some cases this happened, and in others the rabbi resigned after failing, an apparently substantial but undetermined number of Yeshiva University graduates, torn between piety and prosperity, or influenced by American conditions, made peace with mixed seating. In a few cases, they later defended the practice's orthodoxy in court.

Court proceedings dealing with the mixed-seating problem were, as we know from the B'nai Jeshurun affair, nothing new. A series of cases in the 1950s,[69] however, had the effect of solidifying Orthodoxy's position on the issue, while undermining the comfortable arguments of those who insisted that mixed seating and Jewish tradition could be made compatible. Leading Orthodox spokesmen, in concert with the Union of Orthodox Jewish Congregations of America and the Rabbinical Council of America, so vigorously insisted that mixed seating violated *halacha*, that those who supported the opposite position realized that they were clinging to a view that no institutionalized brand of Orthodoxy would agree to legitimate.

Three cases received particular attention. The first involved Congregation Adath Israel in Cincinnati. Founded by Polish Jews in 1853, and for many years the leading non-Reform synagogue in the city, Adath Israel harbored a range of traditional Jews and had for many years walked a tightrope between the Conservative and Orthodox movements. The synagogue's constitution proclaimed adherence to the "forms and traditions of Orthodox Israelites."[70] At the same time, the synagogue belonged to the Conservative United Synagogues of America. Fishel J. Goldfeder, Adath Israel's rabbi, boasted both an Orthodox and a Conservative training. Members sought to appeal to those with Orthodox leanings and Conservative leanings at one and the same time.

Separate seating of some form or other had been the rule at Adath Israel since its inception. At least since 1896, "separate but equal" seating had been deemed sufficient: "Men sit on one side and the women sit on the other side of the first floor of the Synagogue without any curtain or any partition between them."[71] In 1923, apparently in reaction to liberalization moves in many Conservative synagogues, members voted an amendment to their constitution: "that no family pews be established nor may men remove their hats during services; that no organ be used during services; that no female choir be permitted so long as ten (10) members in good standing object thereto."[72]

Beginning in 1952, however, the congregation, which had been expanding rapidly, began to be agitated by demands for optional family seating, many of them from younger members. The board of trustees, with the blessing of Rabbi Goldfeder, voted 17–9 in favor of optional family seating on December 30, 1953, and a congregational meeting subsequently ratified the action by a vote of 289–100.[73]

Opponents claimed that mixed seating violated the synagogue's constitution. They pointed out that more than the necessary ten members objected to family seating, and besides, they insisted that family seating contravened the "forms and traditions of Orthodox Israelites." They, therefore, moved to block the action, and by mutual agreement finally submitted their dispute to a private court. A three-judge panel ("each side to the controversy shall select one Judge of its own choosing and the third Judge shall be selected by agreement of the counsel for both sides") was given binding authority to decide the case.[74]

The court proceedings brought to the fore the deep divisions within Adath Israel that had long simmered beneath the surface. As the judges noted in their decision, "Some witnesses contended that the . . . Synagogue is strictly Orthodox: some said that it is liberal Orthodox, and others believed that it is a Conservative synagogue."[75] Supporters of mixed seating argued, on the one hand, that the congregation was Conservative, since it lacked a formal *mechitsa* (partition), employed a microphone, and confirmed women, and on the other hand, that mixed seating accorded "with the forms and traditions of Orthodox Israelites," as defined by their rabbi. By contrast, opponents of mixed seating argued that the congregation was Orthodox, notwithstanding earlier reforms, and that mixed seating would cause Adath Israel "to lose its status as a proper place of worship."[76] Testimony from leading figures in Orthodox and Conservative Judaism put forth diverging views on mixed seating's *halachic* status, and on the meaning of "Orthodoxy" to different kinds of Jews.

In their decision, Judge Chase M. Davies and Rabbi Joseph P. Sternstein (the third judge, Mr. Sol Goodman, dissented) refused to consider these *halachic* issues at all. Having been instructed to "resolve the controversy involved in the synagogue on a legal basis," they first ruled the 1923 amendment outlawing family pews "not a valid and presently effective amendment to the Constitution and By-Laws of the congregation," since improper procedures had accompanied its adoption. On the more important question of whether family seating violated Orthodox "forms and traditions," the judges, on the basis of American precedents, decided that the issue

> presents a religious question over which a Court of law, and this private Court, which has been instructed to follow legal principles, has no right, power, or jurisdiction. To hold otherwise would be an assumption by this private Court of monitorship of the religious faith of the members of the congregation, since under federal and state Constitutions, there can be no disturbance of or limitation to the power and right of the congregants to exercise that freedom of conscience which is the basis of our liberty.[77]

Given the fact that the board of trustees, the majority of the members, and the rabbi all supported "optional family seating," the judges ruled the practice valid. They took pains to point out, however, that as an opinion of a private court, theirs "should not be considered, or cited, as authority in any other case."[78]

In closing, the judges expressed the hope that their decision would "result in a harmonious and unified worship of God by all members of the congregation."[79] That, however, did not come about. Instead, many of the members who had always considered Adath Israel to be Orthodox and opposed mixed seating, withdrew and joined other synagogues. Those who remained at Adath Israel became more closely aligned with the Conservative

Movement and referred to themselves increasingly as Conservative Jews. The seating controversy thus unwittingly served as a vehicle for clarifying both religious identity and ideology. By taking a stand on one issue, people expressed their views on a host of other issues as well.

*Davis v. Scher*[80] the second mixed-seating case, concerned Congregation Beth Tefilas Moses, an avowedly Orthodox Jewish congregation in Mt. Clemens, Michigan, which voted to introduce family seating into its sanctuary in 1955. Baruch Litvin, a businessman who belonged to the congregation and was cordially disliked by many of its members, took up the battle against this decision,[81] basing himself on an established American legal principle: "A majority of a church congregation may not institute a practice within the church fundamentally opposed to the doctrine to which the church property is dedicated, as against a minority of the congregation who adhere to the established doctrine and practice."[82] Litvin's attorneys, supported by the Union of Orthodox Jewish Congregations, introduced a great deal of evidence to support the claim that mixed seating was "clearly violative of the established Orthodox Jewish law and practice" and argued that if mixed seating were introduced, the Orthodox minority would have to worship elsewhere, "deprived of the right of the use of their property . . . by the majority group contrary to law." The congregation, by contrast, argued that the dispute involved only "doctrinal and ecclesiastical matters," not property rights, and that "it would be inconsistent with complete religious liberty for the court to assume . . . jurisdiction."[83] Despite court urging, the congregation's lawyers refused to cross-examine witnesses or to introduce any testimony of their own in defense of mixed seating, for fear that this would weaken their argument. They did not believe that the secular courtroom was the proper forum for Jewish doctrinal debates.

Lower courts sided with the congregation and refused to become involved, arguing that Congregation Beth Tefilas Moses' majority voice had the power to rule. The Michigan Supreme Court, however, unanimously reversed this decision and accepted the minority's claims. It stressed that "because of defendants' calculated risk of not offering proofs, no dispute exists as to the teaching of Orthodox Judaism as to mixed seating." By the laws governing implied trusts, therefore, the congregation's majority was denied the power to carry property dedicated for use by Orthodox Jews "to the support of a new and conflicting doctrine." "A change of views on religious subjects," the court ruled, did not require those who still held to older views to surrender property originally conveyed to them.[84]

The third case, *Katz v. Singerman*,[85] had much that was seemingly in common with *Davis v. Scher*. Congregation Chevra Thilim of New Orleans voted in 1957 to introduce family pews, and a minority, led by Harry Katz, went to court to thwart the move. Like Baruch Litvin, Katz argued for minority rights, particularly since the Chevra Thilim charter explicitly included "the worship of God according to the orthodox Polish Jewish ritual" as one of its "objects and purposes," and the congregation had accepted the donation of a building upon the stipulation that it "shall only be used as a place of Jewish worship according to the strict ancient and orthodox forms and ceremonies."[86] The issue to be determined by the court was "whether the practice of mixed or family seating in Chevra Thilim Synagogue is contrary to and inconsistent with the 'orthodox Polish Jewish Ritual' and 'Jewish worship according to the strict ancient and orthodox forms and ceremonies,' and therefore in violation of the trust and donation . . . and also the Charter of the Congregation."[87]

Where *Katz v. Singerman* differed was in the strategy employed by defendants. They introduced considerable testimony in support of mixed seating, including evidence supplied by Rabbi Jacob Agus, ordained at Yeshiva University, as well as twenty-seven affidavits testifying that mixed seating "is not contrary to Orthodox Jewish forms and ceremonies."[88] Seventy-five affidavits, and a host of formidable witnesses from across the Orthodox spectrum opposed this testimony, offering abundant evidence in support of separate seating. The court was left to decide who understood Jewish law better.

Lower courts, impressed by the plaintiff's legal display and by the strong pro-Orthodox language employed in the original charter, decided in Katz's favor. The Supreme Court of Louisiana, however, in a decision similar to that rendered in the Adath Israel affair, decided differently. Given the "well-settled rule of law that courts will not interfere with the ecclesiastical questions involving differences of opinion as to religious conduct,"[89] and the famous Supreme Court decision in *Watson v. Jones* (1872), which held that "[i]n such cases where there is a schism which leads to a separation into distinct and conflicting bodies, the rights of such bodies to the use of the property must be determined by the ordinary principles which govern voluntary associations,"[90] the court decided that Chevra Thilim's board of directors alone had the "authority to ascertain and interpret the meaning of 'orthodox Polish Jewish Ritual.'" The fact that Chevra Thilim's rabbi agreed with the board and favored mixed seating held "great weight" with the court, which also cited precedents based on church-state separation and the principle that "churches must in their very nature 'grow with society.'"[91] "This case differs from the case of *Davis v. Scher*," the judges insisted, "for there the evidence was all on one side." Here, with two sides offering conflicting testimony as to what the phrase "orthodox forms and ceremonies" means, the court, following abundant precedent, left the matter for the congregation to decide.[92]

From the point of view of law, *Katz v. Singerman* dealt a severe blow to Orthodoxy, since it made it highly difficult for an Orthodox minority to overturn in court any majority decision, even one found unacceptable in terms of *halacha*. From another point of view, however, the case, like *Davis v. Scher* and the Adath Israel case, actually strengthened Orthodoxy, for it gave publicity to the movement's views and established in the popular mind the fact that "true" Orthodoxy and separate seating went hand in hand. Orthodox Jewish publications denominated those who defended the orthodoxy of mixed seating as "Conservative Jews," and ridiculed "mixed-seating Orthodoxy" as a contradiction in terms.[93] Those who did define modern Orthodox in terms of mixed seating found themselves increasingly isolated. In some cases, congregations that once considered themselves modern Orthodox moved, after adopting mixed seating, firmly into the ranks of the Conservative Movement.[94] In other cases, particularly in congregations served by rabbis from Hebrew Theological College in Chicago, modern Orthodox congregations began to worship under the label of traditional Judaism.[95]

Exceptions notwithstanding, mixed seating, even more than when Marshall Sklare first made the observation, symbolized by the third quarter of the twentieth century that which differentiated Orthodoxy from Jewry's other branches.[96] The symbol that had first signified family togetherness and later came to represent women's equality and religious modernity, had finally evolved into a denominational boundary. Around it American Jews defined where they stood religiously and what values they held most dear.[97]

## NOTES

I am grateful to Rochelle Elstein, Barry Feldman, Robert Shapiro, and Barbara E. Ullman for bringing valuable materials to my attention; to Professors Benny Kraut, Jacob R. Marcus, Michael A.

Meyer, Jeffrey S. Gurock, Robert Handy, Chava Weissler, Jack Wertheimer, and Lance J. Sussman, for commenting on earlier drafts of this chapter; and to the Memorial Foundation for Jewish Culture for its ongoing support of my work.

1. John M. Neale. *The History of Pews*, 2d ed. (Cambridge, U.K., 1842), 3.

2. The best available materials on synagogue seating have been prepared by parties in legal disputes; see Baruch Litvin, ed., *The Sanctity of the Synagogue* (New York, 1959); and the special issue of *Conservative Judaism*, 11 (Fall, 1956), devoted to the Adath Israel affair.

3. For two responsa on this issue, see Bernhard Felsenthal, "Muss Man Sich Beim Beten Nach Osten Wenden?" *Sinai*, 6 (May, 1861), 110–11; and Shaul Yedidyah Shochet, *Tiferet Yedidya*, vol. 2 (St. Louis, 1920), 26–32. See also Franz Landsberger, "The Sacred Direction in Synagogue and Church," *Hebrew Union College Annual*, 28 (1957), 181–203.

4. See Jacob Agus. "Mixed Pews in Jewish Tradition," *Conservative Judaism*, 11 (Fall, 1956), 35–36; and Rachel Wischnitzer, *Synagogue Architecture in the United States* (Philadelphia, 1955), 60.

5. For various perspectives, see Leon A. Jick, *The Americanization of the Synagogue* 1820–1870 (Hanover, N.H., 1976); Moshe Davis, *The Emergence of Conservative Judaism* (Philadelphia, 1965); Nathan Glazer, *American Judaism*, 2d ed. (Chicago, 1972); and Allan Tarshish, "The Rise of American Judaism" (Ph.D. diss., Hebrew Union College, 1938).

6. Ismar Elbogen, *Hatefilah Beyisrael* (Tel Aviv, 1972), 350–352; Andrew Seager, "The Architecture of the Dura and Sardis Synagogues," in *The Synagogue*, ed. Joseph Gutmann (New York, 1975), 156–158, 178 nn. 35–36; Salo W. Baron, *The Jewish Community*, vol. 2 (Philadelphia, 1945), 140; Samuel Kraus, *Korot Bate Hatefilah Beyisrael* (New York: Histadrut Ivrit, 1955), 239–240; *Encyclopedia Judaica*, 11, 134–135; Shaye J. D. Cohen. "Women in the Synagogues of Antiquity," *Conservative Judaism*, 34 (November–December, 1980), 23–29; J. Charles Cox, *Bench-Ends in English Churches* (London, n.d.), 17–27.

7. David Philipson, *The Reform Movement in Judaism* (New York, 1931), 245. A similar seating arrangement may have been in effect as early as 1815 in the Reform congregation that met at the home of Jacob Herz-Beer in Berlin. See Nahum N. Glatzer, "On an Unpublished Letter of Isaak Markus Jost," *Leo Baeck Institute Year Book*, 22 (1977), opposite 132. I owe this reference to Professor Michael A. Meyer.

8. Jacob Sonderling, "Five Gates—Casual Notes for an Autobiography," *American Jewish Archives*, 16 (November 1964), 109. On Budge, see Cyrus Adler, *Jacob H. Schiff: His Life and Letters*, vol. 1 (Garden City, N.J., 1929), 7–8. Rebekah Kohut reports in 1929 that "everywhere in Europe, except in the Reform Temples of Paris and London, men and women still worship separately." *As I Know Them* (New York, 1929), 119.

9. *American Israelite*, 37 (27 November 1890), 4.

10. John Demos, "Images of the American Family, Then and Now," in *Changing Images of the Family*, ed. Virginia Tufte and Barbara Myerhoff (New Haven, 1979), 48; Cox, *Bench-Ends*, 17–19; Robert J. Dinkin, Seating the Meeting House in Early Massachusetts," *New England Quarterly*, 43 (1970), 450–464; Peter Benes and Philip D. Zimmerman, *New England Meeting House and Church, 1630–1850* (Boston, 1979), 55–56; Wischnitzer, *Synagogue Architecture*, 12.

11. Patricia J. Tracy, *Jonathan Edwards, Pastor* (New York, 1980), 128. For a similar contemporary argument, see Morris Max, "Mixed Pews," *Conservative Judaism*, 11 (Fall 1956), 70.

12. Dinkin, "Seating the Meeting House," 456; Tracy, *Jonathan Edwards, Pastor*, 244 n. 9.

13. Alan Graebner, *Uncertain Saints* (Westport, Conn., 1975), 17; "Pews," *The American Quarterly Church Review*, 13 (July 1860), 288–289. See Jacob Angus's discussion of the 1885 mixed-seating controversy in Grace Methodist Church of Dayton, Ohio, in Agus, "Mixed Pews in Jewish Tradition," 41.

14. Demos, "Images of the American Family," 43–60, 49; Carl N. Degler, *At Odds: Women and the Family in America from the Revolution to the Present* (Oxford, 1980), 9; and Carl N. Degler, "Women and the Family," in *The Past Before Us*, ed. Michael Kammen (Ithaca, N.Y., 1980), 317.

15. Hyman B. Grinstein, *The Rise of the Jewish Community of New York* (Philadelphia, 1945), 317–318; see Kenneth L. Ames, "Ideologies in Stone: Meanings in Victorian Gravestones," *Journal of Popular Culture*, 14 (1981), 641–656.

16. James G. Heller, *Isaac M. Wise: His Life, Work and Thought* (New York, 1965), 214.

17. Heller, *Wise*, 124–183; Naphtali J. Rubinger, "Dismissal in Albany," *American Jewish Archives*, 24 (November 1972), 161–162.

18. Isaac M. Wise, *Reminiscences* (1901; 2d ed., New York, 1945), 116–117.

19. Wise, *Reminiscences*, 172.

20. Rubinger, "Dismissal in Albany," 160–183; Heller, *Wise*, 184–234. On the conversion of

churches into synagogues, a phenomenon little
known in Europe, see Wischnitzer, *Synagogue Architecture*, 61–62. Apparently, Wise did not introduce mixed pews immediately upon his arrival in
Cincinnati. They only came to Bene Yeshurun in
1866 when the congregation moved into the Plum
Street temple. See James Heller, *As Yesterday When
It Is Past* (Cincinnati, 1942), 114.

21. Wise, *Reminiscences*, 212.

22. *Occident*, 9 (December, 1851), 477; *As-
monean*, 10 October 1851, 226; 17 October 1851, 240;
see 21 November 1851, 53; 19 December 1851, 83.

23. *American Israelite*, 15 November 1872, 8; 27
November 1890, 4. Naphtali J. Rubinger, "Albany
Jewry of the Nineteenth Century; Historic Roots
and Communal Evolution" (Ph.D. diss., Yeshiva
University, 1970), 120, notes other occasions when
Wise retrospectively exaggerated the extent of the
opposition against him. Such efforts aimed at cre-
ating a personal "hero myth" are common; see
Frank J. Sulloway, *Freud, Biologist of the Mind*.
(New York, 1979), 445–495; Joseph Campbell, *The
Hero With A Thousand Faces* (Princeton, 1968).

24. Myer Stern, *The Rise and Progress of Reform
Judaism* (New York, 1895), 14; *New Era*, 4 (1874),
126; Grinstein, *Jewish Community of New York*, 267;
see also Leopold Mayer's description of Emanu-El
in 1850, in Morris U. Schappes, *A Documentary
History of the Jews in the United States*, 1654–1875
(New York, 1971), 308.

25. Philipson, *Reform Movement*, 183–184,
219–220; see Kaufmann Kohler, *Jewish Theology*
(New York, 1918), 472–473.

26. *See Sinai*, 6 (August 1861), 205–207. For a
sociological perspective on the German debate in
terms of "identity formation and boundary maintenance," see David Ellenson, "The Role of Reform
in selected German-Jewish Orthodox Responsa: A
Sociological Analysis," *Hebrew Union College Annual*, 53 (1982), 357–380.

27. Alexander Hamilton, *Itinerarium*, quoted
in David and Tamar De Sola Pool, *An Old Faith in
the New World* (New York, 1955), 453; *Religious In-
telligencer*, 1 (1817), 556; *Western Monthly Review*,
2 (January 1829), 440; *New York Herald*, 22 September 1836. For other negative notices, see Joseph S.
C. F. Frey, *The Converted Jew* (Boston, 1815), 15;
*The Jew at Home and Abroad* (Philadelphia, 1845),
65; Joseph L. Blau and Salo W. Baron, *The Jews of
the United States, 1790–1840: A Documentary History*, vol. 3 (New York, 1963), 677–680; and Lydia
M. Child, *The History of the Condition of Women in
Various Ages and Nations*, vol. 1 (Boston, 1835), 20.
Cf. I. J. Benjamin's Jewish critique (1859) in his

*Three Years in America*, vol. 1, transl. Charles
Reznikoff (Philadelphia, 1956), 85–89; and see
more broadly Joan Jacobs Brumberg, *Mission for
Life* (New York, 1984), 79–106.

28. *New York Herald*, 28 September 1836; *Sunday Times and Noah's Weekly Messenger* (New
York), 7 July 1850, 26 January 1851; James Parton,
*Topics of the Times* (Boston, 1871), 299, 308. The
leading Jewish apologia, imported from England,
was Grace Aguilar, *The Women of Israel*, 2 vols.
(New York, 1851). For a modern analogue, see Lucy
Davidowicz, *The Jewish Presence* (New York, 1978),
46–57.

29. Louise Abbie Mayo, "The Ambivalent
Image: The Perception of the Jew in Nineteenth
Century America" (Ph.D. diss., City University of
New York, 1977), 93–104.

30. Philipson, *Reform Movement*, 220.

31. *Sinai*, 3 (1858), 824; Isaac M. Fein, *The
Making of an American Jewish Community* (Philadelphia, 1971), 113.

32. *Sinai*, 3 (1858), 818–824; 6 (1861), 205–
207.

33. Bernhard Felsenthal, *The Beginnings of the
Chicago Sinai Congregation* (Chicago, 1898), 23.

34. *Occident*, 18 (1860), 154; Fred Rosenbaum,
*Architects of Reform* (Berkeley, 1980), 26.

35. *New Era*, 1 (February 1871), 193.

36. Jerome W. Grollman, "The Emergence of
Reform Judaism in the United States" (Ord. thesis,
Hebrew Union College, 1948), 18, 43 passim; *A
History of Congregation Beth El, Detroit, Mich.,
1850–1900* (Detroit, 1900), 26–28; Jonathan D.
Sarna, "Innovation and Consolidation: Phases in
the History of Temple Mishkan Israel," *Jews in New
Haven*, vol. 3, ed. Barry E. Herman and Werner S.
Hirsch (New Haven, 1981), 102; Edward N.
Calisch, *The Light Burns On* (Richmond, 1941), 25;
Frank J. Adler, *Roots in a Moving Stream* (Kansas
City, 1972), 22; Isidor Blum, *The Jews of Baltimore*
1910), 23; *New Era*, 5 (1875), 4; Solomon Breibart,
"The Synagogue of Kahal Kadosh Beth Elohim,
Charleston." *South Carolina Historical Magazine*, 80
(July 1979), 228—all describe the adoption of
mixed seating in other nineteenth-century Ameri-
can Reform congregations. For the situation at the
more traditional congregation Sherith Israel of San
Francisco in the 1870s, see Norton B. Stern, "An Or-
thodox Rabbi and a Reforming Congregation in
Nineteenth Century San Francisco," *Western States
Jewish Historical Quarterly*, 15 (April 1983),
275–281.

37. Quoted in Grollman, *Emergence of Reform
Judaism*, 89.

38. Wise, *Reminiscences*, 212.

39. *Occident*, 13 (1855), 417; 21 (1863), 345; 21 (1864), 500.

40. *Occident*, 21 (1863), 407. On Buttenwieser, see A. Z. Friedman, *Tub Taam*, 2d ed. (New York, 1904), introduction.

41. E.g., *American Israelite*, 13 December 1878, 4.

42. Israel Goldstein, *A Century of Judaism in New York: B'nai Jeshurun*, 1825–1925 (New York, 1930), 51–113; see also Grinstein, *Jewish Community of New York*; Moshe Davis, "The Synagogue in American Judaism: A Study of Congregation B'nai Jeshurun, New York City," in *Two Generations in Perspective*, ed. Harry Schneiderman (New York, 1957), 210–235, translated and revised in Moshe Davis, *Beit Yisrael Be-Amerikah* (Jerusalem, 1970), 1–24. On Raphall, see Bertram W. Korn, *Eventful Years and Experiences* (Cincinnati, 1954), 40–41.

43. Goldstein, *B'nai Jeshurun*, 126.

44. Ibid., 126–129; see Jonathan D. Sarna, ed., *People Walk on Their Heads: Moses Weinberger's Jews and Judaism in New York* (New York, 1981), 12–14.

45. Goldstein, *B'nai Jeshurun*, 128, 153–156; *Answers to Questions Propounded by the Ritual Committee on the Subject of the Improvements Intended to Be Introduced in the Synagogue Service of the Cong. "B'nai Jeshurun"* (New York, 1869); Minutes of Congregation B'nai Jeshurun, 1865–1875. Congregation B'nai Jeshurun Papers, microfilm 493c, American Jewish Archives, Cincinnati, Ohio.

46. Goldstein, *B'nai Jeshurun*, 156; Nahum Streisand, *Lilmod Latoim Binah* (New York, 1872); *Jewish Messenger*, 16 July 1875.

47. B'nai Jeshurun Minutes, 8 November 1874.

48. Goldstein, *B'nai Jeshurun*, 157.

49. Ibid., 155; *Answers to Questions*, 1; cf. *New Era*, 1 (1870), 36, for an attack on this phenomenon.

50. *B'nai Jeshurun Minutes*, 8 November 1874, as correlated with the "Register of Congregational Membership," in Goldstein, *B'nai Jeshurun*, 404–436; *Jewish Messenger*, 16 July 1875, 6.

51. William M. Rosenblatt, "The Jews: What They Are Coming To," *Galaxy*, 13 (January 1872), 60; *New Era*, 4 (1874), 14, 513; for a similar later argument (1922), see Aaron Rothkoff, *Bernard Revel* (Philadelphia, 1972), 111.

52. *Jewish Messenger*, 16 July 1875, 6.

53. *Jewish Times*, 21 May 1875, 184.

54. *Jewish Messenger*, 21 May 1875, 21.

55. *American Israelite*, 37 (November 27, 1890), 4, italics added. See Gustav Gottheil, "The Jewish Reformation," *American Journal of Theology*, 6 (April 1902), 279.

56. Jo Renee Fine and Gerald R. Wolfe, *The Synagogues of New York's Lower East Side* (New York, 1978).

57. Pool, *An Old Faith*, 100.

58. Jeffrey S. Gurock, *When Harlem Was Jewish* (New York, 1979), 117; see also Chapter 1 in this volume.

59. Marshall Sklare, *Conservative Judaism* (1955; 2d. ed., New York, 1972), 85–90.

60. *United Synagogue Recorder*, 1 (July 1921), 8.

61. The Cleveland Jewish Center case of 1927, involving Rabbi Solomon Goldman (*Katz v. Goldman*, 33 Ohio A150), drew particular notice. The Ohio Supreme Court ruled in Goldman's favor, refusing to invalidate the changes that he introduced. See Aaron Rakeffet-Rothkoff, *The Silver Era in American Jewish Orthodoxy* (New York, 1981), 112–114, 121 n. 14, 326–347; Jacob J. Weinstein, *Solomon Goldman: A Rabbi's Rabbi* (New York, 1973), 12–17.

62. *Conservative Judaism*, 11 (Fall 1956), 39; Eli Ginzberg, *Keeper of the Law: Louis Ginzberg* (Philadelphia, 1966), 229–230.

63. Sonderling, "Five Gates," 115.

64. Sklare, *Conservative Judaism*, 88; see Rothkoff, *Bernard Revel*, 111; and Norman Lamm, "Separate Pews in the Synagogue [1959]," in *A Treasury of Tradition*, ed. Norman Lamm and Walter S. Wurzberger (New York, 1967), 243–267.

65. *Katz v. Singerman*, 241 Louisiana 154 (1961); Rothkoff, *Bernard Revel*, 164.

66. *Katz v. Singerman*, 241 Louisiana 150.

67. "Opinion in Kahila Kodesh Adath Israel Congregation Matter" (Cincinnati, 1954, mimeographed), 42, Louis Bernstein, *Challenge and Mission: The Emergence of the English Speaking Orthodox Rabbinate* (New York, 1982), 20–21, 36, 46–49, 138–141.

68. Rothkoff, *Bernard Revel*, 164.

69. For the legal background, see Meislin, *Jewish Law in American Tribunals*; and W. E. Shipley, *Change of Denominational Relations or Fundamental Doctrines by Majority Faction of Independent or Congregational Church as Ground for Award of Property to Minority*, 15 ALR 3d 297 (1967). The Supreme Court's ruling in *Presbyterian Church in the United States v. Mary Elizabeth Blue Hull Memorial Presbyterian Church*, 393 U.S. 440 (1969) resolved several important legal questions bearing on mixed seating disputes; see Paul G. Kauper. "Church Autonomy and the First Amendment: The Presbyterian Church Case," in *Church and State: The Supreme Court and the First Amendment*, ed. Philip B. Kurland (Chicago, 1975), 67–98.

70. "Opinion in Adath Israel Matter," 4. In what follows, I cite this version; a slightly abbreviated and variant version of the decision may be found in *Conservative Judaism*, 11 (Fall 1956), 1–31.

71. "Opinion in Adath Israel Matter," 12. David Philipson found this seating pattern when he preached at Adath Israel's dedication in 1927. He predicted that "ere long the women will sit with their husbands and children." *My Life as an American Jew* (Cincinnati, 1941), 378.

72. Philipson, *My Life as an American Jew*, 8.

73. Ibid., 8–12.

74. Ibid., 1–3. On the use of arbitration in cases of this sort, see Jerold S. Auerbach, *Justice without Law?* (New York, 1983), 69–94.

75. Auerbach, *Justice without Law?* 63.

76. Ibid., 30; *Conservative Judaism*, 11 (Fall 1956), 44.

77. *Opinion in Adath Israel Matter*, 43–66; quotations from 47, 45, 66.

78. Ibid., 59.

79. Ibid., 67.

80. The case is reported in 356 Michigan 291, and is described in great detail, with documents, in Litvin, *Sanctity of the Synagogue*. Much of what follows is based on this volume. See also Bernstein, *Challenge and Mission*, 138–141.

81. Litvin, *Sanctity of the Synagogue*, 11–17.

82. Ibid., 378.

83. Ibid., 382, 412, 408.

84. Ibid., 407–418 reproduces the entire Michigan Supreme Court decision; quotations are from 417, 415.

85. The case is reported in 241 Louisiana 103. For early documents, see Litvin, *Sanctity of the Synagogue*, 61–77; see also Bernstein, *Challenge and Mission*, 138–140.

86. *Katz v. Singerman*, 107, 109.

87. Ibid., 114.

88. Ibid., 136–149. Agus's testimony resembled that which he gave in the Adath Israel matter; see *Conservative Judaism*, 11 (1956), 32–41.

89. *Katz v. Singerman*, 116 quoting *Katz v. Goldman*, above n. 73.

90. *Katz v. Singerman*, 118; cf. *Watson v. Jones* 13 Wall. 679, 20 L ed. 666 (1872).

91. *Katz v. Singerman*, 131, 134.

92. Ibid., 151. Shipley, *Change of Denominational Relations*, 324, 331, overlooks this critical point.

93. E.g., Litvin, *Sanctity of the Synagogue*, 73.

94. See Isaac Klein's letter in *Conservative Judaism*, 11 (Winter 1957), 34.

95. E.g., Joseph Schultz, ed., *Mid-America's Promise: A Profile of Kansas City Jewry* (Kansas City, 1982), 42.

96. Cf. Alan J. Yuter, "Mehizah, Midrash and Modernity: A Study in Religious Rhetoric," *Judaism*, 28 (1979), 147–159; Samuel Heilman, *Synagogue Life* (Chicago, 1976), 28. Charles Liebman, "Orthodoxy in American Jewish Life," *Aspects of the Religious Behavior of American Jews* (reprinted from *American Jewish Year Book*, 66; New York, 1974), 146, notes "some 30 synagogues" which once had mixed seating and, since 1955, have installed *mechitsot*—no doubt to maintain their Orthodox affiliation.

97. In a conversation with me, Prof. Sefton D. Temkin quotes a colleague of his as pointing out that whereas American Orthodoxy defined itself in terms of opposition to mixed seating, British Orthodoxy did so in terms of opposition to the mixed choir, German Orthodoxy in terms of opposition to the organ, and Hungarian Orthodoxy in terms of opposition to the raised, forward pulpit. A comparative study elucidating these differences would be of inestimable value.

THE FEMINIST THEOLOGY OF THE

BLACK BAPTIST CHURCH, 1880–1900

*Evelyn Brooks Higginbotham*

In her study of the Women's Convention in the National Baptist Church, Evelyn Brooks Higginbotham goes well beyond previous understandings of both the African-American church and women's religious experience by focusing on the roles of black women within what was the largest organization of African Americans at the turn of the century. While many historians have explored the African-American church, most focus on the leadership of black men and overlook the contribution of the black women who made up most of the church's membership. In contrast, Higginbotham argues that the black Baptist church was not the creation of male ministers but rather "the product and process of male and female interaction." Similarly, while a growing number of scholars have explored the various ways in which men and women shaped and were shaped by the nineteenth-century religious world of the European-American middle class, their studies do not help us understand how women and men beyond the borders of the white middle class appropriated the ideology of separate spheres. Here Higginbotham shows how a rising gender consciousness led black women to be "at once separate and allied with black men in the struggle for racial advancement while separate and allied with white women in the struggle for gender equality." Higginbotham's depiction of black Baptist women who are living within multiple racial and gender realities confounds simplistic renderings of separate men's and women's spheres.

Adapted by permission of the publisher from "Feminist Theology, 1880–1900," in *Righteous Discontent: The Women's Movement in the Black Baptist Church, 1880–1920* by Evelyn Brooks Higginbotham, pp. 120–149, Cambridge, Mass.: Harvard University Press, Copyright 1993 by the President and Fellows of Harvard College.

*What if I am a woman; is not the God of ancient times the God of these modern days: Did he not raise up Deborah, to be a mother and a judge in Israel [Judges 4:4]? Did not queen Esther save the lives of the Jews? And Mary Magdalene first declare the resurrection of Christ from the dead?*

—Maria Stewart, "Farewell Address,"

21 September 1833

# 13

# THE FEMINIST THEOLOGY
# OF THE BLACK BAPTIST CHURCH,
# 1880–1900

## *Evelyn Brooks Higginbotham*

BOSTON BLACK MINISTER Peter Randolph cited gender proscriptions among the "strange customs" that he confronted when he returned to his Virginia birthplace soon after the Civil War to assume the pastorate of Richmond's Ebenezer Baptist Church. Randolph noted the segregated seating for men and women and the men's refusal to permit women at the business meetings of the church. Charles Octavius Boothe, a black Baptist minister in Alabama, recalled that in the early years of freedom women were not accustomed to the right to pray publicly.[1] Even as late as the 1880s in Tennessee and in Arkansas, black women met with virulent hostility in their efforts to establish separate societies.

During the last two decades of the nineteenth century, black Baptist women increasingly challenged such examples of gender inequality. Working within the orthodoxy of the church, they turned to the Bible to argue for their rights—thus holding men accountable to the same text that authenticated their arguments for racial equality. In drawing upon the Bible—the most respected source within their community—they found scriptural precedents for expanding women's rights. Black women expressed their discontent with popular conceptions regarding "woman's place" in the church and society at large. They challenged the "silent helpmate" image of women's church work and set out to convince the men that women were equally obliged to advance not only their race and denomination, but themselves. Thus the black Baptist women developed a theology inclusive of equal gender participation. They articulated this viewpoint before groups of men and women in churches, convention anniversaries, and denominational schools, and in newspapers and other forms of literature.

The religious posture of black Baptist women was contextualized within a racial tradition that conflated private/eschatological witness and public/political stand. Saving souls and proselytizing the unconverted were integral to black women's missions, but their work was not limited to the private sphere of spiritual experience. The public discourse of church leaders and members, both male and female, had historically linked social regeneration, in the specific form of racial advancement, to spiritual regeneration. According to the ethicist Peter Paris, the principle of human freedom and equality under God constituted the "social teaching" of the black churches. This social teaching survived as a "nonracist appropriation of the Christian faith" and as a critique of American racism. The social teaching of human equality distinguished black churches from their white counterparts and represented a liberating principle "justifying and motivating all endeavors by blacks for survival and transformation."[2]

While the "nonracist" principle called attention to a common tradition shared by black churches, it masked the sexism that black churches shared with the dominant white society. Black women reinterpreted the church's social teaching so that human equality embraced gender as well. In the process, they came to assert their own voice through separate women's societies and through their recognition of an evangelical sisterhood that crossed racial lines. Within a female-centered context, they accentuated the image of woman as saving force, rather than woman as victim. They rejected a model of womanhood that was fragile and passive, just as they deplored a type preoccupied with fashion, gossip, or self-indulgence. They argued that women held the key to social transformation, and thus America offered them a vast mission field in which to solicit as never before the active participation of self-disciplined, self-sacrificing workers.[3] Through the convention movement, black Baptist women established a deliberative arena for addressing their own concerns. Indeed, one could say that the black Baptist church represented a sphere for public deliberation and debate precisely because of women.

## ORTHODOXY'S GENDERED VISION

The feminist theology in the black Baptist church during the late nineteenth century conforms to Rosemary Ruether's and Eleanor McLaughlin's concept of a "stance of radical obedience.'" Referring to female leadership in Christianity, Ruether and McLaughlin distinguished women's positions of "loyal dissent" that arose within the mainline churches from women's positions of heresy that completely rejected the doctrines of the traditional denominations. They argued for the wider influence of women inside rather than outside the denominations, since women in the "stance of 'radical obedience'" seized orthodox theology in defense of sexual equality.[4]

If black Baptist women did not break from orthodoxy, they clearly restated it in progressive, indeed liberating language for women. In many respects their gendered vision of orthodoxy was analogous to the progressive racial theology already espoused by black ministers. In the Jim Crow America of the late nineteenth century, the Reverend Rufus Perry's *The Cushites, or the Descendants of Ham as Found in the Sacred Scriptures* (1893) dared to interpret the Bible as a source of ancient black history—as the root upon which race pride should grow.[5] Nor was a progressive, liberating theology new to blacks. For generations under slavery, African Americans rejected scriptural texts in defense of human bondage. Despite the reluctance of the slavemaster to quote the biblical passage "neither bond nor free in Christ Jesus," the slaves expressed its meaning in their spirituals and prayers. However, in the black Baptist church of the late nineteenth century, the women in the leadership called attention to the verse in its more complete form: "Neither bond nor free, neither male nor female in Christ Jesus."

By expounding biblical precedents, black women presented the intellectual and theological justification for their rights. But they expressed, too, a gendered interpretation of the Bible. The multivalent religious symbols within the Bible had obviously caused slavemasters and slaves, whites and blacks, to invoke "orthodoxy" with meanings quite different from one another. It is perhaps less obvious that the Bible served dually to constrain and liberate women's position vis-á-vis men's in society. Caroline Bynum acknowledges gender differences in the way people appropriate and interpret religion in its symbolic and practical forms, inasmuch as people are gendered beings, not humans in the abstract. Bynum calls attention to the radical potential in this acknowledgment: "For if symbols can invert as well as reinforce social values . . . if traditional rituals can evolve to meet the needs of new participants . . . then old symbols can acquire new meanings, and these new meanings might suggest a new society."[6]

Even more important than the multivalent character of biblical symbolism are the very acts of reappropriation and reinterpretation of the Bible by black women themselves. As interpreters of the Bible, black women mediated its effect in relation to their own interests.

## WOMEN'S THEOLOGIZING

Women members of the male-dominated American National Baptist Convention, forerunner of the National Baptist Convention, U.S.A., were the first to question the illusory unity of the convention as the voice of all its people. Within this national body, Virginia Broughton of Tennessee and Mary Cook and Lucy Wilmot Smith of Kentucky were the most vocal in defense of women's rights. Broughton, Cook, and Smith were active in organizing separate Baptist women's conventions in the face of varying levels of male support and hostility. They spoke for an expanding public of women who stood in opposition to exclusive male power and dominance.

All three women were born in the South during the last years of slavery, but Broughton's background was the most privileged. She described her father as an "industrious man" who hired out his time from his master and subsequently bought his wife's and his own freedom. Raised as a free black, Broughton enrolled in a private school taught by a Professor Daniel Watkins during her adolescent years. She graduated from Fisk University in 1875—claiming to be the first woman of any race to gain a collegiate degree from a southern school. She was married to John Broughton, a lawyer active in Republican Party politics in Memphis, although she continued to work as a teacher and full-time missionary throughout her married life. In 1885, Broughton's feminist attitude surfaced when she challenged the appointment of a less experienced, black male teacher over herself. Supported by her husband, she eventually won her case as head teacher in the Kortrecht school—the only black public school in Memphis to have one year of high school instruction.[7]

After working for twelve years as a teacher in the public school system and as a part-time missionary for at least five of those years, Broughton left the school system to become a full-time missionary. She was immensely popular among southern black and northern white Baptist women. Her stature as a national figure among black Baptists continued to rise in the upcoming century.[8] Broughton's gendered appropriation of biblical symbols shaped her understanding of the women of her own day; she traced the Baptist women's movement and its providential evolution to Eve in the Garden of Eden. In *Women's Work, as Gleaned from the Women of the Bible* (1904), Broughton summed up the ideas that had marked her public lectures, correspondence, and house-to-house visitations since the 1880s, and she sought to inspire the church women of her day "to assume their several callings."[9]

Mary Cook was born a slave in Kentucky in 1862. Raised in a very humble environment, she was able to acquire a college education partly through the philanthropy of white Baptist women in New England and partly through the support of the Reverend William J. Simmons, black Baptist minister and president of the State University at Louisville. Cook graduated from the Normal Department of the State University at Louisville in 1883 and subsequently taught Latin and literature at her alma mater.[10] Like Broughton, Cook worked closely with the black Baptist women of her state and enjoyed communication with northern white Baptist women. In 1898 she married the Reverend Charles H. Parrish, a leader among black Baptists in Kentucky. She was active in the national convention of black Baptist women, which was founded in 1900, and also in secular black women's clubs, especially the National Association of Colored Women.

Cook, the most scholarly of the three women, expressed her views in the black press, in an edited anthology, and in speeches before various groups, including the American National Baptist Convention. She served on the executive board of the ANBC and was honored by being selected to speak on women's behalf in the classic statement of black Baptist doctrine, *The Negro Baptist Pulpit* (1890). In often militant language, Cook strove to enlarge women's power in the church. She termed the Bible an "iconoclastic weapon" that would destroy negative images of her sex and overcome the popular misconceptions of woman's place in the church and society. Like Broughton, Cook derived her position from the "array of heroic and saintly women whose virtues have made the world more tolerable."[11]

Although it is not clear whether Lucy Wilmot Smith was born a slave, she is reported to have grown up in a very poor household. Born in 1861, Smith was raised by her mother, who as sole provider struggled to give her daughter an education. Smith graduated from the Normal Department of the State University at Louisville, taught at her alma mater, and also worked as a journalist. She never married. At the time of her premature death in 1890, she was principal of the Model School at the State University at Louisville. A leader in the Baptist Woman's Educational Convention of Kentucky, she sat on its Board of Managers and served as the secretary of its children's division. Like Cook, she was one of very few women to hold an office in the male-dominated American National Baptist Convention. She served as Historian of the ANBC, wrote extensively in the black press, and delivered strong feminist statements at the annual meetings of the ANBC.[12] She ardently supported women's suffrage. Her death in 1890 prevented her from joining Broughton and Cook in the later movement to organize a national women's convention. Cook eulogized her: "She was connected with all the leading interests of her race and denomination. Her pen and voice always designated her position so clearly that no one need mistake her motive."[13]

None of the women was a theologian in any strict or formal sense, and yet their theocentric view of the world in which they lived justifies calling them theologians in the broad spirit that Gordon Kaufman describes:

> Obviously, Christians are involved in theologizing at every turn. Every attempt to discover and reflect upon the real meaning of the Gospel, of a passage in the Bible, of Jesus Christ, is theologizing; every effort to discover the bearing of the Christian faith or the Christian ethic on the problems of personal and social life is theological. For Christian theology is the critical analysis and creative development of the language utilized in apprehending, understanding, and interpreting God's acts, facilitating their communication in word and deed.[14]

As Kaufman implies, the act of theologizing was not limited to the formally trained male clergy. Nor did it extend only to college-educated women such as Broughton, Cook, and Smith. Scriptural interpretation figured significantly in the meetings of ordinary black women's local and state organizations. Virginia Broughton noted a tremendous groundswell of black women engaged in biblical explication in their homes, churches, and associational meetings.[15] In 1884 Lizzie Crittenden, chairman of the board of managers of the women's convention in Kentucky, identified the women's gendered interpretation of orthodoxy as revelation of their continued organizational growth: "It has really been marvelous how much has been found in the sacred word to encourage us that before had been left unsaid and seemed unheeded."[16] The reports of northern white missionaries in southern black communities confirmed these observations. Mary O'Keefe, a white missionary in Tennessee, wrote to her Chicago headquarters that black women in Bible Bands recited and interpreted passages of Scripture at their meetings. O'Keefe was fascinated by their black expressive culture. One elderly black woman, interpreting a scriptural text, became louder and louder in her delivery. "The last word came out with a whoop," O'Keefe recounted, "which was echoed and re-echoed by the others until it was quite evident that her view was accepted."[17] Mary Burdette, a leader of white Baptist women in the Midwest, also found black Baptist women engaged in biblical study during her tour of Tennessee. The women discussed ancient role models in justification of current demands for participatory parity within the denomination. Burdette described their roundtable discussion: "Six sisters added to the interest by brief essays and addresses relating to women's place and work in the church as illustrated by the women of the Bible. Mrs. Broughton spoke of Eve, the mother of us all and the wife given to Adam for a help-meet, and following her we heard of Deborah, and that from her history we could learn that while men might be called to deliver Israel, they could not do it without the presence and assistance of Christian women."[18]

The enthusiasm with which black women of all educational backgrounds and ages claimed their right to theological interpretation was characterized by Virginia Broughton as part of the "general awakening and rallying together of Christian women" of all races. There were other black women who joined Broughton, Cook, and Smith in voicing gender concerns. Black women interpreters of the Bible perceived themselves as part of the vanguard of the movement to present the theological discussion of woman's place.[19] They used the Bible to sanction both domestic and public roles for women. While each of the feminist theologians had her own unique style and emphasis, a textual analysis of their writings reveals their common concern for women's empowerment in the home, the church, social reform, and the labor force. The Baptist women invoked biblical passages that portrayed positive images of women and reinforced their claim to the public realm. This realm, according to the literary critic Sue E. Houchins, provided black religious women like Broughton and others an arena in which they could transcend culturally proscribed gender roles and "could 'function as person[s] of authority,' could resist the pressures of family and society . . . and could achieve legal and structural support from the church for their work as spiritual advisors, teachers, and occasional preachers."[20]

## THE GOSPEL ACCORDING TO WOMAN
The feminist theologians of the black Baptist church did not characterize woman as having a fragile, impressionable nature, but rather as having a capacity to influence man. They

described woman's power of persuasion over the opposite sex as historically positive, for the most part, although they also mentioned a few instances of woman's negative influence, notably the biblical stories of Delilah and Jezebel. But even this discussion emphasized man's vulnerability to woman's strength, albeit sometimes pernicious, and never recognized an innate feminine weakness to fall to temptation. Mary Cook asserted that woman "may send forth healthy, purifying streams which will enlighten the heart and nourish the seeds of virtue; or cast a dim shadow, which will enshroud those upon whom it falls in moral darkness."[21]

According to the feminist theologians, while the Bible depicted women in a dual image, it also portrayed good and evil men, and thus only affirmed woman's likeness to man and her oneness with him in the joint quest for salvation. Virginia Broughton insisted that the Genesis story explicitly denied any right of man to oppress woman. Her interpretation of woman's creation stressed God's not having formed Eve out of the "crude clay" from which he had molded Adam. She reminded her readers that God purposely sprang Eve from a bone, located in Adam's side and under his heart, for woman to be man's companion and helpmate, and she noted that God took the bone neither from Adam's head for woman to reign over him, nor from his foot for man to stand over her. Broughton observed that if woman had been Satan's tool in man's downfall, she was also God's instrument for human regeneration, since God entrusted the germ for human redemption to Eve alone. By commanding that "the seed of woman shall bruise the serpent's head," God had linked redemption inseparably with motherhood and woman's role in the physical deliverance of the Redeemer.[22]

Feminist theologians praised and took pride in the mothers of Isaac, Moses, Samson, and other greater or lesser heroes of the Old Testament. They described the women of the Old Testament as providing far more than the bodily receptacles through which great men were born into the world. They were responsible for rearing and molding the sons who would deliver Israel from its oppressors. The mother's determining hand could extend as far back as the child's prenatal stage—or so concluded Virginia Broughton in a reference to Samson's mother: "An angel appeared to Manoah's wife, told her she should have a son and instructed her how to deport herself after the conception, that Samson might be such a one as God would have him be, to deliver Israel from the oppression of the Philistines."[23]

Since motherhood was regarded as the greatest sanctity, Mary the mother of Jesus personified the highest expression of womanhood. Of all biblical mothers, she assumed the position of the "last and sublimest illustration in this relation."[24] Hers was motherhood in its purest, most emphatically female form, for it was virginal and thus without the intercession of a man. To the feminist theologians of the black Baptist church, Jesus, conceived from the union of woman and the Angel of God, became the fruition of God's commandment in Genesis. Mary Cook used her knowledge of ancient history and the Latin classics to add further insight concerning the virgin mother theme: she revealed its roots in antiquity by calling attention to the concept of virgin mother as a literary motif. Citing parallels with the story of the twins, Remus and Romulus, the mythical founders of Rome, Mary Cook posited, "Silvia became their mother by the God Mars, even as Christ was the son of the Holy Ghost."[25]

Although motherhood remained the salient image in their writings and speeches, Broughton, Cook, and Smith did not find their own personal lives consumed with maternal responsibilities. Lucy Wilmot Smith never had a husband or child, nor did Mary Cook during the period when she wrote her feminist theological texts. Broughton, on the other hand, was married with five children, and even lectured on the subject of "the ideal mother." Yet she spent little time in the actual role of mothering. She admitted taking her son periodically with her on missionary trips, but more often the care of the younger children fell to older siblings, other family members, and a number of "good women secured from time to time." In fact Broughton noted that all her children were taught domestic duties at an early age. The eldest daughter, Elizabeth, fixed suppers for the family and "was always solicitous about her mother's comfort."[26] Although she wrote lovingly of her children in her autobiography, Broughton undoubtedly valued her missionary work above every other responsibility. This is clearly revealed in the case of her daughter's illness. Broughton canceled a missionary engagement to join her sick daughter Selena, who died a few days after her mother's return home. She never again canceled a missionary engagement, for her daughter's death had taught her that "she could stay home and sit by the bedside of her children and have all the assistance that medical skill could render, and yet God could take her children to himself if he so willed it."[27] What may seem callous by today's standards was not viewed as such by Broughton's household. Broughton describes her last hours with her daughter as loving spiritual moments that influenced all of the family members to "think seriously of heavenly things." Her single-minded devotion to missions did not result in censure or condemnation by her community. Broughton commanded the respect of the women in her community and black Baptist women across the nation.

For feminist theologians such as Cook and Broughton, the image of woman as loyal, comforting spouse transcended the husband-wife relationship to embrace that of Jesus and woman. They were quick to point out that no woman betrayed Jesus and noted that a woman had bathed his feet with her tears and wiped them with her hair, while Mary and Martha had soothed him in their home after his long, tiring journey. Biblical women had expressed their faith through acts of succor and kindness much more than had men. Yet Cook and Broughton coupled woman's domestic image as comforter with the public responsibility of prophesying and spreading the gospel. Cook remarked that in Samaria, Jesus engaged in conversation with the woman at the well, "which was unlawful for a man of respect to do," and by so doing set a new standard for encouraging woman's intellect and permitting "her to do good for mankind and the advancement of His cause."[28]

Their emphasis on woman's relationship with Jesus ironically, albeit subtly, shifted women's duties outside the home, since woman's primary obligation was interpreted to be to God rather than husband. This was evident in Virginia Broughton's own marriage. Broughton resisted pressures of family and society by proclaiming her allegiance to God above family. She boldly alluded to her work as independent of her husband's wishes. Not yet converted when she began mission work, Broughton's husband demanded that she cease this endeavor, since it took her away from home and family for several days at a time. When he asked, "When is this business going to stop?" Broughton replied with what she termed a divinely inspired answer. "I don't know," she hurled at him, "I belong to God first, and you next; so you two must settle it." According to Broughton, her husband eventually came around to her way of thinking, "after a desperate struggle with the world, the flesh, and the devil." Broughton was able to convince her husband that she was called by God for missionary work and that "to hinder her would mean death to him."[29]

During the late nineteenth century feminist theology turned to the example of women leaders in the Old and New Testaments as sanction for more aggressive church work. Both

Cook and Broughton reinterpreted biblical passages that had traditionally restricted woman's role—particularly Paul's dictum in the book of Corinthians that women remain silent in church. For Cook, an analysis of the historical context of Paul's statement revealed that his words were addressed specifically "to a few Grecian and Asiatic women who were wholly given up to idolatry and to the fashion of the day." Her exegesis denied the passage universal applicability. Its adoption in the late nineteenth century served as merely a rationalization to overlook and minimize the important contribution and growing force of woman's work in the church. Both Cook and Broughton argued that Paul praised the work of various women and, at times, depended upon them. The feminist theologians particularly enjoyed citing Paul's respect for Phoebe, the deaconess of the church at Cenchrea. Having entrusted Phoebe with an important letter to Rome, Paul demanded that everyone along her route lend assistance if needed. The Baptist women added the names of others who aided Paul, for example, Priscilla, Mary, Lydia, and "quite a number of women who had been co-workers with the apostle."[30]

The black feminist theologians also found biblical precedent for leadership outside the church in charitable philanthropic work. Olive Bird Clanton, wife of the Reverend Solomon T. Clanton of New Orleans, addressed the American National Baptist Convention in 1887 and maintained that Christian doctrine "has placed the wife by the side of her husband, the daughter by the side of her father, the sister by the side of her brother at the table of the Lord, in the congregation of the sanctuary, male and female met together at the cross and will meet in the realms of glory." Unlike Broughton and Cook, Olive Clanton's northern upbringing made her sensitive to the plight of foreign immigrants and to the squalid conditions in urban tenements. She had little faith in ameliorative legislation if unaccompanied by the activity of women in social reform, especially female education, the care of children, and the cause of social purity. Clanton advocated an aggressive, outgoing Christianity to reach the oppressed and needy class of women and children who did not go to church and thus remained outside the purview of the minister. These types could be helped by women, whose kindness and compassion uniquely qualified them for uplift work. In Clanton's opinion, "the wearied wife, and anxious mother, the lonely woman, often feeling that she is forgotten by the world and neglected by the church will open her heart and life to the gentle Christian woman that has taken the trouble to visit her." She encouraged women to organize social purity societies, sewing schools, and other types of unions in order to uplift the downtrodden.[31] The tireless work of Dorcas, who sewed garments for the needy, became a standard biblical reference for women's charitable work.

Proponents of a feminist theology endeavored to broaden employment opportunities for women. Lucy Wilmot Smith, Historian of the American National Baptist Convention, put the issue squarely before her predominantly male audience in 1886 when she decried the difference in training between boys and girls. She noted that the nineteenth-century woman was dependent as never before upon her own resources for economic survival. Smith believed that girls, like boys, must be taught to value the dignity of labor. She rejected views that considered work for women disdainful, or temporarily necessary at best—views that conceded to women only the ultimate goal of dependency on men. "It is," she wrote, "one of the evils of the day that from babyhood girls are taught to look forward to the time when they will be supported by a father, a brother, or somebody else's brother." She encouraged black women to enter fields other than domestic service and suggested that enterprising women try their hand at poultry raising, small fruit gardening, dairying, bee culture, lecturing, newspaper work, photography, and nursing.[32]

Mary Cook suggested that women seek out employment as editors of newspapers or as news correspondents in order to promote women's causes and to reach other mothers, daughters, and sisters. She advocated teaching youths through the development of juvenile literature and urged women in the denomination's schools to move beyond subordinate jobs by training and applying for positions as teachers and administrators. Cook praised women with careers as writers, linguists, and physicians, and she told the gathering of the American National Baptist Convention in 1887 that women must "come from all the professions, from the humble Christian to the expounder of His word; from the obedient citizen to the ruler of the land."[33]

Again, the Baptist women found biblical precedents to bolster their convictions and to inspire the women of their own day. Cook and Broughton pointed to the biblical woman Huldah, wife of Shallum. Huldah studied the law and interpreted the Word of God to priests and others who sought her knowledge. In the Book of Judges another married woman, Deborah, became a judge, prophet, and warrior whom God appointed to lead Israel against its enemies. Depicting Deborah as a woman with a spirit independent of her husband, Cook asserted: "Her work was distinct from her husband who, it seems, took no part whatever in the work of God while Deborah was inspired by the Eternal expressly to do His will and to testify to her countrymen that He recognizes in His followers neither male nor female, heeding neither the 'weakness' of one, nor the strength of the other, but strictly calling those who are perfect at heart and willing to do His bidding."[34]

Biblical examples had revealed that God used women in every capacity and thus proved that there could be no issue of propriety, despite the reluctance of men. Mary Cook urged the spread of women's influence in every cause, place, and institution that respected Christian values, and she admonished her audience that no profession should be recognized by either men or women if it lacked such values. She concluded her argument with an assertion of women's "legal right" to all honest labor, as she challenged her sisters in the following verse:

> Go, and toil in any vineyard
> Do not fear to do and dare;
> If you want a field of labor
> You can find it anywhere.[35]

## AN AGE OF LIBERAL THEOLOGY

The feminist theology of the black Baptist church reflected several intellectual trends of the late nineteenth century. Like other Americans, the Baptist thinkers accepted a priori the notion of certain intrinsic differences between the male and female identity. The dominant thought of the age embraced an essentialist understanding of gender; it ascribed to womanhood a feminine essence that was virtuous, patient, gentle, and compassionate, while it described manhood as rational, aggressive, forceful, and just. Unlike man, woman was considered naturally religious, bound by greater emotionalism, and with a greater capacity to sympathize and forgive. Since the manifestation of the feminine essence became most readily apparent in the act of raising children in the home, feminine virtues were easily equated with maternal qualities.[36] It appeared axiomatic that God and nature had ordained woman's station in life by providing her with a job and workplace incontestably her own.

At the same time, the Baptist feminist theologians were influenced by the secular woman's movement, which rejected the bifurcation of the private sphere of home and family from the public sphere of business and politics. The goals of organizations such as the National American Woman Suffrage Association and other secular clubs gained momentum during the latter decades of the century among white and black women. These organizations sought to steer women's entrance into the public domain by such routes as voting rights and equal educational and employment opportunities. Yet even though their agenda questioned gender-prescribed roles, most adherents of nineteenth-century feminism remained bridled in a gender-specific, "domesticating" politics.[37] They continued to adhere to essentialist conceptions of gender—defining woman's "nature" as separate and distinct from man's. They translated the preeminence of the maternal responsibility for molding the future character of youth into woman's superior ability to shape the destiny of society. Frances Willard, the suffragist and temperance leader, asserted her belief in "social housekeeping" when she maintained that woman carried her "mother-heart" into the public realm and lost none of her femininity in the process. On the contrary, woman's "gentle touch" refined and softened political institutions, professions, indeed every arena it entered.[38]

Even more directly, the writings and speeches of black Baptists formed part of a feminist-theological literary tradition that spanned the entire nineteenth century. Feminist theological literature especially proliferated in the century's latter decades—the years that the historian Sydney Ahlstrom termed the "golden age of liberal theology." Liberal theology emerged in response to Darwinist biological theories of evolution, Social Darwinism, and a host of geological discoveries and historical studies that challenged what had previously appeared to be the timeless infallibility of the Bible. A radical tendency to deny any sacred authority to the Scriptures found advocates among "infidels" such as Robert Ingersoll and the suffragist Elizabeth Cady Stanton. At the other end of the spectrum stood the fundamentalists, many of whom were southern Protestants, holding tenaciously to the literal truth of each biblical statement despite disclosures of particular inaccuracies and contradictions.[39]

Between these extremes were liberals who came from the pulpits and seminaries of northern Protestant denominations—in fact, some of the same groups responsible for establishing institutions of higher learning for black people in the South. The great majority of these liberals attempted to reconcile their traditional religious beliefs with the new social and scientific theories. By articulating a resilient and vibrant orthodoxy, evangelical liberalism, led by such ministers as Henry Ward Beecher, Newman Smyth, William Newton Clarke, and Washington Gladden, effected the survival of traditional Protestantism in an age of questioning and positivistic devotion to accuracy. Discussing the largely "conservative intent" of this liberalizing influence, Winthrop Hudson argued that the primary interest of the evangelical liberals was not to destroy Christian doctrines, but to restate them "in terms that would be intelligible and convincing and thus to establish them on a more secure foundation."[40]

This exact intent may be attributed to the writings of feminist theologians. Frances Willard, also a contributor to feminist theology, reconciled gender equality with the vital spirit of the Bible. She noted that the insistence on "real facts" had changed not only views toward science and medicine but also those toward theology, causing theology to become more flexible and to see the Bible as an expansive work that "grows in breadth and accuracy with the general growth of humanity." Willard advocated the "scientific interpretation of the Holy Scriptures" and urged women to lend a gendered perspective to the modern exegesis of the Bible.[41]

Feminist theologians who emerged in the mainline denominations argued for women's rights from the standpoint of liberal orthodoxy. They stood in dramatic opposition to Elizabeth Cady Stanton's elaborate condemnation of the Bible in *The Woman's Bible* (1895). Stanton rejected orthodoxy, liberal or conservative. A compilation of interpretive essays from many contributors, *The Woman's Bible* critically questioned the Bible as the divinely inspired authority on women's position in society. Although some of the essays called attention to heroines and positive female images, *The Woman's Bible* pointed overwhelmingly to biblical images that were negative. The Bible, according to Stanton, had served historically as a patriarchal instrument for women's oppression. She condemned it for inspiring women only with the goals of obedience to husbands, subordination to men in general, and self-sacrifice at the expense of their own self-development. *The Woman's Bible* challenged women to reject Christian teachings as set forth in the Bible and to assert full equality with men.[42]

Feminist theology within the mainstream Protestant churches differed significantly from that of Stanton. Its goal was to make religion less sexist, not to make women any less religious. While feminist theology did not make converts of all who professed Protestant liberalism, it represented a significant movement within liberal evangelicalism's effort to relate theology to social issues. During the age of liberal theology, religious education and critical theological scholarship grew with unprecedented dynamism. Referring to the term "Christology" as a coinage of his day, Augustus Strong noted in 1884 that the study of Christ had become a science in its own right.[43] As biblical scholars investigated and debated the human and divine nature of Jesus, some of them also drew attention to his masculine and feminine qualities. In doing so they drew upon Protestant discourses that had their origin early in the nineteenth century and indeed can be traced to the eighteenth century's rooting of morality in the sentiments. The historians Ann Douglas and Barbara Welter, for example, have disclosed a wealth of early nineteenth-century religious and literary materials that identified the church and Christ himself with feminine attributes—representing Christ, that is, as soft, gentle, emotional, and passive.[44] The feminization of Christianity, needless to say, did not go unchallenged either before or after the Civil War. In fact, the debate concerning the association of the church and Savior with feminine virtues lost none of its vibrancy after 1875, as feminist theologians and women generally used a feminine image of Christ to justify their struggle for social justice in general and for women's rights in particular.

Opponents of the feminine version of religion often conceded the feminine attributes in Christ but reaffirmed the predominance of the masculine. Gail Bederman argues that movements such as the Men and Religion Forward Movement and other advocates of a "muscular Christianity" adopted cultural constructions of gender in order to reconcile religion to the modern "corporate, consumer-oriented order" of the twentieth century.[45] The masculinist perspective countered efforts to subsume Christ's manliness in the glorification of the feminine by contending that his feminine virtues, namely, tenderness, sympathy, and forgiveness, were subordinate to his masculine attributes of assertive leadership, strong intellect, and business acumen. Defenders of the masculine orientation evoked the image of the "church militant" in the religious conquest of the world, and they offered a "tough Christianity" with stern, uncompromising features as a counterpoint to the softness and emotionalism of a feminized church.[46]

## DOUBLE GENDER CONSCIOUSNESS

Black Baptist men and women did not debate Christ's feminine versus masculine nature, but the duality captured the complexity of images surrounding their own racial and gender identities. A dialogic imagery of Christ as simultaneously feminine and masculine, passive and aggressive, meek and conquering informed African Americans' self-perceptions and self-motivations. This was true for them as individuals and as a group. Black Baptist women continually shifted back and forth from feminine to masculine metaphors as they positioned themselves simultaneously within racial and gendered social space. Whether united with black men, or working separately in their own conventions or cooperatively with white Baptist women, black Baptist women expressed a dual gender consciousness—defining themselves as both homemakers and soldiers. Their multiple consciousness represented a shifting dialogic exchange in which both race and gender were ultimately destabilized and blurred in meaning.

On the one hand, black Baptist women spoke in unambiguous gendered symbols. Virginia Broughton called attention to the feminine symbolism in the Bible (for example, the designation of the church as the "bride" of Christ), and she regarded such metaphors as conveying biblical esteem for women.[47] The black feminist theologians also contextualized women's gains in society within an evolutionary framework that repeatedly referred to the degraded status of women in ancient civilizations and in contemporary non-Christian cultures, and they argued that the standard of womanhood evolved to a higher plane with the spread of Christianity. This view undergirded their emphasis on motherhood and domesticity. Since mothers were considered to be the transmitters of culture, woman's virtue and intelligence within the home measured the progress of African Americans and all of civilization.[48]

Black Baptist women shared common bonds with white Baptist women who worked in similar societies. They were familiar with the history of white Baptist women's societies and praised their work for the freedpeople at the end of the Civil War. The white Baptist missionary Joanna P. Moore played an influential role in the lives of a number of southern black women. Moore cited biblical precedents for women as teachers and church leaders, although her conviction that women should engage in teaching, house-to-house visitation, and temperance work never minimized for her the singular importance of woman's domestic role. Her views coincided with the views of the black feminist theologians whose image of women's religious duties posited them within the traditional home setting, at the same time as they beckoned women into the world to spread the faith.[49]

The feminist theologians of the black Baptist church considered the combined efforts of black and white women critical to the progress of black people and to harmonious race relations. By Christianizing the home and educating the masses, women provided the key to solving the race problem in America. Black women likened their role to that of the biblical Queen Esther, who had acted as an intermediary between the king and her people. They envisioned themselves as intermediaries between white America and their own people. Expressing the biblical analogy, Mrs. H. Davis compared Ida B. Wells to Queen Esther and praised her crusade against lynching on the front page of the *National Baptist World:* "We have found in our race a queen Esther, a woman of high talent, that has sounded the bugle for a defenceless race."[50]

Women such as Virginia Broughton, Mary Cook, and Lucy Wilmot Smith epitomized the high quality of woman's rational powers. Widely read, this educated female elite implicitly and explicitly challenged the conviction that assigned intellect to men and emotionalism to women. Mary Cook explained the cultivation of the female intellect as Christ's special mission to women and blamed sexism, not Christianity, for hindering women's intellectual development. "Emancipate woman," she demanded, "from the chains that now restrain her and who can estimate the part she will play in the work of the denomination."[51]

Yet the feminist sentiments articulated by these black Baptist theologians were neither uniform nor rigid. At times Virginia Broughton appeared to soften her demands for women's presence within the highest denominational councils and to adopt a more conciliatory attitude toward men. She urged, if sometimes with tongue in cheek, complementary work with a deeper sensitivity to what she called man's "long cherished position of being ruler of all he surveys." She referred to the "womanly exercise" of talent, and at a time when woman's role was emergent but not clearly defined, she tended to assure men that women would not seek unauthorized office.[52]

Lucy Wilmot Smith spoke less circumspectly. In strong feminist language, she insisted upon new expectations of women. Smith revealed her outspoken belief in the need for women to adopt attitudes identified as male in outlook: "Even in our own America, in this last quarter of the Nineteenth Century ablaze with the electric light of intelligence, if she [woman] leaves the paths made straight and level by centuries of steady tramp of her sex, she is denominated strong-minded or masculine by those who forget that 'new occasions make new duties.'"[53]

However, Lucy Smith could subordinate easily, almost imperceptibly, her feminist consciousness to that of race. On one such occasion she stated that educated black women held certain advantages over white women. She believed that the identical labor reality for male and female slaves created a solidarity not found in the white race, and she praised the black man of her day for continuing to keep his woman by his side as he moved into new types of work. Smith noted that the white woman "has had to contest with her brother every inch of the ground for recognition."[54] Mary Cook spoke of the freedom women exercised within the Baptist denomination and told the men of the American National Baptist Convention: "I am not unmindful of the kindness you noble brethren have exhibited in not barring us from your platforms and deliberations. All honor I say to such men."[55] Thus racial consciousness equally informed their identity and their understanding of gender.

Racial consciousness placed black women squarely beside black men in a movement for racial self-determination, specifically in the quest for national black Baptist hegemony. From the perspective of racial self-help, this movement so blurred values and behavior exclusively associated with either the masculine or the feminine identity that it implicitly undermined the validity of gender dichotomies. Despite nineteenth-century essentialist assumptions about woman's moral superiority, the black Baptist women's preoccupation with "respectability," as the cornerstone for racial uplift, never tolerated a double standard of behavior on the part of men and women.[56] In the same vein, concepts such as self-sacrifice and patience lost their traditionally feminine connotations and became sources of strength

endorsed by men, not only women. Black ministers championed self-denial as a prerequisite for race development, while they hailed patience as the self-control necessary to build a
strong black denominational force.

For nineteenth-century African Americans, distinctions between the feminine and
masculine identity were complicated by a racial system that superimposed "male" characteristics upon all whites (male and female) and "feminine characteristics" upon all blacks
(male and female). Theories of racial essence, what George Fredrickson termed "romantic
racialism," paralleled and overlapped essentialist gender assumptions. During the nineteenth century and into the twentieth, both blacks and whites subscribed to theories of innate characteristics and behaviorism that captured the soul of each race. Within the
human family, so romantic racialists theorized, black people embodied an essence that was
musical, emotional, meek, and religious. In contrast, the white race was perceived to be intellectual, pragmatic, competitive, and with a disposition to dominate. The counterposing
of the two races paralleled the feminine-masculine dichotomy. During the Civil War, the
white abolitionist Theodore Tilton described blacks as the "feminine race of the world." In
the early twentieth century, Robert Park, the white sociologist, similarly described the
Negro as an "artist, loving life for its own sake. . . . He is, so to speak, the lady of the
races."[57]

Although blacks usually rejected the explicit analogy between their "soul qualities" and
the feminine essence, they invariably re-presented and re-constructed a group identity
with qualities reminiscent of those ascribed to women. Harvard-trained W. E. B. Du Bois
championed theories of racial distinctiveness. In his article "The Conservation of Races,"
published in 1897, Du Bois disclosed his recognition and admiration for what he believed
to be the "spiritual, psychical" uniqueness of his people—their "special gift" to humanity.[58]
In *The Gift of Black Folk* (1924) he opined that the meekness and "sweet spirit" of black
people "has breathed the soul of humility and forgiveness into the formalism and cant of
American religion."[59] For blacks, the idealization of race served to negate notions of white
superiority and, in turn, the legitimacy of white male power and racist institutions. Like
the feminine ideal, the racial ideal valorized a more equitable, inclusive society.[60]

Perceiving themselves to be joined in a struggle for the economic, educational, and
moral advancement of their people, black Baptist men as well as women employed masculine symbols when characterizing black women's efforts to combat the legacy of slavery
and the continued rise of racism at the turn of the twentieth century. By so doing, black
women and men once again confounded interpretations of race and gender essentialism
that had their origins in white discourses. The black women in the Baptist church fused the
rhetoric of war with that of domesticity. They represented themselves as the "home force"
while at the same time exhorting one another to assume the role of valiant "soldier"—to
go out into the "highways and hedges" and forge the "link between the church militant and
the church triumphant."[61] Virginia Broughton looked to both the Bible and history for validation: "But what about man going alone to war? We answer by asking who was it that
drove the nail into Sisera's temple? And what of the heroism of Joan of Arc? War is one of
man's inventions; it is not good in itself, neither is it good for man to go to war alone, most
especially in the Lord's work."[62]

This aggressive attitude, commonly identified with male subjectivity, underlay the black
women's determination to insert their voices boldly into the deliberative arena of the convention movement. The Old Testament figures Deborah and Huldah became the recurrent

reference points illustrating woman's capacity to combine humility and grace with aggressive zeal and strong intellect. The examples of Deborah and Huldah were also cited by the black Baptist women to prove that marriage need not negate public leadership for women.

The feminist theology of the black Baptist church never altered the hierarchical structure of the church by revolutionizing power relations between the sexes, nor did it inhibit ministers from assuming men's intellectual and physical superiority over women.[63] To the ire of black women, the black newspaper *Virginia Baptist* in 1894 presented a two-part series that adopted biblical arguments for restricting women's church work to singing and praying. The newspaper claimed divine authority in denying women the right to teach, preach, and vote.[64] Although the black feminist theologians opposed this line of thought, they did not challenge the basis for male monopoly of the clergy, nor did they demand equal representation in conventions in which both men and women participated. But feminist theology stirred women to find their own voice and create their own sphere of influence.

Feminist theology had significant implications for black Baptist women's future work. It buttressed their demand for more vocal participation and infused their growing ranks with optimism about the dawning twentieth century. It also encouraged women to establish and control their own separate conventions at the state and national levels. Black Baptist women did not, in the end, demand a radical break with all the sexist limitations of their church, but they were surely ingenious in fashioning the Bible as an "iconoclastic weapon" for their particular cause. The feminist theologians had operated "from a stance of 'radical obedience.'" And indeed it was this vantage of orthodoxy that compelled the brethren to listen.

## NOTES

1. Peter Randolph, *From Slave Cabin to the Pulpit: The Autobiography of Rev. Peter Randolph* (Boston: James H. Earle, Publisher, 1893), 89. Charles O. Boothe, *The Cyclopedia of the Colored Baptists of Alabama* (Birmingham: Alabama Publishing Company, 1895), 252; also see Jacqueline Jones, *Labor of Love, Labor of Sorrow: Black Women, Work, and the Family from Slavery to the Present* (New York: Random House, 1985), 67.

2. Peter J. Paris, *The Social Teaching of the Black Churches* (Philadelphia: Fortress Press, 1985), 11–13.

3. Mary V. Cook, "Work for Baptist Women," in Edward M. Brawlet, ed., *The Negro Baptist Pulpit* (Philadelphia: The American Baptist Publication Society, 1890), 271–285; American National Baptist Convention (hereafter ANBC), *Journal and Lectures of the Second Anniversary of the 1887 American National Baptist Convention, Held with the Third Baptist Church, Mobile, Ala., August 25–28, 1887* (n.p., n.d.), 57.

4. Rosemary Ruether and Eleanor McLaughlin, eds., *Women of Spirit: Female Leadership in the Jewish and Christian Traditions* (New York: Simon and Schuster, 1979), 19; also see this argument applied to white women during the Second Great Awakening in Carroll Smith-Rosenberg, "The Cross and the Pedestal: Women, Anti-Ritualism, and the Emergence of the American Bourgeoisie," in Smith-Rosenberg, *Disorderly Conduct: Visions of Gender in Victorian America* (New York: Oxford University Press, 1986), 129–164.

5. Rufus Perry traced the ancestry of black Americans to the biblical Cushites, who were the descendants of Cush, Ham's eldest son. According to Perry, the Cushites were the ancient Ethiopians and indigenous Egyptians whose history exemplified prowess in medicine, war, art, and religious thought. Identifying the Cushite leaders of the Bible, Perry considered the greatness of the African past to be the foundation stone of the African American's future. See Rufus L. Perry, *The Cushites, or the Descendants of Ham as Found in the Sacred Scriptures and in the Writings of Ancient Historians and Poets from Noah to the Christian Era* (Springfield, Mass.: Willey, 1893), 17–18, 158–161.

6. Caroline Walker Bynum, Steven Harrell, and Paula Richman, eds., *Gender and Religion: On the Complexity of Symbols* (Boston: Beacon Press, 1986), 15–16.

7. See Kathleen Berkeley's discussion of the Broughton case. Berkeley argues that the case was more than simply one of gender discrimination, but a power struggle between the white superintendent of schools and a black member of the school board. Kathleen C. Berkeley, "The Politics of Black Education in Memphis, Tennessee, 1868–1891," in Rick Ginsberg and David N. Plank, eds., *Southern Cities, Southern Schools: Public Education in the Urban South* (Westport, Conn.: Greenwood Press, 1990), 215–217.

8. Broughton was elected to office in the Woman's Convention, Auxiliary of the National Baptist Convention, U.S.A., when it was organized in 1990. She held the office of recording secretary in this organization, which represented more than one million black women across the United States. See National Baptist Convention, *Journal of the Twentieth Annual Session of the National Baptist Convention, Held in Richmond, Virginia, September 12–17, 1900* (Nashville: National Baptist Publishing Board, 1900), 195–196. See also Thomas O. Fuller, *History of the Negro Baptists of Tennessee* (Memphis: Haskins Print-Roger Williams College, 1936), 238.

9. Virginia Broughton, *Women's Work, as Gleaned from the Women of the Bible, and Bible Women of Modern Times* (Nashville: National Baptist Publishing Board, 1904), 3, 23, 36.

10. I. Garland Penn, *The Afro-American Press and Its Editors* (Springfield, Mass.: Willey, 1891), 367–374; G. R. Richings, *Evidences of Progress among Colored People*, 12th ed. (Philadelphia: Geo. S. Ferguson, 1905), 224–227; Charles H. Parrish, ed., *Golden Jubilee of the General Association of Colored Baptists in Kentucky* (Louisville, Ky.: Mayes Printing Company, 1915), 284–285; State University Catalogue, 1883–1884, Simmons University Records, Archives Department, University of Louisville.

11. Brawley, ed., *The Negro Baptist Pulpit*, 271–286; ANBC, *Journal and Lectures, 1887*, 49.

12. Penn, *The Afro-American Press*, 376–381.

13. See Mary Cook's eulogy of Lucy Wilmot Smith in *Home Mission Echo* (January 1890): 4–5; Penn, *Afro-American Press*, 378–381; Woman's American Baptist Home Mission Society (hereafter WABHMS), *Twelfth Annual Report of the Woman's American Baptist Home Mission Society with the Report of the Annual Meeting, Held in the First Baptist Church, Hartford, Connecticut, May 7–8, 1890* (Boston: C. H. Simonds, 1890), 26.

14. Gordon D. Kaufman, *Systematic Theology: An Historicist Perspective* (New York: Charles Scribner's Sons, 1968), 57.

15. Virginia W. Broughton, *Twenty Years' Experience of a Missionary* (Chicago: The Pony Press Publishers, 1907), 32.

16. *Minutes of the Baptist Women's Educational Convention of Kentucky. First, Second, Third, Fourth, Fifth Sessions, 1883–1887* (Louisville, Ky.: National Publishing Company, Print, 1887), 13.

17. Miss M. O'Keefe to Mary Burdette, 4 April 1891, Mary Burdette File, Correspondence 1891–1898, WABHMS Archives, American Baptist Archives Center, Valley Forge, Penn.

18. See report of Mary Burdette, "Our Southern Field," *Tidings* (January 1894): 9.

19. Mary Cook stated: "As the Bible is an iconoclastic weapon—it is bound to break down images of error that have been raised. As no one studies it so closely as the Baptists, their women shall take the lead." ANBC, *Journal and Lectures, 1887*, 49.

20. See introduction by Sue E. Houchins, *Spiritual Narratives* (New York: Oxford University Press, 1988), xxxii. *Spiritual Narratives* includes Virginia Broughton's autobiography, *Twenty Years' Experience of a Missionary*, along with those of Maria Stewart, Jarena Lee, Julia A. J. Foote, and Ann Plato.

21. ANBC, *Journal and Lectures, 1887*, 53–54; also see the evaluation of woman's influence by black Baptist minister William Bishop Johnson, editor of *The National Baptist Magazine*, when he stated: "Man may lead unnumbered hosts to victory, he may rend kingdoms, convulse nations, and drench battlefields in blood, but woman with heavenly smiles and pleasant words can outnumber, outweight, and outstrip the noblest efforts of a generation." William Bishop Johnson, *The Scourging of a Race, and Other Sermons and Addresses* (Washington, D.C.: Beresford Printer, 1904), 78.

22. Broughton, *Women's Work*, 5–7.

23. Ibid., 11–16.

24. Ibid., 25.

25. Mary Cook described Mary, the mother of Jesus, as "non-excelled maternal devotion." See ANBC, *Journal and Lectures, 1887*, 47–48.

26. Broughton, *Twenty Years' Experience*, 48–51.

27. Ibid., 42–45, 48.

28. Broughton, *Women's Work*, 31–32; Brawley, ed., *Negro Baptist Pulpit*, 273.

29. Broughton, *Twenty Years' Experience*, 46–47. Sue Houchins argues that Broughton and women like her drew confidence to transcend prescriptive gender roles from belief in the "privileged nature of their relationship with God." See introduction by Houchins, *Spiritual Narratives*, xxxiii.

30. The argument that attempted to restrict Paul's words exclusively to "immoral" women of Corinth was used by both black and white advocates of greater church roles for women. See, for example, Frances Willard, *Women in the Pulpit* (Boston: D. Lothrop, 1888), 159, 164; ANBC, *Journal and Lectures, 1887*, 48–50.

31. Olive Bird Clanton was raised in Decatur, Illinois, where she obtained a high school education. Her husband was elected secretary of the American National Baptist Convention in 1886. In a biographical sketch of Solomon Clanton, William J. Simmons, then president of the American National Baptist Convention, described Olive Clanton as "one of the most discreet, amiable, and accomplished women in the country." See William J. Simmons, *Men of Mark: Eminent, Progressive and Rising* (Cleveland: Geo. M. Rewell, 1887), 419–421; ANBC, *Journal and Lectures, 1887*, 56–57.

32. ANBC, *Minutes and Addresses of the American National Baptist Convention, Held at St. Louis, Mo., August 25–29, 1886 in the First Baptist Church* (Jackson, Miss.: J. J. Spelman, Publisher, 1886), 68–74.

33. ANBC, *Journal and Lectures, 1887*, 50–53, 55–56.

34. Ibid., 47; Broughton, *Women's Work*, 27–28.

35. ANBC, *Journal and Lectures, 1887*, 55–56.

36. For discussions on the cult of motherhood and domesticity, as well as treatment of woman's unique qualities relative to man's, see the following: Ann Douglas, *The Feminization of American Culture* (New York: Alfred A. Knopf, 1977), 87–89; Barbara Welter, "The Cult of True Womanhood, 1820–1860," *American Quarterly*, 18 (Spring 1966): 151–174; Katherine Kish Sklar, *Catherine Beecher: A Study in American Domesticity* (New York: W. W. Norton, 1976), 134–137; Anne Firor Scott, *The Southern Lady: From Pedestal to Politics, 1830* (Chicago: University of Chicago Press, 1970), 37; also see this discussion as part of the evolving themes in women's history in Linda K. Kerber, "Separate Spheres, Female Worlds, Woman's Place: The Rhetoric of Women's History," *Journal of American History*, 75 (June 1988): 9–39.

37. See Paula Baker, "The Domestication of Politics: Women and Political Society, 1780–1920," *American Historical Review* 89 (June 1984): 620–647; Michael McGerr, "Political Style and Women's Power, 1830–1930," *Journal of American History* 77 (December 1990): 864–885.

38. Willard, *Women in the Pulpit*, 54, 64; Douglas, *Feminization of American Culture*, 51–52.

39. Sydney E. Ahlstrom, *A Religious History of the American People* (New Haven: Yale University Press, 1972), 763–787; Arthur Meier Schlesinger, "A Critical Period in American Protestantism, 1875–1900," *Massachusetts Historical Society Proceedings*, 64 (1930–1932): 523–548; Richard Hofstadter, *Social Darwinism in American Thought, 1860–1915* (Philadelphia: University of Pennsylvania Press, 1944), 1–16, 88; Barbara Welter, "Something Remains to Dare," introduction to Elizabeth Cady Stanton et al., *The Woman's Bible* (1895; rpt. New York: Arno Press, 1974), V–XI.

40. The label "progressive orthodoxy," coined by the faculty of Andover Seminary in 1884, characterized the majority of evangelical liberals who sought to retain Christian doctrine as much as possible while allowing for adjustment when necessary. See Winthrop S. Hudson, *Religion in America: An Historical Account of the Development of American Religious Life*, 2nd ed. (New York: Charles Scribner's Sons, 1973), 269–274.; Martin E. Marty, *Modern American Religion*, vol. 1 (Chicago: University of Chicago Press, 1986), 17–43.

41. Mary Cook also encouraged the belief in a living, rather than static doctrine and argued that women's freedom would grow with the "vitalizing principles" of the Baptist denomination. Frances Willard's position was more extreme than Cook's, however. In order to discourage literalism, Willard presented a two-page chart that graphically revealed changing, ambivalent, and contradictory biblical references to women. Willard also rejected literalism's opposite tendency, or what she termed "playing fast and loose." ANBC, *Journal and Lectures, 1887*, 49; Willard, *Woman in the Pulpit*, 17–38, 50.

42. See Matilda Jocelyn Gage, *Woman, Church, and State*, 2nd ed. (New York: The Truth Seeker Company, 1893); and Welter, "Something Remains to Dare," *Woman's Bible*, XXV–XXXIV; Aileen S. Kraditor, ed., *Up From the Pedestal: Selected Writings in the History of American Feminism* (Chicago: Quadrangle Books, 1968), 108–121.

43. Augustus H. Strong, *Philosophy and Religion* (New York: A. C. Armstrong and Son, 1888), 201.

44. Douglas, *Feminization of American Culture*, 9–13; Barbara Welter, "The Feminization of American Religion: 1800–1860," in Mary Hartman and Lois Banner, eds., *Clio's Consciousness Raised: New Perspectives in the History of Women* (New York: Harper and Row, 1974), 137–157.

45. Bederman notes that church membership remained more than 60 percent female for nearly two centuries and that the perceived crisis of a "fem-

inized church" reflected in actuality the "gendered coding of contemporary languages of religion and of power." In short, feminized Protestantism was deemed acceptable to men during the era of laissez-faire capitalism. It went hand in hand with the old middle-class virtues of hard work, thrift, and self-sacrifice. While these values served "an individualistic, producer-oriented middle class," they were rendered anachronistic to the emergent corporate capitalism of the Gilded Age. See Gail Bederman, "'The Women Had Charge of the Church Work Long Enough': The Men and Religion Forward Movement of 1911–1912 and the Masculinization of Middle Class Protestantism," *American Quarterly* 41 (September 1989): 432–461; also T. Jackson Lears, *No Place of Grace: Anti-Modernism and the Transformation of American Culture 1880–1920* (New York: Pantheon Books, 1981), 104.

46. Twenty years before Matheson, a white Baptist minister, the Reverend Augustus Strong, stated that Christ had brought new respect to passive virtues at a time when the world had hitherto exalted only manly virtues. Strong's writings nonetheless insist on Christ's dominant masculinity. Strong incurred the ire of suffragists, since he opposed woman's suffrage and believed in woman's subordination to man in office based on biblical authority. See Strong, *Philosophy and Religion*, 400–416, 549–550. Another white Baptist minister, Jesse Hungate, denied woman's right to ordination, maintaining that the ministry was the divine calling of men. Hungate stressed the necessity of woman's subordination to her husband. Included in his book are the responses of seventy-two Baptist ministers who overwhelmingly agreed with Hungate's opposition to women in the clergy. See Jesse Hungate, *The Ordination of Women to the Pastorate in Baptist Churches* (Hamilton, N.Y.: James B. Grant, University Bookstore, 1899), 4–5, 11, 13–14, 29–36, 46, 69–84, 101–102.

47. Such metaphors could present interesting consequences. For Virginia Broughton, they seemed to offer unambiguous masculine and feminine images: "By no title could our risen Lord endear himself more to women than that of bridegroom and thus it is he likens his return in the parable of the 'Ten Virgins.' " For the sexist, masculine bias of white Baptist Jesse Hungate, the common designation of the church as the "bride" of Christ led him to assert his demand for a manly Christianity, stating: "She is the church militant; who is also the conquering one." See Broughton, *Women's Work*, 43–44; Hungate, *Ordination of Women*, 35.

48. The argument that woman's status evolved with Christianity was advanced by critics for and against woman's rights. It put religious emphasis on the general impetus of Social Darwinism. The anti-women's rights group argued that Christianity's civilizing influence heightened differences between men and women. The higher the culture, the more women were removed from the hardening contact with labor alongside men. Women were able to confine their duties to home and family and thus became more refined and delicate. The black Baptist writers did not stress this particular theme as much as they argued the direct relation between Christianity and the sanctity of marriage and home life. They focused on women's victimization in non-Christian cultures in antiquity and the present. In non-Christian cultures, women were described as merchandise subject to barter, polygamy, and marriage without love or "delicacy." See ANBC, *Minutes and Addresses, 1886*, 69; ANBC, *Journal and Lectures 1887*, 45–46; ANBC, *Journal, Sermons, and Lectures, 1888*, 89–90; also see Hofstadter, *Social Darwinism*, 24–29; Strong, *Philosophy and Religion*, 405–406; Hungate, *Ordination of Women*, 41–42; Case, *The Masculine in Religion*, 5–7.

49. The title of Joanna Moore's autobiography showed that she viewed her own work as surrogate to Christ's. See Joanna P. Moore, *In Christ's Stead* (Chicago: Women's Baptist Home Mission Society, 1895), 131–133, 139–140, 146.

50. Another comparison of Ida B. Wells with Esther in the Bible appeared in H. J. Moore, "Let America Beware," *National Baptist World*, 12 October 1894; [Mrs.] H. Davis, "A Moses Wanted," *National Baptist World*, 5 October 1894.

51. ANBC, *Journal and Lectures 1887*, 48–49.

52. Broughton, *Women's Work*, 37–40, 43.

53. ANBC, *Minutes and Addresses, 1886*, 69, ANBC, *Journal and Lectures, 1887*, 48.

54. Penn, *Afro-American Press*, 380–381.

55. ANBC, *Journal and Lectures, 1887*, 49.

56. Broughton, *Women's Work*, 32.

57. George Fredrickson discusses "romantic racialism" within the context of the "benign" view of black distinctiveness. This view was upheld by romanticism, abolitionism, and evangelical religion and should be distinguished from anti-black sentiments which vilified blacks as beasts and unworthy of human dignity. See *The Black Image in the White Mind: The Debate on the Afro-American Character and Destiny, 1817–1914* (New York: Harper and Row, 1972), 101–115, 125–126; Everett C. Hughes et al., eds., *The Collected Papers of Robert Ezra Park* (Glencoe, Ill.: Free Press, 1950), 280,

quoted in Stanford M. Lyman, *The Black American in Sociological Thought* (New York: Capricorn Books, 1973), 42.

58. Du Bois stated: "But while race differences have followed mainly physical race lines, yet no mere physical distinctions would really define or explain the deeper differences—the cohesiveness and continuity of these groups. The deeper differences are spiritual, psychical, differences—undoubtedly based on the physical but infinitely transcending them." W. E. B. Du Bois, "The Conservation of Races," in Philip S. Foner, ed., *W. E. B. Du Bois Speaks: Speeches and Addresses, 1890–1919* (New York: 1970), 77–79, 84.

59. W. E. Burghardt Du Bois, *The Gift of Black Folk: The Negroes in the Making of America* (New York: Washington Square Press, 1970), 178.

60. Blacks, more often than whites, counterposed a black ideal against white in distinguishing the two races. Outstanding black leaders such as W. E. B. Du Bois, Edward Wilmot Blyden, Benjamin Brawley, son of Baptist leader Edward M. Brawley, and Nannie H. Burroughs, the corresponding secretary of the Woman's Convention of the black Baptist church, expounded theories of "romantic racialism." See James McPherson, *Abolitionist*

*Legacy: From Reconstruction to the NAACP* (Princeton, N.J.: Princeton University Press, 1975), 67–68, 344; Nannie H. Burroughs, "With All Thy Getting," *Southern Workman*, 56 (July 1927): 301.

61. ANBC, *Journal and Lectures, 1887,* 46–47, 49–50, 54–55, 57; Brawley, *The Negro Baptist Pulpit,* 285. Black Baptist minister William Bishop Johnson also used the warfare motif when addressing women, and he challenged them to fulfill their obligations to God "by going forth into the highways and hedges and compelling men to bow allegiance to Calvary's cross." Johnson, *Scourging of a Race,* 78–79.

62. Broughton, "Woman's Work," *National Baptist Magazine* (January 1894): 33.

63. Anthony Binga does not describe women outside the role of homemaker; William Bishop Johnson contended that men did not give women their proper estimation in society, and yet he also assigned to man the qualities of "understanding" and "mind," and to woman, "will" and "soul." See Binga, *Sermons,* 293; Johnson, *Scourging of a Race,* 76.

64. See the response of black club women to the *Virginia Baptist* articles in "Editorial—Woman's Place," *The Woman's Era,* 1 (September 1894).

# THE PRINCE HALL MASONS AND THE AFRICAN AMERICAN CHURCH

*David G. Hackett*

It is still not well known that from the middle to the end of the nineteenth century the feminization of white American Protestantism was paralleled by the growth of white fraternal orders. By 1900, one out of every four white adult male Americans—and a majority of those living in urban settings and working in white-collar occupations— were members of such organizations as the Odd Fellows, Freemasons, Knights of Pythias, Red Men, and hundreds of smaller orders. Among the white urban middle class, the women were in the churches and the men were in the lodges. Even less well known is the importance of fraternal orders among African American men. In the late nineteenth century nearly every prominent African American man was a member of either the black Prince Hall Masons or the Colored Odd Fellows. Unlike white middle-class men who, some scholars have argued, swarmed to the lodges as part of a rite of passage away from the church's maternal "feminine" theology and toward the aggressive "masculine" demands of the workplace, leading black men were actively involved in both the church and the lodge.

In his analysis of the Prince Hall Masons and the African American Church, David Hackett employs a case study of the African Methodist Episcopal Zion bishop and Prince Hall grand master James Walker Hood to explore the nexus of fraternal lodges and African American Christianity at the turn into the twentieth century. Though significantly different in their beliefs and rituals, the black church and the Prince Hall lodge were structurally similar organizations that appealed to the same broad cohort of young African American men. The origins of this relationship are traced to the post-Revolutionary era when both mutual benefit societies and the black church provided resources for black autonomy and barricades against white racism. Following the Civil War, these two interwoven social institutions came to the South offering black Southerners similar "race histories" that countered white racial images while providing meaning and hope for their lives. Though rarely recognized by white Americans, after the Civil War the Prince Hall Masons flourished among African American men, providing, alongside the black church, a separate male sphere that reinforced a collective sense of African American identity and pride.

Reprinted by permission from David G. Hackett, "The Prince Hall Masons and the African American Church: The Labors of Grand Master and Bishop James Walker Hood, 1831–1918." *Church History*, 69:4 (December, 2000), 770–802.

# 14

# THE PRINCE HALL MASONS AND THE AFRICAN AMERICAN CHURCH

## The Labors of Grand Master and Bishop James Walker Hood, 1831–1918

*David G. Hackett*

DURING THE LATE NINETEENTH CENTURY, James Walker Hood was bishop of the North Carolina Conference of the African Methodist Episcopal Zion Church and grand master of the North Carolina Grand Lodge of Prince Hall Masons. In his forty-four years as bishop, half of that time as senior bishop of the denomination, Reverend Hood was instrumental in planting and nurturing his denomination's churches throughout the Carolinas and Virginia. Founder of North Carolina's denominational newspaper and college, author of five books including two histories of the AMEZ Church, appointed assistant superintendent of public instruction and magistrate in his adopted state, Hood's career represented the broad mainstream of black denominational leaders who came to the South from the North during and after the Civil War. Concurrently, Grand Master Hood superintended the southern jurisdiction of the Prince Hall Masonic Grand Lodge of New York and acted as a moving force behind the creation of the region's black Masonic lodges—often founding these secret male societies in the same places as his fledgling churches. At his death in 1918, the Masonic Quarterly Review hailed Hood as "one of the strong pillars of our foundation."[1] If Bishop Hood's life was indeed, according to his recent biographer, "a prism through which to understand black denominational leadership in the South during the period 1860–1920,"[2] then what does his leadership of both the Prince Hall Lodge and the AMEZ Church tell us about the nexus of fraternal lodges and African-American Christianity at the turn of the twentieth century?

Scholars have noted but not substantially investigated the significance of fraternal orders for African American religious life. At the turn of the century, W. E. B. Du Bois saw in these secret societies hope for the uplift of blacks through "mastery of the art of social organized life."[3] In 1910, Howard Odum ranked black fraternal orders equal in membership to the black church and "sometimes" more important.[4] In fact, according to *Who's Who of the Colored Race* for 1915, two-thirds of the most prominent African Americans held membership in both a national fraternal order and the black church. Forty-two percent of those holding joint memberships were Prince Hall Masons, one-third of whom were clergymen or church officers.[5] Subsequent research has explored the economic, class, and political importance of these orders while continuing to document their pervasive presence in

African American society.[6] Yet none of these investigators has ventured into the meaning of fraternal beliefs and rituals for their members and rarely have they explored the relationship between secret societies and the black church.[7]

In addition to the tendency among historians to underemphasize rites and beliefs, the study of the religious life of black fraternal orders has suffered from a paucity of evidence. The otherwise prolific Bishop Hood left few references to his lodge membership. Unlike the study of white lodges, which pose a problem not so much of finding materials as making sense of them,[8] Prince Hall primary materials are harder to locate. This has partly to do with the scarcity of these records and partly with the still enforced "secrecy" of this secret society.[9] Nevertheless, in Hood's case some of the annual proceedings of the North Carolina Grand Lodge are available and these records along with the minutes of the AMEZ North Carolina Conference allow us to observe similarities and differences between the two organizations and the role Hood played in each. Also available are several Prince Hall histories, some state by state proceedings, and a scattered national array of lodge information, members' writings, and newspaper accounts. Together these materials shed light on Hood's Masonic career, while offering insight into the relationship between the lodge and the black church.

This article will argue that for James Walker Hood the activities of the Prince Hall Masons complemented the work of the AMEZ Church. A considerable portion of the membership of Hood's North Carolina Prince Hall fraternity was drawn from the rolls of his North Carolina denomination. Though different in their beliefs and ritual lives, the two organizations were structurally similar. The origins of this relationship can be traced to the post-Revolutionary era when both mutual benefit societies and the black church provided seedbeds of autonomy and bulwarks against the racism of white society. Following the Civil War, these two interwoven social institutions came to the South offering black Southerners similar "race histories" that countered white racial images while providing meaning and hope for their lives. Bishop Hood appropriated from Masonry beliefs which complemented his missionary efforts, while his fraternity's practices created bonds among black men and helped them to become responsible members of the community. This marriage between the church and the lodge was not without conflicts from outsiders in the Holiness movement, between church and lodge members, and between men and women. Still, compared to white Masons, Bishop Hood's Prince Hall members were active supporters of the church in a common struggle against racism and for the self-determination of the African American community.

## CHURCH AND LODGE

In late November of 1874, Bishop James Walker Hood presided over the week-long eleventh annual gathering of the ministers of the North Carolina Conference of the African Methodist Zion Church in New Berne, North Carolina. Reared in Pennsylvania and ordained in New England, Hood was pastor of a congregation in Bridgeport, Connecticut, when he was sent by his denomination as a missionary to the freedpeople in the South. In 1864 he arrived in the city of New Berne in coastal North Carolina, was appointed bishop in 1872, and by 1874 had overseen the planting of 366 churches with over 20,000 members.[10] As a northern missionary and church organizer, Hood operated in a milieu where most of the newly freed slaves were either completely unchurched or, in their exposure to religious teaching under slavery, were in need of additional structure and organization, at least from the northern perspective, in order to purify their Christianity from the distortions of southern white religion.[11] A religious conservative whose social activism stemmed from his belief that Christian conversion would lead to the downfall of oppression and social injustice, Hood urged his followers to pursue a "profound" commitment to Christ. This was especially important for ministerial candidates, whom the Conference examined carefully for their "literary qualifications, their intemperate habits and filthy practices," and to whom the Bishop directly appealed to honor the dignity of the ministry by living "holy and spotless lives." Following these remarks Hood announced that, prior to the evening's "love feast," the Masonic fraternity would lay the cornerstone at New Berne's new brick church.[12]

Five days later, the Zion leader journeyed to Raleigh where he was feted as "Most Worshipful Grand Master" at the fifth annual proceedings of the Prince Hall Grand Lodge of Free and Accepted Ancient York Masons for the State of North Carolina. Shortly after his arrival in New Berne in 1864, Hood followed through on his commission as superintendent of the southern jurisdiction for the Prince Hall Masonic Lodge of New York by establishing King Solomon Lodge No. 1 in the same town where he organized his first AMEZ Church.[13] The next three lodges were organized in the towns of Wilmington, Fayetteville, and Raleigh, sites of the largest AMEZ congregations.[14] In 1870, these four lodges formed themselves into the North Carolina Grand Lodge and unanimously elected Bishop Hood as their grand master. By 1874, there were eighteen Prince Hall lodges in the state, with 478 members. In his address that year to his "dear Brethren," Grand Master Hood sounded notes of encouragement concerning the "state of the craft" that echoed—though in different language—the remarks he made one week earlier to the AMEZ faithful regarding the state of their church. Appealing first to the "Supreme Grand Master" to bless their gathering "within these sacred walls," the Prince Hall leader pronounced that "the state of the craft in this jurisdiction is good." Most lodges were "composed of good, solid material, and, when the master's hammer has given [them] the necessary polish, [they] will form a beautiful structure." A few, notably his namesake J. W. Hood Lodge No. 8 in Goldsboro, "lacked Masonic ability," while the Grand Master reported that his best visit was to Pythagoras Lodge No. 6 in Smithville where most of "its members are professors of Christianity."[15] In assessing candidates for "the mysteries of Masonry" Hood urged that they be "men of active minds" who have, according to the Grand Lodge By-Laws, "a desire for knowledge, and a sincere wish of being serviceable to [their] fellow-creatures." A candidate must also be "free," "of good standing as a citizen," and have no physical deformity "so as to deprive him from honestly acquiring the means of subsistence." On the last day of the gathering, Grand Master Hood prayed to the "Supreme Architect of the Universe" to "guide and govern all we do."[16]

Accompanying Bishop Hood in his journey from New Berne to Raleigh were a number of his ministers who also served under his direction as leaders in Prince Hall Masonry. The 1874 AMEZ Conference Minutes list 192 ministers as members. Sixty-four or one-third of these conference members also appear in the available Prince Hall Proceedings for the 1870s. These include one-third of the conference's ruling elders, some of whom held similar leadership positions within the Grand Lodge. Thomas H. Lomax, for example, was appointed Presiding Elder for the Charlotte district, one of six districts in the conference, by Bishop Hood in 1875. In that same year, Lomax was appointed District Deputy Grand Master for the Charlotte district, one of five districts overseen by the Grand Lodge, by

Grand Master Hood. Similarly, R. H. Simmons, a ruling elder throughout the 1870s, was appointed Grand Pursuivant within the Grand Lodge, in charge of instructing members in the lore and practice of Freemasonry. Several elders held important committee positions within both the conference and Grand Lodge. Still others were both ministers of churches and leaders of their local lodges. In sum, in 1874 one-third of the AMEZ ministers in North Carolina were members and often leaders in Prince Hall Masonry. These sixty-four ministers, in turn, accounted for more than 13 percent of the state's 485 Prince Hall members. Since these figures do not include an untold number of church members who, like their ministers, followed their leader into the lodge, it appears that Grand Master Hood forged a substantial portion of the leadership and membership of North Carolina's Prince Hall lodges from the leaders and members of his North Carolina AMEZ denomination.[17]

Indeed there were similarities between these two organizations. Not only did they share the same leader and an overlapping membership and exist in many of the same towns,[18] but they had similar organizational structures and appealed to the same broad cohort of young African American men. In both instances the annual meetings took place over several days and followed a rhythm of worship, business, and recreation. Central to each meeting was the bishop or grand master's address and report on his preceding year's visit to individual churches or lodges. Both were rational, hierarchical societies governed by by-laws and central committees. Enduring committees within the conference included Credentials, Finance, By-Laws, and Complaints, which had their parallel in the committees on Credentials, Finance, By-Laws, and Grievances within the Grand Lodge. Considerable time in each annual meeting was given over to complaints or grievances concerning existing members. AMEZ complaints revolved around intemperance, adultery, irregular credentials, and "preaching erroneous doctrine." Grand Lodge penitents were more often assailed for being "dull and inactive," holding irregular credentials, or challenging Masonic doctrine. Finally, a major concern of both groups was the recruitment of able young men with "active intellects." AMEZ ministerial candidates were particularly scrutinized for their "clean" habits and Christian learning, while "good citizenship" and adequate employment were important criteria for becoming a Prince Hall Mason.[19] Taken together, the AMEZ Conference and the Prince Hall Grand Lodge were structurally similar organizations.

And yet there were fundamental differences. The AMEZ Conference was the ruling body of a denomination of Christian men and women who believed in the literal gospel and worshipped according to the practices of Methodism. The Grand Lodge, in contrast, was the governing body of a secret group of men whose beliefs stemmed from a variety of medieval, esoteric, and early Christian sources and regularly passed their members through three successive rites of initiation. Hymn-singing and sermons pervaded the Zion Conference activities. Invocations of the Supreme Architect, esoteric rites, and flamboyant public processions distinguished the Grand Lodge gatherings. Church records marked time by the Christian calendar. Lodge minutes predated the Christian calendar by 4,000 years to what Masons believed to be the beginning of time and Masonry. The December 1874 Grand Lodge Proceedings, for example, are actually dated December 5874. The lodges themselves were named Hiram, Pythagoras, Widow's Son, Morning Star, Rising Sun, and even J. W. Hood to recognize important men and moments in Masonic lore. Unlike the Christian churches, which met to worship every Sunday, the lodges enacted their rituals twice a month on a weekday night, sometimes "before the full moon."[20] In moving from Sunday morning church services to weekday evening lodge meetings, Bishop Hood and other leading ministers left their sanctuaries, took off their ecclesial robes, and entered lodge rooms decorated to resemble King Solomon's Temple, donned cloth aprons displaying the "All-Seeing Eye," embroidered collars and jeweled pendants signifying their office, and assumed positions in a rectangle of elders. Despite their apparent structural similarities there were significant differences of belief and ritual that separated the AMEZ church from the Prince Hall Lodge. How did Bishop Hood and his followers come to live in these mingled worlds? To try to answer this question we need first to consider the origins of the Prince Hall Lodge and the AMEZ Church and how each adapted to the needs and desires of African Americans.

## ORIGINS

Both the Prince Hall lodge and the AMEZ Church emerged from the distinctive social milieu of free, urban African Americans following the Revolution. The earliest African American social institutions resulted from a mixture of black initiative and white discrimination. In Philadelphia, for example, Absalom Jones and Richard Allen created the Free African Society in 1787 as a mutual aid organization as well as a nondenominational religious association. Several years later, in perhaps the most famous event in African American religious history, Jones and other black members were forcibly removed from their prayer benches in St. George's Methodist Church. Subsequently, Jones and Allen created the African Episcopal and the African Methodist Episcopal churches. This incident of discrimination has influenced historians to emphasize white racism as the reason for the development of black churches. Albert Raboteau, in contrast, points to the earlier desires on the part of Jones and Allen to create a separate religious association as equally important as white racism in the creation of the black church.[21]

   The close relationship between mutual benefit societies and the black church as both resources for black autonomy and barricades against white racism continued throughout the nineteenth century. African mutual aid societies assisted the needy, especially widows and their children, in return for modest dues. They also provided social networks for a community in flux by offering information on jobs, mobilizing public opinion, and cultivating social bonds. Many of Philadelphia's societies were associated with black churches, and many of their names indicate the continuing identity of blacks with their African heritage—the Daughters of Ethiopia, Daughters of Samaria, Angola Society, Sons of Africa, and the African Lodge of the Prince Hall Masons.[22] By the second quarter of the nineteenth century, Christian names predominated.[23] Out of the post-1820s Baltimore Mutual Aid Society, for example, grew at least three national societies: the Good Samaritans, the Nazarites, and the Galilean Fishermen.[24] By 1848, Philadelphia alone had over 100 variously named small mutual benefit societies with a combined membership of more than 8,000;[25] while in the South, similar groups, like the Burying Ground Society of the Free People of Color of the City of Richmond (1815), had appeared. Many of the later societies, such as the New York Benevolent Branch of Bethel (1843), grew out of churches.[26] Yet the example of the African mutual benefit society preceding the Christian church suggests the weaving of African and Christian, secular and sacred, within and between these two primordial social institutions of African American culture.[27] These mutual influences were again on display in 1797, when Absalom Jones and Richard Allen, founders of the Free African Society and founding bishops of the African Episcopal and African Methodist

Episcopal churches respectively, established Philadelphia's African Lodge of Prince Hall Masons. In 1815, Absalom Jones became Pennsylvania's first grand master.

Masonry among African Americans began in Boston and spread to Philadelphia. In 1785 Prince Hall, an Indies-born artisan, along with fourteen other black Bostonians was inducted into an English army lodge. Though their Masonic credentials were legitimate, the Grand Lodge of Massachusetts denied them admission, after which they applied to the Grand Lodge of England to recognize them as a valid Masonic lodge. Soon thereafter the growing number of black lodges created the African or Prince Hall Grand Lodge and, as their white counterparts had done after the Revolution, declared independence from the Grand Lodge of England.[28] From these beginnings, the Prince Hall lodges developed and, from the outset, both reinforced their claims to authenticity in the eyes of European Americans by largely following the beliefs and practices of European American lodges, while asserting to African Americans the ultimately African origins of the Masonic fraternity.

Whatever their differences, all Masons trace their medieval origins to the time of the Norman Conquest[29] when guilds of stonemasons were essential to the building carried on by kings, nobles, and churchmen. When the first Grand Lodge was formed in London in 1717, "Free," or independent, masonry[30] took on the character of a nobleman's club while retaining the traditional features of medieval institutions connected to an artisan culture. These included a secret brotherhood and the central importance of ritual, initiation, and myths of origin.[31] When it migrated to the Continent and to North America, the newly formulated Masonic order continued to alter its beliefs and practices as it encountered different social and political contexts.[32] By the middle of the eighteenth century, changes in the North American fraternity reflected shifting definitions of power and hierarchy embodied in the American Revolution. Beginning in the 1750s, groups of mechanics, lesser merchants, and military men, some of whom had been rejected by existing lodges, transformed the social and intellectual boundaries of the fraternity. By the 1790s, as the order spread rapidly through the countryside, these ambitious and politically active men began to describe the fraternity as embodying the new republic's values of education, morality, and Christianity.[33]

Like the European Americans who joined this English society and adapted it to their circumstances, African Americans found in the American Masonic fraternity a useful "tool kit"[34] of social forms and ideals for adaptation to their social environment. Like other mutual benefit societies, Prince Hall Masonry offered its members economic aid and social connections. Unlike most other societies, the first black Masons appear to have drawn their members from the most "respectable" black families. The men who joined Philadelphia's First African Lodge, for example, were among the most affluent and longstanding black residents, even if their occupations did not measure up to bourgeois status in their white neighbors' eyes.[35] Moreover, as the black equivalent of a prestigious white society, the public recognition granted to Prince Hall leaders provided a stage for addressing the larger society. Until that time, usually only black ministers received such public acknowledgment. Like the many African American religious leaders who used the Declaration of Independence's trumpeting of equality to challenge racial inequality,[36] Prince Hall and his followers employed the fraternity's ideals of unity and brotherhood across racial and national lines to confront racism. "Live and act as Masons," Prince Hall charged his brothers, "give the right hand of affection and fellowship to whom it justly belongs; let their color and complexion be what it will, let their nation be what it may, for they are your brethren and it is your indispensable duty so to do."[37] By asserting the egalitarian ideals of an international brotherhood, Prince Hall employed its moral authority to confront the contradic-tions of an American society that embraced equality yet denied rights of citizenship and humanity to black people.

At the same time, Prince Hall, the statesman Martin Delaney, and other early Masonic leaders created a history of the order that provided a powerful moral vision for the emerg-ing African American community. While historians see the first Masons emerging from medieval stonemason guilds, Masons themselves, both white and black, trace the mythic origins of the fraternity to King Solomon, whom, they believe, synthesized all previous wisdom into physical science and manifested it through the building of the Temple of Jerusalem. The three Masonic rites of initiation of Entered Apprentice, Fellow Craftsman, and Master Mason are intended to mark a deepening knowledge of the wisdom of this temple and, by analogy, the stages of life's journey. Masons, white and black, generally agree on this basic story and the rites that accompany it. Black Masons, however, claimed that the deeper truths presented by Solomon originated in the African civilization that preceded him. It was "the Africans," said Martin Delaney, "who were the authors of this mysterious and beautiful Order."[38] By this interpretation, black Masons were able to claim the legacy of Masonic history as their own and to contend that it was not a slave heritage but a glorious history in which Masonry was synonymous with freedom, liberty, and dem-ocratic government.

Though we do not know for certain when and where James Walker Hood entered into the "mysteries of Masonry," the evidence suggests that it was in 1855 when, as a young man of twenty-four, he first traveled from rural Pennsylvania to New York City and found work as a waiter. "Soon after I became of lawful age," he states in the North Carolina Grand Lodge Proceedings, "I petitioned a regular Lodge, in due form, and my prayer was granted."[39] In the mid-nineteenth century, New York, Boston, and Philadelphia were the principal centers of the less than thirty Prince Hall lodges then in existence.[40] In joining the fraternity, the young Hood gained entrance into an influential society of African American men that encouraged his self-determination and opposed the racism of white society. Around the same time that the future grand master became a Mason, he also entered the ministry of the black church.

Hood was born in 1831 into a religious family in rural southeastern Pennsylvania. His father, Levi, was a minister in the African Union Church, the very first black denomina-tion, and his mother, Harriet, was a member of Richard Allen's Bethel AME Church. In 1855, during the young Hood's sojourn in New York City, he joined a small congregation of the African Union Church. In 1856, the Reverend Williams Councy, pastor of the con-gregation, granted Hood a preaching license. During the autumn of 1857 Hood relocated once again, to New Haven, Connecticut, but this time he was unable to locate a branch of the African Union Church. So he joined a quarterly conference of the Zion connection, which accepted his license to preach. The following conference year, nearly two years after his affiliation with the New Haven Quarterly Conference, that body recommended to the June 1859 New England Annual Conference that it accept the young minister on a trial basis. The annual conference consented to this request and gave Hood an appointment of two stations in Nova Scotia. The AMEZ Church, like most independent black denomina-tions during these years, was interested in the salvation of African people wherever they might be found. After two years in Nova Scotia, Hood assumed the pastorate of a congre-gation in Bridgeport, Connecticut. Then, in 1863, members of the New Haven Conference, many of whom were from New Berne, North Carolina, called on their bishop to send someone down to New Beme and surrounding areas to serve the newly emancipated people in areas captured by Union forces. Shortly thereafter, in 1864, Reverend Hood set out on his mission to the South.[41]

Like many black denominational leaders, Bishop Hood believed that the black church in the United States had a providential role to play in society. In his 1895 history of the African Methodist Episcopal Zion Church, the Zion leader placed his denomination's story into the larger epic of the African exodus from white churches following the Revolution. The particular history of the AMEZ denomination dates from 1796, when it was organized by a group of black members protesting discrimination in the Methodist John Street Church in New York City. Their first church, Zion, was built in 1800 and from there emerged an African American denomination that continued to follow Methodist polity. Like contemporary scholars, Hood saw the emergence of the African American church as both a reaction to white discrimination and an act of black self-determination. While decrying the particular efforts of white Methodists to "maintain the inferiority of the Negro" in the John Street Church, Bishop Hood also saw the late eighteenth- and early nineteenth-century movement of "colored members of all denominations" into "the Negro Church" as guided by a "divine purpose." As he put it, "In the unfolding of that Providence that underlay the human meanness which produced the general exodus of the Afro-American race from the white Church, there have come and still are coming to the proscribed race benefits so rich, abundant, and glorious that the sufferings incident are not worthy of mention." Without the black church, Hood proclaimed, the black man "would have had no opportunity for the development of his faculties, nor would he have had any platform on which to exhibit his vast possibilities."[42]

Though the founders of the new AMEZ denomination had, according to Hood, "no fault to find with the doctrine or form of government" of Methodism,[43] both he and other nineteenth-century "race historians" adapted the history of the Christian church to serve the needs and desires of African Americans. As Laurie Maffly-Kipp has argued, during the nineteenth century a new genre of "race history" emerged among African Americans intent on providing a significant moral and spiritual purpose to the history and future of the race. Race historians hoped to counter white racial images by reimagining the story of the African American community in such a way that their narratives would provide both prophetic indictments of contemporary racial practices and self-fulfilling prophecies of racial unity.[44] Like most black Christians during his lifetime, Bishop Hood believed in the literal truth of Scripture. Using the genealogical tables of the Bible, the Zion minister identified Ham as the ancestor of blacks and traced the origins of major ancient civilizations, such as Egypt, Ethiopia, and Babylon, to Hamitic ancestry. Indeed, the Zionite insisted that the African race stood at the front ranks of the earliest civilizations of the world.[45] Like the Prince Hall reworking of Masonic history, Hood and other "race historians" employed their understanding of the Bible to provide a positive vision for the emerging black community.

When James Walker Hood left Connecticut for North Carolina he went as an emissary for perhaps the two most prominent and deeply interwoven social institutions of the northern African American community, the Prince Hall Masons and the black church. Both had emerged following the Revolution and each provided the emerging black society with resources for their development and a defense against white racism. Both Hood's Masonic fraternity and his AMEZ denomination continued to observe the doctrines and practices of their white counterparts, yet each adapted their society's history to remove the stigma of slavery and endow their past and future with a significant spiritual and moral purpose. Bishop Hood was among the many northern missionaries who saw the black church as a means through which God was acting in history to uplift the black race. Grand Master Hood, in turn, saw in the Masonic fraternity an opportunity to embrace the dignity and humanity of a universal brotherhood. During the last decades of the nineteenth century, both societies became southern institutions. As senior bishop of the AMEZ Church, Hood presided over the growth of his denomination from 4,600 members in 1860 to 700,000 by 1916. At the same time, Grand Master Hood contributed to the southern expansion of the Prince Hall Masons. By the turn of the century there were over 117,000 Prince Hall Masons nationally with nearly two-thirds of the membership concentrated in the South.[46] Despite the common commitment of each of these prominent social institutions to the "uplift" of black Southerners, there remained substantial differences. What was the relationship between the theology of the black church and the beliefs of Prince Hall Masons? And what was the practice and purpose of Masonic rituals? Here again, James Walker Hood's story provides some insights.

## BELIEFS AND RITES

Bishop Hood's theology reflected the thinking of an era before the rise of science and the professionalization of history when biblical paradigms and sacred histories pervaded the religious worldview. By the 1880s the scientific and intellectual currents that gave rise to Protestant liberalism were filtering into black religious communities through such journals as the AME Church Review, though these new ideas were most frequently met with apologies for Protestant orthodoxy.[47] Hood was one among many of his contemporary black denominational leaders who defended the literal understanding of the Bible and stood against all changes in Christian doctrine. During the post-Civil War period, the Zion leader opposed Darwinian scientific theories, historical and critical study of Scripture, and the idea that salvation was possible outside of Christianity.[48] By the turn of the century, the progressive "New Negro," who had little use for sacred stories and biblical world views, was gaining currency among African American intellectuals.[49] Prior to that time, and outside intellectuals' circles for some time to come, Bishop Hood and his fellow "race historians," many of whom were ordained ministers, provided their congregations with a vision of the historical world that placed the story of African American suffering in a temporal context that gave their lives meaning and hope. Emerging at a time when the power of sacred history had yet to be undercut by historical-critical methods, these histories offered African Americans representations of their race that countered disparaging white narratives.[50]

Like many of these accounts, Bishop Hood's sacred history parted company with European American narratives by asserting "the ancient greatness of the Negro race." The Zion leader began by accusing "modern historians of the Caucasian race" of trying to "rob" the Negro of a "history to which he can point with pride." Against this treachery, Hood proclaimed, "the Holy Bible has stood as an everlasting rock in the black man's defense." Employing the Bible and the work of selected white historians to buttress his case, the Zion leader argued that "Ethiopia and Egypt were the first among the early monarchies and these countries were peopled by the descendants of Ham, through Cush and Mizraim, and were governed by the same for hundreds of years." More than an identification of African people in a white narrative, Hood's history identified the contributions of particular

African cities and heroes to ancient culture. "Caucasian civilization can point to nothing that exceeds" the "gallantry" and "generosity" of the black city of Carthage nor the "persons of St. Augustine and St. Cyprian . . . two of the ablest ministers of which the Christian Church can boast." In this way, the Zion bishop underscored an African historical legacy that refuted white beliefs that Africans were an inferior race.[51]

Although Bishop Hood argued that white people had misrepresented the past by portraying Africans as a degraded race, he did not advise abandoning Christianity because of its contamination by white prejudice. Rather, he outlined what he saw as God's true plan. While realizing the original greatness of the race of Ham, Hood also recognized that Ham, through his son Nimrod, "forsook God and took the world for his portion." In retaliation, God, at Babel, "confounded" the language of Ham's people and "scattered them abroad from thence upon the face of all the earth." Hood's narrative then moved to America, ignored the era of slavery, and asserted the special destiny of the black church. Though God punished the followers of Ham for their idolatry, he also gave them a "promise," Hood told his followers, that the sons of Ham "shall cast aside idolatry and return unto the Lord." The African American church was now leading the way in this redemption. "That this promise is now in the course of fulfillment," he proclaimed, "the Negro Church stands forth as unquestionable evidence." The black church, in sum, was "the morning star which precedes the rising sun," leading all Christians toward the "millennial glory."[52]

Bishop Hood's race history must not be read as the work of an uneducated man. Though largely self-taught, his writings reflect a lifetime of intelligent reading. Yet consistent with his faith in the Bible's literal truth, the Zion bishop interpreted Scripture in a manner that provided encouragement to his people. Beyond the inroads that scientific and biblical criticism were making into religious authority, the black orthodox response to these new intellectual currents was rooted in racial as well as religious concerns. Black religious leaders and other learned African Americans like James W. Hood were additionally burdened with the reality that black history was given insufficient attention by most scholars. Some feared that the Darwinian theory and biblical criticism employed in the liberal assault upon Scripture and traditional Christianity would be used to deny the humanity and rights of the black race.[53] In the face of these difficulties, Hood and his fellow denominational leaders turned to the Bible and found in it a more complete and compassionate presentation of the history and humanity of black people. Despite a reliance on Scripture's literal truth for accurate historical details, black traditionalists' understanding of the Bible as the inerrant word of God played a critical role in a period when there were few professionally trained African American scholars.[54] Beyond the Bible, the bishop turned especially to the race histories of his fellow black churchmen to support his beliefs. The most famous of these, the Baptist Rufus Perry's *The Cushites, or the Descendants of Ham,*[55] he endorsed as a work of "profound learning" that should become essential reading "respecting the ancient greatness of the descendants of Ham, the ancestors of the American Negro."[56] The sacred history of the Prince Hall Masons provided further support for the "truth" of the African American past.

Although Grand Master Hood left no Masonic race history of his own, the history written by Martin Delaney was likely passed down to him by Masonic orators through the lore of the lodge. Delaney's history asserts that the institution of Masonry was created by Africans and "handed down only through the priesthood" in the earliest period of the Egyptian and Ethiopian dynasties "anterior to the Bible record." These early Egyptians, Delaney continued, adduced and believed in a trinity of the Godhead which later became "the Christian doctrine of three persons in one—Father, Son, and Holy Ghost." Moses, "the recorder of the Bible," Delaney states, "learned all of his wisdom and ability from Egypt." "Africans," therefore, "were the authors of this mysterious and beautiful Order" and "did much to bring it to perfection" prior to the writing of the Bible.[57]

Though Bishop Hood never addressed the African origins of Masonry in his public writings, he did import elements of the Masonic tradition into his Christian race history. In his sermon on "Creation's First-Born, or the Earliest Gospel Symbol," for example, he asserted the Masonic belief that the world began 4,000 years before the birth of Christ. "We live in a period, by all accounts, not much less than six thousand years from that in which Jehovah spake and said, 'Let their be light.'"[58] Certain turns of phrase, like the above "morning star" and "rising sun," used to herald the future of the Negro church, held such symbolic significance in the Masonic beliefs that the Grand Master gave them as names to his first North Carolina lodges. The bishop's essay on "God's Purpose in the Negro Church As Seen in the History of the Movement," moreover, refers to the "ancient and honorable" Prince Hall fraternity's maintenance of its "rites and benefits" as part of the larger effort of black people to respond to "Jehovah's plan for the Negro's development."[59] Aside from these and other occasional instances where the bishop mentions the Masonic fraternity, its catch words or ideas, the Zion leader's public writings remain silent on the relationship between his Christian and Masonic beliefs. Within the confines of the lodge, however, Grand Master Hood provided more insight.

In his 1880 annual address to the North Carolina Grand Lodge, the "most worshipful" Grand Master instructed the gathered brethren on the relationship between the beliefs and rites of Masonry and what he considered to be religion. On one hand, Hood stated that he did not believe that Masonry was a religion. Yet, on the other hand, he did hold that the fraternity was older than Christianity and Judaism and—through its oral tradition—passed on an ancient knowledge born at the beginning of time. "Most Masonic writers admit that Masonry does not claim to be a religion. I admit that it is not a religious sect, yet I am fully persuaded that it is the offspring of the only genuine religion known to man in the early history of the world. This I gather from tradition. . . . For hundreds of years tradition was the only channel through which the knowledge of events was handed down from generation to generation. . . . Oral instruction was the universal mode in ancient times. Masonry is the only Order that retains and adheres strictly to the ancient mode."[60] Masonry, then, was heir to an oral transmission of ancient knowledge that originated at the beginning of the world. It was not itself a religion yet it was the "offspring" of the only genuine religion available to ancient peoples. Since nowhere in either his Christian or Masonic writings does Hood speak of a conflict between Christianity and Masonry, the bishop appears to have believed that the orally transmitted, ancient knowledge passed through Masonry was complementary to Christian teachings. Since the content of this knowledge constitutes that which is most "secret" in Masonry, Hood understandably does not divulge it. Yet he does begin to explain the process of its transmission.

According to the beliefs of Masonry, Grand Master Hood proceeded, King Solomon synthesized this esoteric knowledge into physical science and manifested it through the building of the Temple at Jerusalem. The Masonic lodge, in turn, symbolically represented the Temple of Jerusalem. "There are many symbols which identify the Freemason's Lodge with the city and Temple at Jerusalem. (1)—The city was built on the high hills of Zoria and Moria, and near the Valley of Jehosaphat. Our lodge is symbolically situated upon the highest hills and lowest valleys. (2)—The Temple was built due east and west. So is our Lodge. (3)—The Temple was an oblong square, and its ground was holy. Such is the form and ground of our Lodge. . . . Like the Temple, our Lodge is founded on the mercies of Jehovah: consecrated in His name dedicated to His honor; and from the foundation to the capstone it proclaims, 'Glory to God in the highest, peace on earth and good will to man.'"[61] Masonic wisdom was, therefore, symbolically represented in the lodge's replication of King Solomon's Temple in Jerusalem. Access to this knowledge, in turn, came through an understanding of these symbols through participation in rites of initiation.

Though Hood did not believe that Masonry was either a religion or opposed to Christianity, nevertheless, he did believe that "Masonic symbolism, from beginning to end, was capable of instructing us in the truths of evangelical religion."[62] For example, as Hood explained it, when the "candidate was initiated into the ancient mysteries" he was "invested with a white apron in token of his newly attained purity." The Grand Master then interpreted the symbolic meaning of the Mason's lamb skin or white leather apron through biblical references. "From the Book Divine we learn that it was the most ancient piece of apparel ever worn. It was worn by Adam and Eve before they were turned out of the Garden. . . . The apron, or girdle, was universally received as an emblem of truth among the ancients. Paul so styles it. 'Having your loins girded with truth.' . . . He, therefore, who wears the white apron as a badge of a Mason, is continually reminded of that innocence and purity which ought to be the distinguishing characteristic of every Mason."[63] How the brother came truly to understand the apron's symbolic meaning came through "the peculiar circumstances in which he receives it."[64] Here Hood appeared to be saying that the Christian idea of innocence and purity was most deeply apprehended through the Masonic ritual of initiation. The apron was not, however, a token of the initiate's entrance into the Christian community but, rather, a sign through which the novice "was made to feel his relationship to the fraternity."[65] Whether Masonic rituals deepened the candidate's understanding of Christian truths, as Hood stated, or Masonic fellowship, as his remarks might be interpreted, the fraternity's secret ceremonies clearly set the brotherhood apart from the practices of Christian congregations.

Exclusive to all American Masons, white and black, were two or more monthly gatherings on weekday evenings for long and complex rituals of initiation. The three primary rituals of Entered Apprentice, Fellow Craft, and Master Mason were intended to mark a deepening knowledge of the wisdom of Solomon's Temple and, by analogy, the stages of life's journey. A 1903 Prince Hall national inventory highlighted the importance of these stages by categorizing the membership according to which of these three rites they had completed.[66] Each of these ceremonies lasted an hour or more and plunged the candidate into the mysteries of the order. At the moment the lodge was "opened," the initiate lost his sense of time. Ceremonies were said to begin at "daybreak," although meetings were actually held in the evening. While he was prepared, the evening's actors changed into costumes. Others arranged the setting, lit candles, and extinguished the lights. The lodge room itself was rectangular in imitation of the shape of the Ark of the Covenant. The Bible was placed on an altar in the middle of the room beside replicas of a craftsman's square and compass and laid open to a passage appropriate for the evening's "labor." Seated around the room were the members, in formal attire with aprons displaying a picture of the "All-Seeing Eye" (like the one on the American one-dollar bill). The major officers sat in designated chairs, each wearing an embroidered collar and jeweled pendant represent-ing the special insignia of their position. Slowly the present faded from view and before their eyes an imagined scene from the past appeared.

Each major ritual took the form of a journey through the good and evil of human life. As the candidate proceeded in his travels, he was stopped at certain points to hear a lecture, to pray, or to be subjected to a dramatic presentation designed to link his mind and emo-tions through physical stimulation. For example, the Entered Apprentice ritual began when the partially undressed and blindfolded initiate entered the lodge room and was met by the sharp point of the drafter's compass against his exposed left breast accompanied by the senior deacon's stern words not to reveal the secrets of the order. Through similar trials the initiate was taught the history of the order and the meaning of its key symbols and in-structed in his moral responsibilities as a Mason. Following the initiation the lodge was "closed" with a prayer or song and the announcement that, because the sun had set, their Masonic labors had ended. The lodge now returned to ordinary time.[67]

Within each ritual, the candidate learned that the Bible was the "cornerstone" of Ma-sonry and that he must be obedient to God, but the major thrust of the rite was to teach Masonic tenets. As the Methodist minister and Deputy Prince Hall Grand Master William Spencer Carpenter explained in a Masonic sermon, "The traveling as a Master Mason is symbolic of the journey through life to that Celestial Lodge eternal in the Heavens, where God is the Worshipful Master, Jesus Christ is the Senior Warden, and where the Holy Ghost is the Junior Warden, whose duty it is to . . . call the craft [the assembled Masons] from labor to refreshment and from refreshment to labor again at the will and pleasure of the Master."[68] As in Grand Master Hood's explanation of the Mason's apron, Carpenter is not entirely clear whether Christianity or Masonry has the upper hand. In fact, Masonic rituals contained a grab-bag of religious elements. The frequent Masonic references to God as the "Grand Architect of the Universe" underscored the order's embrace of reason and science. Moral laws could be discerned like natural laws and it was the Mason's duty to obey them. Similarly, commitment to the brotherhood of all men and the truth of all religions sug-gested an opposition to sectarian divisions. At the same time, the rituals borrowed exten-sively from the Bible and the Judeo-Christian tradition. As a result Freemasonry contained an ambiguous religious content, open to several interpretations.[69] For many men, the fra-ternity's rituals succeeded primarily in creating a lasting, meaningful bond between mem-bers infused with religious overtones.

In addition to these private rituals, Prince Hall Masons conducted public parades that proclaimed the identity and dignity of the order. These processions were the highlight of the North Carolina Grand Lodge's annual meetings. Preceded by a brass band, the mem-bers of the fraternity, dressed in their regalia, marched through the town's "principal" streets, usually to a Zion Methodist church. There a minister offered prayers, a Masonic anthem was sung, Grand Master Hood addressed "the Craft," the band played some music, all sang a Masonic ode, and a minister offered a benediction. After these "usual cere-monies," the "procession again was formed" and paraded back to the lodge.[70] Prince Hall parades had their origins in the practices of the European American Masonic tradition yet had particular meaning in the African American community.[71] Carried out with the re-hearsed self-consciousness of public theater complete with ornamented clothing and pol-ished gestures, this public performance of fraternal life enacted racial dignity and pride for a people derided as unruly by some white Southerners. Louis Armstrong captured the heart of this positive function for fraternal orders when he remembered watching his father march by as the Grand Marshal of the New Orleans Odd Fellows parade: "I was very proud to see him in his uniform and his high hat with the beautiful streamer hanging down. . . . Yes, he was a fine figure of a man, my Dad. Or, at least that is the way he seemed to me as a kid when he strutted by like a peacock at the head of the Odd Fellows parade."[72] Wearing an apron or sash and making a "show in a procession" was admittedly one of the attractions of fraternal orders but, as Virginia's Grand Master Harrison Harris remarked, "We do not want a Masonry that makes a man anxious to shine in a procession" but a "Masonry that goes into the family and makes a man a better husband, a kinder father, a more devoted patriot and . . . a more liberal and devoted Christian."[73] It was this understanding of Masonry that attracted James Walker Hood.

## COMPLEMENT AND CONFLICT

We cannot say for certain what the significance of Masonic beliefs and rituals was for Bishop Hood. We do know that he spent considerable time throughout his career attending to the fraternity's affairs and presiding over its ritual life. Following thirteen years as Grand Master, he continued to serve in such capacities as Grand Orator and supervisor of Masonic Jurisprudence, guiding the brotherhood's beliefs and practices. Late in life, when he was too feeble to attend the annual Grand Lodge meetings, past Grand Master Hood wrote letters to the assembled brethren that were printed prominently in their Proceedings. Yet despite his annual unanimous reelection, Hood chose to step down from the position of Grand Master due to his more pressing "ecclesial labors."[74] In fact, any time, effort, or output comparison of Hood's work for the church and his labor for the lodge would show that his church work was more important.

What does seem clear is that Bishop Hood appropriated from Masonry beliefs that complemented his missionary efforts. Given his Christian conservatism, it seems unlikely that the Zion leader would have been attracted to the liberal Masonic ideals of interreligious brotherhood or scientific progress which, some scholars have argued, helped bring modernizing late nineteenth-century European American men into the order.[75] In addition to his biblical literalism, Hood remained opposed to non-Christian paths to salvation. He viewed Islam, for example, as a "corrupting influence" operating "against the Christian Church."[76] Instead, Bishop Hood's Masonic teachings emphasized universal values like "purity of heart" and "rectitude of conduct." The Mason was an honest, upright man, a good citizen and a responsible member of the community. Moreover, as one member put it, Masonry, "having fewer doctrines, can reach some that Christianity cannot reach, and not until Christianity shall cover the earth . . . will the demand for Masonry cease."[77] The best lodges, the Grand Master believed, are those in which "all its members are professors of Christianity, and are men whose lives accord with their profession."[78] Further in accord with his evangelical Christian ideals, Hood's Grand Lodge enforced a code of behavior forbidding alcohol, tobacco, and any illegal behavior. Similarly, the Zion leader spoke to his brothers of the need to "soften our hearts" by giving our love to Jesus. In 1885 and at subsequent North Carolina Grand Lodge gatherings, Hood's Masonic hymn "The Feast of Belshazzar" was sung, ending with the following chorus:

See our deeds are all recorded,
There is a Hand that's writing now:

Sinners give your hearts to Jesus
At His royal mandate bow;
For the day is fast approaching
It must come to one and all,
When the sinner's condemnation
Shall be written upon the wall.[79]

In this way, Grand Master Hood emphasized the Christian teachings within Masonic beliefs. Moreover, though he did not share in the Masonic embrace of non-Christian religions, the Prince Hall leader did see the lodge as a vehicle for building Christian unity across black denominational lines. "It was my purpose," he reflected near the end of his life, "to invite the best men in all the Churches in this State into the Masonic Fraternity. In this our success has been all that could have been expected. Every denomination having a considerable membership has been represented in this Grand Lodge. Nearly all have been represented in the office of Grand Officers."[80] Hood's appropriation of Masonic beliefs complemented his Christian efforts to "uplift" and unite his people.

An emphasis on discipline and respectability was similarly central to both organizations. As we have seen, Hood and his fellow northern missionaries who established most Southern black churches brought with them a formal organization, governed by published rules that stipulated adherence to standards of moral conduct and punished those who transgressed. Duty-bound to teach the values of religion, education, and hard work, these "respectable" people equated restrained public behavior with individual self-respect and the advancement of the race. Prince Hall emissaries, again often the same people, imposed a similar organizational structure and had similar behavioral expectations for their members. Admissions committees were looking for intelligent, clean-living, sober, and industrious young men, preferably married and able to provide for their households. In both cases, expectations of "respectable" deportment and threats of expulsion conditioned behavior that encouraged racial "uplift."[81] In these efforts, fraternal members claimed, "Masonry does not aspire to the office of Christianity. It provides no atonement, and consequently cannot save the soul; but it seeks to elevate man, to beautify and adorn his character with domestic virtues. It teaches him the lessons of sobriety, and industry, and integrity. But Christianity teaches him to prepare for a higher life, a future state, and a brighter world."[82]

Taken together, Prince Hall lodges and Christian churches were central to the southern institution building that was demanded by freedom. Following emancipation, African Americans quickly adopted the voluntary associational conventions of American life to suit their specific needs. Both Hood's Masonic fraternity and his AMEZ denomination continued to follow the doctrines and practices of their white counterparts, yet each adapted their society's history to remove the stigma of slavery and empower their past and future with a meaningful spiritual and moral purpose. Moreover, as an institution brought to the South by a northern AMEZ missionary, Hood's North Carolina lodges shared with his churches a desire to bring discipline and respectability to the newly freed slaves. Broadly interdenominational in membership within the framework of the post-Reconstruction South, the North Carolina lodges supported the mainstream churches in this common effort to "purify" the beliefs and "uplift" the practices of black southerners. Though there is little evidence of regional consciousness in Hood's behavior and writings nor of tensions between the North Carolina lodges and their northern elders, further studies of southern fraternalism may reveal a regional distinctiveness and perhaps, as with the churches, disputes over resources and relative power within institutional structures that straddled the regions. Further, studies of other southern black Masonic leaders may suggest a greater willingness to follow liberal Masonic traditions though not at the expense of the church institution, given the critical role it played in the post-1865 black world.

Certainly, the marriage of church and lodge was not without conflicts. By the 1890s, leaders of the new Holiness movement emerging from the Mississippi Delta began to speak out against the involvement of the black church with fraternal orders. Responding to the social estrangement experienced by some African Americans, Holiness leaders attacked "worldly" Baptists and Methodists for their fashionable standards of consumption and their allegiance to secret societies, calling them back to the simplicity of the early Christian church. Followers of Charles Price Jones's new Church of Christ, for example, were encouraged to mark their spiritual birth as sanctified Christians by "pitching their secret order pins . . . out the church windows."[83] Though Bishop Hood did not directly address the Holiness attack on fraternal orders, as we have seen, his Prince Hall lodges followed stringent rules of ethical conduct. At the same time, the Zion bishop resisted a growing worldliness within mainstream black Methodism by retaining earlier emphases on a holy ministry, morally pure and free of scandal. As a participant in the Holiness movement within black Methodism, Hood and his contemporaries insisted that freedom from sin was attainable in this life and that every Christian should strive for this sanctification. Since belief in the possibility of sanctification in one's lifetime was not shared by all Methodists, Hood and other bishops insisted that their candidates for ministry adhere to this teaching.[84] Though the rapid growth of the Holiness movement likely influenced Prince Hall membership elsewhere, Hood's emphasis on high ethical conduct and striving for sanctification may have helped prevent both church and lodge defections in North Carolina.[85]

In addition to these attacks from outside the church-lodge nexus, there is also scattered evidence of tensions within the black church between fraternal members and church leaders. Writing in the *Indianapolis Freeman* in 1891, a Baptist minister complained that fraternal "members took more interest in their societies than their church."[86] Such behavior, echoed Methodist H. T. Keating in the *Christian Recorder*, led secret society members to "neglect their duties" to the church "in order to be regular in their attendance upon lodge meetings."[87] These complaints were often couched in conciliatory language that recognized the power of the orders within the church. "It will be observed that we do not enter into a discussion of whether secret societies are right and good in principle," Keating continued, "but simply protest against the neglect of the church in the slightest degree for these societies. Assuming both church and society right, which is most right and worthy of support?"[88] In response, Mason and AME minister S. H. Coleman, writing in the AME *Church Review*, defended the lodge as "not a substitute for the church but an handmaid of religion." The teachings of the order, he claimed, supplemented rather than replaced the truths of the Bible by teaching "us our social and political duties."[89] Other Prince Hall members pointedly rebuked the church for its criticisms. G. L. Knox specifically warned that "[d]id it so desire, [the lodge] could destroy the power of the pulpit." He then added "but such is not its mission. . . . Instead of being in antagonism with the church, it is content to draw its inspiration from God's holy house, and as an humble handmaiden, to do its Master's work, as it shall see it and understand it."[90] Though this evidence suggests some power struggles in the black church between lodge members and church leaders, these differences can hardly be compared with the successful evangelical effort to shut down the white Masonic order during the anti-Masonic campaign of the 1820s or the late nineteenth-century threat of excommunication posed by conservative white churches against those members who dared join fraternal orders.[91] In comparison with white Masons, who were far less likely than black Masons to be church members,[92] fraternal orders and the black church were deeply interwoven social institutions.

Gender tension between black lodge members and women was another potential area for conflict but, here again, compared to white Masons, there is less evidence of strife. Not only did the rituals of the Prince Hall Masons set them apart from the African American church, exclusive male membership separated the brothers from black women. In his study of the late nineteenth-century black Odd Fellow Amos Webber, Nick Salvatore remarks on Webber's relationship with his wife: "It was not that Amos thought Lizzie unimportant or that, after thirty years of marriage, he did not care for her. Rather his formal distancing from her suggested the overwhelming maleness of the world he inhabited."[93] In bearing witness to the "powerful influence" of nineteenth-century gender roles, black fraternal members inhabited a distinctly male sphere. Fraternal rites, unlike those of the Protestant churches, celebrated a man's bonds with his brothers while neglecting the event of his marriage. Even within the predominantly female churches these distinctions continued, with men controlling the visible, public positions of authority and women providing for the church's social activities through Sunday school, prayer meetings, missionary work, social events, and care for the needy.[94] And yet underlying both the lodge and the church was a tangled thicket of male-female relations, intimately joined by kinship ties between sisters and brothers, wives and husbands, that formed a common social framework for community activities. Within the church, acceptance of male religious leadership did not prevent women from creating their own influential networks; while within the lodge, women's auxiliaries participated in social activities and found meaning in the order's larger purposes.[95]

James Walker Hood was instrumental in efforts to include women in both lodge and church activities. As Mark Carnes has shown, late nineteenth-century white Masons were very reluctant to include women in their affairs, even going so far as to threaten members with fearful punishment if they should "tell their wife the concerns of the order."[96] In contrast, shortly after founding the North Carolina Grand Lodge, Hood encouraged the establishment of a ladies' auxiliary—the Order of the Eastern Star[97]—which became involved in the maintenance and support of the Order.[98] At the same time, Bishop Hood supported the full ministerial rights of women within the AMEZ denomination. He acted on this conviction first by ordaining Mrs. Julia A. J. Foote as deacon at the New York Annual Conference in 1894, and then, during the ultimately successful struggle for women's ordination that engulfed the denomination at the turn of the century, Hood was a leader among those who supported full equality for women in all aspects of church life.[99] All of this is not to deny the probability of gender tensions in an African American community where the male role remained dominant. Evelyn Higginbotham and others have identified some of these tensions within the black church.[100] Doubtless there were conflicts as well between some black women and the Prince Hall Masons. Yet, in contrast, most white Masons were not members of their wives' churches and discouraged the creation of ladies' auxiliaries. [101] Compared to the separation of the male lodge and the female church among the white Protestant middle class, there was substantially more interaction between the male world of Prince Hall men and the activities of black women.

## CONCLUSION

James Walker Hood believed that his labors for the Prince Hall Masons complemented his work for the AME denomination in a common effort to provide encouragement and hope to black Southerners facing debilitating circumstances. In Bishop Hood's view the church was more than a means for spiritual renewal, a providential movement acting in history to uplift the black race. As part of this larger movement of God, the Zion leader appropriated from Masonry beliefs and practices that complemented his missionary efforts. In the effort of African Americans to respond to the indignities and racial violence that formed the fabric of everyday life, the fraternity provided a mediating institution to defy the racism of American society. Membership in the order provided responsible and industrious men with public recognition, moral authority, and an alternative history with which to buffer and respond to potentially disabling images of the black man. Denied all but the most menial jobs and pushed to the margins of white society, the fraternity recognized each man's dignity and nurtured his growth by providing outlets for leadership and avenues for gaining status. At the same time, rites of initiation secured a lasting, meaningful bond with other men, while the fraternity's eclectic ideology provided a framework for a moral commitment that drew broadly upon the spiritual values of the Judeo-Christian tradition. Though rarely recognized by white Americans, after the Civil War the Prince Hall Masons flourished among African American men, providing, alongside the black church, a separate male sphere that reinforced a collective sense of African American identity and pride.

As a fraternal organization whose beliefs and activities intermingled with those of a Christian denomination, this study of the Prince Hall Masons and the AMEZ church has larger implications for the study of Christian history. Since the early 1700s, Masonically inspired fraternal orders spread throughout European and American Christianity, providing men with an eclectic "tool kit" of cultural resources for adapting to their social world. Recent scholarship has begun to explore the ways in which fraternal beliefs and rituals have parallelled, supported, and subverted the activities of Christian churches. Scholars have argued for the inclusion of Masonic resources in efforts to broaden our understanding of the "Christian" religious world, from the appropriation of Masonic practices by upstart Mormons to the creation of a separate "male" sphere of sympathetic feeling.[102] Bishop Hood's Christian conservatism had no difficulty including Masonic beliefs and rites in this larger worldview. More important, Hood's racial identity shaped relationships between lodge and church to serve a larger racial purpose. By including fraternal beliefs and rituals in a larger understanding of religious culture, students of Christianity may continue to find a rich resource for insight into the gender, racial, and ritual dynamics of post-Enlightenment Christianity.

## NOTES

1. "Bishop James W. Hood," *The Masonic Quarterly* 1 (1919): 3.

2. Sandy Dwayne Martin, "Biblical Interpretation, Ecclesiology, and Black Southern Religious Leaders, 1860–1920: A Case Study of AMEZ Bishop James Walker Hood" in *"Ain't Gonna Lay My 'Ligion Down": African American Religion in the South*, eds. Alonzo Johnson and Paul Jerslid (Columbia, S.C.: University of South Carolina Press, 1996),

111. I am indebted to Martin's fine recent biography of Hood for providing me with a great deal of information on Hood's life and career; *For God and Race: The Religious and Political Leadership of AMEZ Bishop James Walker Hood* (Columbia, S.C.: University of South Carolina Press, 1999).

3. W. E. B. Du Bois, *The Philadelphia Negro* (Philadelphia: University of Pennsylvania Press, 1899), 221–24.

4. Howard W. Odum, *Social and Mental Traits of the Negro: Research into the Conditions of the Negro in Southern Towns* (New York: Columbia University Press, 1910), 267. Booker T. Washington praised secret societies for teaching black businessmen how to create capital and thereby "greatly increase property in the hands of members of the race" (*The Story of the Negro*, 2 vols. [New York: Doubleday, 1909] 2:169). By the 1930s, Carter Woodson found that two-thirds of all black physicians and lawyers were members of fraternal orders (*The Negro Professional Man and the Community with special emphasis on the Physician and the Lawyer* [Washington, D.C.: Association for the Study of Negro Life and History, 1934] chaps. 8 and 16). In 1967, John Hope Franklin asserted that the creation of independent fraternal organizations within the antebellum free black communities of the North was central to the struggle to achieve status in an evolving American society (*From Slavery to Freedom: A History of Negro Americans*, 3rd ed. [New York: Knopf, 1967], 165).

5. Frank Lincoln Mather, ed., *Who's Who of the Colored Race* (1915, reprint, Detroit, Mich.: Detroit Gale Research Company, 1976).

6. The most recent analysis of the economic influence of black fraternal orders is by David M. Fahey, *The Black Lodge in White America: "True Reformer Brown" and His Economic Strategy* (Dayton, Ohio: Wright State University Press, 1994). William A. Muraskin's *Middle-Class Blacks in a White Society* (Berkeley, Calif.: University of California Press, 1975) emphasizes class. Other studies that to some degree include black fraternal orders and employ an analysis that weaves together economics, class, and politics include: Earl Lewis, *In Their Own Interests: Race, Class, and Power in Twentieth-Century Norfolk, Virginia* (Berkeley, Calif.: University of California Press, 1991); Joe William Trotter Jr., *Coal, Class, and Color: Blacks in Southern West Virginia 1915–32* (Urbana, Ill.: University of Illinois Press, 1990), 198–213; Peter J. Rachleff, *Black Labor in the South: Richmond, Virginia, 1865–90* (Philadelphia: Temple University Press, 1984; reprinted, Urbana: University of Illinois Press, 1989); David A. Gerber, *Black Ohio and the Color Line, 1860–1915* (Urbana, Ill.: University of Illinois Press, 1976), 162; and the older yet still frequently cited study by Hylan Lewis, *Blackways of Kent* (Chapel Hill, N.C.: University of North Carolina Press, 1955), 259–76.

7. The one exception is Nick Salvatore's recent study of Worcester's Amos Webber, *We All Got History: The Memory Books of Amos Webber* (New York: Times Books, 1996).

8. Steven C. Bullock, *Revolutionary Brotherhood: Freemasonry and the Transformation of the American Social Order, 1730–1840* (Chapel Hill, N.C.: University of North Carolina Press, 1996), 321.

9. Joseph A. Walkes Jr., longterm editor of the Prince Hall research journal *Phylaxis*, frequently laments, in its pages, the absence of comprehensive state-by-state records. More than once in my efforts to gain access to a lodge, I was told that the lodge building and whatever records were there were not available to me because they were "secret." Nevertheless, a fairly large, though hardly comprehensive, public collection of Prince Hall materials can be found at the Iowa Masonic Library in Cedar Rapids, Iowa.

10. *Minutes of the Eleventh Session of the North Carolina Annual Conference of the African Methodist Episcopal Church in America* held in New Berne, N.C., 25 November to 2 December 1874 (Raleigh, N.C.: John Nichols & Co., 1875), 37–47.

11. Recent studies of African American Christianity's expansion in the South during the Civil War and Reconstruction include: Daniel W. Stowell, *Rebuilding Zion: The Religious Reconstruction of the South, 1863–1877* (New York: Oxford University Press, 1998); Paul Harvey, *Redeeming the South: Religious Culture and Racial Identities among Southern Baptists, 1865–1925* (Chapel Hill, N.C.: University of North Carolina Press, 1997); Reginald F. Hildebrand, *The Times Were Strange and Stirring: Methodist Preachers and the Crisis of Emancipation* (Durham, N.C.: Duke University Press, 1995); William E. Montgomery, *Under Their Own Vine and Fig Tree: The African-American Church in the South, 1865–1900* (Baton Rouge, La.: Louisiana State University Press, 1993); Katherine L. Dvorak, *An African-American Exodus: The Segregation of Southern Churches* (Brooklyn, N.Y.: Carlson Publishing Company, 1991); and portions of Forrest G. Wood, *The Arrogance of Faith: Christianity and Race in America from the Colonial Era to the Twentieth Century* (Boston: Northeastern University Press, 1990).

12. *Minutes of the Eleventh Session*, 23.

13. In an address to the North Carolina Grand Lodge in 1917, Hood stated that when he "was appointed by Bishop J. J. Clinton as Superintendent of Missions for the A.M.E. Zion Church, [he] also had an appointment by M. W. G. W. Titus, Grand Master of Masons in New York, a[s] Superintendent of the Southern jurisdiction of the Grand Lodge of New York" (*Proceedings of the Most Worshipful Grand Lodge*, Forty-Eighth Annual Communication held in Salisbury, N.C., 11–13 December 1917 (Nashville, Tenn.: A.M.E. Sunday School Print, 1917), 89. See also William Grimshaw, *Official His-*

*tory of Freemasonry Among the Colored People of North America* (New York, 1903; reprint, Freeport, N.Y.: Books for Libraries, 1971), 258–59.

14. *Proceedings of the Most Worshipful Grand Lodge of Free and Accepted Ancient York Masons for the State of North Carolina* (Raleigh, N.C.: Nichols and Gorman, 1872), 53–55; *Minutes of the Eleventh Session*, 37–47.

15. *Proceedings of the Most Worshipful Grand Lodge . . . Fifth Annual Communication* (1874), 5–9.

16. Ibid.; the by-laws can be found in *Proceedings of the Most Worshipful Grand Lodge of Free and Accepted Ancient York Masons for the State of North Carolina* (Raleigh, N.C.: Nichols and Gorman, 1872), 14–21.

17. This statistical information was compiled from the following sources: AMEZ Church: *Minutes of the Eleventh Session, Minutes of the Twelfth Session of the North Carolina Annual Conference of the African Methodist Episcopal Zion Church* (Raleigh, N.C.: John Nichols and Company, 1875), *Minutes of the Thirteenth Session . . .* (1876), *Minutes of the Fourteenth Session . . .* (1877), and *Minutes of the Fifteenth Session . . .* (1878); Prince Hall Lodge: *Proceedings of the Most Worshipful Grand Lodge of Free and Accepted Ancient York Masons for the State of North Carolina* (Raleigh, N.C.: Nichols and Gorman, 1872), *Proceedings of the Most Worshipful Grand Lodge of Free and Accepted Ancient York Masons for the State of North Carolina at its Fifth Annual Communication* (Raleigh, N.C.: Nichols and Gorman, 1874), Joseph C. Hill, Right Worshipful Grand Secretary, Compiler, *Proceedings of the Most Worshipful Grand Lodge of Free and Accepted Ancient York Masons for the State of North Carolina, Sessions of December 1875, 1876, and 1877* (Wilmington, N.C.: Hall, 1878), and *Proceedings of the Eleventh Annual Communication of the Most Worshipful Grand Lodge of Free and Accepted Ancient York Masons for the State of North Carolina* (Wilmington, N.C.: Warrock, 1881).

18. Both the conference and the Grand Lodge founded societies along the routes of the new railroads that crisscrossed the state following the Civil War. Hood often pointed to the distance from railroad stations as a reason for a church or lodge's dormant state. In his 1874 report to the Grand Lodge, for example, he explained the slow growth of Rising Sun Lodge in Columbus County as due to the Lodge being situated "six or seven miles from the nearest railroad station" (*Proceedings* [1874], 8). For an insightful discussion of the relationship between the expansion of southern railroads and the development of African American social insti-

tutions, see John Giggie, "God's Long Journey: African Americans, Religion, and History in the Mississippi Delta, 1875–1915" (Ph.D. diss., Princeton University, 1997), 92–137.

19. *Minutes of the Eleventh Session* (1874); *Proceedings of the Grand Lodge* (1874).

20. *Proceedings* (1872), 54.

21. Albert J. Raboteau, *A Fire in the Bones: Reflections on African-American Religious History* (Boston: Beacon, 1995), 79–102. See also Gary B. Nash, *Forging Freedom: The Formation of Philadelphia's Black Community* (Cambridge, Mass.: Harvard University Press, 1988), 98–104. For a broader view, see William B. Gravely, "The Rise of African Churches in America (1786–1822): Re-Examining the Contexts," *Journal of Religious Thought* 41 (1984): 58–73.

22. Nash, *Forging Freedom*, 210.

23. James Oliver Horton, *Free People of Color: Inside the African American Community* (Washington, D.C.: Smithsonian Institution, 1993), 153.

24. Monroe N. Work, "Secret Societies as Factors in the Social and Economical Life of the Negro" in *Democracy in Earnest*, ed. James E. McCulloch (Washington, D.C.: Southern Sociological Congress, 1918), 343.

25. Du Bois, The Philadelphia Negro, 222.

26. James B. Browning, "The Beginnings of Insurance Enterprise Among Negroes," *Journal of Negro History* 22 (1937): 421–29.

27. The African origins of these mutual benefit societies remains a field of speculation. Certainly in the South, some of these societies evolved from the hidden, "invisible" institutions and folk culture that slaves developed within their plantation communities. Melville J. Herskovitz probably extrapolated from too little evidence when he held that they could be directly linked to African secret societies. Still, it is logical to assume that prior knowledge of African mutual aid systems would have been applied within the slave community. See Melville J. Herskovitz, *The Myth of the Negro Past* (New York: Harper and Brothers, 1941). Furthermore, structural similarities have been identified between the organization and rituals of the early mutual aid societies and their African counterparts. See Deborah Gray White's study of the "female slave network," which contributed to the collective care of children, the sick, and the elderly, as suggestive of the African origins of this mutual aid system (*Ar'n't I a Woman: Female Slaves in the Plantation* South [New York: Norton, 1985], 119–41). Herbert Gutman believed that this web of social obligations reached back to family and gender responsibilities in Africa (*The Black Family in*

*Slavery and Freedom, 1750–1925* [New York: Pantheon Books, 1976]). Betty Kuyk suggests an even more direct link, noting the African birth of several founders of these American societies ("The African Derivation of Black Fraternal Orders in the United States," *Comparative Studies in Societies and History* 25 [1983]: 559–94). And Susan Greenbaum argues that the earliest African American societies existed before the European organizations had much to offer in the way of a model ("A Comparison of African American and Euro-American Mutual Aid Societies in 19th Century America," *The Journal of Ethnic Studies* 19 [1991]: 111). Still, the traditional emphasis on secrecy and the need to hide organized behavior from their masters has left scant evidence of the existence of these societies among slaves. In contrast, evidence for the existence of northern societies like the Free African Society of Philadelphia is much more "visible." Jon Butler's review of recent work in African American religious history, "Africans' Religions in British America, 1650–1840," *Church History* 68 [1999]: 127–28, summarizes what we know about the persistence of African religions in the United States.

28. Mary Ann Clawson, *Constructing Brotherhood: Class, Gender, and Fraternalism* (Princeton: Princeton University Press, 1989), 131–35.

29. Douglas Knoop and G. P. Jones, *A Short History of Freemasonry to 1730* (Manchester, Ill.: Manchester University Press, 1940), chap. 1.

30. As fully qualified craftsmen, "free" to enjoy the rights and privileges of the guild, masons were referred to as freemasons much as other skilled tradesmen were sometimes called "free carpenters," for example, or men granted the rights of citizenship in a town were called "freemen." The several possible meanings of "free" include references to "freestone," a building material found in Scotland, and "freedom" from feudal serfdom. The term might also have referred to liberality (as in the seven liberal arts), though freemanship is the preferred meaning. See Dudley Wright, ed., *Gould's History of Freemasonry Throughout the World*, 6 vols. (New York: Charles Scribner's Sons, 1936), 1: 249–58; David Stevenson, *The Origins of Freemasonry: Scotland's Century, 1590–1710* (Cambridge, U.K.: Cambridge University Press), 11, and Douglas Knoop and G. P. Jones, *The Genesis of Freemasonry*, (London: Quatuor Coronati Lodge, 1978), 10–15. For changing meanings of the term in later Freemasonry, see Bernard E. Jones, " 'Free' in 'Freemason' and the Idea of Freedom Through Six Centuries," in *The Collected Prestonian Lectures, 1925–1960* (London: Lewis Masonic, 1983), 1: 363–76.

31. Clawson, *Constructing Brotherhood*, 53–83.

32. Concerning migration to the continent, Templarism, for example, originated as an aristocratic and anti-capitalist version of Freemasonry in France, but it achieved its most thorough dominance in Germany, where it developed as part of a wider reaction against the rationalist values of the Enlightenment. See Klaus Epstein, *The Genesis of German Conservatism* (Princeton: Princeton University Press, 1966).

33. Bullock, *Revolutionary Brotherhood*, 85–162.

34. This term was coined by Ann Swidler to refer to a culture's "habits, skills, and styles from which people construct 'strategies of action'" ("Culture in Action: Symbols and Strategies," *American Sociological Review* 51 [1986]: 273).

35. Nash, *Forging Freedom*, 217.

36. See William B. Gravely, "The Dialectic of Double-Consciousness in Black American Freedom Celebrations, 1808–1863," in David G. Hackett, ed. *Religion and American Culture*, second ed. (Routledge: New York, 2003) pp. 111–26.

37. Prince Hall, "A Charge, Delivered to the African Lodge, June 24, 1797," reprinted in *Early Negro Writings, 1760–1837*, ed. Dorothy Porter (Baltimore: Black Classic, 1995), 77.

38. Martin Delaney, *The Origins and Objects of Ancient Masonry, Its Introduction into the United States and Legitimacy Among Colored Men* (Pittsburgh: W. S. Haven, 1853), 18; see also Prince Hall, "A Charge Delivered to the Brethren of the African Lodge on the 25th of June, 1792," reprinted in *Early Negro Writings*, 63–69.

39. *Proceedings* (1872), 27.

40. Grimshaw, *Official History*, 84–130.

41. James Walker Hood, *One Hundred Years of the African Methodist Episcopal Zion Church* (New York: A.M.E. Book Concern, 1895), 85–86; Martin, *For God and Race*, 22–58.

42. Hood, *AMEZ History*, 2–26.

43. Hood, *AMEZ History*, 10.

44. Laurie Maffly-Kipp, "Mapping the World, Mapping the Race: The Negro Race History, 1874–1915," *Church History* 64 (1995): 610–26.

45. Hood, *AMEZ History*, 27–55; Martin, *For God and Race*, 74, 134.

46. Grimshaw, *Official History*, 305; by 1909, 2,600 of 3,336 Prince Hall lodges came from the South. For example, there were 340 Prince Hall lodges in Alabama compared to 70 in Pennsylvania (W. H. Anderson, *Anderson's Masonic Directory* [Richmond, Va.: W. H. Anderson, 1909]). The order continued to grow in the twentieth century, with as many as 150,000 followers in the 1920s and 300,000

by the 1950s, before beginning to decline. See William A. Muraskin, *Middle-Class Blacks in a White Society* (Berkeley, Calif.: University of California Press, 1975), 29. C. Eric Lincoln and Lawrence Mamiya confirm this decline (*The Black Church in the African American Experience* [Durham, N.C.: Duke University Press, 1990], 152).

47. Moses Nathaniel Moore, "Orishatukeh Faduma and the New Theology," *Church History* 63 (1994), 64–66.

48. Throughout his career, Hood remained committed to the belief that the Bible was the pure and infallible word of God. His commentary on the book of Revelation, for example, reflects this literalist understanding (*The Plan of the Apocalypse* [York, Pa: P. Anstadt & Sons, 1900]). His sermon, "Creation's First Born, Or the Earliest Gospel Symbol," takes issue with Darwinian science (in *The Negro in the Christian Pulpit* [Raleigh, N.C.: Edwards, Broughton and Company, 1884], 105–21). For examples of Hood's understanding of the nature of the Christian church in general and the mission of the black church in particular, see *The African Methodist Episcopal Zion Quarterly Review* 8 (1899): 1–9; "The Character and Power of the Christian Religion," *The African Methodist Episcopal Zion Quarterly Review* 13 (1904), 11–19; and *Sketch of the Early History of the African Methodist Episcopal Church*, Vol. 2 (New York: A.M.E. Book Concern, 1914), 66–69. Regarding Hood's position that Christianity is the unique pathway to salvation, see, for example, Hood, *Pulpit*, 105–21.

49. Henry Louis Gates, "The Trope of a New Negro and the Reconstruction of the Image of the Black," *Representations* 24 (1988): 155–99.

50. Maffly-Kipp, "Mapping the World," 617–19.

51. Hood, "The Negro Race" in *One Hundred Years*, 27–52.

52. Hood, "The Negro Race," 53–55. For a discussion of similar race histories see Laurie Maffly-Kipp's forthcoming book, *African-American Communal Narratives: Religion, Race, and Memory in Nineteenth Century America.*

53. See, for example, Benjamin T. Tanner, *The Descent of the Negro* (Philadelphia, 1898). For an insightful discussion of the influence of Darwinian science on race and manhood, see Gail Bederman, *Manliness and Civilization: A Cultural History of Gender and Race in the United States, 1880–1917* (Chicago: University of Chicago Press, 1995).

54. Martin, "Biblical Interpretation," 134.

55. Rufus L. Perry, *The Cushite, or the Descendants of Ham* (New York: Literary Union, 1887). *The A.M.E. Church Review* in 1899 recognized this work as fourth in a list of the most important works of the race (*Life of Frederick Douglass* was first). See *A.M.E. Church Review* 16 (1899): 631.

56. *Star of Zion*, 16 November 1893, 2. James Melvin Washington believed that Perry was not only a Mason but that his history "shows signs of his Masonic influences" (*Frustrated Fellowship: The Black Baptist Quest for Social Power* [Mercer, Ga.: Mercer University Press, 1986], 75, 131).

57. Delaney, *The Origins and Objects of Ancient Freemasonry*, 16–19.

58. Hood, *Christian Pulpit*, 107.

59. James Walker Hood, *Sketch of the Early History of the African Methodist Episcopal Zion Church* (Published by the author, 1914), 60, 62.

60. *Proceedings* (1880), 10.

61. Ibid., (1880), 11.

62. Ibid., (1880), 12.

63. Ibid., (1880), 12–13.

64. Ibid., (1880), 12.

65. Ibid., (1880), 12.

66. In 1903, the national total for members at each degree level was: Entered Apprentice: 30,640; Fellow Craftsman: 20,482; Master Mason: 66,365; TOTAL: 117,487 (Grimshaw, *Official History*, 305).

67. Harrison L. Harris, M.D., Grand Secretary of the Grand Lodge of Virginia, *Harris' Masonic Textbook: A Concise Historical Sketch of Masonry, And the Organization of Masonic Grand Lodges, and especially of Masonry among Colored Men in America; Also, a Compilation of the Illustrations of Masonic Work, As drawn from the Most Reliable Authorities on the subject* (Petersburg, Va.: Masonic Visitor Company, 1902), 134–93; Malcolm C. Duncan, *Duncan's Masonic Ritual and Monitor*, 3d ed. (Philadelphia: Washington Publishing Company, 1880); Grimshaw, *Official History*, 318–28; Anthony Fels, "The Square and the Compass: San Francisco's Freemasons and American Religion, 1870–1900," (Ph.D. diss., Stanford University, 1987), 145; and Mark C. Carries, *Secret Ritual and Manhood in Victorian America* (New Haven, Conn.: Yale University Press, 1989), 29.

68. Reverend William Spencer Carpenter, Right Worshipful Past Grand Master Prince Hall Grand Lodge of Massachusetts, Rector Bridge Street A.M.E. Church, Brooklyn, N.Y., Sermon delivered to the Masons of the Second Masonic District, 16 May 1920 (*Masonic Quarterly Review* 1 [1920]: 3).

69. Steven Bullock's recent study of the early years of the fraternity in America emphasizes Masonry's "multiplication of uses" which "involved Masonry in conflicting and even contradictory activities and ideas" (*Revolutionary Brotherhood*, 2–3).

Although Mary Ann Clawson's focus is on the social construction of class and gender (*Constructing Brotherhood*, 11), Mark Carnes sees Masonry providing young men with rites of passage away from the female-dominated home and to the masculine workplace (*Secret Ritual and Manhood*, ix), and an earlier work by Lynn Dumenil argues that the fraternity provided a "sacred asylum" in a rapidly changing society (*Freemasonry and American Culture, 1880–1939* [Princeton, N.J.: Princeton University Press, 1984], 32–42). All of these scholars, to differing degrees, point out that the fraternity's religious message was ambiguous.

70. *Proceedings* (1872), 34; *Proceedings* (1878), 27–28.

71. *Constitutions of the Freemasons: Containing the History, Charges, Regulations, etc. of the Most Ancient and Right Worshipful Fraternity* (London, 1723; reprint, Philadelphia, 1734). T. O. Haunch, "The Formation, 1717–1751" in *Grand Lodge, 1717–1967* (Oxford: United Grand Lodge of England, 1967), 80. The origins of eighteenth-century public displays, in turn, have been traced to later medieval towns where large religious parades involving most of the townspeople brought together the many layers of the civic hierarchy. Following the Reformation, the civic ceremonies that survived were oriented toward processions of the ruling oligarchy of town leaders to church or court with the townspeople participating only as onlookers (Peter Clark and Paul Slack, *English Towns in Transition, 1500–1700* [London, 1976], 131–71 and E. P. Thompson, "Patrician Society, Plebeian Culture," *Journal of Social History* 7 [1973–1974], 389). For an overview, see Bullock, *Revolutionary Brotherhood*, 43, 52–56, 70, 78–79, 80–82.

72. Louis Armstrong as quoted in Lawrence W. Levine, *Black Culture and Black Consciousness: Afro-American Folk Thought from Slavery to Freedom* (New York: Oxford University Press, 1977), 268–69.

73. Harrison L. Harris, *The Masonic Visitor* (August, 1887), 29.

74. Proceedings of the Nineteenth Annual Communication of the Most Worshipful Grand Lodge (Goldsboro, N.C.: Argus Publishing Company, 1889), 87.

75. See, for example, Don H. Doyle, "The Social Function of Voluntary Associations in a Nineteenth-Century Town," *Social Science History* 1 (1977): 338–43 or Rowland Berthoff, *An Unsettled People: Social Order and Disorder in American History* (New York: Harper and Row, 1971), 273–74.

76. Hood, *Pulpit*, 115.

77. *The Masonic Visitor* (June and July, 1887), 9.

78. *Proceedings . . . Fifth Communication* (1874), 7.

79. *Proceedings* (1886), 42–43.

80. *Proceedings of the Most Worshipful Grand Lodge, Forty-Eighth Communication*, Salisbury, N.C., 11–13 December 1917 (Nashville, Tenn.: A.M.E. Sunday School Union, 1917), 90.

81. On "respectability," see Higginbotham, *Righteous Discontent*, 14–15 and Montgomery, *Under Their Own Vine and Fig Tree*, 36–37.

82. *Masonic Visitor*, (June and July, 1887), 9.

83. Charles Price Jones, as quoted in Otho B. Cobbins, ed., *History of the Church of Christ (Holiness) U.S.A., 1895–1965* (New York: Vantage, 1966), 18.

84. Martin, *For God and Race*, 17–18. For Hood's evangelical and Holiness views, see his *The Negro in the Christian Pulpit*, esp. 33–48 and 247–59. On the emergence of the Holiness movement, see Montgomery, *Under Their Own Vine and Fig Tree*, 345–47.

85. For the Holiness attack on secret societies, see Giggie, *God's Long Journey*, 196–218.

86. Reverend Leonard of Olivet Baptist Church, as paraphrased in an article entitled "An Immense Congregation" in the *Indianapolis Freeman*, 6 June 1891.

87. H. T. Keating, "Secret Societies Among the Negroes," *The Christian Recorder* (Philadelphia: African Methodist Episcopal Church), 12 April 1883.

88. H. T. Keating, "Secret Societies Among the Negroes."

89. S. H. Coleman, "Freemasonry as a Secret Society Defended," *AME Church Review* 14 (1898): 327, 337.

90. G. L. Knox as quoted in "An Immense Congregation," *Indianapolis Freeman*.

91. See Carnes, *Secret Ritual and Manhood*, 24–26, 74–76 and *The History of the National Christian Association* (Chicago: Ezra Cook and Co., 1875), 28–29. In contrast to white Masonry, there is no evidence of an anti-Masonic campaign against Prince Hall Masons, nor of a decline in membership during the 1830s. On the contrary, the 1830s was a period of growth and prosperity for the order. As one Prince Hall historian put it, "perhaps" for the Prince Hall Mason "his subordinate and inconspicuous position permitted the storm [of anti-Masonry] to pass over his head" (Harry E. Davis, *A History of Freemasonry Among Negroes in America* [Published under the Auspices of the Scottish Rite, Northern Jurisdiction, 1946], 187–88).

92. Most white Masons regarded the lodge as their only religious institution. One study of late

nineteenth-century San Francisco reported that an overwhelming majority of all Masons, more than two-thirds, did not belong to any religious institution (Fels, *Square and Compass*, 435). See also Carnes, *Secret Ritual and Manhood*, 77–79.

93. Salvatore, *We All Got History*, 262. See also James Oliver Horton, "Freedom's Yoke: Gender Conventions Among Antebellum Free Blacks," *Feminist Studies* 12 (1986): 51–76.

94. Montgomery, *Under Their Own Vine and Fig Tree*, 114–15.

95. Salvatore, *We All Got History*, 66, 162, 207, 275.

96. Carnes, *Secret Ritual and Manhood*, 79.

97. Grand Lodge Proceedings (1876), 29.

98. Late in life, Hood stated that "[t]here are three important organizations in this State in which I have taken special interest, namely: The A.M.E. Zion Church, the Masonic Fraternity, and the Eastern Star" (*Grand Lodge Proceedings* [1917], 89). In the 1920s the Prince Hall historian Harry A. Williamson remarked that "[u]*nlike the whites*, [his emphasis] Negroes do not appear to understand the great line of demarcation between the two [male and female orders]" ("The Adoptive Rite Ritual," undated, Williamson Papers, Schomburg Library, New York City). Other black orders, like the True Reformers, incorporated women from the outset. See David M. Fahey, "Class, Gender and Race in Fraternal Ritualism: A Review Essay," *Old Northwest* 14 (1988) and *The Black Lodge in White America*, 7.

99. Martin, "The Women's Ordination Controversy, the AMEZ Church, and Hood's Leadership," *For God and Race*, 163–75.

100. Higginbotham, *Righteous Discontent*. See also Cheryl Townsend Gilkes, "The Politics of 'Silence': Dual-sex Political Systems and Women's Traditions of Conflict in African-American Religion," in *African-American Christianity: Essays in History*, ed. Paul E. Johnson (Berkeley, Calif.: University of California Press, 1994), 80–110.

101. Carnes, *Secret Ritual and Manhood*, 81–89.

102. For the Mormon appropriation of Masonry see John L. Brooke, *The Refiner's Fire: The Making of Mormon Cosmology* (Cambridge, U.K.: Cambridge University Press, 1994). Steven Bullock explores the Masonic male private sphere in *Revolutionary Brotherhood*, 239–73. Beyond Christianity, Daniel Soyer has recently explored the relationship between fraternalism and American Judaism in "Entering the 'Tent of Abraham': Fraternal Ritual and American-Jewish Identity, 1880–1920," *Religion and American Culture* 9 (1999): 159–82.

# THE LAKOTA GHOST DANCE

*Raymond J. DeMallie*

For Native American peoples, the nineteenth century was a period of continual change marked by the takeover of their country by white people, the disappearance of the buffalo, and finally, adjustment to reservation life. Until recently the ghost dance that emerged among many tribes in the late nineteenth century (and was most dramatically enacted during the Lakota Sioux massacre at Wounded Knee in 1890), has been interpreted as a reaction by Native Americans to hunger and the loss of their land. In contrast, Raymond DeMallie argues that this interpretation does not do justice to the religious nature of the movement or see it as part of the whole of Lakota culture. Instead, DeMallie sees the Sioux Ghost Dance as a new religious movement that drew upon and reformulated the pre-existing rituals and myths of the Lakota religious tradition.

# 15

## THE LAKOTA GHOST DANCE

An Ethnohistorical Account

*Raymond J. DeMallie*

THE LAKOTA GHOST DANCE (*wanagi wacipi*)[1] has been the subject of extensive study, first by newspapermen, who made it a true media event, and later by anthropologists and historians. The chronology of the contextual events in Lakota history—the 1888 and 1889 land cession commissions and their subsequent delegations to Washington, the beef ration cuts at the agencies, the spread of the ghost dance ritual among the Lakotas in 1890, the death of Sitting Bull, the calling in of U.S. troops, the flight of Lakota camps to the badlands, the blundering massacre at Wounded Knee, and the eventual restoration of peace under U.S. army control of the Sioux agencies—is voluminously detailed in the printed literature.[2]

The historiography of the Lakota ghost dance period begins with two contemporary works drawn primarily from newspaper sources, James P. Boyd's *Recent Indian Wars* (1891) and W. Fletcher Johnson's *Life of Sitting Bull and History of the Indian War of 1890–91* (1891). Despite the sensationalist tone, both volumes compiled a substantial body of important historical material. James Mooney, in his anthropological classic, *The Ghost-Dance Religion and the Sioux Outbreak of 1890* (1896), included a balanced historical discussion based on unpublished government records, newspaper accounts, and interviews with Indians. Mooney stressed the revivalistic aspects of the ghost dance and the hope it offered for regeneration of Indian culture. Subsequently there have been numerous historical studies of the Lakota ghost dance, most of which are partisan, focusing either on the Indian or military point of view. George E. Hyde's *A Sioux Chronicle* (1956) attempted to reconcile both perspectives and present the ghost dance in its political and economic context. The definitive modern historical study is Robert M. Utley's *The Last Days of the Sioux Nation* (1963), the best presentation of the military perspective.[3]

The so-called "Sioux Outbreak" with the associated troop maneuvers and the resultant Wounded Knee massacre were, from the moment they began, linked with the ghost dance. This new religion had come into Sioux country from the West, originating with Jack Wilson (Wovoka), a Paiute prophet living in Nevada. Lakota acceptance of the ritual has been interpreted as a response to the stress caused by military defeat, the disappearance of the buffalo, and confinement on a reservation. The ghost dance religion itself has been seen as an epiphenomenon of social and political unrest. As the redoubtable Dr. Valentine T. McGillycuddy, the former dictatorial agent of Pine Ridge, diagnosed the situation in January 1891: "As for the ghost dance, too much attention has been paid to it. It was only the symptom or surface indication of deep-rooted, long-existing difficulty. . . ."[4]

Such an analysis has become standard in the writings of both historians and anthropologists. Mooney wrote that among the Sioux, "already restless under both old and new grievances, and more lately brought to the edge of starvation by a reduction of rations, the doctrine speedily assumed a hostile meaning."[5] Similarly, Robert H. Lowie asserted in *Indians of the Plains* (1954), a standard text: "Goaded into fury by their grievances, the disciples of Wovoka in the Plains substituted for his policy of amity a holy war in which the Whites were to be exterminated."[6] However, this consensual interpretation of the ghost dance has not gone unchallenged. For example, in an anthropological overview, Omer C. Stewart explicitly rejected the characterization of the ghost dance as a violent, warlike movement.[7] Nonetheless, this is a minority viewpoint in the literature.

Re-evaluation of the ghost dance starts with an examination of the consensual interpretation exemplified in Robert M. Utley's work. He wrote:

> Wovoka preached a peaceful doctrine, blending elements of Christianity with the old native religion. . . . The Ghost Dance gripped most of the western tribes without losing this peaceful focus. Among the Teton Sioux, however, it took on militant overtones. . . . In their bitterness and despair, the Sioux let the Ghost Dance apostles, Short Bull and Kicking Bear, persuade them that the millennium prophesied by Wovoka might be facilitated by destroying the white people. Wearing "ghost shirts" that the priests assured them would turn the white man's bullets, the Sioux threw themselves wholeheartedly into a badly perverted version of the Ghost Dance.[8]

Before this analysis can be evaluated, a number of fundamental assumptions underlying it must be made more explicit. First, the statement that Wovoka's doctrine blended Christianity with "the native religion" implies that there was some fundamental similarity between the native religions of the Paiutes and the Lakotas. This assumption underestimates the significance of the vast cultural differences between these two tribes.

Second, the analysis asserts that the Lakotas perverted a doctrine of peace into one of war. This assertion incorrectly implies that the Lakota ghost dance religion was characterized by a unified body of doctrinal teaching. Lakota accounts of visits to the prophet clearly show that his teachings were not formulated into a creed; each man went away from meeting Wovoka with a personal interpretation of the ghost dance religion. For the Lakotas, this behavior was very much in accord with traditional religious practices, which defined loci of power (*wakan*) in the universe and devised rituals to tap this power, but which left each individual free to contribute to the understanding of the totality of the power (*Wakan Tanka*) through his own individual experiences.[9] Within the context of a non-doctrinal religion, there can be no heretics, only believers and nonbelievers.

Third, the analysis asserts that the leaders of the ghost dance misled their followers for political reasons, even to the point of making false claims that their sacred shirts would ward off bullets. This assertion assumes *a priori* that to its leaders the ghost dance was a political movement merely masquerading as religion.

Fourth, the claims that the ghost dance "gripped" the tribes and that "the Sioux threw themselves wholeheartedly into" the ritual suggests irrational fanaticism. But the historical record makes it clear that the period of Lakota participation in the ghost dance was basically confined to the fall and early winter of 1890 and that the majority of the Lakota people in the ghost dance camps had only gone to them because they feared that an attack from the U.S. army was imminent. This factor explains why these camps fled to the safety of the badlands.

The standard historical interpretation of the Lakota ghost dance takes too narrow a perspective. It treats the ghost dance as an isolated phenomenon, as though it were divorced from the rest of Lakota culture. It also refuses to accept the basic religious nature of the movement. The so-called ghost dance outbreak has broader implications and interconnections than historical studies have indicated. To dismiss the ghost dance as only a reaction to land loss and hunger does not do it justice; to dismiss it as merely a desperate attempt to revitalize a dead or dying culture is equally unsatisfactory. Even though it was borrowed from outside sources, the ghost dance needs to be seen as part of the integral, ongoing whole of Lakota culture and its supression as part of the historical process of religious persecution led by Indian agents and missionaries against the Lakotas living on the Great Sioux Reservation.

The primary reasons why previous historical analyses of the Lakota ghost dance have been inadequate lie in our reluctance to consider seriously the symbolic content of Indian cultures—in this instance, to allow the Lakotas their own legitimate perspective. Instead, empathetic writers have characterized the Lakotas as though they were either uncomprehending children or were motivated by precisely the same political and economic drives as white men. Both attitudes are as demeaning as they are misleading, and they fail to treat Indian culture with the same serious consideration afforded other cultures.

Writing history that deals with the meanings and conflicts of peoples with different cultural systems is a complex task. In recent years historians of the American Indian have turned to ethnohistory to provide methods for understanding the complexities of interactions between participants coming from totally different cultures. In a discussion of the new perspectives available from political, ecological, economic, and psychological anthropology, Calvin Martin has demonstrated the utility and contributions of each to the writing of ethnohistory.[10] Within the discipline of anthropology, however, there is a more general theoretical perspective that may profitably be applied to ethnohistorical study—namely, symbolic anthropology. This method attempts to isolate differing significant symbols—units of meaning—that define perspectives on reality within different cultural systems.[11] In the context of ethnohistory, it attempts to compare epistemological and philosophical bases for action from the perspective of the different cultures involved. Its focus is on ideas systematically reconstructed for each cultural system. It does not reduce history to ideological conflicts, but uses ideology to understand the motivation that underlies behavior.[12]

It must not be assumed that the intention of a symbolic approach to ethnohistory is to penetrate the minds of individuals in the past. Psychological approaches to history are necessarily highly speculative, and any claim to intersubjectivity is no more possible with individuals in the past than with those of the present. Rather, the symbolic approach attempts to delineate collective understandings from each of the cultural perspectives involved, and thus to describe the cognitive worlds of the participants in the events under study. Using this as background, the ethnohistorian has a basis for ascribing motives and meanings to past actions. Robert Berkhofer expressed it well when he wrote: "Historical study, then, in my view, is the combination of the actors' and observers' levels of analysis into a unified representation of past reality."[13]

In attempting to reconcile and combine both Lakota and white perspectives on the ghost dance, it is essential to compare causal notions of change as understood by the two cultures. During the late nineteenth century the basic issues on the Great Sioux Reservation were what kinds of change would occur in Indian culture and social life and who would direct this change. Whites assumed that Indian culture was stagnant and that the Indians could be transformed for the better only by the imposition of Western civilization. Indians, on the other hand, sought to control the process of change themselves.

For the Lakota people, the nineteenth century had been a period of continual changes: further explorations on the Plains, the complete integration of the horse into their culture, the flourishing of the sun dance as the focal point of ritual activity, the slow takeover of their country by the whites, the disappearance of the buffalo, and finally the adjustment to reservation life. A discussion of the Lakota view of the relationship between mankind and the natural world, particularly the buffalo, can help us begin to understand these changes from the Lakotas' perspective.

During the 1860s, when commissioners traveled up the Missouri River to sign treaties with the Indians, they found the attitude of the Lakotas toward the buffalo to be particularly unrealistic. To the commissioners it was evident that the buffalo were being exterminated and would soon be gone from the region. To the Indians this decline did not appear to be an irreversible process. For example, the chiefs told the commissioners that they hoped the whites would take away the roads and steamboats and "return us all the buffalo as it used to be."[14] Baffled at this illogic, the commissioners reported that the Indians "are only too much inclined to regard us possessed of supernatural powers."[15] This complete failure to communicate stemmed from the commissioners' assumption that the facts of the natural world must have appeared the same to the Indians as they did to the whites. Yet the Indians themselves recorded testimony which showed dramatically that the Lakotas thought of the land, the animals, and the people as a single system, no part of which could change without affecting the others. Thus when the commissioners asked if the Indians would consent to live on the Missouri River, they were told: "When the buffalo come close to the river, we come close to it. When the buffaloes go off, we go off after them."[16] The Indians, the animals, and the land were one; while the people lived, talk of buffalo extinction was without meaning. Much later, Black Elk expressed the same attitude when he commented to poet John G. Neihardt: "Perhaps when the wild animals are gone, the Indians will be gone too."[17]

To understand this interrelatedness of man, land, and animals—particularly the buffalo—it is necessary to understand the Lakota view of their origins. During the early twentieth century, the old holy men at Pine Ridge instructed Dr. James R. Walker, the agency physician, in the fundamentals of their religion. A cornerstone of their belief was that both mankind and the buffalo had originated within the earth before they emerged on the surface.[18] When the buffalo became scarce, it was believed that they went back inside the earth because they had been offended, either by Indians or whites. At any given time, this explanation accounted for the scarcity of buffalo. Later, Black Elk told Neihardt about a holy man named Drinks Water who had foretold during the mid-nineteenth century that "the four-leggeds were going back into the earth."[19] But this explanation also allowed for the return of the buffalo. The ghost dance messiah's promise of a new earth, well stocked with buffalo, was completely consistent with the old Lakota system of cause and effect by which they comprehended the ecology. If the buffalo had been driven back into the earth by the white man, they could be released again by the messiah.

The Lakotas' causal model of change was vastly different from the white man's. The Lakota world was a constant, with relationships among its parts varying according to external pressures. As the nineteenth century wore on, these pressures came more and more from the whites. But these pressures were not conceived of by the Lakotas as cumulative or developmental. All that *was* existed in its potentiality before the whites intruded; if they would leave, the world could be again as it had been. From the 1850s through the 1870s the Lakotas tried to get rid of the whites by war; in 1890 they tried ritual dancing and prayer. The white view, of course, was diametrically opposed. This was the age of the developmental social philosophers preaching the doctrine of individual competition for the evolution of humanity. The history of mankind was religiously believed to be progressive; changes were accepted as good and cumulative, leading from earlier stages of savagery and barbarism (in which the Indians still lived) to civilization, which was believed to be becoming progressively better, not only technologically, but morally as well.

It is within this general context of cross-cultural misunderstanding that a symbolic approach can contribute to an analysis of the Lakota ghost dance and subsequent military action. The dance itself, the actual ritual, became the focus of misunderstanding between Indians and whites. Most important, dance was a highly charged symbol. For the Lakotas the dance was a symbol of religion, a ritual means to spiritual and physical betterment. Even Lakota nonbelievers accepted the religious motivation of the ghost dance. For the whites, on the other hand, Indians dancing symbolized impending war. Similarly, Indian and white conceptions of ghosts were different. For the Lakotas, the ghost dance promised a reunion with the souls of their dead relations. For the whites it suggested that the Indians were expecting to die, caught up in a frenzy of reckless fatalism.

This clash over the meaning of the ghost dance is fully documented in the literature. For example, in 1890, according to James Boyd's *Recent Indian Wars*:

> The Indians mingled tales of their hard treatment with their religious songs, and their religious dances assumed more and more the form of war dances. . . . The spirit of fatalism spread and they courted death at the hands of white men, believing that it would be a speedy transport to a happier sphere.[20]

However, Boyd's sources—both Indian and white—do not provide factual support for his interpretation. Nonetheless, this seems to have been the general opinion held by whites living on the frontiers of the Great Sioux Reservation. Boyd wrote:

> Older residents, and those acquainted with Indian warfare, knew well that an outbreak was always preceded by a series of dances. While these men were quite familiar with Indian nature, they failed to discern between a religious ceremony and a war dance.[21]

Boyd reviewed the progress the Sioux had made in Christianity, home building, farming, and ranching, and he raised the question of why they would wish to precipitate war. One possible answer came from Red Cloud, who said in an interview:

> We felt that we were mocked in our misery. . . . There was no hope on earth, and God seemed to have forgotten us. Someone had again been talking of the Son of God, and said He had come. The people did not know; they did not care. They snatched at the hope. They screamed like crazy men to Him for mercy. They caught at the promises they heard He had made.[22]

Towards the end of the book, Boyd revealed his personal interpretation of the cause of the trouble: "The Indians are practically a doomed race, and none realize it better than themselves."[23]

Doubtlessly, some individual Lakotas shared this sense of despair. There were no buffalo; the government systematically broke its promises to support the Sioux until they could provide for themselves; and the Indians were starving. The ghost dance, arising at this opportune time, held out hope for the Lakotas. But if the Lakotas truly had believed themselves to be a doomed people, they would have paid no attention to the ghost dance. The religion was powerful because it nurtured cultural roots that were very much alive—temporarily dormant, perhaps, but not dying.

Is it reasonable to dismiss the Lakota ghost dance as insignificant, the mere "symptom" of other troubles, to use McGillycuddy's medical metaphor? This depiction does not explain the popularity of the ghost dance as a religious movement among other tribes. Perhaps it could be used to explain the warlike twist that the ghost dance took among the Lakotas. But when the record is evaluated objectively, it seems clear that the Lakota ghost dance did not have warlike intentions. Hostility was provoked only when Indian agents demanded that the dance be stopped, and violence came only after extreme provocation—the assassination of Sitting Bull by the Standing Rock Indian Police and the calling in of the army. For all intents and purposes, Sitting Bull's death was unrelated to the ghost dance. Agent McLaughlin had been clamoring for the old chief's arrest and removal from the reservation for some time, ever since Sitting Bull had refused to take up farming and be a model "progressive" Indian, to use McLaughlin's own term.[24]

Lakota ghost dancers were enjoined to put away whatever they could of the white man's manufacture, especially metal objects. George Sword, captain of the Pine Ridge Indian Police, noted that some of the ghost dancers did have guns.[25] When the agent demanded that the dance at No Water's camp cease, he was threatened with guns and retreated to the agency.[26] Apparently, the purpose of the weapons was to ward off outside interference with the ritual. However, Boyd quoted a ghost dancer named Weasel: "We did not carry our guns nor any weapon, but trusted to the Great Spirit to destroy the soldiers." This statement was made after troops had arrived at Pine Ridge. Weasel related: "The priests called upon the young men at the juncture not to become angry but to continue the dance, but have horses ready so that all could flee were the military to charge the village."[27] However, even this precaution was not considered necessary by fervent believers. Short Bull, one of the ghost dance leaders, assured his people that they would be safe from the white soldiers:

> If the soldiers surround you four deep, three of you, on whom I have put holy shirts, will sing a song, which I have taught you, around them, when some of them will drop dead. Then the

rest will start to run, but their horses will sink into the earth. The riders will jump from their horses, but they will sink into the earth also. Then you can do as you desire with them. Now you must know this, that all the soldiers and that race will be dead.[28]

Historical sources provide more information about the ghost dance from Short Bull than from any other of the leaders. Talking to Walker, he outlined his understanding of the prophet's teachings: "It was told that a woman gave birth to a child and this was known in heaven."[29] Short Bull went to meet him. "This man professed to be a great man, next to God." The prophet told Short Bull and the other Lakotas "that he wished to be their intermediator. He said 'Do nothing wrong.'" On another occasion Short Bull said:

> Who would have thought that dancing could have made such trouble? We had no wish to make trouble, nor did we cause it of ourselves. . . . We had no thought of fighting. . . . We went unarmed to the dance. How could we have held weapons? For thus we danced, in a circle, hand in hand, each man's fingers linked in those of his neighbor. . . . The message that I brought was peace.[30]

The messianic and strongly Christian nature of the ghost dance is very clear in Short Bull's teachings:

> The Father had commanded all the world to dance, and we gave the dance to the people as we had been bidden. When they danced they fell dead and went to the spirit-camp and saw those who had died, those whom they had loved. . . .
>
> In this world the Great Father has given to the white man everything and to the Indian nothing. But it will not always be thus: In another world the Indian shall be as the white man and the white man as the Indian. To the Indian will be given wisdom and power, and the white man shall be helpless and unknowing with only the bow and arrow. For ere long this world will be consumed in flame and pass away. Then, in the life after this, to the Indian shall all be given.[31]

Through the teachings of the ghost dance, and statements about it by Lakotas recorded from 1889 until about 1910, it is possible to proliferate evidence to demonstrate the peaceful intentions of the leaders of the ghost dance. The historical record does not support the accusation that the Sioux "perverted" the ghost dance doctrine of peace to one of war.

Simple refutation of the consensual historical interpretation does little to advance an understanding of the ghost dance. Since it had a short life among the Lakotas, at least as far as active performance of the ritual, perhaps it might be dismissed as an isolated reaction to social stress, a revitalization movement that failed. After all, Mooney estimated that only half of the Sioux were affected by the ghost dance, and his sources suggest that of these only a small number were real believers in the religion.[32] But this conclusion ignores the extreme importance that the Lakotas of 1890 placed on the dance, as well as the extent to which its suppression had served in later years as a symbol of white oppression. When Mooney visited Pine Ridge in 1891 as part of his comparative study of the ghost dance, he found the Lakotas uncooperative. He wrote: "To my questions the answer almost invariably was, 'The dance was our religion, but the government sent soldiers to kill us on account of it. We will not talk more about it.'"[33]

The study of Lakota history from 1880 to 1890 suggests that it is a mistake to treat the ghost dance as an isolated phenomenon. Its prohibition was only another step in the systematic suppression of native religious practices that formed an integral part of the U.S. government's program of Indian civilization. Missionary observers felt that the ghost dance was only one more eruption of the "heathenism" that necessarily underlay the Indian pysche, a heathenism to be conquered and dispatched when Indians, as individuals, raised themselves from barbarism to civilization. The evolutionary social theory of the times held sway in the rhetoric of Indian policy.[34] *The Word Carrier*, a Protestant missionary newspaper published at the Santee Agency in Nebraska, argued in 1890 (before Wounded Knee) that it was the government's responsibility to end the ghost dancing because of its political potential. The argument was an insidious one, expressed as follows:

> Their war dances have been suppressed simply as a political measure. The sun dance was forbidden in the name of humanity, as cruel and degrading. The Omaha dances should be summarily suppressed in the name of morality. But all of these alike, as well as all other of their heathen dances, should be prevented as far and as fast as possible until utterly eradicated, because they are potentially dangerous. We ought not to touch them as religious ceremonials, but, as breeders of riot and rebellion, we must.[35]

The callousness of missionary zeal for the suppression of heathenism is nowhere more dramatically revealed than in *The Word Carrier's* editorial on the Wounded Knee massacre printed in the January 1891 issue:

> The slaughter of a whole tribe of Indians at Wounded Knee was an affair which looks worse the more it is investigated. But aside from the question of culpability there is a providential aspect which demands notice. Taking it in its bearings on the whole condition of things among the rebellious Titon [sic] Sioux it was a blessing. It was needful that these people should feel in some sharp terrible way the just consequences of their actions, and be held in wholesome fear from further folly.[36]

Commentary is perhaps unnecessary, but we can suggest that the fanaticism of Christian missionaries was no less than that of the ghost dancers themselves. Stanley Vestal, in his biography of Sitting Bull, takes the Christian aspects of the ghost dance at face value and seizes the opportunity to comment on the missionaries:

> The Ghost dance was entirely Christian—except for the difference in rituals. However, it taught nonresistance and brotherly love in ways that had far more significance for Indians than any the missionaries could offer. No wonder the missionaries became alarmed; they were no longer sure of their converts.[37]

However, the dominant interpretation of the ghost dance, contemporarily and historically, places little significance on Christian parallels.

Some contemporary observers felt that the ghost dance showed striking resemblances to the sun dance, a suggestion that seems at first unfounded, but which gains credibility by reading descriptions of the ritual. Mary Collins, a missionary, witnessed the ghost dance in Sitting Bull's camp and recorded the following description:

I watched all the performance, and I came to the conclusion that the "ghost dance" is nothing more than the sun dance revived. They all looked at the sun as they danced. They stopped going round now and then, and all faced the sun, with uplifted faces and outstretched arms, standing in straight lines and moaning a most horrible sound. Then they raised themselves on the toes, and then lowered themselves, raising and lowering their bodies in this way, and groaning dismally, then joined hands with heads strained backwards, watching the sun and praying to it until, with dizziness and weariness, one after another fell down, some of them wallowing and rolling on the ground and frothing at the mouth, others throwing their arms and running around and whooping like mad men, and all the time, as much as possible, still gazing sunward. They have not yet cut themselves, as in the old sun dance, but yesterday I heard this talk: some said, "If one cuts himself, he is more 'wakan,' and can see and talk with the Messiah."[38]

These similarities to the sun dance—gazing sunward and the dance step of the sun dance—are suggestive. Also, Mooney notes that of all the tribes who adopted the ghost dance, the Sioux were one of the few to dance around a sacred tree (or pole), the structural form of the old sun dance.[39] This element may be superficial, serving only to indicate that when people borrow new ideas, they adapt them to older cultural forms as closely as possible. However, it reinforces the Lakotas' sense of religious loss and their deeply felt need to establish continuity with their past. It seems that the new religion, believed to come from a reincarnated Christ wearied of the faithlessness of the whites and ready to aid his Indian children, was incorporated in a ritual form that merged the circle dance of the Paiutes (in which men and women danced together in a circle, holding hands—an innovation for the Lakotas) with the sacred dance circle and center pole of the traditional Lakota sun dance.

A speech by Short Bull to his people on October 31, 1890, points out the importance of the tree or center pole as defining the sacred space for the ghost dance ritual: "Now, there will be a tree sprout up, and there all the members of our religion and the tribe must gather together. That will be the place where we will see our dead relations." Short Bull's ghost dance preachings incorporated traditional Lakota symbolism of the four directions to suggest the unifying effects of the ghost dance on all Indian tribes. "Our father in heaven has placed a mark at each point of the four winds," indicating a great circle around the central tree. To the west was a pipe, representing the Lakotas; to the north, an arrow, representing the Cheyennes; to the east, hail, representing the Arapahoes; and to the south, a pipe and feather, representing the Crows. "My father has shown me these things, therefore we must continue this dance." He promised that the ghost dance shirts would protect them from the soldiers. "Now, we must gather at Pass Creek where the tree is sprouting. There we will go among our dead relations."[40] Many years later one Lakota who had participated in the ghost dance as a boy commented: "That part about the dead returning was what appealed to me."[41]

In practice, the millennialism of the ghost dance was merged with the symbols of the old religion. The tree, which had symbolized the body of an enemy in the old sun dance, became in the ghost dance symbolic of the Indian people themselves; this tree was dormant, but it was about to sprout and bloom. The tree symbol is best known from Black Elk, who found the outward symbols of the ghost dance so strikingly similar to his own vision during childhood that he was immediately caught up in the new religion. He felt it as a personal call, a reminder that he had not yet begun the work assigned him by his vision. "I was to be intercessor for my people and yet I was not doing my duty. Perhaps it was the Messiah that had appointed me and he might have sent this to remind me to get to work again to bring my people back into the hoop and the old religion."[42]

It seems clear in Black Elk's case that the ghost dance, while seen as a new ritual, inaugurated by a new prophet—perhaps Christ himself—was in no way felt to be a sharp break with the old religion. It was rather a means to bring the old religion to fulfillment. There is no denial that this new hope for religious fulfillment was born of frustration and unhappiness bordering on despair. The ghost dance was to bring about the transformation to a new life on a rejuvenated earth filled with all the Lakota people who had ever lived before—living again in the old ways, hunting buffalo unfettered by the demands of whites, and freed from the cares of the old earth. Years later, one ghost dancer recalled the wonderful promise of the ghost dance visions:

> Waking to the drab and wretched present after such a glowing vision, it was little wonder that they wailed as if their poor hearts would break in two with disillusionment. The people went on and on and could not stop, day or night, hoping perhaps to get a vision of their dead, or at least to hear of the visions of others. They preferred that to rest or food or sleep. And I suppose the authorities did think they were crazy—but they weren't. They were only terribly unhappy.[43]

In order to put the ghost dance in its proper perspective in Lakota religious history, it is imperative to review the process of religious persecution that marked the Lakota experience during the 1880s. At Pine Ridge, from the beginning of the decade, Agent McGillycuddy preached against the evils of the sun dance. Finally, in his annual report for 1884, he wrote that "for the first time in the history of the Ogalalla Sioux and Northern Cheyennes" the sun dance was not held.[44] Though McGillycuddy did not fully understand the reasons why, the prohibition of the sun dance was indeed a drastic blow. As a public festival it brought together Lakotas from all the agencies into old-time encampments, with opportunities for courting and fun. In addition to the actual ritual of the ceremony, the sun dance provided the time and place for many additional rituals, including the acting out of visions, dances by groups of people with shared vision experiences, demonstrations of the powers of medicine men (healers), the piercing of babies' ears (essential for identity as a Lakota), and lavish giveaways. Camped around the sacred circle with the sacred tree at its center, the occasion of the sun dance was a real affirmation of Lakota identity and power, in both physical and spiritual senses. In the words of Little Wound, American Horse, and Lone Star, as they explained their traditional religion to Dr. James R. Walker in 1896: "The Sun Dance is the greatest ceremony that the Oglalas do. It is a sacred ceremony in which all the people have a part. . . . The ceremony of the Sun Dance may embrace all the ceremonies of any kind that are relative to the Gods."[45]

In 1888, as the Oglala winter counts—native pictographic calendars—record, a further government prohibition was enforced on the Lakotas: "Bundles were forbidden."[46] It had been the custom when a beloved person died to cut a lock of his or her hair and save it in a ritual bundle for a year, thus causing the spirit (*wanagi*) to remain with the people. At the end of the period, the spirit was released, and a great giveaway was held; throughout the year goods were amassed to give away in honor of the departed one. In some cases, as upon the death of a first-born son, the parents gave away everything they owned, although, according to tribal customs of sharing, they would in return be given the necessities of life and thus reestablished in a new home to help put the past out of their minds. Agent H. D. Gallagher at Pine Ridge decided in 1888 that although this custom had been allowed unchecked by his predecessors, he would put an immediate stop to it. Yet, he wrote in his annual report, "I found myself opposed by every Indian upon the reservation."[47] To the Lakotas it was a final horror: not even in death was there escape from the white man's restrictions. The giveaway after death was prohibited and became an offense punishable by arrest. Ten years later, in 1898, Short Bull, in his capacity as religious leader, sent a plea to the agent begging for understanding:

> The white people made war on the Lakotas to keep them from practicing their religion. Now the white people wish to make us cause the spirits of our dead to be ashamed. They wish us to be a stingy people and send our spirits to the spirit world as if they had been conquered and robbed by the enemy. They wish us to send our spirits on the spirit trail with nothing so that when they come to the spirit world, they will be like beggars. . . . Tell this to the agent and maybe he will not cause us to make our spirits ashamed.[48]

Such requests fell on deaf ears. From the agents' point of view, every vestige of heathen religion had to be eliminated before civilization could take firm root. The powers of the agents were dictatorial in the matter.

Following the prohibition of public rituals surrounding the sun dance, as well as the rituals of death and mourning, came the prohibition in 1890 against the new ritual of the ghost dance. Then came the murder of Sitting Bull and the massacre at Wounded Knee. It was a period of grave crisis for the Lakota people, physically and emotionally. Their religion had been effective before the whites came, but now the *Wakan Tanka* seemed no longer to hear their prayers. Under the restraints of reservation life, traditional customs relating to war and hunting were abandoned. For spiritual renewal there were only two places to turn: secret rituals of the purification lodge, vision quest, *yuwipi*, and attenuated versions of the sun dance, or alternatively to the various Christian churches which were clamoring for converts.

But the years immediately following the ghost dance were bad ones for missionaries to make new converts. According to Agent Charles G. Penney, in his annual report for 1891, there were yet "a considerable number of very conservative Indians, medicine men and others, who still insist upon a revival of the Messiah craze and the ghost dancing."[49] The following year the missionary John P. Williamson, a perceptive observer, reported from Pine Ridge that "the effect of the ghost dances in the former years was very deleterious to Christianity, and is still felt among the Ogalallas. The excitement of a false religion has left a dead, indifferent feeling about religion."[50]

The Lakota religious leaders at Pine Ridge who shared their thoughts with Dr. Walker at the beginning of the twentieth century were disappointed, but not defeated. Little Wound, after revealing the sacred secrets of the *Hunka* ceremony, said to Walker:

> My friend, I have told you the secrets of the *Hunkayapi*. I fear that I have done wrong. But the spirits of old times do not come to me anymore. Another spirit has come, the Great Spirit of the white man. I do not know him. I do not know how to call him to help me. I have done him no harm, and he should do me no harm. The old life is gone, and I cannot be young again.[51]

Afraid of Bear commented: "The spirits do not come and help us now. The white men have driven them away."[52] Ringing Shield stated: "Now the spirits will not come. This is because the white men have offended the spirits."[53]

One of the most eloquent testimonies comes from a speech by Red Cloud, recorded by Walker, in which he outlined his understanding of the Lakota *Wakan Tanka*. Then he added:

> When the Lakotas believed these things they lived happy and they died satisfied. What more than this can that which the white man offers us give? . . . *Taku Skanskan* [Lakotas' most powerful god] is familiar with my spirit (*nagi*) and when I die I will go with him. Then I will be with my forefathers. If this is not in the heaven of the white man, I shall be satisfied. *Wi* [Sun] is my father. The *Wakan Tanka* of the white man has overcome him. But I shall remain true to him.[54]

Outwardly, the white man's victory over Lakota religion was nearly complete. Inwardly, even among those who—like Red Cloud—accepted Christianity for what it was worth, the recognition of the existence of *wakan* in the life forms of the universe provided foci of belief and hope.

Any meaningful understanding of the Lakota ghost dance period must begin with an analysis of the foundations for cultural conflict. Lakotas and white men operated under radically different epistemologies; what seemed illogical to one was sensible to the other and vice versa. Objects in the natural world symbolized totally different realms of meaning in the two cultures. This difference has important implications for the writing of history. For example, Utley suggests that "when the hostile Sioux came to the reservation, they doubtless understood that the life of the future would differ from that of the past."[55] But we can raise a reasonable doubt that this statement truly characterized the Lakota point of view. When Utley writes: "That the vanishing herds symbolized their own vanishing ways of life cannot have escaped the Sioux,"[56] we must deny the assertion. This is the unbeliever's attitude, totally dependent on acceptance of western philosophy. Similarly, it is necessary to take issue with Utley's claim that "after Wounded Knee . . . the reality of the conquest descended upon the entire Nation with such overwhelming force that it shattered all illusions."[57] This is political rhetoric to justify the defeat of the Indians, not reasoned historical assessment.

The vast difference between the rhetoric of whites and Indians gives special significance to the ghost dance as the last step in a decade-long series of events aimed at crushing every outward expression of Lakota spirituality. From the believer's standpoint, the social and political problems—the so-called outbreak and the Wounded Knee massacre—were but epiphenomena of religious crisis. The ghost dance was inextricably bound to the whole of Lakota culture and to ongoing historical processes in Lakota society. Although it was introduced from the outside, it was rapidly assimilated to the Lakota system of values and ideas, especially because it promised resolution to the grave problems that beset the people. To recognize it as a religious movement in its own right does not deny its interconnection with all other aspects of Lakota life or negate its intended practical consequence to free the Lakotas from white domination. However, such recognition does retain the Lakotas' own focus on the ghost dance as a fundamentally religious movement which was to bring about radical transformation completely through religious means. Virtually all historical data point to the nonviolent intentions of the ghost dance religion and the commitment of the believers to achieving their ends nonviolently. It was the explicit command of the Messiah. In a cultural sense, this understanding of the ghost dance was shared by all Lakotas, believers and nonbelievers alike.

The importance of the ghost dance is not to be measured in the simple number of participants or in the unhappiness or despair that it reflected, but rather as part of the religious history of the Lakota people. For a time it held out such hope to the Lakotas that its ultimate failure, symbolized by the tragic deaths of the believers at Wounded Knee, generated a renewed religious crisis that forced a final realization that the old ways, with the hunting of the buffalo, were actually gone forever. Out of this religious collapse, new beliefs, new philosophies, eventually developed that would entail a major intellectual reworking of the epistemological foundations of Lakota culture.

Among the writers on the Lakota ghost dance, only John G. Neihardt accepted it as a legitimate religious movement and saw it as an attempt by the holy men of the Lakotas to use sacred means to better the condition of their people.[58] A symbolic approach forces examination of the religious aspects of the ghost dance, not only because it *was* primarily religious from the Lakotas' perspective, but also because at least some contemporary white observers—the missionaries—understood that the ritual's true power lay in its religious nature. To the white men the ghost dance was seen as the last gasp of heathenism; to the Indians it offered renewed access to spiritual power.

The ghost dance ritual itself was a powerful symbol, but one on whose meanings the whites and Lakotas were incapable of communicating. They shared no common understandings. That the ghost dance could be a valid religion was incomprehensible to the whites, just as the whites' evolutionary perspective on Lakota destiny—that the barbaric must develop into the civilized—was incomprehensible to the Lakotas. Religion, dancing, ghosts, the processes of social change, and animal ecology were all important symbols to both whites and Indians but the meanings of these symbols in the two cultures were diametrically opposed. By focusing on these symbols it is possible for the ethnohistorian to reconstruct the meanings of events from the perspective of the participants and to arrive at an analysis that has both relevance and insight, and which contributes to an understanding of the historical realities of the Lakota ghost dance.

## NOTES

1. Literally, "spirit dance." The term *wanagi* refers to the immortal spirit of a human and may be translated as "spirit," "ghost," or "soul." See James R. Walker, *Lakota Belief and Ritual*, ed. by Raymond J. DeMallie and Elaine A. Jahner (Lincoln, Neb., 1980), 70–71.

2. For a historiographical survey of the literature on the Lakota ghost dance, see Michael A. Sievers, "The Historiography of 'The Bloody Field . . . That Kept the Secret of the Everlasting Word': Wounded Knee," *South Dakota History*, VI (1975), 33–54.

3. James P. Boyd, *Recent Indian Wars, Under the Lead of Sitting Bull, and Other Chiefs; with A full Account of the Messiah Craze, and Ghost Dances* (Philadelphia, 1891); W. Fletcher Johnson, *Life of Sitting Bull and History of the Indian War of 1890–'91* (Philadelphia, 1891); James Mooney, *The Ghost-Dance Religion and the Sioux Outbreak of 1890*, Bureau of American Ethnology Annual Report 14, pt. 2 (Washington, D.C., 1896); George E. Hyde, *A Sioux Chronicle* (Norman, Okla., 1956); Robert M. Utley, *The Last Days of the Sioux Nation* (New Haven, 1963).

4. Mooney, *Ghost-Dance Religion*, 833.

5. Ibid., 787.

6. Robert H. Lowie, *Indians of the Plains* (New York, 1954), 181.

7. Omer C. Stewart, "The Ghost Dance," in W. Raymond Wood and Margot Liberty, eds., *Anthropology on the Great Plains* (Lincoln, 1980), 184.

8. Robert M. Utley, *Frontier Regulars: The United States Army and the Indian, 1866–1890* (New York, 1973), 402–403,

9. See Walker, *Lakota Belief and Ritual*, 68–73; Raymond J. DeMallie and Robert H. Lavenda, "Wakan: Plains Siouan Concepts of Power," in Richard Adams and Raymond D. Fogelson, eds., *The Anthropology of Power: Ethnographic Studies from Asia, Oceania and the New World* (New York, 1977), 154–165.

10. Calvin Martin, "Ethnohistory: A Better Way to Write Indian History," *Western Historical Quarterly*, IX (1978), 41–56.

11. For an introduction to the field, see Janet L. Dolgin, David S. Kemnitzer, and David M. Schneider, eds., *Symbolic Anthropology: A Reader in the Study of Symbols and Meanings* (New York, 1977) and Clifford Geertz, *The Interpretation of Cultures* (New York, 1973).

12. See, for example, DeMallie, "Touching the Pen: Plains Indian Treaty Councils in Ethnohistorical Perspective," in Frederick C. Luebke, ed., *Ethnicity on the Great Plains* (Lincoln, Neb., 1980), 38–53.

13. Robert E. Berkhofer, Jr., *A Behavioral Approach to Historical Analysis* (New York, 1969), 73.

14. *Proceedings of a Board of Commissioners to Negotiate a Treaty or Treaties with the Hostile Indians of the Upper Missiouri* (Washington, D.C., 1865), 104.

15. Indian Peace Commission, in *Annual Report of the Commissioner of Indian Affairs* (1866), 169.

16. *Proceedings of A Board of Commissioners*, 34.

17. Transcript of interviews of Black Elk by John G. Neihardt, 1931, 3–4, Western History Manuscripts Collection, University of Missouri, Columbia.

18. Walker, *Lakota Belief and Ritual*, 124, 144.

19. Black Elk interview transcripts, 161.

20. Boyd, *Recent Indian Wars*, 198.

21. Ibid., 180.

22. Ibid., 181.

23. Ibid., 289.

24. A good analysis is provided by Stephen D. Youngkin, "Sitting Bull and McLaughlin: Chieftainship Under Siege," (M.A. thesis, University of Wyoming), 1978.

25. Mooney, *Ghost-Dance Religion*, 798.

26. Ibid., 847.

27. Boyd, *Recent Indian Wars*, 194–195.

28. Mooney, *Ghost-Dance Religion*, 789.

29. Walker, *Lakota Belief and Ritual*, 142.

30. Natalie Curtis, *The Indians' Book* (New York, 1935), 45.

31. Ibid., 46–47.

32. Mooney, *Ghost-Dance Religion*, 917, 927.

33. Ibid., 1060.

34. See Francis Paul Prucha, *American Indian Policy in Crisis: Christian Reformers and the Indian, 1865–1900* (Norman, Okla., 1976), 155–158.

35. *The Word Carrier*, XIX, no. 12 (Dec. 1890) 34.

36. Ibid., XX, no. 1 (Jan. 1891), 1.

37. Stanley Vestal, *Sitting Bull: Champion of the Sioux* (new ed., Norman, Okla., 1957), 272.

38. *The Word-Carrier*, XIX, no. 11 (Nov. 1890), 30.

39. Mooney, *Ghost-Dance Religion*, 823.

40. Ibid., 788–789.

41. Ella C. Deloria, *Speaking of Indians* (New York, 1944), 83.

42. Black Elk interview transcripts, 182.

43. Deloria, *Speaking of Indians*, 83.

44. Valentine T. McGillycuddy, in *Annual Report of the Commissioner of Indian Affairs* (1884), 37.

45. Walker, *Lakota Belief and Ritual*, 179–180.

46. James R. Walker, *Lakota Society*, ed. by Raymond J. DeMallie (Lincoln, 1982), 151.

47. H. D. Gallagher, in *Annual Report of the Commissioner of Indian Affairs* (1888), 49.

48. Walker, *Lakota Belief and Ritual*, 141.

49. Charles G. Penney, in *Annual Report of the Commissioner of Indian Affairs* (1891), 410.

50. John P. Williamson, in ibid. (1892), 459.

51. Walker, *Lakota Belief and Ritual*, 198.

52. Ibid., 202.

53. Ibid., 206.

54. Ibid., 140.

55. Utley, *Last Days of the Sioux Nation*, 22.

56. Ibid.

57. Ibid., 5.

58. John G. Neihardt, *The Song of the Messiah* (New York, 1935).

# "HE KEEPS ME GOING"

*Robert A. Orsi*

Despite the fact that by 1890 Roman Catholics numbered more than one-quarter of America's churchgoing population, we still do not know very much about their religious lives. Between 1850 and 1920 successive waves of Irish, German, Italian, Polish, and other immigrants made the Roman Catholic Church by far the largest Christian denomination in the United States. Perceived by turn-of-the-century Protestants as an alien and other-worldly subculture, immigrant Roman Catholicism has also been set apart by scholars as a field of research. Even within the field of American Catholic history most scholarship has privileged the institutional church and its male hierarchy. Though recent work has focused on popular religion and the experience of the laity, the Irish and printed English sources continue to be favored. Among the many largely unexplored areas of the Catholic immigrants' religious life is the intimate relational world of devotional practices that evolved in the United States through the middle years of the twentieth century.

In his study of mid–twentieth century Catholic women's devotions to St. Jude, the saint of hopeless causes, Robert Orsi helps us to see this devotionalism as not only a "place of gender construction," but also a "site of gender contestation in American Catholic culture." Devotion to Saint Jude was shaped by both the intentions of the male hierarchy and the motives of lay women. The Claretian priests who created the shrine saw it primarily as a means of providing financial support for young boys attending the order's seminary. From this perspective, female devotion to Saint Jude reinforced women's submission to men. Women did not only inherit Jude, however, they also created him from the "needs and desires" of their particular life circumstances. The women who first turned to Chicago's new shrine to St. Jude in the late 1920s and 1930s belonged to a transitional generation of American Catholic women. Though still close to the inherited ways of their European mothers and grandmothers, they had to negotiate the new social and economic challenges that emerged from the disintegration of the old immigrant neighborhoods. For these second generation immigrants, Jude was a dependable guide and companion. In contrast to such well-known holy figures as St. Anthony and St. Thérèse of Lisieux, who had definite assignments in the old urban enclaves, Jude was a new presence in the American Catholic world as of 1929. Though formally recognizable, he was less burdened by a tradition of interpretation and therefore more open to the imaginations of immigrants' daughters who called upon him when the effects of changing historical circumstances entered forcefully into their lives. In contrast to the tendency among historians to see women's participation in the cult of saints as evidence of submission, Orsi emphasizes that the women themselves believed that they were empowered by praying to St. Jude.

While it is important to recognize the limitations of such empowerment, what has not been acknowledged is how devotionalism served as a source of power and identity for women. Here, Orsi is careful to warn us, the analysis must be dialectical.

Women did not directly challenge the family structures which they felt were oppressive, nor did they dramatically alter the devotional practices that were given to them. "Still, through the power of their desire and need, and within the flexible perimeters of devotional practice," they were able to re-imagine themselves by reshaping the available symbols of gender.

# 16

# "HE KEEPS ME GOING"

Women's Devotion to Saint Jude Thaddeus
and the Dialectics of Gender in American
Catholicism, 1929–1965

*Robert A. Orsi*

DEVOTION TO SAINT JUDE THADDEUS, patron saint of hopeless causes, began in an incident at Our Lady of Guadalupe Church, a Mexican national parish in South Chicago, in the spring of 1929. Our Lady of Guadalupe was a new church, built in 1928 by Claretian missionaries, a Spanish order of men who had assumed as one of their concerns the care of Spanish-speaking migrants in North American cities. The church was located in an ethnically mixed neighborhood, and representatives of the community's many different Catholic cultures had participated in its dedication ceremonies. South Chicago was dominated in these years by slaughterhouses and steel mills, and crisscrossed by train tracks. In prosperous times, a gritty cloud of cinders and dust darkened the streets even in the middle of the afternoon. These were not prosperous times, however, so the air was clearer, but the neighborhood was shadowed by economic crisis. Shrine historians emphasize the grim mood in South Chicago in the early months of 1929.[1]

Visitors to the church in these hard times could bring their prayers and petitions to two saints whose statues stood on a small side altar to the right of the central image of *Nuestra Señora de Guadalupe*. Saint Thérèse of Liseux, the Little Flower, occupied the place of prominence above this side altar, and off to one side on a detached pedestal stood a large statue of Saint Jude Thaddeus, who was at this time virtually unknown in American Catholicism.[2]

Most of the people kneeling before the two statues were women, although the story of the shrine's origins does not make this explicit. Popular piety in American Catholic culture has largely been the practice and experience of women, just as it has always been publicly dominated by male religious authorities.[3] As the devotion to Saint Jude eventually took shape in Chicago, it too became women's practice. Jude is identified by his devout with particular women in their lives. The minority of men who participate in the cult point back to their mothers, wives, or sisters when they talk about the first times they prayed to the saint. As one man told me, "I lived on Ashland Avenue [in Chicago]. My mother lived on Ashland Avenue for forty-five years. She called on Saint Jude whenever she had a problem, and I have followed in her footsteps."[4] Women have characteristically assumed special responsibilities in the practice of the cult; they were thought to be in a particularly close relationship with Jude not accessible to men, and as a result their prayers were believed to be more powerful and efficacious.

The clergy at various American Catholic shrines, well aware of this feature of the devotions over which they presided, have often seemed embarrassed by it; and they have sometimes worried that they were exploiting women to raise funds for clerical projects.[5] During the 1930s, the founder of Chicago's enormously popular Sorrowful Mother novena tried to goad men into attending services in greater numbers by offering them a reward of cigarettes, and the director of Jude's shrine warned in 1958 that prayer is "not only the practice of pious women and innocent children but a deadly earnest necessity for all equally."[6] But it is mainly women who appear in a pictorial essay on the shrine prepared in 1954.[7] However unacknowledged this participation is officially, the legend of the founding of Jude's shrine takes on new meaning, and raises new questions, when it is glossed with the fact of women's central role in the cult.

Thérèse was a celebrated figure, beloved for her "little way" of sanctity, the path of submission, humility, and silence. Contemporary authors have discovered another Thérèse, fiercely independent and spiritually innovative, but this was not the figure of the Catholic popular imagination in 1929. "Thérèse of Lisieux," writes Monica Furlong, "sweet, childlike, obedient, tragic, has been until recent times a cherished icon of Catholic womanhood," cast in "one of the favorite moulds of traditional female sanctity, the mould of virginity, of suffering, of drastic self-abnegation."[8] It is more difficult to determine how people understood Saint Jude, but I have asked his contemporary devout, many of whom have participated in his cult since its early years, and they most often emphasize his manly qualities. I was told that Jude "is tall, handsome, with a cleft in his chin"; "looks like Saint Joseph"; "[looks like] a very loving big brother or father"; "is quiet, soft-spoken, sure of himself"; "is very handsome—he looks like Jesus." One woman described him as "a great man, who is close to God and has a pull with him." Another said the saint is "a powerful healer. He looks like Christ. He looks like a man who wants you to test him on whatever the petitions may be." A sixty-eight-year-old woman whose devotion to Jude began twenty-five years ago gave me a longer description:

> I picture St Jude as a man to be of 5 feet and between 9 to 11 inches in height with a good and average build. He gives the appearance of a very kindly, loving, and caring person with a Big Heart. He looks like a very humble and courageous man, with a very Fatherly disposition, and compassion for all mankind particularly those who are desperate for help. His very close resemblance to his Cousin Jesus is simply outstanding and beautiful.[9]

The statue of Jude in Chicago, consistent with an older iconographical tradition, shows the saint holding in his arms a small image of Jesus' face, so that when the devout look at Jude they are looking into the faces of two men, a transposition of the familiar depiction of the Madonna and Child. The belief that Jude was an Apostle further identifies him with the church and its male authorities. One of my sources made this identification explicit: "Sometimes when I pray to him for something I need desperately it seems like he is standing right next to me in Mass vestments."[10]

Legends about the origins of devotions to particular saints, in Western and Eastern cultures, point to the supernatural influences determining the site of the devotion, and this is true of the account preserved at the shrine in Chicago as well. During Holy Week of 1929, the story goes, visitors to the church began gathering at the base of Jude's statue in ever greater numbers. So insistent was their devotion to the unknown Apostle that the clergy finally decided, on Holy Saturday, to reverse the two statues, giving Jude the place of prominence over the side altar, where he remains today. The cult of Saint Jude begins in this reversal. According to shrine chroniclers, this spontaneous expression of devotion to Jude was a sign that the saint himself had willed Chicago, an industrial city of immigrants in the middle of the United States, as the location of the modern revival of his cult.

The clergy had less supernatural reasons for preferring Jude to the Little Flower. Jude's cult was founded by Father James Tort, an ambitious and savvy young priest from Barcelona who is described in an early profile as a "little high-pressure" man.[11] The Claretians needed some means of supporting their various enterprises in the United States, and Tort must have realized that only limited help would come from Chicago's formidable Cardinal, George Mundelein, who believed that priests should finance and support their own endeavors.[12] Although there is no evidence of this, Tort surely knew that popular devotions were a well-tried and promising source of funds, but at the same time he also must have been aware that there was already a local cult of the Little Flower at a nearby Carmelite parish in Chicago, as well as a thriving national devotion based in Oklahoma City.[13] Jude, on the other hand, had the singular advantage of truly being the "unknown saint," as he is identified in the early years at the shrine.

Devotion to Saint Jude took shape then somewhere between the desires of the devout and the ambitions of the clergy. For our purposes it is not important whether or not this legend is true: this is how the shrine imagines its founding. The story of the switched statues, however, does raise the two interconnected sets of questions with which this essay is concerned, one having to do with the language and structures of gender in religious traditions and the other with the nature and practice of popular religion. But before I outline these issues, we need to look at how women think about this saint's place in their lives.

## "AN ONGOING RELATIONSHIP"

The most obvious characteristic of devotion to Saint Jude is the impulse of the devout toward narrative. Because Jude is the "hidden saint," as the shrine presents him, obscured in history by the unfortunate popular misidentification of him with Judas, the devout promise that they will make his actions in their lives public so that others will learn of him. This is the reason for all the discursive practices associated with the cult, from the long letters women write to the shrine to the simple thank-you notices that appear in the classified sections of local newspapers around the country. Women entered the world of the cult knowing that their connection with Jude would sooner or later give them the chance to describe in some public forum the most awful experience of their lives.

This transformation of experience into narrative took (and still takes) many forms. Women told their stories to other women, to strangers in hospitals, to family members, to needy colleagues at work. Jude's older devout, the women whose devotion dates to the early years of the cult's history, structure their autobiographies with reference to the saint's place in their lives; Jude has been their constant and trusted companion, they believe, every day, and at every major crisis or turning point in their experience. They reconstruct their lives with reference to Jude, imagining themselves in relation to this Other. Hagiography here takes on a new connotation: these women do not write and talk *about* the saint but about themselves and the saint together.

The following narrative was prepared in response to a request I made through the shrine's mailing list for stories of women's devotion to Jude. The woman writing is sixty-two years old, married, and the mother of two adult children who live close to her in a small New England town.

"I am writing," she begins, "because Saint Jude has been sharing all of my burdens, giving me peace of mind and generally being with me for more than 30 years." She first encountered the devotion in 1954, when "a crippled man" appeared at her door selling religious articles. "At that time I was 29 years old, newly married, pregnant, and living in my husband's family's house with my mother-in-law," a situation that was causing her some unhappiness. Jude's devout typically can remember the circumstances of their initial meeting with the saint, and they privilege this moment in their autobiographies: after encountering Jude, things change; something new happens. As another woman wrote to the shrine about her first meeting with Jude in 1941, "I never heard of this wonderful Saint, and it makes me feel like a different person since I know about him."[14]

Saint Jude intervened in the tense situation developing between the young woman and her mother-in-law. The couple was able to find their own home, and shortly afterwards their first child, a boy, was born. "From that time on, I very seldom made a decision or took any action in my life without asking Saint Jude for his guidance."

"How has he helped my family?" she asks. She has been married for thirty-four years, and even though "our life together was not perfect, all problems were minor and handled quickly by prayer to Saint Jude." Jude helped her raise her son and daughter, "particularly when [they] were teenagers and out on their own. . . . I would ask Saint Jude to care for them while I could not, and he always did!" Although her husband is "not as verbal or demonstrative in his devotion to Saint Jude as I am," he has seen what the saint has done for them and "I feel he also trusts Saint Jude for our future and is thankful for our past."

Jude helped her advance over the years from her first job as a "typist" to the position of managing executive of a town, the post from which she has recently retired. "I could not have accomplished this had Saint Jude not been with me all the way, putting the correct words and actions into my head when I required assistance." She has always told her friends and co-workers about Jude, and she kept shrine prayer cards in her desk to give to people who needed them. She has a statue of Jude on her bedroom dresser, and "in times of great stress I light a vigil light in front of this statue. . . . I feel my prayers are always answered, altho' my requests are not always granted." She closes her story, "I feel I have been very privileged to have Saint Jude with me always to help carry my burdens and share my joys."

The sense here at the end is of a partnership between Jude and this woman: Jude has helped her bear her own burdens, he has not miraculously taken them away. As another woman wrote me, "I am sure I pester Saint Jude too much, but he keeps me going and he never fails, although I try to help myself first."[15]

There was a postscript to the letter of the New England mother, appended three months later. "Before I completed this correspondence last June, my husband was diagnosed as having bladder cancer! I will not go into detail, but with the constant help of Saint Jude we have had the best summer I can remember." Although the future is uncertain, she says at the end, "I have complete confidence that Saint Jude will care for us both."[16]

Since the founding of the devotion in Chicago in 1929, many thousands of American Catholic women have lived in what another correspondent called "an ongoing relationship" with the saint.[17] They have carried his picture in their purses, set his statue up in their homes in places where, as they say, they can look into his "soft, sympathetic," "penetrating," "compassionate" eyes when they need to and have talked to him as they go about their days.[18]

These older women encountered Jude during the "heyday of devotionalism" in American Catholic culture, in Jay Dolan's phrase, from the 1920s to the 1960s, an extraordinarily creative period in the history of American Catholic popular piety, when women and clergy, sometimes together, frequently at odds with each other, experimented with devotional forms and structures in response to the community's changing needs and perceptions.[19] Jude's cult grew rapidly in these years, moving along dispersed tracks of narrative exchange in neighborhoods and across the country. The devotion existed primarily in women's conversations with each other. As one woman explained to me:

> I share my devotion to Saint Jude with all [the] members in my family and try to promote devotion to [among?] my friends and have succeeded. I have a friend who was terrified because the doctor discovered a lump on her breast and she came to me because I just had my right breast removed and I gave her the [Saint Jude] prayerbook and told her she must have faith in Saint Jude and she will come thru.[20]

Jude here is the medium for the exchange of confidences, shared fear and discomfort, and the occasion for the expression of support; and through conversations like this the devotion to Saint Jude became one of American Catholicism's most important and visible popular cults.

## HOPELESS CASES

The women who entered the world of Jude's devotion, seeking his face on medals and prayer cards, addressing his statue on their night tables, were impelled by fear and need. Jude was called upon only when all other help, divine and human, had failed. But what constitutes "hopelessness"? What kind of social or cultural experience is a crisis defined as "desperate"?

The hagiographical autobiography cited above offers some indication of what women meant by a hopeless situation: Jude helped in times of personal transition (from single to married, at the threat of impending widowhood), cultural change (during adolescence in the difficult 1960s), sickness, uncertainty, and when a beloved significant other turned away either in sickness, death, incapacity, powerlessness, or rejection. These were not "private" (as opposed to "public") occasions: Jude was called upon at just those moments when the effects and implications of changing historical circumstances (economic distress, the evolution of new medical models and authorities, and war, to cite just three of the recurring situations described by the devout) were directly and unavoidably experienced within the self and family.

"Crisis"—these situations of hopelessness—always has specific historical coordinates. There has been a tendency in discussions of the cult of saints to construe the entreaties of the devout as perennial: people have always gotten sick, this argument goes, and sick people always desire to be better, and this is why they pray to saints. But "crisis" itself is a cultural construction: people construe their unhappiness, experience their pains, talk about their sicknesses, and search for the appropriate intellectual, moral, and emotional responses to their dilemmas in socially and culturally bound ways. Because Jude stands at the intersection of the "private" and "public," praying to him became the way women encountered, endured, imagined, thought about, and learned the appropriate responses to "crisis." The cult offered women a critical catechesis in ways of living.

Women came to Jude as sisters, daughters, mothers, aunts—in other words, as figures in socially constructed and maintained kinship roles. The women who first turned to the saint in the late 1920s and 1930s belonged to an important transitional generation in American Catholic history. Historians have noted the beginnings of the dissolution in these years of the immigrant enclaves, the intricately constructed honeycombs of mutual responsibility and support in urban Catholic neighborhoods. Once the immigrant family had been the primary source of economic stability and social security, shaping an individual's fundamental choice of job, spouse, and residence; now the children of immigrant parents were confronted with new challenges and possibilities in a changing social and economic world.[21]

This new generation of American-born or raised southern and eastern Europeans had also begun to entertain new kinds of ambitions: the power and authority of immigrant parents, often not explictly denied, had begun to wane as their children entered a work world in which their parents could be of limited support and assistance. The woman whose autobiography we have studied began her work life as a typist, a position which required skills lacking in the immigrant generation. The period was marked by conflict between the generations in these Catholic ethnic communities as younger people sought greater autonomy in choosing companions, work, spouses, residence. In southern and eastern European immigrant communities, tension and anger over changing roles and expectations and distress over the loosening of traditional authority would be most sharply focused on young women.[22]

The letters written by women to the Chicago shrine over the years reflect these particular conflicts and special pressures. Jude was called upon when women were unable successfully to negotiate among contradictory cultural assignments and responsibilities: to help resolve conflicts over the choice of a spouse, for example, or to assist young women in their efforts to live their married lives in a newer, more American idiom as their husbands' partners, to aid them in finding and keeping jobs, and in securing adequate childcare while they worked.[23]

The devotion began in the experience of the Depression, flourished during the Second World War, and continued to grow in the postwar years; this is the public chronology of the cult. But these historical periods were experienced by the devout in particular ways, and the letters of need and gratitude written by women to the shrine and published in the *Voice of Saint Jude* constitute a running gloss on the recent past, disclosing the inner history of these years. During the Depression women wrote about their grief at their husbands' unemployment and their own dismay at not being able adequately to meet the household responsibilities they believed were theirs.[24] Women took their husbands to the shrine and prayed there with them, reestablishing through Jude a bond that was otherwise threatened. "We are praying," one woman wrote, "that my husband will hold his job and make good."[25]

In the late 1940s and throughout the 1950s, women brought to Jude their fears of the pain of childbirth or their terrible unhappiness at not being able to have children. A woman confided to the readers of the letters page of the *Voice of Saint Jude* in April 1952:

> During my pregnancy I was quite ill; and I was in such great fear of the pain I would have to endure when the baby would arrive. Yet with Jude's help I had the strength to see my illness through, and at the actual birth I suffered so little that I could hardly believe it was all over and I was the mother of a beautiful child.[26]

Another woman wrote that she had become "obsessed with fear" before her daughter's birth, but that she "wore [Jude's] medal (even on the delivery table) and put my fear and anguish in his hands."[27] Many women named their children Jude or Judith in gratitude for the saint's help.[28]

During the 1950s, when married women began looking for work outside the home again in greater numbers, the devout turned to Jude for assistance in dealing with the new problems they were facing. This is how one woman understood this particular moment in her life:

> I applied for a secretarial position [after being away from this work for five years] and while on the way to this job I prayed to Saint Jude who granted me this job. To this day and forever I shall thank him. Also granted was the guidance he gave me to get my boy started in kindergarten. For three weeks my boy cried when I took him and attempted to leave him in the room. The teachers and I had given up. One day as I was taking him home a stranger saw me crying and taking my boy home. She told me to pray to Saint Jude for help which I did and on the second day my boy went to class without a fear. I shall always be grateful and say a prayer for this stranger and Saint Jude.[29]

Single women turned to Jude for help in finding good husbands and then for assistance in dealing with the inevitable family tension that erupted over their choices. Younger women wrote that Jude helps "through all the frustrations and problems of being a teenager."[30] Mothers asked him to guide them in responding to the needs and values of their maturing children: "show me the right way to help my son" one woman prayed to the saint during a family crisis.[31] Older women sought Jude's assistance in caring for dying parents, living with the loneliness of widowhood, and facing the problems of aging.

Women understood themselves to be accomplishing something when they turned to Saint Jude: in partnership with him, they changed things, found work, settled problems.[32] The least helpful way of reading this devotion would be to try to account for what happens after prayer in the way that last century's scientists "explained" the cures at Lourdes. More important is to consider how these women created and sustained a world in relation to Jude, how they imagined reality and its alternatives, and how they constructed this world in their devotions. The stories women told about themselves and Saint Jude were not static recapitulations of experience, explained by referring to the economic crisis of the Depression or the physical threats of the social pressure to have children after the war. The narrative process is central here: the letters do not represent the recasting of experience in another, "symbolic," key, but the reexperiencing of experience in a new way.

We have seen that the women believed themselves to be "different persons" after encountering Jude. Without Jude's help, one woman wrote me, "I don't think I would be as a good a person."[33] The world and the self are remade in relation to Jude, but what is the world and who is the self so constituted?

## NEW AND BETTER PERSONS: QUESTIONS OF GENDER IN THE DEVOTION TO SAINT JUDE

Women who say that they became new persons in their encounters with Jude at the most desperate moment in their lives are alerting us to a central feature of devotionalism studied specifically as women's practice. Feminist historians for the last two decades have been struggling with fundamental issues of the study of women's history: Is this the history of domination? Resistance? Of women's culture or women's sphere, as an earlier division had it? Joan Scott has recently suggested that a new approach to women's history entails a new understanding of politics and subjectivity as well as a new analysis of gender. Drawing on poststructuralist understandings of subjectivity, Scott writes that "identities and experiences are variable phenomena . . . discursively organized in particular contexts or configurations." From this perspective gender is defined as culturally sanctioned and maintained "knowledge about gender differences."[34]

Religious traditions, with their considerable institutional and psychological authority, are highly privileged expressions of what is considered true and real (at least to certain segments of modern society), and devotionalism, which was the way most Catholics engaged their tradition in the mid-twentieth century, served as the site of particularly compelling discursive organizations of truth about gender. Religious sanctions were applied and divine approbation given to specific presentations of "maleness" and "femaleness" in the various media, official and popular, of American Catholicism. Women were positioned in a certain way in relation to the sacred, and this position was said to reflect and reveal women's fundamental identity.

What world of meaning, then, did women enter when they turned to Jude and imagined him looking at them with sympathy and understanding? The first task here will be to indicate some of the characteristic patterns of behavior, clusters of symbols, and affective responses (Geertz's "moods and motivations") that comprised American Catholic devotionalism in the middle years of this century. "Woman" was constructed in the tropes and metaphors of devotional culture in specific ways. When women prayed to the saint, practiced the cult, and discovered or created new selves in the process, they were learning by an intimate pedagogy the religiously consecrated cultural grammar of gender, and they were taking shape as selves within the gendered forms and structures with which reality is constituted by religious traditions.

Women entered the world of Jude's devotion at particularly difficult times, as we have seen: in their own perceptions, the world had become unhinged, everything was upside down, and they were feeling desperate, hopeless, and abandoned. Once we have identified some of the levels of meaning in the devotional construction of "woman," can we go on to say that at such desperate moments women were located in (and even located themselves in) a particular ordering of the world? To borrow a term from the structuralist study of ideology, are women "interpellated" here into the organization of gender characteristic of devotional culture?

The second part of the discussion that follows suggests another more dialectical possibility for understanding women and popular religion. Gender is not a static social category into which people are *fitted*. As Scott notes, constructions of gender emerge out of highly conflictual and open-ended cultural processes and so bear the marks of contradiction, dissent, resistance, repression. We will have to consider whether or not devotional culture is marked in this way as well, opening the way for creativity amid its fissures. But we need to begin with the world that women entered through Jude's eyes.

## "WHY SHOULD A VOICE LIKE MINE BE HEARD?" WOMEN IN AMERICAN CATHOLIC DEVOTIONAL CULTURE

The devotion to Saint Jude does seem to have reproduced in another register the character-istic structures of male-female relations during the Depression. Susan Ware observes that there was a clear division of men's and women's roles in the United States in this period, with women assigned primary responsibility for the maintenance, economic and moral, of the home. "Women had complete responsibility for the domestic sphere and played a cru-cial role in holding families together against the disintegrating forces of the Depression."[35] Threatened by their increasing inability to fulfill this sustaining role in hard times, women turned to religion for "consolation," as Ware puts it, and church attendance rose. William Chafe suggests that this inward turning and search for religious consolation and security reinforced women's traditional roles.[36] A number of studies of American working people have shown that workers tend to hold themselves responsible for losing their jobs, even in periods of manifest economic crisis, and evidence from the Depression suggests that women blamed their men for their inadequate support. One man remembers his feelings in Bethlehem, Pennsylvania, in the 1930s: "I think Roosevelt's program saved the self-respect and the sanity of a lot of men."[37]

Seen against this background, Jude appears to be a further expression of the resentment and disorientation women experienced when their husbands lost their jobs, on the one hand, as well as another way of saving male sanity and self-respect, on the other. Nowhere in the published letters (or in my conversations with the devout about these times) is there any expression of anger against an economic system that could make families feel hungry and threatened. Instead, women prayed to Jude for his help in finding work for their hus-bands; and when at last, often after long, sustained periods of searching, the latter did find jobs, their wives explicitly attributed their success to Jude, not to the men's skill, diligence, or dedication, or to changes in the economy. "I started a Novena on Easter Sunday so my husband would find work," one woman informed the shrine. "I am so happy to say that he went to work the other day. I am sure that without Saint Jude's help he would have failed to secure employment."[38] This is the characteristic structure of Depression narratives: they open with an incomprehensible event (unemployment), describe the woman's turning to Saint Jude, and end in an incomprehensible event (finding work), reinforcing—by finding religious meaning in—an alienated understanding of the social process. There is a perva-sive sense of passivity throughout: men are fired, men are hired. "Some time ago," another woman wrote the shrine in 1935, "I asked you to remember my husband in your prayers for the novena [sic] that he might secure work. At the same time I prayed hard and placed Saint Jude's picture in my front window and asked him to call my husband to work. A few days later he was called to work."[39]

Women were turning here to a male to help men, so that the devotion reproduced and confirmed female dependence on, and silent, unobtrusive support of, men. The public life of Jude's cult was male dominated. The Claretian rationale for the devotion was to provide financial support for young boys attending the order's seminary in Momence, Illinois. Pic-tures of seminarians regularly appeared in the *Voice of Saint Jude*, along with photographs of clergy and the other major group of males publicly identified with the cult, the Chicago

Police. Tort founded the Police Branch of the Saint Jude's League in 1932, both to secure Jude's protection for the police and to involve the latter in his various fundraising efforts. Several times a year the Chicago Police marched in full dress uniform around the shrine, or, after 1948 when a special meeting hall was opened for the fraternal organization in the Claretian building in the Loop, around the Claretians' downtown church. One thousand policemen received communion together at the shrine in 1936, five thousand on October 27, 1946. Pictures of these events routinely appeared in the *Voice*.[40]

Women were participating then in a devotion to a male saint, officially understood to derive his power from his kinship relationship with Jesus, a devotion that was publicly represented, not by women (with the unintentional exception of the pictorial history cited earlier), but by priests, boys destined for the clergy, and armed adult men.[41] The devout supported this structure out of a strong sense of duty: once Jude had acted for them, they understood themselves to have acquired a lifelong debt. One man told me that his mother sent a donation to the shrine even during the most difficult days of the Depression in thanksgiving for something Jude had done for her and in support of the boys in the seminary.[42]

American-born or -raised women, the daughters of the immigrants, were thus initiated into understandings of themselves as women common in Irish and southern and eastern European Catholic cultures: bound by duty and need to a male religious figure who was thought to be particularly responsive to their prayers, women acted in the cult as the strong, quiet, invisible centers of emotional, moral, and practical order and stability in their homes.[43] One way of understanding devotionalism in this period is as the disciplining of a new generation of Catholic women. As a priest writing in another popular devotional periodical, *Little Flower Magazine*, warned: "How much then there is for the [Catholic] women of America to do in their own gentle, womanly way. They must be the custodians of modern society to drive from it all sham and sin and falsehood; to scorn evil and love good; women of good lives, of intelligence, of tender feeling; women with pity and mercy, the living images of God's tenderness; an unsparing devotion to the happiness of others."[44]

There was a great deal of uneasiness in devotional culture that young Catholic women "in these days of movies, automobiles, trolleys, golf, sensational magazines, woman suffrage and women in business, sport, etc." (as these days were defined by Martin Scott, S.J., writing in the influential devotional journal *Ave Maria*) were not living up to the ideal of "the Catholic woman." The intensity and venom with which young women were imagined and criticized in devotional culture during these transitional years reflects this fear. "The ranks of the Magdalens will be recruited by numbers all too great," the editors of *Ave Maria* feared in 1927, because of the atmosphere in "stores and shops and factories and offices," and against this they urged "early training and parental control."[45] If women fall, according to Msgr. Thomas Riley, so does culture, because conscience is but "everyman's nagging wife."[46]

The discipline of economic hardship during the Depression was welcomed by some Catholic writers as an antidote to the dreams of young women. Mothers, wrote Nellie Ivancovich in *Ave Maria*, who are responsible for "building that citadel of the Church and of society, the Christian home," have been threatened of late by their own ambitions in "pagan and materialistic culture." But this is changing: "The many reasons that drew a large number of women away from the home—money, pleasure, prosperity—have failed in these days of depression, and people are learning that in the search for advantages something of much greater value has been lost—the proper care and training of the children." Fortunately, although mothers have been failing, the "ideal of perfect motherhood, a memory or a vision of 'Mother' as she was or might have been," has persisted.[47]

There were two categories of women in devotional culture: old women who had been broken by time and labor and young women who needed to be broken by time and labor. Older mothers are always tired, beaten, sad, and silent; young women are always rebellious, dangerous, wild. Rosie, a young bride in "Jim Graney's Wife," a short story published in *Ave Maria* in 1920 by Helen Moriarity, is an idle, rebellious red-haired beauty, "intoxicated with life, vain of the beauty which had captivated sober Jim Graney, selfish with youth's supreme and thoughtless egotism." She is contrasted in the story with Jim's mother, whose life is characterized by "self-sacrifice." One afternoon, Jim comes home and finds Rosie out with friends and his mother lying in a heap on the floor, crushed by overwork. When Rosie comes home, Jim exiles her forever from his house.

Rosie responds by indenturing herself as a servant to her own mother's family, and the transformation of the young woman by suffering begins. "Time . . . laid a devastating hand on her bright hair, ruthlessly took the lilt out of the gay voice, and set the giddy feet on duty's rugged path." She slaves for her family, converting their slovenly home into the cleanest dwelling in the neighborhood, but "in the process she herself became little more than an indistinguishable blur. A bent, pale little drudge, with red work-worn hands, the hair that was once her pride drawn back into a dull knot at the back of her head, she bore slight resemblance to the radiant, round-cheeked beauty that had charmed the heart out of sober Jim Graney."

As it turns out, Jim prefers red hands to red hair. His mother dies, and Jim, wounded in a railroad accident, is lying on his bed when he hears a "timid voice" asking him if he wants supper. At first he cannot recognize his wife, but when he does, he yields to the "tender touch of Rosie's toughened but capable hand." They reunite, raise many children together, and at the end of the story, gay young Rosie has become a "popular and beloved matron."[48]

Rosie and her sisters were treated harshly in devotional culture in these years. Inevitably wild and dangerous, they were frequently shown luring their "sober" men into danger. "Let's live on thrills," a young woman cries in a short story in the *Voice*, taunting her man on to drive recklessly, an adventure which ends with her in the hospital after the car crashes. "Freddy sustained only a broken collar bone. It was Barbara who paid the severe penalty with a crushed chest."[49] Young women are defined by their discontent and ambitions.[50]

They are punished for these things: the stories always end with the young women chastened by grief, pain, sickness—which they admit they have brought on themselves—alone in squalid rooms, abandoned by everyone except the saints and the Virgin, resigned to their new lives. Stories that played with this theme were published regularly in the *Voice*, a striking counterpoint to the expressions of suffering and grief in the letters columns. The plot is always the same: a successful young woman abandons the friends of her childhood in her lust for fame and glory, which she achieves very briefly before disaster strikes, after which she learns the true meaning of life. Susan Grayson, in Anne Tansey's "Will-o'-the-Wisp," was the pet of her teachers and the darling of a fast crowd of friends. After graduation, she seeks glory on the stage (indeed, she changes her name to "Gloria"), which she finds, although "success went to Susan's head." Suddenly, inexplicably, Susan breaks down and is "confined" to a hospital for three years—"careless and extravagant living exacted its toll." Alone, abandoned by the friends of her days of triumph, humiliated, Susan comes to her senses. She turns to the saints for help, but even here Tansey cannot refrain from ridicule, depicting the sad woman as "rushing" frantically "from saint to saint for succor." Susan finally finds Jude and accepts her lot in life: at the end she is living in a "shabby house in a poor section" but she is "placidly happy" and content with the "companionship of no one" other than Jude.[51] Not even young nuns are exempt from this treatment: in another story, when a novice's mother objects to the harsh discipline her daughter is undergoing at the hands of her novice mistress, the young religious replies, "Mother darling! It is only what I deserve, and you know it!"[52]

Women were warned in devotional culture that to make choices for themselves was to risk the certain destruction of their families. Their desires are always corrosive.[53] So dangerous were these women that at times their ambitions are treated as capital offenses: one young woman's murder in a story published in the *Voice* is called "retributive justice" for her having abandoned the "simple shepherd" who loved her as a girl.[54]

But the favorite gender trope of devotional culture was the woman in pain: suffering was understood to be women's true destiny and vocation, and the source of their access to power in the sacred world.[55] Suffering defined the vocation of motherhood. "We are 'two in one flesh,' with [mother] by a far more intimate physical union than she can possibly achieve with her husband," according to a priest writing in *Sign*, allowing the oedipal subtext of official devotionalism periously close to the surface. This is because "she suffers for us as she suffers for no other."

> In a sense, she dies for us that we might live, for it is of her substance, by the destruction of part of her, that our physical substance grows, differentiates, matures, and is delivered. Of all this, father is a silent spectator, quite helpless to do anything for his child.[56]

Mothers, who are always contrasted in devotional culture with wild young women, suffer with and for their children, and in this way redeem them.

The Christological undercurrents in this portrayal of mothers dying, children (sons) rising, is made explicit in the devotional treatment of Mary, who is described as "co-operatrix" in Jesus' work.[57] Mary alone can avert the disaster that God intends for humankind, becoming in this way the model woman standing loyally beside her fallen, depraved children. In a favorite imaginative exercise of devotional literature, a clerical writer asks, "How would your mother feel if she were to meet you on the way to the electric chair or the gallows?" Any good mother would behave in this situation like Mary. "She approaches Him and kneels, wipes the sweat and blood and spit from His face, throws her arms about Him. True mother even in this anguish, she seeks to console, rather than be consoled, to lift Him up rather than be lifted up, to encourage Him rather than be encouraged."[58]

Women are not just called to suffering in devotional culture, however; they are also taught how to suffer as women: cheerfully, resignedly, and above all, silently. A young, very sick female character in a story published in the *Voice* silences herself so as not to ruin "the little haven to which Jimmy [her brother] might come to the rest he had earned by honest toil."[59] When women complain, they bring down spiritual and physical disaster on their families.[60] Instead, they are called upon to imitate Mary, who is held up as the model of silent and resigned suffering. "Be brave then," a priest writing in *St. Anthony's Messenger* urges his women readers, "whoever you are, be silent, in imitation of her whose heart held the sorrows of the world."[61] "Why were you silent?" a character asks Mary in a poem published in *Ave Maria*; the Virgin modestly replies, "Why should a voice like mine be heard?"[62] Injunctions to silence seem particularly perverse in the devotional press because it was precisely here, in their letters of thanksgiving and request, that women broke their silence.

On May 30, 1920, a poor Roman matron, Anna Maria Taigi, was beatified by Benedict XV. She was quickly taken up by American Catholic devotional writers and offered as a model to mothers and wives. Taigi had been a "gay bride," according to Florence Gilmore in a sketch published in *Ave Maria*, until "the grace of God touched her soul." Seeing her "frivolity" now in a new light, Taigi began to wear "the commonest and coarsest clothes," under which she hid a hairshirt. She endured a life of terrible sufferings, which included a violently abusive husband, "cheerfully and smilingly" and sought ways to increase her discomforts. "Hot as Rome often is and hard as she worked, Anna Maria often passed several days without a drink of water." She was "unfailingly patient" with her abusive husband, "silent when he was angry, eager to please him in every way." God rewarded Taigi for her silent and willing suffering with the grace of healing: "the mere touch of her toil-roughened hands cured the sick."[63]

Women's pain/women's power; women in pain/women healers; female silence/male violence—this is the grammar of gender in American Catholic devotionalism in the crucial years after the end of immigration. The path marked out for women was clear: rebellion yielded crushing pain, while suffering and sickness made women powerful matrons, able to heal. All women had to do was keep silent. Broken, they were strong; through their own pain they secured the power to heal others.

This seems to be the logic of Jude's devotion as well. Women assumed all the responsibilities for their families in times of distress. They called on the saint, often in grueling prayer marathons that lasted all night or for days; as one woman put it, she prayed "until my throat ached" for a cure for a relative.[64] When a couple was in trouble, for example, or a man's business failing, it was always the responsibility of the women involved to pray and to make whatever sacrifices were thought necessary to propitiate the sacred. The devout believed that to some extent Jude's response to them was dependent on the quality of their prayer: it must be strong, intense, self-sacrificial.[65] It was women's task to negotiate with the sacred, bartering their own sacrifice and devotion for the welfare of their families. Women also assumed the duty of acknowledging and remembering the saint's intervention: years after a crisis, the women of a family continued to write to the shrine, recalling the moment of Jude's intervention.[66]

Women acted as the centers of prayer, domestic unity and order, success, and health, through their special alliance with Saint Jude: they prayed to Jude constantly, monitored his responses, assumed all responsibilities toward the sacred, wrote the narratives of distress and gratitude, and served as their families' memories. True to the warning against complaint in the devotional image of woman, the devout never expressed anger or resentment in their narratives at the husbands who left them, the doctors who failed to comfort them, or the children who rejected them. Participation in the devotion sealed women's sense of obligation: they were responsible for everything. They were also uniquely positioned to suffering—in some sense, identified with it, responsible for it. Like Mary in the devotional literature, they had assumed responsibility for averting disaster and had devoted themselves to others in need. A new generation of Catholic women seemed trapped in the consequences of devotional fantasies: they have been cast as the hidden figures responsible for holding up the world by the powers that are theirs through suffering, brokenness, and self-sacrifice.

## WHOSE VOICE? THE DIALECTICS OF POPULAR RELIGION

This is as far as a historian can go with the structural study of culture, which fails the social historian when he or she comes to the question of how people live in, with, and against, the discourses which they inherit. Göran Therborn has pointed out that ideology is always dialectical: people are both located in and empowered by particular arrangements of reality.[67] Gianna Pomata has criticized Donzelot's *The Policing of Families* in a way that is useful here. She writes,

> The tutelary "police" is here reconstructed and analyzed through its "knowledge," that is to say, the texts of doctors and philanthropists; but the book lacks, by contrast, a reconstruction of the other "knowledges" which this police encountered and with which it came into conflict, above all the knowledge of popular traditions. In this manner the book privileges the image of social processes and relations of power which emerges from texts linked to the "police," in relation to other possible images, other points of view.[68]

I would prefer to focus not on other knowledges but on the seams, disjunctures, and alternative possibilities within popular Catholicism itself. "The point of the new historical investigation," Joan Scott argues, "is to disrupt the notion of fixity, to discover the nature of the debate or repression that leads to the appearance of timeless permanence in binary gender representation."[69] Our task now is to uncover the polysemy of devotional culture, ritual, and belief.

Consider, as a way of beginning this discussion, whose "voice" was heard at the shrine. According to the official understanding, by narrating his intervention in their lives, women were giving Jude back his voice, which had been muted in history because of his identification with Judas. But the "voice" heard at the shrine was always double: by talking about Jude's actions in their lives, women were also speaking their own experience, finding a voice for themselves. Jude could not speak apart from the devout; his voice could be heard only in theirs. Indeed, the devout treated this as a bond of reciprocity or mutuality between heaven and earth: Jude needed them as much as they needed him. Women were thus enabled through this devotional ventriloquism to articulate aspects of their experience which they might otherwise have been unable to speak. The reciprocity between heaven and earth found its ultimate expression in this identity of voices.

Women did not only inherit Jude; they also invented him out of their needs and desires, and continued to invent him throughout their lives as they faced the successive crises and dilemmas of their experience. Jude's followers believed that when they wrote about the saint they were presenting him to the world for the first time. In this way Jude resembles the nameless spirits Gananath Obeyesekere has studied in the religious imaginations of Sri Lankan Buddhists. Obeyesekere writes that in distinction to the formalized, highly delineated deities of the official pantheon,

> Spirits, by contrast, are a known *category*, but they are not known beings. . . . [T]he individual exercises an option or choice in selecting a spirit from a known cultural category; and he manipulates the spirit. When these conditions obtain . . . the symbol or ideational set is used by the individual to express his personal needs.[70]

Although Jude was certainly in the recognizable and highly valued category of saint, he had had only the most modest prior tradition of popular devotion and the Chicago shrine claimed with some justice to have discovered this hidden figure. Like the spirits Obeyesekere studied, Jude was available for psycho-social improvisation: the blankness of Jude in the tradition became the space for the imaginative work of the devout.

Women imagined Jude as a sympathetic, caring, engaged man, who understood their needs and desires, a figure bound to them by various ties of reciprocity and mutual need and so both constrained and inclined to act on their behalf. Women claimed Jude by imagining him looking at them—in this way they took him away from the shrine and brought him into the centers of their experience. When I asked one woman what Jude looked like, she began by saying that of course he resembled the statue at the shrine, and then went on to offer a powerful, personal, alternative imagining of him.[71] Another woman pointed out that "in enjoying friendship with Saint Jude you feel an intimate personal feeling, almost like you are the only one praying to him."[72]

I have argued that it was a new generation of women who turned to Jude, imagining him into being as much as encountering him in the official cult, when the saints of their various immigrant communities no longer seemed adequate to their needs. The saint that was invented between Chicago and the personal experience of the devout was imagined to have a particular understanding of the special problems of women. He is compassionate and sympathetic, one woman wrote me, and has an "awareness of how we feel when we are going through a desperate situation."[73] Saint Jude, another woman told me, simply, "sees us for what we are."[74]

The intensity with which Jude was imagined, of course, reflected the dire circumstances of need and distress that motivated this imagining. "I was twenty years old, single, and very ill, and scared," a woman described the time of her first meeting with the saint, and went on to picture him as "kind, personable, and loving. I always relate to the picture on my prayercard."[75] Jude appeared then as the object of desire, his image constructed of many different sources, and the intensity of this desire threatened the closure of the discourse of woman and gender in devotional culture.

The initial deep connection between Jude and the devout was most often established through an imagining of his eyes, which one woman described as "penetrating," and more generally of his smiling, attentive, and compassionate face. His eyes are "compassionate and loving," "kind and sad," "soft and pleasing."[76] Jude's face is always turned toward his followers in gentle consideration. The devout say that Jude is: "a gentle, kind, loving person who you would like to embrace"; "kind, generous, and helpful"; and "someone to lean on."[77] Above all, Jude is a powerful friend who is sincerely interested in helping and understanding his devout. The saint, according to one woman, is "a compassionate person that would listen to your problems and intercede for you." Jude is "capable of handling the most serious problems in life." Unlike the living persons in their lives, finally, Jude never "turn[s] his head when I ask him for help."[78]

The conversations women had with this figure, whom they imagined in this way, were private and complex, often kept secret from husbands and children, and understood to be distinct from saying the official prayers published at the shrine.[79] "Oftentimes I carry on a full conversation" with Jude, one woman explained, and added that "periodically I plead and become angry." Women say that they came away from these conversations "full of hope."[80]

The material culture of devotionalism facilitated this process of personal appropriation. Women could send away to the shrine for various objects—statues, medals, prayer cards, oils, car ornaments—which they could then use and manipulate as they wanted, often to the consternation of the shrine clergy. This extensive or detachable quality of shrine culture was an important source both of women's power and improvisatory creativity in the practice of the cult. Women painted Jude's statue in bright colors, hid it in secret places in their homes or displayed it in elaborate home shrines; they sewed his medals into their husbands' and children's clothing and wore them on their underclothes when they went for radiation therapy. Until the early 1960s, when it was discontinued at the shrine, women used holy oil blessed with Jude's relic to heal themselves and their families and friends. The oil became the instrument of their power: they administered it on the bodies of sick kin and passed it on to friends with careful instructions about its proper use. When healings occurred, these women expected to be included in the thanksgiving for Jude's intervention.[81] (Older devout still manage to obtain oil for themselves, mainly from a rival shrine of Saint Jude in Baltimore.)

Women used the objects available at the shrine to create networks of support and assistance among their female relatives and friends similar to those their mothers and grandmothers had relied on in the transition from the old world to the new.[82] As they exchanged prayer cards of Saint Jude with each other in times of trouble, women also shared their stories, perceptions, and problems, and the saint became the privileged medium of communication between mothers and daughters, sisters, and friends. As one woman described this interweaving of voices, "A young lady friend of mine sent me the picture of Saint Jude with [the] prayer on the back. When we write to each other she would tell me her troubles, and I mine."[83] The exchange between women involving Jude was always an exchange of feelings, confidence, trust; it was also an exchange of information, one piece of which was about Jude, but included folk remedies, self-healing practices, advice on dealing with troubled husbands and children, recommendations of doctors, and life stories.

Acting within this network and in relationship with the gentle, powerful, attentive companion saint, women felt themselves to be empowered in new ways. They broke off relationships with "mean" boyfriends, rejected unwanted medical treatments, passed difficult qualifying exams of different sorts, and confronted family crises with newfound confidence.[84] Throughout the 1940s and 1950s, for example, when the official voices of devotional culture were decrying women's return to work, the devout found in their relationship with Jude the strength and confidence to look for, secure, and keep their new jobs.[85] Women have always written to describe problems they are having at work, their hopes of finding better employment, and their struggles with management. They have used prayer cards and medals to create networks of support with other women at work.[86] So central has Jude been to the working lives of women in these years that a contemporary devout has come to believe that the saint is particularly interested in the concerns of working women: "it has been my experience . . . that [Saint Jude] is especially good with finding employment and in solving problems related to employment."[87]

Finally, women resisted through various devotional practices, especially the construction of narratives of crisis, the silence imposed by Catholic devotional culture on women in the "Catholic home." The contrast between the male-articulated culture of innocence, as this has been well described by William Halsey in *The Survival of American Innocence*,[88] and the picture that takes shape in the letters pages is striking: the narratives written to the shrine recount tales of alcoholic husbands, financial struggles that are not glossed by sentimental celebrations of Christian poverty, women's fears of having more babies, and so on.

Women found their own sources of power and support and their own ways of speaking amid the complex possibilities of devotional culture.

## "DEVOTIONAL LIFE CAN BECOME EXUBERANT"

In 1943, Joseph Donovan reflected on one of his colleague's scruples about a new devotional practice in his monthly column of advice for parish clergy in *The Homiletic and Pastoral Review*. Some Irish-American women had taken to eating prayer cards of the Virgin Mary in the hope that this would secure their petitions. Donovan warned his clerical colleague not to be too fussy about such practices. After all, he points out, "devotional life can become exuberant."[89]

Although the clergy were often uneasy with this exuberance, as Donovan's comments suggest they also contributed in these years to an atmosphere of devotional experimentation and creativity. Many voices could be heard in the devotional world, speaking often against each other or from different perspectives, for different audiences. As one woman put it, writing to the shrine in 1949 about her trouble in finding adequate day care for her daughter while she worked, "This may not sound like a difficult problem to you, but. . . ."[90] She seems to be writing past the shrine clergy here to the other women who read and wrote for these pages.

This leads to a new understanding of devotionalism, not only as the place of gender construction, but as the privileged site of gender contestation in American Catholic culture. Devotional culture was polysemous and polyvalent. Women not only "discovered" who they were in the dense devotional world that developed through much of this century in the United States, but created and imagined themselves, manipulating and altering the available grammar of gender. Religious traditions must be understood as zones of improvisation and conflict. The idea of a "tradition" itself is the site of struggle, and historically situated men and women build the traditions and counter-traditions they need or want as they live. Finding meaning in a tradition is a dialectical process: women worked with the forms and structures available to them, and their imaginings were inevitably constrained by the materials they were working with. Still, through the power of their desire and need, and within the flexible perimeters of devotional practice, they were able to do much with what they inherited.

Women believed that they became agents in a new way with Jude's help. Their prayers made things happen in their lives. Then they sat down and wrote out accounts of their experience for publication at the shrine. These narratives must not be understood to provide "closure" to painful experiences in any simple sense. Rather, the narrative process, occurring within the complex world of devotional culture, was a zone of reimagination, a privileged exercise in which frightening experiences were engaged, struggled with, shared, endured, remembered, and in some sense healed. Women used the resources of devotional culture to recreate their world.

Again, the analysis here must always be dialectical. Women did not directly challenge the family arrangements which they experienced as oppressive, more often finding new ways of coordinating their lives within these structures with Jude's help; and I have discussed in this essay some of the ways that Jude's devotion recreated normative structures of gender relations. But these dimensions of the devotion must be read from the perspective of women's own appropriations, manipulations, and recreations of the forms and structures of devotionalism.

Finally, popular religion can now be seen as one of the central intersections of "public" events and "private" experience. Jude appeared as a figure in the space between prayer, desire, and need, on the one hand, and social and cultural structures, authorities, and norms, on the other. Although the devout do not recognize the disciplinary distinction between inner and outer, Jude was both a "public" symbol encountered by women in the language and structures of a particular religious tradition at a particular moment in their social experiences and the creation of private desire and imagination. The saint is a kind of boundary-crossing figure for the devout, serving as a special kind of emissary between levels of their experience. History is always the story of this conjuncture of inner and outer.

## THE STORY OF THE SWITCHED STATUES AGAIN

Why did the daughters of immigrants turn to Saint Jude in the difficult days of 1929? We know how they went on to imagine Jude, and what their lives with this saint looked like. Perhaps they were dissatisfied with the holy figures that their parents prayed to, suspecting that these saints could not understand their new experiences and feelings. Perhaps they were frightened by their fathers' and husbands' difficulties at finding and keeping work, and in response they created a powerful, sympathetic man for themselves who could help them but who was also dependent on them for his own voice.

But I have begun to wonder whether this generation of Catholic women may also have been turning away, perhaps unconsciously, from the model of the Christian woman offered in Thérèse—the saint of "suffering" and "self-abnegation"—in favor of a saint whose existence was rooted in their needs and who would not only understand and comfort them, but empower them as well.

Power in what sense though? Freedom, Sartre said in an interview late in his life, is what a person can make of what has been made of him or herself. This is the dialectic of devotionalism.

## NOTES

1. This paper has benefited from the close scrutiny and generous criticism of two of my friends and colleagues at Indiana University, Jeff Isaac and Rich Miller. I am grateful to both of them for their help.

The history of the founding of the Church of Our Lady of Guadalupe is based on *Dedication of Our Lady of Guadalupe Church*, September 30, 1928. Chicago: John H. Hannigan Publisher; "Necrology: Father James Tort, C.M.F.," a privately printed biographical sketch, 1955; *Our Lady of Guadalupe Church: 50th Anniversary Bulletin, 1924–1974*, privately printed by the Claretian Fathers, 1974; Joachim DePrada, C.M.F., "Our Founder Is Dead," *Voice of Saint Jude* (hereafter cited as *Voice*), June 1955, 34; Frank Smith, "Load of Bricks Stumps Priest Who Fled Bullets," *Voice*, February 1935, 18; James Tort, C.M.F., "Dedication Anniversary of the National Shrine of Saint Jude," *Voice*, February 1935, 12–13; George Hull, "Life Begins at Forty," *Voice*, June 1935, 7–10; John Schneider, C.M.F., "Tenth Anniversary," *Voice*, April 1942, 12–17. The history of the shrine is told in comic-book form in "Jude the Forgotten Saint," published in 1954 by the Catechetical Guild Educational Society.

2. Mary Lee Nolan and Sidney Nolan, in their comprehensive survey of contemporary shrine culture in Western Europe, note that Jude ranked third among the Apostles as a "pilgrimage saint," with at least nine European shrines dedicated to him. They go on to say, however, that "the cult of this apostle, who replaced Judas Iscariot among the original group, developed slowly and became important only in the Twentieth Century." Nolan and Nolan, *Christian Pilgrimage in Modern Western Europe* (Chapel Hill, N. C., and London: 1989), 137.

3. For women's central place in nineteenth-century popular piety see Ann Taves, *The Household of Faith* (Notre Dame, Ind., 1986).

4. Interview with Frank K, sixty-six years old, Los Angeles, California.

5. J. P. Donovan, C.M., takes up the question of clerical scruples on this matter in "Is the Perpetual Novena a Parish Need?" *Homiletic and Pastoral*

*Review* 56, no. 4 (January 1946): 252–57. Donovan, who wrote a regular advice column for his clerical colleagues, says that some clergy had concluded that devotional practices like the perpetual novena were either "rackets" or "sentimentality." For a rather bitter clerical admission of the predominance of women in devotional culture see Francis W. Grey, "The Devout Female Sex," *Ave Maria* 26, no. 20 (November 12, 1927): 609–12.

6. John M. Huels, O.S.M., "The Friday Night Novena: The Growth and Decline of the Sorrowful Mother Novena," privately printed by the Eastern Province of Servites, Berwyn, Illinois, 1977, 21–23; and Joachim DePrada, C.M.F., "To Whom Shall We Turn?" *Voice*, December 1958. In several different gatherings of clergy I have heard it dryly observed that the problem with the ordination of women is that if women take over clerical duties there would be no one left in the pews.

7. "We Visit a Solemn Novena," *Voice*, October 1954, 14–17.

8. Monica Furlong, *Thérèse of Lisieux* (New York, 1987), 1. For an excellent review of the "posthumous history" of the Little Flower, her changing image over time, see Barbara Corrado Pope, "A Heroine without Heroics: The Little Flower of Jesus and Her Times," *Church History* 57 (March 1986): 46–60.

9. Personal communications: FG-F-49-Chicago-M; AC-F-70-Chicago-W; MPD-F-75-So. Chicago-W. MTD-F-27-Haiti-M; AI-F-55-Chicago-D; AG-F-55-Chicago-S; DD-F-62-Whiting, Ind.-M; FA-F-68-Indiana-S. I distinguish in the notes between two kinds of direct communications to me. "Personal communication" refers to women's written responses to twenty very general questions about their devotions to Saint Jude which I distributed at the shrine in Chicago during a novena in the summer of 1987. Seventy women responded. (I did not ask that only women participate, nor do the questions imply that I think men would not pray to Saint Jude, but only five men wrote to me.) Most of the women who responded to my questions did so at length, adding sheets of paper to the form I had distributed. "Personal correspondence" refers to letters sent me about Saint Jude; I received forty of these. I also conducted about thirty-five interviews with the devout, and these are cited in the text as well. These three sources are intended to supplement the letters written to the shrine over the last fifty years.

I will identify my sources by a consistent designation, beginning with fictitious initials, followed by gender, age, residence, and marital status. In the latter category, M=married, S=single, W=widowed, D=divorced.

10. Personal correspondence: MMc-F-89-LaCrosse, Wisc.-W.

11. George Hull, "Life Begins at Forty," *Voice*, June 1935, 8–9.

12. On Mundelein, see Edward R. Kantowicz, *Corporation Sole: Cardinal Mundelein and Chicago Catholicism* (Notre Dame, Ind., 1983), and Charles Shanabruch, *Chicago's Catholics: The Evolution of an American Identity* (Notre Dame, Ind., 1981). According to shrine accounts, Mundelein was an enthusiastic supporter of the cult in its early years, Hull, "Life," 8.

13. Information on this important popular devotion is in *Little Flower Magazine*, published monthly until the mid-1970s by the Carmelite Fathers of Oklahoma City. There is a historical sketch of the origins of the devotion to the Little Flower in Chicago in *The Sword*, May 1948, 106–16.

14. *Voice*, February 1941, p. 18, Mrs. EF, Detroit.

15. Personal correspondence: MCM-F-89-LaCrosse, Wisc.-W.

16. Personal correspondence: RA-F-62-Dracut, Mass.-M.

17. Personal correspondence: AM-F-65+-Carol Stream, Ill.-M.

18. Personal communication: JF-F-49-Chicago-M; BE-F-66-Chicago-M; CD-F-75-Milwaukee-M.

19. There is unfortunately no comprehensive history of this period. Jay Dolan has a short and helpful chapter on the subject in *The American Catholic Experience: A History from Colonial Times to the Present* (Garden City, N.Y., 1985), "The Catholic Ethos," 221–41. The best study of American Catholic popular religion in the nineteenth century is Ann Taves's *Household*, cited earlier. Joseph Chinnici's recent history of piety in the United States, *Living Stones: The History and Structure of Catholic Spiritual Life in the United States* (New York, 1988), is unfortunately not concerned with popular religion.

20. Personal communication: CD-F-75-Milwaukee-M. Another woman wrote me: "I give these prayer cards out all over the U.S. My friends and people are scattered from Cleveland, Ohio, Minnesota, Illinois, Louisiana, Kentucky, Florida, Nevada, Newportnews, Taft, Scranton. I sent for 1000 [prayer cards]. All I can say Where I go my Patron Saint Jude goes with me." Personal correspondence: CG-F-75-Richmond, Va.-W.

21. This sketch of the changing history of immigrant communities is based on a number of studies both of particular ethnic communities as

well as of immigration more generally. I owe a great
deal to John Bodnar's *Workers' World: Kinship,
Community, and Protest in an Industrial Society,
1900–1940* (Baltimore and London, 1982), and *The
Transplanted: A History of Immigrants in Urban
America* (Bloomington, Ind., 1985). These transitions are helpfully discussed in Shanabruch,
*Chicago's Catholics*, 155–87. For studies of particular communities see Judith E. Smith, *Family Con-
nections: A History of Italian and Jewish Immigrant
Lives in Providence, Rhode Island, 1900–1940* (Al-
bany, N.Y., 1985); Humbert Nelli, *Italians in
Chicago, 1880–1930: A Study in Ethnic Mobility*
(Oxford, 1970); Dino Cinel, *From Italy to San Fran-
cisco: The Immigrant Experience* (Stanford, Calif.,
1982); Virginia Yans-McLaughlin, *Family and
Community: Italian Immigrants in Buffalo, 1880–
1930* (Ithaca, N.Y., and London, 1971); Samuel L.
Baily, "The Adjustment of Italian Immigrants in
Buenos Aires and New York, 1870–1914," *American
Historical Review* 88 (April 1983); Joseph John
Parot, *Polish Catholics in Chicago, 1850–1920: A Re-
ligious History* (DeKalb, Ill., 1981); Paul Wrobel,
*Our Way: Family, Parish, and Neighborhood in a
Polish American Community* (Notre Dame, Ind.,
1979); Dennis Clark, *The Irish in Philadelphia: Ten
Generations of Urban Experience* (Philadelphia,
1973); Lawrence McCaffrey, Ellen Skerret, Michael
F. Funchion, and Charles Fanning, *The Irish in
Chicago* (Urbana, Ill., and Chicago, 1987); Peter
d'A. Jones and Melvin G. Holli, *Ethnic Chicago*
(Grand Rapids, Mich., 1981); Audrey S. Olson, *St.
Louis Germans: The Nature of an Immigrant Com-
munity and Its Relation to the Assimilation Process*
(New York, 1980); Josef J. Barton, "Religion and
Cultural Change in Czech Immigrant Communi-
ties, 1850–1920," 3–24, in Randall M. Miller and
Thomas D. Marzik, eds., *Immigrants and Religion
in Urban America* (Philadelphia, 1977); William J.
Galush, "Faith and Fatherland: Dimensions of Polish-
American Ethnoreligion, 1875–1975," 84–102, in
Miller and Marzik, *Immigrants and Religion*; and
M. Mark Stolarik, "Immigration, Education, and
the Social Mobility of Slovaks, 1870–1930," 103–16
in Miller and Marzik, *Immigrants and Religion*.

22. As Linda Gordon has observed of this period in her study of family violence in Boston, although "parental violence against adolescents of
both sexes" in immigrant communities which were
just experiencing the loss of the "family economy,"
was "particularly intense," it was "more so with
girls." Linda Gordon, *Heroes of Their Own Lives:
The Politics and History of Family Violence, Boston,
1880–1960* (New York, 1988), 188.

23. *Catholic Women's World*, a "new type of
Catholic magazine," according to its editors, "designed for the modern woman," began publication
in June 1939. Although intended for a college-
educated, middle-class audience, the magazine is a
useful guide to the changing concerns and needs of
young Catholic women in these years. Of particular
interest here is the treatment of married life in the
magazine: the women in *Catholic Women's World*'s
fiction, advice columns, and true stories all seem
to feel that they must work carefully and conscientiously to make their marriages successful, to
the extent even of taking classes to learn how to
do special things in the kitchen and around the
house. (Adele de Leeuw, "Bookcases and Broccoli,"
*Catholic Women's World* 1, no. 5, [November 1939].)
There are beauty hints each month and pages of
recipes, as well as highly ambivalent advice about
love and work from Jane Frances Downey. Although
Jude's devout came from all social classes, *Catholic
Women's World* points to a broader shift in social
mores among younger Catholic women. The entry
of these women into the culture of expertise, their
need for advice on everything from buying towels
to changing diapers, suggests that they had begun
to feel that their mothers' counsel was of limited
usefulness to them.

24. "My husband and I were married less than
two months," a woman wrote the shrine in October
1936, "when he lost his position. Needless to say, it
brought about a great deal of worry and shattered
our dreams for the future." *Voice*, October 1936,
Mr. and Mrs. MJB, Chicago.

25. *Voice*, September 1936, 15, Mrs. MCG,
Chicago. For relations between men and women in
this period see Susan Ware, *Holding Their Own:
American Women in the 1930s* (Boston, 1982), 8–18,
and William Chafe, *The American Woman: Her
Changing Social, Economic, and Political Roles* (Oxford, 1972), 135ff.

26. *Voice*, April 1952, 32, DD, Detroit.

27. *Voice*, July 1950, 7, PR, Saint Louis.

28. Personal communication: ER-F-74-Chi-
cago-M.

29. *Voice*, July 1953, Mrs. GH, Chicago.

30. *Saint Jude's Journal*, January 1967, 4, Miss
JF, Baltimore. The *Journal*, a small, four-page, simply printed devotional newsletter, began publication in 1960. At the same time, the *Voice of Saint
Jude* was renamed *U.S. Catholic*, and all devotional
material was shifted out of that periodical and into
the newsletter. The *Voice* had been evolving over
the years into a more general Catholic family magazine, which had long been the ambition of its cleri-

cal and lay editors and publishers. But the devotional material had fit quite well into this evolving format through the 1940s and 1950s, and indeed there were important connections between the devotional features of the periodical and the more sophisticated political and social commentary that had begun to appear: Jude, for example, was as stalwart an anti-Communist as any Catholic editor. Something else was happening, though, in Chicago and elsewhere at the end of the fifties: devotionalism, which had flourished in the postwar years, had come under sharp criticism from liturgical reformers, parish clergy, and a new generation of Catholic laity. The repositioning of the devotional material at the shrine reflects this new sensibility.

31. *Voice,* April 1958, DSS, Rosindale, Mass.

32. I discuss this aspect of the devouts' understanding of themselves in "What Did Women Think They Were Doing When They Prayed to Saint Jude," *U.S. Catholic Historian* 8, nos. 1–2, (Winter/Spring 1989): 67–79.

33. Personal correspondence: AS-F-65+-Carol Stream, Ill.-M.

34. Joan Scott, *Gender and the Politics of History* (New York, 1988), 24.

35. Ware, *Holding Their Own,* 2–24.

36. Chafe, *The American Woman,* 135.

37. Bodnar, *Workers' World,* 116.

38. *Voice,* June 1935, 16, SMT, Chicago.

39. *Voice,* January 1935, 16, Mrs. ME, Chicago.

40. On the Police Branch of the Saint Jude's League see: Frank Smith, "Load of Bricks Stumps Priest Who Fled Bullets," *Voice,* February 1935, 18; Father Anthony, C.M.F., "The St. Jude Novena," *Voice,* March 1938, 10; John Schneider, C.M.F., "Tenth Anniversary," *Voice,* April 1942, 12–18; Joseph M. Puigvi, C.M.F., "Jottings on Devotion to Saint Jude," *Voice,* December 1946, 7; "Police Overflow Church for Annual Communion," *Voice,* June 1948, 7; "19th Annual Police Mass," *Voice,* June 1951, 19; Joachim DePrada, "Our Founder Is Dead," *Voice,* June 1955, 34; "Guns and Missals," *Voice,* October 1954, 28–29.

41. A recent shrine director suggested to a reporter from a local Chicago paper that, in the reporter's words, "policemen are logically clients of Saint Jude . . . in that they carry clubs." Peter Schwendener, "The Patron Saint of Hopeless Cases," *Reader,* May 27, 1983, 34. Jude is usually shown holding a thick wooden shaft, the implement of his martyrdom.

42. BC-M-55-Queens, N.Y-M.

43. As John Bodnar writes, "in nearly every immigrant household economy, the central manager of financial resources, children's socialization, and the entire operation, was the married female." *Transplanted,* 81–82.

44. Father Marrison, O.C.D., "The Woman in Social Life," *Little Flower Magazine* 15, no. 9 (December 1934): 5.

45. "The Discipline of Girls," *Ave Maria* 25, no. 26 (June 25, 1927): 821.

46. Joseph McClellan, "Everyman's Nagging Wife," *Ave Maria* 90, no. 13 (September 26, 1959): 5–9.

47. Nellie R. Ivancovich, "Motherhood," *Ave Maria* 35, no. 11 (March 12, 1932): 338–40.

48. Helen Moriarity, "Jim Graney's Wife," *Ave Maria* 12, no. 15 (October 9, 1920): 463–66, and 12, no. 16 (October 16, 1920): 494–98. See also: E. M. Walker, "East End Granny," *Ave Maria* 25, no. 25 (June 18, 1927): 781–83; James A. Dunn, "The Picture," *Sign* 28, no. 8 (March 1949): 20–23; Constance Edgerton, "Desert Love," *Voice,* April 1938, 17–18; Anne Tansey, "Receive This Word," *Voice,* June 1944, 14, 16–17; Pauline Marie Cloton, "Larry's Wife," *Sacred Heart Messenger,* 56, no. 6 (June 1921): 325–32.

49. Tansey, "Receive This Word," 14.

50. P.J.C., "Contentment," *Ave Maria* 35, no. 14 (April 2, 1932): 437.

51. Anne Tansey, "Will-o-the-Wisp," *Voice,* July 1944, 10, 17.

52. Sister M. Marguerite, R.S.M., "Barter and Exchange: For Fathers Only," *Voice,* May 1947, 4, 19, 24.

53. Ben Hurst, "Sibyl's Awakening," *Ave Maria* 26, no. 22 (November 26, 1927): 688–91; Ann Tansey, "Going Home," *Voice,* September 1944, 10, 16.

54. Edgerton, "Desert Love," 18.

55. For a good discussion of the history of women's identification with suffering in the Catholic tradition, and the special place in this story of Augustine's suffering mother, Monica, see Clarissa W. Atkinson, " 'Your Servant, My Mother': The Figure of Saint Monica in the Ideology of Christian Motherhood," 139–72 in Atkinson, Constance H. Buchanan, and Margaret R. Miles, eds., *Immaculate and Powerful: The Female in Sacred Image and Social Reality* (Boston, 1985).

56. Hilary Sweeney, C.P., "When Ignorance is Bliss," *Sign* 28, no. 11 (June 1949): 39–40.

57. "The Union of Jesus and Mary," *Ave Maria* 12, no. 26 (December 25, 1920): 820–21. This theme is most strongly articulated in the widely read work of Don Sharkey. See for example *The Woman Shall Conquer* (New York, 1954), which is a celebration both of Mary's (and in general, women's) powers and of women's suffering.

58. Arthur Tonne, O.F.M., "Swords of Sorrow," *St. Anthony's Messenger* 48, no. 8 (January 1941): 25, 47.

59. Maude Gardner, "The Undaunted Christmas Spirit," *Voice*, December 1937, 15–17.

60. Sister M. Adelaide, R.S.M., "Short Wave to Saint Jude," *Voice*, April 1950, 4.

61. Tonne, "Swords," 31.

62. Alice Pauline Clark, "The Silent Saint," *Ave Maria* 35, no. 12 (March 19, 1932): 353.

63. Florence Gilmore, "Wife, Mother, and Saint," *Ave Maria* 35, no. 8 (February 20, 1932): 240–43; also Countess de Courson, "A New Beata. Anna Maria Taigi," *Ave Maria* 11, no. 25 (June 19, 1920): 782–87.

64. *Voice*, December 1950, 5, MC, Chicago. One female correspondent reports that she made a fifty-four day "rosary novena" while she and her husband were looking for a home. *Voice*, September 1958, ARS, Chicago.

65. *Voice*, May 1955, 34, Mrs. CEN, Bay City, Michigan; ibid., June 1951, 32, RM, St. Louis; personal communication: DH-F-67-Indiana-M.

66. *Voice*, January 1935, Mrs. MB, Chicago; ibid., March 1935, 15, Mrs. EH, Hasbrouck Heights, N.J.; ibid., December 1950, 5, IB, Kent, Conn.; ibid., April 1955, 34, Miss CM, Chicago.

67. Göran Therborn, *The Ideology of Power and the Power of Ideology* (London, 1980), 16–18.

68. Quoted in Peter Dews, *Logics of Disintegration: Post-Structuralist Thought and the Claims of Critical Theory* (London and New York, 1987), 188.

69. Scott, *Gender*, 43.

70. Gananath Obeyesekere, *Medusa's Hair: An Essay on Personal Symbols and Religious Experience* (Chicago, 1984), 115–22.

71. Personal communication: DA-F-54-Chicago-W.

72. Personal communication: EA-F-59-Chicago-M.

73. Personal communication: BC-F-36-Joliet, Ill.-S.

74. Personal communication: BF-F-75-So. Chicago-W.

75. Personal communication: GG-F-55-Chicago-M.

76. Personal communications: BB-F-48-Chicago-S; HH-F-33-Chicago-M; CD-F-75-Milwaukee-M; CH-F-69-Chicago-W.

77. Personal communications: DG-F-76-Chicago-M; AH-F-58-Chicago-M; BE-F-66-Chicago-M.

78. Personal communications: CD-F-67-Chicago-M; EF-F-63-Chicago-W; *Journal*, April 1967, 4, OJB, Forest Park, Ga.

79. Personal communication: BG-F-63-Chicago-M. She writes, "Somehow I would much rather talk [to] him than say the Journal prayers."

80. Personal communications: BD-F-46-Chicago-M; AH-F-58-Chicago-M.

81. See, for example, *Voice*, January 1935, 17, Mrs. CGF, Chicago; ibid., May 1935, 16, Mrs. MHF, Chicago, and Mrs. MK, Chicago; ibid., March 1950, 6, AS, Wyoming, Ohio; ibid., April 1950, 5, LW, Malden, Mass.; ibid., March 1951, 29, DR, Santa Clara, Calif.; ibid., March 1958, Mrs. ERP, Lawrence, Mass.; *Journal*, August 1966, 4, Mrs. PS; ibid., April/May 1964, 4, Mrs. MS.

82. See Bodnar, *Workers' World*, 173.

83. Personal communication: US-F-65+-Michigan-M. On the importance of women's networks see Ellen Ross, "Survival Networks: Women's Neighborhood Sharing in London Before World War I," *History Workshop* 15 (Spring 1983): 4–27; Mary P. Ryan, "The Power of Women's Networks: A Case Study of Female Moral Reform in Antebellum America," *Feminist Studies* 5, no. 1 (Spring 1979): 66–86; and Temma Kaplan, "Female Consciousness and Collective Action: The Case of Barcelona, 1910–1918," *Signs* 7 (1982): 545–66.

84. Personal correspondence: MF-F-60(?)-Yarmouth, England-S; *Voice*, April 1941, 18, Mrs. AG, Chicago; ibid., May 1953, 33, Mrs. PK, Louisville, Ky. "When I have a problem," a correspondent wrote in 1967, "I always say a prayer to Saint Jude and it seems I can face that problem with more courage." *Journal*, August 1967, Miss MP, no location cited.

85. On the consensus in the devotional press against women's working see Joseph McShane, S.J., "And They Lived Catholicly Ever After: A Study of Catholic Periodical Fiction between 1930 and 1950," unpublished paper; on the general social disapproval of this, see Chafe, *American Woman*, 174–89.

86. *Voice*, July 1955, Mrs. MF, Cincinnati.

87. Personal communication: BC-F-36-Joliet, Ill.-S.

88. William Halsey, *The Survival of American Innocence* (Notre Dame, Ind., 1980).

89. Joseph P. Donovan, C.M., "Novenas and Devotional Tastes," *Homiletic and Pastoral Review* 43, no. 7 (April 1943): 643–44.

90. *Voice*, June 1949, 4, MC, Providence, R.I.

# PART FOUR

# CONTEMPORARY LIFE
# 1945–PRESENT

# OLD FISSURES AND NEW FRACTURES IN AMERICAN RELIGIOUS LIFE

*Robert Wuthnow*

Before the Second World War, much of American religious life was divided into the three dominant groups of Protestants, Catholics, and Jews. After the war, this division was replaced by a cross-cutting ideological fracture separating religious conservatives from religious liberals. Unlike older interpretations that saw the principal tensions in American life as those dividing Protestants from Catholics and Christians from Jews, Robert Wuthnow employs a sociological and empirical analysis to document this new mapping of American religious life as polarized along liberal and conservative lines. Conservatives are more likely to go to church or synagogue, believe in the literal truth of the Bible, oppose abortion, and favor prayer in public schools. Liberals, in contrast, are less likely to attend church or synagogue regularly, yet say that religion is important in their lives; they see the Bible as inspired by God, and take liberal positions in moral and political debates. Wuthnow traces the origins of this split to both long-term patterns and recent developments in American religious life. Though neither side is monolithic, he concludes that both conservatives and liberals tend to see the worst in the other, and there are few indications that reconciliation is on the horizon.

Robert Wuthnow, *The Struggle for America's Soul: Evangelicals, Liberals, and Secularism*, 1989: Wm. B. Eerdmans Publishing Company, Grand Rapids, MI. Used by permission.

# 17

# OLD FISSURES AND NEW FRACTURES IN AMERICAN RELIGIOUS LIFE

*Robert Wuthnow*

IN THE OPENING LINES of his hauntingly memorable description of the Battle of Waterloo, Victor Hugo makes a startling observation: "If it had not rained on the night of June 17, 1815, the future of Europe would have been different. A few drops more or less tipped the balance against Napoleon. For Waterloo to be the end of Austerlitz, Providence needed only a little rain, and an unseasonable cloud crossing the sky was enough for the collapse of a world."[1] What is startling is not the idea that the future of Europe, or even the outcome of the battle, hinged on something as seemingly trivial as an unexpected rainstorm.

Such explanations fill the annals of military history. Had not the British expeditionary force been able to evacuate from Dunkirk under cover of heavy fog during the week of May 26, 1940, the German army might well have gone on to win the war. Those who tread the battlefields near Gettysburg, Pennsylvania, view the heights along Culp's Hill and Cemetery Ridge, and wonder what the outcome would have been had Lee's troops occupied those favored positions instead of Meade's. The great turning points of history sometimes appear to hinge less on what people do than the conditions under which they have to do it. The flukes of nature—or the hand of God—intervene willfully at fortuitous moments.

Yet we in contemporary society, schooled as we have been in the complexities of history, know how tenuous these arguments often prove to be. Battles may be won or lost on the basis of a sudden turn of weather, but wars are not and neither is the course of history.

What if, by some chance, Lee's troops had occupied the heights at Gettysburg? Would Meade's then have run the bloody gauntlet that became immortalized as "Pickett's charge"? Or would the Federal army have faded away to fight on more opportune terms? We learn from modern analysts of the battle that Lee was forced to fight, despite the unfavorable terrain, because he desperately needed to win. Supplies were running low and Confederate agents needed to be able to demonstrate to their European creditors that they could win. The reason supplies were running low lay deep in the South's agrarian economy (in contrast with the North's industrial economy) and even deeper in the triangular trade that had developed between the South, Great Britain, and West Africa. Lee was forced to fight; Meade could have slipped away.

As we proceed with Victor Hugo's account, what actually startles us is that he succeeds so well in defending his thesis. A soggy battlefield was indeed a decisive factor. But as so often is the case in Hugo's narratives, it was the larger terrain—and the uncertainties inherent in this terrain—that constituted the framework in which the decisions of the two commanders had to be made. An unexpected rainstorm made it impossible for Napoleon to deploy the full force of his artillery. He could not have anticipated this factor, an element of the battle that in essence remained obscure.

The *quid obscurum* in Hugo's account, though, is at once more simple and straightforward than this and more elusive. Running through the battlefield, interposed directly between the two armies, was a ditch. It extended across the entire line that Napoleon's cavalry would have to charge. It was a deep chasm, made by human hands, the result of a road that had been cut like a knife through the natural terrain. It was hidden from view. The cavalry charged, and then faced the terror. Hugo recounts:

> There was the ravine, unexpected, gaping right at the horses' feet, twelve feet deep between its banks. The second rank pushed in the first, the third pushed in the second; the horses reared, lurched backward, fell onto their rumps, and struggled writhing with their feet in the air, piling up and throwing their riders; no means to retreat; the whole column was nothing but a projectile. The momentum to crush the English crushed the French. The inexorable ravine could not yield until it was filled; riders and horses rolled in together helter-skelter, grinding against each other, making common flesh in this dreadful gulf, and when this grave was full of living men, the rest marched over them and went on. Almost a third of Dubois's brigade sank into the abyss.[2]

The *quid obscurum* was quite literally a hidden fracture with enormous consequences.

The second, and deeper, meaning of Hugo's reference to the *quid obscurum* is that of the broader uncertainties evoked by the clash of two armies. Only in the heat of battle do the unforeseen contingencies become evident; only then do the plans of the commanding generals prove to have missed important features of the broader terrain. In the struggling line of soldiers engaged in hand-to-hand combat one begins to realize that the expenditures are greater than expected. The consequences of seemingly unimportant conditions turn out to be incalculable. It is left to the historian to calculate, with the advantage of hindsight, the role of these previously obscured realities.

## THE GREAT FRACTURE IN AMERICAN RELIGION

My purpose in drawing attention to Hugo's discussion is also twofold. At the more literal level, like the ravine cutting across the plateau of Mont-Saint-Jean, a great fracture runs through the cultural terrain on which the battles of religion and politics are now being fought. It is a fracture that deserves our attention. For it is of recent creation, a human construction, unlike the timeless swells of culture through which it has been cut. It has become a mire of bitter contention, consuming the energies of religious communities and grinding their ideals into the grime of unforeseen animosities. At a broader level, this fracture also symbolizes the unplanned developments in the larger terrain that did not become evident until the battles themselves began to erupt. With the advantage of hindsight, we can now discover the importance of these developments. We can see how the present controversies in American religion were affected by broader changes in the society—the consequences of which remained obscure at the time but have now become painfully transparent.

The ravine running through the culturescape of American religion is as real as the one made by the road between the two villages on the Belgian border, though it differs from that Belgian ravine in one important respect. It is not simply a fissure in the physical environment, a ditch that creates the downfall of one of the protagonists. It is to a much greater extent the product of the battle itself. The chasm dividing American religion into separate communities has emerged largely from the struggle between these two communities. It may have occurred, as I shall suggest shortly, along a fault line already present in the cultural terrain. But it has been dug deeper and wider by the skirmishes that have been launched across it.

Depending on whose lens we use to view it, we can describe this fissure in any number of ways. Television evangelist Jimmy Swaggart has described it as a gulf between those who believe in the Judeo-Christian principles on which our country was founded and those who believe in the "vain philosophies of men." On one side are the "old-fashioned" believers in "the word of Almighty God" who are often maligned as "poor simpletons"; on the other side are the "so-called intelligentsia," those who believe they are great because they "are more intelligent than anyone else," "socialists," believers in "syphilitic Lenin," and the burdened masses who have nothing better to get excited about than football and baseball games.[3] In contrast, a writer for the *New York Times* depicted it as a battle between "churches and church-allied groups" who favor freedom, democracy, and the rights of minorities, on the one hand, and a right-wing fringe interested in setting up a theocracy governed by a "dictatorship of religious values," on the other hand.[4]

Apart from the colors in which the two sides are portrayed, though, one finds general agreement on the following points: (a) the reality of the division between two opposing camps; (b) the predominance of "fundamentalists," "evangelicals," and "religious conservatives" in one and the predominance of "religious liberals," "humanists," and "secularists" in the other; and (c) the presence of deep hostility and misgiving between the two.

An official of the National Council of Churches summarized the two positions, and the views of each toward the other, this way: "Liberals abhor the smugness, the self-righteousness, the absolute certainty, the judgmentalism, the lovelessness of a narrow, dogmatic faith. [Conservatives] scorn the fuzziness, the marshmallow convictions, the inclusiveness that makes membership meaningless—the 'anything goes' attitude that views even Scripture as relative. Both often caricature the worst in one another and fail to perceive the best."[5]

To suggest that American religion is divided neatly into two communities with sharply differentiated views is, of course, to ride roughshod over the countless landmarks, signposts, hills, and gullies that actually constitute the religious landscape. Not only do fundamentalists distinguish themselves from evangelicals, but each brand of religious conservatism is divided into dozens of denominational product lines. Similar distinctions can be made on the religious left. In the popular mind, though, there does seem to be some reality to the cruder, binary way of thinking.

A national survey, conducted several years ago (even before some of the more acrimonious debates over the role of religion in politics had arisen), found both a high level of awareness of the basic division between religious liberals and conservatives and a great deal of genuine hostility between the two. When asked to classify themselves, 43 percent of those surveyed identified themselves as religious liberals and 41 percent said they were religious conservatives. The public is thus divided almost equally between the two categories, and only one person in six was unable or unwilling to use these labels.[6]

The ways in which self-styled liberals and conservatives answered other questions also seem to lend some validity to the two categories. As one would expect, conservatives were much more likely than liberals to identify themselves as evangelicals, to believe in a literal interpretation of the Bible, to say they had had a "born-again" conversion experience, to indicate that they had tried to convert others to their faith, and to hold conservative views on issues such as abortion and prayer in public schools. Liberals were less likely than conservatives to attend church or synagogue regularly, but a majority affirmed the importance of religion in their lives, tended to regard the Bible as divinely inspired (but not to be taken literally), and held liberal views on a variety of political and moral issues.

Some denominations tended to consist of more conservatives than liberals, or vice versa. But generally, the major denominational families and faith traditions—Methodists, Lutherans, Presbyterians, Baptists, Catholics, Jews—were all divided about equally between religious conservatives and religious liberals. In other words, the cleavage between conservatives and liberals tends not, for the most part, to fall along denominational lines. It is a cleavage that divides people within the same denominations—as recent struggles within the Southern Baptist Convention, the Episcopal Church, the Presbyterian Church, U.S.A., and the Roman Catholic Church all attest.

The study also demonstrated the extent to which the relations between religious liberals and religious conservatives have become rife with conflict. A majority of the public surveyed said the conflict between religious liberals and conservatives is an area of "serious tension." A substantial majority of both groups said they had had unpleasant, or at best "mixed," relations with the other group. These relations were said to have taken place in fairly intimate settings: in one's church, among friends and relatives, even within the same Bible study or fellowship groups. Moreover, each side held a number of negative images of the other. Liberals saw conservatives as rigid, intolerant, and fanatical. Conservatives described liberals as shallow, morally loose, unloving, and unsaved.

The study also demonstrated that, unlike other kinds of prejudice and hostility, the ill feelings separating religious liberals and religious conservatives *did not mitigate* as the two groups came into greater contact with one another. The more each side came into contact with the other, and the more knowledge it gained about the other, the less it liked the other.

Viewed normatively, such levels of animosity and tension between religious liberals and conservatives are disturbing. We might expect nothing better from communists and capitalists or Democrats and Republicans. But deep within the Hebrew and Christian traditions lies an ethic of love and forgiveness. In congregation after congregation prayers are routinely offered for unity among the faithful. Creeds are recited stating belief in the one, holy, catholic church. And homilies are delivered on Jesus' injunction to love one's neighbor as oneself.

If these findings are disturbing, they are not, however, surprising. They accord with the way in which American religion is portrayed in the media and in pulpits, and with the way in which American religion seems to function. The major newspapers and television networks routinely publicize the bizarre activities of fundamentalists and evangelicals: the conservative governor who prays with his pastor and hears God tell him to run for the presidency, the television preacher who prays (successfully, it turns out) that an impending hurricane will be averted from the Virginia coast, the fundamentalists in Indiana who deny their children proper schooling and medical care, the evangelical counselor in California who is sued by the family of a patient who committed suicide, the deranged member of a fundamentalist church in Maine who shoots down his fellow parishioners with a shotgun.

Conservative television preachers and conservative religious publications make equally vitriolic comments about their liberal foes: how an Episcopal bishop is condoning sexual permissiveness within his diocese, how Methodist liberals are encouraging homosexuality among the denomination's pastors, how zealous clergy in the nuclear disarmament movement are selling the country out to the Russians, how religious conservatives are being discriminated against in colleges and universities. It is little wonder that the labels begin to stick. Sooner or later it does in fact begin to appear as if the world of faith is divided between two belligerent superpowers.

But this picture of the religious world is not simply a creation of the sensationalist media. At the grass roots, one can readily find denunciations of liberalism from conservative pulpits and diatribes against fundamentalism from liberal pulpits. One can readily observe the split between liberals and conservatives in church meetings and discussion groups. Liberals freely express doubts about the historical authenticity of the Bible. Conservatives appeal for greater faith in the supernatural, the miraculous, and argue for more emphasis on sin and personal salvation. Beneath the innocent statements of each are deeper feelings about right and wrong, truth and error.

Beyond these simple exchanges, the two also isolate themselves in different communities of support and action: liberals in the nurturing environment of the local peace concerns fellowship, the forum on AIDS, the movement to lobby for equitable and affordable housing; conservatives in the womb of Bible study groups and prayer fellowships.

One can also readily observe the polarizing tendencies of national issues on the religious environment. Pick up the latest issue of *Christian Century* or *Christianity Today*; observe the number of articles that deal with politics and note the paucity of material on theology or even personal spirituality. Or open the mail and count the letters from Moral Majority, Christian Voice, People for the American Way, the American Civil Liberties Union. The issues are now national rather than local or regional. They concern an appointment to the Supreme Court, a constitutional amendment on abortion, a preacher running for president. They are supported by one faction of the religious community and opposed by another. They induce polarization.

But to say that the chasm between religious liberals and conservatives exists for many reasons is still only to describe it—to parade the colors of the troops engaged in the great battle of which this conflict consists. It is a chasm deepened and widened by political debate. It is a chasm around which religious communities' participation in public affairs divides. It has become a predictable feature of the contemporary debate over church-state relations. To understand it, though, we must look at broader developments in the social terrain. We must try to discover why this particular fracture line existed in the cultural geography in the first place.

## A CLOSER LOOK AT THE CULTURAL GEOGRAPHY

In one sense, of course, the fracture line can be found in the soil of American religion as far back as the years immediately after the Civil War. Even in the eighteenth century and during the first half of the nineteenth century one can identify the beginnings of a division between religious conservatives and religious liberals insofar as one considers the effects of the Enlightenment on elite culture. Skepticism, atheism, anticlericalism, and of course deism constitute identifiable alternatives to the popular piety of Methodists and Baptists and to the conservative orthodoxy of Roman Catholics, Jews, Presbyterians, and others during this period. But to an important degree, the potential division between conservatism and liberalism before the Civil War is overshadowed by the deeper tensions to which the society is subject. Nationalism and regionalism, differences between the culture of the Eastern seaboard and the expanding Western territories, and increasingly the tensions between North and South provide the major divisions affecting the organization of American religion.

Not until the termination of these hostilities and the resumption of material progress after the Civil War does it become possible for the gap between religious conservatives and liberals to gain importance. Gradually in these years the discoveries of science, the new ideas of Charles Darwin, and by the end of the century the beginnings of a national system of higher education provide the groundwork for a liberal challenge to religious conservatism. Of course, the culmination of these changes comes at the turn of the century in the modernist movement and its increasingly vocal opponent, the fundamentalists.

In the long view, the present division between religious liberals and religious conservatives can be pictured simply as a continuation or outgrowth of this earlier conflict. The inevitable forces of modernization produced a secular tendency in American religion, a tendency that condoned greater individual freedom in matters of the spirit and voiced skepticism toward a faith based in divine revelation, and this tendency evoked a reactionary movement in which religious conservatism was preserved.

That, as I say, is the impression gained from taking a long view of American history. If one takes a more limited perspective, though, a rather different impression emerges. One is able to focus more directly on the immediate contours of the religious environment and to see how these contours are in the short term shaped by specific events. I suppose that this is the advantage of taking the perspective of the sociologist—which seldom extends much before World War II.

At the close of that war, the condition of American religion was quite different than it is now. It contained seeds that were to germinate and grow, like weeds in the concrete, widening the cracks that have now become so visible. But the basic divisions ran along other lines. Tensions between Protestants and Catholics had reached new heights as immigration and natural increase contributed to the growth of the Catholic population. Tensions between Christians and Jews also ran deep, even though they were often less visible than the conflicts dividing Protestants and Catholics. There was, as Will Herberg described it a few years later, a "tripartite division" in American religion: to be American was to be Protestant, Catholic, or Jewish.[7]

In addition, denominational boundaries also played an important role in giving structure to the Protestant branch of this tripartite arrangement. Ecumenical services were beginning to erode some of these boundaries (often for the explicit purpose of displaying Protestant unity against the threat of papal expansion). But ethnic, national, and geographic divisions—as well as theological and liturgical divisions—continued to reinforce denominational separatism.

In all of this, there was little evidence of any basic split between liberals and conservatives. To be sure, fundamentalism was alive and well. But its very success proved in a deeper sense to be its limitation. By the mid-1930s, fundamentalist spokesmen had largely conceded their defeat in the major Protestant denominations and had withdrawn to form their own organizations. As the Great Depression, and then the rationing imposed by the war, made travel more difficult, these organizations also grew farther apart from one another. By the end of the war, they consisted mainly of small, isolated splinter groups on the fringes of the mainline denominations.

Most of the population that continued to believe in such doctrinal tenets as biblical inerrancy, the divinity of Jesus, and the necessity of personal salvation remained within these larger denominations. Even the official policies of these denominations reflected what would now be considered a strong conservative emphasis. Evangelism, door-to-door canvassing of communities, revival meetings, biblical preaching, missions—all received prominent support.

Also of significance was the fact that many of the more outspoken conservative religious leaders were unobtrusively beginning to build their own organizations. At this point, however, these leaders were able to build quietly and were content largely to maintain ties with the major denominations, rather than break away like their fundamentalist counterparts.

There were certainly differences of opinion among believers about such matters as the literal inspiration of the Bible or the role of churches in political affairs. But these were as yet not the subject of mass movements or of widely recognized cultural divisions. Only the terms "fundamentalist" and "liberal" suggest continuity between this period and our own; a more careful examination of issues, personalities, and organizations indicates discontinuity.

## FISSURE LINES IN THE RELIGIOUS LANDSCAPE

In the years immediately following World War II we do find evidence of the conditions that were to predispose American religion to undergo a major transformation in the decades that followed. Three such predisposing conditions stand out.

First, American religion was on the whole extraordinarily strong. The largest churches now counted members in the thousands. Overall, the number of local churches and synagogues ranged in the hundreds of thousands. Some denominations sported budgets in the tens of millions. Collectively, religious organizations took in approximately $800 million annually—as historian Harold Laski observed, this figure exceeded the budget of the entire British government.[8]

In comparison with Europe, the American churches were especially strong. They had not been subjected to the same limitations on government spending that the churches in England, France, and Germany had faced, nor had they encountered the mass withdrawal of the working classes that these churches had experienced; and of course they had not been subject to the extensive destruction resulting from the war. They had been weakened by the Depression and by shortages of building materials during the war. But curiously, perhaps, this very weakness turned out to be a strength as well. It prompted major building programs after the war, allowed the churches to relocate in growing neighborhoods, and generally encouraged what was to become known as the religious revival of the 1950s.

The critical feature of the churches' massive institutional strength for the coming decades was religion's ability to adjust to a changing environment. Rather than simply wither away—or maintain itself in quiet contemplative seclusion—it adapted to the major social developments of the postwar period. In this sense, we owe much of the present controversy in American religion to the simple fact that it had remained a strong institutional force right up to the second half of the twentieth century.

The second predisposing condition was the strong "this-worldly" orientation of American religion. Not only was it able to adapt to changing circumstances; it also engaged itself actively in the social environment by its own initiative. When the war ended, religious leaders looked to the future with great expectancy. They recognized the opportunities that lay ahead. They were also mindful of the recurrent dangers they faced.

Indeed, a prominent theme in their motivational appeals focused on the combination of promise and peril. For instance, a resolution passed by the Federal Council of Churches in 1945 declared: "We are living in a uniquely dangerous and promising time."[9] It was a dangerous time because of the recurrent likelihood of war, the widely anticipated return to a depressed economy after the war-induced boom had ended, and of course the invention of nuclear weapons. It was a promising time because of new opportunities for missionary work and evangelism.

The stakes were high, so persistent activism was the desired response. In the words of a Methodist minister, who reminded his audience of the perilous opportunities facing them: "That requires . . . a great godly company of men and women with no axe to grind, desiring only to save, serve, help and heal."[10] The result was that religious organizations deliberately exposed their flanks to the influences of their environment. Programs were initiated, education was encouraged, preaching confronted issues of the day—all of which, like the rain on Napoleon's troops, would reveal the churches' dependence on the conditions of their terrain.

The third predisposing factor was reflected in the relation understood to prevail between religion and the public sphere. This factor is especially important to understand, because it provides a vivid contrast with the ways in which we now conceive of religion's influence in the political arena. In the 1940s and 1950s there appears to have been a fairly widespread view among religious leaders, theologians, and even social scientists that values and behavior were closely related. Find out what a person's basic values were, and you could pretty well predict that person's behavior. If persons valued democracy, they could be counted on to uphold it in their behavior. If a person worked hard and struggled to get ahead, you could be pretty sure that person valued success and achievement.

More broadly, writers also extended this connection to society. A nation's culture consisted essentially of values, and these values were arranged in a hierarchy of priority. The society was held together by this hierarchy of values. It generated consensus and caused people to behave in similar ways.

For religious leaders, this way of conceiving things was very convenient. It meant that the way to shape people's lives was by shaping their values, and this was what the churches did best: they preached and they taught. They influenced the individual's system of values. They shaped the individual's conscience.

The churches' conduit to the public arena was thus through the individual's conscience. Shape a churchperson's values, and you could rest assured that your influence would be carried into the public sphere. That person would vote according to his or her conscience, would manifest high values in his or her work, would behave charitably, ethically, honestly. All the churches needed to do was preach and teach.

This view also gained support from the public arena itself. Public officials spoke frequently and fervently about their commitment to high moral principles. They lauded the work of religious leaders in reinforcing these principles. Truman, Eisenhower, Dulles, and others spoke of their own religious faith and commended this faith as a source of societal cohesion and strength. It was easy for religious leaders to believe that their efforts were really having an impact.

Already, though, there were signs that this worldview was coming apart. The problem was not that political leaders were suspected of hypocrisy, although this may have been the case. Nor was the problem, as some have suggested, that this was basically a Protestant view, and thus was being undermined by the growing pluralism of the society. Catholic and Jewish leaders in the 1950s articulated it too. The idea was not that religious faith channeled behavior in specifically Protestant or Catholic or Jewish directions. The idea— at least the one expressed in public contexts—was that a deep religious faith gave the individual moral strength, conviction, the will to do what was right.

But the premises on which this worldview itself was based were beginning to be questioned. Doubts were beginning to be expressed about the basic connection between values and behavior. What if one's basic values did not translate into actual behavior? What if one's behavior did not stem from one's convictions but was influenced by other factors?

At this time, these questions were only raised occasionally. But the very fact that they could be raised suggested the presence of a cultural fissure, a fault line along which a more serious fracture could open up. Values constituted one category, behavior another. The two categories were connected—had to be connected closely for arguments about the impact of conscience on public affairs to be credible. But this connection itself was becoming tenuous.

## YEARS OF STRUGGLE

How then did these predisposing conditions in the 1950s become transformed to produce the chasm between religious liberals and conservatives that we experience at the present? How did Herberg's tripartite system, in which the basic religious and *religio-political* divisions occurred between Protestants and Catholics and between Christians and Jews, come to be replaced by what some have called a "two-party system"?

The answer is complex, of course, because it involves not only the relations among all the major religious groupings but also the relations between religion and the forces shaping the broader society. It is, however, enormously important, for it brings together all the decisive factors that have shaped American religion in the period since World War II. We can touch on only the basic contours here.

In picturing the transformation as a tripartite division being replaced by a two-party system, we should not think that the latter simply superimposed itself on the former or that the one led directly into the other. It is helpful to divide the process in two and seek answers for each of its phases separately. The first phase (not chronologically but analytically) amounted to an erosion of the basic divisions constituting the tripartite system. The second phase amounted to developments reinforcing a new, different cleavage between liberals and conservatives. These processes combined to create what many have sensed is a new dynamic in the relations between church and state, or between religion and politics more generally. But they are also analytically separable.

It also helps to identify an interim phase between the two. Three categories of religious organization did not simply meld into two. Thinking of it in those terms causes us to miss the violence associated with any social change as basic as this one. Natural communities were torn asunder, their parts flung into the air and scattered in strange configurations, before the subterranean forces at work in the society finally rearranged them in the patterns we see today. We have to recognize the upheaval and displacement associated with this process if we are to tap the wellsprings from which much of the present political fury arises.

The erosion of the divisions separating Protestants and Catholics, Jews and Christians, and members of different denominations came about gradually. It was legitimated from within by norms of love and humility that promoted interfaith cooperation. It was reinforced from without by changes in the larger society. Rising educational levels, memories of the Holocaust, and the civil rights movement all contributed to an increasing emphasis on tolerance. Regional migration brought Catholics and Protestants, and Christians and Jews, into closer physical proximity with one another. Denominational ghettos, forged by immigration and ethnic ties, were gradually replaced by religiously and ethnically plural communities. Rates of interreligious marriage went up. It became increasingly common for members of all religious groups to have grown up in other groups, to have friends from other groups, and to have attended other groups.

The denominational hierarchies, seminaries, pension plans, and so forth still played a significant role in the organization of American religion. But the ground was in a sense cleared of old demarcations, thereby making new alliances and cleavages easier to emerge.

For those who had spent their entire lives within particular denominational ghettos, these changes in themselves represented major disruptions, of course, especially when it was their pastor who began welcoming outsiders, their denomination that lost its identity by merging with another, or their child who married outside the faith.

Most of the upheaval, though, came during the 1960s and was closely associated with the upheaval that pervaded the society in general. Young people were particularly subject to this upheaval. Many were the first ever in their families to attend college. For many, attending college meant leaving the ethno-religious ghetto for the first time. The campuses themselves were growing so rapidly that alienation and social isolation were common experiences. Of course, the civil rights movement and antiwar protests added to the turmoil.

Among the many ways in which this upheaval affected religion, two are especially important. First, the tensions of the 1960s significantly widened the gap between values and behavior that was mentioned earlier. The two major social movements of this period were the civil rights movement and the antiwar movement, and significantly, both dramatized the disjuncture between values and behavior. The civil rights movement brought into sharp relief what Gunnar Myrdal had called the "American dilemma"—the dilemma of subscribing to egalitarian values in principle but engaging in racial discrimination in practice.[11] Here was a clear example of values and behavior being out of joint.

The antiwar movement pointed up a similar disjuncture. On the one hand, Americans supposedly believed deeply in such values as democracy and the right of people to determine their own destiny. On the other hand, the country was engaged in a war in Southeast Asia that to many seemed to deny these principles. Military force was being used, at best, in an effort to determine another people's destiny for them, or at worst, to prop up an ineffective non-democratic regime. Both movements drove home, often implicitly, the more general point that people of high values and good consciences could not always be counted on to manifest those virtues in their day-to-day behavior.

The wedge that these movements drove into the earlier connection between values and behavior was to prove increasingly important in separating religious liberals from religious conservatives. Although this picture was to be modified somewhat by the 1980s, in the late 1960s it essentially consisted of conservatives grasping the values side of the equation and liberals seizing the behavioral side. That is, conservatives continued to emphasize preaching and teaching, the shaping of high personal moral standards, and above all the personally redemptive experience of salvation. Whether behavior would result that could alleviate racial discrimination or the war in Southeast Asia was not the issue; the issue was what one believed in one's heart and the motives from which one acted. In contrast, liberals increasingly attached importance to behavior. Believe what one will, it does not matter, they said, unless one puts one's faith on the line, takes action, helps bring about change. Changing social institutions was especially important, because they were the reason values and behavior did not correspond. People with good intentions were caught up in evil systems that needed to be overthrown.

For the time being at least, liberals argued for religious organizations' taking direct action in politics, while conservatives remained aloof from politics entirely, preferring instead to concentrate on matters of personal belief. Indeed, the two often gave lip service to the higher principles held by the other but expressed disagreement over the tactics being used. Thus, conservatives often expressed sympathy with the ideal of racial equality, but argued against the direct-action techniques in which liberal clergy were becoming involved. Liberals often continued to express sympathy with the ideal of personal salvation, but argued that personal salvation alone was not enough of a witness if church people did not become actively involved in working for social justice as well.

The second consequence of the turmoil of the 1960s that stands out is the increasing role of higher education in differentiating styles of religious commitment. In the 1950s, perhaps surprisingly so in retrospect, those who had been to college and those who had not were remarkably similar on most items of religious belief and practice. By the early 1970s, a considerable education gap had emerged between the two.

The college educated were much less likely, even than the college educated of the previous decade, to attend religious services regularly. Their belief in a literal interpretation of the Bible had eroded dramatically. They were more tolerant of other religions, and they were more interested in experimenting with the so-called new religions, such as Zen, Transcendental Meditation, Hare Krishna, and the human potential movement. Those who had not been to college remained more committed to traditional views of the Bible, were more strongly interested in religion in general, continued to attend religious services regularly, and expressed doubt about other faiths, including the new religions.

In short, educational differences were becoming more significant for religion, just as they were being emphasized more generally in the society. Higher education was becoming a more significant basis for creating social and cultural distinctions. In regard to religion, education was beginning to reinforce the cleavage between religious liberals and religious conservatives.

For a time, perhaps even as recently as 1976, it appeared that the gap between religious liberals and conservatives might be bridged by a significant segment of the evangelical community. Many of its leaders had participated in the educational expansion of the previous decade. They were exposed to the current thinking in higher education, had been influenced by their own participation in the civil rights movement and the antiwar movement, and had come to hold liberal views on many political issues, and yet retained a strong commitment to the biblical tradition, including an emphasis on personal faith.

Their voice, however, was soon drowned out by the more strident voices of the religious right. Television hookups and direct-mail solicitations replaced the evangelical periodical, seminary, and scholarly conference as more effective means of forging a large following and extracting revenue from that following. Issues such as abortion and feminism provided platforms on which the religious right could organize.

Educational differences continued to separate the more conservative from the more liberal. But other issues began to reinforce these differences. Issues arose that also reflected the experience of women in gaining higher education and becoming employed in professional careers, or the exposure one gained in college to the social sciences and humanities as opposed to more narrowly technical educations in engineering or business.

The religious right also borrowed the more activist style of political confrontation that the left had used during the 1960s. It began to renew the connection between values and behavior. Its commitment to personal morality remained strong, but it now urged believers to take political action, to organize themselves, to infuse their morality into the basic institutions of government. Each side developed special purpose groups to gain its objectives, either within more narrow denominational contexts or in the national arena.

Thus, deeper features of the social and cultural terrain underlie the present fracture between religious liberals and religious conservatives. Had it simply been, say, the Supreme Court's 1973 decision on abortion that elicited different responses from liberals and conservatives, we might well have seen a temporary flurry of activity followed by a gradual progression of interest to other matters. Instead, the religious environment is characterized by two clearly identified communities. Each has developed through the events spanning at least a quarter of a century. The two are located differently with respect to the basic social division that has been produced by the growth of higher education. Other bases of differentiation, such as regionalism, ethnicity, and denominationalism, that might have mitigated this basic division have subsided in importance. Each side has mobilized its resources around special purpose groups.

It is, therefore, highly likely that specific issues concerning the relations between church and state, cases in the federal courts involving religion, and religious issues in electoral campaigns will continue to evoke strong—and opposing—responses from these two communities.

## FACTORS MITIGATING THE STRUGGLE

At the same time, we should not avoid mentioning several forces that may work to contain or reduce this polarization of religion in the public arena. One is the fact that neither community is actually organized as a single party. Each side is still divided into dozens of denominations, is represented by dozens of different national leaders, has mobilized its political efforts through dozens of special purpose groups, and at the grass roots consists of thousands of separate congregations. For either side to operate effectively as a political bloc, it must forge coalitions among these various organizations. And, despite the fact that both sides have been able to transcend old divisions, still, matters of theology, of liturgical tradition, and even of region present formidable barriers to be overcome.

Another mitigating factor is that both sides continue to register, at least at the grass roots, a healthy suspicion of government. It sometimes appears that each side is anxious to use government to achieve its goals. But grass-roots mobilization of church people, whether liberals or conservatives, has been more effective in opposing government than in cooperating with government.

During the civil rights movement, churchgoers who became most active in politics at the grass roots were those who opposed the actions being taken by the government. During the Vietnam War, churchgoers most active in politics were again those who opposed the government's actions. In recent years, the most politically active churchgoers have been those who opposed the government's role on abortion and welfare spending. In each of these periods, moreover, churchgoers who felt government was becoming too powerful were more likely to become politically active than churchgoers who did not feel this way. I suspect that the reason for this political activism lies in the fact that there is a long history of concern, expressed specifically in the First Amendment to the Constitution, over the threat that government poses to religious freedom. In any case, this suspicion of government seems likely to dampen enthusiasm for any strong theocratic orientation of the kind that has sometimes been projected.

Finally, we must remember that the involvement of either religious faction in political life cannot succeed without active support from leaders in the political arena itself. During the 1980s, under the Reagan administration, at least an impression of such support was often taken for granted. At the same time, officials of both political parties have often expressed consternation over the activities of religious groups. Lack of political experience, extremist rhetoric, disinterest in routine party activities, and single-issue orientations have been cited as reasons for this consternation.

Moreover, religious liberals and religious conservatives have often been courted by factions within the political community for entirely secular purposes: because they supported stronger defense initiatives, or because they favored a freeze on nuclear weapons, or because they wanted a tougher policy against communism in Latin America. Either military or economic changes in the larger international arena can radically alter the nature of these issues, and therefore the likelihood of religious factions being courted.

I return, then, to the point at which I began. The relations between faith and politics are contingent on the broader terrain on which they occur. Like the Battle of Waterloo, the battle between religious conservatives and religious liberals is subject to its environment. A deep cultural ravine appears to separate the two communities. Whether this ravine can be bridged depends on raising it from obscurity, bringing it into consciousness, and recognizing the surrounding contours on which these efforts must rest.

## NOTES

1. Victor Hugo, *Les Miserables* (New York: New American Library, 1987), 309.

2. Ibid., 328–29.

3. From a broadcast in February 1987 titled "What is the Foundation for Our Philosophy of Christianity?" I wish to thank Victoria Chapman for the transcription of this sermon.

4. E. J. Dionne, Jr., "Religion and Politics," *New York Times*, 15 September 1987.

5. Peggy L. Shriver, "The Paradox of Inclusiveness-that-Divides," *Christian Century* (January 21, 1984): 194.

6. At the extremes, the public was also about equally divided: 19 percent said they were very liberal; 18 percent, very conservative. These figures are from a survey conducted in June 1984 by the Gallup Organization under a grant from the Robert Schuller Ministries. Some of the study's findings were reported in the May and June, 1986, issues of *Emerging Trends*, a publication edited by George Gallup, Jr. The results of additional analyses of these data appear in Robert Wuthnow, *The Restructuring of American Religion: Society and Faith since World War II* (Princeton: Princeton University Press, 1988).

7. Will Herberg, *Protestant-Catholic-Jew* (Garden City, N.Y.: Doubleday-Anchor, 1955).

8. Harold Laski, *The American Democracy* (New York: Viking, 1948), 283.

9. "The Churches and World Order," reprinted in *Christian Century* (February 7, 1945): 174–77.

10. C. Stanley Lowell, "The Conversion of America," *Christian Century* (September 29, 1949): 1134.

11. Gunnar Myrdal, *An American Dilemma* (New York: Harper & Brothers, 1944).

SEEKING JEWISH SPIRITUAL ROOTS IN MIAMI AND LOS ANGELES

*Deborah Dash Moore*

Following the Second World War, large numbers of Jews from New York and Chicago joined the migrations of people from the Northeast and Midwest to the sunbelt cities of Miami and Los Angeles. Cut loose from the older European religious cultures of their families, these "permanent tourists," as Deborah Dash Moore calls them, created a new and distinctly American Jewish identity in the loosely structured Jewish communities of Miami and Los Angeles. In this fresh look at transformations within modern American Judaism, Moore directs our attention to the young, ambitious rabbis who, like their fellow migrants, were eager to break out of the patterns of belief and behavior that had been established in the Northeast. In a world with few enduring traditions or social hierarchies, these pioneering rabbis created new religious traditions and reclaimed old ones. They understood implicitly that in order to attract a town of rootless migrants to their synagogues they needed to offer Jews a social and religious identity. In this new environment, the common denominational distinctions between Orthodoxy and Conservatism, and Conservatism and Reform, became less visible and, instead, "an easy eclecticism took hold." By imagining religion as a form of "spiritual recreation" that complemented the leisure lifestyle, sunbelt Judaism distinguished itself from the older, European Judaism of the Northeast and Midwest.

*Here there are no vested interests, here there are no sacred cows, here there is no cold hand of the past. There is an opportunity to develop new forms of Jewish communal living geared in a realistic fashion to the actual needs of the Jewish community.*

—Charles Brown, Head of the Los Angeles
Jewish Community Council, 1952 (quoted in
Max Vorspan and Lloyd P. Gartner, *A History of the Jews of Los Angeles*)

# 18

# SEEKING JEWISH SPIRITUAL ROOTS IN MIAMI AND LOS ANGELES

## *Deborah Dash Moore*

AS JEWS PULLED UP THEIR ROOTS and turned their backs on the old home and neighborhood to migrate across the continent, many left their parents' religious traditions behind, those familial religious and ethnic practices that seemed an integral part of the northern urban life and territory. Some, growing up in secular Jewish households, had only known religious tradition from their neighbors and the synagogue down the street. Others remembered sabbaths and seders from childhood in another time and place. Upon arrival in the open golden spaces of Miami and L.A., these childhood religious traditions seemed less appropriate, more of an anachronism. As one self-styled upper-middle-class San Fernando Valley Jewish mother explained, "Our children know and appreciate their heritage, but the realities of university academic competition, part-time jobs, and family and household obligations cannot be ignored. Nor can my husband and I set aside the rigorous full-time effort we must put forward to provide the home, education and general lifestyle we've chosen for ourselves" in order to "return to the kind of practicing Judaism we knew as youngsters. Anyway," she cheerfully confessed, "let's be really honest and admit that those practices were forcibly imposed upon us by our parents, and this was the case for most of our peers."[1]

Jews in Miami and L.A. embraced a kind of rootlessness that proved even more pervasive than the upbeat confession of one San Fernando mother would suggest. Their apparently casual abandonment of religious tradition left them more open to an innovative personalism and eclecticism than would be countenanced by their more rooted relatives in the Northeast and Midwest, many of whom also discarded parental religious traditions. The permanent tourist mentality bred insecurity as well as the sense that every day was a holiday; it undermined the significance of religious traditions by changing their social and cultural context. In the diffuse and loosely structured Jewish communities of Miami and L.A., communities that lacked any real authority, those seeking religious roots necessarily engaged in an individual, personal quest, not a collective endeavor.

Without familiar institutional guides or fixed patterns of living derived from close-knit Jewish families and neighborhoods, newcomers turned to new and ambitious leaders eager to teach and inspire them. A handful of religious entrepreneurs felt the magnetic pull of

Los Angeles to be irresistible. Like their fellow Jewish migrants, they liked the atmo-sphere—often discovered during a stint as chaplain in the armed services—and sought to escape stifling family ties. Many of these young rabbis were more liberal than their peers and possessed a flair for showmanship, a skill vital to those who wish to attract widely dis-persed people with no institutional loyalties to join a congregation. They saw in the City of Angels a market economy in religious culture that encouraged inventiveness and sales-manship and placed few restraints upon them. Self-reliant, flexible, and self-confident, they knew how to mobilize people to build a congregation around themselves. Seeking new lives for themselves and dissatisfied with established rabbinical patterns of behavior and belief, they were eager to break out of the rabbinic mold that had been established in the Northeast. Many also were willing to take risks, to experiment with new forms of Ju-daism, to start with the individual and his or her desires, to craft religious practices in re-sponse to the needs of their rootless fellow newcomers.[2]

In the freewheeling atmosphere of Los Angeles, Jews invented new religious traditions and rediscovered old ones. Denominational distinctions common between Orthodoxy and Conservatism, and Conservatism and Reform lacked clarity in L.A. In the North-east and Midwest, Orthodoxy's emphasis upon the immutability of sacred law, the divine character of the oral and written Torah, and the necessity of upholding ritual obser-vance—especially separate seating of men and women in the synagogue—set it apart from Conservatism, which stressed the changing character of Jewish law, evidenced a willing-ness to modify ritual observance through mixed seating, and staunchly supported Zion-ism. Reform championed modernity, rejected most rituals and laws as outdated, argued for a form of Judaism without an ethnic dimension, and took a non-Zionist posture.[3] But in L.A., where Jews were unconstrained by the past, an easy eclecticism took hold, based in more congenial peer group structures than in traditional hierarchies. Rabbis mixed old and new, invented and restored, to see what would work, what would attract other Jews, what would bring people into the fold.

As a new generation of pioneer rabbis settled in this outpost of American Jewry, they transformed the prevalent rabbinic image by their flexibility and adaptiveness to the new climate. The older view considered L.A. a desolate place where only desperate circum-stances would force a rabbi to settle. Jews used to joke that the only rabbis who were attracted to such a city as Los Angeles—known for its clean air, offbeat society, meager numbers of Jews, and lackluster Jewish religious life—were those with either one lung or two wives. Nevertheless, the arrival of thousands of newcomers every month created enor-mous opportunities for empire building and changed L.A.'s reputation into an attractive one. Most rabbis who came, however, departed from patterns of rabbinic leadership estab-lished in the Northeast. Los Angeles was still a town for the rebellious and outrageous.

Los Angeles's preeminent rabbi, whose unbroken tenure at the city's most prestigious Reform temple gave him enormous prominence within the community, viewed many of the changes brought by newcomers with alarm. He disdained the innovations and eclecti-cism, the mixture of ethnicity and religion that characterized the newcomers' search for re-ligious roots. A blunt, outspoken man, who personified a type of rabbi rarely found in the northeastern and midwestern centers of Jewish life, Edgar Magnin of the Wilshire Boule-vard Temple looked back at the changes since the end of World War II. "This is a different ballgame today," he told reporters; "you've got another Brooklyn here. When I came here, it was Los Angeles." Magnin had more than the Dodgers' franchise in mind. Were the Jewish mores of Brooklyn infesting the palm trees of Los Angeles? The newcomers' persistent and public search for a Jewish identity in the era of ethnic revival irked Magnin. "I see these guys with their yarmulkes eating bacon on their salads at the [Hillcrest Country] club. They want to become more Jewish, whatever that means. It's not religious, it's an ethnic thing. What virtue is there in ethnic emphasis?" he asked. "You know," he concluded, "it's insecurity, the whole thing is insecurity. Roots, roots, roots—baloney!"[4]

Magnin's outrageous and improbable juxtaposition of yarmulkes and bacon spoke to potential contradictions in the newcomers' experimental and eclectic approach. Associating yarmulkes with visibly orthodox, ethnic, East European, and, for Magnin, Brooklyn Jews, he scoffed at the inappropriateness of eating any food in a *tref* (unkosher) country club.[5] But in Los Angeles, who possessed the authority to say that such contradictions mattered?

Rabbis with a vision welcomed the challenge of an unformed Jewish community and its religious contradictions. They saw an opportunity to unify Jews and develop a community around a synagogue. Their vision usually included distinctive traditions, which they designed and nurtured. Once they glimpsed the possibilities of shaping their own congregation, they found it hard to leave; they were "built into the bricks," as one rabbi put it. Under these circumstances, the identity of rabbi and congregation gradually merged. "[I have] become too involved with too many people in the life of Temple Isaiah," Rabbi Albert Lewis wrote, trying to explain to Maurice Eisendrath, the head of the Reform Union of American Hebrew Congregations (UAHC) in New York City, why he was turning down a much more prestigious position with a Detroit congregation. "Essentially it is a close-knit group and many of us have been working together for more than five years. We are just now at the fruition of a part of our program as our Temple nears completion. We have laid plans for the future and these people are looking to me to carry them out." The intimacy and commitment, the opportunity to lead people who really cared and who depended upon a spiritual leader, and the potential to shape a meaningful Jewish religious community from scratch tempted young, imaginative, and aggressive men more than did traditional paths of professional mobility in the established communities left behind.[6]

Miami too had the attraction of being practically virgin territory for eager young rabbis. Its promise enticed in particular three who left their strong imprints on the community's religious life. Irving Lehrman, Joseph Narot, and Leon Kronish successfully built distinctive synagogues and crafted a Jewish tradition that spoke to their congregants' rootlessness. Despite their allegiance to different religious ideologies—Narot to Reform, Kronish to a version of Reform that he called Liberal Judaism, and Lehrman to Conservatism—the synagogues they created exhibited surprising similarities. Kronish and Lehrman arrived during the war, a few years after the founding of the congregations they came to lead. They began, as it were, from scratch. Narot came after the war to the oldest, and for many years the only, Reform congregation in Miami. All initiated and oversaw the physical, spiritual, and educational institutions in which to shelter and sustain their congregations.

These three rabbis presided over substantial construction programs, determining thereby the physical appearance of the synagogues and their attached schools and community buildings. All three assiduously pursued members. Kronish organized his temple into "congregational commandos" to enlist unaffiliated Jews. Lehrman regularly carried membership blanks in his pocket, prepared, for example, to sign up new members at a *simha* (a festivity). As membership grew, so did the programs offered by the congregations. That the rabbis were remarkably effective preachers was attested to by the crowds that regularly came to hear them. Each used his pulpit as a base to participate in the wider world of city and national affairs. All three expected to become leaders of American Jewry as had their mentor, Stephen Wise, yet their individual stories reveal widely different values, styles, and outlooks.[7]

Lehrman arrived in Miami in 1943, thirty-two years old and fresh out of rabbinical school. The son of Abraham Lehrman, an Orthodox rabbi, Irving graduated from the high school program of the Orthodox Rabbi Isaac Elchanan Theological Seminary (RIETS) and studied at City College.[8] He married Bella Goldfarb, daughter of a prominent Brooklyn rabbi. Despite the presence of ten generations of rabbis in his family, Lehrman initially decided to go to law school. However, drawn by his father's friendship with the Talmudic scholar Chaim Tchernowitz, Lehrman entered the Jewish Institute of Religion (JIR), the rabbinical school established by the liberal Zionist rabbi Stephen Wise. Wise had designed the Jewish Institute of Religion to train rabbis for all Jews, across the denominational spectrum, but few fully observant Jews studied there. The institute emphasized Zionism and Jewish peoplehood, especially the common ethnic bonds uniting Jews despite their religious and ideological differences, and encouraged in its students an openness to religious innovation and a disregard for denominational labels. Students tended to model themselves on Wise, and like him, they imagined the rabbinate as committed to Zionism, the Jewish people, and social justice. The school's flexibility provided ideal training for pioneering among Jews without religious roots.[9]

Wise's close connections to the Miami Beach Jewish Center brought young Lehrman to the attention of leading men in the congregation who wanted a Conservative rather than an Orthodox synagogue (at least, they wanted men and women to sit together). Invited to apply for the position—but only on the condition that he pay his own way down to Miami Beach for the interview—Lehrman agreed to take the gamble. He arrived in August with his wife and two children and never left.[10]

Lehrman rapidly began to shape the congregation. Most of the men came from immigrant Orthodox backgrounds familiar to him. Financial success in business encouraged them to embrace a more modern traditionalism. As observant Jews and accomplished businessmen, they wanted their synagogue to blend Jewish traditionalism and American success. Lehrman decided to steer toward Conservatism, a middle path between his father's Orthodoxy and his liberal rabbinical training, a choice that would be especially acceptable to his congregants. He started the late Friday evening service that had become a hallmark of Conservatism. Earlier the congregation had only held a traditional Friday eve service before the festive sabbath meal. Now they enjoyed Lehrman's persuasive sermons and a musical service that occurred after dinner, extending the joyful sabbath spirit. On Shabbat Shuva, the sabbath of return that falls between the High Holidays of Rosh Hashanah and Yom Kippur, he introduced the Conservative prayerbook in place of the Orthodox *siddur*. Its more contemporary English translation of the standard prayer service signaled the congregation's new modern posture.[11]

Lehrman's engaging good looks and effective oratory drew one hundred additional members to the center within a few months of his arrival. One early congregant, who grew up in Brooklyn, remembered how she fell in love with him as a young woman. "Pearls came out of his mouth!"[12] Lehrman initiated popular breakfast services for teenagers on Sunday morning in an attempt to foster a peer group community within the synagogue's orbit and to inspire adolescents to become committed Jews. An enthusiastic congregation raised his four thousand dollar salary after two months in appreciation of his unanticipated success.

By the end of the year, Lehrman elicited a commitment from his congregants to build a synagogue north of 14th Street, in the affluent part of Miami Beach where the synagogue's dome would stand out as a religious symbol among the glitter of the hotels.[13] The men of the synagogue, threatened with Lehrman's departure if he did not get his way, pledged $200,000 toward the million dollars needed.

When the war ended and the center unveiled its plans to build a new synagogue, Lehrman came under attack for misguided priorities. How could a synagogue launch a major fundraising drive at a time when Jewish survivors in the DP camps desperately needed help? Although shaken by the attacks, Lehrman defended the drive. Those who give to build a synagogue would be the same to give to rescue survivors, he argued. One gift did not preclude the other. The sermon was effective, but the controversy reflected the sometimes conflicting pulls of past and future, Europe and Miami Beach, on these pioneering communities. Trying to build anew, they were often seen as self-absorbed and indifferent to the past. The epic struggle for nationhood, by contrast, galvanized Jews in Miami Beach; Zionist rhetoric inspired thousands as well as politicizing and secularizing their faith. Beside the heroic battle to rescue survivors of the Holocaust languishing in DP camps and bring them to the newborn State of Israel, a drive to build a bigger synagogue paled in comparison. The Miami Beach Jewish Center moved into its impressive new synagogue on Washington Avenue and 17th Street in 1948. Further construction and fundraising occupied the leadership throughout the 1950s due to the ever-expanding Jewish population and the synagogue's increased membership.

Lehrman's influence could be measured by the constant construction of elegant facilities for worship as well as for festive events and even meetings, or by the crowds that snaked around the block waiting with their tickets to get in to hear him preach on Friday evenings, or by the steadily increasing numbers who joined the synagogue, or by the life tenure awarded him by a deeply grateful congregation—all signs of Lehrman's success in building a Jewish religious community within the brief span of the postwar period.[14] Seeking to establish Judaism in America's popular playground, Lehrman made synagogue life an acceptable leisure activity for Jews in Miami Beach, both residents and regular visitors. After an elegant meal at one of the many restaurants on the Beach, well-dressed congregants strolled over to the synagogue to hear Lehrman preach on topics of the day. Others joined many of the clubs sponsored by the Miami Beach Jewish Center, including a popular little theater group that "included people from all walks of life, rich and poor."[15] Its entertainments extended the synagogue's reach, bringing both secular and religious leisure activity under congregational auspices.

One of Lehrman's most significant innovations concerned the position and education of women within his synagogue. Here Lehrman worked with Bella, his wife, who helped to pioneer a distinctive role for the rabbi's wife beyond her traditional supportive position. Prewar Conservative congregations had taken tentative steps toward expanding the religious participation of women and enhancing the education of girls. Lehrman went further and encouraged his congregants to treat the supplementary Jewish education of their daughters with the same seriousness as that of their sons. If he was going to build anew, he would incorporate the postwar appreciation of women as active workers in all causes and missions. Man's work, even in such a domain as the synagogue, which traditionally excluded women from active participation, was no longer for men alone. Lehrman reminded members that "the Jewish girl of today is the Jewish mother of tomorrow and it is most important that she receive an intensive education." At the beginning of the school year, which corresponded to the start of the Jewish year, Lehrman regularly urged: "Give your children a Jewish education! Do not disinherit them from the wealth of knowledge and tradition that is rightfully theirs!" Education, he noted, offered children "stability by giving them roots!"[16]

Educating girls and boys together implicitly diminished traditional distinctions between the roles of men and women in Judaism. Women played a secondary role in Jewish public religious observance; the home was their religious realm. But intensive education without participation in synagogue ritual suggested empty promises. Though boys continued to outnumber girls in the afternoon Hebrew school, Lehrman moved toward equality of women within the synagogue.[17] In 1952 he instituted a custom of asking the entire congregation to rise on *Simhat Torah* during the Torah reading, in contrast to the usual practice of calling individuals to receive the honor of an *aliyah* (literally, "going up"; that is to read from the Torah). The entire congregation then repeated the blessings said by the one given an *aliyah*, and as Lehrman explained, each member should consider himself or herself personally called to the Torah in the Jewish tradition. To his surprise he received a letter of thanks from Bess Gersten for the "thrill" of having been called to the Torah for the first time in her life. Gersten also enclosed a check for fifty dollars, the usual practice upon receiving such an honor.[18]

Later that year the congregation celebrated its first bat mitzvah, a new religious ceremony for girls modeled on the bar mitzvah ritual for boys who reach the age of thirteen. A bat mitzvah recognized the accomplishments of girls in mastering a more intensive educational program by honoring them within the synagogue and inviting them to accept their religious responsibilities as Jewish adults. Among the first to become bat mitzvah was Marjorie Friedland, daughter of the synagogue's president, a major supporter of Lehrman and the center. Despite the encouragement, only a devoted few gave their daughters a bat mitzvah though all parents wanted their sons to become bar mitzvah.[19] The introduction of so radical an innovation occurred as the men leading the congregation debated whether to continue the venerable practice of *shnoddering*, or bidding competitively for the honor of an *aliyah*.[20] Thus, old and new, tradition and innovation, coexisted at the center.

Lehrman wanted his congregants to pray, to *daven*, to become intoxicated with Judaism. He wanted them to embrace a personal spirituality. He started a junior congregation run by children at the school, in which "the girls, too, have an opportunity to participate." He admitted that he was "envious" of the thirty thousand young Christians who turned out for a Miami revival meeting of Billy Graham's Youth for Christ movement "to participate in a most moving demonstration of prayer." Lehrman compared Graham's movement to "our synagogue youth organizations . . . our young people who are given all sorts of lectures and forums and discussion groups—everything except good old-fashioned prayer." Despite the attraction of Protestant evangelicalism, Lehrman stopped short of transforming his congregation into a center of fundamentalist fervor. Crowds of four thousand on the High Holidays was his limit. Yet his recognition of a deep need for Jews to find meaning in a Judaism that spoke to them as individuals, comparable to the personal spirituality of Protestant evangelicalism, suggests how attuned he was to what might motivate his fellow permanent tourists in Miami Beach.[21]

If he eschewed a crusading pietism, he and Bella did try to teach congregants the art of Jewish living. They sought, that is, to instruct women in the kind of experiential spirituality associated in the past with the woman's role in Judaism. Through women they hoped to spiritualize the entire family. By the 1950s it was apparent that mothers, previously responsible for home ritual, no longer knew what to do. Somehow—perhaps through neglect or disinterest, perhaps as a result of migration—women had lost the skills to celebrate home rituals. The pious home had all but vanished in this city by the sea. Prodded by the rabbi and his wife, the religious school PTA and synagogue sisterhood sponsored workshops explaining how to observe holidays at home. The workshops demonstrated how to set the table, what food to cook, what blessings to say. Women learned by actually doing. The workshops began with the Hanukkah holiday with its focus on children, but soon expanded to include Pesach (Passover), with its elaborate home seder ritual, and Rosh Hashanah.[22]

Bella Lehrman introduced into the center a novel and entrepreneurial institution: the sisterhood gift shop. The gift shop addressed simultaneously several congregational needs: It provided a steady source of income for the synagogue; it made available ritual objects not easily purchased in Miami; and it helped to link the congregation's younger and older married women. It encouraged as well the development of the women's business skills because running the gift shop required knowledge of purchasing, bookkeeping, and merchandising. Since very few married women worked in an era that promoted women's domestic nature and role and many had maids to help take care of housework, the gift shop provided a rare workplace outside the home for their entrepreneurial energies and skills. Many Jewish women actively sought such volunteer work.[23]

The women running the gift shop sold merchandise that they thought would appeal to other women, their target audience, as the chief purchaser for the household, but they also tried to expand their customers' repertoire of ritual objects. Jews do not actually need all of the ceremonial objects that they possess, although many reflect a desire to beautify ritual activity. Most of the required items—like *tallit*, the prayer shawl, and *tefillin*, the small leather boxes holding scriptural inscriptions that are strapped with thongs to the forehead and arm—belong in the almost exclusive domain of men. The gift shop encouraged Jewish women to change their attitude toward ritual objects, to see them as decorative, functional, and experiential. Women were invited to explore a world of possibilities opened up by postwar affluence, to beautify their homes with Jewish symbols. A pair of silver candlesticks, for example, might decorate a mantlepiece during the week, hold a pair of candles, and even stimulate a woman to kindle and bless the sabbath lights. The shop enhanced the art of living Jewishly even as it contributed to the buying and selling of Jewish culture.[24]

The shop highlighted the commonality of Jews, a people with its own crafts and decorative arts. It became a means to showcase Israeli ceremonial and art objects, linking Israel to American Jews by encouraging women to consume these products of the new Jewish state. Like a miniature museum, the shop displayed artifacts of Jewish culture. Visitors to the shop implicitly learned that Judaism concerned itself with aesthetic issues. The shop's location within the synagogue symbolically placed a religious seal of approval upon its contents. For some a gift shop visit became part of a ritual associated with the synagogue or with shepherding children to religious school. A purchase satisfied both the customer and individual who received the present, creating a Jewish network linking them with the synagogue. The profit from sales contributed to a worthwhile congregational endeavor, such as the synagogue library.

The shop began, as did the workshops, with Hanukkah and bar mitzvah, offering gifts of toys, books, and records for children, jewelry from Israel, and items to decorate the house.[25] It soon expanded to include bride's Bibles and *kiddush* cups for weddings, tie clips and ID bracelets for bar mitzvahs, Israeli menorahs and art objects, and cookbooks for the housewife. By the late 1950s the gift shop contained such elegant items for the home as sterling silver trays, candy dishes, and Israeli coffee spoons that had merely tangential Jewish symbolic significance. In addition, it included specialized ritual objects used only by more observant Jews, like silver spice boxes for the *havdala* ceremony marking the end of the sabbath and matzo covers for Pesach. With an eye on the ornamental, women also bought *mezuzot*, small cases holding scriptural inscriptions that are placed on door lintels to fulfill a religious commandment, and spice boxes to decorate their home. But the shop never became exclusive in its merchandise and continued to carry such American inventions as Jewish New Year's greeting cards and personalized bar mitzvah napkins. The wide range of items available for purchase, in terms of cost, quality, and religious culture, suggested the diversity of commercial Jewish symbols and the eclecticism of popular piety. Although not an exclusive feature of the Miami Beach Jewish Center, the sisterhood gift shop found a broad audience in this innovative and adaptable community because it offered all types of portable, symbolic insignia of roots that newcomers welcomed.[26]

A year after Lehrman found his place in the sun, Leon Kronish and his wife, Lillian, arrived in the "spiritual wilderness" of Miami Beach. A New York native like Lehrman, Kronish also graduated from JIR. Unlike Lehrman, neither he nor his wife came from a rabbinical family, although like Bella, Lillian was a college graduate. Without the pull of parental Orthodoxy, Kronish moved easily toward liberalism, not Conservatism. When he came to the Beth Sholom Center, it had perhaps forty members in good standing. The fledgling synagogue had been established only three years earlier, and despite its name, which meant "house of peace," it was weakened by internal conflict. The handful of founding members, like those of the Miami Beach Jewish Center, thought, but could not agree, to have an Orthodox-Conservative congregation. They hired Kronish in the summer of 1944, and by the fall he was telling the first general congregational meeting of the new year that they were "a Modern Conservative Jewish organization."[27]

Like Lehrman, Kronish immediately made an impact upon the congregation. A tall, handsome man and a persuasive speaker with a good sense of humor—he often began his sermons with a joke—Kronish rapidly attracted followers. He regularly greeted each congregant after services and quickly learned the names of all. Within a few months one hundred new members joined—the new rabbi actively solicited them—and by the spring Kronish was encouraging the board to give the center a more specifically religious name.[28] With the change from Beth Sholom Center to Temple Beth Sholom came a commitment to become a "liberal congregation" that would guarantee freedom of the pulpit.[29] The congregation minutes suggest that Kronish desired to follow his mentor Stephen Wise's path to Reform Judaism, accompanied by a strong commitment to Zionism, Jewish peoplehood, and social justice. During the summer Kronish returned to New York City, charged by the temple's religious committee with purchasing prayer books published by the Reform UAHC. Despite the decision to become a liberal congregation, members continued to quarrel over whether that actually meant what the label *Reform* implied. Many associated *Reform* not with liberalism, social justice, and openness but with elitism, non-Zionism, and a religious service devoid of Hebrew that resembled high-church Protestantism with its organ music, strict rules of decorum, and formal quality of worship.[30]

The issue of denominational labels irritated Temple Beth Sholom throughout the 1940s. Although Kronish urged the board to affiliate with the UAHC, several men resisted the stigma associated with *Reform*.[31] They preferred *liberal* because it lacked the ideological freight associated with *Reform*, especially Reform's long opposition to Zionism and the establishment of a Jewish state, a position that had changed only under the pressures of World War II. Kronish, however, carried his congregation into the Reform Union.[32] When issues arose that might have aligned Temple Beth Sholom with more Conservative practices—such as how many days of a Jewish holiday to observe—Kronish persuaded the board to follow Reform custom, though he rarely justified his argument by referring to Reform authority.[33] By the 1950s, once the hurdle of affiliation was overcome, Kronish pointedly referred to Temple Beth Sholom as a liberal congregation, not a Reform one, since he, too, disliked Reform's lukewarm support of Israel.

Kronish gradually began to give both form and substance to *liberal* through the Friday night and sabbath services and an extensive educational program. The late Friday eve services were largely in English, accompanied by an organ and dominated by the sermon. After the crowds departed, Kronish and his family, often with a few of his devoted followers, would go to Juniors Restaurant, located on Collins Avenue not far from the Temple, to discuss the sermon, an indication of the vigorous debate and enthusiasm generated by the young rabbi. Saturday mornings Kronish reserved for a more traditional service that included the weekly reading of several chapters of the Torah as well as a sermon, or *d'var Torah*, designed to explain some aspect of sacred scriptures; he also used more Hebrew prayers in that service. The congregation left the decision regarding the wearing of prayer shawls up to individuals but insisted that anyone ascending the pulpit for the honor of an *aliyah* don one.[34]

Kronish started to experiment with the religious content of such holiday services as Shavuot, which celebrates the time when the Israelites received the Torah from God at Mount Sinai, and Purim, which commemorates the Jews' rescue from an anti-Semitic pogrom. For Shavuot, he wrote a cantata on the theme of Israel Reborn; for Purim he crafted a new megillah, that is, he retold the story found in the biblical Book of Esther in a modern idiom. Kronish also experimented with the popular holiday of Hanukkah, writing a poetic dramalogue. Touched by the positive response to his innovations, he thanked his congregants for their "understanding spirit which makes possible these creative experiments in religious worship." Many of the men leading Temple Beth Sholom were second generation Jews, familiar with religious changes introduced by Conservatism during the interwar years. Thus they accepted the young rabbi's innovations and supported his efforts to develop "a dynamic ritual that is traditional in spirit, rich in Jewish warmth, and liberal in form." Kronish wanted to create a new *minhag*, or rites, for American Jews, that would be the substance of a religious ritual "that would win the hearts of the masses." Miami Beach, with its cross section of Jews drawn from all corners of the United States, provided an ideal setting for such an ambitious national endeavor. Kronish rapidly filled the temple to capacity, supervised a successful building expansion program, and received recognition from the Miami Jewish community.[35]

Given his articulate and self-conscious religious liberalism, Kronish moved openly and rapidly to enhance the status of women within the congregation. He instituted some innovations even a few years before Lehrman did. Although an early proposal that women be guaranteed places on the board of directors did not change the congregation's governance, Kronish announced in 1948 a special bat mitzvah class. "Mothers are the cornerstone of the Jewish family," he explained. "Women, too, are becoming more prominent in Jewish community life. To provide intelligent leadership and to equip our girls for these responsibilities, we are instituting this year a special BAT MITZVAH program" with a newly designed ceremony. The following year, when members complained about the presence of women on the pulpit during the High Holidays, he recommended that they enroll in his adult education classes to learn the reasons behind Beth Sholom's practices.[36]

Lillian Kronish, like Bella Lehrman, introduced a sisterhood gift shop and holiday workshops. The gift shop started in 1947 with presents appropriate for bar mitzvahs, weddings, holidays, and, of course, Hanukkah. "Gracious Living Means Giving," the sisterhood advertised. "Make it a habit to choose your gifts at the Sisterhood Gift Shop." The shop was open daily from nine to five and on Sunday mornings when children came to school. Holiday workshops began the same year. The rabbi helped guide families in planning their own home seder for the second night of Pesach, following the congregational seder on the first night. He urged members to "make Passover an unforgettable experience, a joyous experience, a family get-together. Children will subconsciously know that God and Israel, freedom and family joy are all one." Herein lay the true art of Jewish living, an experience that was joyous, spiritual, homey, and aesthetically appealing.[37]

Kronish practiced what he preached. "Undoubtedly, the most lasting legacy that I have from my father, the educator, is that Jewish education begins in the home," recalled his daughter. In describing her childhood home, Maxine Kronish Snyder portrayed the art of Jewish living that the rabbi and his wife tried to inspire in their congregants. "The walls, with the Jewish art and books, convey Jewish learning and Jewish feeling; the music on the stereo is Jewish, and it has helped link us to our roots in Europe and Israel," she wrote; "the conversations at the Shabbat and holiday meals are experientially Jewish, and they helped us keep Judaism, Israel, and especially Jerusalem, uppermost in our minds; the kitchen"— not a kosher one but Jewish nonetheless, "where my mother has always been in charge—is intensely Jewish, not just in its delicious foods and smells, but also in its human atmosphere, brimming with caring, concern and sensitivity." This vision of the Jewish home as the source of Jewish spirituality animated efforts to educate Jewish women. Maxine considered herself "fortunate" to have been able "to learn and experience" as she grew up "the power and value of a Jewish education that is centered in an intensely Jewish home."[38]

Given the similarities of the synagogues that Lehrman and Kronish built—of Temple Emanu-El (the more religious name adopted by the Miami Beach Jewish Center in 1954) and Temple Beth Sholom—wherein lay the differences? Jews living on Miami Beach during the 1950s used to point to the fact that worshippers needed a ticket to attend Friday night services at Temple Emanu-El whereas they could just walk in to the services at Temple Beth Sholom. Indeed, Beth Sholom made a commitment to such democratic practices part of its creed. An early membership brochure affirmed: "We demand that [the synagogue] be Democratic. That means an equitable dues system."[39] It also meant no financial barriers to membership, no assigned pews, and no tuition fees. Temple Beth Sholom's modern low-profile brick buildings, recessed from the street, physically expressed similar liberal democratic sentiments and presented a contrast with the tall, elegantly appointed buildings of Temple Emanu-El, especially its multistoried, domed synagogue that sat diagonally at the corner intersection.

The Jewish religious ideals of the congregations also differed, reflecting their rabbis' perspective. In 1948 Temple Beth Sholom published in its bulletin a definition of a good Jew. Such a person was impatient with the sociopolitical ills plaguing society and eagerly sought remedies for them. The definition assumed both marriage and family because it listed educating one's children Jewishly as part of being a good Jew. The good Jew was seen to respond to the needs of his people, read Jewish books, and not be demoralized by anti-Semitism. Such a Jew is intelligently Jewish, affiliates with a synagogue, and has self-knowledge. Compare this to the Miami Beach Jewish Center's checklist for Jewish adults published in 1951. Its minimum rating scale of Jewish practice included a "fair knowledge" of synagogue ritual, familiarity with the background of Jewish observances, knowledge of general Jewish history, a "working knowledge" of Hebrew, and familiarity with Jewish music. A Jewish adult with this background ideally attends every sabbath service he can, enrolls his children in a Jewish school, reads at least five books of Jewish content each year, and fluently expresses ideas about Judaism. Finally, a Jew should both know and recite the kiddush and blessing for his children each sabbath eve. The concern with specific Jewish knowledge and ritual behavior versus liberal values and general Jewish commitment in part distinguished Conservatism from liberalism in postwar Miami.[40]

Despite these differences, not to mention those of style and temperament, Lehrman and Kronish had more in common with each other, especially their strong Zionist commitment to Israel, than they did with the third influential Miami rabbi, Joseph Narot. Ironically, Kronish and Narot joined the Reform rabbinical association, and both led congregations affiliated with the UAHC. Yet the two stood poles apart on many of the most important issues facing American Jews.

Narot came to Miami in 1950 at the age of thirty-seven with ten years of experience as a rabbi of a Reform congregation in Atlantic City. Born in a small town near Vilna, Lithuania, Narot grew up in poverty in Warren, Ohio. He received a traditional Jewish education from his Orthodox parents. In 1969 Narot looked back upon his life in an extraordinary sermon, a personal confession rarely made by rabbis before their congregants. The sermon revealed some of the motives driving these pioneering rabbis. Surveying the rows upon rows of over four thousand congregants gathered in the Miami Beach Convention Center on the eve of Rosh Hashanah, Narot began to preach.[41] "Where shall I begin?" he asked, addressing the thousands sitting before him. What have I learned from my life? "My parents never left the old world—spiritually speaking. They always referred to Europe as 'home'— '*in der haym.*' For that reason I thought that the gap between them and me was due to culture and language," he admitted. "Years later, when I confronted my own children, I learned how mistaken I had been." Narot rebelled against his father and his father's Orthodoxy. When he was eighteen, he discovered Reform Judaism and "took to it with the zeal of the convert." This zeal never abated. "Reform's fervor for social justice, its loyalty to all knowledge and experience, its readiness to innovate and modify, its faith in reason, filled my imagination."

But Narot confessed to more than a fervent devotion to Reform. He acknowledged as well that the Reform rabbinate promised a poor boy a way out of Warren and a chance to earn a decent livelihood. Narot characterized himself as "a self-made man," a vision that drew upon American frontier imagery but discarded any notion of tradition handed down through the generations, a notion that was critical to Jewish continuity and that Jews usually assumed animated their rabbis. Yet in Miami, a city without traditions and roots,

Narot's vision of self-creation hardly outraged his congregants. Perhaps more shocking, he admitted learning "that a man can never get enough money. There is no end to the wanting of things." He confessed, too, "in my secret depths I have yearned to be the world-renowned rabbi and have even envied the acclaim which other colleagues seem to get." Such ambitions, appropriate to secular newcomers, rarely came from a rabbi. Narot's decision to confess his eagerness for fame and fortune, measured by conventional standards, set him apart from his northeastern and midwestern peers, who often proclaimed learning, piety, communal service, and spiritual sacrifice as their motivations for serving in the rabbinate.

As the oldest and most prestigious Reform congregation in Miami, Temple Israel did not suffer from the chaotic conditions of newness faced by Lehrman and Kronish. When Narot arrived to take the pulpit there, he could build upon a solid base, and build he did. Like Lehrman and Kronish, Narot was a handsome man. (Good looks appeared to be a requisite for the Miami rabbinate; it certainly helped attract congregants.) Narot expanded the Temple's membership, constructed new school buildings, and attracted increased attendance at Friday evening services—the main sabbath services for Reform congregations. He also strengthened Temple Israel's position as the representative Jewish institution to Miami's Christian religious world. Though in perhaps less dramatic fashion than the congregations on the Beach, Temple Israel grew rapidly under Narot despite the heavy membership turnover typical of established synagogues. Measured by the same criteria of numbers, buildings, attendance, congregational support, and communal recognition used to gauge Lehrman's and Kronish's achievements, Narot's success was considerable.[42]

But Narot did not change the position of women or the education of girls. Temple Israel fixed minimal educational requirements of several hours once a week for both boys and girls that Narot considered appropriate. He steadfastly opposed using Jews' desire to see their sons become bar mitzvah as a means of encouraging them to give their children more Jewish education, and he attacked this process sharply, ridiculing such synagogue schools as bar mitzvah "factories." Similarly, the radically reduced home rituals of Reform, consisting of a festive meal on the High Holidays and, occasionally, Hanukkah celebrations, sufficed. There were no workshops in the art of Jewish living. Narot urged, instead, making attendance at Friday night services a "fashionable" weekly activity.[43]

Narot managed to leave his stamp upon the synagogue, a more formidable task than that faced by his Miami Beach peers since Temple Israel had a number of local traditions from its previous quarter century.[44] He adamantly adhered to the radical teachings of classic Reform Judaism, especially its rejection of religious ritual and Jewish law, its emphasis upon ethics and the primacy of belief in monotheism, its non-Zionism and lukewarm acceptance of Israel, and its opposition to Jewish ethnicity associated with the idea of Jewish peoplehood. He resisted congregants' efforts to give centrality to bar mitzvah, relegating Hebrew instruction to voluntary weekday classes. He also insisted that such religious symbols as prayer shawls and head covering for men be eliminated as they were in classic Reform temples. Finally, Narot championed the right of Reform Jews not to observe more than one day of each Jewish holiday, since classic Reform had eliminated the traditional second day. In sermons and in printed "letters to my congregation," Narot explained the modern vision of Reform Judaism, its rational religious message, its aesthetic and ethical ideals. Some members thought he apologized for Reform Judaism too much and that he was forever rejecting his own non-Reform origins. But perhaps this psychological spur gave his personal charisma its attractive edge.[45]

This hint of insecurity suggested the drive of the self-selected pioneer to carve out his own domain. Narot's passion for radical Reform was integral to his leadership. He could not take his faith for granted but abrasively and defensively wore it on his sleeve. When he went to the racetrack on Saturday—an unusual Shabbat activity for a Reform rabbi—he defended his sport as legitimate: "Relaxation and recreation must . . . be part of our Sabbath regimen, along with study, prayer, and synagogue attendance."[46] Indeed, his demand that congregants choose Reform as he had chosen it identified him as akin to Lehrman or Kronish in his desire to found a distinctive congregation in his own image.

In the mid-1960s Narot invited a well-known sociologist to survey Temple Israel's Sunday School, Miami's largest.[47] The survey delineated the Jewish values held by the students. Most essential, they said, was a belief in God, in order to be "a good Jew." This emphasis upon belief in God contrasted with the values encouraged by Kronish, who stressed the pursuit of social justice as critical, or by Lehrman, who focused on observing Jewish religious ritual. Neither Kronish's nor Lehrman's congregation bothered to include belief in God as part of their definition of a good Jew. Narot's students, however, learned effectively his interpretation of Judaism, for following their faith statement was an affirmation of identity, that is, accepting oneself as a Jew and not trying to hide one's Jewishness. The students ranked worshipping God, knowing the fundamentals of Judaism, attending services on the High Holidays, and leading an ethical life after these two fundamentals of being a good Jew. Over half thought it essential to gain the respect of their Christian neighbors, thus exhibiting Jews' traditional concern with their Christian neighbors' attitudes toward them. Other issues so central to the congregations of Kronish and Lehrman, including support for Israel, synagogue membership, contributions to Jewish philanthropies, efforts in behalf of equality for all minority groups, and marriage "within the Jewish faith" received recognition as desirable but not essential.

Like the programmatic statements of the two Miami Beach congregations, this list faithfully reflects Narot's concerns and the values of radical Reform. Its focus on belief in God and one's social identity as a Jew, coupled with concern for basic Jewish beliefs and how Jews appeared before their Christian neighbors, indicates Temple Israel's distinctiveness in Miami.

Narot's dedication to Reform, Kronish's commitment to liberal Judaism, and Lehrman's attachment to Conservatism set these three rabbis apart, but their extraordinary ambition, drive, and success in the business of the rabbinate united them. They understood implicitly that in a town of rootless Jews, a rabbi had to be a showman to draw crowds into his synagogue. He had to offer Jews a social as well as a religious identity, political values as well as moral ones. They shared a similar vision of the place of the synagogue in Jewish life: It was a broad, all-encompassing, representative Jewish institution. And despite their different interpretations of Judaism, they imagined religion as spiritual recreation, an opportunity to enjoy learning and working together, men and women, boys and girls, the ideal complement to Miami's leisure lifestyle. These values distinguished them from many of their fellow rabbis but linked them with the characteristic rabbinic figures of Los Angeles.

Edgar Magnin, Los Angeles's leading rabbi for over half a century, was perhaps prototypical of the pioneer American rabbi. Born and raised in San Francisco, Magnin attended the University of Cincinnati and Hebrew Union College (HUC). Like Narot, he saw the rabbinate as a vehicle for social mobility; he wanted to be a Reform rabbi because "the class of people were more refined." Unlike Narot, Magnin inclined toward tradition and away from classic Reform. When Magnin came to Los Angeles in 1920 as rabbi of the city's leading Reform congregation, he opposed changing the Jewish sabbath to Sunday, an action that had been championed by several leading classical Reform rabbis. He consistently leaned toward Conservatism in the context of Reform and thus reintroduced abandoned traditions. Magnin restored the bar mitzvah ritual that classic Reform had rejected in favor of a new ceremony of confirmation and reinstituted blowing the shofar rather than a trumpet on the High Holidays.[48]

Magnin built an impressive sphere of influence for himself. He oversaw the construction of an imposing new synagogue building with "proportions like a theater" on a prestigious site on Wilshire Boulevard, and he urged his congregation to change its name to the Wilshire Boulevard Temple. "I wanted people to know the location," he remarked. He socialized with his wealthy congregants, joining the Hillcrest Country Club at a time when no other rabbis were members in pursuit of the power and influence he needed to build his synagogue and its importance. A large, gregarious man who spoke colloquially, Magnin symbolized the rabbinate in Los Angeles for many years; most non-Jews knew of no other. Neal Gabler dubbed him "rabbi to the stars."[49]

Magnin spoke bluntly about his own singular accomplishment: over fifty years in one pulpit at a prestigious synagogue. His self-assessment and perspective offer insight into the values of pioneer rabbis and their contrast to prevalent American rabbinic norms. Magnin castigated the misplaced rabbinic agenda of the eastern establishment. At annual national meetings, he felt, rabbis discussed silly things like theology or Jewish survival rather than talking about the purpose of the rabbinate or how to succeed in religion, which was, to Magnin's way of thinking, a business like lawyering. When Jews go to a synagogue service, he explained, "they must come out touched. If they don't come out laughing or crying, then there's something wrong." He elaborated: "You should go *away* with some *feeling* of lift and some feeling of 'I'm glad I'm a Jew. There is something to life, some meaning.'" The rabbi produced this effect through his preaching. Magnin, who taught homiletics, saw the rabbinate as "a leadership job." It was his duty to inspire his congregants and give them pride in their Judaism, not to make pronouncements. He disdained those eastern "rabbis who compare themselves to prophets" as "idiots and phonies" and much preferred his own pioneering type of rabbi, who enjoyed the good life. Prophets, after all, "never received a salary, they never had a pension, they never lived in nice homes, they never ate at Perinos or the Bistro out in Beverly Hills."[50] Nor, one might add, did they ever go to racetracks.

Magnin's pragmatic and personal approach to the rabbinate did not preclude a commitment to more intensive and advanced Jewish education or to a more experiential form of Judaism than had traditionally been available in Reform. In 1954 he criticized Reform's tendency to become static and its failure to make demands upon its adherents. Under his guidance Wilshire Boulevard Temple continued to grow and to make new demands upon its members, especially its youth.[51] In the two most significant developments—the College of Jewish Studies and Camp Hess Kramer—Magnin recognized and encouraged the vision of another Reform rabbi eager to draw uprooted Jews into a community around the congregation, Alfred Wolf.

Wolf had come to Los Angeles in 1946 to organize the West Coast Region of the UAHC and collaborated with Magnin and other Reform rabbis in establishing the College of Jewish Studies, which was aimed at Reform Sunday School teachers and interested adults. In 1949 Magnin encouraged Wolf to initiate a camping program under Wilshire Boulevard Temple auspices. Wolf first discovered camping as a teenager in Nazi Germany. "Called upon to organize Jewish youth groups in Heidelberg," he reflected, "I realized how much of Jewish values I could get across to young people as we were hiking or camping together under the open sky." Exposure to American Protestant church groups' use of camp meetings confirmed Wolf's convictions that Jews could learn from them. That fall Wolf presented his idea for "camping in the spirit of Reform Judaism" to the temple's men's club. The men agreed to sponsor the program.[52]

While well established prior to World War II as a Jewish summer activity, camping under specifically religious auspices—especially sponsored by a synagogue—was a new, postwar innovation. Wolf recalled that "there was no tradition then of any temple activity after Confirmation."[53] Even a temple leader like J. Robert Arkush, head of the men's club and a supporter of the camp project, had difficulty convincing his daughter to go. Once the teenagers got to the primitive campsite in the Pacific Palisades, however, they discovered the friendship and closeness camp could engender. Their enthusiasm for camping convinced several temple members to provide their children with a decent campsite.

The decision to purchase property for a camp revealed a serious rift between those who saw religious school as ideal for Jewish youth and camp as a commercial gimmick and those who considered Sunday School ineffective and camp an inspiring Jewish communal alternative. Wolf tried to mediate by suggesting that camp and school could complement each other. School provided "periodic religious reminders in an otherwise secular week" while camp represented the integration of Jewish "religious principles and practices with daily living."[54] It also allowed teenagers to remain connected with the temple after confirmation and it strengthened loyalty to Reform institutions. Despite lack of enthusiasm among some members, an absence of qualified camp directors, and the problem of time for supervision by the rabbis, the men's club directors in 1951 voted to purchase a campsite. The following year Camp Hess Kramer opened on 110 acres in Ventura County.

Magnin never spent a night at camp—he was a "Waldorf Astoria camper"—but he supported the venture. He thought that the camp provided an ideal setting to cultivate religious feelings. Several hundred campers and their counselors experienced Judaism within a surrogate home. "You can give the kids all the tools in the Religious School that you want," an early camping convert argued. "But until they actually have an opportunity to live what they've learned, they just don't get the relationship, they don't get the values. At Camp the kids *live* the Sabbath and they find out it works."[55] Some were inspired to participate more actively in temple educational activities and to exercise youth leadership after their camp experience. Occasionally individuals recruited for positions in camp moved over to full-time employment at the temple as youth directors, teachers, and even cantors. Camp also offered a venue for year-round conferences. Its separate incorporation as a temple subsidiary allowed it to initiate community projects that asserted Reform Judaism's importance in Los Angeles. In 1953 the camp started its annual interracial and interreligious weekend conference on human relations for university students and faculty. Camp Hess Kramer brought influence, personnel, leadership, and, of course, members to Wilshire Boulevard

Temple.[56] Its creation expanded the synagogue's orbit as it taught youth how to be Jewish. Like gift shops and holiday workshops, summer camping under synagogue auspices sought to fill space left by absent religious traditions in Miami and L.A.

Facing the disruptive effects of migration, admitting the absence of a "natural" public Jewish environment in Los Angeles, and unable to depend upon transmission of a pattern of Jewish living by newcomers to their children, ambitious and pragmatic rabbis, eager to experiment, initiated novel programs to fit needs of potential members. On the way they built their own distinctive congregations, establishing their sphere of influence. They borrowed the idea of summer camps from youth leaders in Y's, community centers, and settlement houses, from innovative Jewish educators, from Zionists, Socialists, and Communists in order to nurture and incorporate their own youthful elite.[57] Camping under synagogue sponsorship would show Jews how to live as religious Jews by giving them at least a minimum ritual competence and allowing them to enjoy a Jewish spirituality. It would imbue youngsters with loyalty toward their brand of Judaism, a loyalty that might even extend beyond devotion to "their" rabbi. Though a rabbi like Magnin preferred Judaism without any Jewish ethnicity, camping inevitably introduced elements of shared sociability associated with a sense of family, belonging, and peoplehood.

Wolf's success in carving out his own domain under the institutional umbrella of Temple Wilshire was unusual—a tribute both to his and Magnin's abilities. Magnin's willingness to share his power was exceptional. More often, an ambitious rabbi coming to Los Angeles built his own synagogue and imprinted his personality on the institution. Like their peers in Miami, most Los Angeles rabbis yoked their congregations to a national denominational movement. A few tried to promote what they considered to be a unique Los Angeles vision.[58] "Since its inception the Valley Jewish Community Center has refused to adopt any label other than that of 'Jewish,'" proclaimed its rabbi, Sidney Goldstein. A graduate of the Jewish Institute of Religion, Goldstein championed an inclusive vision for the center. "Its services are traditional yet liberal and its program is many faceted. It seeks to serve all the Jews in the Valley." But most rabbis did not follow his lead. Goldstein himself left the center less than six months later after fighting with members who disputed the substance of his sermons and disagreed with his interpretation of the rabbi's prophetic role.[59]

Deciding to throw "its lot in with the Conservative Movement" and to reject a nondenominational vision, the center board recognized that "naturally, there are many in our midst who do not know what Conservatism represents. . . . This confusion exists in many parts of the country but reaches its acme here on the West Coast." The board solved its dilemma by employing a new rabbi, Aaron Wise. In those years "they accepted whatever I recommended and whatever I did because I was their spiritual leader," Wise recalled.[60] Not only did Wise oversee all the details of building a congregation, but he also linked his efforts and the resources of the Valley Jewish Community Center (VJCC) to the growth of Conservative institutions in Los Angeles, specifically the fledgling University of Judaism. Less than three months after he arrived, Wise praised plans announced by the Conservative Jewish Theological Seminary (JTS) to establish a branch in Los Angeles. "We who have faith that the Jewry of Southern California has a great future are reassured by the Seminary's program," he told his congregants. "Not only will we become a great physical center for Jewish life but also a spiritual and cultural center." Even before his formal installation, the board voted unanimously to support the seminary. As Kronish had affiliated with the Reform UAHC in Miami, so Wise supported the University of Judaism in Los Angeles. He grabbed hold of the national movement to clarify the center's identity as a Conservative synagogue.[61]

Wise discovered California in 1945 when he spent a summer in Santa Barbara as a civilian chaplain. He came to the Valley Jewish Community Center with his wife, Miriam, and children in the summer of 1947 at the age of thirty-four because he wanted to work with his own peers, congregants who "were my age, and not the age of my parents and grandparents."[62] The center had almost ten years of history when Wise arrived. As the first congregation in the San Fernando Valley, it was ideally situated to benefit from the large numbers of Jews finding new homes there. The center also attracted Jews who worked in the motion picture industry. Their impact registered most visibly in the center's music program. However, despite a membership of approximately three hundred, the center was located on a dead end street in a modest building. Like the Miami Beach Jewish Center, the Valley Jewish Community Center possessed unrealized potential.

Wise quickly began to shape the center into a Conservative synagogue, koshering the kitchen and insisting that men cover their heads during worship. He started regular sabbath morning services and required all bar mitzvah and confirmation candidates to attend. After the short (one hour), largely English service, Wise told stories drawn from Jewish folklore. Soon membership began to grow. Like his Miami peers, Wise rapidly achieved success. By 1958 the center had the reputation of being *the* synagogue in the Valley; so many had joined that, with a surplus of funds, it temporarily closed membership. Wise used the center's bulletin to reach out to and educate members, supplementing its schedule of events and personal notices with didactic messages. "A cardinal tenet of our faith is Zionism, and its hope for the rebirth of the Jewish people on its own soil, for the renascence of Hebrew culture and art," he wrote on one occasion. Conservatism, he explained, respects Reform for its innovation and is drawn to the tradition of Orthodoxy, but it loves America. "In this, of all nations on earth, we are native-born: for American democracy is in a profound sense the child of the Judaic tradition."[63]

Yet Wise recognized that the Judaic tradition had "faded from the lives of most" of his congregants. "You would expect that an individual Jew, a father, a grandfather, would belong to a synagogue and have so much to communicate to his children, his own family in the home. But most of that is lost now," he reflected. Wise suggested compensating for the absence of a male Judaic heritage by expanding women's religious education. These innovations resembled those introduced by Lehrman and Kronish in Miami. Like them, Wise relied on his wife to develop new roles for women. Before the first Hanukkah, Aaron and Miriam Wise started a "novel book and gift shop service" under sisterhood supervision. Among the initial items offered for sale were *mezuzahs* and Magen Davids—six-pointed Jewish stars—as well as Hanukkah gifts and books for children and adults. A year later the merchandise included a larger array of ceremonial objects, such as yarmulkes, *tallithim* (prayer shawls), candlesticks, menorahs, and *yarzeit* (annual memorial) bulbs to honor the dead, along with games, Bible coloring books, and statuettes. A poster promoting the shop proclaimed "Make your Jewish home beautiful."[64]

The sisterhood continued to expand the possibilities of making a Jewish home beautiful. Upon completion of construction of a new synagogue building with its stained glass windows by Mischa Kallis, an artist working for Universal Pictures, the sisterhood transferred the design of the stained glass windows to plates. These they offered for sale, inviting members to decorate their homes with the beauty—and, implicitly, the spirituality—of the synagogue by purchasing the dishes. In 1948 the sisterhood introduced a competitive note by sponsoring a contest for the most beautiful Hanukkah home decorations. Over sixty families participated. By 1949 it was clear that these measures were insufficient. Recognizing "a definite need in our Jewish homes to know how to celebrate Hanukkah," the sisterhood initiated a workshop. Over ninety women came to learn how to cook *latkes*, sing songs and blessings, and decorate their homes while they heard the story of the Maccabees and discovered the holiday's contemporary meaning. One workshop's success led to another one for Rosh Hashanah so that members wouldn't feel lost on the "Days of Awe." This workshop, a joint venture of PTA and the sisterhood, included model table settings, explanations of prayers, the design and creation of New Year's greeting cards, and even a skit on High Holiday etiquette. These activities bespoke a determined effort by Aaron and Miriam Wise to create among their congregants a distinctive Jewish lifestyle in a place where such natural rhythms of Jewish living were not part of the landscape.[65]

Wise encountered more difficulty convincing members to give their daughters an intensive religious education. The year he arrived, only one girl out of forty-five students attended Hebrew school. The following year saw little improvement: four out of sixty-two students were female. In 1950 Wise introduced a bat mitzvah program for the four girls. That June, on a Friday night, Connie Chais became the center's first bat mitzvah. The daughter of Zionist activists George and Ruth Chais, Connie read some prayers and spoke on the founder of Hadassah, Henrietta Szold. Although the bulletin noted that "the equality of women in Jewish religious life has been emphasized," the Friday night bat mitzvah ritual hardly approached equality with a sabbath morning bar mitzvah. Wise soon closed the gap by calling women to the Torah during sabbath morning services—as is done for a bar mitzvah—giving them the honor of an *aliyah* in recognition of their learning how to read from the Torah scrolls.[66]

Miriam Wise took bolder and more innovative steps to encourage women's equality within the synagogue. Like her Miami peers, she had received an advanced Jewish and secular education. Like them, she consciously positioned herself as an authoritative model for women congregants, opening possibilities for voluntary synagogue leadership while raising her children. She regularly reviewed books of Jewish interest, and she fostered an appreciation of Jewish learning. Most significant, however, she recruited five women to study Hebrew and Torah together. The four years of study culminated in an adult bat mitzvah in which the group of women were called up to the *bimah*, the raised platform where the Torah scroll was read, in order to read from the Torah. They were not the first women to receive such an honor of an *aliyah*, however. That occurred in the mid-1950s during High Holiday services in the El Portal Theater, rented for the occasion. "I was standing in the lobby," remembered Irma Lee Ettinger, the center's administrator, "when all of a sudden the doors opened and several hundred people streamed out. I stopped one of them," she recounted, "and asked him what was happening. He said, 'There's a woman on the bimah and she has an aliyah.' I said, 'Who is the woman?' and he said, 'Miriam Wise.' The crowd gathered in front of the theater, discussed the major change in religious policy and after they calmed down, they returned to the services," she recalled. "That was the rabbi's rather unique way of advising VJCC that women were going to be given equal rights," she observed.[67] In Los Angeles, a rabbi like Wise could pursue equal rights for women without waiting for congregants to confer.

In Miami as in Los Angeles, rabbis and their wives did their best to whet an appetite for things Jewish, to awaken a desire to experience Judaism, to develop an experiential spirituality, to encourage Jews to choose the art of Jewish living. The cities' Jewish frontier setting drew rabbis seeking fame and influence, men willing to take risks and to innovate in order to pull newcomers to the cities into their synagogues. Seeking to further Judaism, rabbis hitched their personal ambition to the migrants' inchoate desires and needs. They intuitively grasped the mentality of permanent tourists and offered a form of Judaism that fit a leisure lifestyle. Entertaining, uplifting, enriching, such a Judaism appealed to uprooted men and women. Rabbis like Lehrman, Kronish, and Narot in Miami, Wise and Wolf in Los Angeles, along with Albert Lewis and Jacob Pressman and later Isaiah Zeldin and Harold Schulweis, joined earlier figures like Magnin and Max Nussbaum in pioneering new types of congregations. In a world with few constraints, traditions, or established patterns of deference, the eclectic possibilities depended largely upon the imaginations of ambitious pioneer rabbis. Eager to build synagogues of their own, they experimented to create new liturgies, to give Judaism an aesthetic dimension, to fashion novel educational programs. They brought the American Jewish culture of the East, of their upbringing and education, to the South and West where they adapted it to new circumstances.

These men and their wives seized the opportunity to experiment with new ways to be Jewish and to pioneer self-consciously in a world where "the very meaning of Jewishness is changing."[68] The entrepreneurial spirit moved rabbis as much as other Jews. They saw the promise of a frontier society—its openness, venturesomeness, and willingness to tolerate innovation. Rabbis grasped this promise, each in his own way, and offered a personalized path to Jewish fulfillment to the engaged minority seeking religious roots.

## NOTES

1. Letter to the editor of the *Los Angeles Times* in 1970, quoted in Stephen J. Sass, "Southern California," *Present Tense*, 9 (Spring 1982): 33.

2. I am grateful for insights regarding characteristics of L.A. rabbis to Wolfe Kelman, who oversaw the placement of Conservative rabbis in the postwar era. Wolfe Kelman, interview with author, 5 March 1988. Bruce Phillips, lecture at a conference on Jews in Los Angeles, UCLA, 6 May 1990.

3. Marc Lee Raphael, *Profiles in American Judaism: The Reform Conservative, Orthodox, and Reconstructionist Traditions in Historical Perspective* (San Francisco: Harper & Row, 1984).

4. Quoted in "The Jews of Los Angeles: Pursuing the American Dream," *Los Angeles Times*, 29 January 1978.

5. "Yarmulke comes from Poland to Brooklyn to Los Angeles. It's Brooklynese and Polish. Since the founding of the State of Israel it's become kind of a badge to some Jews." Edgar F. Magnin, "Leader and Personality," an oral history conducted 1972–1974 by Malca Chall, 10, Regional Oral History Office, The Bancroft Library, University of California, Berkeley, 1975. Courtesy of The Bancroft Library.

6. Irving Lehrman quoted in Paul S. George, "An Enduring Covenant" in *Event of the Decade*

(1988), 19; Albert Lewis to Maurice Eisendrath, 30 December 1952, General Correspondence, 1/7, Box 212, Albert M. Lewis MSS, AJA.

7. *Temple Beth Sholom Bulletin*, 10 December 1948; Report of Leon Ell, Membership Committee, 24 April 1945; Minutes of Meeting of Board of Directors of Temple Emanu-El, 21 August 1958. Lehrman and Kronish studied at Wise's Jewish Institute of Religion; Narot learned from Wise during the years Narot served as rabbi in Atlantic City. See Joseph R. Narot, "First Teachers in Last Resorts," *CCAR Journal*, Winter 1978: 46–47.

8. He also frequently attended the Brooklyn Jewish Center, one of the foremost and most innovative Conservative synagogue centers in the borough, to hear the preaching of its rabbi, Dr. Israel Levinthal. Irving Lehrman, "The Sermon," in *In the Name of God* (New York, 1979), 216.

9. *Center Review*, 23 September 1943: 4; Helen Goldman, telephone conversation, 10 January 1993; Michael A. Meyer, "A Centennial History," *Hebrew Union College-Jewish Institute of Religion at One-Hundred Years*, ed. Samuel E. Karff (Hebrew Union College Press, 1976), 150, 159.

10. George, "An Enduring Covenant," 9–78. Unless otherwise noted, material is drawn from this commissioned history.

11. This was the first sabbath observed in the new synagogue building. *Center Review*, 21 October 1948: 3.

12. Elaine Glickman, interview with author, 19 March 1991.

13. Lehrman found the architect Charles Greco, who had designed a large synagogue in Cleveland. George, "An Enduring Covenant," 19; Polly Redford, *Billion Dollar Sandbar* (New York: E. P. Dutton, 1970), 274.

14. The board of directors unanimously voted to give Lehrman life tenure in January 1951, less than ten years after his arrival. *Center Review*, 19 January 1951: 5.

15. Glickman, interview; quote from George, "An Enduring Covenant," 48.

16. See, for example, *Center Review*, 15 October 1947 and 5 October 1951. By 1952 the *Review* reported many more girls enrolling in the more intensive Hebrew department of the school, rather than just in the once-a-week Sunday school; 19 September 1952. See also *Jewish Center Review*, 8 May 1953 and 17 September 1954.

17. In 1961–62, after more than a decade of exhortation, there were still over twice as many boys (194) as girls (74) enrolled in the afternoon Hebrew school. Girls, on the other hand, dominated the Sunday school, 155 to 91. Louis Schwartzman, *Seventeenth Annual Report*, Bureau of Jewish Education, Miami, Florida (July 1961–1962), n.p., Rosen files.

18. *Jewish Center Review*, 17 October 1952.

19. *Jewish Center Review*, 4 December 1953; Glickman, interview.

20. Lehrman had convinced the congregation to eliminate *shnoddering*, which was considered undignified, but those who were given an *aliyah* were expected to announce their contribution from the *bimah*. The men leading the congregation did not want to forgo this traditional source of synagogue income. See "President's Report" in the *Review*, 7 April 1948, and Minutes of the Executive Committee Meeting, 14 November 1954.

21. *Jewish Center Review*, 11 January 1952; Irving Lehrman, "The 'Power of Prayer,'" in *In The Name of God*, 197. Graham did invite Lehrman to speak at the 1961 Crusade held in the Miami Beach Convention Center. George, "An Enduring Covenant," 61.

22. See *Temple Emanu-El Review*, 17 September 1954, 10 December 1954, 17 December 1954, 24 March 1955, 31 March 1955, 5 September 1956.

23. Glickman, interview.

24. I appreciate Richard Cohen's insights on the multiple meanings of ritual objects. For an early perceptive discussion see Abraham G. Duker, "Emerging Culture Patterns in American Jewish Life," *Publications of the American Jewish Historical Society* 39:4 (June 1950), 351–88.

25. *Jewish Center Review*, 7 December 1951, 3 December 1954.

26. *Temple Emanu-El Review*, 19 October 1956, 4 January 1957, 8 March 1957, 22 March 1957, 9 September 1957.

27. Letter from Morris Berick to officers and members of Temple Beth Sholom, 27 March 1946, Minutes of Temple Beth Sholom; History in Minutes of the Beth Sholom Center, 6 April 1942; Temple Beth Sholom, *Twentieth Anniversary, 1942–1962*, Jubilee Book and Calendar (1962–63), n.p.; Minutes of the First General Meeting of the 1944–45 Season, 8 November 1944, in Minutes of Temple Beth Sholom.

28. See instructions in temple etiquette, *Beth Sholom Bulletin*, 11 February 1949; also Maxine Kronish Snyder, "My Father and My Family: Growing Up Jewish," in *Towards the Twenty-First Century: Judaism and the Jewish People in Israel and America*, ed. Ronald Kronish (Hoboken, N.J.: KTAV, 1988), 332; report of Leon Ell, Membership Committee, Minutes of Meeting of Board of Directors of Beth Sholem Center, 24 April 1945.

29. Constitution, n.d., in back of Minutes of Temple Beth Sholom. The Miami Beach Jewish Center also changed its name to Temple Emanu-El, but not until 1954.

30. He didn't actually purchase them, and when he returned, he thought "out loud" about using another prayer book. However, the religious committee did order the prayer books, although the temple declined for several years to join the UAHC because of the vehement opposition of one member who thought that such membership would label it Reform. See letter from Morris Berick, 27 March 1946. On the UAHC issue see Minutes of Meeting of Board of Directors of Temple Beth Sholom, 27 December 1945, 22 January 1948, 29 January 1948, 9 March 1950.

31. See Minutes of Special Meeting of Board of Directors of Temple Beth Sholom, 29 January 1949; also, Minutes of Regular Meeting of Board of Directors of Temple Beth Sholom, 24 May 1945, 6 August 1945, 27 December 1945, 21 March 1946, 22 January 1948, 9 March 1950.

32. *Temple Beth Sholom Bulletin*, 10 December 1948. Kronish actually anticipated an American Union of Liberal Synagogues that would absorb Conservative, Reform, and unaffiliated into a renascent *klal yisroel*.

33. In this case Kronish argued that the congregation should follow the pattern of the State of Israel. There are interesting theological implications of such an argument, but Kronish did not discuss them. Minutes of Regular Meeting of Board of Directors of Temple Beth Sholom, 17 March 1949. See also an earlier argument in *Temple Beth Sholom Bulletin*, 15 September 1947. "Since Palestine is now THE CENTER of our spiritual and cultural life, and can safely be said to determine the norm of Jewish existence, as a gesture of Jewish solidarity, we deem it important to follow the Palestinian custom."

34. Ronald Kronish, interview with author, 2 March 1992; Minutes of Meeting of Board of Directors of Temple Beth Sholom, 1 October 1945.

35. *Temple Beth Sholom Bulletin*, 14 March 1947, 23 May 1947, 14 January 1949, 17 September 1948, 1 September 1947.

36. Minutes of General Membership Meeting, 27 March 1946, Minutes of Temple Beth Sholom; *Temple Beth Sholom Bulletin*, 17 September 1948; Minutes of the Regular Meeting of the Board of Directors of Temple Beth Sholom, 20 October 1949.

37. *Temple Beth Sholom Bulletin*, 5 December 1947, 14 January 1949, 4 April 1947.

38. Maxine Kronish Snyder, "My Father and My Family," 329.

39. Included in *Temple Beth Sholom Bulletin*, 17 October 1947.

40. *Temple Beth Sholom Bulletin*, 17 September 1948; *Jewish Center Review*, 16 November 1951.

41. Biographical details and quotes from Joseph R. Narot, "The Meaning of My Life," in *High Holy Day Sermons Preached at Temple Israel of Greater Miami, 1969/5730*, Joseph R. Narot and Steven B. Jacobs (n.d.), 1–5.

42. Narot's concern to expand the membership appears regularly in Minutes of the Meeting of the Board of Trustees of Temple Israel of Miami, 6 November 1951, 4 December 1951, 6 May 1952, 11 November 1952, 10 August 1953, 12 October 1954. See also Joseph R. Narot, "The Earnestness of Being Important," in *Letters to My Congregation* (1959–60), 3.

43. The sisterhood did open a gift shop. Minutes of the Meeting of the Board of Trustees of Temple Israel of Miami, 4 December 1951.

44. For example, in the matter of synagogue ritual, Temple Israel only had mourners stand to say kaddish, the traditional practice. Narot convinced the board to have the entire congregation stand for the kaddish, an innovation of classical Reform. Minutes of the Meeting of the Board of Trustees of Temple Israel, 9 September 1952, for reaffirmation of earlier policy; Minutes of the Regular Meeting of the Board of Trustees of Temple Israel of Greater Miami, 9 February 1959, for the change.

45. Joseph R. Narot, "What I Believe About Bar Mitzvo," in *An Introduction to a Faith* (Miami, n.d.), n.p., and "Bar Mitzvo Again—Once Over Heavily," in *Letters to My Congregation* V (Miami, 1962), 2; Minutes of the Regular Meeting of the Board of Trustees of Temple Israel of Miami, 12 September 1955, 14 February 1955; Joseph R. Narot, *Letters to My Congregation* (Miami, n.d. [1960?]), *An Introduction to a Faith* (Miami, n.d. [1961?]), *A Primer for Temple Life* (Miami, n.d.), "Do I Protest Too Much?" in *Letters to My Congregation* (Miami, n.d.), 15.

46. See Joseph R. Narot, "Horse Races, Barber Shops, and Reform Judaism," in which he defends his decision to go to the races and get his hair cut on the sabbath. *Letters to My Congregation* V, 34.

47. Morris Janowitz, *Judaism of the Next Generation* (Miami: Rostrum Books, 1969), 37, Table 3.2.

48. Magnin, Oral History, 27.

49. Magnin, Oral History, 85, 89; Neal Gabler, *An Empire of Their Own* (New York: Crown, 1988), chapter 8.

50. Magnin, Oral History, 126–27, 186 (emphasis in the original), 56, 53.

51. Magnin, Oral History, 259. Wilshire Boulevard Temple introduced a High School department and a Hebrew department, the former requiring additional study after confirmation and the latter requiring more intensive study for two and a half more hours per week. In 1960 the Academy School for gifted children was started, an even more intensive program in religious education. The academy enrolled thirty children in its first year and required attendance three days each week. See Wilshire Boulevard Temple, President's Annual Report (1961), 3, Wilshire Boulevard Temple, Box 841, George Piness MSS, AJA.

52. The account is drawn from Alfred Wolf and Dan Wolf, "Wilshire Boulevard Temple Camps, 1949–1974," in *Wilshire Boulevard Temple Camps*, ed. Alfred Wolf (Los Angeles: Wilshire Boulevard Temple, 1975), 5–17, quote on 5, Los Angeles, Wilshire Boulevard Temple Camps, Nearprint Box—Geography, AJA. *Bulletin of the Valley Jewish Community Center*, 6 December 1946.

53. Wolf and Wolf, "Wilshire Boulevard Temple Camps," 6.

54. Wolf and Wolf, "Wilshire Boulevard Temple Camps," 8.

55. Tom Redler quoted in Wolf and Wolf, "Wilshire Boulevard Temple Camps," 17.

56. One needed to be a temple member to send one's child to camp. Occasionally this requirement generated resentment. Ellie Hudson, interview with author, 10 July 1989.

57. See Jenna Weissman Joselit, ed., *A Worthy Use of Summer: American Jewish Summer Camping, 1900–1950* (Philadelphia: National Museum of American Jewish History, 1993).

58. Jacob Sonderling followed a similar path. He founded the Society for Jewish Culture that offered dramatic lectures in worship and "conservative reform." Vorspan and Gartner, *Jews of Los Angeles*, 235.

59. *Bulletin of the Valley Jewish Community Center*, 3 January 1947, 21 March 1947, 28 March 1947, 18 April 1947.

60. The account, unless otherwise noted, is drawn from Cynthia and Robert Rawitch, *The First Fifty Years, Adat Ari El* (North Hollywood, 1988), quote on 55.

61. *Bulletin of the Valley Jewish Community Center*, 3 October 1947, 10 October 1947, 5 December 1947.

62. Quoted in Rawitch and Rawitch, *Adat Ari El*, 9.

63. Biography of Irma Lee Ettinger by Elaine Brown, *Adat Ari-El Yearbook* (1981), n.p.; *Bulletin of the Valley Jewish Community Center*, 24 October 1947. For other explanations of Conservatism, see 31 October 1947, 7 November 1947, 21 November 1947.

64. Wise quoted in Rawitch and Rawitch, *Adat Ari El*, 56; *Bulletin of the Valley Jewish Community Center*, 24 October 1947, 1 December 1948.

65. *Bulletin of the Valley Jewish Community Center*, 1 November 1951, 1 January 1949, 15 September 1951.

66. *Bulletin of the Valley Jewish Community Center*, 1 January 1949, 1 June 1950.

67. Quoted in Rawitch and Rawitch, *Adat Ari El*, 70–71.

68. Fred Massarik, "The Jewish Population of Los Angeles: A Panorama of Change," *Reconstructionist* 18:15 (28 Nov. 1952): 14.

# MARTIN AND MALCOLM

*James H. Cone*

Since their deaths in the 1960s, Martin Luther King, Jr. and Malcolm X have symbolized for many people two distinct and conflicting black perspectives on America. King, the nonviolent advocate of equal rights, has been honored as an American hero with his own national holiday. Malcolm, the symbol of defiant self-defense, has become the patron saint of angry young people. Rather than emphasize the conflict between these two men, James Cone argues instead that Martin and Malcolm represent two broad streams of thought within a common African American struggle against racism and for the freedom of black people. Aspects of both perspectives have appeared in the writings of black intellectuals throughout African American history. When it has appeared that blacks would soon be included in American society on an equal basis with whites, Martin's integrationist views have been foreshadowed. In contrast, harbingers of Malcolm's nationalist thinking can be heard whenever despair over the possibility of genuine equality has been warranted. "To understand Martin Luther King's and Malcolm X's perspectives on America and their relation to each other," Cone believes, "it is important to see them in the light of these two different but interdependent streams of black thought."

Reprinted by permission from James H. Cone, "America: A Dream or a Nightmare?" in his *Martin & Malcolm & America: A Dream or a Nightmare* (New York: Orbis, 1991), 1–18.

*I have a dream that one day this nation will rise up and live out the true meaning of its creed, "We hold these truths to be self-evident, that all men are created equal." I have a dream that one day . . . sons of former slaves and the sons of former slave owners will be able to sit down together at the table of brotherhood. . . . This is our hope. . . . With this faith we will be able to work together, to pray together, to struggle together, to go to jail together, to stand up for freedom together, knowing that we will be free one day. . . . This will be the day when all God's children will be able to sing with new meaning, "My country 'tis of thee, sweet land of liberty, of thee I sing."*

—Martin Luther King, Jr.

March on Washington

Washington, D.C.

August 28, 1963

*No, I'm not an American. I'm one of the 22 million black people who are the victims of Americanism. One of the . . . victims of democracy, nothing but disguised hypocrisy. So, I'm not standing here speaking to you as an American, or a patriot, or a flag-saluter, or a flag-waver, no, not I! I'm speaking as a victim of this American system. And I see America through the eyes of the victim. I don't see any American dream; I see an American nightmare!*

—Malcolm X

Cory Methodist Church

Cleveland, Ohio

April 3, 1964

# 19

# MARTIN AND MALCOLM

## Integrationism and Nationalism in African American Religious History

*James H. Cone*

**THE MEETING OF MALCOLM AND MARTIN**

"Well Malcolm, good to see you," Martin said. "Good to see you," Malcolm replied.

After nearly eight years of verbal sparring through the media, two great African American leaders, Martin Luther King, Jr., and Malcolm X, finally met for the first and only time in Washington, D.C., on March 26, 1964. Both were attending the U.S. Senate's debate of the Civil Rights Bill. Initiated by Malcolm following Martin's press conference, the meeting was coincidental and brief. There was no time for substantive discussions between the two. They were photographed greeting each other warmly, smiling and shaking hands. The slim, six-foot three-inch Malcolm towered over the stocky, five-foot eight-inch Martin. They walked together a few paces through the corridor, whispering to each other, as their followers and the media looked on with great interest. As they departed, Malcolm teasingly said, "Now you're going to get investigated."

Although the media portrayed them as adversaries, Martin and Malcolm were actually fond of each other. There was no animosity between them. They saw each other as fellow justice-fighters, struggling against the same evil—racism—and for the same goal—freedom for African Americans.

"I'm throwing myself into the heart of the civil rights struggle and will be in it from now on," Malcolm told James Booker of the *Amsterdam News* the day before he departed for the nation's capital. Recently expelled from the Black Muslim movement, he was trying to develop a new image of himself so he could join the mainstream of the civil rights movement. In Washington, Malcolm observed the debate from the Senate gallery and held impromptu press conferences during much of the day. He was pleased that the Senate voted against sending the bill to the Judiciary Committee and then voted to start debate on the bill in the full Senate. He told the media that the Senate should pass the House-passed bill "exactly as it is, with no changes." But he predicted glumly, "If passed, it will never be enforced. . . . You can't legislate good will—that comes through education."[1]

In another section of the Senate gallery, Martin King was observing the same debate. Like Malcolm, he also held several press conferences and cheered the Senate's decision to take up the bill. But he expressed concern about the southern filibuster which threatened to weaken it. Martin told the media that a month of "legitimate debate" was acceptable. But he vowed that "if the Senate is still talking about the bill after the first week of May," he would initiate a creative direct-action program in Washington and throughout the country "to dramatize the abuse of the legislative process." He did not rule out civil disobedience. "At first we would seek to persuade with our words and then with our deeds." Martin also promised that he would fight for more civil rights legislation the following year. "We cannot stop till Negroes have absolute and complete freedom."[2]

The meeting of Martin and Malcolm has profound, symbolic meaning for the black freedom movement. It was more than a meeting of two prominent leaders in the African American community. It was a meeting of two great resistance traditions in African American history, integrationism and nationalism. Together Martin, a Christian integrationist, and Malcolm, a Muslim nationalist, would have been a powerful force against racial injustice. When they were separated, their enemies were successful in pitting them against each other and thereby diluting the effectiveness of the black freedom movement. Both Martin and Malcolm were acutely aware of the dangers of disunity among African Americans. They frequently spoke out against it and urged African Americans to forget their differences and to unite in a common struggle for justice and freedom. Why then did Martin and Malcolm not set an example by joining their forces together into a black united front against racism? The answer to this question is found partly in the interrelationship of integrationism and nationalism in African American history. These two resistance traditions also provide the historical context for a deeper understanding of Martin's dream and Malcolm's nightmare.

## INTEGRATIONISM AND NATIONALISM IN AFRICAN AMERICAN INTELLECTUAL HISTORY

No one stated the dilemma that slavery and segregation created for Africans in the United States as sharply and poignantly as W. E. B. Du Bois. In his classic statement of the problem, he spoke of it as a "peculiar sensation," a "double-consciousness," "two souls, two thoughts, two unreconciled strivings; two warring ideals in one dark body, whose dogged strength alone keeps it from being torn asunder." The "twoness" that Du Bois was describing stemmed from being an African *in* America. "Here, then, is the dilemma," he wrote in "The Conservation of Races." "What, after all, am I? Am I an American or am I a Negro? Can I be both?"[3]

Integrationist thinkers may be defined as those who answer "Yes" to the question, "Can I be both?" They believe it is possible to achieve justice in the United States and to create wholesome relations with the white community. This optimism has been based upon the "American creed," the tradition of freedom and democracy as articulated in the Declaration of Independence and the Constitution, and is supported, they believe, by the Jewish and Christian Scriptures. The integrationist line of thought goes something like this: If whites really believe their political and religious documents, then they know that black people should not be enslaved and segregated but rather integrated into the mainstream of the society. After all, blacks are Americans, having arrived even before the Pilgrims. They have worked the land, obeyed the laws, paid their taxes, and defended America in every war. They built the nation as much as white people did. Therefore, the integrationists argue, it is the task of African American leaders to prick the conscience of whites, showing the contradictions between their professed values and their actual treatment of blacks.

Then whites will be embarrassed by their hypocrisy and will grant blacks the same freedom that they themselves enjoy.

On the other hand, nationalist thinkers have rejected the American side of their identity and affirmed the African side, saying "No, we can't be both." They have contended that 244 years of slavery, followed by legal segregation, social degradation, political disfranchisement, and economic exploitation means that blacks will never be recognized as human beings in white society. America isn't for blacks; blacks can't be for America. The nationalists argue that blacks don't belong with whites, that whites are killing blacks, generation after generation. Blacks should, therefore, separate from America, either by returning to Africa or by going to some other place where they can create sociopolitical structures that are derived from their own history and culture.

Integrationism and nationalism represent the two broad streams of black thought in response to the problem of slavery and segregation in America. Of course, no black thinker has been a pure integrationist or a pure nationalist, but rather all black intellectuals have represented aspects of each, with emphasis moving in one direction or the other, usually at different periods of their lives. What emphasis any black thinker made was usually determined by his or her perspective on America, that is, whether he or she believed that blacks would soon be included in the mainstream of American life on a par with whites. When blacks have been optimistic about America—believing that they could achieve full equality through moral suasion and legal argument— they have been integrationists and have minimized their nationalist tendencies. On the other hand, despair about America—believing that genuine equality is impossible because whites have no moral conscience or any intention to apply the laws fairly—has always been the seedbed of nationalism. To understand Martin King's and Malcolm X's perspectives on America and their relation to each other, it is important to see them in the light of these two different but interdependent streams of black thought.

## INTEGRATIONISM BEFORE MARTIN KING

Integrationists have had many able advocates since the founding of the republic. Among them were the great abolitionist Frederick Douglass, many prominent black preachers, and representatives of the National Association for the Advancement of Colored People (NAACP), the National Urban League, and the Congress of Racial Equality (CORE).

Frederick Douglass was the outstanding advocate of integrationism during the nineteenth century. Born a slave, Douglass escaped from slavery and became an international figure with his powerful speeches and writings in defense of the full citizenship rights of blacks. For him the existence of slavery was a staggering contradiction of the principles of the Constitution and the concept of humanity.

Unlike the white abolitionist William Lloyd Garrison, who denied his allegiance to a Constitution ratified by slaveholders, Douglass embraced it as an "anti-slavery document" and then proceeded to quote it as supporting evidence for the abolition of slavery. The Constitution reads, " 'We the people'; not we the white people," Douglass proclaimed; "and if Negroes are people, they are included in the benefits for which the Constitution of America was ordained and established."[4]

No one was as persuasive as Frederick Douglass in pointing out to whites the hypocrisy of extolling the "principles of political freedom and of natural justice" articulated in the Declaration of Independence while holding blacks as slaves. His well-known Independence

Day speech in Rochester, New York, on the topic "What to the Slave Is the Fourth of July?" was calculated to cut deeply into the conscience of whites who thought of themselves as civilized. "To [the slave], your celebration is a sham," he proclaimed to a stunned white audience. "Your denunciation of tyrants, brass-fronted impudence; your shouts of liberty and equality, hollow mockery. . . . There is not a nation on the earth guilty of practices more shocking and bloody than are the people of the United States."[5]

Douglass's scathing words did not mean that he had given up on America and would accordingly seek separation from the land of his birth. He was offered an opportunity to stay in England where he was given many honors, but he rejected the idea. Douglass believed that blacks could find justice in the United States and safely intertwine their future with that of the white majority. He was severely critical of blacks and whites who proposed the colonization of blacks in Africa or some other place. "It's all nonsense to talk about the removal of eight million of the American people from their homes in America to Africa," he said. "The destiny of the colored Americans . . . is the destiny of America. We shall never leave you. . . . We are here. . . . To imagine that we should ever be eradicated is absurd and ridiculous. We can be modified, changed, assimilated, but never extinguished. . . . This is our country; and the question for the philosophers and statesmen of the land ought to be, What principle should dictate the policy of the nation toward us?"[6]

Although Douglass experienced many disappointments in his fight for justice, he never lost his love for America or his belief that blacks would soon achieve full freedom in the land of their birth. "I expect to see the colored people of this country enjoying the same freedom [as whites]," he said in 1865, "voting at the same ballot-box . . . going to the same schools, attending the same churches, traveling the same street cars, in the same railroad cars . . . proud of the same country, fighting the same foe, and enjoying the same peace, and all its advantages."[7]

Optimism about blacks achieving full citizenship rights in America has always been the hallmark of integrationism. This optimism has been based not only on the political ideals of America but also upon its claim to be founded on Christian principles. Blacks have believed that the Christian faith requires that whites treat them as equals before God. No group articulated this point with more religious conviction and fervor than black preachers.

According to black preachers, Christianity is a gospel of justice and love. Believers, therefore, must treat all people justly and lovingly—that is, as brothers and sisters. Why? Because God, the creator of all, is no respecter of persons. Out of one blood God has created all people. On the cross Jesus Christ died for all—whites and blacks alike. Our oneness in creation and redemption means that no Christian can condone slavery or segregation in the churches or the society. The integration of whites and blacks into one community, therefore, is the only option open for Christians.

As early as 1787, Richard Allen (an ex-slave and a Methodist minister) led a group of blacks out of St. George Methodist Church in Philadelphia, and in 1816 he founded the African Methodist Episcopal (AME) Church. He did this because he and his followers refused to accept segregation in the "Lord's house." A few years later, James Varick and other blacks in New York took similar action and organized the African Methodist Episcopal Zion (AMEZ) Church. Black Baptists also formed separate congregations.

Independent black churches were not separatist in the strict sense. They were not separating themselves from whites because they held a different doctrinal view of Christianity. Without exception, blacks used the same articles of faith and polity for their churches as the white denominations from which they separated. Separation, for blacks, meant that they were rejecting the *ethical* behavior of whites—they were rejecting racism that was based on the assumption that God created blacks inferior to whites. Blacks also wanted to prove that they had the capability to organize and to operate a denomination just like whites. In short, black Christians were bearing witness to their humanity, which they believed God created equal to that of whites. The motto of the AME Church reflected that conviction: "God our Father, Christ our Redeemer, Man our Brother." "When these sentiments are universal in theory and practice," the AME bishops said in 1896, "then the mission of the distinctive colored organization will cease."[8]

Not all black Christians chose the strategy of separation. Instead, some decided to stay in white denominations and use them as platforms from which to prick the conscience of whites regarding the demands of the gospel and to encourage blacks to strike a blow for freedom. "Liberty is a spirit sent out from God," proclaimed Henry Highland Garnet, a Presbyterian minister, "and like its great Author, is no respecter of persons."[9]

Following the Civil War, the great majority of black Christians joined black-led churches among the Methodists and Baptists. The independence of these churches enabled their pastors to become prominent leaders in the black struggle for integration in society. Prominent Baptists included Adam Clayton Powell, Sr., and Jr., of the Abyssinian Baptist Church (New York), Martin Luther King, Sr., of Ebenezer Baptist Church (Atlanta), William Holmes Borders of the Wheat Street Baptist Church (Atlanta), and Vernon Johns of the Dexter Avenue Baptist Church (Montgomery). Reverdy C. Ransom, an AME minister, was a "pioneer black social gospeler." Other significant voices included Benjamin E. Mays, president of Morehouse College, and Howard Thurman, dean of Rankin Chapel and professor of theology at Howard University. All spoke out against segregation and racism in the white churches and the society, insisting that the integration of blacks and whites into one community was the demand of the Christian faith. In his book *Marching Blacks*, Adam Powell, Jr., accused white churches of turning Christianity into "churchianity," thereby distorting its essential message of "equality" and "brotherhood." "No one can say that Christianity has failed," he said. "It has never been tried."[10]

How can whites claim to be Christians and still hold blacks as slaves or segregate them in their churches and society? That has been the great paradox for black Christians. Since whites attended their churches regularly, with an air of reverence for God, and studied the Bible conscientiously, blacks expected them to see the truth of the gospel and thereby accept them into their churches and society as brothers and sisters. Many black Christians believed that it was only a matter of a little time before Jesus would reveal the gospel truth to whites, and slavery and segregation would come tumbling down like the walls of Jericho. That was the basis of the optimism among black Christians.

Too much confidence in what God is going to do often creates an otherworldly perspective which encourages passivity in the face of injustice and suffering. That happened to the great majority of blacks from the time of the Civil War to the coming of Martin Luther King, Jr. The organized fight for justice was transferred from the churches to secular groups, commonly known as civil rights organizations, especially the NAACP, the National Urban League, and CORE. Each came into existence for the sole purpose of achieving full citizenship rights for African Americans in every aspect of American society. They often have used different tactics and have worked in different areas, but the goal has been the same—the integration of blacks into the mainstream of American society so that color will no longer be a determining factor for success or failure in any human endeavor.

Founded by prominent whites and blacks in 1909, the NAACP was the first and has been the most influential civil rights organization. Branded as radical before the 1960s, it has been a strong advocate of integration, using the courts as the primary arena in which to protest segregation. The NAACP is best known for its successful argument before the United States Supreme Court against the doctrine of "separate but equal" schools for blacks and whites, claiming that such schools are inherently unequal and therefore unconstitutional. The May 17, 1954, school desegregation decision has often been called the beginning of the black freedom movement of the 1950s and 1960s.

One year after the founding of the NAACP, the National Urban League was organized. Less aggressive than the NAACP, the Urban League was founded "for the specific purpose of easing the transition of the Southern rural Negro into an urban way of life. It stated clearly that its role was to help these people, who were essentially rural agrarian serf-peasants, adjust to Northern city life." Using the techniques of persuasion and conciliation, the Urban League appealed to the "enlightened self-interest" of white business leaders "to ease the movement of Negroes into middle class status."[11]

A generation later, in 1942, the Congress of Racial Equality was founded in Chicago. The smallest and most radical of the three groups, CORE is best known for introducing the method of nonviolent direct action, staging sit-ins in restaurants and freedom rides on buses. This new dimension of the black struggle for equality had a profound effect on the civil rights movement in the 1950s and 1960s and particularly on Martin King.

Unlike the black churches, which had few white members and no white leaders, the civil rights organizations included whites in every level of their operations. For example, a white person has often served as the president of the NAACP, and each of the three organizations has had a significant number of whites serve on its board of directors. They claimed that the implementation of integration must apply to every aspect of the society, including their own organizations. The inclusion of whites also limited their independence and made them vulnerable to the nationalist critique that no black revolution can be successful as long as its leadership is dependent upon white support.


## BLACK NATIONALISM BEFORE MALCOLM X

The roots of black nationalism go back to the seventeenth-century slave conspiracies, when Africans, longing for their homeland, banded together in a common struggle against slavery, because they knew that they were not created for servitude. In the absence of historical data, it is not possible to describe the precise ideology behind the early slave revolts. What we know for sure is that the Africans deeply abhorred slavery and were willing to take great risks to gain their freedom.

This nationalist spirit was given high visibility in the slave revolts led by Gabriel Prosser, Denmark Vesey, and Nat Turner during the first third of the nineteenth century. But it was also found in the rise of mutual-aid societies, in the birth and growth of black-led churches and conventions, and in black-led emigration schemes. Unity as a people, pride in African heritage, the creation of autonomous institutions, and the search for a territory to build a nation were the central ingredients which shaped the early development of the nationalist consciousness.

There have been many articulate voices and important movements of black nationalism throughout African American history. Among them were David Walker and Martin Delany during the antebellum period and Henry McNeal Turner, Marcus Garvey, Noble Drew Ali, and Elijah Muhammad during the late nineteenth and early twentieth centuries.

The central claim of all black nationalists, past and present, is that black people are primarily Africans and not Americans. Unlike integrationists, nationalists do not define their significance and purpose as a people by appealing to the Declaration of Independence, the Constitution, Lincoln's Emancipation Proclamation, or even the white man's religion of Christianity. On the contrary, nationalists define their identity by their resistance to America and their determination to create a society based on their own African history and culture. The posture of rejecting America and accepting Africa is sometimes symbolized with such words as "African," "black," and "blackness." For example, Martin Delany, often called the father of black nationalism, boasted that there lived "none blacker" than himself. While Douglass, in typical integrationist style, said, "I thank God for making me a man simply," he reported that "Delany always thanks Him for making him a black man."[12]

The issue for nationalists was not only human slavery or oppression. It was also the oppression of *black* people by *white* people. Nothing aroused the fury of nationalists more than the racial factor in human exploitation. Their identity as black touched the very core of their being and affected their thoughts and feelings regarding everything, especially their relations with white people. Nationalists, unlike integrationists, could not separate their resentment of servitude from the racial identity of the people responsible for it. "White Americans [are] our *natural enemies*," wrote David Walker in his Appeal in 1829. "By treating us so cruel," we "see them acting more like devils than accountable men." According to Walker, "whites have always been an unjust, jealous, unmerciful, avaricious and bloodthirsty set of beings, always seeking after power and authority."[13]

Black nationalism was defined by a loss of hope in America. Its advocates did not believe that white people could ever imagine humanity in a way that would place black people on a par with them. "I am not in favor of caste, nor a separation of the brotherhood of mankind, and would as willingly live among white men as black, if I had an *equal possession and enjoyment* of privileges," Delany wrote in 1852 to the white abolitionist William Lloyd Garrison; he went on: "but [I] shall never be reconciled to live among them, subservient to their will—existing by mere *sufferance*, as we, the colored people, do, in this country. . . . I have no hopes in this country—no confidence in the American people."[14]

This difference in emotional orientation between nationalists and integrationists led to disagreement in their definition of freedom and their strategies for achieving it. For nationalists, freedom was not black people pleading for integration into white society; rather it was separation from white people so that blacks could govern themselves. For many nationalists, separation meant emigration from the United States to some place in Africa or Latin America. "Every people should be the originators of their own designs, the projectors of their own schemes, and creators of the events that lead to their destiny—the consummation of their own desires," Delany wrote in his best-known work, *The Condition, Elevation, Emigration, and Destiny of the Colored People of the United States* (1852). "No people can be free who themselves do not constitute an essential part of the *ruling element* of the country in which they live," said Delany. "The liberty of no man is secure, who controls not his political destiny. . . . To suppose otherwise, is that delusion which at once induces its victim, through a period of long suffering, patiently to submit to every species of wrong;

trusting against probability, and hoping against all reasonable grounds of expectation, for the granting of privileges and enjoyment of rights, that will never be attained."[15]

The ebb and flow of black nationalism, during the nineteenth century and thereafter, was influenced by the decline and rise of black expectations of equality in the United States. When blacks felt that the achievement of equality was impossible, the nationalist sentiment among them always increased. Such was the case during the 1840s and 1850s, largely due to the Fugitive Slave Act (1850) and the Dred Scott Decision (1857).

During the Civil War and the Reconstruction that followed it, black hopes soared and even Delany stopped talking about the emigration of blacks and began to participate in the political process in South Carolina, running for the office of lieutenant-governor.

Black expectations of achieving full citizenship rights, however, were short-lived. The infamous Hayes Compromise of 1877 led to the withdrawal of federal troops from the South, thereby allowing former white slaveholders to deal with their former slaves in any manner they chose. The destructive consequences for blacks were severe politically, economically, and psychologically. Accommodationism emerged as the dominant black philosophy, and Booker T. Washington became its most prominent advocate. Washington replaced Frederick Douglass as the chief spokesperson for blacks, and ministers were his most ardent supporters.

During the period of the "nadir" and the "long dark night" of black people's struggle for justice in America, Henry McNeal Turner, a bishop in the AME Church, and Marcus Garvey of the Universal Negro Improvement Association (UNIA) articulated nationalist perspectives that were more directly linked with the subsequent philosophy of Malcolm X. Like Malcolm's, their perspectives on America were derived from the bottom of the black experience. They spoke a language that was full of racial pride and denunciation of white America. It was intended to elevate the cultural and psychological well-being of downtrodden blacks burdened with low self-esteem in a society dominated by the violence of white hate groups and the sophisticated racism of the Social Darwinists.

A native of South Carolina, Turner grew up on the cotton fields with slaves and learned to read by his own efforts. He was a proud and fearless man, and his nationalism was deepened as he observed the continued exploitation of blacks by whites, North and South, during and following Reconstruction. When the Supreme Court ruled in 1883 that the Civil Rights Act of 1875 was unconstitutional, Turner felt that that "barbarous decision" dissolved the allegiance of black people to the United States. "If the decision is correct," he wrote, "the United States Constitution is a dirty rag, a cheat, a libel, and ought to be spit upon by every negro in the land."[16]

The betrayal of Reconstruction, the "enactment of cruel and revolting laws," lynching and other atrocities, reenslavement through peonage, and political disfranchisement encouraged Turner to conclude that blacks would never achieve equality in the United States. He became an ardent advocate of emigration to Africa. "There is no more doubt in my mind," Turner said, "that we have ultimately to return to Africa than there is of the existence of God."[17]

Although Turner was elected a bishop in the AME Church, he was not the typical holder of that office. The more whites demeaned blackness as a mark of inferiority, the more Turner glorified it. At a time when black and white Christians identified God with European images and the AME Church leaders were debating whether to replace the word "African" in their name with "American," Turner shocked everyone with his declaration that "God is a Negro."[18]

Although Turner addressed his message to the sociopolitical problems of the black masses in the rural South, he did not create an organization to implement his African dream. That distinction fell to Marcus Garvey.

On March 23, 1916, one year after Turner's death, Marcus Garvey came to the United States from his native Jamaica. While Turner's base was the rural South, Garvey worked in the urban North, mainly in Harlem. While the geography was different, the people were essentially the same, being mostly immigrants from the South in search of the American dream of economic security, social advancement, and political justice. Instead they entered a nightmare of racism and poverty which they thought they had left behind in the South.

Garvey understood the pain of color discrimination because he experienced it personally and observed it in the lives of other blacks in Jamaica and also during his travels in Central America, Europe, and the United States. It seemed that everywhere he traveled blacks were being dominated by others. "Where is the black man's Government?" he asked. "Where is his King and his kingdom? Where is his President, his country, and his ambassador, his army, his navy, his men of big affairs?" Unable to find them, Garvey, with the self-assurance of a proud black man, then declared: "I will help to make them."[19]

Garvey knew that without racial pride no people could make leaders and build a nation that would command the respect of the world. This was particularly true of blacks who had been enslaved and segregated for three hundred years. In a world where blackness was a badge of degradation and shame, Garvey transformed it into a symbol of honor and distinction. "To be a Negro is no disgrace, but an honor, and we of the Universal Negro Improvement Association do not want to become white."[20] He made blacks feel that they were somebody and that they could do great things as a people. "Up, you mighty race," Garvey proclaimed, "you can accomplish what you will," and black people believed him.

As whites ruled Europe and America, Garvey was certain blacks should and would rule Africa. To implement his African dream, he organized the UNIA, first in Kingston, Jamaica, and later in New York. "Africa for the Africans" was the heart of his message. In 1920 Garvey called the first International Convention of Negro Peoples of the World, and 25,000 delegates from twenty-five countries met in New York City. A redeemed Africa, governed by a united black race proud of its history, was the theme which dominated Garvey's speeches. "Wake up Ethiopia! Wake up Africa!" he proclaimed. "Let us work towards the one glorious end of a free, redeemed and mighty nation. Let Africa be a bright star among the constellation of nations. . . . A race without authority and power is a race without respect."[21]

No one exceeded Garvey in his criticisms of the philosophy of integration, as represented by the members of the NAACP and other middle-class black leaders and intellectuals. He believed that any black organization that depended upon white philanthropy was detrimental to the cause of Africa's redemption and the uplifting of the black race. "No man will do as much for you as you will do for yourself."[22] By depending on whites, blacks were saying that they could not do it alone, thereby creating a sense of inferiority in themselves.

According to Garvey, integration is a self-defeating philosophy that is promoted by pseudo-black intellectuals and leaders. He accused integrationists of wanting to be white and completely ignoring the socioeconomic well-being of poor blacks at the bottom. W. E. B. Du Bois, then the editor of the NAACP's *Crisis* magazine, was one of Garvey's favorite targets of criticism. Garvey told his followers that "we must never, even under the severest pressure, hate or dislike ourselves."[23] His criticism of the NAACP and Du Bois was very similar to Malcolm X's attack upon the same organization and its executive director, Roy Wilkins, during the 1960s. Black nationalists are defined by race confidence and solidarity, and they are often intemperate in their criticisms of black integrationists, for they believe integrationists compromise the self respect and dignity of the race by wanting to mingle and marry white people—the enemy.

In 1920, Garvey's UNIA claimed a membership of four million and a year later six million, with nine hundred branches. While most scholars insist that the numbers were inflated, no one denies that Garvey organized the largest and most successful mass movement of blacks in the history of the United States. Garvey did what all black nationalists after him have merely dreamed of doing, and that is why they continue to study his life and message for direction and inspiration.

Concerned about Garvey's popularity, the government, with the help of black integrationist leaders, convicted him of mail fraud. Upon his imprisonment and deportation, black nationalism entered a period of decline. But the problems of oppression and identity which gave rise to it did not disappear.

In addition to Marcus Garvey's UNIA, two movements were important in defining the nationalism that influenced Malcolm X: the Moorish Science Temple founded by Noble Drew Ali in Newark, New Jersey, and the Nation of Islam—the "Black Muslims"—founded in Detroit in 1930 by the mysterious Wallace D. Fard and later headed by his disciple, Elijah Poole, a former Baptist minister from Sandersville, Georgia. Elijah Poole, as Elijah Muhammad, achieved his authority in the Black Muslim religion because he convinced Black Muslim believers, including Malcolm, that Allah came to North America "in the person of Wallace D. Fard," taught him for three and a half years, and then chose him as his Messenger.

Both movements rejected Christianity and white people and affirmed the religion of Islam and an African-Asian identity. Both movements were primarily religious, having less political emphasis than Garvey's UNIA. Although the Moorish Science Temple is still in existence, it was important mainly as a forerunner of the Nation of Islam. The Nation of Islam received many members from the Moorish Science Temple following the assassination of Noble Drew Ali.

The Nation of Islam was the most important influence on the life and thought of Malcolm X. Its importance for Malcolm was similar to the role of the black church in the life of Martin King. While Garvey influenced Malcolm's political consciousness, Elijah Muhammad defined his religious commitment. Elijah Muhammad was the sole and absolute authority in defining the doctrine and practice of the Nation of Islam. While affirming solidarity with worldwide Islam, he proclaimed distinctive doctrines. The most important and controversial one was his contention that whites were by nature evil. They were snakes who were incapable of doing right, devils who would soon be destroyed by God's righteous judgment. White people, therefore, were identified as the sole cause of black oppression.

In Black Muslim theology the almighty black God is the source of all good and power. To explain the origin of the evil of black oppression, Muhammad rejected the Christian recourse to divine mystery or God's permissive will, instead setting forth his own distinctive explanation, which focused on the myth of Yacob. Out of the weak individuals of the black race, Yacob, a renegade black scientist, created the white race, thereby causing all of the evil which has flowed from their hands: "The human beast—the serpent, the dragon, the devil, and Satan—all mean one and the same: the people or race known as the white or Caucasian race, sometimes called the European race. Since by nature they were created liars and murderers, they are the enemies of truth and righteousness, and the enemies of those who seek the truth."[24] This myth was important for Malcolm's view that the whites are evil by nature. The myth and its doctrinal development came exclusively from Elijah Muhammad.

The logical extension of this doctrine is that since black people are by nature good and divine they must be separated from whites so they can avoid the latter's hour of total destruction. The solution to the problem of black oppression in America, therefore, is territorial separation, either by whites financing black people's return to Africa or by providing separate states in America.

Although the Nation of Islam and other nationalist movements (especially Garvey's) were the dominant influence in shaping Malcolm's life and thought, he was also indebted to the integrationist protest tradition. The same kind of cross current of nationalist and integrationist influences bore upon the career of Martin King, though he was indebted far less to the nationalist tradition. No sharp distinction can be drawn between the traditions, because representatives of both were fighting the same problems—the power of "white over black" and its psychological impact upon the self-esteem of its victims. Nationalists and integrationists were aware of the truth of each other's viewpoint, even though they did not always acknowledge it. Integrationists realized the danger of complete assimilation into American society. Like nationalists, they did not want to destroy the cultural and spiritual identity of blacks. That was perhaps the major reason why black churches and fraternal and sororal organizations remained separate from whites. Despite their repeated claim about 11:00 A.M. on Sunday morning being the most segregated hour of the week, black ministers in black denominations made no real efforts to integrate their churches. They knew that if they did, their power as blacks would be greatly curtailed and their own cultural and spiritual identity destroyed. The advocates of integration, therefore, focused their energies primarily on the political and economic life of America. They believed that justice was possible if whites treated blacks as equals under the law.

Likewise, black nationalists realized the danger of complete isolation from the political and economic life of America. That was perhaps the major reason for the frequent shifts in their philosophy. Black nationalism was not primarily a Western, "rational" philosophy, but rather a black philosophy in search of its African roots. It was a cry for self-esteem, for the right to be recognized and accepted as human beings. Its advocates knew that blacks could not survive politically or economically in complete separation from others, especially whites in the United States. Neither could any other people (including whites) survive in isolation from the rest of the world. Everyone was interdependent. The black masses, therefore, did not follow nationalists because of their call for separation from America. Rather it was because of the nationalists' ability to speak to their "gut level" experience, that is, to express what it *felt* like to be black in white America.

Integrationists and nationalists complemented each other. Both philosophies were needed if America was going to come to terms with the truth of the black experience. Either philosophy alone was a half-truth and thus a distortion of the black reality in America. Integrationists were *practical*. They advocated what they thought could be achieved at a given time. They knew that justice demanded more. But why demand it if you can't get it? Why demand it if the demand itself blocks the achievement of other desirable and achievable goals? In their struggle for justice, they were careful not to arouse the genocidal instincts inherent in racism. Thus they chose goals and methods which many whites accepted as reasonable and just. The strengths and weaknesses of the integrationist view are reflected in the life and ministry of Martin King.

Nationalists were *desperate*. They spoke for that segment of the African American community which was hurting the most. Thus, they often did not consider carefully the consequences of their words and actions. The suffering of the black poor was so great that practical or rational philosophies did not arouse their allegiance. They needed a philosophy that could speak to their existence as black people, living in a white society that did not recognize their humanity. They needed a philosophy that empowered them to "respect black" by being prepared to die for it. Overwhelmed by misery, the black poor cried out for relief, for a word or an act that would lift them to another realm of existence, where they would be treated as human beings. In place of an American dream, nationalists gave the black poor an African dream. The strengths and the weaknesses of this perspective were reflected in the life and ministry of Malcolm X.

Martin King and Malcolm X were shaped by what Vincent Harding has called the "Great Tradition of Black Protest,"[25] a tradition that comprised many variations of nationalism and integrationism. Their perspectives on America were influenced by both, even though they placed primary emphasis on only one of them. Both integrationism and nationalism readied Martin and Malcolm for leadership in the black freedom movement of the 1950s and 1960s—with Martin proclaiming an American dream from the steps of the Lincoln Memorial and Malcolm reminding him of an American nightmare in the streets of Harlem.

## NOTES

1. *Amsterdam News, 28 March 1964, 50;* Washington Post, 27 March 1964, 4, 6; *New York Times,* 27 March 1964, 10; "Integration: Long Day," *Newsweek,* 6 April 1964, 22; Peter Goldman, *The Death and Life of Malcolm X,* 2d ed. (Urbana: University of Illinois Press, 1979), 95; "The Time Has Come, 1964–66," pt. 2 of *Eyes on the Prize,* Channel 13, New York, 15 January 1990.

2. *WP,* 27 March 1964, 6; *NYT,* 27 March 1964, 10.

3. W. E. B. Du Bois, *The Souls of Black Folk* (1903; reprint, New York: Fawcett Premier Book, 1968), 16, 17; idem, "The Conservation of Races" (1897), in Julius Lester, ed., *The Seventh Son: The Thought and Writings of W. E. B. Du Bois* (New York: Vintage Book, 1971), vol. 1, 182.

4. Philip S. Foner, ed., *Frederick Douglass: Selections from His Writings* (New York: International Publishers, 1964), 57.

5. Ibid., 52–53.

6. Cited in Lerone Bennett, Jr., *Pioneers in Protest* (Chicago: Johnson Publishing Co., 1968), 208–9.

7. Foner, ed., *Frederick Douglass,* 44.

8. Cited in Peter J. Paris, *The Social Teaching of the Black Churches* (Philadelphia: Fortress Press, 1985), 25, n. 26.

9. Henry Highland Garnet, *An Address to the Slaves of the United States of America* (1843), reprinted with David Walker's *Appeal* (1829) in *Walker's Appeal & Garnet's Address to the Slaves of the United States of America* (New York: Arno Press/New York Times, 1969), 93.

10. Adam Clayton Powell, Jr., *Marching Blacks,* rev. ed. (New York: Dial Press, 1973), 194.

11. Kenneth B. Clark, "The Civil Rights Movement: Momentum and Organization," *Daedalus,* 95 (Winter 1966), 245.

12. Cited in Theodore Draper, *The Rediscovery of Black Nationalism* (New York: Viking Press, 1970), 22; for an interpretation of the origin of black nationalism, see August Meier, "The Emergence of Negro Nationalism," Parts I and II, *Midwest Journal,* 45 (Winter 1951 and Summer 1953), 96–104 and 95–111.

13. *Walker's Appeal and Garnet's Address,* 71, 73, 27–28; see also Sterling Stuckey, *The Ideological Origins of Black Nationalism* (Boston: Beacon Press, 1972), 97, 99, 55–56.

14. Carter G. Woodson, ed., *The Mind of the Negro as Reflected in Letters Written during the Crisis, 1800–1860* (1926; reprint, New York: Russell & Russell, 1969), 293.

15. Martin Robison Delany, *The Condition, Elevation, Emigration, and Destiny of the Colored People of the United States* (1855; reprint, New York: Arno Press/New York Times, 1969), 209; see also John H. Bracey, Jr., August Meier, and Elliott Rudwick, eds., *Black Nationalism in America* (Indianapolis: Bobbs-Merrill Co., 1970), 89.

16. Henry McNeal Turner, "The Barbarous Decision of the Supreme Court" (1883), in Edwin S. Redkey, ed., *Respect Black: The Writings and Speeches of Henry McNeal Turner* (New York: Arno Press/New York Times, 1971), 63.

17. Ibid., 165; Edwin S. Redkey, *Black Exodus: Black Nationalist and the Back-to-Africa Movements, 1890–1910* (New Haven: Yale University Press, 1969), 29.

18. Henry McNeal Turner, "God Is a Negro" (1898), in Redkey, ed., *Respect Black*, 176–77.

19. Amy Jacques Garvey, ed., Philosophy and Opinions of Marcus Garvey (New York: Arno Press/New York Times, 1969), vol. 2, 126.

20. Ibid., 325–26.

21. Ibid., vol. 1, 5, 2.

22. Cited in E. David Cronon, *Black Moses: The Story of Marcus Garvey and the Negro Improvement Association* (Madison: University of Wisconsin Press, 1955), 173.

23. Garvey, ed., *Philosophy and Opinions*, vol. 2, 326.

24. Cited in Louis E. Lomax, *When the Word is Given . . .* New York: Signet Book, 1964), 56. The classic study on the Nation of Islam is C. Eric Lincoln, *The Black Muslims in America* (Boston: Beacon Press, 1961, Rev. ed., 1973). See also E. U. Essien-Udom, *Black Nationalism: The Search for an Identity in America* (Chicago: University of Chicago Press, 1962); James Baldwin, *The Fire Next Time* (New York: Dell, 1962). An early significant study is Erdmann Doane Beynon, "The Voodoo Cult Among Negro Migrants in Detroit," *American Journal of Sociology* (May 1938), 894–907. See also Monroe Berger, "The Black Muslims," *Horizon* (Winter, 1964), 48–65. The best source for the teaching of Elijah Muhammad is his *The Supreme Wisdom: The Solution to the So-Called Negroes' Problem* (Chicago: University of Islam, 1957); also his *Message to the Blackman* (Chicago: Muhammad's Temple No. 2).

25. Vincent Harding, *There Is a River: The Black Struggle for Freedom in America* (New York: Harcourt Brace Jovanovich, 1981), 83.

SEARCHING FOR EDEN WITH A SATELLITE DISH

*Grant Wacker*

Pentecostal Christianity began at the beginning of this century and now has more than 30 million American adherents and a worldwide following of 430 million. These numbers rank Pentecostals behind only Roman Catholics as the largest gathering of Christians in the world. Though considerable attention has been given to the public ministries of Jim Bakker, Jimmy Swaggert, and Pat Robertson, and to the extraordinary practice of speaking in tongues, relatively little is known about ordinary Pentecostal church members. In the following essay, Grant Wacker traces the mushrooming growth of Pentecostalism to two impulses that have continually struggled for the movement's soul: primitivism and pragmatism. As Wacker states, the primitive impulse is "a powerfully destructive urge to smash all human-made traditions in order to return to a first century world where . . . dreams and visions exercised normative authority, and the Bible stood free of higher criticism." The pragmatic impulse, in contrast, is a desire to do whatever is needed to meet the movement's goals. By the end of the twentieth century, Wacker argues, these two impulses have resulted in a movement whose primitivism has meant that Pentecostal theology and worship patterns have remained "largely untouched by the assumptions of the secular culture" and yet whose pragmatism has led a rush "to embrace the therapeutic rewards and technological amenities of modernity with scarcely a second thought."

# 20

# SEARCHING FOR EDEN WITH A SATELLITE DISH

## Primitivism, Pragmatism, and the Pentecostal Character

*Grant Wacker*

THE DATE, Monday, April 9, 1906. The place, a four-room house on Bonnie Brae Street in downtown industrial Los Angeles. After the supper dishes had been cleared away, black saints gathered to seek the Baptism of the Holy Ghost. They assumed that when the power fell they would be enabled to speak an array of unlearned foreign languages, just as the apostles had done in the *Book of Acts*. In the preceding weeks the little band had met many times without success. But on that memorable spring evening the Spirit finally moved. First one, then another, and then another began to stammer in unfamiliar tongues. Before the night was over nearly all found themselves singing and shouting in the mysterious cadences of Africa, Asia, and the South Sea Islands. The worshippers concluded, naturally enough, that after a spiritual drought of nearly two thousand years the wonder-working power of the Holy Ghost once again had fallen upon Christ's humblest followers.

Word raced through the black community. Visitors gathered night after night, spilling out onto the porch and front lawn. Tradition has it that the weight of the enthusiasts soon crushed the porch. Realizing that they needed larger quarters, the band scraped together funds to lease an abandoned meeting house several blocks away on a short dirt road called Azusa Street. The following Tuesday evening, eight days after the initial manifestation of tongues, the Lord chose to advertise the mission through a most unsuspecting instrument, a secular newspaper reporter who may have been strolling home from work at the nearby *Los Angeles Times* building. "The night is made hideous . . . by the howlings of the worshipers," he wrote. "The devotees of the weird doctrine practice the most fanatical rites, preach the wildest theories and work themselves into a state of mad excitement." Not surprisingly, the devotees of the weird doctrine saw things differently. Within a week the San Andreas fault shifted, San Francisco lay in shambles, and anyone with a pure heart and an open mind could see that the long-awaited worldwide revival had finally begun.[1]

The tinder that caught fire in that ramshackle mission on Azusa Street is commonly said to have been the beginning of the worldwide pentecostal movement. Whether the revival really started among blacks at Azusa, or among whites in faith healing services in

Topeka, Kansas, years earlier, or even in a series of white-hot meetings among North Carolina hill folk in the 1890s, as various historians have contended, there can be little dispute that the pentecostal insurgence mushroomed into one of the most powerful religious upheavals of the twentieth century. A 1979 Gallup poll revealed that in the United States alone, nineteen percent—or twenty-nine million—adult Americans called themselves "Pentecostal or charismatic Christians."[2] Twelve years later the Assemblies of God, the largest and strongest of the pentecostal denominations, posted two million American adherents and another twenty-two million in affiliated bodies in other parts of the world.[3] In 1993, according to David Barrett, a leading scholar of world Christianity, the movement registered 430 million converts worldwide. Except for Roman Catholics, it ranked as the largest aggregation of Christians on the planet. Barrett projected that the revival would claim 560 million adherents by the year 2000 and well over a billion by the year 2025.[4] Almost certainly those figures swelled in the telling, perhaps wildly so, yet other studies consistently confirmed that within a century of its beginnings pentecostals had managed to claim a massive slice of the religious pie, both at home and abroad.[5]

Exactly who were the Christians who called themselves pentecostals? In the early 1990s scores of denominations—or fellowships, as they preferred to be called—claimed the label. The best known was the Assemblies of God, which was national in scope but strongest in the Sunbelt states. Other well-known bodies included the mostly black Church of God in Christ, clustered in the states of the Old South; the Church of God, concentrated in the Southern Highlands; the Pentecostal Holiness Church, centered in the Southeast; and the International Church of the Foursquare Gospel, most visible on the West Coast. The United Pentecostal Church and the largely black Pentecostal Assemblies of the World, commonly known as "Oneness" groups because of their insistence that Jesus alone was God, identified themselves as pentecostal but maintained (or were allowed to maintain) few relations with other pentecostal bodies. Both were concentrated in the urban Midwest. Literally scores of smaller sects, many of which were non-English speaking, dotted the religious landscape.[6]

What did pentecostals believe and practice? In the early days they often dubbed their missions Full Gospel Tabernacles, which meant that they preached the "full" or "foursquare" gospel of 1) salvation through faith in Jesus Christ, 2) baptism of the Holy Spirit with the evidence of speaking in unknown tongues, 3) divine healing, and 4) the promise of the Lord's soon return. Late twentieth-century adherents still shared those notions but in other ways they had grown extremely diverse. Rundown urban missions competed with opulent suburban churches; rough-tongued country preachers vied with unctuous television celebrities. More important, after World War II an emphasis upon the supernatural gifts of the Spirit as described in *I Corinthians* 12 and 14—preeminently the casting out of demons, divine healing, speaking in tongues, and the interpretation of tongues—penetrated some of the long established Protestant denominations and the Roman Catholic Church. The newer enthusiasts commonly called themselves charismatic Christians, partly to distinguish themselves from their unscrubbed pentecostal cousins.[7] Virtually every week in the 1980s and early 1990s the secular press carried an article about pentecostals or charismatics. Often those items focused upon the avarice of a Jim Bakker, the antics of a Jimmy Swaggert, or the presidential ambitions of a Pat Robertson. Yet behind those very public and often sorry tales lay the private stories of millions of ordinary believers whose commitment to the work of the church typically dwarfed the involvement of non-pentecostal mainline Christians.

Scholars have offered various explanations for pentecostalism's apparent success. Some historians have pointed to the numerous continuities between the Wesleyan holiness and the pentecostal traditions back at the turn of the century, noting that the latter got a head start, so to speak, by appropriating the vast network of periodicals, churches, campmeetings, Bible schools, and faith homes that holiness folk had carefully cemented in place decades earlier. Other historians have suggested that pentecostalism provided spiritual compensations for the material good things that believers felt they had been denied this side of heaven's gate. Sociologists in turn have focused upon pentecostals' aptitude for providing a place in the sun for ordinary folk displaced by social disorganization or cast adrift by cultural dislocations. Friendly theologians have pointed to the revival's ability to meet enduring needs of the human spirit, while unfriendly ones have suggested that it exploited the gullibility of the masses, offering bogus cures for incurable diseases.[8]

All of these explanations bear a measure of truth, yet none seems entirely adequate.[9] In this essay I wish to offer an additional possibility. I do not propose that it supplants any of the others, but I do think that it illuminates a neglected dimension of the question.

Simply stated, pentecostalism flourished because two impulses perennially warred for mastery of its soul. I shall call the first the *primitivist* and the second the *pragmatic*. The labels themselves are not crucial, but they seem as useful as any in suggesting a range of meanings that we shall explore more fully in a few moments. Here it suffices to say that the primitivist impulse represented a powerfully destructive urge to smash all human-made traditions in order to return to a first century world where the Holy Spirit alone reigned. In that realm supernatural signs and wonders formed the stuff of daily life, dreams and visions exercised normative authority, and the Bible stood free of higher criticism. The pragmatic impulse, in contrast, reflected an eagerness to do whatever was necessary in order to accomplish the movement's purposes. Though pragmatism did not logically require acceptance of the technological achievements and governing social arrangements of the post-industrial West—structural differentiation, procedural rationality, centralized management, and the like—as a practical matter that is the way things usually worked out. Moreover, once pentecostals learned that pragmatic attitudes not only worked but also paid large dividends in subjective well-being, they found themselves drawn inch by inch into the assumptions of the therapeutic society where the quest for personal fulfillment reigned supreme.[10]

There are numerous ways to make this argument. In this essay I shall try to achieve this by asking a simple question: What kind of persons joined the revival in the first place? The answer—to jump way ahead in the story—is that the pioneer generation evinced, to a striking degree, *both* primitive and pragmatic character traits. More significantly, they displayed those traits at the same time, without compromise, in a knot of behavior patterns so tangled and matted as to be nearly inseparable. Not everyone fit the prototype of course. As with any large social aggregation—fifty thousand by 1910, maybe twice that number by 1920[11]—a great rainbow of human types joined the revival. Some exhibited consistently primitivist urges, while others found more pragmatic values congenial. Thus the doubleness of the pentecostal character did not necessarily manifest itself with equal force within the same persons all of the time. But within the aggregate it did.

Before turning to those early materials one caveat is needed. Exactly how the founding figures came to acquire these traits falls outside the scope of this essay. Some clearly brought them to the movement.[12] But others just as clearly absorbed them after they joined.[13] Probably most fell somewhere in between, discovering something like an elective affinity between longstanding predispositions on one hand and newly acquired ideals on the other. At this distance it is hard to sort out the exact mix, and probably matters little if we could. The main point is that apparently conflicting impulses energized the initial generation as a whole, and that pattern persisted into the 1990s. The clue lies in the faces of the day laborers and washerwomen who crowded the Azusa mission. In their determination to see the lame healed and the dead raised, whatever the cost—and that is the key phrase: *whatever the cost*—they proved themselves as worldly-wise as their well-heeled great-grandchildren who frequented the glass and steel Christian Life Centers scattered along the Interstate bypasses.

## THE PRIMITIVIST IMPULSE

Pentecostals themselves acknowledged only the primitivist side of their lives, so we shall begin with that part of their story. Primitivism has borne a score of meanings in the historical and theoretical literature of religious studies.[14] I shall define it quite simply as a yearning somehow to return to a time before time, to a space outside of space, to a mythical realm that Alexander Campbell memorably called the "ancient order of things." It is important to note that among early pentecostals primitivism was not simply restorationism, or at least what is commonly called restorationism. The latter suggested a rather self-conscious effort to sit down, figure out what the New Testament blueprint called for, then quite rationally reproduce it in the modern world. Campbellites, Mormons, Landmark Baptists, and other so-called restorationist sects of the nineteenth century readily come to mind.[15] Pentecostal primitivism certainly included all of that, but it was more. It was the dark subsoil in which restorationist and, for that matter, millenarian visions germinated. It was the urge to destroy all recently-made traditions in order to return to the ancient tradition of the New Testament where the Holy Ghost, and only the Holy Ghost, ruled the hearts and minds of the faithful. That long-lost world was, in a sense, an Edenic realm pulsating with supernatural signs and wonders, yet it was also an apocalyptic realm regimented by the timeless truths and universal values of Scripture. First generation stalwarts sought to re-enter that world as literally as possible by breathing its holy air, smelling its sacred fragrances, luxuriating in its spiritual delights. In the process, they fashioned their own social networks, cultural symbols, and religious rituals. To a remarkable extent they succeeded in creating a primitive garden in a modern wilderness.

On first reading, early pentecostals' rhetoric suggests that they were, above all, heavenly-minded pilgrims pursuing other-worldly satisfactions because they harbored little interest in this-worldly delights. Their storefront missions and backlot tents served as sequestered havens where they found inestimable rewards, at least by any ordinary calculus of things. What emerges from the literature is an image of questers determined to exchange the fleeting pleasures of life in the present world for the enduring fulfillments of life in the world to come. Of course they never explained themselves exactly that way. Indeed, they rarely explained themselves at all. But they did leave a long trail of hints, mostly in letters, diaries, and testimonials, suggesting the kind of satisfactions they sought in the sweat-soaked bedlam of the meeting. Those hints enable us to infer the sort of people they were, the hurts they endured, the aspirations they nurtured.

Examples surface everywhere we look in the primary literature. One Chicago partisan put it as plainly as language permitted: "Those who speak in tongues seem to live in another world."[16] Living in another world took a number of forms, however. For some, it engendered something like a sixth sense, a fundamentally new way of seeing even the natural landscape around them. "It seemed as if human joys vanished," a Florida advocate wrote. "It seemed as if the whole world and the people looked a different color."[17] A Wesleyan Methodist pastor in Toronto spoke of a surge of feelings she had never known: "overwhelming power," "absence of fleshly effort," a sensation of walking "softly with God."[18] Some devotees appear to have entered into a sacred zone where time itself was calibrated according to divine rather than human standards. Looking back to the first blush of the revival from the vantage point of the mid 1920s, evangelist Frank Bartleman judged that he would "*rather live six months at that time than fifty years of ordinary time.*"[19] Members commonly spoke of spending hour after hour, sometimes entire days, in prayer and singing without thought of food.[20] Many had no awareness that night had fallen or that daylight had dawned.[21] Converts found themselves in a breathtaking era of history where the old structures had been swept away and new ones erected. In their nightly prayer meetings, a Webb City, Missouri, devotee wrote, "it seemed impossible to distinguish between the earthly and the heavenly anthems. . . . The celestial glory . . . filled the room with a halo of glory. [Some] could scarcely endure the 'weight of glory' that rested upon them."[22] Another recalled that when he underwent the baptism experience, "the fire fell and burned up all that would burn and what would not burn was caught up into heaven. . . . It [was] a salvation indescribable. . . . My spirit long[ed] to be free from a sin-cursed world and be at home with Jesus."[23] One venerable pentecostal historian may have said more than he intended but surely touched an essential chord when he wrote that many onlookers believed they were "either insane over religion, or drunk on some glorious dream."[24]

If the other world of supernatural delights and timeless truths functioned as the all-consuming locus of interest, it is hardly surprising that pentecostals betrayed little interest in earthly affairs such as presidential elections or local politics. Their response to the war then raging in Europe is instructive. A few forthrightly supported American entry into the conflict and a handful opposed it, but the great majority held no opinion at all. What they worried about in letters to the editors was not bloodshed but the likelihood that the conflict would open up new opportunities for sin. "War is a feeder of hell," stormed the *Church of God Evangel.* "This last awful struggle has been the cause of millions of mother's boys dropping into the region of the damned where they are entering their eternal tortures."[25] Peace proved no more interesting than war. The November 1918 issue of Aimee Semple McPherson's *Bridal Call* characteristically said nothing about the Armistice that had just been signed. Six months elapsed before McPherson finally got around to reminding her readers that there was a Red Cross hospital atop Calvary's hill too.

Spirit-filled believers lost interest in the kind of day-to-day activities that most evangelical Protestants regarded as simple and legitimate pleasures of life. I am not thinking here of a pipe by the fireplace on a winter's night, or a frosty beer out on the front porch on a summer afternoon. Worldly enjoyments of that sort remained inconceivable. Rather, the point is that even officially sanctioned satisfactions such as family, children, and marital sex often lost all appeal.

Diaries and autobiographies reveal a good deal. Aimee Semple McPherson may not have cared much about the war, but she did care about Holy Ghost revivals. She boasted that she kept on traveling and preaching, month after month, even though her young daughter back at home seemed to be dying of influenza. The reason? Abraham had never hesitated to sacrifice Isaac.[26] The journal of pioneer educator D. C. O. Opperman, which carefully chronicled his ceaseless travels back and forth across the South between 1905 and 1912, displayed a man so preoccupied with the work at hand that he gave only perfunctory notice to his marriage and the birth of his first two children. He even failed to note the name of his third child.[27] The diary of Pentecostal Holiness Church leader George Floyd Taylor revealed a similar pattern: a litany of reports on sermons preached, biblical passages meditated upon, Sunday School classes taught, cronies talked with, prayer meetings attended. The entry for August 27, 1908, taken virtually at random, proclaimed, "My soul is a sea of glass. . . . Glory! Glory! . . . My soul secretly cries out for God to hide me away in His presence."[28] Except for a daily report on the weather, Taylor's journal avoided any hint of mundane detail. One would never suspect that this husband and father had ever suffered a trace of disappointment, a pang of hunger, or a tug of lust.

Even in death the pattern persisted. Just before his own death, Richard G. Spurling, Jr., a founder of the Church of God, asked that he not be buried facing east, as the custom was among his people, but buried facing his homeplace. With that gesture Spurling meant to signal that he had spent too much time caring for his family and not enough time doing the only thing that really mattered, preaching the gospel.[29]

Enthusiasts subordinated romance to a calculus of heavenly rewards. Neither the wedding nor the wedding night could be taken as events memorable or pleasurable in their own right. The notice of an Inglewood, California, ceremony reported that it was preceded by a time of "rejoicing and praise before God." Many were saved.[30] A newspaper published by a pentecostal band in San Francisco happily observed that when two of its members married, the ritual concluded with an impassioned "exhortation for sinners to seek the Lord."[31] Things were no different in Britain. In the Welsh hamlet of Llandilo, one paper reported, celebrants carved up the wedding home into a prayer room and a food room. To everyone's joy one "brother received the baptism of the Holy Ghost" in the prayer room— while the rest presumably attended to their appetites in the food room.[32] Back in Oklahoma, a new husband-wife evangelist team trumpeted that their wedding had been a "glorious occasion" because it reminded all present of "Jesus our Heavenly Bridegroom coming in the air."[33] Evangelist Howard Goss primly recorded that his bride Ethel spent their wedding night preaching a fiery sermon at a revival in Eureka Springs, Arkansas, with telling effect upon local sinners.[34] A young brother from Canada begged the readers of the *Christian Evangel* to pray that "God will give me the girl of my choice—a baptized saint— for a wife." Why? For love? For family? Perish the thought! If they married, he solemnly explained, they could start a rest home for missionaries.[35]

If pentecostals discountenanced the routine pleasures of life, they were equally prepared to forgo the bonds that tethered them to earth. This helps explain why believers could dismiss digging a storm cellar, an act that surely seemed prudent enough, as a "habit of the flesh."[36] It also helps explain why a sister who claimed to be heaven-bound yet worried about the eternal fate of her children could become a target of ridicule. If a mother were *truly* heaven-bound, the argument ran, she would not be compromised by any earthly interest, even a concern for the souls of her offspring.[37]

Night after night enthusiasts lustily sang, "Take the world, but give me Jesus." But there really was not much to take. They were already living on that distant shore.


## THE PRAGMATIC IMPULSE

If an initial reading of the letters, diaries, and testimonial columns of early pentecostalism leaves an image of pilgrims singlemindedly trekking toward heaven's gate, a second reading creates a strikingly different image. The latter suggests that first generation converts are better interpreted as eminently practical-minded folk who used the limited resources at their disposal to gain their purposes, sacred or otherwise. According to this second perspective, when all was said and done, pentecostals proved themselves a persistently ambitious lot, considerably less interested in what was said than in what was done. A scenario of mundane sagacity and this-worldly hardheadedness dominates the picture.

Admittedly, it requires a bit of reading between the lines to see how prevalent the pragmatic character trait really was. Pentecostals almost never described themselves with the repertoire of words we associate with this-worldliness: shrewdness, adroitness, savvy, and the like. Indeed, they typically went to great lengths to suggest the opposite. They wanted to believe and, more important, they wanted the world to believe, that the Holy Spirit alone governed all aspects of their lives. They also hoped to convince themselves and their neighbors that they never gave a second thought to their own interests. But if we turn the data under the light just a little, they tell a very different story. It was no accident that Aimee McPherson, a pentecostal barnstormer, put up the first religious radio station in the United States, nor that two generations later Pat Robertson, a pentecostal TV preacher, launched the first privately owned communications satellite in the world. That sure sense of knowing the ropes, knowing how to get things done, knowing how to negotiate with local power brokers, existed from the beginning, always poised just beneath the surface.

As a deeply rooted character trait, mundane sagacity manifested itself in countless ways. For brevity I shall discuss only two. The first was a maverick streak so pronounced that it bordered on outright rebelliousness. Historian Timothy L. Smith once wrote that nineteenth-century holiness come-outers typically found themselves "unable to accept much real discipline save their own."[38] That characterization fit early pentecostals even better than their holiness parents. Thumbing through the biographical data, one is struck by pentecostals' self-taught inventiveness, their stubborn unwillingness to be instructed, much less bound, by the conventions of the past. While they were never as theologically unbuttoned as other homegrown sects like Mormons and Jehovah's Witnesses, they routinely winked at or even discarded inherited orthodoxies whenever it suited their purposes. Indeed, the tradition's cardinal doctrinal distinctive—namely, that speaking in tongues invariably accompanied the baptism of the Holy Spirit—stood unprecedented in the entire history of Judaism and Christianity. From time to time individual partisans espoused highly imaginative positions, to put it as charitably as possible, on matters as diverse as the origin of the human species, the destiny of Israel, the gold standard, and much else. Standing alone like that may have taken a toll at some deep psychological level. But on the surface pentecostals seem not to have suffered a twinge of self-consciousness, let alone embarrassment, as they marched in solitary zeal across the theological landscape.

The point I wish to emphasize here is not so much the singularity of pentecostals' theological ideas as such, but the frame of mind they brought to the task of formulating those ideas. The fundamental animus can be described as exuberant creativity, a kind of swash-buckling inventiveness that prompted them to draw their own conclusions from their own sources in their own way, the devil and the established churches be damned. To take one of countless examples, probably only a small minority ever shared founder Charles Fox Parham's view that the unregenerate dead suffered annihilation rather than eternal torment. But the way that he came to that conclusion was altogether typical. Parham had been reared and schooled as an orthodox Methodist. Upon marriage, his wife's grandfather, a Quaker with annihilationist leanings, challenged him to read the Bible without commentaries in hand or creeds in mind. Parham did, and soon reached an annihilationist position himself, which he stubbornly upheld the rest of his life despite relentless vilification from other evangelicals.[39]

The maverick disposition manifested itself in other ways. A disproportionate number of the early leaders had been voluntary immigrants to the United States to begin with, typically coming from Australia, Britain, or Western Europe. Most came over not to escape penury or military service in the Old World but either to do better financially or to find ampler scope for their ministries in the rolling religious spaces of the New World.[40] Many proved inveterate travelers, crisscrossing the United States and frequently the Atlantic and Pacific oceans year in, year out. For example A. A. Boddy, sometimes hailed as the father of British pentecostalism, sailed the ocean at least fourteen times, not counting side trips to Africa, Siberia, and the European continent.[41] Some of course were forced to travel constantly, whether they liked it or not, because they were overseers or itinerant preachers by trade.[42] But autobiographies make clear that the opposite dynamic often dominated: many became overseers or itinerants in the first place because they could not abide the confinement of a settled pastorate for more than a few weeks at a stretch.[43] Some clearly became foreign missionaries for pretty much the same reason. China missionaries Alfred and Lillian Garr wrote that they gladly suffered the loss of their "old Holiness friends" in order to be the first to herald the pentecostal message in Asia. One can almost feel their expansionist exuberance: "It was like beginning life over, a new ministry . . . not limited to a small fraction of the Holiness people, nor to one country . . . but the 'World our parish.'"[44] Sometimes globe-trotting obviously got out of hand. Complaints about the needlessly peripatetic ways of overseas missionaries regularly spiked the editorial columns of early newspapers.[45]

The maverick demon in the pentecostal soul recoiled at the specter of regularization. For the better part of a decade zealots fought off efforts to standardize the funding of missionaries, or to impose even minimal rules of financial accountability upon evangelists or local churches.[46] Until after World War I the majority of periodicals were launched, edited, and run as one-man or, equally often, as one-woman operations.[47] A remarkable number of those editors continued to publish and jealously guard their subscription lists long after joining a pentecostal denomination with its own official publication.[48] Pentecostals were never as prone to put up schools as they were to float periodicals. Yet at least a score of elementary and secondary academies and Bible institutes, originally founded and run largely as one-person operations, persisted long after the founder had joined a body with its own centrally-sponsored institutions. These independent schools sorely irked denominational bureaucrats determined to rein in such endeavors.[49] Yet in their heart of hearts they too knew that the movement had been born of a defiant temper. In later years patriarch Howard Goss, a denominational bureaucrat himself, acknowledged that the very "foundation for the vast Pentecostal Movement" had been laid by loners and free-lancers, by missionaries without board support and pastors without degrees or salaries or "restful holidays."[50]

Besides a maverick disposition, the evidence discloses another pragmatic character trait. Any number of adjectives will do: intrepid, audacious, assertive, pushy. I shall lump them all under the rubric of willfulness. What these terms all suggest, rightly enough, is a singleminded determination to gain the goal at hand, regardless of the obstacles or even of the human cost. One nameless writer hit the nail squarely on the head when he or she judged that the baptism experience steeled believers with "holy boldness."[51] And they were plenty proud of it too. For Church of God General Overseer A. J. Tomlinson, the lassitude that came with "long study and . . . deep tiresome thinking" had grievously undermined established Christianity. In his mind it was high time for Christians to get moving, "fired up with holy zeal and undaunted courage."[52] The faint-hearted might lament the rush of technology or the secular world's obsession with progress, but not Tomlinson. Why should we, he demanded, allow others, "by going hungry and arising early, to win the prize for energy, wit, longsuffering, perseverance, grit and determination?"[53]

For most enthusiasts holy boldness was as much a practical as a spiritual mandate. Thus M. L. Ryan, pastor of a flock in Spokane, Washington, and editor of one of the earliest periodicals, *Apostolic Light*, led a band of eighteen missionaries to Japan in the summer of 1907 without the endorsement of any board or denomination, and apparently without any certain destination in mind or clear notion of how they would support themselves when they got there. No matter. When the band reached Tokyo, Ryan discovered that he would have to pay high customs fees. Undeterred, he offered his typewriter and tent as collateral, somehow secured a two-masted lifeboat and immediately proceeded to sail around Tokyo harbor preaching the pentecostal message (presumably with an interpreter in tow). Within days Ryan had managed to turn out two issues of an English-and-Japanese edition of *Apostolic Light*.[54]

Pentecostals' notorious anti-intellectualism was more stereotypical than typical. Yet insofar as they were anti-intellectual, much of that trait can be attributed to impatience, to a brash determination to get on with the job at hand rather than waste time on pointless theorizing. One leader probably revealed more than he intended when he declared that "God made grappling hooks of His Pentecostal preachers rather than bookworms."[55] Not all preachers and certainly not all laypersons were grappling hooks. As in any large social movement, pentecostalism also attracted the timid and the bookish.[56] But no one thought to preserve their memory in the evidence because it did not fit the ideal. What we read about, rather, are leaders variously described as "vivid, magnetic . . . incisive."[57] Many are "erect, clear-eyed, tense and enthusiastic."[58] Others are "[filled with] intense dogmatic zeal [and] a firm determination to rule or ruin."[59]

Willfulness fired stamina. Though the evidence is too spotty to warrant confident generalizations about the rank and file, pentecostal leaders appear remarkably vigorous. To be sure, most had experienced serious illness before converting to the movement and many suffered recurring bouts afterward. Yet there is good reason to believe that significantly fewer of them endured debilitating illness than the national norm. Moreover, virtually all enjoyed stunning divine healings in their own bodies.[60] Those landmark events not only brought physical restoration but also stirred converts to proclaim the pentecostal message with renewed vigor. Thus willfulness—defined in this case as a determination to believe that one had been healed, regardless of symptoms, or the certainty that one had been divinely commissioned to do the Lord's work, come what may—ignited and sustained extraordinary levels of physical exertion.

Again, examples readily come to hand. One thinks of missionary heroes like Victor Plymire, who toiled forty-one years on the Tibetan-Chinese border, despite hardship, disease, and persecution from local magistrates, with only a handful of converts to show for his life's work.[61] Yet the exertions of less heralded leaders illustrate the point better precisely *because* they were less heralded. One evangelist remembered that if workers could not afford trains or carriages, "they rode bicycles, or in lumber wagons; some went horseback, some walked. Often they waded creeks. Often men removed their clothes, tied their bundles above their heads and swam rivers" to get to the next night's meeting.[62] In 1908 Winnipeg pastor and businessman A. H. Argue casually remarked that he had led nine services per week every week for the past nine months.[63] Mary "Mother" Barnes achieved local notoriety for shepherding a revival in Thayer, Missouri, from nine A.M. until midnight, seven days a week, for eight months straight.[64] In 1912 E. N. Bell proudly grumbled that as sole editor of *Word and Witness*, he had mailed out nineteen thousand copies of the paper each month, personally answered six to seven hundred letters each month, and held down a full time pastorate in Malvern, Arkansas, where he preached five times per week and maintained a regular hospital visitation ministry.[65] The diary of A. J. Tomlinson stands as a chronicle of tireless travel on foot, mule, train, auto, ship—whatever was available—and the preaching on the average of one sermon a day for nearly forty years. The entries for a July 1925 weekend were typical. At age sixty-five, between Thursday and Sunday, he delivered ten sermons amidst swarming mosquitoes and drenching humidity. "The only rest I got," he added in a telling postscript, "was while the saints were shouting, dancing and talking in tongues."[66]

Allowing for some forgivable exaggeration in such accounts, it is clear that extraordinary faith—read willfulness—prompted extraordinary activity. To be sure, common sense tells us that men and women who could ford rivers and shout the devil into submission were blessed with a tough constitution to begin with. But it was an iron-willed frame of mind that put that constitution rightly to work. One author allowed that feeling blue from time to time was to be expected, yet immediately added that melancholy was a sin to be borne and fought off like any other temptation. "[The Christian] is never to be sorrowful for a moment, but to be ALWAYS REJOICING."[67] The steel rod that stiffened the pentecostal spinal column revealed itself in India missionary Elizabeth Sisson. In the dentist's chair, Sisson boasted, she had never used Novocaine because she was determined to retain complete control of her mind and body at all times.[68] That last statement is particularly significant given that Sisson also wrote with luxuriant detail about the frequency and intensity of her ecstatic experiences, events that outsiders would readily categorize as disassociative if not pathological.[69]

Willfulness manifested itself in other ways. Sometimes pentecostal writers sounded like hawkers for a Dale Carnegie course. "It is always better to encourage people to do what they can for themselves," one averred. "People are pauperized by teaching them . . . to ask the Lord to do for us many things which we ought to do for ourselves."[70] Often willfulness expressed itself in a simple syllogism that outsiders found scandalous if not blasphemous. The syllogism ran like this. God has uttered certain promises in Scripture. If believers act in the prescribed manner, God has bound himself to respond in the prescribed manner.

"Getting things from God is like playing checkers," wrote F. F. Bosworth, the most respected healing evangelist of the 1920s. "He always moves when it is His turn. . . . Our move is to expect what he promises."[71]

Pentecostals applied that reasoning most frequently to the matter of physical health. Since God had promised to heal the body if one prayed with genuine faith, the only possible result was immediate and complete restoration of the body. Carrie Judd Montgomery, one of the most prolific and articulate figures in the early history of the movement, made the case with memorable clarity: "If, after prayer for physical healing, we reckon the work as already accomplished in our bodies, we shall not fear to act out that faith, and to make physical exertions which will justify our professed belief in the healing." Then came the knock-out punch: "I have never failed to receive according to my faith."[72] The import was as clear and hard as glass: the genuineness of one's faith was directly and exactly commensurate with one's ability to get up and subdue the afflicting disease. If the symptoms persisted that meant either that one's faith was weak or that they were nothing but "counterfeit symptoms" to begin with. As one physician convert put it, "[You must not] wait to see the evidence of your healing. There will be no evidence until it is done, and it will not be done until you believe without visible or tangible evidence of any sort."[73] One nameless grandmother, who had worn eyeglasses for twenty years, tossed them out when she decided to pray for restoration of her eyesight. From that point on, she forced herself to read ten chapters of her Bible each day without glasses because God had promised that he would answer the prayer of faith. Therefore He *did*. "Why, salt water is good for the eyes," she wrote, tears tumbling onto the page.[74]

Express your needs in prayer. Assume that you possess your healing the instant you pray for it. Get up and act on that assumption. If counterfeit symptoms persist, disregard them. After all, the Lord promised: " 'I'll do anything you want me to do.' "[75]

The formula worked every time—if one possessed the grit and the moxie to make it work.

## CONCLUSION

The better part of a century has passed since that nameless grandmother flung her glasses aside. The world has changed dramatically since then, and in many ways pentecostals have changed with it. But only superficially.

At the end of the twentieth century the essential structural tension between the primitive and the pragmatic persisted as acutely as ever. On one hand, the theology and worship patterns or what religion scholars might call the myths and rituals that energized the movement's inner life survived largely untouched by the assumptions of the secular culture. Biblical inerrancy and literalism hovered as close to the ground as they did at the turn of the century. Darwin, Marx, and Freud, not to mention more recent icons of the secular academy such as Mary Daly, Richard Rorty, and Stephen Jay Gould, remained wholly outside the horizon of pentecostal consciousness. More significantly, the longing for vital manifestations of the supernatural gifts of the Holy Spirit flourished with unabated fervor. Pentecostal periodicals brimmed with stories of stunning healings and divine interventions in daily life. Miracles may not have danced before believers' eyes quite as often as they once did, but one thing was sure: No child of the revival would have counted it a good thing if it were true.[76]

At the same time, however, latter day enthusiasts rushed to embrace the therapeutic rewards and technological amenities of modernity with scarcely a second thought. Although a few still gathered in storefront missions and avoided the trappings of the good life, the majority worshipped in carpeted, air-conditioned buildings indistinguishable from the local United Methodist Church. Adherents propagated their message with state-of-the-art publishing and communications technology. They hobnobbed with the rich and the powerful. Indeed, many of them *were* the rich and the powerful. On the whole, then, they dressed, worked, and played like anyone else who hailed from the same region and occupied the same position in the social system. Sometimes it appeared that the only difference between pentecostal Christians and mainline Christians was that the former got there first and did it bigger, better, and less tastefully.[77]

Taken together, then, pentecostals of the 1990s presented an arresting spectacle. They appeared to believe and worship by one set of rules but to work and play by quite another. Stalwarts spent their evenings at full gospel rallies rapturously speaking in tongues, and spent their days in university computer labs unraveling mysteries of another sort. Spirit-filled medical missionaries cast out demons in the morning and adjusted CAT scanners in the afternoon. Partisans asked the Holy Spirit to help them find their car keys as nonchalantly as they invited a neighbor to drop by for coffee. Though scenarios of this sort could have been witnessed in virtually any large urban pentecostal church—and for that matter a great many small rural ones too—we are not limited to impressions. The hard data sniffed out by social scientists told very much the same story. Case studies of pentecostal converts strongly suggested that the primitive and the pragmatic actually co-varied: the more fervent the former, the more determined the latter.[78]

Any number of outsiders looked at this spectacle and came away scratching their heads, wondering how it all fit together. In their minds it was nothing short of remarkable that pentecostals' taste for other-worldly ecstasies and for ahistorical dogmatisms had survived as long as it had. Surely it could not last indefinitely, they supposed. Surely pentecostals were destined either to go the way of the United Methodists—that is, move uptown culturally as well as socially—or, like Old Order Mennonites, to recede to a picturesque but obscure corner of contemporary life.[79] What most of those observers presupposed, of course, was that cultural modernism and social modernization came together as a package deal, something like a solid-state appliance with no customer-removable parts.

But that is precisely where the problem arises. Recent history proves that no one owns the franchise on modernity. Everywhere we look we see ardent Christians selectively shopping in the warehouse of the times, choosing what they like, ignoring what they do not like, and rarely giving the matter a second thought. The plain fact is that religious folk put their lives together in a dizzying variety of ways.

Examples abound. In the mid-nineteenth century Oneida Perfectionists, fired by a potent mix of apocalyptic Scripture readings and ecstatic religious experience, implemented systematic work habits and careful accounting procedures that led to the redoubtable Oneida Silverware Company. In the late nineteenth century, evangelical missionaries fanned out around the world heralding a darkly primitivist vision of the imminent fiery climax of history. Yet the very urgency of their message also impelled them to adopt the most efficient means of transportation and publication known, along with a streamlining of mission boards at home that should have made Wall Street envious. Anyone familiar with the corpus of missionary biographies and autobiographies of the last two centuries knows how often the primitive and the pragmatic, or at least facsimiles thereof, presented themselves in the same souls. "A strange compound of fiercely practical common sense and profound mysticism," was the way that Pearl Buck described her China missionary mother.[80] After World War II ultra-traditionalist insurrectionaries around the world distinguished themselves by their deployment of the best and latest in mass communications technology—not to mention weaponry. And lest anyone doubt that all sorts of primitivisms could promenade arm-in-arm with the most advanced forms of social modernization, we need only observe the daily lives of millions of mainline Christians in the 1990s. Episcopalians confronted the mystery of the Eucharist on Sunday mornings and ran corporate board meetings on Monday afternoons. Roman Catholics earnestly confessed the Apostles' Creed one day and negotiated high priced real estate deals the next.

All of this is to say that at one time or another virtually every tradition within the Christian family (and for that matter a good many *outside* the Christian family) confronted a roughly similar set of polarities: piety versus intellect, supernature versus nature, prophetic critique versus priestly legitimation, ancient wisdom versus modern insight, right belief versus right results. In this respect, Spirit-filled believers proved themselves no different from countless faithful before them.

But the story does not end there. In other ways first-, second-, and third-generation pentecostals consistently showed themselves very different indeed. If they drew threads of inspiration from the heritage of Christian belief and behavior, they also wove those threads into a distinctive tapestry that was very much of their own making. And one feature of that distinctiveness was the sheer bravura with which they maintained *both* the primitive and the pragmatic sides of their identity at once. Though it would be difficult to prove, looking back over the twentieth century, it is at least arguable that the contrast between transcendent visions and mundane sagacity manifested itself more dramatically among pentecostals than among any other large group of Christians of modern times (except perhaps the Mormons). That was particularly true in the Third World where, especially after World War II, the transcendent and the mundane flourished side by side with riotous abandon.[81]

To be sure, the exact nature of the interaction between the primitive and the pragmatic in the pentecostal subculture is not entirely clear. We grope for metaphors. Is that relationship best construed as a struggle between antagonists? Or as an alliance between partners? Or is it more accurate to picture it as both at once—something like the inexplicable chemistry of a combative yet invigorating marriage?

Subtler images that intimate more complex modes of interaction also come to mind. The trickster figure of American folklore offers one possibility. In those stories a mythic character such as Br'er Rabbit presents itself in one form in one context, but in a dramatically different form in another context. This analogy suggests that perhaps we should think of the primitive and the pragmatic not as two distinct impulses at all, but rather as a single reflex that changed faces according to situation. The signal benefit of the trickster construct is that it reminds us that a given act, such as obliviousness to conventional family ties, may have served primitive ends in one setting and pragmatic ones in another.[82]

Another possibility presents itself. Literary critics have taught us that all texts can be read at two levels (or at *least* at two levels.) Wherever there is a surface text there is always a submerged text; what is said gains force and meaning when we peel back the explicit words, so to speak, and expose the implicit ones beneath. Religious cultures too can be read as "texts." In that case, pentecostals' primitivist behavior can be construed as the surface text, while their pragmatic inclinations can be construed as the submerged text. The task then is not to prove that one was more real or even more important than the other, but to recognize that the revivals' spiritual power and cultural meaning emerged from the perennial interplay of the two.[83]

A metaphor drawn from the realm of the theater offers one more option and, given the intractable doubleness of the evidence, a particularly compelling one. By this reckoning the primitive invariably stood front and center stage, carrying the burden of the plot, reveling in the applause of the faithful and, of course, bravely bearing the jeers of the faithless. The pragmatic, on the other hand, normally served as the stage manager, standing behind the curtains, orchestrating all of the moves—but with the cash till never far from mind. This scenario suggests that when pentecostals were wearing their primitivist garb, they may have been, first and foremost, following a script: a pre-approved story carefully designed to edify the committed and win the uncommitted. It also suggests that if believers played to the galleries more often than they admitted, journalists and historians bought the ruse more often than they knew.[84]

All of these metaphors may well help us conceptualize the inner workings of pentecostal culture, but they also pose risks, for they may beguile us into thinking that the primitive and the pragmatic were somehow substantive things in themselves. Obviously they were not; they are only labels that we apply to conspicuous and persistent patterns of behavior. Thus pinning down the exact configuration of the interaction—be it antagonistic, complementary, competitive, invertible, dialectical, theatrical, or whatever—seems less important than recognizing its pervasive and vital presence in the movement's life. The real task before us then is to divine the functions that the interaction performed in the lives of ordinary believers.

At least two functions come to mind. The first might be called institutional success, the second ethical immaturity.

Institutional success arose from a delicate balancing of primitive and pragmatic energies. On one side, the primitive fueled the revival by offering certitude about the truthfulness of inherited theological claims and the reality of the supernatural. It gave ordinary Christians life-giving energies. It guaranteed that the pentecostal message would not fall into the deadening routines of pragmatic implementation or, worse, of self-serving manipulation. Moreover, other-worldly yearnings distanced the tradition from the conventions of the surrounding culture, making it possible for believers to chart their own spiritual course in a world that was not so much hostile as simply uncomprehending. The pragmatic, in contrast, stabilized the movement by keeping adherents from squandering their energies in ecstatic excesses. It imposed standards of efficiency, economy, and institutional order. It kept the revival from rendering itself, in Emerson's fine words, "frivolous and ungirt." Most important, perhaps, the pragmatic enabled believers to reproduce their culture among succeeding generations by fostering stable educational structures. If primitivist aspirations inspired a vision of life as it might be, pragmatic values afforded the means for preserving it.

Less happily, the interplay of impulses also engendered ethical immaturity. The primitive freed enthusiasts from worrying very much about the propriety of their social attitudes. To be sure, they avoided personal vices such as drinking and smoking and, except for the question of conscription during World War I, they took pride in their obedience to the laws of the land. But until very recently at least, pentecostals displayed little or no concern with larger questions of responsible social and political behavior. It almost never occurred to them that a Christian ought to take a thoughtful stand, or *any* stand, regarding suffrage, prohibition, civil rights, environmental pollution, or famine in other countries. Only the Holy Spirit reigned in their lives, they wanted to believe, and because the Holy Spirit had nothing to say about those pesky questions, there was no reason to trouble themselves with them either. In the meantime, the pragmatic impulse spurred pentecostals to build the biggest and buy the best of everything, mainly for the Lord of course, but sometimes a little for themselves too. Where other more historically seasoned Christians had learned that it was not so easy to live godly lives in a godless world, pentecostals experienced few qualms about their ability to shuttle from celestial heights to terrestrial plains and back again. The impregnable conviction that they—and often enough, that they alone—had seen the Promised Land enabled them to relish the satisfactions of spiritual separation from modern life and, at the same time, to savor most of its benefits without a trace of guilt. The formula proved golden, in more ways than one.[85]

As the movement matures, of course, some of this may change. We need not accept the conclusions of extreme cultural evolutionists who expect the primitive side of the pentecostal character to wither up and die in the bright sun of modern civilization in order to suppose that time and experience will temper the wildest of visionaries. And in the process, pentecostals are sure to tumble into the dark turbulences of history, where life is not simple nor solutions clear cut. Awareness that the movement did not fall from the skies like a sacred meteorite but emerged at a particular time and place, and thus bore the earmarks of its time and place, may make it more difficult to sustain the power of first century signs and wonders. But if immersion in the messy details of history threatens a slowdown of institutional growth, it also promises a deepening of ethical self-awareness.[86]

At the same time, modern secular culture, smugly secure in its relativist premises and its quest for personal gratification, may find that unruly movements like pentecostalism really do have something to say that is worth hearing. "The Lord hath more light yet to break forth out of his Holy Word," Pilgrim John Robinson observed four centuries ago.[87] Pentecostals were not the first and almost certainly will not be the last of American-born sectarians to capture the religious world's attention. But they may demonstrate, in ways that other Christians have not often matched, that the ancient book and the ecstatic visions it harbored still bears the power to change lives and to transform cultures.

## NOTES

A number of colleagues critiqued earlier versions of this essay. Among those I especially wish to thank William R. Hutchison and George M. Marsden.

1. *Los Angeles Times*, April 18, 1906, 1.

2. The Gallup poll is described in Kenneth S. Kantzer, "The Charismatics among Us," *Christianity Today*, February 22, 1980, 24–29.

3. *The Assemblies of God: Current Facts 1991*, a pamphlet published by that body's Office of Information in Springfield, Missouri, in 1992, claims a U.S. constituency of 2,234,708, a U.S. membership of 1,324,800, and a world constituency of 22,723, 215.

4. David B. Barrett, "Annual Statistical Table on Global Mission: 1993," *International Bulletin of Missionary Research*, 17 (January 1993): 23. It should be remembered that many charismatics are Roman Catholics.

5. In 1991 membership for the major pentecostal bodies in the United States totaled 7,698,547. *Yearbook of American and Canadian Churches, 1991* (Nashville: Abingdon, 1991), 258–264. A research assistant and I compiled these figures by adding up the totals for all of the groups that are traditionally categorized as pentecostal. Random telephone sampling of the adult United States population in

1990 yielded adherence figures of 4,032,000. *Research Report, the National Survey of Religious Identification, 1989–90, The Graduate School and University Center of the City University of New York.* (I have not included 442,000 self-professed adherents of the "Church of God," since there are several decidedly non-pentecostal Wesleyan holiness bodies that go by the same name.)

6. For a concise, perceptive overview of the history of American pentecostalism, see R. G. Robins, "Pentecostal Movement," in *Dictionary of Christianity in America*, edited by Daniel G. Reid and others (Downers Grove, Ill.: Inter Varsity Press, 1990).

7. The insurgence of the world charismatic movement is ably described in Vinson Synan, *The Twentieth-Century Pentecostal Explosion* (Altamonte Springs, Fla.: Creation House, 1987).

8. I have briefly addressed the range of explanations that have been offered by scholars in "Bibliography and Historiography of Pentecostalism (US)," in *Dictionary of Pentecostal and Charismatic Movements*, edited by Stanley M. Burgess and Gary B. McGee (Grand Rapids, Mich.: Zondervan, 1988), 65–76.

9. Reductionist approaches predominate, at least in the non-theological scholarly literature. For critiques of such see Virginia H. Hine, "The Deprivation and Disorganization Theories of Religious Movements," in *Religious Movements in Contemporary America*, edited by Irving I. Zaretsky and Mark Leone (Princeton, N.J.: Princeton University Press, 1974), 646–664; Margaret M. Poloma, "An Empirical Study of Perceptions of Healing Among Assemblies of God Members," *Pneuma: The Journal of the Society for Pentecostal Studies*, 7 (Spring 1985): 61–77; and Grant Wacker, "Taking Another Look at the Vision of the Disinherited," *Religious Studies Review*, 8 (1982): 15–22. See also the fine survey of the assumptions and conclusions of the dominant social scientific literature in H. Newton Malony and A. Adams Lovekin, *Glossolalia: Behavioral Science Perspectives on Speaking in Tongues* (New York: Oxford University Press, 1985), chapter 7. More generally see R. Stephen Warner, "Theoretical Barriers to the Understanding of Evangelical Christianity," *Sociological Analysis*, 15 (Spring 1979): 1–9.

10. My understanding of the differences between cultural modernism on one hand and technological and social modernization on the other has been informed by Mary Douglas, "The Effects of Modernization on Religious Change," *Daedalus*, 3 (Winter, 1982): 1–19; Bruce B. Lawrence, *Defenders of God: The Fundamentalist Revolt Against the Mod-*

*ern Age* (San Francisco: Harper & Row, 1989), especially chapter 1; and John F. Wilson, "Modernity and Religion: A Problem of Perspective," in *Modernity and Religion*, edited by William Nicholls (Waterloo, Ontario: Wilfrid Laurier University Press, 1987), 9–18. Obviously there is no necessary link between pragmatism and modernity. Many ancients displayed highly pragmatic behavior and many moderns do not. But the present point is that pentecostals' pragmatic behavior *normally* led to an appropriation of the technological achievements and social arrangements of the post-industrial West.

11. Reliable figures on the size of the movement in the early years of the century are hard to come by, to say the least. In 1908, in the first attempt to construct a historical overview, India missionary Max Wood Moorhead estimated 50,000 adherents in the United States alone. Two years later Arthur S. Booth-Clibborn, a thoughtful and widely-traveled early leader, put the figure at 60,000 to 80,000 fully committed members, plus another 20,000 to 40,000 active supporters worldwide. Moorhead, "A Short History of the Pentecostal Movement," *Cloud of Witnesses*, 1908, 16; Booth-Clibborn, *Confidence*, August, 1910, 182. In 1936 the United States Bureau of the Census, listed 356,329 members for 26 known pentecostal sects. Given pentecostals' propensity to worship in homes, skid row missions, and rural meeting houses, many of which surely escaped the eye of the enumerators, it is safe to assume that the actual number was greater. I have taken these census figures from Robert Mapes Anderson's *Vision of the Disinherited: The Making of American Pentecostalism* (New York: Oxford University Press, 1979), 117.

12. The entwining of primitivist and of pragmatic strains revealed itself in the behavior of holiness pastor A. G. Garr years before his conversion to pentecostalism. See for example the wide-eyed supernaturalism *and* the streetwise bravura of Garr's actions at a 1903 street meeting in Dillon, Mont., in *Burning Bush*, September 10, 1903, 7.

13. Some of the faithful acquired the signature blending of primitive and pragmatic traits only after they converted. Consider for example one missionary correspondent in China who wrote to Nazarene leader A. M. Hills about the personality transformation that overtook holiness defectors to pentecostalism: "Quiet, retiring, teachable natures, who were charitable to a fault, were transformed into dogmatic, unteachable, schismatic and anathema-breathing souls." A. M. Hills, *The Tongues Movement* (Manchester [U.K.]: Star Hall, no date [presumably 1914]), 26.

14. "Primitivism," by George Boas, in *Dictionary of the History of Ideas*, edited by Philip Wiener (New York: Scribners, 1973).

15. The story of these and other explicitly restorationist bodies is ably told by Richard T. Hughes and C. Leonard Allen in *Illusions of Innocence: Protestant Primitivism in America, 1630–1875* (Chicago: University of Chicago Press, 1988).

16. *The Apostolic Faith* [Los Angeles], June-September 1907, 3.

17. *The Apostolic Faith* [Los Angeles], January 1907, 1, quoted in Edith L. Blumhofer, *The Assemblies of God: A Chapter in the Story of American Pentecostalism* (Springfield, Mo.: Gospel Publishing House, 1989), 1:143.

18. Addie A. Knowlton, *The New Acts*, June 1907, 8.

19. Frank Bartleman, *Azusa Street* (Plainfield, N.J.: Logos International, 1980), 21, Bartleman's emphasis. The main body of this work is an unaltered reprint of Bartleman's 1925 classic, *How "Pentecost" Came to Los Angeles—How It Was in the Beginning.*

20. Ardell K. Mead, *The Apostolic Faith* [Los Angeles], November 1906, 3; A. A. Boddy, quoting the letter of "a working-man," *The Christian* [U.K.], August 1, 1907, page number unreadable; Mrs. Hebden, *The Promise* [Toronto], May 1907, 2.

21. *Word and Work*, May 1910, 14; *The Apostolic Faith* [Los Angeles], December 1906, 3; typescript of interview with Azusa pioneer A. G. Osterberg, "Second Tape," Assemblies of God Archives, Springfield, Mo.

22. A. R. Haughawout, *The Apostolic Faith* [Baxter Springs, Kan.], June 1914, 3.

23. J. M. Vawter, *The New Acts*, August 16, 1906, 6.

24. Howard A. Goss, *The Winds of God: The Story of the Early Pentecostal Days (1901–1914) in the Life of Howard A. Goss, As Told by Ethel E. Goss* (New York: Comet Press Books, 1958), 78.

25. *The Church of God Evangel*, February 24, 1917, 1.

26. Aimee Semple McPherson, *This Is That: Personal Experiences, Sermons and Writings* (New York: Garland Publishing, 1985, unaltered reprint of 1919 original), 205–7.

27. Daniel C. O. Opperman, "Diary," 1905–1912, Assemblies of God Archives, Springfield, Mo.

28. George Floyd Taylor, "Diary," North Carolina State History Archives, Raleigh, N.C. This diary was kept for the years 1896, 1901, and 1908. Of course pentecostals' autobiographies and diaries, like all such texts, may have been penned more for the edification of potential readers than as a record of actual experiences. If so, that would make my argument stronger, for it shows that they regarded singleminded other-worldliness as the ideal.

29. James and June Glover Marshall, "R. G. Spurling Jr.: The Origins of the Church of God," *Reflections . . . Church of God Heritage*, Winter, 1990, 3.

30. *Glad Tidings* [San Francisco], July 1928, 10.

31. *Glad Tidings* [San Francisco], May 1926, 8.

32. *Showers of Blessings*, #8 [about 1910], 9.

33. Agnes N. O. LaBerge, *What God Hath Wrought: Life and Work of Mrs. Agnes N. O. LaBerge* (New York: Garland Publishing, 1985, unaltered reprint of 1920 original), 54.

34. Goss, *Winds*, 136.

35. *Christian Evangel*, October 17, 1914, 2.

36. *The Pentecostal Evangel*, April 4, 1914, 6.

37. *The Pentecostal Evangel*, November 1, 1919, 5.

38. Timothy L. Smith, *Called Unto Holiness: The Story of the Nazarenes: The Formative Years* (Kansas City, Mo.: Nazarene Publishing House, 1962), 37.

39. Charles Fox Parham, *The Life of Charles F. Parham Founder of The Apostolic Faith Movement*, compiled by Mrs. Charles Fox Parham (Baxter Springs, Kan.: The Apostolic Faith, 1930), 14.

40. For example, John Alexander Dowie, Fred Vogler, and Frank Ewart emigrated from Australia; Stanley Frodsham, A. W. Frodsham, Noel Perkin, and George T. Studd from Britain; Andrew Urshan from Persia.

41. A. A. Boddy, *Confidence*, September 1914, 176. For Boddy's incessant globe-trotting, which was, if not typical, at least not rare among early leaders, see the typescript biography by his daughter, Mother Joanna Mary Boddy, "Alexander Alfred Boddy, 1854–1930," Assemblies of God Archives, Springfield, Mo.

42. See for example the fat file of newspaper clippings tracking the continental crisscrossings of evangelists John S. and Hattie McConnell, Assemblies of God Archives, Springfield, Mo.

43. Bartleman, *Azusa*, 146–7.

44. Alfred and Lillian Garr, quoted in B. F. Lawrence, *The Apostolic Faith Restored* (St. Louis: Gospel Publishing House, 1916), 98.

45. Gary B. McGee, *"This Gospel . . . Shall Be Preached": A History and Theology of Assemblies of God Foreign Missions to 1959* (Springfield, Mo.: Gospel Publishing House, 1986), 77.

46. For missionaries, see Joseph H. and Blanch L. King, *Yet Speaketh: Memoirs of the Late Bishop Joseph H. King* (Franklin Springs, GA: Pentecostal Publishing House, 1949), 191. For local churches see *Glad Tidings* (Kenedy [correctly spelled], Tex.]) September 1924, 1–2. See also the verbal altercation between patriarchs J. R. Flower and George Brinkman over financial accountability, recounted from one perspective in *The Pentecostal Evangel*, November 15, 1918, 7, and from the opposite in *The Pentecostal Herald*, October 1919, 3.

47. See Wayne E. Warner, "Publications," in *Dictionary of Pentecostal and Charismatic Movements*. Examples of publications launched by women include *The Apostolic Faith* [Portland, Ore.], edited by Florence Crawford and Clara Lum; *The Bridal Call* edited by Aimee Semple McPherson with assistance from her mother, Minnie Kennedy; *Bridegroom's Messenger*, edited by Elizabeth A. Sexton; *Elbethel*, edited by Cora McIlray; *The Latter Rain Evangel*, edited by Lydia Piper and Anna C. Reiff; *Triumphs of Faith*, edited by Carrie Judd Montgomery; and *Trust* edited by Elizabeth V. Baker and Susan Duncan.

48. For example, D. W. Kerr edited and published *The Pentecostal Missionary Report* out of his church in Cleveland, Ohio; Robert Craig edited and published *Glad Tidings* out of his church in San Francisco; Samuel G. Otis edited and published *Word and Work* at the campmeeting grounds in Framingham, Mass.

49. Michael G. Owen, "Preparing Students for the First Harvest," *Assemblies of God Heritage*, Winter, 1989–90, 3–5, 16–18; Lewis Wilson, "Bible Institutes, Colleges, Universities," in *Dictionary of Pentecostal and Charismatic Movements*.

50. Goss, *Winds*, 154.

51. *The Apostolic Faith* [Los Angeles], October 1906, 2.

52. A. J. Tomlinson, *The Last Great Conflict* (New York: Garland Publishing, 1985, unaltered reprint of 1913 original), 68–69.

53. Tomlinson, *Last*, 38.

54. *The Apostolic Faith* [Houston], October, 1908, 2; *Midnight Cry*, November, 1907, 2; *Pentecost*, April–May, 1909, 4, *Seattle Post-Intelligencer* August 29, 1907, 6, and September 3, 1907, 4. There is no reason to believe that Ryan knew a word of Japanese, which makes his venture to Japan all the more audacious. I owe the *The Pentecost* reference to Wayne Warner, and the *Post-Intelligencer* references to Professor Cecil M. Robeck of Fuller Seminary.

55. Goss, *Winds*, 65.

56. Stanley F. Frodsham, long-time editor of the Assemblies of God's *The Pentecostal Evangel*, won lasting notoriety for remaining lost in the heavenlies. "Brother Frodsham had many gifts," a colleague recalled years later, "but discernment was never one of them." Interview with Wayne Warner, August 29, 1992.

57. Goss, *Winds*, 17, regarding Parham.

58. Lewiston, Maine, newspaper reporter describing Frank S. Sandford, quoted in Shirley Nelson, *Fair, Clear, and Terrible: The Story of Shiloh, Maine* ([Lathan, NY]: British American Publishing, 1989), 78.

59. Charles William Shumway, "A Study of 'The Gift of Tongues,'" A.B. thesis, University of Southern California, 1914, 179, regarding William H. Durham.

60. Anderson, *Vision*, 103–104. It is difficult to determine the life expectancy of first generation leaders, partly because the records are spotty, and partly because there is no consensus as to who should be included. With those qualifications in mind, I selected one hundred persons from the *Dictionary of Pentecostal and Charismatic Movements* whose birth and death dates are known and who, in my judgment, served as pathfinders during the formative years from 1905 to 1920. The median birth and death dates for those leaders was 1869 and 1943, yielding a life-span of seventy-four years. In contrast, the typical American born in 1866 (the year closest to 1869 for which census figures are available) lived only fifty-four years. Though this is hardly a scientific sampling, these figures do suggest that far from being sickly, as charged, pentecostal trail blazers exhibited unusual vigor. See "Years of Life Expected at Birth," compiled by National Center for Health Statistics, in *The World Almanac and Book of Facts 1992* (New York: World Almanac, 1992), 956.

61. Victor G. Plymire, typed autobiography, no title, Assemblies of God Archives, Springfield, Mo.

62. Goss, *Winds*, 73.

63. *The Apostolic Messenger*, February–March 1908, 2? (page number not clear).

64. *The Pentecost*, August 1909, page number not available.

65. *Word and Witness*, December 20, 1912, 2. Bell did not acknowledge that volunteers helped him mail out the periodical—which may say a good deal about the image he desired to project. Interview with Wayne Warner, August 31, 1992.

66. *Diary of A. J. Tomlinson*, edited by Homer A. Tomlinson (Jamaica, N.Y.: Erhardt Press, 1955), III: 104–5. See also 140.

67. Henry Proctor, *Trust*, May–June 1930, 14.

68. Elizabeth Sisson, *The Latter Rain Evangel*, May 1909, 6–10. Members of the quasi-pentecostal

Shiloh community near Durham, Maine, routinely refused Novocaine for the same reason. Nelson, *Fair*, 332 of publisher's galley edition, omitted from published edition.

69. See for example Elizabeth Sisson, *The Latter Rain Evangel*, May 1909, 10. A graduate student who read this paper responded that Sisson's willfulness in the dentist's chair seemed more a reflection of primitivist other-worldliness than of pragmatic this-worldliness. Perhaps so. At the margins the two traits blended and often it is hard to know where to draw the line.

70. Anonymous, *Living Water*, reprinted without further citation in *Triumphs of Faith*, June, 1908, 123.

71. F. F. Bosworth, *Christ the Healer: Sermons on Divine Healing* (published by author, 1924), 98–99.

72. Carrie Judd Montgomery, *Faith's Reckonings* [tract], no date [about 1920], 9.

73. Dr. J. A. Krumrine, *Trust*, September 1915, 12–13.

74. Anecdote related by the daughter, Mildred Edwards, *Trust*, February 1915, 13.

75. Maude Craig, *Tongues of Fire*, August 15, 1900, 146, "me" emphasized in the original. This periodical, which bore the subtitle *From "The Church of the Living God The Pillar and Ground of the Truth*," was published by the quasi-pentecostal Shiloh community.

76. Margaret Poloma, *The Assemblies of God at the Crossroads: Charisma and Institutional Dilemmas* (Knoxville: University of Tennessee Press, 1989), chapter 9, especially 161, and Arthur E. Paris, *Black Pentecostalism: Southern Religion in an Urban World* (Amherst: University of Massachusetts Press, 1982), throughout.

77. Edith L. Blumhofer, *Restoring the Faith: The Assemblies of God, Pentecostalism, and American Culture* (Urbana, Ill.: University of Illinois Press, 1993), 254–260; Mickey Crews, *The Church of God: A Social History* (Knoxville: University of Tennessee Press, 1990), throughout, but especially chapter 7, "From Back Alleys to Uptown." For a one-sided though partly defensible exposé of pentecostals' relentless pursuit of the good life, see Robert Johnson, "Heavenly Gifts," *Wall Street Journal*, December 11, 1990, 1. See also Poloma, *Assemblies of God*, 153.

78. See for example Poloma, *Assemblies of God*, 48–49; William J. Samarin, *Tongues of Men and Angels: The Religious Language of Pentecostalism* (New York: Macmillan, 1972), 213; Luther Gerlach and Virginia H. Hine, *People, Power, Change: Movements of Social Transformation* (Indianapolis:

Bobbs-Merrill, 1970), 4–5; H. Newton Malony, "Debunking Some of the Myths about Glossolalia," in *Charismatic Experiences in History*, edited by Cecil M. Robeck, Jr. (Peabody, Mass.: Hendrickson, 1985), 105–106. This article was originally published in the *Journal for the Scientific Study of Religion*, 34 (1982): 144–148. According to this data, better educated and more prosperous adherents are *more*, not less, likely to speak in tongues and to espouse first century (or at least what outside journalists and academics like to think are first century) assumptions in religious matters than their less accomplished counterparts. Admittedly, these studies tested for the correlation between speaking in tongues and position in the social system, which is not exactly the same as pragmatism as I have defined it (that is, a willingness to appropriate the technological achievements and social arrangements of the modern West whenever it suits their purposes). But it is plausible to assume that above average education and wealth normally betoken a measure of pragmatic aptitude for getting along in the modern social system.

79. See for example Vance Packard, "The Long Road from Pentecostal to Episcopal," in *The Status Seekers* (New York: David McKay, 1959), 200–201, described in Martin E. Marty, *A Nation of Behavers* (Chicago: University of Chicago Press, 106). The same outlook undergirds Robert Anderson's otherwise superior study of pentecostal origins, *Vision of the Disinherited*. Anderson claims that pentecostals sought redress for the various deprivations they suffered in "other-worldly, symbolic, and psychotherapeutic" measures. By implication, once those deprivations disappear, the otherworldly measures will disappear too. See especially 229. See also James Davison Hunter, *American Evangelicalism: Conservative Religion and the Quandary of Modernity* (New Brunswick, N.J.: Rutgers University Press, 1983), especially 5–6, 131, and, for a sophisticated reworking of the argument, see *Evangelicalism: The Coming Generation* (Chicago: University of Chicago Press, 1987), especially 238–241. William G. McLoughlin used a different path to arrive at the same destination. He claimed that pentecostals, however numerically impressive, would remain mere "effluvia" incapable of "seriously threatening the old order" as long as they distanced themselves from modern mainstream culture. McLoughlin, "Is There a Third Force in Christendom?," in *Religion in America*, edited by McLoughlin and Robert N. Bellah (Boston: Beacon Press, 1968, first edition 1966), 45–72, especially 47, and McLoughlin, *Revivals, Awakenings, and Reform: An Essay on Religion and Social Change in America, 1607–1977*

(Chicago: University of Chicago Press, 1978), chapter 6, especially 212–216.

80. Pearl S. Buck, *The Exile* (New York: John Day, 1936), 58.

81. David Martin, *Tongues of Fire: The Explosion of Protestantism in Latin America* (Cambridge, Mass.: Basil Blackwell, 1990), 122, 140, 164; David Stoll, *Is Latin America Turning Protestant? The Politics of Evangelical Growth* (Berkeley, Calif.: University of California Press, 1990), 13, 36, 94; Everett A. Wilson, "Sanguine Saints: Pentecostalism in El Salvador," *Church History* 52 (1983): 186–198; Everett A. Wilson, "The Central American Evangelicals: From Protest to Pragmatism," *International Review of Mission*, January 1988, 93–106. More generally see Martin E. Marty's astute assessment of the functions of the interaction of primitivism and pragmatism in "Sophisticated Primitives Then, Primitive Sophisticates Now," *The Christian Century*, June 7–14, 1989, 586–591.

82. See for example Catherine Albanese, *America: Religions and Religion* (Belmont, Calif.: Wadsworth, 1992, second edition), 28–32.

83. See for example Virginia Lieson Brereton, *From Sin to Salvation: American Women's Conversion Narratives, 1800–1980* (Bloomington: Indiana University Press, 1991), chapters 3 and 7.

84. I owe this insight to David D. Hall, *Worlds of Wonder, Days of Judgment: Popular Religious Belief in Early New England* (New York: Alfred A. Knopf, 1989), 239–245. The signal exception to my generalization about historians of pentecostalism is Robert Mapes Anderson who, in *Vision of the Disinherited*, moved to the other extreme, discountenancing the approved script almost entirely.

85. Dan Morgan, *Rising in the West* (New York: Alfred K. Knopf, 1992), offers an intriguing case study of an extended family of sharecroppers who migrated from Oklahoma to California in the 1930s and quite literally made a fortune in construction, junk dealing, real estate, sports franchises, and retirement homes in the burgeoning economy of the Southwest. Morgan shows that the family's fervent pentecostal faith provided spiritual and communal legitimation for their perfectly legal yet financially aggressive (if not avaricious) behavior every step of the way.

To be fair, pentecostals often responded to the material needs of their own members at least by providing food, clothing, rent money, and the like, when those privations arose. But typically they acted on a purely case by case basis, uninformed by any systematic social ethic or recognition of the structural dislocations that might have caused such problems in the first place. More significantly, their leaders consistently refused to permit self-criticism of ease of lifestyle or the use of money by themselves or by the rank and file. In the 1970s and 1980s a few "mainline" pentecostal writers critiqued the "Faith Confession" movement, a subtradition that explicitly sanctified the pursuit of boundless personal wealth. But that critique proves my larger point precisely because it focused upon—and only upon—egregious and flaunted excess, not routine preoccupation with the good life. A signal exception to all of this is the work of pentecostal ethicist Murray Dempster of Southern California College. See for example his "Pentecostal Social Concern and the Biblical Mandate of Social Justice," *Pneuma: The Journal of the Society for Pentecostal Studies*, 9 (Fall 1987): 129–154, and "Christian Social Concern in Pentecostal Perspective: Reformulating Pentecostal Eschatology," *Journal of Pentecostal Theology*, 2 (1993): 51–64.

86. A profounder ethical sense may be coming into being. Pentecostals' preoccupation with laws pertaining to abortion and homosexuality in the 1980s and 1990s betokened a narrow yet very important entry into the broader sphere of public policy.

87. Robinson is quoted in Winthrop S. Hudson and John Corrigan, *Religion in America* (New York: Macmillan, 1992, fifth edition), 32–33.

SUBMISSIVE WIVES, WOUNDED DAUGHTERS,
AND FEMALE SOLDIERS

*R. Marie Griffith*

Stereotypes of conservative Christian women as submissive victims of patriarchal religious teachings have for too long blinded us from understanding their actual religious
experience. In this essay, Marie Griffith examines the multiple ways in which members
of the Women's Aglow Fellowship—an interdenominational charismatic women's
group—assert authority and exercise power even as they remain devoted to a religion
that propounds a conservative ideology of gender. Evangelical teachings on gender have
always varied, Griffith argues, so that even the most conservative women have available to them a variety of ways of interpreting such ideals as female submission to male
authority. In fact, Aglow women have been able to create and maintain an ideal of
Christian womanhood that is neither timidly passive nor aggressively "unfeminine."
While critical of the woman's movement for repudiating male authority, Aglow members also boldly assert the power of women to do great things in the world and, recently,
appear to be moving toward gender equality. Through the power of prayer, telling their
stories, and changing their behavior, Griffith concludes, Aglow women have created "a
variety of substantial yet flexible meanings through which they experience some degree
of control over their lives, however deflected it may often appear." By taking evangelical
women's religious experience seriously, Griffith's essay challenges feminists to recognize
the common ground shared by these overlapping female cultures.

# 21 🙣

# SUBMISSIVE WIVES, WOUNDED DAUGHTERS, AND FEMALE SOLDIERS

## Prayer and Christian Womanhood in Women's Aglow Fellowship

### R. Marie Griffith

DOROTHY WAS A YOUNG WIFE and the mother of two preschool boys in 1965, when she found herself wishing that her husband Elmer "could be someone different." "Overnight, by some quirk in my mental osmosis," she later wrote, "I became obsessed with the thought that my healthy, happy, needed-to-be-changed-in-my-sight husband was going to die." Believing her vision represented "a revelation from God," Dorothy began spending most of her time alone, brooding over her husband's imminent death. She "withdrew" from all social activities, "making excuses against participating in any endeavor that would take me from the house." She closed the drapes in her home to avoid visits from neighbors and was in bed by nine every night "to dwell undisturbed in my other world." She went so far in her preoccupation as to plan the details of Elmer's funeral service, "even to the hymns that would be sung." Yet she concealed her thoughts so well that Elmer "had no idea anything was wrong with me." Later describing this time as one of great illness in which she "subconsciously" wished for her husband to die, Dorothy noted emphatically, "Oh, God, how sick I was!"

Eventually, Dorothy broke her long isolation by confiding in a friend, who told her that her thoughts represented a delusion from Satan. Realizing that she "had been deceived" and that "God would [n]ever work in this way," Dorothy prayed. "As I prayed," Dorothy explained, "I realized the depth of that deception. The truth was, I wanted my husband more than I wanted anything else, whether he changed or not." She "gladly . . . renounced Satan and his lies and his hold on my life," then confessed everything to Elmer. Elmer's response to Dorothy's confession affirmed the rightness of her decision, for he became "a man I had never seen before. He had every right to slap me in the face but instead he took me in his arms. With tears streaming down his face he whispered, 'Honey, all I care about is that you get well.'" Dorothy began to recuperate from what she later called her "mental illness" by returning to the Bible and praying regularly for healing from her fear and guilt. After a few weeks, she felt Jesus speak to her the words of Luke 8:48: "Daughter, be of good comfort: thy faith hath made thee whole; go in peace." Surrendering herself to those words, she experienced release from the guilt and pain that had plagued her for so long.

Ten years later, Dorothy testified in print to the changes that occurred in her life following her confession and surrender:

> My life has been so utterly transformed that I can't find words to express it. My husband, who showed me his real strength the night he forgave me, became the man I had always longed for when I began to appreciate him. I had longed for a husband who would be my spiritual head; I have him. I had longed for a man who would counsel me spiritually rather than I, him; I've been blessed with one. I had longed for a husband who could pray down the power of God with believing prayer; I stand amazed now when I see Elmer's faith.

Finally in total submission both to God and to her husband, Dorothy felt herself to be healed from her terrible sickness and to be living a new life of joyous certainty and peace. In 1975, when her story was published in *Aglow* magazine, Dorothy was praying "constantly," thanking God for her "wonderful man" and for the friend who was "bold enough" to confront her with the fact of her delusion.[1]

Jerry grew up with an alcoholic, emotionally distant father. According to her account, printed in *Aglow* in 1974, she felt hostile toward him from a very young age and continued to resent him throughout much of her adult life, as his drinking worsened considerably. In 1971, when Jerry learned her father had cancer, she and her husband postponed their long-awaited vacation to visit him just prior to his major surgery; as she later testified, however, "I went to him, not from love, but because he was old, alone, and it was my duty." Seeing the care he would need following surgery, Jerry reluctantly moved her father close to her home and resigned as youth director at her church. Throughout his radiation therapy, he continued to drink every day, while Jerry bitterly contemplated the sacrifices she had made in her life for this man she did not love.

As her unhappiness increased, Jerry discussed the situation with her doctor and then her pastor, who told her she must rid herself of the hostilities in her life so that she "could be the effective Christian God wanted [her] to be." The minister prayed with her but she still felt despondent and burdened, not knowing "where to leave those hostilities." She began to pray daily that God would remove her bitterness toward her father and give her "a clean heart." She asked forgiveness for her disgust with her father's drunkenness and pleaded with God to help her love him as he was. On the fifth day of praying these forlorn prayers, she began to feel "totally immersed in God's love from the head to toe"; suddenly, "cleansing tears" flowed down her cheeks as she "began to laugh and praise the Lord." Surrendering herself to this unexpected, consoling experience of "such peace and love," she felt freed from her anger, "able to love freely and reach out for love."

From that time on, Jerry wrote, her obligation to her father became "a joy." As he lost strength, she "grew to love him so much." Shortly before he died, her father took her hand and for the first time said to her the words she had longed for all her life: "Jerry, honey, I love you." She told him she loved him too and, released from her anger and the suffering it had brought her, Jerry reportedly continued to feel the joyous inner peace that came to her during prayer. Jerry concluded her story: "It was a gift from God that I will always treasure, but a gift He could only give after He had taken away the hostilities in my heart."[2]

Dorothy and Jerry crafted their narratives for an audience consisting of participants in Women's Aglow Fellowship International, an organization that emerged out of the Full Gospel Business Men's Fellowship in 1967 as an interdenominational group "where those coming into the charismatic renewal could meet to pray, fellowship, and listen to the testimonies of other Christian women."[3] Known first as the Full Gospel Women's Fellowship, the group adhered to a twofold purpose, combining evangelization of non-Christian women with encouragement for Christian women perceived as starving from the so-called deadness of American mainline churches.[4] Although Aglow was originally a small, local fellowship based in Seattle, Washington, it grew quickly and steadily into an extensive national organization. In 1969, the group's leaders began publishing a newsletter, *Aglow*, which would eventually turn into a glossy magazine with over 75,000 subscribers. The magazine's growth, in turn, stimulated the global expansion of the fellowship itself, which has continued to spread across the United States and throughout much of the world into the 1990s.[5]

In the early days, as now, testimony and prayer were central devotional practices within the Aglow organization, enacted at local gatherings and worship services as well as transmitted in stories published in *Aglow* magazine and other printed texts. Whether experienced in public settings as oral communication or privately as written literature, both testimony and prayer provided women with means for sharing their everyday experiences—the sorrows as well as the successes—and for learning coping strategies from one another. Both in magazine articles and in local monthly fellowship meetings, Aglow members described their trials as wives and mothers, testifying to the misery of a life without Jesus and to the joy and peace received through prayer and complete surrender to God's will. Such stories were not simply or primarily confessional; rather, they were told in hopes that other women would find relief and truth in them, by feeling their own needs expressed in another woman's narrative and envisioning solutions to their own crises based on the lessons of the victorious narrator.

The stories of Dorothy and Jerry provide a useful point of departure for examining Aglow narratives and the devotional practices such narratives describe. Like so many other women in Aglow, these authors had experienced crises within their families and were struggling to love in the face of intense disappointment, frustration, and anger. In each case, the woman was challenged by other Christians to pray for release, and through prayer experienced, first, a change in her own attitude and, second, a change in her circumstances that eradicated the suffering. Surrendering to God, these stories proclaim, leads to freedom from depression, guilt, and hostility; submission brings victory.

Such stories begin to illuminate the complex meanings embedded in notions of "home" and "family" and the ways in which evangelical women who participate in Aglow have used prayer to alleviate the conflicts and contradictions that arise within their households. Incorporating powerful themes both from the broader evangelical culture and from contemporary therapeutic idioms, narratives like those of Dorothy and Jerry explicitly counsel their female audience to surrender their wills to God and to submit themselves to God's hierarchy of earthly representatives, particularly clergymen and husbands. According to narrative conventions, domestic unhappiness stems largely from stubborn willfulness, so that healing can only occur when the wife pliantly consents to obey her husband and allows him to reign as the leader of the home. While further analysis of the stories reveals multiple possibilities for reinterpreting and even subverting the doctrine of submission to women's own ends, it remains the case that most stories in this genre prescribe an exceptionally conservative model of traditional gender roles.

Examined over a much longer range and trajectory of narratives, however, these stories also open to us a medium for perceiving significant shifts over time in Aglow's teachings about women, submission, and power. Stories like that of Dorothy in particular recall other stories from Aglow texts printed in the 1970s, yet they differ in substantial ways from many stories printed from the mid-1980s on, when a perceptibly wider range of options around female submission and power gradually emerged. In order to unfold these shifting notions of Christian womanhood, this essay explores the range of meanings that Aglow women attach to female submission and surrender, historical changes in these meanings along with challenges to former attitudes, and the strategic uses of such meanings in reworking family relationships and responsibilities. Prayer, the turning point in Aglow stories, marks the moment when all attempts to assert control over the conditions in one's family life are willingly dissolved in favor of sacrificial obedience. In this way, prayer works as a kind of axis for the fashioning of practical Christian womanhood, enabling religious identity to be formed and reformed even as domestic life is presumably transformed as well.

### "THE MAN I'D ALWAYS LONGED FOR"

Many Aglow stories invoke the theme of marital disappointment, describing in explicit detail the authors' frustrations as wives. Like the women interviewed in studies conducted by sociologists Mirra Komarovsky and Lillian Rubin, and the survey respondents in the Kelly Longitudinal Study analyzed by historian Elaine Tyler May, women in Aglow have often expressed dissatisfaction with their husbands and have spent much time and effort sharing advice for dealing with difficult home lives.[6] Aglow magazines and books are filled with stories from women articulating lives of domestic pain, described variously in terms of abuse, neglect, lack of love, or simply boredom. Fantasies of suicide and divorce abound and are richly elaborated, as the authors tell of falling into bleak despair and of longing to escape through death. Only after reaching this final point of grim desperation is the path to healing revealed, a path that begins with a prayer of surrender and ends with a joyful commitment to wifely submission.[7]

While few evangelical women express fantasies about their husbands' deaths in terms as explicit as Dorothy's, her story is typical in the meanings she draws from her situation and in the messages she conveys about coping with an unhappy home life. Like Dorothy, writers typically describe domestic misery in terms of both sickness and sin, construing their despair as caused by Satan but deepened by their own acquiescence to it. Their lives feel isolated and they fail at their wifely roles because they wish for their husbands to be, in Dorothy's words, "someone different." In order to be healed, then, they must repent of their error and realize the "deception" behind it, taking full responsibility for their unhappiness and accepting their husbands without expecting them to change. Giving up all hopes or expectations of marital satisfaction and simply accepting the duties bestowed by their supposedly God-given role of wife as help-meet, these women describe the pleasant surprise of discovering the greater happiness that is the reward for this sacrificial obedience, some finding their husbands to be "the man I had always longed for." Two more stories will help illustrate this process as it is typically described in Aglow literature.

Mary, deeply disappointed in her marriage, was planning a divorce from her unappreciative husband, Cal, who frequently snapped at her with such cutting remarks as "Can't you ever be happy?" and "Just once I'd like to have a meal on time." Miserable and near despair, Mary asked Jesus to come into her heart, forgive her sins, and be the master of her life. Grimly, she prayed: "If you don't do it there's no point in going on with life. You aren't getting any bargain, but if you can use me, here I am." Shortly afterward she was baptized in the Holy Spirit and seemingly miraculous changes began occurring in all areas of her life, most significantly in her marriage:

> A few weeks later when again Cal said, "Where's lunch?" I began screaming and then stopped midway and prayed, "Jesus, I'm losing my temper, I'm sorry. Forgive me and help me." Once again Cal came in at noon and said, "Where's lunch?" I felt the old anger starting to rise in my body. I clenched my jaws shut so I wouldn't cry out. I prayed, "I'm losing it again, Jesus. Forgive me and help me." No bitter words came out and the anger backed down and disappeared. I was able to say later, "Cal, I've irritated you by not having your lunch ready. I'm sorry." He was amazed. From that time on we began to grow in love for each other and for Jesus until now, five years later, we are able to minister to others.

As Mary learned to surrender her anger to Jesus and submit herself lovingly to her husband, she writes, her misery dissolved and, without any apparent changes in Cal, her bleak marriage was transformed. As she felt herself filled to overflowing with the loving warmth and comfort of the Holy Spirit, the domestic tasks that once made her life feel like drudgery became "a joy."[8]

Donna, who once felt lost and disconsolate in her marriage, recalled that earlier period as her own "state of rebellion." Her bitter conclusion at the time, however, was that she "had married the wrong man. At least that was a good excuse for my being in such a mess." Resentful of her husband's constant changes in career plans, she began criticizing Doug and telling him what to do. "I felt my ministry was to constantly let my husband know how backslidden he was, how unspiritually-minded he was, and that I was doing all I could to hang on in the hope that some day he would wake up and see the light." From Doug's point of view, she later realized, she was not being "a help-meet for his needs": "Unaware of my position as a wife I thought God had made me a leader and that my husband was not making a very good follower."

Finally, after God reprimanded her, Donna says she realized that she needed to surrender to Jesus. When she did, she later wrote, "it seemed a lot of the blame I had put on my husband for things just disappeared. God completed the healing he had begun in our marriage." Her lesson for her readers is to follow her example in submitting themselves to God and husband:

> You may never be able to change your circumstances. If you have five children, you have five children. If your husband is a doctor, your husband is a doctor. If your husband works as a plumber, that is his job. Quit saying, "If my circumstances were only different, then I know God could use me." But begin to pray, "Jesus, help me to allow You to use me in the circumstances in which You have seen fit to place me."

Accepting the circumstances of one's life, even the aspects that seem least appealing, and then striving to fulfill one's God-given roles within those circumstances: these steps constitute the presumed recipe for a happy life, supplying the means for achieving contentment in the midst of daily struggles.[9]

The stories of Mary and Donna, like that of Dorothy, assure their readers that good results will follow a wife's willing acquiescence: once women's attitudes are transformed and they accept their submissive role, their husbands also become happier and more benevolent, reflecting the benevolence of God. Importantly, such stories are indicative of the ways personal power may be encoded in the doctrine of submission, as the women center their narratives on their own capacity to initiate personal healing and cultivate domestic harmony. While not viewed as essential to the woman's healing, changes in a husband's behavior furnish added confirmation that such a healing has indeed taken place. For instance, the fact that Dorothy's husband actually wept when she told him of her illness is highly significant to her story. Rather than slapping her in the face, as she says he had "every right" to do, Elmer embraced her lovingly and expressed his concern that she be healed. Likewise, Mary's husband, Cal, responded to her newfound submission with love and appreciation, and Donna's husband, Doug, was transformed even as she was. Such changes, these writers assert, occurred in large part as the result of the decisive actions of the wives.

These narratives are meant to convince *Aglow* readers of the sincerity of the husbands' love for their wives and the assurance of their manly protection; as Dorothy writes of Elmer, he "showed me his real strength the night he forgave me." Such husbands represent the ideal Christian man, upholding the image of a loving Father God: strong yet gentle, a dynamic leader who is unafraid to express tender feeling, stern and rugged in his righteousness yet willing to forgive and to respond in benevolence. Dorothy, Mary, and Donna are in submission to their husbands' authority, but that authority, like Jesus', is depicted as compassionate and wise, never dominating or cruelly oppressive. Submit to your husband, the authors instruct their readers, and you, too, will discover the man you've always longed for, his seeming harshness softened by your willing obedience to his demands.

This message may be reassuring to women whose husbands are Spirit-filled Christian men, holding a similarly benevolent perspective on male authority, but for women whose husbands are "unsaved" or "backslidden," as is often the case, exhortations to wifely submission may be more ambivalently received. This problem has been repeatedly addressed in the Aglow literature as a common dilemma. In 1974, an anonymous writer, her own "heart ach[ing]" as the wife of an "unbeliever," offered this somewhat gloomy advice:

> Sometimes a Christian wife is under bondage in her home. It is not her own to do with as she pleases. In God's divine order, the wife is placed under the authority and direction of the husband whether he is saved or not. If he does not wish her to accept visits from her minister or have church meetings there, then according to Scripture, she should abide by his wishes. . . . At times you may feel that you can't bear another week, another month—and you will be right; you can't. However, you can live for today and this is all that you are asked to do.

Urging her readers to do all they can to love and serve their husbands, she concludes with great hopefulness that "[T]he Christian wife, by her trust, her prayers, her life and her love, can loose the Holy Spirit and the grace of God to do a special work in her husband's life."[10]

This lesson of submitting to one's non-Christian husband, in hopes that he will eventually be saved through the good example of his wife, is extended frequently in Aglow literature into a lesson on surrendering more fully to God. Another anonymous wife of an unsaved husband articulated this dynamic in poignant terms: "Each time Ralph has failed me, I have grown closer to the Lord and have learned to love my husband more." Over the years, she says, she has learned to be patient and to await God's plan for her husband, who—she is certain—will someday be saved.

> At first I prayed for my husband's salvation; now I simply and gratefully thank God for it. . . . Often I get specific in my prayers concerning events I want my husband to attend, things I'd like him to read, facts I want him to hear. But I have learned not to be disappointed if these prayers are not answered the way I want them to be. God knows more about it than I do.

Acknowledging the continuing temptation to despair, she notes:

> Sometimes even now circumstances seem so bad that I can't pray. During these times, the Lord has taught me to say, "Lord, I don't understand. I'm weary, but Your Word says You'll never fail me or forsake me, so it's up to You, Father." As soon as I start to pray in this way in difficult times, peace comes over me. I know He understands and I can wait for Ralph's salvation with the assurance that everything is under control.

The only option for dealing with an unsaved husband in these Aglow stories is cheerful submission to his will in mundane things, construed as an act of surrender to God's will. When the will of God and the will of the husband conflict, as they inevitably do, the wife must simply trust that her necessary obedience to her husband enables God to deal directly and swiftly with him.[11] In other words, as a male fundamentalist minister put it, "[S]ubmission is the wife learning to duck, so God can hit the husband."[12]

Informing these doctrines of male authority and female submission, as Dorothy and other Aglow women describe them, are meanings attached to the ideals of home and family, meanings formed out of desire for the pleasure and security that these ideals so invitingly promise. The significance of the family in American evangelical culture, long analyzed by historians of American religion, has been helpfully illuminated in anthropologist Carol Greenhouse's description of one community's understanding of the family as representing not simply "a set of relationships (as anthropologists might see the family, for example)" but rather "a set of interlocking roles, or identities."[13] The essential goal for individuals holding this view of family life is to perfect the various roles expected of them— wife, mother, daughter, sister, husband, father, son, brother—and then to feel those roles as authentic and natural. She concludes that "family life, while all-important as a model for society itself, is also crucial to the cultural formation of individuals by isolating them within relationships over which they believe they have no control."[14]

What such a conceptualization of the family means, as Greenhouse observes, is that family harmony hinges on the expectation that each member will perform his or her God-ordained role properly, accepting and following the prescriptions that each role carries within it. When conflict arises, the purported solution is the restoration of proper, rule-governed behavior. Like other groups rooted historically and socially in pentecostal, fundamentalist, or evangelical culture, Women's Aglow has always idealized the family and, like Greenhouse's community, has taught that the antidote to family disharmony is renewed clarification of precisely defined roles.[15] Thus, even as Aglow stories and prayers have been filled with references to the pain of marriage, motherhood, and domestic life generally, they emphasize how such pain may be healed through a submissive and disciplined commitment to what is perceived as true Christian womanhood. The stories recounted here suggest a context in which women describe neglectful parents, distant husbands, and delinquent children, but whose relationships are eventually transformed and made whole because of a woman's submissive behavior. Yet it is evident from these accounts that the family continues to be a source of great suffering; no family manages fully to live up to the expectations and ideals promoted by the popular idealization of the "Christian home."

In her important study of evangelical family life, sociologist Judith Stacey examines the complexities and often unacknowledged contradictions within the "widespread nostalgia for eroding family forms" currently prominent in many varieties of political and religious conservatism. Her research, which uncovers the ordinariness and frequency of divorce behind the rhetoric upholding the "traditional family," is suggestive of the negotiations made by those whose own family patterns clash with their religious ideals.[16] As with Stacey's families, the hope of Aglow women and their sisters of creating a perfect family inevitably remains at least partially unrealized. In cases where even moderate domestic happiness seems impossible, an alternative family may be constructed, taking the place of the disappointingly real family at home. Where no loving father is present, there is a protective, nurturing Father in heaven; for those whose husbands are uncommunicative and generally inadequate, God or Jesus may act as the romantic lover-husband, ever faithful and solicitous of His beloved's needs. Books published by Aglow Publications confirm these possibilities, encouraging readers to "experience the nurturing side of God's character" and to become the "chosen bride" of Jesus.[17]

Several Aglow writers have fruitfully utilized a passage from the book of Isaiah: "For your Maker is your husband—the Lord Almighty is his name."[18] Jo Anne, a single mother of two, appeals to her readers' desires for a perfect husband when she writes, "How would you like to be married to a husband who is always faithful, ever concerned for your welfare, who wants only the best for you and who will love you no matter what you do?" Quoting Isaiah, she responds to her own question: "Surprise! The Bible says we've already got exactly that kind of husband. The God of the Universe my Husband! What a mind-blowing idea." Recounting various stories of learning gratefully to accept this notion and to submit to God as her husband, Jo Anne offers other unmarried women the "opportunity" to "take [God] seriously" and to receive Him as the perfect husband.[19]

Another woman, widowed only three weeks at the time she wrote her story, tells of receiving a dozen long-stemmed roses, with a card saying they are from friends.

> I hold them in my arms and smell their sweetness. As I lift my face from them, I know without any hesitation or doubt that despite the card, these roses have come from Jesus. He knew I needed such a gift at this precious moment: the type of gift that a man sends a woman, a husband gives a wife. It is just one more way that Jesus has become my husband, one more way He is saying, "I love you."[20]

Having God as a husband does not necessarily preclude having an earthly husband as well, however; as another widow writes after her remarriage: "God said that He would be my husband, revealing Himself to me as the Lord of Hosts, the powerful present One in the time of need . . . but on top of that He sent me a flesh-and-blood husband, Andy."[21] Whether a woman is widowed or divorced, married or remarried, God acts as the perfect husband for her, wisely guiding and protecting her in a perfectly ordered "love relationship."

The characterizations of God as perfect husband closely resemble the heroes of contemporary romance literature analyzed by literary critic Janice Radway in *Reading the Romance.* "Strong and masculine" yet "equally capable of unusual tenderness, gentleness, and concern for [the heroine's] pleasure," the ideal romantic hero for the Smithton readers interviewed by Radway is one who recognizes "deep feelings" of love for the heroine and who realizes that "he could not live without her." Like Radway's readers, who want their hero to be both protector of the heroine and dependent on her love, Aglow women desire their divine hero-husband both to lead and look after them and to be nurtured by the mutually gratifying relationship between them. Following God's commands, doing everything He asks of them and more, flattering Him continually by "just telling Him how wonderful He is and how much we love Him," Aglow women fulfill their visions of perfect love relationships, satisfying their unfulfilled needs for affection, protection, and self-esteem through a perceived marital relationship with God.[22]

In addition to the alternative "marriage" provided by a relationship with God, the Aglow community, acting as "a network of caring women" (the organization's slogan), becomes a kind of surrogate family for the women who participate, at least ideally. Members frequently refer to each other as "my sisters," a common enough appellation in evangelical circles but one with distinctive meanings in the Aglow context. For women who have experienced painful estrangement from their own families, and who have perhaps failed to find fulfillment in recovery groups, a local Aglow fellowship may provide a satisfying form of intimacy, although, as I have observed elsewhere, such closeness may carry the cost of lost privacy or undesired reinterpretation of one's story.[23] More specifically, the organization may allow for the reinvention of one's personal identity, as one joins in a collective process of narrative construction. The relatively recent creation of Aglow "support groups," advertised as providing "safe places" for hurting women, contributes to the sense of Aglow as a refuge within which women share their feelings of pain and frustration and find love.[24] Feeling herself to be in relationship with God, a woman may come to feel a part of the Aglow "family," her felt need for love potentially nourished within the sisterhood offered there.

As women come to feel closely bonded with other Aglow members, conflict may arise in the home. Many women speak of conflicts between their religious lives and their family lives, describing husbands jealous and resentful of the time their wives devote to Aglow activities as well as their new devotion directed toward God and time spent on religious practices such as daily Bible reading and prayer. Women teach each other how to deal with those kinds of pressures: by attending to one's husband more willingly, for instance, and trying to include him and other family members in daily devotions without "forcing" anything on them; or, as one Aglow speaker recommended to her listeners, by staying home from church and "lying in bed" with one's husband on occasional Sunday mornings, making sure he feels cared for and loved.[25] Predictably, however, tensions in this area are not easily resolved. The doctrine of submission, which applies equally whether one's husband is a "Spirit-filled Christian" or not, may in fact increase these tensions, as already suspicious husbands mistrust the motives behind their wives' new and seemingly inexplicable behavior. As Aglow women share strategies with one another, they address these and related concerns about balancing domestic duties with spiritual responsibilities, committing themselves fully to both as they believe God requires.

Praying together helps Aglow women create alternative families and ease the conflicts that may occur when such alternatives supplant one's earthly family at home. Praying aloud before an audience that includes many others dealing with similarly conflicted situations allows the women both to articulate the felt crises of their lives—and perhaps gain sympathy and support from the other women who hear their stories—and to begin to resolve these crises by surrendering their own will and asking God to take control. Perhaps the most important role prayer plays is to turn Aglow women toward accepting the limitations of the family and the need to work unceasingly at improving their capacities as wives and homemakers. Through an intricate and highly ritualized process, guilt and anger are reportedly transformed into surrender and acceptance, and possibilities for redemptive healing emerge.[26]

## THE POWER OF SUBMISSION

Surrendering one's will to an authority is a vital meaning of submission, but this is not its sole meaning for evangelical women; in fact, submission is in no way a transparent, unidimensional, or static concept but is rather a doctrine with a discernible, fluid history, even in the relatively short time period examined here. Far from being a fixed entity churning out traditional teachings on gender roles, evangelical theology has always been varied, so that even a group as apparently conservative as Aglow contains a broad repertoire of choices and mutable scripts around such ideals as female submission to male authority. While many outsiders might readily assume that conservative Christian women such as those who belong to Aglow are merely participating in their own victimization, internalizing patriarchal ideas about female submission that confirm and increase their sense of personal inferiority, the women themselves claim that the doctrine of submission leads both to freedom and to transformation, as God rewards His obedient daughters by healing their sorrows and easing their pain. Thus interpreted, the doctrine of submission becomes a means of having power over bad situations, including circumstances over which they otherwise may have no control. As close attention to both oral and written narratives suggests, the apparent simplicity of the ideology of submission masks a rich variety of meanings that, once enacted in devotional practice, prove to be more intricate and subtle than they initially seem.

One text that illuminates these intricacies and complicates the notion of submission as passivity or meek subordination is a kind of evangelical self-help book for women, written by Darien B. Cooper, entitled *You Can Be the Wife of a Happy Husband*. First published in 1974, this book is still in print and is used and revered by Aglow women to this day. While teaching submission as "God's role for you as a woman and a wife," Cooper assures her female readers that in becoming submissive wives they will also see changes in their husbands, and that they will find the greatest happiness possible fulfilling their role:

> I believe the role of the wife in the marital relationship is the choice role. . . . Submission never means that your personality, abilities, talents, or individuality are buried, but that they will be channeled to operate to the maximum. . . . Submission never imprisons you. It liberates you, giving you the freedom to be creative under the protection of divinely appointed authority.[27]

Cooper supports this perspective by insisting on women's need for "protection" in a dangerous world, claiming that within this protected sphere women may enjoy the flourishing of their God-given creativity.

According to Cooper, a woman's marital dissatisfaction stems from "preconceived ideas of how her husband should act." She writes, "When he fails to live up to your expectations, you may be hurt, irritated, and disappointed. You and your husband will only be contented and free when you quit setting goals and stop expecting him to be who he is not." Cooper tells women to display pride in their husbands rather than shame, to accept them as they are rather than "ridiculing" or "belittling" them. Instead of trying to manipulate a husband, she advises, "Respond to his leadership in a relaxed manner, and you will find that your husband usually wants to please you." She recounts story after story of women whose wifely submission improved their marriages by bringing their husbands closer to Jesus. The husband will respond lovingly to a submissive attitude, Cooper asserts: "As God's Word fills and controls your heart, you will gain the praise of your man. Wait for it; do not demand it." Throughout her book Cooper enjoins women to "Accept him as he is!"[28]

In Cooper's view, then, submission brings benefits not only or even primarily to the husband, but also and equally to the wife. Submission is not about grimly resigning oneself to a subordinate position but rather is about "freedom." She addresses women's concerns about submission: "Many women are afraid that they will lose their individuality if they subject themselves to their husbands. . . . Paradoxically, only when you submit to God—in any area—do you know the fullest freedom and power."[29] Submission may be about dependency and compliance, but it is not about helplessness, according to Cooper. Of course, the very fact that she feels compelled to make submission seem more palatable for women evidences conflict over the notion, a point to which I will return.

Cooper's book, as I have noted, is widely used among Aglow women, and she continues to speak to Aglow groups around the country on how to have "happy husbands." Her claim—that the doctrine of submission is ultimately beneficial to women—gets added energy from the belief that men's natural passions need to be domesticated and contained; left unchecked, these passions will rage out of control and may cause injury to women. According to Cooper, men's sexual appetites must be satisfied lest they revert to savagery or adultery. She advises her readers to satisfy their husbands sexually and warns, "If you do not fulfill your husband's sexual needs, you may be a stumbling block in his life and cause him to be led away from spiritual truths instead of toward God." She concludes this section: "Your husband will be the happy man you want him to be when he feels that you accept him as he is, admire him for his masculinity, and put him first and foremost (after God) in your life. He will feel needed at home because he knows he is respected as the family leader, provider, and protector."[30] The wife's influence is also her responsibility; it is up to her to see that her man is kept satisfied as well as contained, assuring him of his worth by admiring his virility.[31]

Such advice has long been articulated by antifeminist women, among others, to diverse ends. In *The Power of the Positive Woman*, for instance, antifeminist activist Phyllis Schlafly writes: "A wife must appreciate and admire her husband," observing that the marriage will fail unless "she is willing to give him the appreciation and admiration his manhood craves." Feminist writer Barbara Ehrenreich rightly notes that Schlafly's analysis, here and throughout her spoken and written pronouncements on similar matters, betrays a deeply distrustful and contemptuous image of men as variously weak or monstrous in contrast to women viewed as active and loving.[32] From this perspective, wifely submission is good for wives as well as husbands because it works as a strategy of containment. It is what men need to bolster their fragile egos, and women should ostensibly comply in order to maintain domestic harmony as well as their own security. If done properly, all parties benefit. Thus the author of a 1976 Aglow booklet, *Quiz for Christian Wives*, tells of the healing that took place in her unhappy marriage when she realized the importance of openly admiring the "good qualities" in her husband, Arthur: that is, the qualities for which *he* wanted to be admired, such as his "broad shoulders" and his "big strong hands." "Such a simple little thing," she remarks, was the turning point in their relationship and the beginning of her new life of love and joy.[33]

Nancy, a local Aglow leader whom I asked about wifely submission, repeatedly declared that she was a "former feminist" who had finally learned "to move beyond all that" into God's true purpose for her life. Having realized that feminism was "bad for [her] marriage," Nancy gave up trying to "compete" against her husband and learned to follow the "marriage principles" of wifely submission to male authority. When I pressed her to explain, Nancy brought up the Hollywood movie, *War of the Roses*, as an example of what happens when men and women do not obey God's prescribed roles and persist in doing things their own way: they hate, hurt, and ultimately destroy each other. Nancy's own marriage, in contrast, was allegedly saved when she committed herself to submitting to her husband, a commitment which, she admitted with a chuckle, she did not always manage to keep. In any case, Nancy assured me that her husband had in fact stopped drinking along the way and now made a conscientious effort to ensure that she felt happy and loved, a transformation that she attributed in great part to her obedience to the principle of wifely submission to the husband's authority.[34]

Related to this tactical notion of submission as a means for turning men into happy husbands who then want to please their wives is the notion of what may be termed "sacred housework," wherein surrendering to one's ordained tasks is seen as an act of worship that also leads to greater happiness in the home. This idea is frequently articulated in Aglow literature, as in *Aglow in the Kitchen*, a cookbook for Christian wives. The author of that book writes of being "stunned" when her husband taught her that "cooking and homemaking are ministries *to the Lord*." Recalling the kinds of "homey tasks" that Jesus had performed during His time on earth, she tells of getting the lettuce from the refrigerator, tearing it up for salad, and "talk[ing] to the Lord": "Jesus, thank You for showing me that housework is sacred. Help me to realize while I am cooking and cleaning that I am doing them for You because You are living here and my husband is Your representative." In this way, what was once drudgery is ostensibly transformed into worship, service, and domestic happiness.[35]

When housework is perceived as sacred, it may also become an important source of self-esteem. As a young housewife and mother whose husband was a traveling evangelist, Betty found herself "very dissatisfied" and "depressed." Finally, she was healed from her misery when Jesus gave her a "vision" of her "role in the home as a happy wife and mother." She began to see that if she were happy, her husband and her children would also be happy, a notion that allowed her to begin to see herself as "the 'hub' of the wheel," around which "everything revolves." She notes, "I began to see myself as VERY IMPORTANT to the members of my family." Her concluding words suggest the continuing ambivalence she feels toward this state, along with her hopeful determination to feel good about herself as a housewife: "I know from experience that I will not always be staying at home, but I also know that with God's help I can have that real contentment WHEREVER I AM."[36]

Here again the lesson disseminated is that surrendering to the roles of housewife and mother brings joy to everyone, most significantly to the submissive woman herself. As Betty tells her readers, women find joy and learn that they are "VERY IMPORTANT" when they simply yield to God's expectations of them, transforming housework from a source of boredom and depression into a wellspring of joy and self-esteem. The frequent admissions by Aglow authors that they find such work as cooking and cleaning and running errands mind-numbingly dull show that such a transformation is anything but easy. Still, in their description of submission and surrender as "natural" and in the reminder that other members of the family could not get along without them, the women of Aglow formulate what they perceive as a workable solution to a persistent dilemma, achieving a kind of pride and self-respect in the most mundane tasks.

Once again, the meanings of submission and surrender for these evangelical women prove to represent far more than simple passivity. They are central notions around which the women of Aglow rework their identities, creatively balancing compliance with strength as they transform themselves into ideal Christian women. At the same time, submission holds instrumental value, by containing husbands and thereby regulating the home, and is capable of being subtly modified or subverted, so that the women retain a kind of mediated agency through their reliance on the omnipotent God. Out of a doctrine that could seem to leave them helpless, evangelical women have generated a variety of substantial yet flexible meanings through which they experience some degree of control, however deflected it may often appear.

The story does not end here, however, as a mere tale of creative acceptance of the doctrine of wifely submission. Since the mid-1980s, discussions of the subject have significantly dropped off in Aglow literature, more or less quietly. While wifely submission continues to receive scattered mention, the general message has perceptibly shifted toward a notion of modified or "mutual submission." Writers often emphasize that while the Bible clearly dictates female submission to male authority, earthly men have not infrequently abused that doctrine to their own selfish ends, rather than accepting their own authority as the kind of Christ-like responsibility intended by God. The chronological shift in meanings around wifely submission is most clearly seen in the popular Aglow Bible study, *God's Daughter*. Written by Aglow staff member Eadie Goodboy and first published in 1974, this booklet has been widely used by Aglow participants; by 1991, it had gone through fourteen printings. The tenth chapter of this text comprises the most comprehensive and sustained examination in Aglow literature of the biblical doctrine of submission, and the important changes that have taken place in this chapter over time indicate shifting notions of Christian womanhood in Aglow, as in American evangelicalism at large.[37]

In 1974, this chapter began by emphasizing the difficulty women face in accepting the doctrine of submission: "The area of submission in the Christian walk has been widely neglected and ignored. To many women it may carry threatening overtones. We visualize Jesus as our Shepherd and ourselves as sheep under His loving care, and we find it easier to yield to His Lordship spiritually than physically to people in authority over us." The passage goes on to observe that "our natural tendency is to confuse submission with servitude, and picture one who is submissive as downtrodden and abused, a 'doormat.'" Yet, the writer suggests, the opposite is the case. Just as the sacrifice made by Jesus on the cross was a "willing" act for the benefit of others, so too should the marriage relationship reflect that same willing self-sacrifice. Thus, "Submissiveness is not an outward form or a role of foolish servitude, but an attitude of the heart."

In this view, woman's particular vulnerability requires protection from man, which is why God places her under the headship of her husband (or, in the case of an unmarried woman, her father). The result is not imprisonment but just the opposite: "Since everything which comes to us from God is meant for our good, we find that coming into an attitude of submission produces freedom. A train is created to run on a track. As long as the train stays on its track, it is free to fulfill that for which it was made. When it jumps the track, chaos results." Rather than participating in the "role-reversal so common in society today," the author concludes, women are to find the vast "service and creativity in our God-ordained roles" as wives, mothers, and homemakers.

In 1985, this chapter was substantially altered. Now, rather than suggesting that teaching submission is like giving medicine to an unwilling child, the author places the idea of submission in the context of previous lessons about the joy of following God's will: "The emphasis of these lessons has been on the subject of yieldedness: letting or allowing the Lordship of Jesus to have total expression through our lives. We have been renewing our minds, unlearning old behavior patterns, tuning in to hear what the Father is saying, studying what He desires, becoming sensitive to sin and to the joy of obedience." She invites readers to "look again at this area of ministry of submission" which, though "often misunderstood or questioned," is the "root of all things spiritual, because it alone takes the proper attitude before God and others." Now, in place of the biblical passages emphasized in the earlier edition, verses are noted in which Jesus spoke of His own total submission to God; rather than turning this immediately into a lesson about wifely submission, moreover, the author points to Jesus' relationship with God as "the pattern for *us* to follow in our personal relationship with God." The chapter then moves into a detailed discussion of humility and of the choice entailed in making this commitment to God, a choice that seemingly has nothing to do with gender but is required of all people, men and women, as children of God.

Finally, the last third of the chapter turns to Ephesians 5:22, the passage about wifely submission that was the centerpiece for the earlier edition of this booklet. The author notes, "This may seem to be a difficult position for some of us who are married women to joyfully agree with, especially in an age when misunderstanding of this verse may have caused some abuse. We need to understand, however, what God desires and how He perceives it." Placing this verse in the context of the larger passage from which it is taken, the author notes that there are various scriptural "counterbalance(s)" to the notion of wifely submission and argues: "[S]ubmission to our husbands does *not* make us 'second class citizens' or those who are ranked 'lower on the totem pole' as lesser beings than the husband. As viewed by God, we have a side-by-side relationship. He looks at us as equally important, but each is designed to function for His glory, in his or her role." Urging a far more limited version of wifely submission to male authority than that earlier affirmed, the chapter ends by asserting that "The entire Christian life is to be a submitted life." Though still affirming gender role differences, this passage has excised the stress on female vulnerability, rebellion, and rigidly defined female roles so central to the original study.

What these different versions suggest is a range of variable notions pertaining to "power" and thus also to "surrender," a range that is confirmed by analysis of the larger literature of Aglow. There is, first, the most immediately apparent meaning of a surrender to God as a way of releasing divine power, enacted in (and only in) prayer; second, complete submission to the husband as God's representative and leader of the home; third, a more carefully nuanced form of the latter, which accepts the husband *as he is* while retaining some room for private critique of his behavior; and fourth, what I have termed "containment," that is, submitting more in word than in deed and celebrating the power to influence—or, in less flattering terms, manipulate—a husband to one's own ends.[38] Although Aglow writers often jumble together these assorted meanings, the categories hold very different implications for thinking about the resources one has at hand for dealing with familial relationships, and for thinking about one's own capabilities in the larger world. As teachings on proper gender roles have fluctuated over time, the strictest of these interpretations has gradually given way to those that are more lenient, flexible, and centered on women's capacity to release divine power and effect change.

Both submission and surrender, then, turn out to be far more slippery concepts than they first appear. Out of the hodgepodge of meanings embedded within them may emerge diverse and even contradictory attitudes toward the peculiar obligations and freedoms bestowed on women by an omnipotent God. While the repressive potential is unmistakable, the possibility also exists for what feminist theologian Sarah Coakley has approvingly termed "power in vulnerability," that is, "the willed effacement to a gentle omnipotence which, far from 'complementing' masculinism, acts as its undoing."[39] In between these two options is the more commonly stated objective, that submission is most valuable for wives, that by means of willing and joyous submission, a man may be domesticated, his will to power contained and transformed into loving protection of his wife. In the latter case, submission provides a strategy for getting what a woman wants, which in these cases appears to be the taming of men's naturally monstrous urges into gentleness, appreciation, and affection and the creation of ideal Christian families. In this sense, submission may work as a tactic of the relatively powerless to recover their power and to create a space within which they may feel both fulfilled and free.[40]

## "UNABLE TO LIKE AND YET COMPELLED TO LOVE": FROM WIFELY SUBMISSION TO DAUGHTERLY ANGER

The disillusionment and disappointment Aglow women have felt toward their own families is repeatedly apparent in Aglow narratives from the 1970s to the 1990s, as is the desire to replace disappointment with happiness and bring greater familial harmony into their homes. The homes women increasingly seek to correct are, however, not only the ones they find themselves in at the moment but also the ones they recall experiencing as children. An examination of Aglow literature shows that growing numbers of women since the 1970s have described the families they grew up in as debilitating for them when they later tried to form families of their own. Stories are filled with accounts of abusive, alcoholic parents who did not attend lovingly to their children and whose violent methods of coping with their own misery wounded those around them. Like Jerry, whose story I recounted at the beginning of this essay, countless women tell about wretchedly unhappy childhoods in which they were bereft of nurturing and grew up unaware or mistrustful of parental love.[41]

Becky, writing in 1985, told of her parents' divorcing when she was two years old. By her senior year in high school, she had seen her father only once. "It was obvious he didn't care about pursuing a relationship with me or my younger sister. I tried not to dwell on it, but whenever I found myself in an uncomfortable position . . . I would fall to pieces."[42] Jessica, writing her testimony for *Aglow* magazine in 1990, recounted her pain at being the daughter of a severely alcoholic mother and her longing for a "shared-love relationship with Mom" that was not to be. When her rage, "a too-long-dormant volcano," finally erupted at her mother, Jessica was tormented by guilt and fear until she begged God to help her heal and understand her mother's own pain. Even now, she writes, "the tears begin to fall again. But now tears of release mix with those of pain; release for what might have been, but is not; for the devastation alcoholism has caused; and for my mom—the woman I am unable to like and yet compelled to love."[43]

Accounts such as these have spawned an outpouring of self-help books published by Aglow since the mid-1980s, all centered on healing from the childhood traumas of neglect and abuse. In *Daddy, Where Were You?: Healing for the Father-Deprived Daughter*, the author writes vividly of her own pain when her father deserted her at a young age, and of the healing she received from learning that God is her true Father.[44] Another, *When Love Is Not Perfect: Discover God's Re-Parenting Process*, discusses issues surrounding child abuse—emotional, physical, and sexual—and provides "a biblical framework to help victims experience God's re-parenting."[45] Others, such as *Healing the Angry Heart: A Strategy for Confident Mothering*, further describe the "tragic cycle" of child abuse and low self-esteem, offering help for those who have been caught in this cycle as children and, later, as mothers.[46] All authors advocate prayer for healing and counsel their readers to ask God to help them forgive and love their abusive parents, as difficult as such an act may seem. In practicing this kind of forgiveness, readers are told, victims of abuse will in turn be free to love their own children more fully. It is not a forgiveness easily achieved, writers agree, but rather one that must be sought with determination and, once attained, carefully guarded. As one Aglow author urges, "Pledge to pray for your parents every day."[47]

Childhood shame, rooted in emotional, physical, or sexual abuse, continues to be of great concern to Aglow women today. Glenda, a local Aglow officer, angrily recounted during our interview the ways in which her mother constantly made her feel like a "bad girl" as a child by incessantly criticizing her behavior, mocking her blemished complexion and frizzy hair, and ridiculing her awkwardness in front of other people. Glenda observed that her main problem throughout her life has been low self-esteem, noting, "I felt like I never measured up." Only when a woman prayed with her at an Aglow meeting did she begin to realize, in her words, "the idiocy of everything I had pointed out [about myself]—none of us are worthy. That's why Jesus died on the cross!" After a long and painful process, Glenda says her relationship with her mother has been healed, yet throughout our conversations she constantly lambasted herself for being "a terrible mother" and always spoke in self-deprecating terms about herself. The persistent effects of Glenda's childhood shame were all too evident.[48]

This theme of looking at one's childhood for the causes of adult frustrations and unhappiness, then learning to forgive one's parents as the first step in healing, is repeatedly echoed by popular speakers at Aglow events. An example is Quin Sherrer, a longtime member of Aglow's international board, prolific writer of books and articles on prayer, and popular speaker at Aglow conferences, who publicly speaks about being deserted by her father at the age of twelve. At the time her father left, she says, she "closed off" her heart to him and vowed silently, "I'll never forgive him." Years of bitterness and "stuffing" her feelings of anger and hurt down inside herself changed after she was told by a minister to repent of her anger against her father and to forgive him. She was then able to go to her

father and experience the restoration of their relationship. Quin's story has become para-
digmatic for many women in Aglow dealing with similar feelings of hatred, as they struggle
to follow her example and hope for similarly miraculous results.[49]

As common as accounts of abandonment and abuse are in Aglow narratives, it would be
incorrect to identify Aglow as composed only of women who were abused as children or
whose primary concern is healing from parental neglect. Many narratives, in fact, do not
directly address such issues, while some women praise their parents as models of love and
virtue. Still, vast energy among Aglow women is given to teaching each other to pray for
and forgive parents for their shortcomings and to work through the anger caused by their
mistakes. The introduction of Aglow "support groups" in 1989 and their explosion since
that time give evidence of this theme, illustrated in the following passage describing
women in pain:

> They live next door, they jog past you in the park, brush against you in the express elevator of
> the downtown office building, and hand you your prescription from the pharmacy. The cu-
> mulative effects of dysfunctional homes, divorces, abuse, addictions, compulsions, financial
> stress, and multiple role expectations have gripped the lives of countless millions of women,
> imprisoning them in hopelessness, isolation, shame, depression, and fear.[50]

Whatever the extent of actual abuse in these women's lives, it is evident that one function
of the narratives recounted in *Aglow* magazines and at their meetings, and of the prayers
described in these narratives, is to bring about healing from the pain and anger of perceived mistreatment at the hands of parents and husbands.

Two points bear emphasis. First, Aglow narratives have from the beginning contained
seemingly endless permutations on a common theme: the pain of family life. While a shift
in emphasis from marital problems to childhood traumas—and thus from the sin of wifely
disobedience to the pain of daughterly victimization—has apparently taken place, that
shift should not obscure the fact that both narrative scripts have been present from the beginning and continue to be articulated today, as women struggle to cope with various
forms of domestic unhappiness. Second, within the Aglow organization, there is a certain
cachet (as well as pathos) to having a bad family life. Expressions of sorrow are not simply
allowed but are in fact encouraged and take on scripted forms within the narrative context.
Like the recovery movement to which it is so intricately connected, Aglow fosters a certain
kind of victimology in which women's suffering is attributed to the family—often construed today as "dysfunctional"—yet becomes meaningful for Aglow women when domestic crises are identified as opportunities for personal atonement and growth. In this way,
the meaning of "bad parents" or a "bad husband" changes when women leave their homes
and enter Aglow: while living in an unhappy home might well be a terrible experience,
Aglow offers women the chance to reinterpret family crises in ways that replace the burden
of guilt and shame with redemption and hope for healing.

Although the notion of victimization and the conviction that one's "sickness" is one's
own burden of sin apparently contradict one another, these beliefs are held together
through an avowal of the need for prayer and surrender. In all the narratives, the key to restoration of the family is a prayer in which one confesses one's total impotence and begs for
help from God. Relinquishing her desire to control the circumstances of her life, the
woman surrenders her will to that of God and may submit to her husband or begin to

work through her anger at her parents. The result, which can occur only after the woman accepts responsibility for her situation, expresses repentance, and forgives her husband and any others toward whom she has felt anger, is a presumably transformed home life. Her surrender enables the woman to believe her sins have been forgiven, but it also works to rid her of her earlier sense of injustice and victimhood, bringing her out of bitter disappointment and depression into a sense of her own responsible agency. She is, according to the narrative formula, no longer victim but victor.

## "BEAUTIFUL BOLDNESS": WOMEN CALLED TO SPIRITUAL WARFARE

In 1980, Aglow President Jane Hansen heard a message from God, saying, "Aglow will be a network of praying, warring, interceding women, covering the face of the earth."[51] Since that time, spiritual warfare has occupied an increasingly important role in Aglow, as leaders and members have intensified their engagement in the putative battle being waged between God and Satan, as interpreted within the "third wave" movement of the Spirit to which Aglow is intimately connected.[52] Hansen is an active member of the Spiritual Warfare Network, a group "specializing in intercession specifically directed to weaken the territorial spirits or principalities and powers which obstruct the spread of the Gospel."[53] Most of Aglow's International Advisors and Advisors-at-Large are also members of the Spiritual Warfare Network, including David (formerly Paul) Yonggi Cho, leader of the world's largest church; George Otis Jr., author of several books on spiritual warfare and "spiritual mapping" and a leader in the A.D. 2000 and Beyond movement; John Dawson, director of Youth with a Mission and author of *Taking Our Cities for God*; Dick Eastman, member of the Spiritual Warfare Network; Cindy Jacobs, president of Generals of Intercession and member of the executive council of the National Prayer Embassy; and C. Peter Wagner, professor of church growth at Fuller Theological Seminary and coordinator of the Spiritual Warfare Network. All are active participants in the "third wave of the Holy Spirit," a term Wagner describes in his 1983 book by the same name. Having already sent the "first wave" as Pentecostalism and the "second wave" in the form of the charismatic movement, Wagner writes, God has now sent an even more powerful "third wave" of spiritual work, distinguished by a new emphasis on healing, spiritual warfare, and what John Wimber has termed "power evangelism," as well as a persistently premillennial theology.[54]

Under Jane Hansen's leadership, Aglow has increasingly moved in this direction, an intensification of its long adherence to the belief that we are living in the "end times" or "last days" and that Christ's return to earth to usher in the Kingdom of God is imminent. From its leaders, Aglow has also adopted some rather controversial spiritual warfare strategies in the form of "spiritual mapping," in which warfare prayers are made over maps—particularly the "10/40 Window," a rectangle between 10° and 40° latitude in which over 90 percent of the world's unsaved population is supposedly located—of areas across the earth where evil spirits and "strongholds" are believed to exert force against the gospel. Throughout these spiritual warfare networks, particularly in Aglow, women are seen as having a crucial role, called by God not only to evangelize in traditional ways but also to "do battle" against the evil forces thought to be at work in the world. Even as they insist that they are merely "ordinary women," then, they have found for themselves a role with extraordinary implications.[55]

Notions pertaining to spiritual warfare have a long history in millennial theology and evangelicalism and are rooted in scriptural passages such as the following: "Put on the full armor of God so that you can take your stand against the devil's schemes. For our struggle is not against flesh and blood, but against the rulers, against the authorities, against the powers of this dark world and against the spiritual forces of evil in the heavenly realms" (Ephesians 6:11–12).[56] Aglow's emphasis on women's important roles in this battle, a seemingly sharp contrast to the stress on submissive femininity and loving nurture, requires some explanation. Here, unlike actual military war, men are not perceived as the primary combat soldiers, with women at the sidelines cheering them on. Nor are men and women envisioned as precisely equal in either responsibility or power. Rather, Aglow teaches that women must be at the frontlines of the war, with a role that sometimes appears more central than that of Christian men.[57]

Two women affiliated with Aglow, Quin Sherrer and Ruthanne Garlock, have co-authored a prescriptive book, published in 1991, entitled *A Woman's Guide to Spiritual Warfare*. After describing the battle against "discouragement, fear, harassment, and other ploys of the evil one," they defend women's role in the spiritual war: "Sure, men are also called to duty, but women have a special interest in this battle." Admonishing their female readers who perceive themselves as weak and helpless, the authors note, "Why is it that we are so influential? Perhaps because women often feel things deeply. We are readily moved with compassion." Moreover: "Quin's theory is that because women were created to give birth in the natural realm, we know more about travailing to give birth in the spiritual realm. We have a high tolerance for pain. We have the tenacity to stick it out until the birthing is done and our loved ones are brought from darkness into the light of Jesus." The lesson resounds: Christian women, not despite but actually because of their "feminine" emotionalism, are called to a position of great responsibility, in which they must fight against evil by enlisting as loyal and vigorous soldiers in God's army.[58]

As Aglow women describe and practice it, spiritual warfare involves "*intercession*," mediating between God and the person one is praying for, as well as standing between that person and Satan to "restrict satanic forces." This is a process of "binding" Satan by forbidding him, in the name of Jesus, to tempt or destroy human beings who rightfully belong to God. As performed in Aglow groups, spiritual warfare is a loud and vigorous process, involving shouting—in tongues and in English—and dramatic bodily gestures that indicate combat with unseen yet powerful forces. By fighting against Satan and constantly praying to God for assistance, Satan's evil power can be blocked and ultimately conquered: "The enemy's attempt to draw us into sin causes our inner conflict. But if we choose to obey God, he gives us success in these skirmishes. Then we are empowered to battle outwardly, dispelling the powers of darkness and setting other captives free."[59] This passage reveals once again the doctrine of surrender connected to implications of power. In choosing to obey God's will rather than give in to Satan's temptations, women are rewarded with the God-given authority to banish Satan and to render him virtually powerless.

Satan's attacks on women include destroying their marriages and bringing misery into their homes, and Aglow literature contains frequent illustrations explaining how spiritual warfare may be waged against the sinful actions of children and husbands. Alicia, whose husband, Carl, appeared to be having an extramarital affair, sought advice from her Aglow friend, Ruthanne, who recounted the story in print:

> I told Alicia that I felt Satan was using this woman's attention as a snare to ruin her husband's testimony and his marriage. I advised her to renounce her hurt and anger, then forgive both of

them. Alicia prayed and forgave Carl and the woman involved. Then we bound the spirits of deception, pride, and lust in both of them. We declared in the name of Jesus that all ties of sexual attraction between Carl and this woman, or any other woman he had lusted after, were broken. We asked the Holy Spirit to reveal truth to him, to expose the enemy's snare, and to bring Carl to repentance.

Afterward, Ruthanne told Alicia that she should no longer argue with her husband about the situation; instead, she advised, "Just ask the Lord to help you express love to him." That very night Ruthanne saw a "radiant" Alicia, who exclaimed, "I can't believe the change in Carl! . . . The Lord must have dealt with him . . . because he . . . apologized to me for his involvement with that woman and for hurting me. I told him I forgave him. His whole attitude has changed, and I know the Lord will help us work everything out."[60]

While not directly challenging the doctrine of wifely submission, Alicia subverts it through a legitimate means; rather than confronting Carl with her pain and anger at his infidelity, she went straight to the authority of God, who, in her view, took control of the situation and transformed Carl's heart. The story of Alicia represents a rather different alternative from that taken by Dorothy; whereas Dorothy took responsibility for her marital unhappiness upon herself, Alicia perceives the problem as her husband's acquiescence to the power of Satan. This difference in the two stories, printed sixteen years apart, represents a similar shift in emphasis as that described previously: a growing willingness to articulate the sins of the husbands (and parents) rather than taking the full burden of blame upon oneself.

Also intriguing are the ways that the language of spiritual warfare may work to undercut the claim to have surrendered fully to the will of God. Certainly God is believed to be the source of women's power, and yet it sometimes appears as if God takes a backseat while the women themselves do battle against the demonic forces in the world. While prayers for assistance are incorporated into the practice of warring against Satan, for instance, the women take matters into their own hands by fighting him themselves as they "command" him to yield to their will. In their surrender, they do not limit their actions to praying for God to take charge of the situation but rather "come against" the enemy as soldiers waging war. Although the battle is always fought "in Jesus' name," the women's insistence on their own agency is apparent. As I heard one Aglow leader exclaim at a spiritual warfare workshop in 1993, "I just want to be a prayer warrior, and I'm going to pray until I win! Because our God is a winning God, and we are winning women!"[61]

Besides forces tearing apart families, there are various other "strongholds" or "spirits" that Aglow women attack by means of spiritual warfare. These include witchcraft, Freemasonry, and "occult" phenomena that are believed to lurk menacingly in the world and to induce people to act immorally. Such forces are believed to seep into one's life and home even without one's knowing it, as when one woman recounted discovering a book she had purchased secondhand was tainted by witchcraft because of the sins of its previous owner.[62] By fighting these spirits through practices of spiritual warfare, Aglow women believe that they play not only a significant role but a truly necessary one in the lives of their families, their neighborhoods, and the nation as a whole, protecting the safety of innocent people who may well be unaware that such spirits exist. More visible targets of spiritual warfare may include illegal drugs, homosexuality, and abortion, all of which are believed to be forces of Satan that are contributing to a precipitous moral decay in American society.

Sending prayers to God about these issues is considered at least as important—and in some ways more so—than doing actual political work against them, for the women believe that their prayers may help change people's hearts and cleanse society from even the most threatening forms of evil. Here and elsewhere, Aglow women assume that their prayers are powerful religious, social, and even political weapons and that they as Christian women have a tremendous responsibility to make warfare prayers and be loyal soldiers of the cross.

The discourse of spiritual warfare prayer is distinct from that of submission, emphasizing female power and authority rather than meek surrender and extending women's realm of activism beyond home and church into the broader society. Like evangelical members of the Woman's Christian Temperance Union at the end of the nineteenth century, whose commitment to "Home Protection" impelled them to broaden the female sphere and revise the ideal of the True Woman, many evangelical women at the end of the twentieth century have seemingly undergone what historian Carolyn DeSwarte Gifford has termed "re-conversion," a renewed conviction of God's great expectations for women to be prayer warriors in the public sphere. Called to be Deborahs and Esthers, both groups of women gradually reimagined Christian womanhood as involving the God-given authority to fight the principalities and powers of the world.[63] As Aglow women frequently declare, they aspire to the "beautiful boldness" to which they avow God has called them.

## REINVENTING CHRISTIAN WOMANHOOD

For the women of Aglow, there is power in prayer, and its reach is not confined to the home but spreads outward into "the world." Through acts of surrender as well as through the tactics of spiritual warfare, these women believe that they may contain enemy forces—the lust of a husband, perhaps, or even such perceived evils as certain social and political policies affecting the "traditional family." These "warfare" strategies also provide a means by which female submission may be subverted and transformed into a tool of authority. Understanding how this process works may lead to greater understanding of the meanings of healing, transformation, and liberation that are so deeply a part of their faith and piety and may also challenge the flat interpretation made by some observers (including many feminists) that female submission is no more than "a delicately balanced commingling of resourcefulness and lack of self-respect."[64] What Aglow women feel (or say they feel) to be liberation or even "empowerment" may, of course, look like something very different to those whose experiences of power bear little resemblance to those of the women I have described here. The task is to bring these perspectives together—hearing the women's narratives on many levels or, in Janice Radway's terms, viewing them from multiple lenses—so as to create a richer account of religion as it is lived by the women of Aglow.

This discussion of the family, prayer, and notions of submission and surrender in Aglow indicates the complex and varied meanings of Christian womanhood for evangelical women. Being a Christian woman involves compliance to male authority, but it also demands the strength and stamina to do battle against Satan. To be a Christian wife is to be privileged with God's choicest role, in the words of Darien Cooper: a role enacted by holding the family together as a stable, happy unit. The ideal of Christian womanhood that charismatic women create and maintain is constructed between a kind of timid passivity, on the one hand, and "unfeminine" assertiveness, on the other. This ideal is articulated by Aglow President Jane Hansen, who warns against a facile interpretation of total submission to an authoritarian husband even as she rejects "the banner of women's lib, ERA and

NOW": "I love being a housewife, a mother and all that goes with that. . . . That's part of who God created me to be. But he also created me to be more than that."[65] Repeatedly criticizing "the women's movement" for rejecting the notion that men should be heads of the household and for stirring up distrust and dissent between men and women, still Aglow participants continue to emphasize women's power to do great things in the world and, in very recent years, seem perceptibly to be moving toward egalitarianism. Admitting that the emphasis on female submission has changed a lot within Aglow, many women, including Hansen, now speak of "mutual submission" between husbands and wives as the ideal, an ideal long distorted, in their view, by church leaders but presently coming into its own.[66]

Historian Margaret Bendroth's observation about fundamentalism, that its "continuing attraction for women ensured that gender questions would arise over and over," remains true in the modern world, and not only for fundamentalism but for other forms of conservative or "traditional" religion as well.[67] In the case of Aglow, older ideals have gradually mixed with modern realities to produce collage-like results. By the mid-1990s, Aglow publications not only recognized that a high percentage of their readership was comprised of women who worked at jobs outside the home, but authors actually provided models for career women, in that few of them described themselves as full-time homemakers (as earlier writers almost inevitably had). Thus, a passage from the Aglow Bible study *God's Daughter* that originally read, "Because we, as women, are the homemakers, we have the blessing of opening our homes to God's people," was revised in 1985 to read more simply, "We, women, have the blessing of opening our homes to God's people."[68] Evangelical ideals of Christian womanhood, then, while always containing multiple possibilities for revision and even subversion, perceptibly shifted after the mid-1980s, as notions of submission were modified by other notions of female occupation as well as female power.

Over time, as increasing numbers of charismatic women have become divorced, single mothers, the older ideal of the happy, submissive wife has given way to newer models of women warriors battling the forces of Satan and helping each other surmount the apparent wreckage of their lives. Admissions of childhood abuse and alcohol-drenched marriages have tempered any remaining optimism about squeaky clean and happy families, yet the tone of victory still resounds as the women create alternative family relationships with God and with their evangelical sisters. Unlike most of the earliest stories published in *Aglow* magazine, written by women who assumed their audience to be mostly, like them, housewives with children, the Aglow literature produced in the 1990s assumes little about their readers' domestic status except that their lives are probably full of grief and confusion over their roles as Christian women, a condition reputedly connected to women's enduring quest for self-esteem. Changing ideals of Christian womanhood in Aglow literature are thus intricately connected to changing social patterns in American marriage and family life since the 1960s, and the array of such ideals reflects choice as well as confusion about dissolving gender role boundaries.

Religious practices provide further insight into the processes of negotiation that occur as Aglow participants reshape and refine their identities as Christian women. Such practices create moments of active engagement with beliefs and assumptions that may conflict in unseen ways. Prayer is a particularly illuminating practice in the case of Aglow because of the doubleness of its operation, serving simultaneously as a means of articulating the pain and frustration felt in daily life and as a tool for solving these crises. As a mode of both direct and indirect communication, prayer brings to light all kinds of conflicts and contradictions that could otherwise remain hidden in Aglow women's lives and illuminates how really very difficult submission, surrender, and forgiveness can be. Yet the women persevere, struggling to practice these ideals and hoping that in this case, practice can make perfect.

Central to this study, as in other analyses of lived religion, are questions about how particular religious practices actually work for those who enact them, the relation of such practices to broader social matrices, and the impact of such practices on ordinary life. By highlighting the workings of power in the Aglow organization, I have aimed at discerning whether practices such as prayer and storytelling about prayer effectively oppose or conserve norms of discipline and authority. Do, that is, such apparently conventional rituals hold potential for resistance or do they, tangibly as well as covertly, merely replicate the hierarchical status quo and ultimately perpetuate female subordination?[69] My own reading of these materials suggests that these practices work in double ways so as both to conserve particular meanings and to oppose others, upholding various power arrangements and even instilling them in newcomers while allowing other arrangements to be challenged and possibly reshaped.

This analysis may offer some insights for reconsidering the practical effects of activities such as prayer; it may prompt, in other words, a strategy for avoiding the either/or dilemma in which practices are viewed as *either* opposing *or* conserving certain meanings and values in grand terms. One way of articulating such a strategy might be to think in metaphoric terms of "making room." What practices such as prayer and, even more, telling stories about prayer do for the women of Aglow is to open up space in areas that once were tightly bounded, limited, constrained. By "making room" for new ways of imagining their situations, prayer makes those boundaries appear wider and less constraining than before. Dorothy opens up the drapes in her living room and imagines her world expanding. Darien Cooper's readers discover that they have the power to make their husbands happy and thereby enhance or ameliorate conditions at home. Alicia, doing battle against the "powers of darkness" that have attacked her husband, receives assurance that her marriage has been healed. Although problems may well persist and other hardships are sure to transpire, there is always room for hope, opening up new space within which one's sense of self may be transformed. What emerge into view are not simply glib or superficial solutions to life's perduring trials but spaces of calm assurance, expectation, and possibility.

The boundaries are not demolished, however. They shift, tightening in spots that are not always immediately evident. The capacity for active protest and dissent shrinks drastically; the sanctions against "rebellion"—including rebellion against conventions strictly upheld within Aglow—are great. Dissatisfaction and unhappiness with one's life may only be voiced as a way of illuminating one's own weaknesses and recognizing the responsibility to surrender and accept whatever comes. The potential abdication of personal will and desire is not only individually stifling but also, and perhaps more ominously, politically immobilizing. Surrendering one's will in Aglow all too often seems to include the surrender of one's willingness to think independently and of the capacity to protect oneself, a capacity that these women cannot afford to lose.

In the end, then, the room these women make for themselves may be negated by the room they lose; nevertheless, the notions of submission and surrender, enacted through prayer, through narrative, and through changed behavior in everyday life, provide Aglow women with a means of reinventing themselves, of "making room" for themselves within a familial or larger social context that they also believe to be transformed. The larger political implications of this process are unclear, but at the very least, the willful determination these women manifest in reworking their lives seems to suggest possibilities for further changes in the future. Aglow prayer narratives hinge on moments when new possibilities for identity are realized, and it is in the surrender to such possibilities that new selves may be born.

## NOTES

1. "My Husband's Going to Die," *Aglow* 22 (Summer 1975): 9–11.

2. "Daddy Never Said, 'I Love You!'" *Aglow* 16 (Winter 1974): 24–26.

3. "Reflections on Aglow's twenty-year ministry to women around the world" (brochure printed by Aglow Publications, 1987, 4). Historical studies of the charismatic movement include David Edwin Harrell Jr., *All Things Are Possible: The Healing and Charismatic Revivals in Modern America* (Bloomington: Indiana University Press, 1975); and Richard Quebedeaux, *The New Charismatics* (New York: Doubleday, 1976), completely revised and published as *The New Charismatics II: How a Christian Renewal Movement Became Part of the American Religious Mainstream* (San Francisco: Harper and Row, 1983). On the Full Gospel Businessmen's Fellowship, see Vinson Synan, *Under His Banner: History of Full Gospel Business Men's Fellowship International* (Costa Mesa, Calif.: Gift Publications, 1992).

4. Today local meetings attract up to one hundred women. Individual chapters are interdenominational and convene monthly for prayer and worship, often in church sanctuaries, civic centers, or public auditoriums. Each chapter is part of a larger regional group with its own board of officers, who together oversee the meetings and the chapter leaders. At one time Aglow claimed to serve over a half million women in the United States; however, in September 1993, their membership was down to 19,717 women in the United States, with supposedly thousands more throughout the world. The organization discontinued publication of *Aglow* magazine in 1991, but has continued to publish a variety of newsletters, Bible studies, and Christian self-help books since that time.

5. I have outlined the history and current configuration of Women's Aglow elsewhere; see Griffith, *God's Daughters: Evangelical Women and the Power of Submission* (Berkeley: University of California Press, 1997), esp. ch. 1.

6. Mirra Komarovsky with Jane H. Philips, *Blue-Collar Marriage* (New Haven, Conn.: Yale University Press, 10th printing, 1987); Lillian Breslow Rubin, *Worlds of Pain: Life in the Working-Class Family* (New York: Basic Books, 1976); Elaine Tyler May, *Homeward Bound: American Families in the Cold War Era* (New York: Basic Books, 1988). See also Brett Harvey, *The Fifties: A Woman's Oral History* (New York: HarperCollins, 1993); William Chafe, *The American Woman: Her Changing Social, Economic and Political Role, 1920–1970* (New York: Oxford University Press, 1972); Carl Degler, *At Odds: Women and the Family in America from the Revolution to the Present* (New York: Oxford University Press, 1980); Benita Eisler, *Private Lives: Men and Women of the Fifties* (New York: Franklin Watts, 1986); Eugenia Kaledin, *Mothers and More: American Women in the 1950s* (Boston: Twayne, 1984); and Leila Rupp and Verta Taylor, *Survival in the Doldrums: The American Women's Rights Movement, 1945 to the 1960s* (New York: Oxford University Press, 1987).

7. Sociologist Susan D. Rose, writing about similar narrative scripts among charismatic women, observes that whereas feminists would interpret the illnesses of Dorothy and other women as encoding both surrender and rebellion against their prescribed female roles, the women themselves perceive such illnesses as warning signs that they stepped out of their proper place. See Rose, "Women Warriors: The Negotiation of Gender in a Charismatic Community," *Sociological Analysis* 48, no. 3 (1987): 245–58.

8. "Master of My Life," *Aglow* 13 (Spring 1973): 20–23.

9. "Pieces of the Puzzle," *Aglow* 11 (Fall 1972): 20–23, 27.

10. "The Wife of the Unbeliever," *Aglow* 19 (Fall 1974): 29–31.

11. "My Non-Christian Husband," *Aglow* 29 (Spring 1977): 20–23. See also "Glad You Asked That," *Aglow* 15 (Winter 1974): 17. For success sto-

ries of converting a previously unsaved husband, see "He Gave Me Love," *Aglow* 28 (Winter 1977): 3–6; and "We've Made It," *Aglow* 35 (July-August 1978): 12–14.

12. Ed Hindson, "The Total Family," *Faith Aflame* 4, no. 1 (January-February 1979): 12; cited in Joan Jacobs Brumberg, *Mission for Life: The Story of the Family of Adoniram Judson, the Dramatic Events of the First American Foreign Mission, and the Course of Evangelical Religion in the Nineteenth Century* (New York: The Free Press, 1980), 222.

13. Carol Greenhouse, *Praying for Justice: Faith, Order, and Community in an American Town* (Ithaca, N.Y.: Cornell University Press, 1986), 48.

14. Ibid., 49.

15. Particularly since World War II, this religious concern for family life has taken on an increasingly anxious tone among conservative evangelicals and fundamentalists. David Harrington Watt and Margaret Lamberts Bendroth have separately argued that there was a shift after the war from the earlier fundamentalist preoccupation with apocalyptic speculation to increased attention to "practical issues of moral conduct." In particular, the new emphasis turned, often quite fiercely, to the issue of the Christian home. Bendroth describes this shift as initiated by "a desire within fundamentalism for more uniform standards of feminine conduct and a movement toward greater structure in gender relationships." The new emphasis on female submission to masculine headship reshaped notions of hierarchy and had a significant impact on evangelical ideals of family life. See Bendroth, *Fundamentalism and Gender, 1875 to the Present* (New Haven, Conn.: Yale University Press, 1993), 98–99; Watt, *A Transforming Faith: Explorations of Twentieth-Century American Evangelicalism* (New Brunswick, N.J.: Rutgers University Press, 1991), 84–91.

16. Judith Stacey, *Brave New Families: Stories of Domestic Upheaval in Late Twentieth Century America* (New York: Basic Books, 1991).

17. Sontag, *When Love Is Not Perfect*, 78; Newbrough, *Support Group Leader's Guide*, 36.

18. Isaiah 54:5.

19. "A Christian Road Map for Women Traveling Alone," *Aglow* 20 (Winter 1975): 8–11, 15.

20. "'I Shall Not Fear,'" *Aglow* 31 (Fall 1977): 16.

21. "Testimony: A Story of God's Care," *Aglow* 33 (March-April 1978): 21–23.

22. Janice Radway, *Reading the Romance: Women, Patriarchy, and Popular Literature* (Chapel Hill: University of North Carolina Press, 1991), 81; "A Christian Road Map," 10.

23. Griffith, *God's Daughters*.

24. See Newbrough, *Support Group Leader's Guide*, 7.

25. February 1994. The speaker made the recommendation during a conference workshop for women with non-Christian husbands.

26. Nancy T. Ammerman has discussed this process in *Bible Believers: Fundamentalists in the Modern World* (New Brunswick, N.J.: Rutgers University Press, 1987), esp. 134–46. See also Stacey, *Brave New Families*, 113–46.

27. Cooper, *You Can Be the Wife of a Happy Husband: By Discovering the Key to Marital Success* (Wheaton, Ill.: Victor Books, 1974), 17.

28. Ibid., 30, 78, 119, 138.

29. Ibid., 139.

30. Ibid., 153.

31. This image of men as naturally out of control and so needing constraint is common in contemporary evangelical teachings on the family, as in the following passage from Christian family guru James Dobson: "The single male is often a threat to society. His aggressive tendencies are largely unbridled and potentially destructive. . . . When a man falls in love with a woman, dedicating himself to care for her, protect her, and support her, he suddenly becomes the mainstay of the social order. Instead of using his energies to pursue his own lusts and desires, he sweats to build a home, save for the future, and seek the best job available. His selfish impulses are inhibited. His sexual passions are channeled. He discovers a sense of pride—yes, masculine pride—because he is needed by his wife and children. Everyone benefits from the relationship." "A New Look at Masculinity and Femininity," *Moody Monthly* 82 (June 1982): 54.

32. Schlafly, *The Power of the Positive Woman* (New Rochelle, N.Y.: Arlington House, 1977), 54–55; cited in Ehrenreich, *The Hearts of Men: American Dreams and the Flight from Commitment* (New York: Anchor Press/Doubleday, 1986), 163.

33. Mae Erickson, *Quiz for Christian Wives* (Lynnwood, Wash.: Aglow Publications, 1976), 6–8.

34. Interview, January 27, 1994.

35. *Aglow in the Kitchen*, ed. Agnes Lawless and Ann Thomas (Lynnwood, Wash.: Aglow Publications, 1976), 7. Another author, in a prayer printed for "my son's partner," writes: "If housework ever seems to be a monotonous chore to her, help her realize that whatever she does in word or deed, she should do it with all her heart as working for You." (Quin Sherrer, *How to Pray for Your Children*, [Lynnwood, Wash. Aglow Publications, 1986], 34).

36. "My Home: My Ministry," *Aglow* 11 (Fall 1972): 25–26.

37. For this discussion, I compared three versions of this booklet by Eadie V. Goodboy: the original (*God's Daughter: A Study of Practical Christian Living for Women*, 1974); a version slightly revised in 1976 and reprinted in 1981 (*God's Daughter: Practical Aspects of a Christian Woman's Life*); and a version revised in 1985 and reprinted in 1991.

38. I am indebted to theologian Sarah Coakley for helping me distinguish between these forms of power and surrender.

39. Coakley, "*Kenosis* and Subversion: On the Repression of 'Vulnerability' in Christian Feminist Writing," in *Swallowing a Fishbone?: Feminist Theologians Debate Christianity*, ed. Daphne Hampson (London: SPCK, 1996), 110.

40. Michel de Certeau, *The Practice of Everyday Life* (Berkeley: University of California Press, 1984), esp. xviii–xx, 24–28, 29–42.

41. Shirley Dobson, wife of well-known evangelical psychologist James C. Dobson, has described her own childhood in an alcoholic home and its after-effects. See, for instance, "Shirley Dobson: From Shaky Childhood to Secure Womanhood," in Helen Hoosier Kooiman, *Living Cameos* (Old Tappan, N.J.: Revell, 1971), 30–38.

42. "The Best Choice," *Aglow* 76 (May-June 1985): 7.

43. "Mom's an Alcoholic!" *Aglow* 21, no. 1 (January-February 1990): 10–12.

44. Heather Harpham, *Daddy, Where Were You?: Healing for the Father-Deprived Daughter* (Lynnwood, Wash.: Aglow Publications, 1991).

45. Marie Sontag, *When Love Is Not Perfect: Discover God's Re-Parenting Process* (Lynnwood, Wash.: Aglow Publications, 1991). Sontag writes that "as many as one out of four adults" are victims of some form of child abuse (14).

46. Kathy Collard Miller, *Healing the Angry Heart: A Strategy for Confident Mothering* (Lynnwood, Wash.: Aglow Publications, 1984), esp. 39–46 (quote from 39).

47. Ibid., 46. Another example of this genre published by Aglow Publications is Stanley C. Baldwin, *If I'm Created in God's Image Why Does It Hurt to Look in the Mirror?: A True View of You* (1989); see also "When You Hurt: A Study of God's Comfort" (Aglow Encourager Bible Study series, 1987).

48. Interview, May 18, 1993.

49. Quin Sherrer first published her narrative in "The Song That Changed: A Story of Forgiveness," *Aglow* 76 (May-June 1985): 18–20 (quotes from 19); she also told this story in a workshop at the U.S. Women's Aglow Conference in November 1994.

50. Jennie Newbrough [with Carol Greenwood], *Support Group Leader's Guide* (Lynnwood, Wash.: Aglow Publications, 1993), 26.

51. This prophecy has been recounted in numerous places, including the Women's Aglow Prayer Map and *Women of Prayer Released to the Nations* (Lynnwood, Wash.: Aglow Publications, 1993), 9.

52. Metaphors of warfare have been utilized by a wide variety of cultural fundamentalists. See David Snowball, *Continuity and Change in the Rhetoric of the Moral Majority* (New York: Praeger, 1991), esp. 123–49. As Snowball notes, the effectiveness of prowar rhetoric requires optimism that the war can indeed be won (135).

53. Brochure of the Spiritual Warfare Network, coordinated by C. Peter Wagner. This network is part of the United Prayer Track of the A.D. 2000 and Beyond movement and is supported by Global Harvest Ministries, Pasadena, Calif.

54. C. Peter Wagner, *The Third Wave of the Holy Spirit: Encountering the Power of Signs and Wonders* (Ann Arbor, Mich.: Servant Publications, 1988); John Wimber (with Kevin Springer), *Power Evangelism* (San Francisco: Harper and Row, 1986). See also Wimber and Springer, *Power Healing* (San Francisco: HarperCollins, 1987). An evangelical critique of this movement is Michael G. Moriarty, *The New Charismatics: A Concerned Voice Responds to Dangerous New Trends* (Grand Rapids, Mich.: Zondervan, 1992).

55. For recent elaborations of this view by international Aglow leaders, see the essays in *Women of Prayer Released to the Nations*.

56. The passage continues: "Therefore put on the full armor of God, so that when the day of evil comes, you may be able to stand your ground, and after you have done everything, to stand. Stand firm then, with the belt of truth buckled around your waist, with the breastplate of righteousness in place, and with your feet fitted with the readiness that comes from the gospel of peace. In addition to all this, take up the shield of faith, with which you can extinguish all the flaming arrows of the evil one. Take the helmet of salvation and the sword of the Spirit, which is the word of God. And pray in the Spirit on all occasions with all kinds of prayers and requests. With this in mind, be alert and always keep on praying for all the saints" (13–18).

57. Other evangelical groups that utilize military imagery have emphasized women as warriors, notably the Salvation Army; see Diane H. Winston, "Boozers, Brass Bands, and Hallelujah Lassies: The Salvation Army and Commercial Culture in New

York City, 1880–1918" (Ph.D. diss. Princeton University, 1996). Women have been dramatized as warriors in other cultural and historical settings as well; a particularly interesting study is Dianne Dugaw, *Warrior Women and Popular Balladry, 1650–1850* (Chicago: University of Chicago Press, 1996; orig. pub. by Cambridge University Press, 1989).

58. Quin Sherrer and Ruthanne Garlock, *A Woman's Guide to Spiritual Warfare: A Woman's Guide to Battle* (Ann Arbor, Mich.: Servant Publications, 1991), 12, 58.

59. Ibid., 41.

60. Ibid., 164–65.

61. February 1993. The speaker made this comment during the inspirational talk to a group of about one hundred women.

62. April 21, 1993. This statement was made in an informal group discussion with approximately fifteen women present.

63. Gifford, "Home Protection: The WCTU's Conversion to Woman Suffrage," in *Gender, Ideol-* ogy, and Action: Historical Perspectives on Women's Public Lives, ed. Janet Sharistanian (Westport, Conn.: Greenwood, 1986), 95–120.

64. Andrea Dworkin, *Right-Wing Women* (New York: G. P. Putnam's Sons, 1983 [1979]), 26.

65. "Jane Hansen: Waking Up from the American Dream," *Charisma & Christian Life* (November 1987): 18–23 (quote from 23).

66. Interviews, September 14, 1993; May 18, 1993; May 14, 1993. Hansen is currently writing a book on this very subject, according to my conversation with her in August 1996. In contrast, some elderly women who were early members of Aglow but are no longer affiliated with the organization emphasized the doctrine of female submission in much stronger terms. Phone interviews, September 16, 1993.

67. Bendroth, *Fundamentalism and Gender*, 7.

68. Goodboy, *God's Daughter*, 27 (in original version) and 29 (in 1991 version).

69. See Radway, *Reading the Romance*, 209–22.

# THE CHURCH OF BASEBALL, THE FETISH OF COCA-COLA, AND THE POTLATCH OF ROCK 'N' ROLL

*David Chidester*

Isn't religion part of American popular culture? Do we find it only in churches, synagogues, mosques, and temples or is it also present in our everyday lives? What if we were to take seriously seemingly casual assertions that baseball operates like a church, that Coca-Cola is a sacred object, or that the pop song "Louie, Louie" offers us religious meaning? In recent years scholars have turned to the analysis of religion in popular American culture to help us understand not only the character of religion but the ways in which the very term "religion" is continually redefined, applied, and extended in cultural discourses and practices. Through this attempt to account for religion's role in popular American culture, academic models of religion are undergoing revision and their application expanded. In this essay, David Chidester explores popular accounts of baseball, Coca-Cola, and rock 'n' roll as representing three different theoretical models—church, fetish, and potlatch—for analyzing religion in American popular culture. He shows us how each of these models helps us to see the degree to which baseball, Coca-Cola, and rock 'n' roll might be seen as manifestations of religion. Through this analysis, religion is revealed not only as an intellectual concept but also as a figure of speech whose meaning is continually subject to metaphorical play.

Reprinted by permission from David Chidester, "The Church of Baseball, the Fetish of Coca-Cola, and the Potlatch of Rock 'n' Roll: Theoretical Models for the Study of Religion in American Popular Culture." *Journal of the American Academy of Religion* 64:4 (1996), 743–765. Reprinted by permission of the American Academy of Religion.

# 22 🙿

# THE CHURCH OF BASEBALL, THE FETISH OF COCA-COLA, AND THE POTLATCH OF ROCK 'N' ROLL

Theoretical Models for the Study of Religion

in American Popular Culture

## *David Chidester*

CONSIDERABLE ACADEMIC ATTENTION has recently been directed towards the analysis of religion in American popular culture. Although much of this academic industry has successfully marked out exciting new areas of inquiry, we still need to ask: What are we talking about? What do we mean by "religion" in the study of religion in American popular culture?

Consider this: "What has a lifetime of baseball taught you?" Buck O'Neil is asked in an interview for Ken Burns's television series on the history of the American national pastime. "It is a religion," O'Neil responds. "For me," he adds. "You understand?"

Not exactly, of course, because we have no idea what Buck O'Neil, the great first baseman of the Kansas City Monarchs in the 1930s, who served baseball for over six decades as player, coach, manager, and scout, means by the term "religion." What does he mean? As Ken Burns would have it, baseball is a religion because it operates in American culture like a church, "The Church of Baseball." Is that how we should understand "religion" in American popular culture, as an organized human activity that functions like the more familiar religious institution of the Christian church?

To complicate the matter, however, consider this: A religion is not a specific institution; rather, a religion is "a system of symbols. . . ." So says anthropologist Clifford Geertz; so also says author Mark Pendergrast in his account of a new religion that was founded in America but eventually achieved truly global scope, the religion of Coca-Cola.

In his popular history *For God, Country, and Coca-Cola*, Pendergrast concludes that the fizzy, caramel-colored sugar water stands as a "sacred symbol" that induces "worshipful" moods that animate an "all-inclusive world view espousing perennial values such as love, peace, and universal brotherhood." According to this reading, therefore, religion is about sacred symbols and systems of sacred symbols that endow the world with meaning and value. As Pendergrast argues, Coca-Cola—the sacred name, the sacred formula, the sacred image, the sacred object—has been the fetish at the center of a popular American system of religious symbolism.

But we can complicate things even further by considering this: "Let's Give It to 'Em, Right Now!" screams singer Joe Ely before the instrumental break in the Kingsmen's 1963 rock 'n' roll classic, "Louie, Louie." In the midst of the clashing, crashing cacophony, with lyrics that are unintelligible at any speed, we are struck by the strained screech of Ely's exhortation, "Let's Give It to 'Em, Right Now!" What kind of a "gift" is this?

In his book-length history of the song, which explores "the Secret" of "Louie, Louie," rock critic Dave Marsh proposes that one useful model for understanding this kind of gift-giving appears in the ritualized display, presentation, and destruction of property associated with the potlatch ritual performed by indigenous American societies in the Pacific Northwest. This analogy with a Native American ritual, Marsh argues, can illuminate what he calls the "socioreligious" character of "Louie, Louie" in American culture. In this sense, however, religion is not an institution; it is not a system of symbols; it is the gift.

Church, fetish, potlatch—these three terms represent different theoretical models for analyzing religion in American popular culture. By examining their recent deployment in popular accounts of baseball, Coca-Cola, and rock 'n' roll, I hope to explore some of the consequences of these theoretical models for the study of religion. Among those consequences, I will highlight the force of metaphoric transference in theory-building; the implications of these three metaphors, representing, respectively, the institutional formation of the church, the powerful but artificial making of the fetish, and the non-productive expenditure of the potlatch, for our understanding of the character of religion; and the ways in which the very term "religion," including its definition, application, and extension, does not, in fact, belong solely to the academy but is constantly at stake in the interchanges of cultural discourses and practices.

## THE CHURCH OF BASEBALL

To return to the testimony of Buck O'Neil, baseball is a religion because it is an enduring institution that is governed by established rules. "If you go by the rules," he explains, "it is right." Baseball is a religion, according to Buck O'Neil, because "it taught me and it teaches everyone else to live by the rules, to abide by the rules."[1]

This definition of religion as rule-governed behavior, however, is not sufficiently comprehensive or detailed to capture what Ken Burns presents as the religious character of baseball. The "church of baseball" is much more than merely the rule book. It is a religious institution that maintains the continuity, uniformity, sacred space, and sacred time of American life. As the "faith of fifty million people," baseball does everything that we conventionally understand to be done by the institution of the church.

First, baseball ensures a sense of continuity in the midst of a constantly changing America through the forces of tradition, heritage, and collective memory. As Donald Hall suggests, "Baseball, because of its continuity over the space of America and the time of America, is a place where memory gathers."[2] Certainly, this emphasis on collective memory dominates Burns's documentary on baseball. But it also seems to characterize the religious character of the sport in American culture. Like a church, Major League Baseball institutionalizes a sacred memory of the past that informs the present.

Second, baseball supports a sense of uniformity, a sense of belonging to a vast, extended American family that attends the same church. As journalist Thomas Boswell reports in his detailed discussion of "The Church of Baseball," his mother was devoted to baseball because "it made her feel like she was in church." Like her church, Boswell explains, baseball provided his mother with "a place where she could—by sharing a fabric of beliefs, symbols, and mutual agreements with those around her—feel calm and whole."[3] Boswell draws out a series of analogies between baseball and his mother's church: both feature organs; both encourage hand clapping to their hymns; both have distinctive robes and vestments; and in both everyone is equal before God. Although his analogy between the basepaths of a diamond and the Christian Cross seems a bit strained, Boswell provides sufficient justification for asserting that his mother regarded her attendance of baseball games as roughly equivalent to belonging to a church.

Third, the religion of baseball represents the sacred space of home. In this respect, baseball is a religion of the domestic, of the familiar, and even of the obvious. As Boswell explains, "Baseball is a religion that worships the obvious and gives thanks that things are exactly as they seem. Instead of celebrating mysteries, baseball rejoices in the absence of mysteries and trusts that, if we watch what is laid before our eyes, down to the last detail, we will cultivate the gift of seeing things as they really are." The vision of reality that baseball affords, therefore, is a kind of normality, the ordinary viewed through a prism that only enhances its familiarity. While many religions point to a perfect world beyond this world, Boswell observes, baseball creates a "perfect universe in microcosm within the real world."[4] By producing such a ritualized space within the world, baseball domesticates the sacred and gives it a home.

Fourth, the religion of baseball represents the sacred time of ritual. "Everything is high-polish ritual and full-dress procession," Boswell notes. The entire proceedings of the game are coordinated through a ritualization of time. But baseball also affords those extraordinary moments of ecstasy and enthusiasm, revelation and inspiration, that seem to stand outside of the ordinary temporal flow. In church, according to Boswell, his mother experienced those moments of "ritual epiphany." "Basically," he reports, "that's how she felt about baseball, too."[5] Through ritual and revelation baseball provides an experience of sacred time that liberates its devotees from time's constraints.

In these terms, therefore, baseball is a church, a "community of believers." Certainly, the church of baseball is confronted by the presence of unbelievers within the larger society. As Thomas Boswell reports, his father failed to find his rightful place among the faithful in the church of baseball. "The appeal of baseball mystified him," Boswell explains, "just as all religions confound the innocent bewildered atheist." Like any church, however, baseball has its committed faithful, its true believers. The opening speech of Annie Savoy in the film *Bull Durham* can be invoked as a passionate statement of religious devotion to baseball. "I believe in the church of baseball," she declares. She testifies that she has experimented with all other forms of religious worship, including the worship of Buddha, Allah, Brahma, Vishnu, Siva, trees, mushrooms, and Isadora Duncan, but those religions did not satisfy. Even the worship of Jesus, she confesses, did not work out, because the Christian religion involves too much guilt. The religion of baseball, however, promises a freedom beyond guilt. Although she observes the analogy between baseball and the Christian church, which is supported by the curious equivalence between 108 beads on the rosary and 108 stitches on a baseball, Annie Savoy proclaims baseball as a church in its own right. "I've tried them all, I really have," she concludes, "and the only church that truly feeds the soul, day in, day out, is the church of baseball."[6]

"What nonsense!" an unbeliever might understandably conclude in response to all this testimony about the church of baseball. Baseball is not a religion. It is recreation; it is entertainment; and, supported by the monopoly granted to Major League Baseball, it is big business. All this religious language merely mystifies the genuine character of the sport in American society.

For all the apparent mystification, strained analogies, and improbable statements of faith, however, the depiction of baseball as a church represents a highly significant development in attempts to locate religion in American popular culture. In earlier anthropological accounts, especially those produced by the anthropologist-from-Mars school of cultural anthropology that gave us the "Nacirema" (America-spelled-backwards) tribe, baseball registers as "magic" rather than "religion."[7] For example, a frequently anthologized article on "Baseball Magic" records the magical techniques employed by baseball players to manipulate unseen forces and control events.[8] Using various kinds of amulets for good luck, players engage in specific practices—never stepping on the foul line, always spitting before entering the batter's box—that appear, in Freudian terms, just like "what are called obsessive acts in neurotics." In their magical practices, baseball players display an obsession with "little preoccupations, performances, restrictions and arrangements in certain activities of everyday life which have to be carried out always in the same or in a methodically varied way."[9] Although Sigmund Freud held that such "obsessive acts" characterized the practice of both ritual and magic, the author of "Baseball Magic" implicitly upholds the familiar analytical distinction between the two. Instead of interpreting baseball as religion, however, he highlights its superstitious practices of magic.

This account of baseball magic raises two theoretical problems. First, by characterizing baseball as magic the author pushes us back to the basic opposition between "religion" and "superstition" that has been crucial to the very definition of religion in Western culture. As the linguist Emile Benveniste observed, "the notion of 'religion' requires, so to speak, by opposition, that of 'superstition.'"[10] The ancient Latin term *religio*, indicating an authentic, careful, and faithful way of acting, was defined by its opposite *superstitio*, a kind of conduct that was allegedly based on ignorance, fear, or fraud. In these terms, *we* have religion; *they* have superstition. Only rarely has the inherently oppositional character of the notion of "religion" been recognized. Thomas Hobbes, for example, observed that the "fear of things invisible is the natural seed of that, which everyone in himself calleth religion; and in them that worship or fear that power otherwise than they do, superstition."[11] Baseball magic, therefore, is not religion. It is a repertoire of superstitious beliefs and practices that stands as the defining opposite of authentic religion. From the perspective of the anthropologist who stands outside and observes, baseball magic is clearly something very strange that they do; it is not our religion.

Second, by focusing on baseball magic, the author recalls the tension between the individual and society that has characterized academic reflections on the difference between magic and religion. Following Emile Durkheim's classic formulation, magic is essentially individualistic and potentially anti-social. Unlike religious ritual, which affirms and reinforces the social solidarity of a community, magic manipulates unseen forces in the service of self-interest. As Durkheim insisted, there can be no "church of magic." Accordingly, if baseball is magic, there can be no "church of baseball."

Ken Burns intervenes in these theoretical problems by reversing their terms. He presents baseball as religion rather than magic and thereby represents the game as an authentic religious affirmation of the traditional continuity, uniformity, and solidarity of American society. Adopting a functional definition of religion, Burns documents the ways in which baseball operates like a church by meeting personal needs and reinforcing social integration. In fact, his implicit theoretical model of religion seems to be informed by the kind of functional assumptions found in J. Milton Yinger's definition of a universal church as "a religious structure that is relatively successful in supporting the integration of society, while at the same time satisfying, by its pattern of beliefs and observances, many of the personality needs of individuals on all levels of society."[12] Like a church, with its orthodoxy and heresies, its canonical myths and professions of faith, its rites of communion and excommunication, baseball appears in these terms as the functional religion of America.

Of course, this account of the church of baseball is positioned in an historical moment of great public disillusionment with the professional game. Feeling betrayed by both greedy players and arrogant owners, many devotees have become apostates of the religion of baseball. In this context the phrase "church of baseball" shifts from metaphor to irony; it becomes a figure of ironic displacement as collective memory is transformed from commemoration of an enduring tradition to nostalgia for a lost world. From this vantage point, the continuity and uniformity of baseball tradition, the sacred time and sacred space of the baseball religion, can only be recreated in memory.

## THE FETISH OF COCA-COLA

A very different theoretical model of religion is developed in Mark Pendergrast's *For God, Country, and Coca-Cola*. Drawing upon the familiar definition of religion provided by Clifford Geertz, Pendergrast proposes that Coca-Cola is a religion because it is "a system of symbols which acts to establish powerful, pervasive, and long-lasting moods and motivations in men by formulating conceptions of a general order of existence and clothing these conceptions in such an aura of factuality that the moods and motivations seem uniquely realistic."[13] To his credit, Pendergrast does not force his history of Coca-Cola into the mold of Geertz's definition. Rather, he allows the major actors in the drama to evoke their religious moods and motivations in their own voices. Here we need to recall only the most striking examples:

From the beginning, the beverage was enveloped in a sacred aura, as its inventor, John Pemberton, referred to one of Coca-Cola's original ingredients, cocaine (which remained in the mix from 1886 until 1902) as "the greatest blessing to the human family, Nature's (God's) best gift in medicine" (27). During the 1890s Coca-Cola emerged as a popular tonic in the soda fountains that a contemporary commentator described as "temples resplendent in crystal, marble and silver" (16). Eventually, however, the blessings of Coca-Cola moved out of the temple and into the world.

Company executives, advertisers, bottlers, and distributors displayed distinctively religious moods and motivations in relation to the sacred beverage. Asa Candler, the Atlanta entrepreneur who started the Coca-Cola empire, was described by his son as regarding the drink with "an almost mystical faith" (68). Candler eventually "initiated" his son "into the mysteries of the secret flavoring formula" as if he were inducting him into the "Holy of Holies" (61). Robert Woodruff, who became president of the company in 1923, "demonstrated a devotion to Coca-Cola which approached idolatry" (160). Harrison Jones, the leading bottler of the 1920s, often referred to the beverage as "holy water" (146). Even the bottle itself was a sacred object that could not be changed. At a 1936 bottlers convention Harrison Jones declared, "The Four Horsemen of the Apocalypse may charge over the earth and back again—and Coca-Cola will remain!" (178). Archie Lee, who assumed direction of Coca-Cola advertising in the 1920s, complained that the "doctrines of our churches are meaningless words," but he speculated that "some great thinker may arise with a new religion" (147). Apparently, Archie Lee, along with many other "Coca-Cola men," found that new religion in Coca-Cola.

Throughout the second half of the twentieth century the Coca-Cola religion inspired a missionary fervor. At the first international convention at Atlantic City in 1948 an executive prayed, "May Providence give us the faith . . . to serve those two billion customers who are only waiting for us to bring our product to them" (238). As advertising director in the early 1950s Delony Sledge proclaimed, "Our work is a religion rather than a business" (261). Obviously, the Coca-Cola Company has imagined its enterprise as a religious mission.

For the consumer, however, Coca-Cola has also assumed religious significance. It has "entered the lives of more people," as one executive put it, "than any other product or ideology, including the Christian religion" (406). In the jive vocabulary of the 1930s Coca-Cola was known as "heavenly dew" (178). But the religious significance of Coca-Cola extended far beyond the scope of such a playful invocation. It gave America its orthodox image of Santa Claus in 1931 by presenting a fat, bearded, jolly old character dressed up in Coca-Cola red; it became the most important icon of the American way of life for U.S. soldiers during World War II; it represented an extraordinary sacred time—the "pause that refreshes"—that was redeemed from the ordinary postwar routines of work and consumption; and from the 1960s it promised to build a better world in perfect harmony. As one indication of the popular religious devotion to the drink, public outcry at the changed formula of "New Coke" in 1985 caused one executive to exclaim, "They talk as if Coca-Cola had just killed God" (364). In these profoundly religious terms, as editor William Allen White observed in 1938, Coca-Cola became a potent symbol of the "sublimated essence of America" (198).

Although the religion of Coca-Cola has pervaded American society, that popular religion has also been global. Represented in over 185 countries, more countries, Pendergrast notes, than are included in the United Nations, the Coca-Cola Company has extended its religion all over the world. As company president Roberto Goizueta put it, "Our success will largely depend on the degree to which we make it impossible for the consumer around the globe to escape Coca-Cola" (397). Suggesting the impossibility of escaping the religion of Coca-Cola, the 1980s film *The Gods Must Be Crazy* presented an absurd parable of its effect among a remote community of Bushmen in southern Africa. As Mark Pendergrast notes, the film opens as "the totemic bottle falls out of the sky onto the sands of the Kalahari Desert, where it completely transforms the lives of the innocent Bushmen as surely as Eve's apple in Eden" (406). Here we find Coca-Cola as a sacred sign, a sign subject to local misreading, perhaps, but nevertheless the fetish of a global religion, an icon of the West, a symbol that can mark an initiatory entry into modernity. Through massive global exchanges and specific local effects, the religion of Coca-Cola has placed its sacred fetish "within arm's reach of desire" all over the world.

"What utter nonsense!" a skeptic might justifiably conclude after reviewing this alleged evidence for the existence of a Coca-Cola religion. Coca-Cola is not a religion. It is a consumer product that has been successfully advertised, marketed, and distributed. In the best tradition of American advertising, the Coca-Cola Company has created the desire for a product that no one needs. Even if it has led to the "Coca-colonization" of the world, this manipulation of desire through effective advertising has nothing to do with religion.

In the study of popular culture, however, the religious character of advertising, consumerism, and commodity fetishism has often been noted. "That advertising may have become 'the new religion of modern capitalist society,'" Marshall W. Fishwick has recently observed, "has become one of the clichés of our time."[14] Advertising-as-religion has transformed the "fetishism of commodities" into a redundant phrase. In the symbolic system of modern capitalist society that is animated by advertising, the commodity is a fetish object.

As a model for defining and locating religion, the fetish raises its own theoretical problems. As William Pietz has shown in a series of articles, the term "fetish" has focused ongoing controversies in Western culture over what counts as authentic *making*. From the Latin *facere*, "to make or to do," the term has carried the semantic burden of indicating artificial, illicit, or evil making, especially in the production of objects of uncertain meaning or unstable value. In this respect, the fetish is not an object; it is a subject for arguments about meaning and value in human relations.

As a modern dilemma the problem of the fetish arises in complex relations of encounter and exchange between "us" and "them." On the one hand, the fetish is something "they" make. Recalling the evil making—the *maleficium*—of black magic, Portuguese traders on the west coast of Africa in the seventeenth century found that Africans made *fetissos*, objects beyond rational comprehension or economic evaluation. Likewise, for generations of anthropologists the fetish was an object that "they" make, a sign of their "primitive" uncertainty over meaning and inability to evaluate objects. On the other hand, Marx, Freud, and their intellectual descendants have found that the fetish is something "we" make—the desired object, the objectification of desire—that is integral to the making of modern subjectivities and social relations.[15]

Drawing upon this ambivalent genealogy of the fetish in western culture, Michael Taussig has recently emphasized the importance of "State Fetishism" in both making and masking the rationality and terror of the modern political order.[16] This recognition of the role of fetishized making in the production and reinforcement of the state resonates with recent research on the making of those collective subjectivities—the imagined communities, the invented traditions, the political mythologies—that animate the modern world.[17] All of these things are made, not found, but they are made in the ways in which only the sacred or society can be produced.

Unlike the historical continuity and social solidarity represented by the church, therefore, the fetish provides a model for religion in which religion is inherently unstable. As an object of indeterminate meaning and variable value, the fetish represents an unstable center for a shifting constellation of religious symbols. Although the fetishized object might inspire religious moods and motivations, it is constantly at risk of being unmasked as something made and therefore as an artificial focus for religious desire. The study of religion in popular culture is faced with the challenge of exploring and explicating the ways in which such "artificial" religious constructions can generate genuine enthusiasms and produce real effects in the world.

## THE POTLATCH OF ROCK 'N' ROLL

As if it were not enough to bestow religious status on baseball and Coca-Cola, we now have to confront the possibility that rock 'n' roll should also count as religion. Certainly the ambivalent relations between rock and religion have often been noticed. As Jay R. Howard has observed, "Religion and rock music have long had a love/hate relationship."[18] On the one hand, rock 'n' roll has occasionally converged with religion. Rock music has sometimes embraced explicitly religious themes, serving as a vehicle for a diversity of religious interests that ranges from heavy metal Satanism to contemporary Christian evangelism.[19] On the other hand, rock 'n' roll has often been the target of Christian crusades against the evils that allegedly threaten religion in American society. From this perspective, rock music appears as the antithesis of religion, not merely as an offensive art form but as a blasphemous, sacrilegious, and anti-religious force in society.[20]

Rock's ambivalent relationship with religion is obvious. Less apparent, perhaps, is the inherently religious character of rock 'n' roll. How do we theorize rock 'n' roll as religion? Attempts have been made. For example, rock 'n' roll has given rise to "a religion without beliefs"; it has given scope for the emergence of a new kind of "divinely inspired shaman"; rock has revived nineteenth-century Romantic pantheism; rock music, concerts, and videos have provided occasions for what might be called, in Durkheimian terms, "ecstasy ritual"; and a new academic discipline—"theomusicology"—has included rock 'n' roll in its mission "to examine secular music for its religiosity."[21] From various perspectives, therefore, rock 'n' roll has approximated some of the elementary forms of the religious life.

In one of the most sustained and insightful analyses of the religious character of rock 'n' roll, Dave Marsh has undertaken a cultural analysis of the archetypal rock song, "Louie, Louie," in order to explore the secret of its meaning, power, and rhythm, the "sacred *duh duh duh. duh duh*."[22] Marsh issues a daunting assessment of all previous attempts to address his topic. The "academic study of the magic and majesty of *duh duh duh. duh duh*," as Marsh puts it bluntly, "sucks." To avoid this condemnation, we must proceed, not with caution, but with the recklessness that the song requires. We must say, with the song's African American composer Richard Berry, who first recorded "Louie, Louie" as a calypso tune in 1956, "Me gotta go now," and see where that going takes us.

As Dave Marsh follows the sacred rhythm of "Louie, Louie," especially as it was incarnated by the Kingsmen in 1963, he dismisses previous attempts to explain the secret of the song's appeal as the result of effective marketing or as the effect of the intentional mystification that is produced by its unintelligible lyrics.

As an example of the first type of explanation, Marsh cites the commentary of Geoffrey Stokes, who authored the section on the 1960s in *Rock of Ages: The Rolling Stone History of Rock 'n' Roll*. "It's almost embarrassing to speak of 'significance' in any discussion of 'Louie Louie,'" Stokes claimed, "for the song surely resists learned exegesis."[23] Its success can only be attributed to aggressive marketing and efficient distribution.

Illustrating the second type of explanation, Marsh invokes the analysis provided by Robert B. Ray, Professor of Film Studies at the University of Florida, who has earned his rock credentials by serving as songwriter and singer for the band the Vulgar Boatman. According to Ray, the Kingsmen rendered "Louie, Louie" in a way that revealed that they had "intuited a classic strategy of all intellectual vanguards: the use of tantalizing mystification." Like Lacan and Derrida, for example, the Kingsmen employed terms and phrases that "remained elusive, inchoate, quasi-oral charms."[24] The result—alluring but ultimately incoherent—was the strategic production of mystery.

In rejecting these economic and rhetorical explanations, Marsh advances an analysis of the secret of "Louie, Louie" in explicitly religious terms. His analysis uncovers layers of religious significance that are all associated with the gift. Although his discussion is inspired by the dramatic prelude to the instrumental break—"Let's Give It to 'Em, Right Now!"—it is also directly related to the power of giving and receiving in the history of religions.

The song might be regarded as if it were a divine gift. As Marsh's colleague Greil Marcus puts it, by the 1980s "the tune was all pervasive, like a law of nature or an act of God." Marsh plays upon this theme: If the song was a gift from God or the gods, he observes, "he, she, or they chose a vehicle cut from strange cloth, indeed—*deus ex cartoona*."[25] However, the sacred gift of "Louie, Louie," the hierophany of incoherence, three chords, and a cloud of dust, cannot be accounted for in the conventional terms of any orthodox theology. Accordingly, Marsh turns to a passage in the Gnostic Gospel of Thomas that seems to capture the "holy heartbeat" of "Louie, Louie."

> Jesus said, "If you bring forth what is within you, what you bring forth will save you. If you do not bring forth what is within you, what you do not bring forth will destroy you."

Bringing forth all that is within them, the gnostic celebrants of "Louie, Louie" are saved, if not "eternally," as Marsh clarifies, then at least temporarily during the liberating moment in which they participate in the rhythm of the "sacred *duh duh duh. duh duh*" and the "magical incantation" of "Let's Give It to 'Em, Right Now!"[26]

Ultimately, however, the religious significance of the gift must be located in relations of exchange. Here a Native American ritual—the potlatch—provides a model for giving and receiving in which the gift assumes a sacred aura. From a Chinook term meaning simply "to give," the potlatch practiced by indigenous communities of the Pacific Northwest signifies the ritualized display, distribution, and sometimes destruction of valued objects at ceremonial occasions.[27]

Although potlatch has variously been interpreted in the ethnographic literature as religious ritual, as status competition, as a kind of banking system, or even as a periodic outburst of "unabashed megalomania," Marsh focuses on three aspects: First, the gift is total. The potlatch demands giving "everything you had: your food, your clothing, your house, your name, your rank and title." As a ritual occasion for giving everything away, the potlatch demonstrates an "insane exuberance of generosity." Second, the gift is competitive. In ritual relations of exchange, tribes compete with each other to move to the "next higher plane of value." Third, the sacred secret of the gift is ultimately revealed in destruction. As the ritualized exchanges of ceremonial gift-giving escalate in value, the supreme value of the gift is realized by destroying valued objects, so that, as Marsh concludes, "eventually a whole village might be burned to the ground in order that the rules of the ceremony could be properly honored."[28]

By odd coincidence the Pacific Northwest was home to both the Native American societies that performed the potlatch and the rock 'n' roll bands of the early 1960s that played the song "Louie, Louie." In Marsh's account, both demonstrate the religious "Secret" of the gift, especially as it was revealed in acts of conspicuous destruction, in ritual acts that "violated every moral and legal tenet of non-Native American civilization, encumbered as it was with the even stranger socioreligious assumption that God most honored men by allowing them to accumulate possessions beyond all utility in this life, let alone the next."[29] In these "socioreligious" terms the "modern day electronic potlatch" of rock 'n' roll violates Euroamerican religious commitments to capitalist production and accumulation, to property rights and propriety, by reviving the sacred secret of the gift.

In defense of the capitalist order J. Edgar Hoover's FBI pursued a four-year investigation of "Louie, Louie" during the 1960s in search of evidence of subversion and obscenity in the song and its performers. As Marsh recalls, Hoover's mission "consisted precisely of visiting the plague of federal surveillance upon any revival of the potlatch mentality."[30] But "Louie, Louie" survived this state-sponsored inquisition. Defying all attempts to suppress it, the song remains the archetype of the sacred gift at the religious heart of the potlatch of rock 'n' roll.

"What utter, absolute, and perverse nonsense!" anyone might conclude after being subjected to this tortuous exposition of the religion of rock music. Rock 'n' roll is not religion. Besides the obvious fact that it is a major part of the entertainment industry, rock 'n' roll is a cultural medium in which all the "anarchistic, nihilistic impulses of perverse modernism have been grafted onto popular music." As a result, it is not a religion; it is a "cult of obscenity, brutality, and sonic abuse."[31]

The model of the potlatch, however, refocuses the definition of religion. As exemplified most clearly by rituals of giving and receiving, religion is a repertoire of cultural practices and performances, of human relations and exchanges, in which people conduct symbolic negotiations over material objects and material negotiations over sacred symbols. If this theoretical model of religion as symbolic, material practice seems to blur the boundaries separating religious, social, and economic activity, then that is a function of the gift itself, which, as Marcel Mauss insists in his classic treatment, is a "total" social phenomenon in which "all kinds of institutions find simultaneous expression: religious, legal, moral, and economic."[32] According to Mauss, the potlatch, as ritual event, social contest, and economic exchange, displays the complex symbolic and material interests that are inevitably interwoven in religion. Similar interests, as Dave Marsh and Greil Marcus argue, can be located in rock 'n' roll.

In the performance of the potlatch, Mauss observes, the contested nature of symbolic and material negotiations becomes particularly apparent; the "agonistic character of the presentation," he notes, "is pronounced."[33] If contests over the ownership of sacred symbols characterize the potlatch, what is the contest that is conducted in the potlatch of rock 'n' roll? It is not merely the competition among musical groups, a competition waged in the "battle of the bands" that Marsh identifies as an important element of the history of "Louie, Louie." It is a contest with a distinctively religious character. In broad agreement with rock critics Marsh and Marcus, anthropologist Victor Turner proposes that rock 'n' roll is engaged in a contest over something as basic as what it means to be a human being in a human society. "Rock is clearly a cultural expression and instrumentality of that style of communitas," Turner suggests, "which has arisen as the antithesis of the 'square,' 'organization man' type of bureaucratic social structure of mid-twentieth-century America."[34] By this account, rock 'n' roll, as anti-structure to the dominant American social structure, achieves the human solidarity, mutuality, and spontaneity that Turner captures in the term, *communitas*. It happens in religious ritual; it happens in rock 'n' roll.

This "agonistic character" of the potlatch of rock 'n' roll, however, is not only evident in America. As Greil Marcus has proposed, the potlatch might unlock the "secret history of the twentieth century."[35] Tracking a disconnected narrative that links dada, surrealism, litterists, situationists, and performance art, Marcus rewrites the cultural history of the twentieth century from the vantage point of the punk rock that was epitomized in 1976 by the Sex Pistols. Surprisingly, perhaps, that revised history depends heavily upon a sociology of religion that is implicitly rooted in the foundational work of Emile Durkheim and extended by Marcel Mauss's seminal essay on the gift; but it is a left-hand sociology of religion that takes an unexpected turn through the world of the French social critic, surrealist, and student of religion Georges Bataille.

In his 1933 essay "The Notion of Expenditure," Bataille takes up the topic of the potlatch to draw a distinction between two kinds of economic activity, production and expenditure. While production represents "the minimum necessary for the continuation of life," expenditure is premised on excess and extravagance, on loss and destruction, or, in a word, on the gift. This alternative range of economic activity "is represented by so-called unproductive expenditures: luxury, mourning, war, cults, the construction of sumptuary monuments, spectacles, arts, perverse sexual activity (i.e., deflected from genital finality)—all these represent activities which, at least in primitive circumstances, have no end beyond themselves." While productive economic activity is directed towards goals of subsistence, gain, and accumulation, expenditure is devoted to achieving dramatic, spectacular loss. In expenditure, according to Bataille, "the accent is placed on a loss that must be as great as possible in order for the activity to take on its true meaning."[36] In the performance of the potlatch, especially when gift giving escalates to the destruction of property, Bataille finds a model of expenditure that informs his entire theory of religion.

As exemplified by the potlatch, religion intersects with rock 'n' roll because they are both cultural practices of expenditure. The gift, as in "Let's Give It To 'Em, Right Now," reopens the complex ritual negotiations over meaning and power, over place and position, over contested issues of value in modern American society. In that context, religion in American popular culture is not a church; nor is it a symbolic system revolving around a fetish. Beyond the constraints of any institution or the play of any desire, religion is defined as religion by the practices, performances, relations, and exchanges that rise and fall and rise again through the ritualized giving and receiving of the gift.

## RELIGION IN AMERICAN POPULAR CULTURE

So now where are we? After this long journey through the religious contours and contents of baseball, Coca-Cola, and rock 'n' roll, we are still left with the question: Where is religion in American popular culture? How do we answer that question? Where do we look? If we only relied upon the standard academic definitions of religion, those definitions that have tried to identify the essence of religion, we would certainly be informed by the wisdom of classic scholarship, but we would also still be lost.

In the history of the academic study of religion, religion has been defined, following the minimal definition of religion proposed in the 1870s by E. B. Tylor, as beliefs and practices relating to spiritual, supernatural, or superhuman beings.[37] This approach to defining religion continues to find its advocates. The assumption that religion is about beliefs in supernatural beings also appears in the discourse of popular culture. For example, the extraordinary athlete can easily become the focus of religion to the extent that he or she is regarded as a superhuman being. When Michael Jordan returned to basketball in 1995, his "second coming" was portrayed in precisely these superhuman terms. "When it is perceived as religion," Jordan complained, "that's when I'm embarrassed by it." While *Sports Illustrated* recorded Michael Jordan's embarrassment at being regarded as the superhuman focus of religious regard, it also added that this reservation was expressed by "the holy Bull himself" about "the attention his second coming has attracted." Adding to the embarrassment, the same article quoted Brad Riggert, head of merchandising at Chicago's United

Center, who celebrated the return of Michael Jordan by declaring, "The god of merchandising broke all our records for sales."[38] In this case, therefore, Michael Jordan—the "holy Bull," the "god of merchandising"—registers as a superhuman being that should satisfy Tylor's minimal definition of religion.

In a second classic attempt to define religion, Emile Durkheim in 1912 stipulated that religion was constituted by beliefs and practices that revolve around a sacred focus, a sacred focus that serves to unify a community.[39] In this approach to defining religion, which also continues to have its proponents, religion depends upon beliefs and practices that identify and maintain a distinction between the sacred and its opposite, the profane. That distinction between the sacred and the profane has also appeared in the discourse of American popular culture. For example, during the long and difficult development of a crucial new software product, Microsoft hired a project manager who undertook the task with religious conviction. According to the unofficial historian of this project, that manager "divided the world into Us and Them. This opposition echoed the profound distinction between sacred and profane: We are clean; they are dirty. We are the chosen people; they are the scorned. We will succeed; they will fail."[40] According to this account, therefore, the cutting edge of religion—the radical rift between the sacred and the profane—appears at the cutting edge of American technology.

Like church, fetish, and potlatch, these classic definitions of religion—belief in supernatural beings, the distinction between sacred and profane—are at play in American culture. As a result, religion is revealed, once again, not only as a cluster concept or a fuzzy set but also as a figure of speech that is subject to journalistic license, rhetorical excess, and intellectual sleight of hand.[41] For the study of religion, however, this realization bears an important lesson: The entire history of academic effort in defining religion has been subject to precisely such vagaries of metaphorical play.

As I argue in detail elsewhere, the study of religion and religious diversity can be seen to have originated in the surprising discovery by Europeans of people who have no religion. During the eras of exploration and colonization Europeans found indigenous populations all over the world who supposedly lacked any trace of religion. Gradually, however, European observers found ways to recognize—by comparison, by analogy, and by metaphoric transference from the familiar to the strange—the religious character of beliefs and practices among people all over the world. This discovery did not depend upon intellectual innovations in defining the essence of religion; it depended upon localized European initiatives that extended the familiar metaphors that were already associated with religion, such as the belief in God, rites of worship, or the maintenance of moral order, to the strange beliefs and practices of other human populations.[42] In the study of religion in American popular culture, I would suggest, we are confronted with the same theoretical dilemma of mediating between the familiar and the strange.

The theoretical models of religion that we have considered allow some of the strangely religious forms of popular culture—baseball, Coca-Cola, and rock 'n' roll—to become refamiliarized as if they were religion. They allow them to appear as the church, the fetish, and the sacred gift of the ritual potlatch in American popular culture. Why not? Why should these cultural forms not be regarded as religion?

The determination of what counts as religion is not the sole preserve of academics. The very term "religion" is contested and at stake in the discourses and practices of popular culture. Recall, for instance, the disdain expressed by the critic who dismissed rock 'n' roll as a "cult of obscenity, brutality, and sonic abuse." In this formulation the term "cult" signifies the absence of religion. "Cult," in this regard, is the opposite of "religion." The usage of the term "cult," however it might be intended, inevitably resonates with the discourse of an extensive and pervasive anti-cult campaign that has endeavored to deny the status of "religion" to a variety of new religious movements by labeling them as entrepreneurial businesses, politically subversive movements, or coercive, mind-controlling, and brainwashing "cults." In that context, if we should ever speak about the "cult" of baseball, Coca-Cola, or rock 'n' roll, we could be certain about one thing: We would not be speaking about religion.

The very definition of religion, therefore, continues to be contested in American popular culture. However, if we look again at the privileged examples that we have considered—baseball, Coca-Cola, and rock 'n' roll—they seem to encompass a wildly diverse but somehow representative range of possibilities for what might count as religion. They evoke familiar metaphors—the religious institution of the church, the religious desires attached to the fetish, and the religious exchanges surrounding the sacred gift—that resonate with other discourses, practices, experiences, and social formations that we are prepared to include within the ambit of religion. Why do they not count as religion?

In the end, we will need to answer that question. By saying "we," however, I refer in this case to all of us who are in one way or another engaged in the professionalized and institutionalized academic study of religion. Participants in American popular culture have advanced their own answers. As a baseball player, Buck O'Neil certainly had an answer: "It's a religion." As a Coca-Cola executive, Delony Sledge definitely had an answer: "Our work is a religion." As a rock 'n' roller, John Lennon had his own distinctive and controversial answer: "Christianity will go. It will vanish and shrink. I needn't argue about that. I'm right and I will be proved right. We're more popular than Jesus now."[43] From the church of baseball, through the fetish of Coca-Cola, to the sacred and sanctifying gift-giving of the potlatch of rock 'n' roll, the discourses and practices of popular culture raise problems of definition and analysis for the study of religion. In different ways, as I have tried to suggest, these three terms—church, fetish, and potlatch—signify both the problem of defining religion and the complex presence of religion in American popular culture.

## NOTES

1. Geoffrey C. Ward and Ken Burns, eds., *Baseball: An Illustrated History* (New York: Alfred A. Knopf, 1994): 231

2. Ibid., xviii.

3. Thomas Boswell, "The Church of Baseball," in Geoffrey C. Ward and Ken Burns, eds., *Baseball: An Illustrated History* (New York: Alfred A. Knopf, 1994): 189.

4. Ibid., 193

5. Ibid., 189–90.

6. Ibid., 189.

7. Horace Miner, "Body Ritual Among the Nacirema," *American Anthropologist* 58/3 (1956): 503–507.

8. George Gmelch, "Baseball Magic," in James P. Spradley and David W. McCurdy, eds., *Conformity and Conflict: Readings in Cultural Anthropology* (Glenview, Ill.: Scot, Foresman, 1978): 373–383.

9. Sigmund Freud, "Obsessive Acts and Religious Practices," in James Strachey, ed., *The Standard Edition of the Complete Psychological Works of Sigmund Freud* (London: Hogarth Press, 1953): 9: 117–127.

10. Emile Benveniste, *Indo-European Language and Society*, trans. Elizabeth Palmer (London: Faber and Faber, 1973): 522.

11. Thomas Hobbes, *Leviathan*, ed. Michael Oakeshot (New York: Collier Books, 1962): 69.

12. Milton J. Yinger, *Religion, Society, and the Individual* (New York: Macmillan, 1957): 147.

13. Mark Pendergrast, *For God, Country, and Coca-Cola: The Unauthorized History of the World's Most Popular Soft Drink* (New York: Charles Scribner's Sons, 1993). All subsequent references to this text are cited by page number in the body of the essay.

14. Marshall Fishwick, "Review: Sut Jhally, *The Codes of Advertising*," *Journal of Popular Culture* 26/2 (1992): 155.

15. William Pietz, "The Problem of the Fetish, I," *Res: Anthropology and Aesthetics* 9 (Spring 1985): 5–17; "The Problem of the Fetish, II," *Res: Anthropology and Aesthetics* 13 (Spring 1987): 23–45; "The Problem of the Fetish, IIIa," *Res: Anthropology and Aesthetics* 16 (Autumn 1988): 105–123. See Emily Apter and William Pietz, eds., *Fetishism as Cultural Discourse* (Ithaca, N.Y.: Cornell University Press, 1993).

16. Michael Taussig, "Maleficium: State Fetishism," *The Nervous System* (London: Routledge, 1992).

17. Benedict Anderson, *Imagined Communities: Reflections on the Origin and Spread of Nationalism* (London: Verso, 1991); Eric Hobsbawm and Terrence Ranger, eds., *The Invention of Tradition* (Cambridge: Cambridge University Press, 1985); Leonard Thompson, *The Political Mythology of Apartheid* (New Haven: Yale University Press, 1985).

18. Jay R. Howard, "Contemporary Christian Music: Where Rock Meets Religion," *Journal of Popular Culture* 26/1 (1992): 123.

19. Gross, Robert L. "Heavy Metal Music: A New Subculture in American Society," *Journal of Popular Culture* 24/1 (1990): 119–130; Davin Seay and Mary Neely, *Stairway to Heaven: The Spiritual Roots of Rock 'n' Roll* (New York: Ballantine, 1986).

20. Bob Larson, *Rock and Roll: The Devil's Diversion* (McCook, NB: Larson, 1967); Linda Martin and Kerry Segrave, *Anti-Rock: The Opposition to Rock 'n' Roll* (Hamden, Conn.: Archon Books, 1988); Dan Peters, Steve Peters, and Cher Merrill, *What About Christian Rock?* (Minneapolis: Bethany, 1986).

21. David Shenk and Steve Silberman, *Skeleton Key: A Dictionary for Deadheads* (New York: Doubleday, 1994): ix; Tony Magistrale, "Wild Child: Jim Morrison's Poetic Journeys," *Journal of Popular Culture* 26/3 (1992): 133–144; Robert Pattison, *The Triumph of Vulgarity: Rock Music in the Mirror of Romanticism* (Oxford: Oxford University Press, 1987); Lisa St. Clair Harvey, "Temporary Insanity: Fun, Games, and Transformational Ritual in American Music Video," *Journal of Popular Culture* 24/1 (1990): 39–64; Jon Michael Spencer, "Overview of American Popular Music in a Theological Perspective," in Spencer, ed., *Theomusicology* (Durham, N.C.: Duke University Press, 1994): 205.

22. Dave Marsh, *Louie, Louie* (New York: Hyperion, 1993): 74.

23. Ibid., 77.

24. Ibid., 78.

25. Ibid., 78

26. Ibid., 73–74.

27. For a useful review of literature on the potlatch, see Steven Vertovec, "Potlatching and the Mythic Past: A Re-evaluation of the Traditional Northwest Coast American Indian Complex," *Religion* 13 (1983): 323–344.

28. Marsh, *Louie, Louie,* 79–80.

29. Ibid., 80.

30. Ibid.

31. Martha Bayles, *Hole in Our Soul: The Loss of Beauty and Meaning in American Popular Music* (New York: Free Press, 1994): 12.

32. Marcel Mauss, *The Gift: Forms and Functions of Exchange in Archaic Societies.* Trans. Ian Cunnison (London: Cohen & West, 1969): 1.

33. Ibid., 4.

34. Victor Turner, *Dramas, Fields, and Metaphors: Symbolic Action in Human Society* (Ithaca, N.Y.: Cornell University Press, 1974): 262.

35. Greil Marcus, *Lipstick Traces: A Secret History of the Twentieth Century* (Cambridge, Mass.: Harvard University Press, 1989).

36. Georges Bataille, "The Notion of Expenditure," in *Visions of Excess: Selected Writings, 1927–1939*, ed. Allan Stoekly, trans. Allan Stoekly, Carl R. Lovitt, and Donald M. Lesie, Jr. (Minneapolis: University of Minnesota Press, 1985): 118.

37. E. B. Tylor, *Primitive Culture.* 2 vols. (London: John Murray, 1870): 1:424.

38. *Sports Illustrated* 82/14 (April 10, 1995): 92.

39. Emile Durkheim, *The Elementary Forms of the Religious Life*, trans. Joseph Ward Swain. (New York: Free Press, 1965): 62.

40. G. Pascal Zachary, *Showstopper: The Breakneck Race to Create Windows NT and the Next Generation at Microsoft* (New York: Free Press, 1994): 281.

41. On the significance of the polythetic categories of "cluster concepts" and "fuzzy sets" for the study of religion, see Fitz John Porter Poole, "Metaphors and Maps: Towards Comparison in the Anthropology of Religion," *Journal of the American Academy of Religion* 54 (1986): 428; and Jonathan Z. Smith, *Drudgery Divine: On the Comparison of Early Christianities and the Religions of Late Antiquity* (Chicago: University of Chicago Press, 1990): 50.

42. David Chidester, *Savage Systems: Colonialism and Comparative Religion in Southern Africa* (Charlottesville: University Press of Virginia, 1996).

43. Fred Bronson, *The Billboard Book of Number One Hits* (New York: Billboard Publications, 1985): 201.

SPIRITUALITY FOR SALE

*Christopher Ronwanièn:te Jocks*

Can Native American religious beliefs and practices be written about without exploitation? In "Spirituality for Sale," Chris Jocks, a Native American scholar, alerts us to the growing traffic in indigenous spirituality at a time when discrimination against Native peoples continues. What is wrong with interpretations of Native American knowledge that are written for general as well as academic markets, Jocks argues, is that they are often inaccurate or they reveal privileged information without permission. In either case, the use of "sacred knowledge" can be not only unethical but deeply offensive to indigenous peoples, regardless of whether the author is an "insider" or an "outsider" to the tradition being interpreted. In response to this situation, Jocks calls for all writers to not only explain the motivations behind their research but substantially contribute to the welfare of the communities they study.

Reprinted from the *American Indian Quarterly*, volume 20, numbers 3 and 4 (summer/fall 1996), by permission of the University of Nebraska Press. Copyright 1997 by the University of Nebraska Press.

# 23

# SPIRITUALITY FOR SALE

## Sacred Knowledge in the Consumer Age

*Christopher Ronwanièn:te Jocks*

A FRIEND OF MINE, a traditional Kanien'kehá:ka (Mohawk) woman, tells about being ap-proached by members of a foundation dedicated to "New Age" spirituality. As she tells the story, they introduced themselves, described their various spiritual pursuits, and on the basis of these credentials requested to be allowed to participate in some kind of American Indian ceremony. "They were really insistent," she said. "They were convinced they were ready and deserving of this thing." She told them she would oblige them.

"This is what you do," my friend told them. "First, you prepare the feast. Cook up lots and lots of food. We Mohawks make corn soup, but you can substitute tofu stir-fry if you like. As you're cooking it, think about the people you'll be inviting, about their lives, and about your own. Think about the ingredients too, where they come from, and who helped bring them to you. Then invite everyone you know to come over. Make sure you have enough food. Everybody that comes, you feed them. And you listen to them, pay attention to their advice, their problems. Hold their hands, if that's what they need. If any of them needs to stay over, make a place for them. Then, next month, you do the same thing again. And again, four times, the same way. That's it! You've done an Indian ceremony!"

This friend of mine was not being facetious or making fun of these seekers. Her advice was completely earnest. Nor was she asserting that somehow hospitality is the essence of ceremony. Rather, as I understand it, her reply was based on a critical distinction between what might constitute a ceremony for members of the participating ceremonial commu-nity—in this case, an Iroquois Longhouse community—and those aspects of it that are considered useful or accessible or teachable to others. It had the further merit of politely but clearly unmasking the arrogant assumption that one can prepare to participate in cer-emony, and in fact can earn the right to do so, in any way other than by *becoming a member* of the community enacting the ceremony.

I can discern at least two bases upon which an American Indian community might de-cide what is or is not to be shared with outsiders, in relation to traditional thought and practice. One is moral and political, and concerns the "unequal power relations," to put it politely, that continue to exist between American Indian peoples and Euroamericans. Here, the issue is this: sharing of spiritual practices and knowledge can only rightly take place among equals, in a discourse of mutual respect, with the permission of both parties. By contrast, today an entire industry has sprung up in which indigenous spirituality is appropriated, distorted, used, and sold without respect or permission, *even while* physical assaults on Native people, lands, and ways of life, continue. The best intentions and most heartfelt rejection of injustice by Euroamerican *individuals* are simply not very relevant here as long as they remain mere sentiment; hard work and real change from within the larger society, not escapism, are requisite. In many variations, this is the most frequently heard critique by Native people of attempts to appropriate their spiritual lives.

The other distinction is perhaps less often articulated, and concerns not what *should* be taught, but what *can* be taught; or, what can be translated accurately out of a Native context into a non-Native one. The issues here are not only linguistic, but epistemological and ontological as well, coming together under the title of hermeneutics. They concern the very nature of knowledge, and of the reality enacted or enhanced by American Indian ceremonies. These are matters about which Native traditionalists cultivate and maintain vastly different perceptions from those familiar to Euroamerican intellectual and religious history.

For the remainder of this text I will do three things: First, I will briefly review and summarize the first of these two critiques, the moral-political. I say briefly because these matters have been amply addressed elsewhere. Second, I will extend my discussion of the second distinction, the hermeneutical, drawing on the remarks of Indian and non-Indian commentators, as well as events related to a tradition with which I am a little familiar. Last, I will engage in some reflection about the relationship between appropriations attempted by New Age enthusiasts and other "seekers," on the one hand, and the work of anthropologists and other seekers of comparative social and cultural "data," on the other. My thesis is that without firmly grounded and enacted knowledge about the internally prescribed limits of externally available knowledge, such "data" is liable to be not only ethically clouded, but logically and intellectually unreliable.

Before proceeding, however, I should clarify my own place in relation to this thesis: Although I am Kanien'kehá:ka as well as Euroamerican by birth and by law, and although I have participated in Longhouse ceremonies, my academic career and placement have prevented me from being a regular participant in any Longhouse community. Thus I write, compile, and arrange these comments not as a representative, official or otherwise, of any Native tradition. Rather, I write from an in-between perspective, as a member of the academic community who at the same time seeks to maintain and build relationships with my own and other Native communities. Based on these relationships, I am committed to clearing open ground for new kinds of discourse between this hemisphere's First Peoples and Euroamerican intellectual tradition, in which the former are active, critical participants rather than passive specimens or curiosities.

## THE MORAL-POLITICAL ARGUMENT

Some of the most colorful and energetic attacks on the appropriation of American Indian identity and "wisdom" are those by Ward Churchill. Especially pronounced in them is the impression shared by many people involved with Indian communities, that most of these "adaptations" are patently ludicrous. Anger or outrage are later responses; the initial reaction is usually to laugh in disbelief at the depth of human gullibility. As, for instance, when

Lynn Andrews claims that she was forced to strip naked and enter a luminous tipi in order to be initiated by "the grandmothers" into a planetary/cosmic "Sisterhood of the Shields" (Andrews 1981:49). Churchill describes the ridiculous nature of these revelations:

> In her version of events, [these women] had apparently been waiting their entire lives for just such an opportunity to unburden themselves of every innermost secret of their people's spiritual knowledge. They immediately acquainted her with such previously unknown "facts" as the presence of kachinas in the Arctic Circle and the power of "Jaguar Women," charged her with serving as their "messenger," and sent her forth to write a series of books so outlandish in their pretensions as to make [Carlos] Castaneda seem a model of propriety by comparison. (Churchill 1992a: 189)[1]

There comes a point, however, when amusement gives way to indignation. Churchill's comic caricature of some forms of the "men's movement" inspired by the writings of Robert Bly is perhaps his least restrained satire (Churchill 1994: 207–72), in which a sense of outrage renders all but transparent the veneer of amusement at such doings. The source of this anger, at least in part, is the astounding success of these and like enterprises, and the fact that this success often displaces, distorts, marginalizes, and belittles Native people's own cultural production. Churchill, as well as Wendy Rose (1992) and other commentators, has described this not only as cultural imperialism, but cultural genocide. Readers can easily consult these sources for more detailed discussion and examples of these critiques. I summarize them as follows:

1.   Commercial adaptations and academic interpretations of American Indian knowledge and practice are often plainly inaccurate. Such inaccuracy can take several forms:
     *Outright falsification*: In some cases events or people are described as representing or embodying authentic traditional practices and thinking, but are later shown to have been simply made up. The works of Carlos Castaneda and Lynn Andrews are most often mentioned under this category.[2]
     *Distortion*: Descriptions of events and people considered authentic by the community to which they belong and by scholars as well can nonetheless distort through the use of inappropriate external categories or frames of interpretation. This is a particular problem in academic writing that has assumed congruence between American Indian religious understandings and European religious categories such as "the supernatural," "Supreme Being," "evil," and even such borrowings as the northern Eurasian "shamanism."[3]
     *Violation of context*: There are numerous examples of descriptions that distort by selecting only the most pleasing (read, "marketable") elements of Native experience to "reveal." Typically, practices that seem to involve "mystical" individual experiences are promoted, while other elements considered equally or more important by Native participants are ignored: elements such as kinship obligations, hard work, suffering, and the sometimes crazy realities of everyday reservation life. Especially guilty in this regard are various how-to books that purport to teach individuals how to replicate Indian ceremonies on their own.[4]

2.   Conversely, adaptations or interpretations can be *too* accurate, in the sense that they are too revealing. They can violate Native rules of privilege, designed to protect aspects of specialized knowledge and practice from dangerous exposure or misuse. This is rarely the case in popular writing, but has been an issue in anthropology at least since Frank Cushing threatened his way into the kivas at Zuñi.[5]

3.   In either case, such adaptations or interpretations can be severely unethical, in that perpetrators use knowledge without proper Native permission or attribution, and often do so as part of alien and deeply offensive commercial enterprises. To say that traditional ceremonies are not intended to be performed for cash or for profit is to miss the more fundamental point, which is that traditional American Indian ceremonial work is of a piece with traditional economic structures which, in turn, are based on reciprocal relationships within a community.

     Thus a sacred practitioner is, by definition, a person integrated into the place and the community out of which she or he works. I have been fortunate enough to meet a handful of such people and to know a couple of them well, and in each case I have the feeling I am meeting not only a remarkable individual, but a kind of epitome of the community they serve. As I have witnessed, when traditional exchanges are offered in return for ceremonial work, within days this "payment" is usually spread in one way or another among relatives and friends, into and across an entire district.[6]

4.   All such behavior demonstrates to the legitimate practitioners of these traditions that those who abuse ceremony in these ways do not actually believe in the power and efficacy involved. In a gesture of profound disrespect, powerful and potentially dangerous techniques whose use in the Indian context often requires years of study and training are treated as if they were merely edifying symbolic or meditative exercises. I can think of no clearer example than Thomas Mails's *Secret Native American Pathways: A Guide to Inner Peace* (1988), in which artificial versions of pieces of Hopi, Cherokee, Apache, and "Sioux" prayer forms are taught to unseen readers as "The native American way and your way to lasting inner peace" (226).[7]

Note that these critiques apply equally to those who write books about Native knowledge and practice—whether packaged as poetry, academic or popular non-fiction, or fiction based on privileged information—and those who profess to actually practice, teach, and perform such things in workshops and the like. Wendy Rose, for instance, treats both under the category of "whiteshamanism." Again, those unfamiliar with these arguments are referred to the sources mentioned. Note too that from an Indian perspective, while primary responsibility for such violations must be assigned to those who perpetrate them knowingly, once a follower is aware of the objections of Native communities, she or he is called upon to respond accordingly. However nobly an individual may understand her or his own motives, it is simply not up to anyone other than the members of the practicing community to decide what these limits should be.

## THE HERMENEUTICAL ARGUMENT

It is my contention that each of the above abuses of American Indian religious integrity renders its product not only reprehensible but meaningless, to the extent that it poses an interpreted part for the original whole. This assertion follows logically from what I proposed originally as an Iroquois Longhouse epistemological framework, extended here as a general theory:

> In American Indian contexts, the only knowledge that is meaningful is that which is enacted ("walk your talk"). It is enacted by individuals, but individuals act, whether they are aware of it or not, only as part of a community, and thus, a participant in that community's history.[8]

To the extent that this is true, the history and intentions of a speaker, or by extension a writer, are an integral and inescapable component of the message she or he expresses.[9] Thus, knowledge as a timeless, preexisting abstraction, or data that can be transmitted independent of the "accidents" of its encodation, is simply undefined, unverifiable, unapproachable. From this perspective knowledge cannot be traded in some imagined neutral "marketplace of ideas," as if it were itself a neutral, disembodied object. A falsified claim of identity or authority, then, can render the message moot just as in many traditions a mistake either of execution or of attitude can render a ceremony ineffective.

Responding to a paper at a recent academic conference, I found myself searching for an image with which to convey a sense of this intimate approach to knowledge. I ended up speaking about skin. "For Indians," I said, "these ceremonies and the knowledge they express are like our skin. That's how close to us they are. When people we don't know, or people we do, pretend to use these ceremonies away from their proper setting, it really is like stealing the 'skin off our backs.' " The Center for the Support and Protection of Indian Religions and Indigenous Traditions (CSPIRIT) put it this way in 1993;

> Traditional ceremonies and spiritual practices . . . are precious gifts given to Indian people by our Creator. These sacred ways have enabled us as Indian people to survive—miraculously— the onslaught of five centuries of continuous effort by non-Indians and their government to exterminate us by extinguishing all traces of our traditional ways of life. Today, these precious sacred traditions continue to afford American Indian people of all [nations] the strength and vitality we need in the struggle we face every day; they also offer us our best hope for a stable and vibrant future. These sacred traditions are an enduring and indispensable "life raft" without which we would be quickly overwhelmed by the adversities that still threaten our survival. Because our sacred traditions are so precious to us, we cannot allow them to be desecrated and abused. (CSPIRIT 1993)

Such language further supports Churchill's own remarks criticizing the casual approach of many New Age enthusiasts who dabble in multiple "spiritualities":

> I thought about protesting that spiritual traditions cannot be used as some sort of Whitman's Sampler of ceremonial form, mixed and matched—here a little Druid, there a touch of Nordic mythology followed by a regimen of Hindu vegetarianism, a mishmash of American Indian rituals somewhere else—at the whim of people who are part of none of them. I knew I should say that to play at ritual potluck is to debase all spiritual traditions, voiding their internal coherence and leaving nothing usably sacrosanct as a cultural anchor for the peoples who conceived and developed them, and who have consequently organized their societies around them. (Churchill 1994: 213)

At the very least, then, this places a necessity on anyone writing about such matters to state clearly and accurately the kinds of experience, collaboration, and authorization upon which statements are based. Interpretations of, say, Iroquois spirituality, produced by other than duly recognized representatives of Iroquois communities, need to be identified as such, and the relationship between such interpreters and those communities specified. It is even more important for publishers, both academic and popular, to adhere to standards along these lines in evaluating submissions, and to refuse to publish work that violates them.[10]

None of this should be construed as if to suggest a "party line" of Indian political (or spiritual) correctness, however, in which only those with the most complete or pedigreed knowledge have any right to speak. Such authoritarianism is completely antithetical to all the North American traditions I know of. Sit around Indian campfires or kitchen stoves very long and one is bound to hear differences of opinion, of interpretation, even on spiritual matters, enjoyed and passed around, chewed over and disputed, once the anthropologists have gone home and the tape recorders are turned off—at least among those interested in such things. In fact it would be yet another mark of racism, smacking of nineteenth-century stereotypes of communal "primitive mentality," to expect drab uniformity or inarticulateness of belief around these fires.

We simply need to demand that those who put forth their interpretive opinions in public fora, printed and otherwise, stand up and tell their stories fully—"put their belly out before us," in Frank Waters's memorable phrase—and not hide behind cloaks of holier-than-thou, or more-learned-than-thou, arrogance. Once they have stood up, they must expect the same kind of sharp, even combative, scrutiny that visitors sometimes experience when visiting Indian communities. In my experience, bearing such attacks, showing what one is made of, can be the best way to make friends.

This is the case whether the "authority" in question is of Indian descent or not.[11] A number of the most sharply attacked "plastic medicine men" are of Native blood, and some of them can recount deep connections to their Indian contexts earlier in their lives. Once they have started on the road of selling their Native spirituality to paying customers elsewhere, however, relations back home invariably go bad. Some, like Ed McGaa (also known as "Eagle Man"; 1990 and 1992), assert nonetheless that their "mission" to the wider world was the result of visionary experience, a claim that leaves nonparticipant readers as well as many Indian people in something of a quandary. The line between authenticity and quackery is not always easy to draw, and in fact many of the most traditional-minded will simply refrain from doing so as a matter of policy.

As a teacher, I am not interested in silencing anyone, not even a Lynn Andrews. Yet when I am faced with strong evidence that an author's claims are deceptive, or if their interpretation of a community's religious life is far askew of what is known from those people's own perspectives, I will work to call such an author to account. If the accusing evidence is clear, I will urge others not to buy the book, not to pay for the workshop—not only for ethical reasons, but because what is being sold is probably not "the real thing" anyway; won't do what it is claimed to do, and might just do harm instead. Then there is one other judgment I am forced to make: Which books or articles will I have my students read, and how will I present them? In these decisions I will always prefer works that show strong evidence of real, ongoing connections within a community. An author may dispute predominant interpretations or attitudes in a community; I will only insist that she or he do so from a basis of demonstrated understanding of and familiarity with the life of that community.

## THE PRIVILEGES OF SCHOLARSHIP?

The same Kanien'kehá:ka woman whose story begins this essay was preparing to begin her graduate work in religious studies when she was contacted by the professor she would mainly be working with and asked to bring with her whatever information she could gather from Longhouse elders on the so-called "False Face" society—in Mohawk, *ato'wíhtshera*—who play an important but highly privileged and protected role in Longhouse spiritual work. This "data" the professor hoped to include in a comparative study of "masking." My friend protested that as a traditional person, she could not do this. As far as she was concerned, the work of this society was real; the power its members associate with, potentially dangerous. As someone not initiated into the society, for her even to inquire about it would be to invite harm. This much she said to her professor; but I think she would agree with me that even if she had been a member, the same harm would result from giving out elements of that understanding—in effect, selling it—to outsiders who are, by definition, unprepared to understand and respect it. Thus, the accuracy of the information she might or might not have been able to obtain, from the narrow standpoint of academic/scientific "data," was never the issue. The whole network of context and intention, was.

Unfortunately, at least as this graduate student recounted the story to me, her reply initiated an increasingly hostile exchange with her professor that ended in the termination of their working relationship.[12] According to her understanding, this representative of the academic establishment refused ultimately to credit or respect her conviction that academic inquiry be limited by, and thus in some sense subject to, the demands of Iroquois traditionalists, the "subjects" of this proposed study. The question then becomes, does this kind of external limitation damage the integrity of such a study? Can an academic discipline privilege the authority of religious stricture in the formulation of its own research, as indeed has been demanded recently by the Hopi Tribal Council?[13]

In a recent assessment of the academic study of religion, Sam Gill, once recognized as an authority on Native American religion in particular, strongly criticizes what he sees as the emphasis of the entire discipline on "discourse conducted on the authority of vision, insight, or experience," rather than on "rational discourse, hypothetical inference, and the application of scientific method"; claims that the discipline has thus abandoned its academic foundations to become "the religious study of religion"; in other words, that "the academic study of religion has often failed to acknowledge what it is. It is academic; it is *Western*; it is intellectual" (Gill 1994: 967–68; emphasis mine).[14]

The same conflict my graduate student friend encountered, over academic self-limitation in the face of Native community demands and concerns, is implied in this critique. As a scholar I have no interest in promoting *irrational* discourse; but as an Indian I would counter that the religious discourse of any Native people responds to its own rationality. Yet if we ask to whose rationality academic work ought to respond, Gill's answer is clear: *Western* rationality must continue to be the norm.

I respond that cross-cultural study can never break out of its "ghetto" in this way. Under this regime, rather than contributing to and broadening theory, method, or epistemology, *they*—meaning the "other" culture—become merely another "subject," another kind of specimen, for Euroamerican intellectual frames, categories, or tools. The stipulation of Iroquois elders that *ato'wíhtshera* is out of bounds for academic research thus becomes merely an impediment without intrinsic merit, to be overcome if possible. This too is appropriation, dressed up a bit but just as offensive to Native thought and practice as the ludicrous concoctions of commercial would-be shamans.

Dealing with these real and substantive issues involves the very theoretical basis—the *what* and *how*—of cross-cultural academic work. Professor Gill, by contrast, shifts the focus to questions of *who*. He asserts that the field at present is hopelessly sidetracked by issues of academic qualification; more specifically, whether work in the field should be restricted to those with fieldwork and linguistic competency in the community under study, or even more narrowly, to those who are ethnically Native American. Thus, he asserts that participation in the field is being dictated by Indian people (scholars?) along ethnic and racial lines, so that graduate programs "encourage primarily those who are ethnically Native American," producing scholars who "engage only cultural materials absent of conversation with any academic community whatsoever" (Gill 1994: 971–73).

As an Indian scholar of religion who has been active in the field for five years, I must report I have never encountered a single incident in which such an exclusionary strategy has been promoted. Furthermore, any survey of the small body of literature on American Indian traditions in religious studies journals will find that Native scholars are in fact *underrepresented*. The issue is not and has never been whether non-Natives should "be allowed" to work in this field, and no Native scholar I know has ever insisted that one must be Indian in order to understand or study Indian communities. To do so would embrace notions of "wisdom in the blood" that carry cultural and philosophical relativism to its untenable extreme.

Rather, the issue is how the work is to be done. Again, the crux of the matter is both hermeneutical and political. It is hermeneutical in that one simply cannot gain an accurate understanding of what goes on in Indian Country without living in and around an Indian community for a long time. American Indian life does not work by the same rules or categories as life in the "mainstream," and it usually takes years to become aware of the subtleties of perception, history, and communication that inform it. In fact, one really needs not just to reside, but to reside *as a relative*, since there are vast dimensions of meaning that are only acted out in this way. Even this is not a matter of blood, however. There are fullblood Indians who have lost this ability to participate in kinship, and yet in every Indian community I have ever visited there have been one or two whites who have gained it.

And the issue is political in that power, status, money, and sometimes passionate mainstream public emotions continue to surround Indian issues, and hinge on their resolution. In the current American climate of racial and economic tension, these supposedly intellectual arguments quickly reveal their provocative political undersides. This is no news to Indian people, who have been eyewitnesses from the beginning to the confluence of Western intellectual history and the inescapable reality of the genocidal invasion of the Americas. It is news to many scholars, however, and not very welcome news at that. For example, Sam Gill laments that "the matter [of academic qualification in the study of American Indian religions] has become almost purely political and has failed to raise any substantive academic issues" (Gill 1994: 971). In fact, by disdainfully ignoring the presence of political history at the academic table, Gill is led to an odd but telling non sequitur. He writes:

> The question of whether or not one ought to know one's subject in terms of the language and cultural setting seems to be the question of whether or not the area of study is an academic one. For there to be any discussion is evidence that it is not. (Gill 1994: 971)

In other words, the discipline itself—which, again, Gill understands as dominated by ethnic American Indians—is to be discredited as non-academic and thus blamed for even raising the issue of research competence. No mention is made of the fact that it is the in-competence and inaccuracy of generations of mostly non-Native "authorities" on Indian religion, as perceived by Native people, that has necessitated the focus on this issue.

In a larger sense, however, the hermeneutical and the political domains of this response merge. Traditional American Indian communities do not conceive of "religious knowl-edge" apart from its complex relations with other domains, including economics and poli-tics. There is no knowledge other than what is lived out, and there is no living out that is not political and historical. In other words if, as a colleague has written, "being born Indian is being born into politics" (Alfred 1995: 1), then how can any attempt to study Indian life avoid the political? How can any study of adaptations to "modernity" in Native religious life ignore the direct and indirect attacks that modern Euroamerican institutions have made and continue to make on Indian ways of life? To put it bluntly, while academicians may pretend to cloak themselves in a pure mantle of scientific detachment, virtually all the institutions we work for, in one way or another are connected to and supported by—in fact were built on—enterprises involving the exploitation of American Indian land and lives.

Of course historical study is the only way to achieve depth in the analysis of religious, political, or other developments and questions. I often tell people that I have never en-countered a people more attuned to and interested in historical questions than those in my ancestral Mohawk community of Kahnawà:ke. My inquiries there were not even taken se-riously until I was able to demonstrate knowledge of, and opinions about, Kahnawà:ke's history. Thus I would find highly suspect a synchronic community study that lacked his-torical depth. Conversely, historical studies that exhibit no relationship with the present, no input from today's descendants of that history, strike me as pallid and decapitated.

In fact, strong political disputes are often sparked and churned up around historical questions. A particularly difficult pass is reached when historical documents dispute an In-dian community's own perception, in oral tradition, of its history. This is tricky ground for any scholar who cares about her or his standing in the community. But again, I would argue against choices that smother disagreement and enforce conformity to a party line. Rather, the best answer might be to focus on presentation. Such contradictions need not be reported simply because they have been found, first of all—this calls up the question of motivation; the purpose of the study in the first place. But even when the choice is to pres-ent the contradiction, I have found that it can be done in such a way as to *explain* it; to sug-gest reasons for the discrepancy; to see it in larger frames, and thus usually to some degree to turn it into an occasion for thoughtful exchange rather than polemics.

At the very least, therefore, those involved in academic inquiry ought to reexamine both the means and the ends of research involving Native peoples. How did the academic tradi-tion of prying and cajoling and tricking "information" out of Native "informants"—then expertly demonstrating the real, hidden reasons and motivations for such outlandish be-havior and beliefs—arise? What has motivated it, and how much of that motivation remains? Rather than scientist interpreting specimen, can we imagine a model in which Indigenous and Euroamerican intellectual histories meet and conduct authentic exchanges in a context of real respect?

If scholars of religion continue to insist that such a model surrenders too much control to believers, tainting scientific method with theology—becoming "the religious study of religion"—then scholars and traditional practitioners will continue to inhabit largely un-related worlds. Such scholars will find themselves increasingly placed by angry Indians on the same platform with a whole crowd of commercial neo-Native "hucksters" whom the scholars themselves once dismissed and scorned. As an alternative, I list a few bare suggestions toward building the kind of model I am hoping for:

1. If an academic career built on the study of an American Indian community provides a living for a scholar and the scholar's family, she or he should feel obliged to reciprocate in some substantial way toward that community. This is especially true if that community faces imminent threats to its survival, which few Indian communities today do not.

2. As stated above, scholars need to provide clear and comprehensive accounts of their relationships with the Indian communities they study. Moreover, the issue of motivation—*why* they are involved in this work—ought to be considered an integral part of its justification. Mere curiosity or filling in lacunae in "the research record" should not be thought of as adequate reasons to probe into peoples' lives.

3. Scholarship ought to look on American Indian systems of knowledge and practice not as new, untried fields of data with which to test existing Amer-European essentialist theories; but as sources for new theories, new categories—even new frameworks with which to study and evaluate aspects of non-Indian life.

4. Indigenous sacred work and Native interpretations of such work ought to be considered as intellectual property, subject to all the appropriate permissions and credits.[15]

5. Given the profound linguistic, philosophical, historical, and political chasms between modern, literate, Amer-European civilization and the oral world of traditional American Indian communities, no written source, whether the author is Indian or not, should be exempted from the closest critical evaluation.

In this essay I have tried to demonstrate two things: first, how the appropriation of American Indian religious or spiritual systems involves not only ethical but political and hermeneutical failures; and second, how these same issues, which can appear in such exaggerated, obvious, cartoon form in some manifestations of popular enthusiasm, lie also more subtly beneath the rarefied realm of academic inquiry. But in my estimation, if we are to speak in general of "contemporary issues in Native American spirituality," as this collection of essays attempts to do, this issue of appropriation and intrusion by academics and "New Age" enthusiasts is but one of perhaps three areas of deepest concern to Native traditionalists these days. The other two are (1) continuing threats to Indian landholdings and land use, especially in relation to sacred places—although all Indian land is understood as sacred in a basic sense; and (2) continuing economic and cultural invasion of Native communities, causing erosion of self-sufficiency and the decay of *integrity* in ceremonial work.

Current land issues include the conflict over the University of Arizona's Mount Graham observatory complex, as well as such longstanding issues as the Big Mountain relocation; the Lakota, Dakota, and Nakota claim to the Black Hills; and a long list of other Native land claims, large and small.[16] Examples of economic and cultural invasion issues include the forced imposition of educational methods and programs antithetical to traditional values, language, and ways of life; the invasion of consumer culture via television, alcohol, and most brands of Christian missionization; ongoing lobbying by powerful private and gov-

ernment entities to locate radioactive waste dumps and other toxic byproducts of technological excess on Indian land; and of course, the long history of the reservation system, the
removal of Native children to boarding schools, and other forms of economic and cultural
exploitation that make these new get-rich-quick schemes so attractive to many Indian
communities. How can ceremonial life fail to suffer degradation when the natural environment is degraded, when economic demands upon time spiral out of control, when Native
languages rapidly erode, and when a whole gamut of market-driven alien substitutes
crowd around every Indian home?

Of these areas of concern, the focus of this essay is probably the most abstract in terms
of its actual threat to Indian ways of life, yet its importance to Indian communities is apparent from the sustained intensity of their response. Even so, because of its secular and
scientific foundations, the non-Indian Euroamerican world continues to respond cynically
to all protests based on traditional indigenous values, characterizing such activism as
merely political—as public relations strategy—rather than religious or spiritual.[17]

All these matters particularly implicate scholarly research and publication, which is why
I thought it important to include at least a brief treatment of them in this collection. The
point is that if academic research on "contemporary issues in Native American spirituality," in whatever specific context, is to be of any use or relevance to Indian people, and if it
is to move beyond the kinds of controversies and friction that have characterized it recently, it cannot but concern itself with these issues, as well as with internal issues involving
cross-cultural methods, theory, and motivation. Rather than impeding, compromising, or
polluting pure academic inquiry, however, these matters ought to be embraced as enliven-
ing it. This is the fertile theoretical ground to which Sam Gill points when he remarks that
"nearly everything about [small-scale exclusively oral] cultures and their religions questions the assumptions and approaches of the academic study of religion" (Gill 1994: 970).
In a sense, I am only advocating additions, primarily political, to his understanding of this
challenge, and pointing out that it is a challenge to expand and deepen the "assumptions
and approaches" not only of one relatively small sub-discipline, but of all cross-cultural
academic work.

## NOTES

1. I am aware of the questions raised in the last few years about Churchill's own claim to "Creek/ Cherokee Métis" identity. I am not in a position to evaluate either the questions or his response, but quote his writing because I find it useful. Certainly the irony of these accusations in light of his stance on the issue is lost on few who are aware of it. The issue of politics, scholarship, and Indian identity are addressed further along in this essay.

2. Castañeda's series of immensely successful popular books began with his *The Teachings of Don Juan: A Yaqui Way of Knowledge* (1968), a revised version of his dissertation in anthropology from UCLA. The evidence against its authenticity is pre-sented in de Mille 1976 and 1980. I am aware of no such exposé regarding the equally popular Andrews

titles, beginning with her *Medicine Woman* in 1976, although Wendy Rose dismisses a few of Andrews' boldest assertions in her critique mentioned above (1992). Pointedly, despite their transparent falsity, both these series of works continue to be listed in libraries and bookstore shelves as works of anthro-pology, ethnography, or religious studies, rather than as fiction.

3. Sometimes the scholar writes as if proving the existence of the phenomenon named by the cat-egory, such as Åke Hultkrantz's work on "the High God" in American Indian traditions (1971; 1979: ch. 2). The alternative is always the absence of the phenomenon; the very applicability of the category is not seriously questioned. Thus, in a real sense what was to be proven is assumed.

4. Two excellent examples are Michael Harner's trademark "Harner® Method" of do-it-yourself "core shamanism," described in his *Way of the Shaman* (1982), and the instructions included in Thomas Mails's *Secret Native American Pathways* (1988).

5. For a recent review of Cushing's odd career, see Green 1990. See also Don Talayesva's passionate Hopi attack on the depredations of the missionary, photographer, and "ethnological collector" Henry R. Voth (Talayesva 1942: 6, 41, and 252). Talayesva is less diplomatic than scholars have been, describing Voth as a brutish, acquisitive thief. He writes, for instance: "The land was very dry, the crops suffered, and even the Snake Dance failed to bring much rain. We tried to discover the reason for our plight, and remembered the Rev. Voth who had stolen so many of our ceremonial secrets and had even carried off sacred images and altars to equip a museum and become a rich man." (Talayesva 1942: 252)

6. In a humorous but entirely typical case, I remember an occasion when a friend of mine gave a respected Singer a fine new western shirt in appreciation for the knowledge he had shared with her over the years. Minutes later he was trying it on when a relative appeared, a middle-aged man somewhat the worse for wear. Sure enough, a few minutes later this "uncle" left, the proud owner of the same flashy new shirt, leaving my friend temporarily nonplused.

7. In an almost unbelievable display of either ignorance or arrogance, Mails continues, "Remember that different approaches will suit different people. In this respect, we are more fortunate than the native Americans were, for while they had only their own pathways to follow, we can choose from those of four different tribes. . . . Test the ways and make your own choices" (Mails 1988: 228–29).

8. This theory is stated more elaborately in Chapter 1 of my dissertation, "Relationship Structures in Longhouse Tradition at Kahnawà:ke" (1994). As I note therein, "knowledge about traditional procedures is but a pale shadow of the active ability to perform them—to rekindle them, in the Longhouse idiom" (Jocks 1994: 5). Gary Witherspoon makes a similar observation in a different context: "Navajos taught me that anything you cannot remember without writing down is something you do not know or understand well enough to *use* effectively" (Witherspoon 1977: 7; emphasis mine).

9. Something very similar in a much wider context seems to be articulated in philosopher Donald Davidson's work on "propositional attitudes," as summarized by Hans Penner in his presentation of "holistic analysis" (Penner 1994). Penner writes, for instance, that "what a person says or does is not just dependent upon what she believes, but also on what she desires, and hopes for" (980).

10. Unfortunately, given the power of market incentives, this is unlikely in the absence of any significant legal means for Native communities to protect the intellectual, emotional, and spiritual rights inherent in their traditional knowledge and practices.

11. The other side of this coin—the question of legitimate participation in American Indian religious life by non-Natives—is taken up in the next section of this essay.

12. Out of courtesy and because I have never taken the opportunity to speak with this professor about the matter, I refrain from naming either of these two parties. My purpose in mentioning it at all is not to accuse an individual, after all, but to illustrate an attitude that seems to me obviously characteristic of much academic inquiry.

13. As I understand it, the Hopi Tribal Council has announced that it must approve and review all future academic research involving Hopi people, land, or culture.

14. Portions of the remainder of this section have been submitted in somewhat different form to the *Journal of the American Academy of Religion*, as a response to Gill's article. Professor Gill announced several years ago that he would no longer teach or publish in the study of American Indian religions, as I understand it for many of the same reasons mentioned in his critique. I regret his departure, having admired much of his work in the field, especially that done before 1987.

15. In a curious twist, I recently encountered a situation in which academic appropriation involved giving more credit than was due to a Native contributor. The latter was listed as co-author of an article, but in fact his contribution was the telling of a traditional narrative whose interpretation was left almost entirely to the other, non-Indian, co-author. In today's market, having a Native co-author listed on the cover will sell more books; yet the product may not be substantively Native at all.

16. An overview of many of these issues can be found in Jaimes 1992. I recently encountered a worthwhile overview of the Mount Graham issue in *High Country News* 27 (13), dated July 24, 1995; its address is: P.O. Box 1090, Paonia CO 81428.

17. For example, see the collection of mainstream critiques Clifton 1990. See also Ward Churchill's evaluation of the book (1992b).

# REFERENCES

Alfred, Gerald R. 1995. *Heeding the Voices of our Ancestors: Kahnawake Mohawk Politics and the Rise of Native Nationalism.* New York: Oxford University Press.

Andrews, Lynn. 1981. *Medicine Woman.* San Francisco: Harper and Row.

Castañeda, Carlos. 1968. *The Teachings of Don Juan: A Yaqui Way of Knowledge.* Berkeley: University of California Press.

Churchill, Ward. 1992a. *Fantasies of the Master Race: Literature, Cinema and the Colonization of American Indians.* Ed. M. Annette Jaimes. Monroe, Maine: Common Courage Press.

———. 1992b. "The New Racism: A Critique of James A. Clifton's The Invented Indian." In Churchill 1992a: 163–84.

———. 1994. *Indians Are Us?: Culture and Genocide in Native North America.* Monroe, Maine: Common Courage Press.

Clifton, James, ed. 1990. *The Invented Indian: Cultural Fictions and Government Policies.* New Brunswick N.J.: Transaction Books.

CSPIRIT (Center for the Support and Protection of Indian Religions and Indigenous Traditions). 1993. "Alert Concerning the Abuse and Exploitation of American Indian Sacred Traditions." Press Release (?), quoted in Churchill 1994: 279–80.

de Mille, Richard. 1976. *Castaneda's Journey: The Power and the Allegory.* Santa Barbara, Calif.: Capra Press.

———. 1980. *The Don Juan Papers: Further Castaneda Controversies.* Santa Barbara, Calif.: Ross-Erikson.

Gill, Sam. 1994. "The Academic Study of Religion." *Journal of the American Academy of Religion* 62: 965–75.

Green, Jesse, ed. 1990. *Cushing at Zuni: The Correspondence and Journals of Frank Hamilton Cushing, 1879–84.* Albuquerque: University of New Mexico Press.

Harner, Michael. 1982. *Way of the Shaman.* New York: Bantam.

Hultkrantz, Åke. 1971. "The Structure of Theistic Beliefs among North American Plains Indians." *Temenos* 7: 66–74.

———. 1979. *The Religions of the American Indians.* Trans. Monica Setterwall. Hermeneutics: Studies in the History of Religions, no. 7. Berkeley: University of California Press.

Jaimes, M. Annette, ed. 1992. *The State of Native America: Genocide, Colonization and Resistance.* Race and Resistance Series. Boston: South End Press.

Jocks, Christopher Ronwanièn:te. 1994. "Relationship Structures in Longhouse Tradition at Kahnawà:ke." (Ph.D. diss., University of California, Santa Barbara.)

Mails, Thomas E. 1988. *Secret Native American Pathways: A Guide to Inner Peace.* Tulsa, Okla.: Council Oak Books.

McGaa, Ed (Eagle Man). 1990. *Mother Earth Spirituality: Native American Paths to Healing Ourselves and Our World.* San Francisco: Harper & Row.

———. 1992. *Rainbow Tribe: Ordinary People Journeying on the Red Road.* San Francisco: Harper San Francisco.

Penner, Hans H. 1994. "Holistic Analysis: Conjectures and Refutations." *Journal of the American Academy of Religion* 62: 977–96.

Rose, Wendy. 1992. "The Great Pretenders: Further Reflections on Whiteshamanism." In Jaimes 1992: 403–21.

Talayesva, Don C. 1942. *Sun Chief: The Autobiography of a Hopi Indian.* Ed. Leo W. Simmons. New Haven: Yale University Press.

Witherspoon, Gary. 1977. *Language and Art in the Navajo Universe.* Ann Arbor: University of Michigan Press.

DIASPORIC NATIONALISM AND URBAN LANDSCAPE

*Thomas A. Tweed*

Since 1970 the number of Hispanic immigrants from Mexico, Cuba, Puerto Rico, and other Latin American countries to the United States has more than doubled to 35.3 million or more than 12 percent of the U.S. population. Hispanics now constitute the largest minority group in the nation. Within the Catholic Church, Hispanic Catholics are the single largest ethnic group. Despite this phenomenal growth, very little is known about the Hispanic Catholic experience of immigration and assimilation to North American culture. In this study of Cuban-American Catholicism, Thomas Tweed analyzes devotion to Our Lady of Charity as an expression of Cuban diasporic nationalism.

The story of Cuban-exile Catholicism begins in 1961 on the feast day of Our Lady of Charity, when a replica statue of Cuba's patron saint was smuggled out of the island and reunited with the Cuban diaspora in a Miami baseball stadium. By 1973, a newly built shrine dedicated to the saint and looking over to Cuba across the waters of Biscayne Bay had become the sacred center of the exiled community. The great majority of the devotees are older, white, middle-class Cubans who see the shrine as a symbol of pre-Castro Cuban nationalism. Tweed's analysis, however, teases out undercurrents of conflicted and contested meanings. A minority of the shrine's visitors, for example, are Afro-Cuban followers of Santería who see Our Lady of Charity as a manifestation of the African Yoruba goddess Ochún. While both groups celebrate a common Cuban national identity, Tweed demonstrates through interviews, participant-observation, and material artifacts how the shrine's Santería devotees give different meanings to the Virgin's appearance, the uses of holy water, and annual rites which de-emphasize the majority's emphasis on war and patriotism. Within this contested national identity, moreover, is a struggle over religious identity, tellingly illustrated by the Cuban clergy's use of the shrine as a means to purify nominal Catholics of the residue of Santería that survives in their popular devotions.

Tweed's essay is both a contribution to our understanding of Cuban-American Catholicism and a theoretical reflection on the interconnections of religion, identity, and place. Diasporic religion, Tweed argues, involves an ongoing process wherein individuals map, construct, and inhabit worlds of meaning. For first and second generation migrants this cultural process is "translocative" and "transtemporal" in its tendency to move the exile community back and forth in place and time between the homeland and the new land. Tweed shows the many ways the new immigrants transform their homes and neighborhoods to look, sound, and even smell like "the Cuba of memory and desire." Correspondingly, Our Lady of Charity is seen as a place that celebrates "Cubanness" more than Catholicism, for the shrine has few rites of baptism, marriage, or death. But this is the place where newborns are brought to visit the Virgin and be blessed by the priests, and the dead are remembered in prayers. Despite different understandings of what the shrine's symbols ultimately mean, all the devotees are joined

by an attachment to the traditions and geography of the homeland. As pluralism en-
riches our present and is increasingly discovered in our past, Tweed's focus on the
theme of place—and the related sub-themes of mapping, meeting, and migration—
may prove to be indispensable for narrating religion in the United States and the
Western Hemisphere.

Reprinted by permission from Thomas A. Tweed, "Diasporic Nationalism and Urban Landscape:
Cuban Immigrants at a Catholic Shrine in Miami" in Robert Orsi, ed. *Gods of the City* (Bloomington:
Indiana University Press, 1999), 131–154.

# 24

# DIASPORIC NATIONALISM AND URBAN LANDSCAPE
## Cuban Immigrants at a Catholic Shrine in Miami

*Thomas A. Tweed*

> *Diasporas always leave a trail of collective memory about another place and time and create new maps of desire and attachment.*[1]

FIDEL CASTRO'S REVOLUTIONARY ARMY victoriously entered Havana on January 8, 1959, and thereby transformed the cultural landscape of Miami. In 1960, only 29,500 Cubans lived in Miami, where they constituted only 3 percent of the local population. Jews had migrated earlier, and they had some public power. Yet the region was still largely Southern and Protestant in character. By 1990, however, more than 561,000 Cubans had arrived, and they made up almost 30 percent of the local residents.[2]

The Cubans who have so abruptly and radically altered the cultural landscape of Miami have viewed themselves above all as members of an exiled community, citizens of a dispersed nation. Yet collective identity becomes especially problematic for exiles. Most immigrants experience disorientation, and most retain fondness for their native land. For exiles, however, those feelings are intensified. As the geographer Yi-Fu Tuan has suggested, "To be forcibly evicted from one's home and neighborhood is to be stripped of a sheathing, which in its familiarity protects the human being from the bewilderments of the outside world." The diaspora's sense of meaning and identity is threatened because it has lost contact with the natal landscape, which is "personal and tribal history made visible."[3]

As political exiles, Cubans have experienced the expected disorientation and shown a singleminded passion for their homeland. As Cuban Americans boast, and some non-Latino blacks and "Anglos" complain, the diaspora tenaciously holds to the Cuban past and continually plans its future. In voting, most ask first about the candidate's stance toward Castro. Musicians and singers who have visited Cuba have been banned from performing in the city. Even those who are not as consumed with these issues scan the news for signs of instability in Castro's government or for stories about the latest *balsero*, or rafter, found bobbing in the Straits of Florida. Spanish-language radio stations hold contests to guess the date that Castro will fall; and paramilitary groups, as well as associations of business and education leaders, plan for the future in a democratic and capitalist Cuba. According to recent surveys, less than one-quarter of exiles say they definitely would return to Cuba to live if democracy and capitalism were restored. But even those who might not return to a "liberated" homeland still repeat the expression commonly heard at Christmas Eve family gatherings: "La próxima Nochebuena nos comeremos el lechoncito en Cuba!" (Next Christmas Eve, we shall eat the traditional roast pork dinner in Cuba).[4]

This attachment to homeland, or nationalism, has a distinctive character for exiles in general and Cubans in particular. For them, "nation" cannot refer to a state or territory: Castro's socialist government is seen as the main problem, and the displaced live outside their homeland's political boundaries. Yet exiles in Miami continue to refer to themselves as part of the Cuban "nation." Nation, in this context, becomes an imaginative construct, even more than is usually the case. The exile group's identity is created, not given; dynamic, not fixed. Relying on memories of the past and hopes for the future, exiles define themselves. In the process, they deterritorialize the nation. For them, nation becomes a supralocal or transregional cultural form, an imagined moral community formed by the diaspora and the oppressed who remain in the homeland.[5]

Diasporic nationalism, then, comes to mean attachment to the traditions and geography of the homeland, but with a twist. Cuban exiles are attached to the utopia of memory and desire, not to the dystopia of the contemporary socialist state. On the one hand, diasporic nationalism entails "geopiety," or an attachment to the natal landscape. This includes feelings for the natural terrain, the built environment, and the mental map of neighborhood, town, province, and country. Diasporic nationalism also involves attachment to the imagined contours of the liberated homeland as well as affection for the remembered traditions. In this case, it means passionate concern for democracy, capitalism, and various components of Cuban culture, including its music, fashion, architecture, language, and food. Some of these cultural components remain only slightly altered in contemporary Cuba; others exist now only in the exilic imagination.[6]

As part of the imaginative process of creating collective identity, diasporas often shape their new environment in the image of the old. Most Cuban exiles, like other immigrants, have lived in cities; so it is in urban spaces—alleys, streets, stores, apartments, and parks—that the imaginative processes linked with diasporic nationalism have taken place. In Miami, where most Cuban immigrants live, exiles have transformed the built environment. Cuban restaurants and businesses dot the landscape, and streets and parks named after Cuban leaders define space in the predominantly Cuban neighborhoods that spread out in a V-shaped pattern from the port of Miami. One small park in Little Havana that fills with older men playing dominoes, smoking cigars, and discussing politics is named after Antonio Maceo, a hero of the Cuban war for independence. Two blocks east of that park is a monument that has the emotional power for Cuban Americans that the Vietnam War Memorial holds for other Americans. The cylindrical stone monument remembers the men of Brigade 2506 who died during the failed Bay of Pigs invasion.[7]

At the same time, exiles also have drawn new mental maps. They imaginatively have mapped the history and geography of the homeland onto the new urban landscape. For instance, prerevolutionary Cuba had been divided into six provinces and 126 municipalities or townships. In Miami, local organizations called Cuban Municipalities in Exile preserve and intensify old regional and local affiliations. There are 110 officially recognized *municipios en el exilio*. Twenty of them have permanent buildings. Two of the larger ones, Havana and Santiago de Cuba, list almost a thousand members and hold monthly meetings. Most have a few hundred members and meet a few times each year. In their official headquarters, or in rented halls or restaurants, those who hail from the same Cuban township regularly are invited to congregate to sip Cuban coffee and converse about Cuban politics.[8]

Religion has played an important role in the process of transforming the cultural land-scape and creating collective identity. In this chapter I explore the role of religion in the con-struction of "national" identity among Cuban immigrants in their new urban setting. For reasons that will become clear, I focus on devotion to Our Lady of Charity, the patroness of Cuba, at the shrine erected in her honor in Miami. I suggest—and this is my main point—that exiles struggle over the meaning of symbols, but almost all Cuban American visitors to the shrine see it above all as a place to express diasporic nationalism. There, exiles map the landscape and history of the homeland onto the new urban environment through architec-ture and ritual. Through symbols at the shrine, the diaspora imaginatively constructs its collective identity and transports itself to the Cuba of memory and desire.[9]

I divide this chapter into four sections. I first describe my method and sources and then offer a brief history of devotion to Our Lady of Charity, in Cuba and Miami. Next I con-sider some of the ways that the meanings of symbols are *contested*. Finally, I explore the *shared* meaning of the architecture and ritual.

## METHODS AND SOURCES

I use a combination of historical and ethnographic methods. I have analyzed contempo-rary and archival written sources. As a means of tracing changes over time, I also have re-viewed statistical information on the religious life of Cubans before and after Castro's revolution. I have studied the exile community's material culture as well—architecture, yard shrines, murals, holy cards, and statues.

To understand the contemporary situation, I relied on observation and interviews. Most important, I conducted 304 structured interviews in which shrine visitors answered twenty questions on a questionnaire. I conducted research at all days and times. I stood outside the steps near one of the three exits. As pilgrims left, I told them that I was writing a book about devotion to the Virgin at the shrine, and I asked if they had time to answer some questions. This method did not ensure a random sample, of course, even though it yielded responses from a diverse group in terms of gender, region, and age. But it did provide rich detail about how some visitors understood devotion at the shrine. Most of those who spoke to me were middle-aged, and slightly more women than men visited the shrine. Yet often, especially on weekends, extended families would arrive together, kneel at the altar, buy a souvenir, take group photographs, stroll the grounds, and pile back into the minivan for the ride home.

Half of the twenty questions that visitors answered were open-ended. I asked, for exam-ple, not only about their arrival date and native region, but also about their impressions of the mural and the reasons for their devotion. Most of the questionnaires were self-adminis-tered, but occasionally those who were infirm, aged, or illiterate asked me to read the ques-tions to them. In either case, I stood beside them as they answered. This allowed me to clarify ambiguities in the questions and encouraged them to explain their answers. It also led to a very high response rate. As we went along, I often asked them for elaboration or clarification, and often they volunteered more than I requested, sometimes telling long, and usually sad, stories about their life in Cuba and their exile in America. After they answered the standard questions, I asked visitors if they had time to talk further. Many did. Although I encountered the members of the Confraternity of Our Lady of Charity often, I spoke with most pilgrims once, and the conversations lasted approximately thirty minutes. Some were shorter, as devotees rushed home to make dinner, scurried to gather relatives, or hurried back to the office. Other conversations lasted much longer, even several hours. Except when pilgrims requested otherwise, the interviews were in Spanish. Even when some visitors would begin in English, they would return to their native tongue to express a deeply held belief—and, I learned, many Cuban pilgrims had deeply held religious beliefs.[10]

## OUR LADY OF CHARITY AND THE SHRINE

Prerevolutionary Cuba was a relatively unchurched nation, especially in rural areas. In 1954, a few years before Castro's revolution, Cuba had the lowest percentage of nominal Catholics and practicing Catholics in Latin America. There were relatively few priests. In a 1957 survey of four hundred rural heads of families, only half identified themselves as Catholics. The vast majority (88.8 percent) never attended services, and only 4 percent attended three or more times a year. In fact, only slightly more than half (53.5 percent) had ever seen a priest.[11]

All this is not to say, of course, that Cubans were not religious. They simply were not linked closely with formal religious institutions. It was the church and the priests with whom many were not familiar; they felt quite comfortable with the Christian God and the Catholic saints, many even with the African *orishas* of Santería. Folk Catholicism was vigorous. The home and the streets were the preferred places of worship. As in other regions of North and South America, religious festivals played a significant part in devotional life. Many of the older exiles I interviewed told me that they had rarely gone to mass: they lived too far away from the churches. But they reported attending the primary public celebrations—on Good Friday, on the Epiphany, and on the feast days of the three main objects of popular veneration: Saint Barbara, Saint Lazarus, and Our Lady of Charity. They also recalled fondly the religion of the home. One sixty-four-year-old man from a rural township who had rarely gone to church as a child told me, trembling with emotion, that his strong devotion to Our Lady of Charity began with the family and in the home. Each night before bedtime, as his mother had instructed, he knelt to kiss the feet of the statue enshrined in their living room.

Cuban devotion to Our Lady of Charity has a long history, and especially since the nineteenth century she has been linked with national identity. "Cuba and the Virgin are the same thing," explained one shrine visitor. This middle-aged woman, who was born in Havana and arrived in Miami in 1960, expressed a common feeling among immigrants, laity and clergy. One exiled Cuban priest, for instance, suggested that "to look at [the image of] the Virgin of Charity is to think about Cuba, because she has been inexorably linked with our nationality and our history." The connection goes back to the beginning of the seventeenth century, when, according to popular legend, three laborers paddling in a small boat found the statue of the Virgin floating in the sea off the eastern coast of the island. This image later was enshrined in Cobre, a town in the easternmost province, Oriente. For two centuries, devotion was intense in that region, and over time it spread westward to the five other provinces of Cuba.[12]

It was during the late-nineteenth-century wars for independence from Spain that the Virgin became almost inseparable from the land and nation. A number of the soldiers who fought for independence (*los mambises*) adopted her as their patroness. Some carried her image with them into battle; others wore it on their shirts. Still others simply asked her to intercede for them and their nation. Because of her participation in the fight for freedom, the people still refer to her as *la Virgen Mambisa*.[13]

The nationalistic elements of devotion to Our Lady of Charity escalated still further after independence was won in 1902. Indeed, it was the veterans of the wars for independence who successfully petitioned the pope in 1915 to name her the patroness of Cuba, and the Virgin's link with national identity and political resistance reemerged clearly just after the socialist revolution. In 1961, when government officials tried to undermine Havana's traditional procession on the feast day of Our Lady of Charity, thousands of devotees defiantly filled the streets near the church. The spontaneous religious procession developed into a political protest, and violence broke out, with one young leader of the protest being shot. The government, sensing the Virgin's significance and the concomitant political threat, prohibited religious processions. One hundred and thirty-two priests were arrested and expelled from the island a week later. Many of the exiled priests landed in Miami, and the Virgin emigrated as well. Although the original statue remains in Cobre, a replica was secretly transported from Havana to Miami on her feast day in 1961. The Virgin, now an exile herself, finally found a new home in Miami when the shrine was dedicated twelve years later.[14]

Exile has preserved and intensified devotion to Our Lady of Charity. The number of pilgrims to the shrine in Miami has risen over the years. By the 1990s, the urban shrine, the sixth-largest Catholic pilgrimage site in the United States, attracted hundreds of thousands of visitors annually. The large number who make the journey, the vast majority of whom are Cuban, attest to its importance to the diaspora.[15]

The shrine, which was dedicated December 2, 1973, rests on an acre of land on the shore of Biscayne Bay, a short distance south of the skyscrapers of downtown Miami. It is hidden from the view of motorists driving to and from the downtown area; only a small sign by the road, in Spanish, announces its location. As you turn down the winding road that leads from the main street, you pass a parish church and youth center. To the right is the parking lot of a Catholic hospital. Two rows of palm trees and a small sign, again in Spanish, mark the entrance. The wide brick path between the palms leads to the steps of the conical shrine. As you face the shrine, picnic tables and a convent/administrative building sit to the left. A few hundred yards to the right is the hospital. Behind the shrine, the cobalt blue of Biscayne Bay stretches toward the horizon. The shrine itself, with a white base and bronze cap, stands ninety feet high and eighty feet wide. Its verticality is emphasized not only by the cross on its peak but also because its foundation rests fourteen feet above sea level. Inside, hovering in front of the mural, the statue of Our Lady of Charity is raised on a pedestal at the center of the altar.

Several priests and nuns, almost all of Cuban descent, help Agustín A. Román, auxiliary bishop of Miami, oversee the shrine's activities. Román, the director of the shrine, was a moving force in building the edifice, and he remains one of the most beloved leaders of the exile community. One woman in her forties repeated what many others had told me: "He's a saint."

The members of the confraternity, and the other visitors, come at all times; but there are three main public rituals. First, there are weekday masses. On Monday, Wednesday, and Friday evenings masses are scheduled, in turn, for each of the 126 Cuban municipalities or townships. Also, once a year the former residents of each of the six Cuban provinces are invited to return for a *romería*, a festival in which residents from a particular region journey to the local shrine. On the day of the *romería*, exiles from the same Cuban province eat, drink, chat, and worship together. The day, usually a Sunday, begins just after noon with lunch and ends with a rosary and procession around the shrine in the early evening. Finally, on September 8, thousands of exiles also take part in the annual feast day activities. They last all day and into the night. The most important part of those activities is the rosary and mass. Before Hurricane Andrew damaged the structure in 1992, this event usually was held in Miami Marine Stadium, only a short distance from the shrine. Those in the outdoor stadium, which overlooks the downtown skyline, say the rosary first. Later, as darkness falls, the mass begins. A flotilla of boats, all privately owned by exiles, escort the boat carrying the icon on her journey by water from the shrine. At the climax of the mass, that boat motors slowly to the side of the stage by the water's edge. Then several men balancing on the bow reverently lift the Virgin to others standing on the stage. They place the image near the right front of the stage. When the mass concludes, the same men carry the icon up the steep aisles of the stadium so that everyone can get a closer look. Finally, the clergy, choir, and lay readers file off the stage, led by the Virgin. The statue is then placed on the back of a flatbed truck in the parking lot. Devotees crowd close, encircling the unpretentious vehicle, to get another glimpse and to gather the fallen flowers as souvenirs. The truck, with the image secured by several male members of the confraternity, drives the three and a half miles over Rickenbacker Causeway and down a main street to the shrine. Most pilgrims go home as the Virgin leaves the stadium parking lot, but some follow her back to the shrine and remain for an hour or more, praying, singing, and talking.[16]

## CONTESTED MEANINGS

I highlight the shared nationalistic significance of the symbols connected with the shrine; but first it is important to acknowledge that their meaning is, to some degree, contested. There are, for instance, differences in interpretation and attitude between the Cuban American clergy and laity. Even though the exile community feels more positively toward the clergy—and especially Bishop Román—than prerevolutionary Cubans did, "religion as practiced" is partly in tension with "religion as prescribed."[17]

When I asked Bishop Román about the main problem facing the Cuban Catholic community in Miami, he said that it was "evangelization." He elaborated by drawing three concentric circles on note paper. The smallest circle at the center, he explained, represented the minority of exiles who are devoted members of the "liturgical community" and attend mass regularly at their parish. The next-larger circle represented those who were nominal Catholics, the majority of Cuban Americans. The final circle, farthest from the center, represented those who were not officially Catholic. Bishop Román's concern was with the second group, the nominal Catholics who were not active and orthodox members of their parishes.[18]

I thought that I understood, until he explained further: The real challenge, he said, was to eliminate the "confusions." He suggested, "Those evangelizing the Cubans need to realize that one zone in need of purification is that in which the influence of Santería is significant." "Deficiencies in evangelization" have allowed the *orishas* of Santería to be confused with the saints of Catholicism. The number of officially initiated adherents is, he argued, rather small. But many, he claimed, dabble: "What is rather numerous is the amount of people belonging to the baptized multitudes of our Church who sporadically visit the *santero* or minister of that religion looking for good luck, health, protection, or wanting to know the future."[19]

The shrine, the clergy believe, provides the means of "purifying" nominal Cuban Catholicism of the residue of Santería. In the bishop's words, it offers a "pedagogical opportunity." He admitted, indeed, that "the shrine of Our Lady of Charity has been designed with this pedagogical idea in mind." Cubans, who were never as fully integrated into the liturgical community as the clergy would have liked, have had an intense devotion to Our Lady of Charity. So the clergy hoped to use the Virgin to reach the unchurched masses, especially but not exclusively those influenced by Santería. Once they got their attention, they could begin to "catechize," as another Cuban American exiled priest told me.[20]

That catechetical concern is clear in the clergy's attempts to distinguish Our Lady of Charity from Ochún, the Yoruba goddess of the river, with whom she sometimes is "confused." Both are affiliated with water, yellow, and love. Santería initiates, especially devotees of Ochún, still sometimes come to the Miami shrine, even though clerical and lay officials occasionally ask them to leave. One prominent member of the confraternity told me that when they encounter initiates at the shrine, usually dressed in white and throwing pennies, they "chase them off." Yet those Santería followers still find much that is familiar and affirming at the shrine. It is, after all, by the water. Like Ochún, the Virgin is associated with fertility and love, and prayer cards on the souvenir table in the back petition her for a safe and successful pregnancy. Finally, yellow rosebushes and painted yellow stones encircle the left side of the shrine's exterior. For those who know the references, all these elements link the Virgin and the *orisha*. Yet the clergy do their best to separate the two. In these and other ways, Catholic clergy and some laity struggle over the meaning of symbols.[21]

There also is significant diversity among those in the pews: Cuban lay followers struggle among themselves over the meaning of symbols. Gender, class, and race differentiate devotees of Our Lady of Charity, and age seems to be one of the most decisive distinguishing factors. Most studies of urban immigrants have found intergenerational differences in the practice of religion. Cubans seem typical in this regard. The intensity of devotion to Our Lady of Charity declines slightly among those who were born in exile or who came here as young children, those under forty years of age. There seems to be a still more precipitous drop in devotion for those under twenty. One devotee, who arrived at age thirty-three in 1963, put it this way when discussing those who had been born in America or had arrived as young children: "The young people do not believe as we do because they don't know the Virgin of Charity as the patroness of Cuba."[22]

Age was not the only factor dividing Cuban American pilgrims, and nationalistic sentiment was not the only element in their devotion. Respondents of all ages indicated, for instance, that "personal devotions" were more important to them than any scheduled rituals connected with the shrine. Most of the shrine visitors I spoke with suggested that the Virgin provided some sort of spiritual reward: they used words such as "peace," "strength," "confidence," "faith," and "hope." Some of my informants claimed that the Virgin provided material comforts of one sort or another. Pilgrims offered various instrumental prayers, which seek a response about a particular problem. One lower-class woman who arrived from Havana in 1991 did not elaborate but said only that Our Lady "grants me miracles." Many others were more specific. A twenty-eight-year-old woman claimed that the Virgin heals her children when they are sick. Some claimed that the Virgin helped them financially.[23]

Instrumental prayers to the Virgin often are linked with vows that specify the reciprocal action the pledger will take in the event of a favorable outcome, and many shrine visitors come to express gratitude or fulfill a vow. That is what drew one middle-aged man born in

Oriente, who traveled all the way from Los Angeles. I first encountered his daughter, aged twenty-four, in the parking lot that Monday afternoon. After talking with her for twenty minutes or so, I was puzzled. She confessed to a complete lack of piety, but that made her presence at the shrine inexplicable. It turned out that she was waiting, not very patiently, by the rental car for her father to emerge. When he did, I asked him the usual questions. But this was no ordinary interview. He was fighting back tears the whole time. I asked if he had come to fulfill a vow. "Yes, I had some kind of problem with her," he said, pointing to his daughter, who by now had turned on the car radio to pass the time as she waited in the white convertible. His eyes filled with tears again, and he indicated that he had to stop the interview. Whatever the problem, the Virgin had resolved it, and now this man had expressed his gratitude and kept his promise. Tomorrow they would fly back to Southern California.[24]

## SHARED MEANING: DIASPORIC NATIONALISM

As with this Cuban American from California, devotees' petitions often concerned not only their fate and that of their family but also that of their homeland. The pilgrim from Los Angeles, for example, also forcefully expressed his attachment to his native country. He, like most visitors, reported that his devotion to the patroness of Cuba had increased in exile, and he summarized the significance of that devotion this way: "It is that which maintains my hope to see my country free, and to return to it is very important." The nationalistic significance of the symbols was central for him and the other pilgrims. This is the shared meaning of the symbols. Through artifacts and rituals at the shrine, the diaspora maps the history and geography of the homeland onto the landscape of Miami and imaginatively constructs the moral community that constitutes the "true" Cuban nation.[25]

## ARCHITECTURE

Exiles express personal attachment to their homeland and create collective identity in and through the natural landscape and built environment of the shrine. Some of the nationalistic elements are clear and available to most Cuban American visitors. A Cuban flag—in red, blue, and white—has been painted on stones on the left exterior of the shrine. At the rear are busts of José Martí, the leader of the fight for independence from Spain, and Félix Varela, one of the most important Cuban religious leaders.[26]

Both figures also appear on the huge mural, called *La historia de Cuba en una mirada*, which is painted in brown and covers the area behind the altar. The central place in that painting by Teok Carrasco is reserved for the Virgin herself and the rowboat with the three laborers. The shrine's statue of the small dark-haired Virgin, with her cloak of white, is elevated on a pedestal just below the much larger painted image and immediately in front of the boat. From the traditional Cuban chairs that fill the shrine's interior, the statue appears to be standing in the painted boat, so that through *trompe l'oeil* the recovery of the statue at sea is vividly and three-dimensionally recreated.[27]

Martí is joined on the mural by other Cuban military, cultural, and political leaders. His portrait, which is the largest, rests immediately to the right of the painted Virgin. Just below him is Jesus Rabí, major general of the war for independence, who also presided at the important veterans' reunion in Cobre in 1915, when the former soldiers decided to petition the pope. Above and to the right of Martí is another general of the war for independence, Máximo Gómez. In the top right-hand corner, the painter placed the author of the Cuban national anthem, Pedro Figueredo. At the zenith of the mural, two angels ascend to heaven through clouds, wrapped in the Cuban flag. There is nothing subtle about all this, and few Cuban American visitors to the shrine fail to notice the links established between the Virgin and Cuban soil.[28]

There are less explicit but still powerful expressions of attachment to homeland embedded in the shrine's natural and built environment. The shrine stands only yards from the bay, and water recalls both the geography of their island nation and the legend of their patroness. The shrine also was designed so that the statue of the Virgin would stand in a direct line with Cuba. Many of the visitors told me they noticed these more subtle messages.[29]

Bishop Román explained to me and his people other symbolic dimensions of the building. The cornerstone beneath the altar contains sand from the different Cuban provinces that was mixed with water found in a raft on which fifteen people died before they could find American shores. The triangular shape of the building's exterior recreates the contours of the Virgin's cloak, so that the shrine is an architectural expression of a popular Cuban prayer: "*Virgen Santísima, cúbrenos bajo tu manto*" (Most Holy Virgin, cover us with your mantle). The shrine, then, offers protection to the exiles who gather under her cloak. The Virgin's enveloping care is extended to all Cubans, as another architectural feature signifies. The six evenly spaced buttresses that run down the exterior walls of the conical shrine represent the six Cuban provinces.[30]

A few pilgrims noted the symbolic significance of the six columns and the building's shape. One woman, who was born in Cuba in 1937 and has lived in Miami since 1966, repeated the bishop's interpretation: "It is the mantle of the Virgin which protects her sons." Other visitors remained unaware of these meanings, although they still reported in large numbers that they liked both the site and the building. Some even found other, unintended, significance there. One sixty-six-year-old man, for example, used an analogy that no one else mentioned. "For me," he said, "the shrine is like the Statue of Liberty." A woman from Oriente, the province of the original shrine, offered another distinctive interpretation: "It is symbolic. Since we are not able to have a temple on a mountain as in Cobre, the architecture of the shrine is like a symbol of elevation." Like other visitors, she linked the architecture with the landscape of her homeland.[31]

## RITUAL

The meanings and feelings evoked by the architectural space arise, in part, from the practices associated with it, and Cuban exiles also form their national identity as they map the natal landscape onto the new urban environment through ritual. The nationalistic significance is clear in the three primary collective rituals connected with the shrine—*las peregrinaciones*, the weekday masses for the townships; the annual *romerías*, which are organized around provincial rather than municipal affiliation; and *la festividad*, the annual festival on the Virgin's feast day, September 8.[32]

Because space is limited, I discuss only the latter here. The pilgrims I interviewed indicated that the annual festival was the most important collective act of devotion, even though many managed to attend only "occasionally." The festival, and especially the mass, is important for the exile community because it allows for the fullest expression of their diasporic nationalism.

The festival's location has changed over the years, but the ceremony and its nationalist significance have not. For example, consider the 1991 festival. As the clergy reminded the audience, it was the eve of the five-hundredth anniversary of the "evangelization" of the

New World. More important to those in the stands, the date also marked the thirtieth anniversary of the Virgin's arrival in Miami. At the same time, the recent transformation of communist nations in Eastern Europe added a millennialist fervor to the proceedings, and many in the crowd and on the stage seemed to believe that democracy and capitalism soon would be restored in Cuba. At various times that night, clergy repeated the familiar prediction that the exiles would "spend next Christmas in Havana."[33]

The usual large and animated crowd filled the stadium on the bay. All 6,536 seats were filled. The head of security for the stadium estimated that the crowd actually numbered 10,000. As far as I could tell, there were few, if any, Anglos there, and as I walked among the participants, I heard no English spoken. This also was true during the other, smaller events at the shrine. I had thought that the festival might draw a wider audience, maybe even some visitors from outside the local Cuban community, but this seems not to have been the case. It was a Spanish-speaking crowd; and, as their passionate responses to the patriotic messages of the evening indicated, it was overwhelmingly Cuban.[34]

The nationalistic significance of the evening's rituals was as obvious as that of the shrine's mural. This theme was expressed clearly on the program I was handed as I entered the stadium. On the top left of the printed page was the phrase "Virgen de la Caridad"; on the right was a petition, "Salva a Cuba!" (Save Cuba). At the center of the blue program cover was an image of the Virgin. Below her, five *balseros* floated on the sea in a makeshift raft, their arms raised to the Virgin. The message seemed to be that as the Virgin had brought the exiles safely to American shores, she also can help those who remain in Cuba. Most important—and this theme was emphasized throughout the evening—she could help "liberate" Cuba from communism. As one woman told a local reporter before activities began, "The Virgin is the patroness of Cuba, and above all we want to petition her to make Cuba free."[35]

Exiles expressed their attachment to homeland in other ways. Several of the songs and prayers—including "Plegaria a la Virgen de la Caridad," "Caridad del Cobre," and "Virgen Mambisa"—recalled the Virgin's historical connection with Cuban land and history and repeated the call for the liberation of contemporary Cuba. Later, after the Virgin's image had been lifted from the boat and onto the stage, some in the crowd waved Cuban flags, and all stood to sing the Cuban national anthem.

During the evening's activities, which were broadcast to Cuba by federally funded Radio Martí, the clergy led the participants in several chants—all of which expressed nationalist sentiment. Perhaps most surprising (at least to me), Father Luis Pérez, a Cuban American parish priest, stopped in the middle of the rosary to urge all to chant "Our Lady of Charity, Save Cuba." At his prompting, the crowd jubilantly shouted it three times. Then, like a cheerleader at a sporting event or a keynote speaker at a political convention, the priest asked the crowd over and over, "What do we want?" "Save Cuba!" was the loud reply each time. The same sort of chants erupted, again encouraged by the clergy, during the sermon. The speaker, another exiled Cuban priest, skillfully stirred the crowd with a poetic and passionate homily filled with patriotic references, interrupting his remarks several times so that he, and most of the participants, could chant "Cuba será libre" (Cuba will be free). He ended his sermon, to the most thunderous applause of the evening, with a prayer to the Virgin: "Our Lady of Charity, save Cuba and bring liberty."

This collective ritual and the natural and built environment of the shrine have both a vertical and a horizontal dimension; and the latter is especially important for the exiles' construction of national identity. On the one hand, the rituals and architecture create a vertical opposition between superior and inferior and lift the Cuban community to another, transcendent dimension. The Virgin, for all her accessibility to devotees, still resides in a realm beyond this world. She can approach us, and we can approach her. Some movement, however, is necessary to establish contact; and the shrine and the devotions held within it provide that, as they also elicit the accompanying emotions—humility, gratitude, and reverence.[36]

More important for visitors to the shrine, the symbolic spaces and practices also have a horizontal dimension. They highlight, and finally overcome, opposition between here and there, us and them. In this sense, exiles are propelled horizontally, not vertically. They move out, not up. The shrine's rituals and architecture unite the Virgin's devotees in Miami with other Cubans, in exile and on the island, creating an imagined moral community and generating feelings of nostalgia, hopefulness, and commonalty. The symbols bridge the water that separates exiles from their homeland and transport the diaspora to the Cuba of memory and desire. By appropriating the Cuban flag at the shrine, narrating Cuban history in the mural, placing Cuban sand in the cornerstone, organizing devotions by Cuban regional affiliation, and ritually aligning the Cuban patroness with their cause, the displaced community simultaneously reclaims Havana and re-maps Miami. Although Cuban American pilgrims struggle to some extent over the meaning of rituals and artifacts, the symbols' shared nationalistic significance allows exiles to imaginatively construct their collective identity as they map the history and geography of their homeland onto the new urban landscape.

## NOTES

I gratefully acknowledge the support of the National Endowment for the Humanities. A number of scholars offered helpful comments on earlier drafts, including Ruth Behar, Matthew Glass, Robert Levine, Robert Orsi, and Yi-Fu Tuan. Of course, it is not their fault if errors remain.

1. Carol Breckenridge and Arjun Appadurai, "On Moving Targets," *Public Culture* 2 (1989): i.

2. By the term "Miami" I refer to the greater metropolitan area, or Dade County. Thomas D. Boswell and James R. Curtis, "The Hispanization of Metropolitan Miami," in *South Florida: Winds of Change*, ed. Thomas D. Boswell, prepared for the annual conference of the Association of American Geographers (Miami, 1991), 140–61.

3. Yi-Fu Tuan, *Topophilia: A Study of Environmental Perception, Attitudes, and Values* (Englewood Cliffs, N.J.: Prentice-Hall, 1974), 99; Yi-Fu Tuan, *Space and Place: The Perspective of Experience* (Minneapolis: University of Minnesota Press, 1977), 157.

4. Two surveys in 1992 reported on Cubans' attitudes about returning to their homeland. The first was conducted by pollsters with Bendixen and Associates for a local Spanish-language television station (WLTV). The second was designed by sociologist Juan Clark of Miami Dade Community College and conducted under the auspices of the Archdiocese of Miami. The first survey found that 24 percent said they would return to a free Cuba. The second reported that 45 percent were unsure, and only 10 percent said they definitely would do so. "Poll: Optimism Dips over Quick Castro Fall," *Miami Herald*, May 5, 1992, B1–2; "Sumario de la encuesta de la reflexion Cubana en la Diaspora," *Ideal* 261 (1992): 4–5. The expression about Christmas dinner was mentioned by my consultants and is discussed briefly in María Cristina Herrera, "The Cuban Ecclesiastical Enclave in Miami: A Critical Profile," *U.S. Catholic Historian* 9 (Spring 1990): 212.

5. As far as I can tell, the term "diaspora nationalism" was coined by Ernest Gellner. See Ernest Gellner, *Nations and Nationalism* (Ithaca, N.Y.: Cornell University Press, 1983), 101–109. My understanding of nation and nationalism has been shaped by that work and several others. Benedict Anderson, *Imagined Communities: Reflections on the Origin and Spread of Nationalism* (London and New York: Verso, 1983); Liisa Malkki, *Purity and Exile: Violence, Memory, and National Cosmology among Hutu Refugees in Tanzania* (Chicago: University of Chicago Press, 1995). Several articles in a

special issue of *Cultural Anthropology* also were useful, including Akhil Gupta and James Ferguson, "Beyond 'Culture': Space, Identity, and the Politics of Difference," *Cultural Anthropology* 7 (February 1992): 6–23; Liisa Malkki, "National Geographic: The Rooting of Peoples and the Territorialization of National Identity among Scholars and Refugees," *Cultural Anthropology* 7 (February 1992): 24–44.

6. Breckenridge and Appadurai, "On Moving Targets," i. My understanding of attachment to homeland has been shaped by the writings of cultural geographers. The geographer John Kirkland Wright coined the term "geopiety" to describe the religious dimension of this attachment. See John K. Wright, "Notes on Early American Geopiety," in *Human Nature in Geography: Fourteen Papers, 1925–65* (Cambridge: Harvard University Press, 1966), 250–85. Others have modified and applied the concept. See, for instance, Yi-Fu Tuan, "Geopiety: A Theme in Man's Attachment to Nature and Place," in *Geographies of the Mind: Essays on Historical Geosophy*, ed. David Lowenthal and Martyn J. Bowden (New York: Oxford University Press, 1976), 11–39; and Tuan, *Space and Place*, 149–60.

7. Thomas D. Boswell and James R. Curtis, *The Cuban-American Experience: Culture, Images, and Perspectives* (Totowa, N.J.: Rowman and Allanheld, 1983), 89–96. On immigrants' experiences in American cities, see John Bodnar, *The Transplanted: A History of Immigrants in Urban America* (Bloomington: Indiana University Press, 1985), and Bayrd Still, ed., *Urban America: A History with Documents* (Boston: Little, Brown, 1974), 116–26, 194–203, 392–405. On the role of ethnicity in shaping the American landscape, see Michael P. Conzen, "Ethnicity on the Land," in *The Making of the American Landscape*, ed. Michael P. Conzen (Boston and London: Unwin Hyman, 1990), 221–48. Latino Catholics have received some attention in recent years. Only one history of the Latino church in the United States has been published, but two new book series help fill some gaps. Half of one of those volumes focuses on Cuban American Catholics, but for the most part Cubans remain understudied. The book series on Latino religion are the Notre Dame History of Hispanic Catholics in the U.S. Series, which is associated with the University of Notre Dame Press, and the Program for the Analysis of Religion among Latinos (PARAL) Studies Series, which is sponsored by the Bildner Center for Western Hemispheric Studies at the Graduate School and University Center of the City University of New York. The former has published three books, and the latter, four. Two edited volumes in these series offer useful perspectives on the larger issues

that arise in the study of Latino religion: see Anthony M. Stevens-Arroyo and Gilbert R. Cadena, eds., *Old Masks, New Faces: Religion and Latino Identities*, Program for the Analysis of Religion among Latinos (New York: Bildner Center for Western Hemispheric Studies, 1995); and Jay P. Dolan and Allan Figueroa Deck, S.J., eds., *Hispanic Catholic Culture in the U.S.: Issues and Concerns*, Notre Dame History of Hispanic Catholics in the U.S. Series (Notre Dame: University of Notre Dame Press, 1994). The contribution on Cubans in the Notre Dame series was written by a Cubanist who was trained in sociology, Lisandro Pérez, not a specialist in Roman Catholicism or U.S. religion. Lisandro Pérez, "Cuban Catholics in the United States," in Jay P. Dolan and Jaime R. Vidal, eds., *Puerto Rican and Cuban Catholics in the U.S., 1900–1965* (Notre Dame: Notre Dame University Press, 1994), 147–207. The only book-length study of Latino Catholics devotes less than three pages to Cubans: Moises Sandoval, *On the Move: A History of the Hispanic Church in the United States* (Maryknoll, N.Y.: Orbis, 1990), 87, 106–108. Some useful information about Cuban American Catholicism appears in Michael J. McNally, *Catholicism in South Florida, 1868–1968* (Gainesville: University Press of Florida, 1982), 127–66. On immigrants' transformation of the Miami social landscape, see Alejandro Portes and Alex Stepick, *City on the Edge: The Transformation of Miami* (Berkeley and Los Angeles: University of California Press, 1993).

8. Recent information on the municipalities in exile has been published in Boswell and Curtis, "Hispanization of Miami," 54.

9. For a fuller account, see Thomas A. Tweed, *Our Lady of the Exile: Diasporic Religion at a Cuban Catholic Shrine in Miami* (New York and Oxford: Oxford University Press, 1997).

10. I had help with some of the interviews. My research assistants included two Cuban American students at the University of Miami, Ivonne Hernandez and David Sosa. Two other Cuban American assistants, Emilia Aguilera and Ada Orlando, helped in countless ways. In a related project, one of my students, Roxanna Sosa, conducted interviews with yard shrine owners. I am grateful for their aid.

11. The comparison with other Latin American countries and a summary of the 1957 survey are found in Margaret Crahan, *Religion and Revolution: Cuba and Nicaragua*, Working Paper No. 174, Latin American Program, Wilson Center (Washington, D.C.: Smithsonian Institution, 1987), 4. For a historical overview of Cuban Catholicism that includes primary sources, see Ismael Testé, *Historia Eclesias-*

*tica de Cuba*, 3 vols. (Burgos, Spain: Editorial El Monte Carmelo, 1969). See also Conferencia Episcopal Cubana, *Encuentro nacional eclesial cubano* (Havana: Conferencia Episcopal Cubana, 1987), 33–49. A solid overview of Cuban religion before 1959 appears as the first two chapters in John M. Kirk, *Between God and the Party: Religion and Politics in Revolutionary Cuba* (Tampa: University of South Florida Press, 1989), 3–62. At least ten dissertations on religion in Cuba were written between 1945 and 1991, but only two focused on Catholicism. The others analyze Protestantism or Santería. See Jesse J. Dossick, *Cuba, Cubans, and Cuban-Americans, 1902–1991: A Bibliography* (Miami: University of Miami North-South Center, 1992), 80–81.

12. On national Virgins, see Victor Turner and Edith Turner, *Image and Pilgrimage in Christian Culture: Anthropological Perspectives* (New York: Columbia University Press, 1978). On the history of Cuban devotion to Our Lady of Charity, see Testé, *Historia Eclesiastica*, vol. 3, 346–411, and José Tremols, *Historia de la devoción de la Virgen de la Caridad* (Miami: Album de America, [1962?]). See also Delia Díaz de Villar, "Historia de la devoción a la Virgen de la Caridad," in *Ermita de la Caridad*, n.p., n.d. [Miami: La Ermita de la Caridad], 12–20; and Olga Portuondo Zúñiga, *La Virgen de la Caridad del Cobre: Símbolo de cubanía* (Santiago de Cuba: Editorial oriente, 1995). For evidence of the continuing influence of Our Lady of Charity in the homeland, see the recent pastoral letter from the bishops: Conferencia Episcopal Cubana, *Encuentro nacional eclesial cubano*, 43–45, 265–66. The testimony of Juan Moreno, one of the three laborers who claimed to have found the statue in the sea, has survived. Archivo General de Indias, Sevilla, Audiencia de Santo Domingo, legajo 363. This document was rediscovered by Leví Marreo and published in his *Cuba: Economía y sociedad: El Siglo XVII*, vol. 5 (Madrid: Editorial Playor, 1976), 92–93. Interview #83, August 1, 1991, female, age 51, born Havana, arrived 1960. Eduardo Boza-Masvidal, "Una imagen que es un símbolo," in *Ermita de la Caridad*, 9–10.

13. One interesting sign of the increased nationalistic significance of the Virgin after the war for independence comes from two novenas to Our Lady of Charity published in Havana in 1880 and 1950. The second, published after she had officially become patroness, reprinted exactly the novena of 1880, but the editors affixed a thirty-one-page historical overview that emphasized her ties with the veterans and her link with the nation. Compare the two: *Novena a la Virgen santisima de la Caridad del Cobre* (Havana: Pedro Martinez, 1880) and *Nuestra Señora de la Caridad del Cobre, Patrona de Cuba: Historia, Devocion, Novena* (Havana: Liga de Damas de Acción Católica Cubana Consejo Nacional, 1950). Other Virgins, so important in Latin American cultures, have played a similar role. Our Lady of Guadalupe, for instance, has been associated with rebellions and revolutions. See David Carrasco, *Religions of Mesoamerica: Cosmovisions and Ceremonial Centers* (San Francisco: Harper and Row, 1990), 135–38.

14. The letter to the pope has been reprinted in several works. See "Petición de los veteranos de la independencia de Cuba," in *Ermita de la Caridad*, 42–43. Juan Clark, *Religious Repression in Cuba* (Miami: University of Miami North-South Center, 1986), 10–12. Agustín A. Román, "The Popular Piety of the Cuban People," master's thesis, Barry University, 1976, 81.

15. A German geographer has discussed the shrine in a survey of Catholic pilgrimage places in the United States. On the number of annual visitors and other matters, see Gisbert Rinschede, "Catholic Pilgrimage Places in the United States," in *Pilgrimage in the United States, Geographia Religionum*, Band 5 (Berlin: Dietrich Reimer, 1990), 69, 82–83. The number of visitors in 1992, as estimated by the confraternity, was 750,000: T.N., confraternity member, interview with the author, Miami, Florida, June 23, 1992. Of course, without further study it is difficult to assess the accuracy of these figures. There can be no doubt, however, that the shrine attracts large numbers of visitors and that it is a crucial pilgrimage site for Cuban Americans.

16. The feast-day masses have been held at various sites since 1991: Bayfront Park (1992), Dinner Key Auditorium (1993), and Hialeah Racetrack (1994–97). Wherever they are held, the ceremonies are very similar.

17. William A. Christian, Jr., made the distinction between "religion as practiced" and "religion as prescribed." See William A. Christian, Jr., *Local Religion in Sixteenth-Century Spain* (Princeton: Princeton University Press, 1981), 178. For reasons I have noted above, Cuban Americans do talk about the "humanity" of the clergy, but they display somewhat less "anti-clericalism" than the subjects of other studies of "popular" Catholicism in Europe. Compare Ruth Behar, *Santa María del Monte: The Presence of the Past in a Spanish Village* (Princeton: Princeton University Press, 1986); Eric R. Wolf, ed., *Religion, Power, and Protest in Local Communities: The North Shore of the Mediterranean* (Berlin and New York: Mouton, 1984); and Ellen Badone, ed., *Religious Orthodoxy and Popular Faith in European Society* (Princeton: Princeton University Press, 1990).

18. Agustín A. Román, interview with the author, July 15, 1991, Shrine of Our Lady of Charity, Miami.

19. Román, "Popular Piety," 48, 46, 47, 78. On Santería, see Lydia Cabrera, *El Monte* (Miami: Ediciones Universal, 1975); George Brandon, *Santeria from Africa to the New World: The Dead Sell Memories* (Bloomington: Indiana University Press, 1993); David Hilary Brown, "Garden in the Machine: Afro-Cuban Sacred Art and Performance in Urban New Jersey and New York," 2 vols., Ph.D. dissertation, Yale University, 1989; and Joseph M. Murphy, *Santería: An African Religion in America* (Boston: Beacon, 1988). There are no full-length studies yet, but on Santería in Miami, see Stephan Palmié, "Afro-Cuban Religion in Exile: Santería in South Florida," *Journal of Caribbean Studies* 5 (Fall 1986): 171–79, and Diana González Kirby and Sara Maria Sánchez, "Santería: From Africa to Miami via Cuba—Five Hundred Years of Worship," *Tequesta* 48 (1988): 36–48.

20. Román, "Popular Piety," 57, 98. Father Romeo Rivas, interview with the author, February 3, 1992, Shrine of Our Lady of Charity, Miami. The concern to "purify" Cuban Catholicism of the influences of Santería is evident in periodicals published by the Archdiocese of Miami for Spanish-speaking laity and clergy. For example, see Eduardo Boza Masvidal, "Conservemos la pureza de nuestra fe," *Cuba Diáspora* (1978): 13–14. One priest, Juan J. Sosa, has addressed the issue many times. For an example, see Juan J. Sosa, "Devociones Populares: Santa Barbara and San Lazaro," *Cuba Diáspora* (1976): 101–103.

21. Román, "Popular Piety," 41. Murphy, *Santería*, 42–43, 67. T.N., interview with the author, June 23, 1992, Miami. *Verdades de la fe Cristiana*, pamphlet (Miami: Ermita de la Caridad, n.d.).

22. Interview #104, February 4, 1992, female, age 22, born U.S.; Interview #136, March 3, 1992, female, age 60, born Hoguín, arrived 1965; Interview #43, March 1, 1992, female, age 17, born Cuba [municipality not given], arrived 1980; and Interview #44, March 1, 1992, female, age 16, born Spain, arrived 1991; Interview #1, January 26, 1992, female, age 63, born Guanajay, arrived 1949; Interview #114, February 15, 1992, female, age 62, born Havana, arrived 1963.

23. William A. Christian, Jr., *Person and God in a Spanish Valley* (New York and London: Seminar Press, 1972), 118–19. Interview #89, January 18, 1992, male, age 24, born Havana, arrived 1991; Interview #115, February 15, 1992, female, age 28, born Colombia, arrived 1980; Interview #20, February 3, 1992, male, age 33, born Havana, arrived 1967.

24. Interview #17 (the daughter), February 3, 1992, female, age 24, born U.S.; Interview #18 (the father), February 3, 1992, male, age 48, born Cienfuegos, arrived 1961. As William A. Christian, Jr., has noted, the vow is the prototypical prayer of Mediterranean Roman Catholicism. Christian, *Person and God*, 119.

25. Interview #18; Interview #20; Interview #1. Note that half of those who answered the question indicated that their devotion to Our Lady of Charity had increased in exile. Only two said that it had declined.

26. José Martí apparently had some devotion to Our Lady of Charity, since he wrote a poem in her honor. That poem has been reprinted: "Un Poema de Martí a la Virgen," *Cuba Diáspora* (1978): 77–78. He also approved of worshipping "God-*Patria*." But as one biographer has argued, he was very suspicious of religious institutions and their tendency to assume secular control. He had strong "anti-clerical" impulses. For these reasons, it is not clear how Martí would have felt about being enshrined. John Kirk, *José Martí Mentor of the Cuban Nation* (Tampa: University Presses of Florida, 1983), 119–25. Varela, on the other hand, probably would have been pleased. Some of Varela's philosophical and religious writings have been translated into English. See Felipe J. Estévez, ed., *Félix Varela: Letters to Elpidio* (New York: Paulist Press, 1989).

27. The title of the mural in English is "The History of Cuba in a Glance." For a description of the contents and history of the mural, see the pamphlet published by the shrine, *El mural de la Ermita* (Miami: Ermita de la Caridad, n.d.). For the artist's account, see Teok Carrasco, "Descripción del Mural," in *Ermita de la Caridad*, 38–41.

28. Interview #84, July 31, 1991, female, age 48, born Havana, arrived 1955.

29. When asked if the site had any special significance for them, a quarter of those who answered mentioned that it was situated by the sea. Others noted that the site had some link with Cuba, and a surprising number of informants even mentioned that the shrine was situated in a line with their homeland. The majority of visitors who answered the question found some nationalistic significance in the site itself.

30. Agustín A. Román, "La Virgen de la Caridad en Miami," in *Ermita de la Caridad*, 6–8.

31. Interview #48, March 1, 1992, female, age 52, born municipality of Trinidad (Cuba), arrived 1971; Interview #109, February 11, 1992, female, age 55, born Guanajay, arrived 1966; Interview #69, January 3, 1992, male, age 66, born Santiago de las

Vegas, arrived 1962; Interview #137, March 3, 1992, female, age 51, born Puerto Padre, arrived 1960.

32. I refer here to the "architectonics" of the building, as anthropologist James W. Fernandez has used the term in his study of religion among the Fang in Equatorial Africa. James W. Fernandez, *Bwiti: An Ethnography of the Religious Imagination in Africa* (Princeton: Princeton University Press, 1982), 377, 408–12. Rinschede has reported that "around 10% of all pilgrimage places are visited exclusively by one specific ethnic group only." Besides the shrines in Miami and Doylestown, he mentions four others, two associated with Ukrainian Americans, one with Hungarian Americans, and one with Mexican Americans. Rinschede, "Catholic Pilgrimage Places," 91.

33. For an analysis of later festivals, see Tweed, *Our Lady of the Exile*, 116–18, 125–31.

34. "Miles aclaman a la Caridad del Cobre," *El Nuevo Herald*, September 8, 1991. See also "La apari-

ción de 'la Virgen mambisa' a los cubanos," *El Nuevo Herald*, September 8, 1991; "La Ermita de la Caridad: el sexto santuario más importante de EU," *El Nuevo Herald*, September 8, 1991; and "Exilio reafirma fe en la Caridad," *Diario Las Americas*, September 10, 1991.

35. "Virgen de la Caridad: Salva Cuba!" Program for the Festival of Our Lady of Charity, September 7, 1991 (Miami: La Officina de Liturgia y Vida Espiritual de la Arquidiócesis de Miami, 1991). "Miles aclaman a la Caridad del Cobre," 1B.

36. My analysis of the vertical and horizontal dimensions of the shrine's architecture and ritual has been informed, in part, by Fernandez's discussion of the architectonics of the *Bwiti* chapel and Catherine Bell's treatment of the spatial dimensions of ritualization. Fernandez, *Bwiti*, 371–412. Catherine Bell, *Ritual Theory, Ritual Practice* (New York: Oxford University Press, 1992), 125.

## THE HINDU GODS IN A SPLIT-LEVEL WORLD

*Joanne Punzo Waghorne*

The dramatic growth of the world's religions in America during the past quarter century remains a little noticed phenomena. Since the 1965 immigration act lifted national quotas and restrictions on Asian immigration, the ethnic make-up of the United States has come to include many more immigrants from Asia, the Pacific, and the Middle East. Today Muslim mosques and Hindu and Buddhist temples can be found in nearly every American city, though most are hard to see because they are in homes, former churches, or movie theaters. Soon, if not already, there will be more Muslims than Jews in the United States. In some parts of the United States, like New York and California, followers of Asian religions now outnumber Episcopalians and Presbyterians. In the past decade scholars have begun to investigate the very different experiences of these new immigrant communities through close examination of their religious lives.

Joanne Waghorne relates the experience of one new immigrant group in their attempt to establish their religious institution in America. In contrast to earlier, less affluent immigrants to America who joined inner city ethnic enclaves and gradually worked their way up the occupational ladder, the wave of highly educated elite Indians, who began coming to the United States in the late 1960s and early 1970s, settled among their suburban peers from major technological industries, hospitals, and universities and were soon successful. During the last two decades, many of these prosperous overseas Indians have contributed to the creation of "authentic" Hindu temples that stand, Waghorne argues, "on a highly complex space that is at once American, Indian, and global, but at the same time also middle-class and suburban." Situating their temple on a site selected for its easy access to highways and not for any traditional coordinates, the leaders of the Sri Vishnu Temple—like those of other major American Hindu temples and newer temples in urban India—build on the foundations of global commerce and a middle-class ethos a contemporary configuration of ancient sacred space. Waghorne's essay deftly explores the construction of the Sri Vishnu Temple as an occasion for reworking Hindu identity and practice, gender, relations between generations, and ultimately for engaging the struggle to define the emerging global Hinduism.

Reprinted by permission from Joanne Punzo Waghorne, "The Hindu Gods in a Split-Level World: The Sri Siva-Vishnu Temple in Suburban Washington, D.C." in Robert A. Orsi, ed. *Gods of the City* (Bloomington: Indiana University Press, 1999), 105–130.

# 25

# THE HINDU GODS IN
# A SPLIT-LEVEL WORLD

## The Sri Siva-Vishnu Temple
## in Suburban Washington, D.C.

*Joanne Punzo Waghorne*

A "COUNTRY" MAILBOX, metal encased in wood, stands on the road in front of an arche-typical suburban split-level house. Wrought iron letters read SSVT. Behind this symbol of American family life rise the ornate *vimanas* or spires of the largest Hindu temple in the United States. The temple stands on fourteen acres of former Maryland farmland at the edge of the sprawling suburbs of the nation's capital. Its congregation is made up of the first generation of a new wave of immigrants. Neither tired nor poor nor huddled masses, the technological and scientific elite of India began coming to the United States in the late 1960s and early 1970s, when changes in the immigration laws removed odious restrictions against Asians. Unlike immigrants from the past who began their life on American shores far lower on the occupational hierarchy, these educated newcomers quickly prospered and chose to settle in the suburbs, new cities, and edge cities, among their colleagues from major technological corporations, hospitals, and universities.

The Sri Siva-Vishnu Temple is located on Cipriano Road, the local route to the NASA Goddard Space Center less than a mile away. It shares that same road with two churches. Just next door is another split-level used by a gospel study group, the Victory World Out-reach. Another house, now used as a Hindu temple for those devoted more exclusively to the god Murugan, is in the vicinity. Homes in this neighborhood range from modest 1950s ranch-styles of the first suburban inroads onto this once virgin Maryland farmland to newer and larger split-level subdivisions. A garden apartment complex and modern new industrial buildings now impinge on the large tracts of farmland that remain within two miles of this fast-growing outpost of metropolitan Washington. On Saturday mornings, East Asian Americans, African Americans, and European Americans can be seen mowing their lawns. Cipriano Road reflects a multi-layered suburban community with an eco-nomic, racial, and ethnic mix that reflects its layers of growth. Lanham, Maryland, is united only, it seems, by its middle-class ethos marked by good fences, good houses, and the good jobs that make home ownership a reality.

Indians around Washington, as in other parts of the country,[1] have not settled in any one neighborhood, although Arlington and Silver Springs do have a larger proportion of

South Asians than other areas. The only temple located near a "little India" is, not surprisingly, in New York City. The Hindu Temple Society of North America created the first temple in the United States in the early 1970s by reconstructing an old Greek Orthodox Church in Flushing, now down the road from an Indian shopping center that functions less as a residential neighborhood than as a center of commerce. The larger Hindu temples built in the last two decades, however, rise from suburban landscapes convenient to major interstate highways in Pittsburgh, Houston, Boston, Chicago, and Nashville. The Sri Siva-Vishnu Temple, like other major American Hindu temples, is in many ways both more incongruous with its particular environment and yet more a part of the generic mainstream American landscape than older religious centers in the many Little Italies, Little Polands, and Chinatowns that anchor ethnic space in the inner cities.

Unlike the earlier waves of immigrants at the turn of the century, many of these recent arrivals left urban environments in India that better prepared them for life in the United States. Many Indians came here from middle-class homes—not affluent, but fluent in English and familiar with the business-suit world of modern urban commerce inherited from two hundred years of British rule. The parents or even the grandparents of migrants especially from South India who make up the majority of the trustees and devotees of the Sri Siva-Vishnu Temple belonged in India to the mobile and multilingual civil service, university, and scientific communities. The traditional ties that bound persons to particular places in India had been severed, then, a generation earlier in the families of many of the new Indian Americans. In urban centers such as Madras and Bangalore, *enka ur*, "our town," is usually somewhere away from *enka vitu*, "our house." Many Indians, certainly many of those most active in the SSVT, came to the United States already "twice-migrated,"[2] with a history of dis-placement: a heritage of multiple meanings for "our land," "our home," and "our place" in the world.

This pattern of "double migration," however, is complicated by the two decades of rapid technological change (1960s–1980s) that brought many of the earliest Indian immigrants to the United States, often as agents of that change. They moved with their degrees from India's institutes of technology and schools of medicine to highly specialized jobs at institutions such as NASA, at university research institutes and hospitals, or at large corporations such as IBM and Burroughs-Wellcome.[3] But in this postmodern era, the technology that lured them from India at the same time holds them close to each other and to the mother country through a global network of telephones, modems, jetliners, and now international newspapers, including *Hinduism Today*, *India Today*, *Accent*, and *The Indian American*. Under the headline "Trend to Watch," *Hinduism Today*, published in California, proudly quoted Joel Kotkin's forecast in *Tribes: How Race, Religion and Identity Determine Success in the New Global Economy*: "The more than twenty million overseas Indian today represent one of the best-educated, affluent groupings in the world . . . The Indian may prove to be the next diaspora to emerge as a great economic force."[4] This newspaper, which proclaims its task as "Recording the Modern History of Nearly a Billion Members of a Global Religion in Renaissance," touted the suggestion that a tight network of the Indian "tribe" in the new global village may be the key to its success in this age of transnational economics.

But as prepared as Indian Americans may be to take up their role as the newest diaspora, an ideology of journey and wandering was never at the heart of their ancient culture. Unlike the Jews, who are often mentioned by Indian Americans as a model for economic acculturation with continuing community cohesion,[5] Indians have been conquered but never forcefully driven from their soil. The gods of the Hindus, unlike the Lord God of Israel, have no strong tradition of moving about in a tent for their dwelling[6] or of residing solely inside their holy word: they live in temples. Thus over the last decade, many of the most successful of the new "tribe" of overseas Indians—many now American citizens— have given the money derived from their great success along with their boundless energy to once again construct "authentic" Hindu temples that nonetheless stand on a highly complex space that is at once American, Indian, and global, but at the same time also middle-class and suburban. The Hindu gods of metropolitan Washington, D.C., like the Hindu gods of the cities of Houston or Pittsburgh or Nashville, live in a substantive holy house that nonetheless *is* and yet *is not* at home on the land on which it stands.

## MIDDLE-CLASS AND HINDU: AN INDIAN MATRIX, A GLOBAL CONTEXT, AN AMERICAN VENUE

Indian Americans at the Sri Siva-Vishnu Temple, like others in this new diaspora, express a continuing bond to the mother country. Some equation of their Hinduism with India always remains. But at the same time, these diaspora Indians openly acknowledge that they felt forced to leave this mother as too old, too tired, and too slow to nurture the ambition and the skills that so many possessed. When they differentiate America from India, India is the "spiritual and unchanging" place, while America is the land of "material" success, recently given the Sanskrit name *karmabhumi*, meaning "the land of action, the place of work."[7] At a classical Indian dance recital in Raleigh, North Carolina, in the early 1990s, a prominent Indian guru now settled in the United States told his largely Indian American audience that they should combine "the East with the West." From the West, said the guru, they could learn "punctuality and how to succeed materially." Implied, of course, was that the East held all the cultural riches. Yet in spite of the continued sense of deep kinship with family and old colleagues left behind, the particular character of the interconnection between India and its diaspora is, as Amitav Ghosh points out, "a very peculiar, almost inexplicable phenomenon."[8]

In an article written in 1989, Ghosh points to the curious lack of any real institutional structures that could unite India with overseas Indians. The economic links are insubstantial, the marriage ties weak, the political connections fragmented. Pointing to the international fame of diaspora writers like V. S. Naipaul, A. K. Ramanujan, and Salman Rushdie, Ghosh instead suggests that the strongest cultural bonds are "lived within the imagination" in the space of literature. And, indeed, the construction of a "spiritual India" among many Indian Americans echoes the broad, often mystified sense of the homeland developed by the most famous of India's long-absent sons, Mahatma Gandhi, who spent his early career among Indian migrants in Africa. This imagined India is the *Area of Darkness* that Trinidadian V. S. Naipaul so stunningly contrasted with the shocking reality of his first "return" to the country he had never seen.[9]

However, very recent evidence of the rapidly developing institutions that now mediate between diaspora Indians and India, including political parties and organizations with a conservative religious message, suggests the rise of a more structured solidarity with the motherland. Conspicuously active in the United States is the VHP (Vishwa Hindu Parishad, "World Hindu Council"), the religious wing of India's right-wing party, the BJP (Bharatiya Janata Party, "the Indian People's Party"). The VHP in 1993 sponsored "Global

Vision 2000" in Washington, D.C., to celebrate Swami Vivekananda's famous presentation of Hinduism before the World Parliament of Religions in 1893.[10] The event drew Indo-American enthusiasts, but also others protesting the disguised conservative agenda.[11] These same organizations are part of an increasingly popular Hindu "fundamentalism" within India that defines Indians—over and against the "foreign" Christians and Muslims—as citizens *native* to the soil who put no other gods, no other holy places before Bharat Mata, mother India. The *India Times*, published in Washington, D.C., has become a voice for this new strident nationalism of some Indians, permanent residents of the United States and sometimes citizens, who nonetheless write editorials urging an electoral platform for the BJP that would create "India as a strong economic power . . . India as a strong military power . . . India as a nation with an unwavering sense of identity with the secular Vedic-Hindu civilization."[12]

This very visceral attachment to the land rises from a definition of India as *the* Hindu nation whose "Vedic-Hindu" civilization emanates so naturally from the soil that it should not be called "a religion" like the foreign-made Islam. Hence Hinduism is truly the "secular" civilization of India. This Hindu mother India now exists as another model of the home country among diaspora Indians alongside the more easily portable, less controversial "spiritual India" of art and sacred literature. So difficult and dense are these questions defining the place of so many of the world's most recent immigrants in this new age of global migration and multiple identities that the problem has precipitated three new academic journals: *Diaspora: A Journal of Transnational Studies; Transition: An International Review;* and *Public Culture: Bulletin of the Center for Transnational Cultural Studies.*

This ambiguity involved in defining a place for "India" in the Hinduism of the diaspora has much to do with the equally puzzling problem of defining the place of "Hinduism" within modern India, especially for the mobile, middle-class professionals who were the parents and are often the stay-at-home brothers and the sisters of the new Indian Americans. While the BJP tries to forge an unbreakable link between Hinduism and India as a nation, the urban middle class has a history of a different solution to the sense of religious and personal dislocation felt in a new urban environment. The problem is complicated by the paucity of studies on religion among the urban middle class, whose workaday habits in Bombay offices or Madras bureaucracies could never attract the anthropological eye from the exotic and more dazzling bells and smoke-filled rituals of their country and tribal cousins. The available studies of modern trends in religion within India have tended to stress the ways that the modern middle class in India's new industrial cities adapted older forms of Hinduism to their own needs through what Max Weber first identified as the intensive emotional surrender to the charismaticguru, the divine teacher, which he assumed "quite naturally became the primary form of holy seeking for the aliterary middle classes."[13]

In *Redemptive Encounters*, Lawrence Babb investigated three modern religious movements in India's capital city of New Delhi that centered on founding saints. Babb found that disconnection between person and the daily place of residence or place of work in these movements was so radical that "interactions with deities and deitylike persons" became "a way in which a very special sense of self and the world, which has little basis in the experience of everyday life, can be assimilated to a devotee's inner life."[14] In describing the sense of community in one such movement formed around this common ethos of a split between inner and outer life and absolute belief in the founding spiritual teacher, Babb doubts if it can be called "a community in any normal sense because its territorial dispersion mitigates against the formation of anything resembling corporate ties. The group is probably best conceived as a loose 'congregation.'"[15] The contemporary middle class in India, then, are not strangers to social and economic factors that demand a relocation— often a radical relocation—of the self in a seemingly fragmented world.

Several of these same guru-centered organizations have become international, and their "congregations" spread over the globe.[16] For many middle-class Hindus in the United States, these guru-centered global communities continue to provide a sense of relocation and reidentification of the self with a spiritual network that connects—sometimes by telepathy or telephone, letter, or fax—the devout with the guru while transcending national boundaries.[17] To fully understand where "India," "America," and "Britain" are on the map of their spiritual life is difficult, but one thing is certain: Where the guru is, there is holy space. However, the temple builders in Lanham, Maryland, or Flushing, New York, or Houston, Texas, by envisioning and constructing temples they consider authentic, have chosen to center their religious life in the temple itself, and therefore to adopt/adapt a tradition that has connected making a holy house with sanctifiying the land.

Amid all the complexity of the place of "India" within diaspora Hinduism and the place of "Hinduism" within middle-class India stands the new Hindu temple in America as a marker of what John Fenton, in a study of South Asian immigrants to the United States, calls "the process of becoming at home (having a *desh* or place where one belongs) on the foreign soil of America."[18] Other scholars of contemporary temple building in America verify the almost literal sense of the "transplantation" of Hinduism onto American soil,[19] and of the process that makes God "immediate; this land, holy."[20] But amid this process of implantation (the ceremony to consecrate a Hindu temple creates strong analogies between planting a seed and "planting" a temple) remain the shifting borders of modern life—the transfers and new assignments and career advances that necessitate continued mobility. The Hindu temple is in "America" and stands as a marker of the acceptance of a new place for the growth of Hinduism; but at the same time, this holy house cannot be easily associated with a new stable group of people now permanently (re)tied to this land. "America's" place in the temple and the temple's place in America is a far more complex issue than the traditional place of the temple in India—even in modern India.

In *Space and Place*, Yi-Fu Tuan reminds his readers that "the original inspiration for building a city was to consort with the gods." Gods live in traditional Hindu temples quite literally embodied in iconic form and firmly fixed in a specific locality. The most common words for temple in classic Sanskrit texts, according to Stella Kramrisch, are *vimama*, "measured out," and *prasada*, "seat." Both words emphasize the fixing, seating, settling of the divine in a constructed abode.[21] The most familiar contemporary words for "temple" in both Sanskrit and vernacular languages translate as "palace," "house of God," "place of God," "abode of God." As S. S. Janaki puts it, "synonyms like *alayam*, *mandiram* and *grha* are in a general way applicable to the dwelling place of both human beings and divinities."[22] The Indian city then continues as a place where humans and divine inhabitants share the same space—each in their own respective houses. Stella Kramrisch, in her now-classic study of the Hindu temple, quotes texts which state that the installation of divine icons in temples should be made, "in forts; in auspicious cities, at the head of shop-lined streets."[23] And indeed in many of the still-living temple cities of South India, the most exclusive shops are located on the four streets that surround the urban temple complex, the *mada* streets. Here the finest silk weaving, the best brassware and jewelry can be found.

The Sri Siva-Vishnu Temple, however, is not defined by the patterns of interconnected yet bounded communities that historians of modern India have described as characterizing Indian cities even at the turn of the century. The model of little villages within a larger urban corporation marked Indian cities until the mid-nineteenth century, when British residents of colonial port cities such as Madras began to move their personal residences from the trading and governmental centers to new garden suburbs.[24] The rising middle-class Indians in Madras city, for example, began to build new neighborhoods like their British overlords, but they always re-created an older Indian sense of urban space: a central temple surrounded by a combination of houses and stores. The Mylapore area of Madras is a perfect example of this older urban model that continues even today.[25] Only after independence in 1947 did Madrasis begin to create purely residential suburbs in the American sense of bedroom communities. In the Indian context, the oft-quoted maxim "Do not live where there is no temple" is taken seriously in the new suburbs, which have seen the rise of small temples built by new multi-caste and multi-ethnic constituencies that are within residential neighborhoods but no longer at their literal center.

In the new American context, devotees of the Sri Siva-Vishnu temple, have built and now maintain a multi-million-dollar temple complex that is even less the center of a new neighborhood than its Indian counterparts. They have moved one step beyond the Indian urban middle class. Their temple is not even contiguous to their residential neighborhood. The temple takes on even greater importance, then, as the only concrete embodiment of the community. Ironically, it rests on land in a non-Hindu neighborhood and yet remains the focal point for a Hindu community that itself has no clear edges except its sprawling middle-class suburbanness. There is as yet no obvious—visibly created and theoretically formulated—relationship between the space of the temple and the land of Maryland and the life that it supports. The "space" of the Sri Siva-Vishnu Temple exists somewhere amid the concreteness of the traditional temple, the ethereal space of "spiritual" India, the newer creation of an ideological motherland, and the shifting space of the everywhere/nowhere/everybody's/nobody's split-level world of the migrating international middle class. Without acknowledgment and understanding of that conundrum, the *place* of the temple among Hindu Americans would be lost.

Suburban areas such as Lanham, Maryland, must not be ignored as an important environment for building newer dimensions to modern Hinduism. New Hindu temples in Boston, Los Angeles, Pittsburgh, Chicago, and Nashville rise up at the very edge of urban centers in the same way that new temples now complete the suburban landscape of Madras, Bangalore,[26] New Delhi, London,[27] Singapore,[28] Sidney,[29] and Durban.[30] Indeed, the same English-speaking and highly articulate architects trained at government-sponsored schools of religious architecture in Mahabalipuram outside Madras city and in the famous temple city of Tirupati in Andhra Pradesh have provided designs and guided the construction of new temples in suburban India and the United States. Thus the sacred homes built for these Hindu gods of the American city are at the same time a part of strongly contested definitions of an emerging global Hinduism. The questions of what is India-Indian, what is America-American, where *is* the temple, and who belongs there are all written, I will argue, on the walls, into the design, and throughout the ritual life of this temple. Rather than debating the definition of Hinduism in a public forum, as does the VHP, or quietly setting aside a place in their minds or spirits for a new internalized Hinduism, as do many middle-class Indians, the patrons and devotees of this temple are finding and founding a place to shape their answers to this new "world of crisscrossed economies, intersecting systems of meanings, and fragmented identities," as an advertisement for the new journal *Diaspora* describes it.

## INSIDE/OUTSIDE: THE MODERN HINDU TEMPLE IN A SUBURBAN WORLD
A carefully designed brochure used to solicit donations in 1989 for the first permanent building of the Sri Siva-Vishnu Temple provided a brief history of the temple along with construction plans, estimated costs, and an explanation of the organization of the Sri Siva-Vishnu Temple Trust:

> The dream of setting up a Hindu Temple, in the Nation's Capital, where religious services are performed in the time-honored tradition, was conceived in January, 1980. The SRI SIVA-VISHNU (SSVT) TRUST was formed and registered in the state of Maryland for religious, educational and charitable purposes. The primary aim of the trust is to build and maintain an authentic Hindu temple for performing various religious functions.

The establishment of the trust was followed four years later by the purchase of a modest split-level house on four acres. The split-level became the first temple with the installation of the *balalaya*, literally the "baby" images—the wooden prototypes of the gods that would eventually be remade in stone and housed in the permanent temple. When the trust purchased the ten adjacent acres, plans for construction began in earnest under the direction of a famous *sthapati*, a traditional temple architect, Sri V. Ganapathi Sthapati, from an ancient center of traditional Hindu artisans, Mahabalipuram near Madras city. By September 26, 1990, the basic structure was finished and the final round of inspections completed on the very eve of this major celebration, as the November 1990 temple newsletter later divulged.

The first stone images of three of the fourteen gods and goddesses that the SSVT planned to install in the new temple had made the long journey from the sculptors in Madras to arrive in Lanham for the elaborate rituals of consecration—also, as I was later told, at the last moment. Priests from other Hindu temples in Albany, Los Angeles, and New York joined the resident priest on Cipriano Road for the four-day *pranapratistha* rituals which "fix" (*prastistha*) the "life breath" (*prana*) into the stone sculpture, transforming it from a work of art into a visible embodiment of a god.

I first saw the temple and met the trustees at this point as part of a visual documentation of contemporary temple rituals that my husband, photographer Dick Waghorne, and I had started in Madras two years earlier. We have returned each summer since then to photograph and participate in a series of consecration rituals that have marked the growth of this temple.

On July 3–7, the first *mahakumbabhisekam*, was carefully performed. The *vimana*s, the ornate spires that covered the sanctum of the major god Siva and his son Murugan, were sanctified along with the divine images of these deities by pouring holy water (*abhisekam*, "sprinkling") from a sacred vessel (*kumba*, "pot") simultaneously over the gold finial of the *vimana* and the divine image fixed in the chamber just below. On July 9–12, 1992, a second *mahakumbabhisekam* consecrated the *vimanas* and a monumental reclining stone image of Vishnu in his form as Padmanabha, the deity awaking from rest at the moment of creation. A new wing was added to the temple and dedicated to the god Venkateeswara in the summer of 1993. The consecration ceremonies in 1993 were on Memorial Day weekend, May 28–30. Fundraising was already moving quickly to build a new wing on the temple to house an image of the god Aiyyappa. The cost of this temple in this early period exceeded two million dollars, as not only the deities but also extensive external ornamentation has been added by sculptors who have come and gone from Madras to Lanham in continual rotation so that the bare cinderblock is now fully dressed in unmistakable Indian garb.

To anyone familiar with Hindu deities, the particular selection of gods and the general style of the temple would immediately reveal the South Indian origins of most of the trustees and the devotees of SSVT. Thus I, like the majority of the trustees, came to this temple from the context of the urban temples I have known in South India. As a steady migrant in the opposite direction over the last twenty years, I have lived in or near the neighborhoods from which many of the SSVT devotees came, and I know families like theirs as neighbors and friends in Madras with cousins, brothers, sons, and daughters in America. We are all part of a generation of crisscrossings and multiple heres and theres. The detailed description that follows is grounded in this shared experience on two continents, the numerous conversations I have had here and there, and observations of similar rituals in suburban Madras and suburban Washington, D.C.

On the first day of the scheduled activities for the week of July 4, 1991, when the second of the four-year cycle of consecration rituals occurred, the front yard in Lanham still held several crates containing the sacred stone sculptures of the temple's major deities, which had been transported from the hands of their *silpis* (sculptors) in southern India to their new guardians in America. Several *silpis* had come from Madras prior to the sculptures' arrival to complete their installation in the temple as part of this five-day-long, *mahakumbabhisekam* ritual, which would fully consecrate the images. The details of this July 4 week when the Hindu gods were fully manifest near the U.S. capital will serve as the text for a careful consideration of the nature of the space that was first sanctified that day.

The temple at this point still lacked its exterior decoration, thus exposing the basic form of its architecture. The temple's base unit is the traditional square, in this case 90 by 90 feet. The two stories, however, are very untraditional. The upper floor, which is actually on the ground level at the rear, houses the divine images; the lower story, which opens from the side to the parking lot in the front, contains a large auditorium for cultural performances, the dance and music that has long been part of Hindu temple practice. This central auditorium is ringed by a modern kitchen, restrooms, classrooms, a library, an office, and meeting rooms. Families gathered on the first day of consecration week in the auditorium, eating lunch while keeping an eye on the video monitor that carried every moment of the ongoing five-day ritual in progress upstairs.

The board of trustees of this impressive religious institution expressed great pride that this temple was designed by one of India's leading temple architects, Sri Ganapathi Sthapati. "Sthapati" is a title borne by certain families who, like priests, know and control a special set of sacred texts that give careful guidelines as to the proper forms and methods of their work.[31] Within these formal parameters, however, there is always latitude for change, provided the architect himself commands respect for his own knowledge and personal religiosity, since in Hindu traditions, authority ultimately rests with authoritative people, not books. Thus devotees can rightly claim that this temple is thoroughly "authentic" in spite of the considerable and obvious innovations.

The most striking distinctions between this modern American temple and its older urban counterparts in India are its use of levels and its manner of enclosing space. The Kapaleeswara Temple, for example, in the Mylapore section of Madras, not twenty miles from Mahabalipuram where Sri Ganapathi Sthapati works, has no basement level. The idea of a basement would normally be unthinkable because the deities should always be in unbroken contact with the ground. During the consecration rituals, the stone images are literally glued to their base, and the base is firmly fixed into the temple floor and thus to the earth. When I asked Ganapathi Sthapati about this seemingly unorthodox practice in building the temple in Lanham, he explained that under each of the images is a separate hollow pillar that is filled with dirt. From the basement level these look like supporting pillars, but in fact they serve fundamentally to provide each image the requisite contact with earth. The columns allow the temple to remain orthodox, with a basement.

In the Kapaleeswara Temple in Mylapore, all functions occur at ground level, but not under one roof as in the temple in Lanham. The Madras temple is actually a walled courtyard enclosing many smaller structures. Musicians often perform under the *mandapam*, the pillared pavilions. They do not use an auditorium with a stage but perform close to the gods in their holy sanctums; their music is directed to the gods and only overheard by devotees. The gods' several shrines can be recognized by their ornate domes. The kitchens and the business offices, which are built onto the inner walls of the temple, are where the temple's daily routine occurs. Outside, the four surrounding streets are lined with shops, but on festival days the streets become the gods' royal roads when the divine images are processed around the temple borders. Thus the Kapaleeswara Temple, like the Sri Siva-Vishnu Temple, provides space for music, for daily office-keeping chores, and for preparing the *prashad* (sanctified food that is offered to the gods, then eaten by devotees). However, while the Sri Siva-Vishnu Temple divides these functions from the actual seats of the gods in one two-storied building, the Kapaleeswara Temple remains a single-level complex of buildings.

Climatic differences alone cannot account for this change in architecture from a walled compound in India to a single structure in America. The design of the Sri Siva-Vishnu Temple openly articulates theological changes that have occurred in the transplanting of India's gods to America. The community of devotees in the Washington area chose to construct a temple that would unite the two major Hindu traditions, Vaishnavism and Shaivism, "under one roof," as one member of the board of trustees aptly put it. Thus the gods Siva and Vishnu are each housed in their own shrines, but within this single building. Other deities associated with each tradition have smaller shrines along the sides and the back of the first floor. A large shrine to Lord Murugan is at the center of the temple. The cupola over his image seems to blossom out of the temple's roof. He is flanked on the right and left by shrines of Siva and Vishnu respectively. The *vimanas* of their shrines likewise burst through the roof. The *vimanas* of other shrines are confined to the interior of the building.

A member of the board of trustees explained to me that the temple was carefully designed to exactly balance the two cosmic forces embodied in Siva and Vishnu. Thus, while the divine image of the powerful goddess Durga rests on the north wall of the temple next to the Siva shrine, an image of the powerful Rama, an incarnation of Vishnu, was to balance her power on the east next to Vishnu's shrine in the original plans. Now Hanuman stands in this place as a deity of dimensions expansive enough to balance the goddess's own staggering force. These stone images of Durga and Hanuman were the first to be consecrated, on September 27–30, 1990.

The choice of the divine occupants for these shrines was much discussed by the trustees and community of devotees here and remains in flux. The original plans for the temple, included in the early fundraising brochure, called for a shrine to Rama, an incarnation of Vishnu, to be placed next to another shrine housing Nataraja, Siva as the cosmic dancer. Now Hanuman occupies the place next to Rama, as is traditional. The large wing dedicated to Lord Venkateeswara was proposed by a committee formed within the larger congregation, who then gained the support of the trustees. The board of trustees announced in the temple newsletter that "in response to the overwhelming desire of the devotees," it had decided to build a Sri Venkateeswara shrine as another extension to the present temple at the cost of $240,000. I received notice of the formal proposal to raise $300,000 to construct a shrine to Ayyappa as "an extension of the existing structure with the traditional 18 steps."

These decisions to include certain images reflect the creation of what could be called a new American Hindu pantheon. While traditional temples in South India often house several deities, and some major temples have substituted or subordinated one major deity for another in their thousand-year history, the choice of such an eclectic mix of deities from different regions in India and from once more distinct theologies is a phenomenon of modern times—especially of the rapid pace of temple growth in America. This new model is crucial because in America all the gods live in the same house.

This new model of a single enclosed space holding a group of different shrines is yet another architectural innovation within the boundaries of authenticity. The changes were explained to me by the member of the board of trustees who was the liaison between the board, Ganapathi Sthapati, his Indian crew, and the American contractors who actually built the basic structure. What appears in Lanham to be the outer wall of the temple actually functions like the outer wall that normally surrounds the open courtyard of a Hindu temple in South India. Thus inside this enclosure each deity continues to occupy his or her own shrine. The cupolas of the shrines of the three major deities actually protrude from the roof, and it is these three ornate *vimana*s that neighbors in Lanham see as they pass the temple. There are plans to put the *gopara*, the traditional massive gates at the cardinal directions in a temple's surrounding wall, onto the walls of this temple. But in the American context, these gates will appear as doors into this enclosed space. Hence the plurality of gods here live under the same roof, but nonetheless in their own rooms. Devotees tell me that this conglomerate space allows them either to see the temple as a unified divine area or to concentrate their devotion on one deity. As one said, "I can feel as though I am only with one god if I want, or with all."

The curious feature of this great effort at unity within the diversity of Hinduism, however, is the concomitant separation of sacred from secular in the use of two levels. Music, eating, office work, and education are now "downstairs" functions, while upstairs is reserved for the holy rituals and ceremonies. Further, no festival actually spills out into the streets of this quiet suburban neighborhood. When the gods are first processed, they are carried inside around the first floor. During important rituals, like the recent consecration rites, the priest carries holy water in sacred pots around an outer promenade which forms a railed porch circling the entire first floor and opening out onto a grand staircase leading down to the lower parking lot. Processions around this outer promenade are the only public display of Hindu rituals that Lanham, Maryland, will normally see.

The only god whose eyes turn to Cipriano Road is Ganesa, who can be seen looking out from his niche in the exterior wall. Ganesa, as the divine guardian of doors, is by his very nature a border-ward and thus looks out to the world. The other deities will live their lives on the upper level within these cinderblock walls. And more important, the devotees have chosen to demarcate the holy life of the gods above from the music, education, and business carried on below. Thus dance and education will not be conducted in front of the very eyes of the gods, as is the case in India. The Hindu gods in America truly live in a split-level suburban world, with its inside/outside, upstairs/downstairs dichotomies.

The transplantation of Hinduism to America in the case of the Sri Siva-Vishnu temple is not just a matter of finding a home and feeling at home, as John Fenton so well describes; it is a matter of building and maintaining a house. The crucial clue revealed in the design of the temple and its place on Cipriano Road is that ultimate marker of the American dream—home ownership. In India, ancient temples were built and maintained by kings. During the colonial period, this royal function passed to the new British government, which created a system of temple trusts both independent of and yet part of the state governments, a system, much like our federal reserve, which remains today. In modern India the very wealthy build temples, and the state still has a hand in their maintenance and construction. In Lanham, on the other hand, the devotees own the temple as a joint trust. Several members of the board of trustees pointed out that the model of administration by elected and appointed trustees supported by hundreds of individual contributions is new. They would agree with the way the chairman of the board of trustees of a Hindu temple in Nashville described the situation: "We found ourselves, a bunch of amateurs, trying to manage the complexities of a religious institution." Through their trustees, devotees pay the mortgage each month, and all the other problems of home ownership must be met without fail.

But this house belongs to the whole community and marks the true rise of the middle-class Indian. As they moved close to the deity, or climbed up on the roof to see the *vimana*s, or sat right next to or even entered the sanctum during the rituals, members of the board of trustees and many devotees said to me, "We could never get this close to the ritual in India; we could never see such things there; we could never take such an important part in this ritual." In owning a temple, thus, the middle class has thrown down the rights of kings, the rights of the British Raj, and the rights of the state over such structures. The fact was not lost on devotees that as the fireworks blasted above Washington on July 4, 1991, the Sri Siva-Vishnu Temple was installing its gods! In 1993, I heard a legend that a famous psychic at the turn of the century had predicted that Hindu temples would come to America on a Fourth of July holiday.

But what does this phenomenon of home ownership have to do with the issues of the universality and particularity of the Hindu temple that began this essay? The point here can be stated simply: The mobile middle class in the world now goes from house to house, not place to place! The temple stands amid other houses, but it is not related to them in any way other than that this suburban world allows such a temple to exist as a house among houses. Even the zoning laws in such areas recognize such houses of God as residential and not commercial property. In this sense, only such neutral areas that are not bounded neighborhoods could so easily tolerate such diversity. The Indian community at the temple takes great care not to disturb its close neighbors and those whose houses border the temple. Devotees have invited their neighbors to participate in important activities, and a few of these folks do drop by as good but somewhat bewildered neighbors. I found myself explaining the rituals to an African American neighbor who had come by to see her new neighbors. She quietly asked me the pressing question for her as a Muslim, "Do they believe in God?" When I said yes, she left satisfied, saying that was all that really counted.

Suburban land on the borders of the metropolitan area remains segmented into plots. Like their neighbors, the devotees of the Sri Siva-Vishnu Temple do not bring their private religious life out into the streets. Religious practice is carried on within the confines of their own castle—in a very middle-class sense of that term. Here is one structure that is to hold the new Hindu family in America under one roof, separate but equal with the other religions of America. The gods of India have a new home, a foothold on the western shore, a life beyond the borders of India but yet a life confined to a house. Is this not the quintessential characteristic of the suburban home? Family on the inside facing out. Diversities living side by side but never infringing on the other—a patchwork quilt, a cut-and-paste world of multiculturalism that is stitched together by neighborliness and good fences. Yet within the walls of each square lives a private world, as the old song goes, "with a plot of, not a lot of land."

Thus as a house, the Sri Siva-Vishnu Temple becomes a very particular and concrete entity, while as a place, Lanham, Maryland, remains seemingly neutral—the location a plot on a surveyor's chart of streets and houses. But this American Hindu holy house also contains two levels. What are the upstairs and downstairs of this world? Certainly the downstairs is not completely situated in Lanham, Maryland, but it is also not identical to the orthodox upstairs where the priests imported from India do their holy work. Ultimately, the split-level world of this suburban Washington temple provides an apt image for the cultural world of the affluent Indian American community here. In America, Indians live in a split-level universe that is "traditional" above but with a lower floor that is the space of the worldwide modern middle-class family life—from which Indians came in India, but which is now enhanced by their move to America.

## UPSTAIRS/DOWNSTAIRS: NEGOTIATING GENDER AND GENERATIONS

In the attractive brochure introducing the temple to prospective donors, the temple lists its services as "religious," "cultural," and "philosophical." The category "religious" is confined to the celebration of festival, group worship, the performance of wedding and other life-cycle rites, and classes on "Sanskrit, Vedas, and Hindu rituals." The term "religious," in other words, now belongs only to the ritual performances of the priests. These are the upstairs activities. Philosophical talks and discussions—the preaching activities of Hinduism—now belong downstairs with such teaching activities as summer camps for youth and adults, yoga classes, dance classes, and lessons in the various vernacular languages of India. Although such an upstairs/downstairs division of the temple (reserving the word "religion" for the upstairs) is quite out of step with Hindu tradition, the division makes sense in America. Sacred is not really divided from secular here, and middle-class family life has actually invaded what were once professional and priestly realms. The family is now on the lower floor of the temple. The middle-class world has been reconstructed within the temple as it is known in the homes of recent immigrants. These are not sanctuaries *from* America, because the suburban outside has been integrated into both floors of the temple, though as an Indo-American, not a Euro-American, phenomenon.

The case of dance is instructive here. Until the early part of this century, dancers in India were temple servants who worked alongside the priests to provide comfort and pleasure to the gods embodied in the temple. A rigorous reform movement accused these *devadasis*, slaves of God, of being nothing more than glorified prostitutes and corrupting the temple, and they were soon expelled. But within two decades, Indians realized that they had thrown out an important cultural performance in the name of an ostensible moral purity. Dance was revived outside the temple as an art to be cultivated by the daughters of the rising upper middle class, and so it remains in performance halls in India. But in America it has returned to the temple, while acquiring much the same place that ballet lessons have in the Euro-American home, as a matter of family pride in the accomplishments of a daughter who, nonetheless, is rarely encouraged to become a full-time professional dancer.

Pride in the "culture" of the homeland frequently marks the middle-class first and second generation's most permanent tie to the mother country in the American context. For the secular Indian, the categories of "culture" and "philosophy" have become neutral terms with few religious overtones. A great Carnatic vocal performed in the common room is like the Ave Maria sung in a concert hall, not at the altar in a Catholic church. Similarly, discussions of the meaning of religious texts are "philosophy" and fully congruent with the modern rational world, whereas the same text chanted in ritual might seem an embarrassing incantation. There are many in the Indian American community who are not supportive of religious ritual, but they do want to keep up family values and to retain Hinduism as a moral and aesthetic force in their life. The lower-floor auditorium is for them.

The lower floor is also for the second generation, for whom the activities upstairs often seem as confusing as for any American youth. John Fenton summarizes the dilemma for the generation who pledged much of their lives and even their fortune to help build this temple: "The irony of Hindu temple-building activity in America is that it emphasizes that aspect of Hindu religion that so far has the least meaning and that is the most opaque to second generation Indian immigrants."[32] "We have built this for the sake of our children," said one older devotee while pointing to this grand edifice in the nation's capital. "Are we building it for nothing?" A telling scene in the movie *Mississippi Masala* shows two young second-generation children playing cowboys and Indians (the Native American variety) in the midst of the celebration of the holy Hindu wedding rites in a small town in Mississippi. Several young boys with baseball bats in hand, ready to "play ball," can be spotted outside the holy *yagasala*, the tent constructed to build the sacred fires needed to awaken the gods during the great installation rituals in July.

Such "youths," at quite a loss on the upper floor, are more at home in the classrooms below. In the first National Indian American Students Conference, hosted by Sangam, the Indian students' association at the University of North Carolina/Chapel Hill, Indian American college students from almost fifty institutions articulated their discomfort with religion "as a show" and with ritual that they could not and were not asked to understand.[33] An essay in *Sanyog: South Asian Expressions* poses the dilemma of ritual for the second generation: "You can't give god a granola bar."[34] Here in Washington, those families who chose to watch the ritual on video downstairs sat in congenial groups, as mother-father-children, while upstairs the South Indian proprieties were tacitly observed, with gender-segregated seating. An active group of young people who were trying to get into the spirit of things during this *mahakumbabhisekam* ritual nonetheless did not remain upstairs for the rituals but sold "Om Shanti" T-shirts on the lower floor, while their mothers cooked a phenomenal amount of food, which they sold downstairs at nominal cost to raise money for the temple.

Women in the kitchen downstairs and men carrying out priestly functions (now defined as "religious") upstairs, is the source of low-level but palpable, tension in the temple. This gender dichotomy in part reflects traditional Indian society, but it also is created by the up-stairs/downstairs spatial division. There are some real ironies here. For American femi-nists, women in the kitchen marks gender segregation and subordination, but these South Asian women work in the temple kitchens, a task reserved in India for Brahmin men, whose ritual purity was a prerequisite for handling the holy food which was always served first to God. When women now make this *prashad*, sanctified meals eaten by devotees as a sacrament, they are assuming a priestly role; their domestic task has expanded in America into temple service. The downstairs of the temple now has become a true home where the housewife cooks and serves the larger family of devotees. Sharing this home-space with young people, women find their status at once enhanced by their greater role but also diminished because that role is no longer on a level (literally) with the other ritual func-tions of the temple. In American fashion, food, now only vaguely sacralized as the *prashad*, is served as "lunch" on Styrofoam plates by exhausted volunteers and eaten with plastic spoons.

Women grumble about this aspect of the new split-level world. Many of these women work and succeed in America, as do their spouses. Yet here in this space, the division could be seen as even more segregated than in the "control" temple Kapaleeswara in Madras, where the cooking is left to the Brahmins and women are not behind kitchen walls. I heard discontent in the American temple; women mentioned to me that they have no real say in serious decision making. Yet women were forceful and very active not only in cooking but also in decorating the temple upstairs and in organizing fund raising; most important, I heard a number of women chanting in Sanskrit along with the priest as they sat "listening." I suspected a desire for an increased ritual role, and my suspicions were realized late on the last holy night of the installation rituals that July. After a long, quite beautiful marriage rit-ual for the god Murugan and his wives, while the congregation chanted the wedding vows for the divine couples, the lovely palanquins with the bronze images of the deities inside were lifted by male devotees for the ride around the borders of the interior of the temple. When they reached the shrine of the goddesses Sarada and Parvati, however, the two palan-quins apparently changed hands—for when the procession came out the other side of the temple, they were being carried by some joyous women. I asked one female palanquin bearer if it was usual in India for women to do this. She replied immediately, "In India they are male chauvinists, but this is America." As the palanquins turned the corner, one mid-dle-aged woman grumbled about seeing women behave in this manner, but the faces of the hijackers revealed the glee of women taking their first steps toward a new role in their rit-ual and managerial positions in the temple.

Upstairs/downstairs may be solid architectural space, but it is not, then, stable social space. The more domesticated the temple becomes, the more its overarching model becomes the family, the more the tensions in middle-class family life will explode through the seemingly solid floors. By adopting the suburbs as the location of the temple, by opting for the suburban split of domestic life from public life, the founders of the Sri Siva-Vishnu Temple sought to create a Hindu family within the American world of family life and family values. American life has not been factored out; it has been invited in to rest right under the Hindu holy sanctums. But as the women here have already shown, the space between the floors is not airtight.

## BETWEEN UPSTAIRS/DOWNSTAIRS: TECHNOLOGY AS THE THIRD STREAM

The moment when the priests awakened the gods to their new life in America by pouring the holy waters, the *abhishekam*, over the stone images, was viewed by many devotees on video monitors carefully placed alongside each sanctum. In the earlier Pranapratistha ceremonies which awakened Durga, Hanuman, and Ganesa, the *abhishekam* for each deity was performed in rapid sequence in each sanctum. Devotees sat facing the deity whose rituals they had sponsored through donation. The video monitors allowed devotees to get the closest view of the ritual in front of them and to witness each of the consecutive consecrations; the chief engineer for this complex technology switched from camera to camera to catch the crucial moments at each shrine. A telling moment in this conflation of authentic ritual with advanced technology occurred when I was seated with a large group of devotees in front of Hanuman, with another group of devotees at our rear facing the Durga shrine in the opposite direction. At the moment when the holy waters awakened Durga, my Hanuman group raised their folded hands in the sign of devotion to the to the image on the video monitor in front, when a simple twist of the head would have revealed Durga the actual goddess. The image on the video monitor was an acceptable double for the image to the rear.

In the consecration ritual, this video system operated by an African American crew and director became an ever-present symbol of the modernity of these rituals. Although few non-Indians participated, the video crew was afforded the clearest vision of the holiest of sights by virtue of their skill in the new medium of imaging. This use of video cameras is by no means new to the Hindu temple. The cameras now have the first view of the holiest of rituals in the sanctums of major temples in India when there is no other way to accommodate the desire of the vast crowd of devotees to share in these holy sights. But new in America was the choice to put these cameras in non-Hindu hands. The crew remained patient and respectful through the long days of these rituals. The remark of one tired "grip" showed how well the presence of the video cameras had made the translation of this temple ritual to an American idiom: "This is the longest church service I ever attended," he sighed on the fifth straight day of the rituals.

The non-Hindu community was again directly incorporated into the ritual at the point of another technical skill. The African American mason who carefully cut and fixed the marble on the walls of the interior of the sanctum, the very place where the divine images would reside, became an important participant in the consecration ritual. On the first day of the rituals in July, this mason found himself standing with his shirt and shoes removed in front of the sacred fire. Minutes later, with a turban on his head, this obviously serious but delighted mason pulled a burning straw man through each of the interiors of the new sanctums in the temple. His was the final act of purification to make the sanctums ready for their divine residents. His work as mason had taken on its full ritual significance.

The Sri Siva-Vishnu Temple lives with its doors open to its neighbors. No one is excluded; an announcement of the consecration rituals in July invited "all Hindus and non-Hindus alike to join in this unique event." Some non-Hindu Indians, some non-Hindu Americans, and some Hindu Euro-Americans came. But they were not as openly representative of the greater American community as the mason who was seen to stand for the many non-Hindus who had a hand in constructing the temple.

There are non-Hindus who now figure in the stories told about the monumental five-year task of constructing this temple. I heard particular praise for the Italian American master stonecutter who worked with his Indian counterparts, the *silpis* from Madras. Their common love of stone led to an exchange of ideas and techniques. The American stonecutter introduced the *silpis* to the ideas of laser cutting and developing computer patterns for their decorative work. He marveled at the style and skill of their work. The exchanges took place on the level of seeing and doing, because many of the *silpis* know little English. Another much-praised non-Hindu company were the movers who successfully brought the two-ton stone sculpture of Vishnu into his sanctum inch by inch without harming a speck of his body. Their technical skill, but also their quiet and innate sense of the sacredness of the piece, impressed the Indian crew. It is in such stories of a shared love of craft and the technology of construction, the mutual awe at skills and design, that Hindus and non-Hindus meet in this temple, just as it is in front of the video that families of all generations are able to sit together. Technology, in this temple, is the third space where differences of generation and even of ethnic and religious origins are increasingly able to find a meeting ground.

## CONCLUSION: A HOUSE WITH MANY ROOMS

Trustees and devotees of the Sri Siva-Vishnu Temple live with and talk openly about the many tensions in their new lives in the United States. Husbands and wives worry about the loss of Indian culture in their children. The "children" who are now adults in college wonder about the meaning of this Hinduism that they see reconstructed in front of them. At a time of rising Hindu nationalism in India, these Hindus away from India wonder how to react to the new Indian political-religious parties now coming here for their support. Men remain worried about their chances for ultimate success in a highly competitive global market. Discussions of an economic "glass ceiling" are part of the ethos of those who also worry about the economics of keeping a roof over the gods. But this congregation has built the dialogue, the tensions, and the uncertainty of their lives into the space of a temple in suburban Washington, D.C. In a move that was at once as characteristically American as it was Indian, they offered their prosperity as a down payment, mortgaged their fears, and built a house.

This temple as a *house*, however, has fixed nothing for these Indian Americans—and, I would argue, was never meant to *fix* anything. This building made of concrete, these gods formed from stone, are not inanimate objects that are riveted motionless. The temple and the gods are "vibrating," as Ganapathi Sthapati told the devotees at the moment of the consecration of the temple in July, 1991. Once the houses—of the gods and of humanity—are freed from their status as inanimate things, their power to transform and to recreate their creators becomes clear. In this sense of the *power* of space, the American home and the Hindu holy house live as analogues in the modern world.

In a dramatic statement in *The Poetics of Space*, Gaston Bachelard declares, "the house remodels man."[35] David Knipe, in a striking conclusion to a volume of cross-cultural essays on the temple in society, also ends with the suggestion that temples are ultimately places for and models of "transformation" both for the self and for an entire culture.[36] In these approaches to constructed space, the human house and the divine temple are alive with power; those who associate the construction of buildings only with finding security or with engraving meanings in stone do not understand the tensile, active, "vibrating" nature of holy stones or sacred rocks or even houses. Bachelard's houses are built out of wood and stone and imagination to re-place the human soul into a built life in this world.

But just as Bachelard constructed his musings on space in the middle of this century out of his experiences with the house, so the house in the contemporary world may be the primary model and space for middle-class imaginings of the saved. "The City" as a place of dreams may well have been replaced by "the house." Certainly children "grow up" in houses, and old people hope to "pass away" in the heart of their own homes; the magazine rack at the grocery store is filled with photos of "dream houses." The Sri Siva-Vishnu Temple in America may prove to be the kind of contemporary house—with enough rooms, staircases, twists and turns—to hold a very diverse family made up of gods and humans, men and women, parents and children, Indians and Americans, while giving them all space enough to grow.

## NOTES

1. Surinder M. Bhardwaj, "Asian Indians in the United States: A Geographic Appraisal" in *South Asians Overseas: Migration and Ethnicity*, edited by Colin Clark (Cambridge: Cambridge University Press, 1990), 195–217.

2. See Parminder Bhashu, "New Cultural Forms and Transnational Women in the Diaspora: Culture, Class, and Consumption Among British Asian Women," paper presented at "The Expanding Landscape: South Asians in Diaspora," sponsored by the Independent Scholars of South Asia and Southern Asian Institute, Columbia University, March 5–6, 1993.

3. Raymond B. Williams, *Religions of Immigrants from India* (Cambridge: Cambridge University Press, 1988), 14–23.

4. New York: Random House, 1993. Quoted in *Hinduism Today*, September 1993, 27.

5. Priya Agarwal, *Passage from India: Post 1965 Indian Immigrants and their Children* (Palos Verdes, Calif.: Yuvat, 1991), 67–68.

6. Bible, 2 Samuel 8:6.

7. Vasudha Narayanan, "Creating South Indian Hindu Experience in the United States," in *A Sacred Thread: Modern Transmission of Hindu Traditions in India and Abroad* ed. Raymond Brady Williams (Chambersburg, Penn.: Anima, 1992), 164.

8. Amitav Ghosh, "The Diaspora in Indian Culture," *Public Culture* 2 (Fall 1989): 76.

9. V. S. Naipaul, *An Area of Darkness* (London: Andre Deutsch, 1964).

10. Richard Hughes Seager, ed., *The Dawn of Religious Pluralism: Voices from the World's Parliament of Religions, 1893.* (La Salle, Ill.: Open Court, 1993), 421–32.

11. *India Today*, North American edition, August 31, 1993, 48C.

12. *India Times*, June 30, 1993, 4.

13. Max Weber, *The Religion of India*, trans. by Hans H. Gerth and Don Martindale (Glencoe, Ill.: The Free Press, 1958 [1921]), 309. See J. N. Farquhar, *Modern Religious Movements In India* (reprint; Delhi: Munshiram Manoharlal, 1977 [1914]); Stephen Fuchs, *Rebellious Prophets: A Study of Messianic Movements in Indian Religions* (Bombay: Asia Publishing House, 1965).

14. Lawrence Alan Babb, *Redemptive Encounters: Three Modern Styles in Hindu Religion* (Berkeley and Los Angeles: University of California Press, 1986) 186, 224–25.

15. Ibid., 18.

16. Raymond. B. Williams, *A New Face of Hinduism: The Swaminarayanan Religion* (Cambridge: Cambridge University Press, 1984); Williams,

*Religions of Immigrants from India,* 129–85; Mark Juergensmeyer, *Radhasoami Reality: The Logic of a Modern Faith* (Princeton: Princeton University Press, 1991).

17. Williams, *Religions of Immigrants from India,* 173–85.

18. John Y. Fenton, *Transplanting Religious Traditions: Asian Indians in America.* (New York: Praeger, 1988), 171.

19. Fred W. Clothey, "The Construction of a Temple in an American City and the Acculturation Process," in *Rhythm and Intent: Ritual Studies from South India* (Madras: Blackie, 1983).

20. Narayanan, "Creating South Indian Hindu Experience in the United States," 18.

21. Stella Kramrisch, *The Hindu Temples,* 2 vols. (Delhi: Motilal Banarsidass, 1976 [1946]), 131–44.

22. S. S. Janaki, "Dhvaja-Stambba: Critical Account of its Structural and Ritualistic Details," in *Siva Temple and Temple Rituals,* ed. S. S. Janaki (Madras, 1988), 122–181.

23. Kramrisch, *The Hindu Temples,* 5.

24. Susan Lewandowski, "Changing Form and Function in the Ceremonial and the Colonial Port City in India: An Historical Analysis of Madurai and Madras," *Modern Asian Studies* 2 (1974): 183–212.

25. Joanne Punzo Waghorne, "Mylapore," in *Temple Towns of Tamil Nadu,* ed. George Michell (Bombay: Marg Publications, 1993), 114–28

26. Philip Lutgendorf, "My Hanuman is Bigger Than Yours," *History of Religions* 33 (February 1994).

27. Kim Knott, "Hindu Temple Rituals in Britain: The Reinterpretation of Tradition," in *Hinduism in Great Britain* ed. Richard Burkhart (London and New York: Tavistock, 1987); Robert Jackson, "The Shree Krishna Temple and the Gujarati Hindu Community in Coventry," in *Hin-*

*duism in England* ed. David G. Bowen (Bradford, West Yorkshire: Bradford College, 1981); Steven Vertovec, "Community and Congregation in London Hindu Temples: Divergent Trends," *New Community* 18 (January 1992): 251–64; Susan Nowikowski and Robin Ward, "Middle Class and British? An Analysis of South Asians in Suburbia," *New Community* 8 (Winter 1978–79): 1–10.

28. Fred W. Clothey, "Rituals and Reinterpretations: South Indians in Southeast Asia," in *A Sacred Thread: Modern Transmission of Hindu Traditions in India and Abroad,* ed. Raymond Brady Williams (Chambersburg, Penn.: Anima, 1992).

29. Purushottama Bilimoria of Deakin University is working extensively on new Hindu temples in Australia.

30. Paul Mikula, Brian Kearney, and Rodney Harber, *Traditional Hindu Temples in South Africa* (Durban: Hindu Temple Publications, 1982).

31. V. Ganapathi Sthapati, "Symbolism of Vimana and Gopura," in *Siva Temple and Temple Rituals,* ed. S. S. Janaki (Madras: The Kuppuswami Sastri Research Institute 1988), 114.

32. Fenton, *Transplanting Religious Traditions,* 179.

33. Research Triangle Park, August 6–9, 1992

34. Anuradha Mannar, "You Can't Give God a Granola Bar," *Sanyog: South Asian Expressions* (Durham, N.C.) 3 (Fall 1992): 28–29.

35. Gaston Bachelard, *The Poetics of Space,* trans. Maria Jolas (Boston: Beacon, 1969), 47. The study of space was introduced to American scholarship by Yi-Fu Tuan, *Space and Place: The Perspective of Experience* (Minneapolis: University of Minnesota Press, 1977).

36. David M. Knipe, "The Temple in Image and Reality," in *Temple in Society,* ed. Michael V. Fox (Winona Lake: Eisenbrauns, 1988), 132–33.

IS THERE A COMMON AMERICAN CULTURE?

*Robert N. Bellah*

Given the growing multiculturalism of American society is there still a common American culture? Robert N. Bellah's answer is an emphatic yes, but it is probably not the common culture we are seeking. What is common to American culture, Bellah argues, is individualism. We are a people who place our individual needs to advance ourselves, often economically but also in "spiritual" quests to "find ourselves," ahead of the communal and religious ties that bind us together as a society. Elsewhere, in Habits of the Heart, Bellah traces the historical roots of this utilitarian and expressive individualism; here he locates perhaps its deepest tributary in the Protestant sectarian insistence upon the sacredness of the individual conscience. What is most disturbing about our common culture of individualism, Bellah argues, is that despite our insistence on individual difference, it has made us all the same. Whether African, Asian, Native American, European, or whatever in our cultural origins, the more time we have spent in this market-driven American culture the less we know about our separate cultural pasts and the more we speak the same language, watch the same television shows, and buy the latest fashions. Television and education, and increasingly the Internet are the agencies of socialization to this common culture prescribed to us by the state and the market. In the face of such powerful forces, how is it possible for any group in America to withstand these pressures and sustain genuine cultural difference? Though "the hour is late and the problems mount," Bellah urges us to become more connected to the world around us through religious involvement and collective social action.

Reprinted by permission from Robert N. Bellah, "Is There a Common Culture?" *Journal for the American Academy of Religion* 66: 3 (1998), 613–625. Used by permission of the American Academy of Religion.

# 26

# IS THERE A COMMON
# AMERICAN CULTURE?

*Robert N. Bellah*

I MIGHT BEGIN MY TALK this morning somewhat facetiously by asking the question, not whether there is a common American culture, but how is it that a plenary session of the American Academy of Religion is devoted to this question in a society with so powerful and monolithic a common culture as ours? The answer, however, is obvious: it has become part of the common culture to ask whether there is a common culture in America.

K. Anthony Appiah, Professor of Afro-American Studies and Philosophy at Harvard, in a review of Nathan Glazer's recent book *We Are All Multiculturalists Now* (whose very title makes the point), quotes the book as saying "The Nexis data base of major newspapers shows no reference to multiculturalism as late as 1988, a mere 33 items in 1989, and only after that a rapid rise—more than 100 items in 1990, more than 600 in 1991, almost 900 in 1992, 1200 in 1993, and 1500 in 1994. . . ."(7) Appiah adds, "When it comes to diversity it seems we all march to the beat of a single drummer." (32) There is something very congenial to multiculturalism in common American culture, but such congeniality is not to be assumed as natural or shared in all societies today. It is worth looking at the contrasting case of France. Rodney Benson, a graduate student in my department, is writing a most interesting dissertation which, among other things compares the fate of multiculturalism in France and the U.S. Benson describes a nascent French multiculturalism of the late 1970s and early 1980s as ultimately being rejected by virtually the entire ideological spectrum in favor of a universalistic republicanism in the late 1980s, just when multiculturalism in the U.S. was taking off. Why American culture has been so singularly receptive to multiculturalism as an ideology is a point to which I will return.

But first, a sociological point about why there not only is but has to be a common culture in America: culture does not float free from institutions. A powerful institutional order will carry a powerful common culture. An example of just how important this relation between culture and institutions is comes from the recent reunification of Germany. In the last days of the German Democratic Republic, the protesters chanted "*Wir sind ein Volk*," and the chant stirred euphoria among West Germans as well. But the painful and unexpected experience of living together, as made vivid to me by an outstanding Harvard doctoral dissertation filed earlier this year by Andreas Glaeser, using the integration of East and West German police officers into a unified police force in Berlin as a microcosm, showed that they were not, after all "*ein Volk*," but indeed "*zwei*." It wasn't just that the "*Ossies*" and the "*Wessies*" ("Easterners" and "Westerners") had different views on common problems, they had different and to some degree mutually unintelligible ways of thinking about the world altogether. Forty-five years of radically different institutional orders had created two cultures which to this day are very far from united, although the experience of a unified institutional order will, almost certainly, though not without time and pain, ultimately reunite them.

The United States, surely, has an exceptionally powerful institutional order. The state in America, even though it is multi-leveled and, to a degree, decentralized, has an enormous impact on all our lives. For example, the shift in marriage law in the late sixties and early seventies toward "no-fault divorce" was a response to, but also an impetus for, the emergence of "divorce culture" in America as a serious competitor to "marriage culture." The state is even responsible to a degree for the construction of multiculturalism through the little boxes that must be checked on a myriad of forms. Haven't you ever been tempted to check them all or to leave them all empty? If the state intrudes in our lives in a thousand ways, the market is even more intrusive. There is very little that Americans need that we can produce for ourselves any more. We are dependent on the market not only for goods but for many kinds of service. Our cultural understanding of the world is shaped every time we enter a supermarket or a mall. I taught a senior seminar of about 20 students this spring, roughly divided into one-fourth Asian American, one-fourth Hispanic, one-fourth African American, and one-fourth Anglo. What was remarkable was how easily they talked because of how much they shared. Beyond the ever-present state and market, they shared the immediate experience of coping with a vast state university, with its demands and its incoherence.

Education, which is linked largely though not exclusively to the state, and television (and increasingly the Internet) linked to the market, are enormously powerful purveyors of common culture, socializers not only of children but of all of us most of our lives. Not only are we exposed from infancy to a monoculture, we are exposed to it monolingually. The cultural power of American English is overwhelming and no language, except under the most unusual circumstances, has ever been able to withstand it, which is what makes the English Only movement such a joke. As Appiah notes, 90 percent of California-born Hispanic children of immigrant parents have native fluency in English and in the next generation only 50 percent of them still speak Spanish. One more generation and you can forget about Spanish. When third generation Asian Americans come to college they have to learn Chinese or Japanese in language classes just like anyone else—they don't bring those languages with them. Appiah contrasts our society with his own experience growing up in Ghana where there were three languages spoken in the household: English, Twi, and Navrongo. "Ghana," he writes, "with a population smaller than that of New York State, has several dozen languages in active daily use and no one language that is spoken at home— or even fluently understood—by a majority of the population." (31) Ghana is multilingual and therefore multicultural, in a way that we, except for first generation immigrants, have never been. When language, which is the heart of culture, goes, then so, in any deep sense, does cultural difference. I don't say identity, which is something I will come back to, but culture. Serious multicultural education would begin by teaching native English speakers a second language, but, unlike most of the rest of the world, that almost never happens in the

United States. The half-hearted effort to teach Spanish in California public schools results in very few native English speakers with a secondary fluency in Spanish. Why don't most Americans speak another language? Because we don't have to—everyone in the world speaks English—or so we think. Tell me about multiculturalism. (The truth is that American culture and American English are putting their stamp on every other culture in the world today.)

There are exceptions, though they are statistically small, but I had better talk about them. Enclaves of genuine cultural difference, centered on a language different from English, can persist, or even emerge, under special conditions: where socio-economic status is low and residential segregation is effective. A particularly poignant example is the emergence among one of the oldest groups of English speakers in America, African Americans, of enclaves of black English dialects in a few inner cities in the northeastern U.S. that are mutually unintelligible with standard American English. This can happen under conditions of hypersegregation where opportunities to participate in the larger society are almost completely denied. Native American languages survive on a few reservations, though many are dying out, even with strenuous efforts to maintain them. Since there is much less hypersegretation of Hispanics or Asians than of blacks, enclaves of Spanish or Korean, or other Asian languages, have the generational transience of, say, Polish or Italian a hundred years ago.

If I am right, there is an enormously powerful common culture in America and it is carried predominantly by the market and the state and by their agencies of socialization: television and education. What institutions might withstand that pressure and sustain genuine cultural difference? In simpler societies kinship and religious communities might do so, but in our society families and churches or synagogues are too colonized by the market and the state to provide much of a buffer. They may give a nuance, an inflection, to the common culture, but families and even religious communities are almost always too fragile to provide a radical alternative. Nevertheless such nuances and inflections are important, not only in their own right, but because they can provide the wedge through which criticism of the common culture, and the possibility of altering it, can occur.

What, then, is the content of this common culture? If we realize that the market and the state in America are not and have never been antithetical, and that the state has had the primary function, for conservatives and liberals alike, of maximizing market opportunities, I believe I can safely borrow terminology from *Habits of the Heart* and say that a dominant element of the common culture is what we called utilitarian individualism. In terms of historical roots this orientation can be traced to a powerful Anglo-American utilitarian tradition going back at least as far as Hobbes and Locke, although it operates today quite autonomously, without any necessary reference to intellectual history. Utilitarian individualism has always been moderated by what we called expressive individualism, which has its roots in Anglo-American Romanticism, but which has picked up many influences along the way from European ethnic, African American, Hispanic, and Asian influences. Here, too, the bland presentism of contemporary American culture obliterates its own history. Our Anglo students do not come to college with a deep knowledge of Jane Austen or Nathaniel Hawthorne any more than our Japanese American students bring a knowledge of Lady Murasaki or Natsume Soseki. What they bring, they bring in common: Oprah Winfrey, *ER*, *Seinfeld*, Nike, Microsoft, the NBA, and the NFL. If the common culture is predominantly Euro-American, or, more accurately, Anglo-American, in its roots, the enormous pressure of the market economy, and the mass media and mass education oriented to it, obliterate the genuine heritage of Anglo-American, European, African, and Asian culture with equal thoroughness.

And yet, and yet. . . . Nestled in the very core of utilitarian and expressive individualism is something very deep, very genuine, very old, very American, something we did not quite see or say in *Habits*. Here I come to something that will be of especial interest to this audience, for that core is religious. In *Habits* we quoted a famous passage in Tocqueville's *Democracy in America*: "I think I can see the whole destiny of America contained in the first Puritan who landed on those shores." (279) Then we went on to name John Winthrop, following Tocqueville's own predilection, as the likeliest candidate for being that first Puritan. Now I am ready to admit, although regretfully, that we, and Tocqueville, were probably wrong. That first Puritan who contained our whole destiny might have been, as we also half intimated in *Habits*, Anne Hutchinson, but the stronger candidate, because we know so much more about him, is Roger Williams.

Roger Williams, banished from the Massachusetts Bay Colony by John Winthrop, founder of Providence and of the Rhode Island Colony, was, as everyone knows, a Baptist. The Baptists in seventeenth-century New England were a distinct minority, but they went on to become, together with other sectarian Protestants, a majority in American religious culture from the early nineteenth century. As Seymour Martin Lipset has recently pointed out, we are the only North Atlantic society whose predominant religious tradition is sectarian rather than an established church. (1996: 19–20; for a detailed contrast of the influence of church and sect religion in America see Baltzell 1979.) I think this is something enormously important about our culture and that it has, believe it or not, a great deal to do with why our society is so hospitable to the ideology, if not the reality, of multiculturalism.

What was so important about the Baptists, and other sectarians such as the Quakers, was the absolute centrality of religious freedom, of the sacredness of individual conscience in matters of religious belief. We generally think of religious freedom as one of many kinds of freedom, many kinds of human rights, first voiced in the European Enlightenment, and echoing around the world ever since. But Georg Jellinek, Max Weber's friend, and, on these matters, his teacher, published a book in 1895 called *Die Erklärung der Menschen- und Bürgerrechte*, translated into English in 1901 as *The Declaration of the Rights of Man and of Citizens*, which argued that the ultimate source of all modern notions of human rights is to  be found in the radical sects of the Protestant Reformation, particularly the Quakers andBaptists. Of this development Weber writes, "Thus the consistent sect gives rise to an inalienable personal right of the governed as against any power, whether political, hierocratic or patriarchal. Such freedom of conscience may be the oldest Right of Man—as Jellinek has argued convincingly, at any rate it is the most basic Right of Man because it comprises all ethically conditioned action and guarantees freedom from compulsion, especially from the power of the state. In this sense the concept was as unknown to antiquity and the Middle Ages as it was to Rousseau. . . ." Weber then goes on to say that the other Rights of Man were later joined to this basic right, "especially the right to pursue one's own economic interests, which includes the inviolability of individual property, the freedom of contract, and vocational choice." (1978: 1209) I will have to return to the link to economic freedom, but first I want to talk about the relation between the sectarian notion of the sacredness of conscience and what we mean by multiculturalism today, starting with the Baptist Roger Williams.

It is worth remembering that one of the sources of Williams's problems was his unhappiness with John Winthrop's assertion that the Massachusetts Bay colonists were building "a city upon a hill," because, in Williams's view, it was *somebody else's hill!* The hill belonged to the Native Americans, and if the other Puritans were inclined to overlook that, Roger Williams wasn't.

When Williams was banished from Massachusetts Bay in January of 1636, he probably would not have survived the winter in Rhode Island without the "courtesy" of the Indians, with whom he had, not surprisingly, an excellent relationship. Of this courtesy he wrote, in his charming doggerel:

> The courteous pagan shall condemn
>> Uncourteous Englishmen,
> Who live like foxes, bears and wolves,
>> Or lion in his den.
>
> Let none sing blessings to their souls,
>> For that they courteous are:
> The wild barbarians with no more
>> Than nature go so far.
>
> If nature's sons both wild and tame
>> Humane and courteous be,
> How ill becomes it sons of God
>> To want humanity. (Miller: 61–62)

Williams would have nothing to do with the idea that Europeans were superior to Indians. He wrote, "Nature knows no difference between Europe and Americans [that is, Native Americans] in blood, birth, bodies, God having of one blood made all mankind (Acts 17) and all by nature being children of wrath (Ephesians 2)." (Miller: 64) And he admonished his fellow Englishmen:

> Boast not, proud English, of thy birth and blood,
>> Thy brother Indian is by birth as good.
> Of one blood God made him and thee and all,
>> As wise, as fair, as strong, as personal.
>
> By nature, wrath's his portion, thine no more,
>> Till grace his soul and thine restore.
> Make sure thy second birth, else thou shalt see
>> Heaven ope to Indians wild, but shut to thee. (Miller: 64)

We know that the passage of the Virginia Act for religious freedom and of the First Amendment to the Constitution (and it was no accident, following Jellinek and Weber, that it was indeed the *First* Amendment), of which I will have more to say in a moment, depended on an alliance of enlightenment Deists like Jefferson and Madison, and sectarians, largely Baptists. The fundamental Baptist position on the sacredness of conscience relative to government action is brought out in a passage discovered by Lipset in *The First New Nation.* The idea must seem quaint to us today, but in 1810 Congress passed a law decreeing that mail should be delivered on Sundays. In 1830 a Senate committee reported negatively on a bill to abolish Sunday mail delivery. The report, written by Richard Johnson, a Kentucky senator and an active Baptist leader, argued that laws prohibiting the government from providing service on Sunday would be an injustice to irreligious people or non-Christians, and would constitute a special favor to Christians. The report spelled out these principles:

> The constitution regards the conscience of the Jew as sacred as that of the Christian, and gives no more authority to adopt a measure affecting the conscience of a solitary individual than that of a whole community. . . . If Congress shall declare the first day of the week holy, it will not satisfy the Jew nor the Sabbatarian. It will dissatisfy both and, consequently, convert neither . . . It must be recollected that, in the earliest settlement of this country, the spirit of persecution, which drove the pilgrims from their native homes, was brought with them to their new habitations; and that some Christians were scourged and others put to death for no other crime than dissenting from the dogmas of their rulers. . . .
>
> If a solemn act of legislation shall in *one* point define the God or point out to the citizen one religious duty, it may with equal propriety define *every* part of divine revelation and enforce *every* religious obligation, even to the forms and ceremonies of worship; the endowment of the church, and the support of the clergy. . . .
>
> It is the duty of this government to affirm to all—to the Jew or Gentile, Pagan, or Christian—the protection and advantages of our benignant institutions on *Sunday*, as well as every day of the week. (Lipset 1963: 164–165)

My fellow sociologist of religion, Phillip E. Hammond, has written a remarkable book, *With Liberty for All: Freedom of Religion in the United States*, which I have been privileged to see in manuscript, detailing the vicissitudes of this sectarian Protestant concern for the sacredness of the individual conscience as it was embodied in the First Amendment to the Constitution and has been given ever wider meaning by the judicial system, especially the Supreme Court, ever since. For Hammond, the key move was to extend the sacredness of conscience from religious belief to any seriously held conviction whatever. A key moment in this transformation was the Court's decision to extend the right of conscientious objection to military service to those whose beliefs were not in any traditional sense religious, but were fervently held nonetheless. Individual conviction and conscience have become the standards relative to which even long-established practices can be overturned. Hammond argues that *Roe v. Wade* is an example of the extension of this principle, and that its logic will ultimately lead to the legitimation of gay marriage. In the course of the extension of the sacredness of individual conscience from religion to the entire range of belief, Hammond argues, the sacred core of the *conscience collective*, the very sacred center of our society, what might even be called our civil religion, has moved from the churches to the judiciary. Whether we need to go that far with Hammond could be argued, but he has surely uncovered something very important about our society, something deeper than utilitarian or expressive individualism, the sacredness of the individual conscience, the individual person. And, I might add as an aside, here, in the city of San Francisco, where you can probably do almost anything within reason and still not raise an eyebrow, it is all ultimately thanks to the Baptists, even though some Baptists today find it rather upsetting!

It is with this background in mind that I think we can understand why multiculturalism as an ideology is so appealing to Americans today, but why the emphasis on culture is so misleading. A common culture does not mean that we are all the same. Common cultures are normally riven with argument, controversy, and conflict. Those who imagine that in *Habits of the Heart* we were arguing for homogeneous "communities" languishing in bland consensus could hardly have gotten us more wrong. Difference between communities (and we must also remember that there are differences within communities, starting with the family, which someone recently defined as "the place we go to fight"), even when the cultural differences between them are remarkably thin, can give rise to significant differences in identity. Identity is not the same thing as culture, but it can be just as important. Remember Bosnia, where Serbs, Croats, and Muslims share a common language and probably 99 percent of their culture, but where the memory of ancestral religion, in a highly secularized society, has led to murderous conflicts of quite recently constructed political identities.[1]

And yet in America the rise of identity politics on a local or a national scale probably signifies something else, something much closer to the core of our common culture. Again, Anthony Appiah has put it well:

> But if we explore these moments of tension [between groups in contemporary America] we discover an interesting paradox. The growing salience of race and gender as social irritants, which may seem to reflect the call of collective identities, is a reflection, as much as anything else, of the individual's concern for dignity and respect. As our society slouches on toward a fuller realization of its ideal of social equality, everyone wants to be taken seriously—to be respected, not "dissed." Because on many occasions disrespect still flows from racism, sexism, and homophobia, we respond, in the name of all black people, all women, all gays, as the case may be. . . . But the truth is that what mostly irritates us in these moments is that we, as individuals, feel diminished.
>
> And the trouble with appeal to cultural difference is that it obscures rather than diminishes this situation. It is not black culture that the racist disdains, but blacks. There is no conflict of visions between black and white cultures that is the source of racial discord. No amount of knowledge of the architectural achievements of Nubia or Kush guarantees respect for African Americans. No African American is entitled to greater concern because he is descended from a people who created jazz or produced Toni Morrison. Culture is not the problem, and it is not the solution. (35–36)

If the problem is disrespect for the dignity of the person, then the solution is to go back to that deepest core of our tradition, the sacredness of the conscience and person of every individual. And that is what a great deal of the ideology of multiculturalism is really saying: We are all different; we are all unique. Respect that.

But there is another problem, a very big problem, and its solution is hard to envision. Just when we are moving to an ever greater validation of the sacredness of the individual person, our capacity to imagine a social fabric that would hold individuals together is vanishing. This is in part because of the fact that the religious individualism that I have been describing is linked to an economic individualism which, ironically, knows nothing of the sacredness of the individual. Its only standard is money, and the only thing more sacred than money is more money. What economic individualism destroys and what our kind of religious individualism cannot restore, is solidarity, a sense of being members of the same body. In most other North Atlantic societies a tradition of an established church, however secularized, provides some notion that we are in this thing together, that we need each other, that our precious and unique selves aren't going to make it all alone. That is a tradition singularly weak in our country, though Catholics and some high church Protestants have tried to provide it. The trouble is, as Chesterton put it, in America even the Catholics are Protestants. And we also lack a tradition of Social Democracy such as most European nations possess, not unrelated to the established church tradition, in which there is some notion of a government that bears responsibility for its people. But here it was not Washington and Hamilton who won but Jefferson and Madison, with their rabid hatred of the state, who carried the day.

Roger Williams was a moral genius but he was a sociological catastrophe. After he founded the First Baptist church he left it for a smaller and purer one. That, too, he found inadequate, so he founded a church that consisted only of himself, his wife, and one other person. One wonders how he stood even those two. Since Williams ignored secular society, money took over in Rhode Island in a way that would not be true in Massachusetts or Connecticut for a long time. Rhode Island under Williams gives us an early and local example of what happens when the sacredness of the individual is not balanced by any sense of the whole or concern for the common good. In *Habits of the Heart* we spoke of the second languages that must complement our language of individualism if we are not to slip into total incoherence. I was not very optimistic then; I am even less so today. Almost the only time this society has ever gotten itself together has been in time of war, and I am sure that my understanding of America is deeply formed by experiencing the depression as a child and the Second World War as an adolescent. It is not easy to hear those second languages today and some of those who are too young to have shared my experiences seem hardly able to recognize them even when they hear them. But the poignant reality is that, without a minimal degree of solidarity, the project of ever greater recognition of individual dignity will collapse in on itself. Under the ideological facade of individual freedom, the reality will be, is already becoming, a society in which wealth, ever more concentrated in a small minority, is the only access to real freedom. "The market" will determine the lives of everyone else. So, much as we owe the Baptists, and I would be the first to affirm it, we cannot look to them for a way out. All you have to do is look at the two Baptists in the last White House to see that. And yes, I know Hillary is a Methodist—I meant Clinton and Gore.

But, if I can pull myself back from the abyss, which sometimes in my Jeremiah mood is almost the only thing I can see, I can describe even now resources and possibilities for a different outcome than the one toward which we seem to be heading. By the time we came to publish the 1996 edition of *Habits of the Heart* we realized that even the biblical and civic republican traditions, which we had called "second languages," had made their own contribution to the kind of individualism that we had largely blamed on utilitarianism and expressivism in the first edition. This does not mean, however, that the second languages haven't still much to teach us, even if what we have to learn from them must pass through the fires of self-criticism from within these traditions themselves.  Our situation is curiously similar to that of post-Communist Eastern Europe. Vaclav Havel and others have opposed an effort to distinguish too sharply between the guilty and the innocent in the former Communist regimes, since it was the very nature of those regimes to draw almost everyone into some kind of complicity. The line between guilt and innocence ran through rather than between individuals, it was argued. I think of the banner in an East German church shortly after the fall of the Berlin Wall which read: "We are Cain *and* Abel." With respect to our American individualism, even in its most destructive forms, it is useless to try to sort out the good guys from the bad guys. We are all complicit, yet change is never impossible.

Here I would like to return to the reference to nuances and inflections in our common culture that I made early in this paper. Recognizing that we are all, of whatever race and gender, tempted to exalt our own imperial egos above all else, we can still find those social contexts and those traditions of interpretation, which can moderate that egoism and offer a different understanding of personal fulfillment. Every church and synagogue that reminds us that it is through love of God and neighbor that we will find ourselves helps to mitigate our isolation. Every time we engage in activities that help to feed the hungry, clothe the naked, give shelter to the homeless, we are becoming more connected to the world. Every time we act politically to keep the profit principle out of spheres where it ought not to set the norms of action we help to preserve what Jürgen Habermas calls the lifeworld (1987), and, incidentally, to prevent the market from destroying the moral foundations which make it possible. It must be obvious from the example of recent history that without the legal and ethical culture of public morality a market economy turns into Mafia gangsterism. We still have more of what has come to be called "social capital" than many other nations, but it cannot be taken for granted. It survives only when we in our religious and civic groups work strenuously to conserve and increase it.

It is the special responsibility of those of us who are intellectuals to appropriate and develop our cultural resources, even while criticizing them. William Dean, in his *The Religious Critic in American Culture*, has given us a splendid example of the work that needs to be done. He draws heavily from the tradition of American Pragmatism, especially William James, and from contemporary thinkers as diverse as George Lindbeck and Cornel West, to argue for the necessity of conventions, and indeed sacred conventions, for a viable culture. He speaks of the "religious critic" as a public intellectual, situated not just in the university but in third sector institutions, including churches, working to criticize but also to reclaim a viable myth of America.

Thus, I still believe that there are places in the churches, and other religious and civic organizations, and even nooks and crannies in the universities, to which we might look. But the hour is late and the problems mount. In this hour of need in our strange republic, it is up to us to teach the truth as we discern it.

## NOTES

1. William Finnegan in a fascinating article (1997) describes the hunger for identity but the shallowness of cultural resources for it in Antelope Valley, a recently developed suburb of Los Angeles. For example he mentions a girl named Mindy who became a Mormon but before that she had "wanted to become Jewish. But that had turned out to be too much work. Becoming a Mormon was relatively easy. All this was before Mindy got addicted to crystal methamphetamine and became a Nazi, in the ninth grade." (62–63) Finnegan's article concludes: "Martha Wengert, a sociologist at Antelope Valley College, said, 'This area has grown so fast that neighborhoods are not yet communities. Kids are left with this intense longing for identification.' Gangs, race nationalism, and all manner of 'beliefs' arise from this longing. I thought of Debbie Turner's inability to comprehend Mindy's enthusiasm for the likes of Charles Manson and Adolf Hitler. 'The kids reach out to these historical figures,' Dr. Wengert said. 'But it's through TV, through comic books, through word-of-mouth. There are no books at home, no ideas, no sense of history.' "(78) These identities that lack any cultural depth are nonetheless powerful enough to be literally matters of life and death for the young people involved.

## REFERENCES

Appiah, K. Anthony. 1997. "The Multiculturalist Misunderstanding." *The New York Review of Books*, 44/15, October 9: 30–36.

Baltzell, E. Digby. 1979. *Puritan Boston and Quaker Philadelphia*. New York: Free Press.

Bellah, Robert N., Richard Madsen, William M. Sullivan, Ann Swidler and Steven M. Tipton. 1985. *Habits of the Heart: Individualism and Commitment in American Life*. Berkeley: University of California Press.

Benson, Rodney D. 1997. "Constructing and Dismantling a French 'Right to Difference': A Social Constructionist Re-interpretation." Paper presented at the Harvard University Conference on Politics and Identity Formation in Contemporary Europe. April 12, 1997.

Dean, William. 1994. *The Religious Critic in American culture*. Albany, N.Y.: State University of New York Press.

Finnegan, William. 1997. "The Unwanted." *The New Yorker* 73/37, December 1: 60–78.

Glaeser, Andreas. 1997. "Divided in Unity: The Hermeneutics of Self and Other in the Post-unification Berlin Police." Doctoral Dissertation, Department of Sociology, Harvard University.

Glazer, Nathan. 1997. *We Are All Multiculturalists Now*. Cambridge, Mass: Harvard University Press.

Habermas, Jürgen. 1987. *The Theory of communicative Action*. Vol. II. *Lifeworld and System: A Critique of Functionalist Reason*. Boston: Beacon.

Hammond, Phillip E. 1998. *With Liberty for All: Freedom of Religion in the United States*. Louisville, Ky.: Westminster John Knox Press.

Jellinek, Georg. 1901. *The Declaration of the Rights of Man and of Citizens [Die Erklärung der Menschen- und Bürgerrechte]*. New York: Holt.

Lipset, Seymour Martin. 1963. *The First New Nation: The United States in Historical and Comparative Perspective*. New York: Basic.

——1996. *American Exceptionalism: A Double-Edged Sword*. New York: Norton.

Miller, Perry. 1953. *Roger Williams: His Contribution to the American Tradition*. Indianapolis: Bobbs-Merrill.

Tocqueville, Alexis de. 1969 [1835, 1840]. *Democracy in America*. Trans. by George Lawrence and ed.. by J. P. Meyer. Garden City, N.Y.: Doubleday.

Weber, Max. 1978 [1921–1922]. *Economy and Society*. Ed. by Guenther Roth and Claus Wittich. Berkeley: University of California Press.

# CONTRIBUTORS

**Robert N. Bellah** is Elliott Professor of Sociology, Emeritus, at the University of California, Berkeley. His many publications include: *Beyond Belief* (1970), *The Broken Covenant* (1975), and with Ann Swidler, Richard Madsen, William Sullivan, and Steven Tipton *Habits of the Heart* (1985) and *The Good Society* (1991). In 2003 the University of California Press published his *Imagining Japan: The Japanese Tradition and Its Modern Interpretation*. In 2000 Bellah was awarded the National Humanities Medal.

**Ann Braude** is Director of the Women's Studies in Religion Program and Senior Lecturer in American Religious History at Harvard University. She is the author of *Radical Spirits: Spiritualism and Women's Rights in Nineteenth Century America* (1989) and *Women and American Religion* (2000). Her current work is on the intersection between the changing roles of women and the changing roles of religion in American society since the 1960s.

**David Chidester** is Professor of Religious Studies at the University of Cape Town, South Africa, Director of the Institute for Comparative Religion in Southern Africa, and Co-Director of the International Human Rights Exchange. His publications include *Salvation and Suicide: An Interpretation of Jim Jones, the Peoples Temple, and Jonestown* (1988), *American Sacred Space* (with Edward Linenthal, 1995), *Savage Systems: Colonialism and Comparative Religion in Southern Africa* (1996), and *Christianity: A Global History* (2000).

**James H. Cone** is Charles A. Briggs Distinguished Professor of Systematic Theology at Union Theological Seminary. His books include *Black Theology and Black Power* (1969), *A Black Theology of Liberation* (2d ed. 1986) and *Martin & Malcolm & America* (1991).

**Raymond J. DeMallie** is Professor of Anthropology and Director of the American Studies Research Institute at Indiana University. He is the editor (with Elaine A. Jahner) of James R. Walker, *Lakota Belief and Ritual* (1980), the editor of *The Sixth Grandfather: Black Elk's Teachings Given to John Neihardt* (1984), and the editor (with Douglas R. Parks) of *Sioux Indian Religion: Tradition and Innovation* (1987). He is completing a translation and edition of the writings of the early-twentieth-century Oglala religious and political leader George Sword.

**William B. Gravely** retired in 2000 as Professor of Religious Studies at the University of Denver. He is the author of *Gilbert Haven, Methodist Abolitionist* (1973) and of many journal articles concerning African American religion, abolitionism, and Methodist studies. He is completing an interpretive study of the 1947 lynching of Willie Earle, the last lynching in South Carolina.

**R. Marie Griffith** is Lecturer in Religion and Associate Director of the Center of the Study of Religion at Princeton University. She is the author of *God's Daughters: Evangelical Women and the Power of Submission* (1997). She is writing a book on American Christianity and the body.

**Ramón A. Gutiérrez** is Professor of Ethnic Studies and History at the University of California, San Diego. He is the author of *When Jesus Came, the Corn Mothers Went Away: Marriage, Sexuality, and Power in New Mexico, 1500–1846* (1991) and coeditor of *Feasts* *and Celebrations in North American Ethnic Communities* (1995), *Contested Eden: California before the Gold Rush* (1998), and *Mexican Home Altars* (New Mexico, 1997). He is working on a social and cultural history of Indian slavery.

**David G. Hackett** is Associate Professor of Religion at the University of Florida. The author of *The Rude Hand of Innovation: Religion and Social Order in Albany, New York 1652–1836* (1991), he is completing a book on fraternalism and religion in American religious history.

**David D. Hall** is Professor of American Religious History at Harvard Divinity School. He is the editor of *The Antinomian Controversy: A Documentary History, 1636–1638* (1968) and the author of *Worlds of Wonder, Days of Judgment: Popular Religious Belief in Early New England* (1989). He is completing a source book on Puritanism in New England that is attentive to diversities of several kinds.

**Evelyn Brooks Higginbotham** is Professor of History and Afro-American Studies at Harvard University. Her published work covers a number of topics—race theory, women's history, religion, and civil rights. She is the editor-in-chief of the comprehensive guide to sources, *The Harvard Guide to African-American History* (2000) and the author of the prize-winning book *Righteous Discontent: The Women's Movement in the Black Baptist Church 1880–1920* (1993).

**Christopher Ronwanièn:te Jocks** is Assistant Professor in the Religion Department and Native American Studies Program at Dartmouth College. He belongs to the Native American diaspora, rooted in the Mohawk community of Kahnawà:ke. He is finishing a general study of Native American religious traditions to be published in 2003. His next project relates four seemingly separate topics that are important in traditional Iroquois communities today: creation stories, addiction, river systems and the damage done to them by twentieth-century dam and diversion projects, and child-rearing.

**Charles Joyner** is Burroughs Distinguished Professor of History and Culture at Coastal Carolina University. He is the author of *Down By the Riverside: A South Carolina Slave Community* (1984) and *Shared Traditions: Southern History and Folk Culture* (1999). He is writing a book on the various forms of Southern music.

**Joel W. Martin** holds the Rupert Costo Endowed Chair in American Indian Affairs at the University of California, Riverside, where he is Professor of History and Religious Studies. He co-edited *Screening the Sacred: Religion, Myth and Ideology in Popular American Film* (1995) and authored *Sacred Revolt: The Muskogees' Struggle for a New World* (1991), *The Land Looks After Us: A History of Native American Religion* (2001), and other publications. His current research projects focus on sacred sites in America, encounters among Cherokees and missionaries, and contemporary Native American revitalization movements.

**Deborah Dash Moore** is Professor of Religion and Director of the Jewish Studies Program at Vassar College. She is the author of *At Home in America: Second Generation New York Jews* (1981) and *To the Golden Cities: Pursuing the American Jewish Dream in Miami and L.A.* (1994). With Paula Hyman, she is co-editor of *Jewish Women in America: An Historical*

*Encyclopedia* (1997). She is completing a book on the experience of Jews in the American armed forces during World War II, "When Jews Were GI's."

**Robert A. Orsi** is Charles Warren Professor of the History of Religion in America at Harvard University. He is the author of *The Madonna of 115th Street* (1985) and *Thank-You St. Jude: Women's Devotion to the Patron Saint of Hopeless Causes* (1996). He is working on a social and cultural history of growing up Catholic in the United States in the twentieth century.

**Albert J. Raboteau** is Henry W. Putnam Professor of Religion at Princeton University. He is the author of *Slave Religion: The "Invisible Institution" in the Antebellum South* (1978), *Fire in the Bones* (1995), and *A Sorrowful Joy* (2002). With David Wills, he is co-editing "A Documentary History of African-American Religion."

**Daniel K. Richter** is Professor of History and the Richard S. Dunn Director of the McNeil Center for Early American Studies at the University of Pennsylvania. He is the author of *The Ordeal of the Longhouse: The Peoples of the Iroquois League in the Era of European Colonization* (1992) and *Facing East from Indian Country: A Native History of Early America* (2001).

**Jonathan D. Sarna** is Joseph H. and Belle R. Braun Professor of American Jewish History at Brandeis University. His publications include *Jacksonian Jew: The Two Worlds of Mordecai Noah* (1981) and *JPS: The Americanization of Jewish Culture* (1989). His new history of American Judaism will appear in 2004.

**Leigh Eric Schmidt** is Professor of Religion at Princeton University. He is the author of *Holy Fairs: Scottish Communions and American Revivals in the Early Modern Period* (1989; 2001); *Consumer Rites: The Buying and Selling of American Holidays* (1995); and *Hearing Things: Religion, Illusion, and the American Enlightenment* (2000). He is researching the history of the study of religion in American culture as well as the history of American mysticism and spirituality.

**Thomas A. Tweed** is Zachary Smith Distinguished Professor of Religious Studies at the University of North Carolina at Chapel Hill. He is the author of *The American Encounter with Buddhism, 1844–1912* (1992, rev. ed. 2000) and *Our Lady of the Exile: Diasporic Religion at a Cuban Catholic Shrine in Miami*, which won the American Academy of Religion's award for excellence (1997). He is also the editor of *Retelling U.S. Religious History* (1997) and the co-editor of *Asian Religions in America: A Documentary History* (1999). He is co-editing *The Oxford Companion to Religion in America*.

**Grant Wacker** is Professor of Church History at Duke University. He is the author of *Augustus H. Strong and the Dilemma of Historical Consciousness* (1985) and *Heaven Below: Early Pentecostals and American Culture* (2001). He is working on a study of Billy Graham and modern America.

**Joanne Punzo Waghorne** is Professor of Religion at Syracuse University. She is the author of *The Raja's Magic Clothes: Re-visioning Kingship and Divinity in England's India* (1994). She is completing a book on the construction of Hindu temples in modern urban India and abroad, *Diaspora of the Gods: The Hindu Temple in a Global Context*.

**Rachel Wheeler** is Assistant Professor in the Department of Religious Studies at Lewis and Clark College. She is completing a book comparing the Mahican experience with Congregational and Moravian missionaries.

**Charles Reagan Wilson** is Professor of History and Southern Studies and Director of the Center for Southern Culture at the University of Mississippi. He is the author of *Baptized in Blood: The Religion of the Lost Cause, 1865–1920* (1980) and *Judgment and Grace in Dixie: Southern Faiths from Faulkner to Elvis* (1995). He is writing "The Southern Way of Life," a history of regional culture and consciousness.

**Robert Wuthnow** is the Gerhard R. Andlinger '52 Professor of Sociology and Director of the Center for the Study of Religion. His recent publications include *Loose Connections: Joining Together in America's Fragmented Communities* (1998); *After Heaven: Spirituality in America Since the 1950s* (1998); and, as editor, *The Encyclopedia of Politics and Religion* (1998). His current research projects focus on religion and the arts, contemporary spiritual practices, faith-based nonprofit service organizations, social capital, and the public role of American Protestantism.